Fourth Edition

D0477955

AWAKENING

AN INTRODUCTION TO THE HISTORY
OF EASTERN THOUGHT

Patrick S. Bresnan
De Anza College

Prentice Hall
Boston   Columbus   Indianapolis   New York   San Francisco
Upper Saddle River   Amsterdam   Cape Town   Dubai   London   Madrid
Milan   Munich   Paris   Montreal   Toronto   Delhi   Mexico City   Sao Paulo
Sydney   Hong Kong   Seoul   Singapore   Taipei   Tokyo

Editorial Director: Leah Jewell
Editor in Chief: Dickson Musslewhite
Publisher: Nancy Roberts
Editorial Assistant: Nart Varoqua
Director of Marketing: Brandy Dawson
Senior Marketing Manager: Laura Lee Manley
Marketing Assistant: Patrick Walsh
Production Manager: Fran Russello
Manager, Visual Research: Beth Brenzel
Manager, Rights and Permissions: Zina Arabia
Image Permission Coordinator: Nancy Seise

Manager, Cover Visual Research & Permissions: Karen Sanatar
Creative Director: Jayne Conte
Cover Designer: Bruce Kenselaar
Cover Art: Water H. Hodge/Peter Arnold, Inc.
Full-Service Project Management: Sadagoban Balaji
Composition: Integra Software Services, Ltd.
Printer/Binder: Bind-Rite Robbinsville
Text Font: Garamond

Credits and acknowledgments borrowed from other sources and reproduced, with permission, in this textbook appear on appropriate page within text.

Library of Congress Cataloging-in-Publication Data

Bresnan, Patrick,
  Awakening: an introduction to the history of Eastern thought/Patrick S. Bresnan.—4th ed.
    p. cm.
Includes bibliographical references and index.
ISBN-13: 978-0-205-73909-7 (alk. paper)
ISBN-10: 0-205-73909-1 (alk. paper)
  1. Asia—Religion.   2. Philosophy, Asian.   I. Title.
BL1033.B74 2010
200.95—dc22

                                                            2009029155

10 9 8 7 6 5 4 3 2 1

Prentice Hall
is an imprint of

PEARSON

www.pearsonhighered.com

ISBN 13: 978-0-205-73909-7
ISBN 10:   0-205-73909-1

CONTENTS

PREFACE

PREFACE TO THE FIRST EDITION

We humans struggle to make sense out of a world that often seems chaotic and meaningless. In every age, men and women—at least some men and women—have sought to go beyond the appearances of everyday life and discover a transcendent truth in which reality is seen as it really is. Such an experience is often called "awakening"—it is the opening of consciousness to the light of perfect understanding.

This great quest has been an important part of the history of both East and West, and in both worlds, much attention has been given to uncovering a fundamental principle of unity that underlies the manifold expressions of nature. There has, however, been a difference in emphasis. Speaking very broadly, the West has emphasized the rational and scientific approach, whereas the East, again speaking very broadly, has tended to emphasize the introspective approach, an intuitive opening of consciousness that goes beyond the limits of the rational mind. Such a state of consciousness, in which the underlying oneness of Being is personally experienced, is known as the "unitive state." The search for a way of life that will result in this kind of awakening is at the heart of the history of Eastern thought.

This book tells the story of that search. It is a search that unfolds slowly over nearly four millennia—and, of course, it is still unfolding today; the present age is merely the cutting edge. There is something especially exciting about the present age, though. As the global village takes form, the traditions of East and West are coming together. Who can imagine what wondrous offspring may result from this marriage?

The evolution of Eastern thought grows from many roots. Those of India and China are especially strong and deep, both reaching back before the beginnings of recorded history. We will take up this study at the source of the tradition in India. It is appropriate to begin in India because so much of the spiritual and philosophical foundation of Eastern thought is to be found there. And, it was out of the amazingly fertile Hindu tradition that Buddhism was born. From India, Buddhism would spread to all parts of the Eastern world, sometimes merging with other evolving traditions to create new directions of growth. In China, Buddhism would confront the already established traditions of Confucianism and Daoism, and in Japan, the ancient tradition of Shinto. These too are important parts of this study.

The history of the development of Eastern thought is far too vast to be reduced to the pages of any single volume. The purpose of this work, therefore, is not to tell everything; that would be impossible. Rather, in this book my primary aim is to help you form a comprehensive overview of the subject, a Big Picture. In the pages that follow, I will introduce you to this important part of the story of humankind's search for awakening. It is my goal to include all that is essential to a broad understanding of the subject, and to clarify all major concepts no matter how complex they may be, in a way that is clear and engaging. It is my deepest hope that you, the reader, will come away from this book hungry for more and that you will choose to become a lifelong student of this fascinating subject.

Patrick Bresnan

Los Gatos, California
August, 1997

PREFACE TO THE FOURTH EDITION

Welcome to the fourth edition of *Awakening*. It's been more than ten years since the writing of the Preface to the First Edition. What a decade it has been! This world order that we all live within has taken some mighty blows—and it's still on its feet—but you have to wonder how much more it can take. Clearly, the need for compassionate understanding among the various communities that make up modern global society becomes more urgent all the time. The overarching goal of this book is to awaken you, the reader, to the great riches of the traditions examined in this book, and hopefully to motivate you to choose to become a part of the solution to the challenges we can expect to encounter as the undoubtedly very exciting twenty-first century unfolds.

In this fourth edition, you will find some new sections, some expanded and rewritten sections, and a thoroughgoing overhaul of the entire book. Among the new and expanded sections are those dealing with the Four Noble Truths, Nyaya, Tantra, Madhyamaka, Yogacara, and Tiantai. You will also find a somewhat new organization based on four major "parts," rather than two. All in all, I am satisfied that the Fourth edition represents a sweeping improvement over all that has come before.

Patrick Bresnan
Los Gatos, California
July, 2009

I would genuinely love to hear from you. Don't be reluctant to write.

Patrick Bresnan
bresnanpatrick@yahoo.com

ACKNOWLEDGMENTS

Many people are involved in the publication of a book of this sort. It would take too many pages to thank everyone involved, but I do wish to single out a special few. Among the folks at Prentice Hall. I want to thank, first and foremost, Nancy Roberts (Publisher, Anthropology/Philosophy/Religion), whose help and support have been, in a word, crucial. And thanks, again, to Bruce Kenselaar at Prentice Hall. Bruce has created the cover design for all four editions of Awakening. His design for the fourth edition is, as usual, outstanding. I am grateful for the contribution of Fran Russello in product management. Fran has been the Prentice Hall liaison person working with Sadagoban Balaji of Integra Software Solutions. A very special thanks to Sadagoban, the Project Manager, and to his associate, Pradheeba Balasubramanian, the Copy Editor. The book now in your hands owes a lot to Sadagoban. The high quality of his work and his professionalism are much appreciated.

A NOTE ABOUT PUNCTUATION AND TRANSLITERATION

Generally speaking, proper usage calls for foreign words to be italicized. However, because of the frequent repetition of foreign language words that this study necessitates, I have chosen not to encumber the text with a multitude of italicized words. Instead, I will follow the practice of italicizing the first use only for such words and italicize others as seems appropriate.

Two systems exist for spelling Chinese words in the Western alphabet, pinyin and Wade-Giles. Pinyin, the more recently developed of the two, attempts to overcome some of the phonetic and spelling problems of the Wade-Giles system. In Wade-Giles, for example, Tao is spelled with a "T" even though it is meant to be pronounced more like a "D," which is the correct spelling in pinyin. Pinyin is rapidly replacing Wade-Giles and is the system of choice in this book. In instances where it seems appropriate, I will include the Wade-Giles spelling in parentheses.

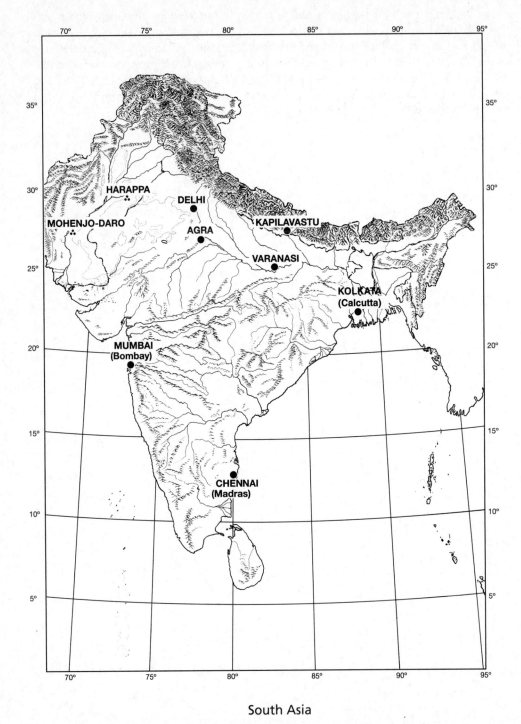

South Asia

Source: Map reprinted with permission of Hammond World Atlas Corporation.

PART ONE

Hinduism
and Related Traditions
of South Asia

Hinduism is a hard word to pin down. It refers to far more than a specific religion or philosophy. Some argue that the word *Hinduism* refers to the entire culture and traditional way of life of the people of India. For our purposes, the word *Hinduism* designates that tradition of thought that arises from, and accepts the sacred authority of, the Vedas, the earliest spiritual and philosophical compositions of Indian civilization. This leaves room for other "non-Hindu" traditions within the history of Indian thought, and we shall examine the most important of these in Chapter 5. The greatest part of the story, though, concerns the evolving tradition that began in the Vedas and progressed through stages to the sublime mystic philosophy expressed in the *Upanishads* and the *Bhagavad Gita*. In Part I, we will concentrate on this main line of development.

CHAPTER 1

India Before the Vedas

Veda is a powerful word. It is derived from the ancient Sanskrit word *vid*, which means "to know," as in the sense of knowing the truth. *Veda* thus means knowledge of truth. More specifically, it refers to a higher, infallible truth, available to only a gifted few, who transmit this knowledge for the benefit of all.

In ancient times, the Brahmin priests were the custodians of Veda; it was their responsibility to preserve this sacred knowledge and to use it for the well-being of the entire community. To a large degree, this was accomplished through the performance of religious ritual. Over time, these ritual celebrations grew to include long chants, which came to be known as the Vedas, religious compositions that expressed the essential truths of Veda. The Vedas, composed more than 3,000 years ago, are the earliest recorded expressions of the Indian tradition. They were, nonetheless, the product of a culture that was far older still.

The earliest evidence of urban civilization in India appeared approximately 5,000 years ago and even that grew out of still older roots. Of course, history knows little of what was going on in those early days. Our *historical* knowledge of this emerging tradition starts with the Vedas, and it is thus with the Vedas that our study properly begins. But before we get to that, it would be valuable to travel back in time and take a somewhat closer look at the background out of which the Vedas took form and that influenced them in many important ways. Most fundamental of all is the physical character of the Indian subcontinent—the stage, so to speak, on which the great drama would take place. And that is where we shall begin.

THE LAY OF THE LAND

The huge subcontinent of India appears on the map to hang gracefully from the southern flank of Eurasia. Its generally triangular shape extends for 1,000 miles into the Indian Ocean, dividing that sea into the Arabian Sea on the west and the Bay of Bengal to the east. Just off the southern tip of India, and almost connected to it by a land bridge, is the beautiful teardrop-shaped island of Sri Lanka. Called Ceylon for centuries, Sri Lanka has always been intimately connected geographically and culturally with India.

Approximately one-half the size of the United States, the Indian subcontinent is effectively isolated by geography from the rest of the Eurasian continent. In the south, India confronts the sea; in the north, it is divided from what lies beyond by the greatest system of mountains on Earth. The vast Himalayas and their associated ranges stretch out across the entire northern frontier from west to east. On a map, the northern mountains have the appearance of a great curtain gracefully draped across the entire reach of the Indian subcontinent. The mountains and the sea have defined India geographically and have, to a degree, isolated it from the rest of the world.

India has not always been a part of the Eurasian continent. Many millions of years ago all of the present-day continents were joined into one great landmass. At that time, India was an integral part of what would become both Africa and Antarctica. The ceaseless movement of the plates that form the earth's crust eventually broke loose the land we know as India, just as today the great rift system of East Africa is evidence that the slow process of plate movement is again separating another piece of that continent from the mainland.

Over millions of years, the Indian plate moved in a generally northward direction, eventually colliding with the southern side of Asia. There were no great mountains then, but as the Indian plate pressed relentlessly against the Asian plate, the upper layers at the interface began to slowly fold and crumple into nascent mountain ridges, while the lower part of the Indian plate (many geologists believe) tunneled under the Asian plate, and the land began to rise.* In time, the high plateau of Tibet took form. The leading edge of what had once been a low coastal plain was eventually thrust almost 30,000 feet into the sky. Over the ages, the forces of erosion have sculpted this geology into the magnificent chain of mountains we know as the Himalayas, which literally means "abode of snow."

Where there are great mountains, there are great rivers. Many rivers flow out of the northern mountains. Eventually they merge into two great river systems. In the west is the Indus system, from which India derives its name. Several rivers gather in the northwest to form the Indus, which then flows to the south emptying into the Arabian Sea near the modern city of Karachi. In modern times, the Indus flows entirely within the nation of Pakistan.

The other great river system is the Ganges, "Ganga" as the people of India call it. The Ganges gathers several major tributaries and flows in a generally eastward direction across the north of India, finally meeting the sea not far from the modern city of Kolkata (formerly known as Calcutta). For more than 1,500 miles, this great river winds its way through the fertile plain of North India. It is in the enormous Ganges plain that much of the history and most of the people of India are to be found. The Ganges, "Mother Ganga," is a sacred river in the Hindu tradition. Along its banks are to be found many hallowed sites in the history of Hinduism, including the holy city of Varanasi.

The great Ganges basin is known to geographers as the North Indian Plain. South of it the land rises somewhat, becoming a hilly plateau that extends for 1,000 miles, all the way to the southern tip of India. This plateau, which encompasses almost all of southern India, is called the Deccan. It rises gently in elevation from east to west extending almost all the way to the west coast, near which the Deccan abruptly erupts into a long line of low coastal mountains known as the Western Ghats.

---

* The great Indian Ocean earthquake and tsunami of 2006 was dramatic evidence that the plate movement is still going on.

India is, for the most part, a tropical country. It knows great heat. In the south, the environment is lushly tropical and hot, but in the mountainous north a totally different environment is to be found. In fact, just about every kind of climate is to be found somewhere in India, but tropical heat is definitely the most common environment. From June to October, the wet monsoon winds from the south bring almost constant rainfall to much of India. But during the rest of the year, dry winds from the north are the rule.

After merging with Eurasia, India became an integral part of its geology. For many millions of years, this varied and beautiful subcontinent evolved in a perfect state of nature. Every conceivable kind of flora and fauna flourished in this land— every kind but one; and in the course of time that one too would come to India and establish itself there.

SOUTH ASIA BEFORE THE VEDIC AGE

No one knows when the first of our human ancestors entered India. Over the ages, there must have been many waves of migrations. Eventually, a more or less stable human population took form. Aboriginal Indian culture was undoubtedly made up of many discrete groupings, with different customs and distinctly different languages. One large language family, though, known as *Dravidian*, became widely distributed in the subcontinent, and hence it is often used as a label for the entire aboriginal Indian culture.

With the exception of one region, practically nothing is known about the life and history of these people. The aboriginal Indians were a preliterate people; there is no historical record to turn to. We can surmise that they lived out their lives in small, widely dispersed communities living close to the earth. Apparently they practiced a simple form of agriculture, undoubtedly supplemented by hunting and gathering. About their religious beliefs, their art, and their philosophy of life, we can only make wild guesses. We can be sure, though, that some of their religious beliefs and practices have left a large and permanent influence on Indian culture.

The one exception referred to above was indeed impressive. In the northwestern part of the subcontinent, in the Indus and associated river valleys, social evolution did not languish at the level of the small farming community. Here, urban life germinated. Genuine cities took form, with well-laid-out streets and strong defensive walls. Beginning in the 1920s, archaeologists have been uncovering numerous urban sites, not only in the vicinity of the Indus and its tributaries, but also along the banks of the Sarasvati, east of the Indus. The Sarasvati, now almost entirely dried up, was a great river in ancient times and is mentioned prominently in the Vedas. Although not technically accurate, it is customary to lump all of these sites together, referring to the whole as Harappan Civilization, or Indus Valley Civilization. *Harappa* is the name modern scholars have assigned to one of the principal urban excavation sites.

What is most exciting to the historian about these Indus Valley cities is the time when they came into being; they were among the earliest in human history. Much is known about early civilization in the Tigris–Euphrates Valley of Mesopotamia and in the nearby Nile Valley of Egypt. City life and the accompanying elements of civilization had taken shape in Mesopotamia before 3000 B.C.E. and somewhat later in Egypt. Archaeological excavations in the Indus River Valley at such sites as Mohenjo-Daro and Harappa are now revealing that early civilization in the Indus Valley was contemporaneous with those of Mesopotamia and Egypt. Mesopotamia is often referred to as the "cradle of civilization"; Egypt joined it in the cradle very early on. We are now discovering that there was a third baby in that cradle—the early civilization of the Indus Valley.

The excavations at Mohenjo-Daro and Harappa give us a fascinating glimpse into the culture of these people, but only a glimpse. They did possess a pictographic form of writing, but it stubbornly, and maddeningly, resists being deciphered. Nevertheless, some things are clear. Their cities, constructed mostly of mud brick and fired brick, were marvels of engineering. They were especially clever in the technology of water management with municipal drainage systems that surpassed anything the world would see again until Roman times. The streets were broad and brick paved and laid out in a way that divided the city into an efficient pattern of blocks. It seems that the standard of living was generally high. Many decorative pieces have been recovered from these sites. A few of them suggest yogic themes that would become important later on in Indian history. The Indologist Romila Thapar makes reference to

> . . . cities with a grid pattern in their town plan, extensive mud-brick platforms as a base for large structures, monumental buildings, complex fortifications, elaborate drainage systems, the use of mud bricks and fired bricks in buildings, granaries, or warehouses, a tank [sacred pool] for rituals, and remains associated with extensive craft activity related to the manufacturing of copper ingots, etched carnelian beads, the cutting of steatite seals, terracotta female figurines thought to be goddesses, and suchlike. (110)

It is a sad fact of history that this exciting and promising beginning in the Indus Valley eventually declined and almost died out. Civilization in the Middle East continued to flourish and spread, but in the Indus Valley it declined, and by the end of the third millennium B.C.E. the once great cities were mostly abandoned and disintegrating. What happened? There are many possible explanations for this decline. One of the more plausible theories concerns the slow but relentless destruction of the natural environment by the generations of people who lived in these cities and towns. As the population continuously grew, and the resources of the environment were plundered without being restored, the time must eventually have come when urban life would no longer have been tenable. (Sound familiar?)

The decline of the Harappan period was apparently accompanied by a deep cultural depression, but it was to be relatively short-lived. A new age was about to dawn in North India, and its defining feature would be the composition of the Vedas. The cities of the Harappan period were in their final stage of decline around 1900 B.C.E. Scholars are in pretty general agreement that the composition of the Vedas began sometime around 1500 B.C.E. (though it should be noted that some would put this date as late as 1200 B.C.E.). The big question, then, is: What accounts for the rise of this new cultural age, the "Vedic Age"? Was the Vedic Age basically a continuation of the Harappan Age, albeit with far less emphasis on urban development? Were the Vedas a composite expression of the religious beliefs and practices of the Harappan city builders? Were the gods featured in the Vedas the same gods worshipped by the pre-Vedic Dravidians? Were the creators of the Vedas the biological and linguistic descendents of the Harappans?

The majority of Indian scholars would certainly answer these questions in the affirmative. In fact, they are virtually unanimous in agreeing that the early history of India proceeded smoothly from the Harappan Age into the Vedic Age: Both were created by an indigenous people who spoke a similar language and worshipped the same gods. In this scenario, the Vedas are the spiritual capstone of a native religious tradition that had been evolving for ages in India.

THE THEORY OF INDO-ARYAN MIGRATIONS

There are some reasonable arguments in support of the above position. Nevertheless, a large majority of non-Indian scholars hold to a very different position. The majority view holds that large numbers of a nonindigenous pastoral people, known as Indo-Aryans, migrated into the northwestern part of the Indian subcontinent in successive waves beginning in the early part of the third millennium B.C.E. These Indo-Aryan people, though presumably opposed by the indigenous population, were ultimately successful in settling permanently throughout much of North India, and established themselves in a dominant position in relation to the native peoples. Their Indo-Aryan culture and their language (Sanskrit)—though much influenced by, and to some degree mixed with, the native culture and languages—became the dominant elements in defining the character of the Vedic Age.

Indeed the majority of scholars worldwide accept the plausibility of the Indo-Aryan Migration Theory, but certainly not all do. As mentioned, within India itself the majority of scholars reject the migration theory in favor of what is known as the Indigenous Aryanism Theory. This can be explained in part as an understandable reaction to the earlier expression of the Indo-Aryan Migration Theory, which has come to be know as the theory of the "Aryan Conquest." Given the tremendous importance of the Vedas to this study, I feel that it is appropriate that we briefly examine this controversy regarding the origin of the Vedas, India's first readable historical written record. And what's more, it is a fascinating story.

Let's begin the story with a now-famous quote from an address delivered in 1786 to the Royal Asiatic Society of Bengal, India. The speaker was the Indologist, and Judge of the High Court of the British East India Company, Sir William Jones:

> The Sanskrit language [the language of the Vedas], whatever may be its antiquity, is of a wonderful structure; more perfect than the Greek, more copious than the Latin, and more exquisitely refined than either, yet bearing to both of them a stronger affinity, both in the roots of verbs and in the form of grammar, than could possibly have been produced by accident; so strong, indeed, that no philologer could examine them all three, without believing them to have sprung from some common source which, perhaps, no longer exists. (quoted in Bryant, 15)

This address helped to open the eyes of linguists to the amazing fact that a huge family of related languages exists, stretching all the way from Europe across parts of the Middle East, and on to northern India. Sanskrit, for example, was seen to be a distant cousin of English. The name given to this aggregation was the Indo-European language family.* But a family implies a family tree, and a family tree implies a time and place where and when it all had a beginning. And so began the long search for the *Ursprache* and the *Urheim*, the mother tongue and the original source place of it all. Many theories have risen, and fallen, over the years; the search continues still. But one general theory, much respected by scholars, deserves our special attention. It does a good job of answering many of the most vexing questions. We have to go back in time a bit, though, to pick up the beginning of its thread.

The last great ice age ended roughly 10,000 years ago. Before that time, it had been impossible for human migrations to penetrate very far north of the subtropics. But as the ice retreated, the climate became milder, and the animal herds roamed farther north, human populations followed. Migrations would eventually radiate throughout all of Eurasia, but the area that most concerns us is the region north of the Caucasus Mountains, between the Black and Caspian seas and the vast grasslands that spread out just above these two seas in what is today southern Russia and Kazakhstan.

This broad region, known as the Pontic-Caspian area, was settled by a pastoral, nomadic people, who, though widely distributed, were presumably interconnected enough to maintain contacts among themselves and communicate using a common language. It is widely believed (though by no means universally) that it was this rough language that was destined to become the mother tongue of the Indo-European language family. This parent language, which no longer exists, is referred to as proto-Indo-European. Today, its descendants are the native languages of more than two billion people:

> We may imagine, then, that during the Mesolithic some of the communities occupying the banks of the great river valleys of the southern part of the European USSR [Russia] probably spoke languages that would later evolve into Proto-Indo-European. (Mallory, 187)

These proto-Indo-Europeans were a hardy, pastoral folk. Although it would seem that they raised a little barley from time to time, agriculture was not to their liking; they preferred the nomadic lifestyle, following the herds. In time, they came to possess herds of their own. They were horse breeders—which would give them a tremendous advantage in later struggles—and they raised cattle. At that time, wealth was measured in horses and cattle. This way of life bred a strong and adaptable people. With the passage of time, the very success of their way of life bred its own set of problems, most notably overpopulation. Their solution would be the same as countless other nomadic peoples facing the same problem: migration.

For centuries, slow-moving waves of migration rolled out into the regions adjoining the ancestral herding lands. Later migrants would often push the descendants of earlier migrations farther on. Beginning in the Balkan Peninsula, wave after wave eventually filled all of the European subcontinent. The Greeks of ancient times were their descendants; so too were the Romans, the Celts, the Slavs, and the Germanic people. Other proto-Indo-European

---

* There are a great many cognates of Sanskrit words in English. The Sanskrit *namen*, for example, becomes "name" in English. *Tri* (three) is related to "triple." *Dama* in Sanskrit becomes "domus" in Latin and "domestic" in English. *Pad* (foot) becomes "pedis" in Latin and "pedal" in English. My favorite is *hekki*, the Sanskrit word for "hiccup" (but that's probably just onomatopoeia).

peoples migrated south through the mountain passes and the eastern shore of the Caspian Sea into Asia Minor and the high plateau of Iran and Afghanistan. Where possible, they continued the old herding way of life. Where this was not possible, they adapted to the new conditions. It was from the Iranian-Afghan highlands that the migration routes would have continued on into northern India. Their route would undoubtedly have followed the Khyber Pass, that famous pass through the Hindu Kush mountains that has witnessed the passage of so many would-be conquerors over the ages. Those Indo-Europeans who allegedly migrated into India are known specifically as the Indo-Aryans. And this is where the story becomes a bit problematic. What follows may help to explain why the majority of Indian scholars support the alternative explanation, the Indigenous Aryanism Theory.

In the nineteenth century, when so much of the early research in this subject was being done, the nations of western Europe were enjoying their golden age of imperialism. Almost every part of the globe was divided up into one or another European colonial empire, and that included the subcontinent of India. European ethnocentrism was a fact of life, and the migration theory felt its effect. An epic story came to be widely accepted in the West that was known as the theory of "The Aryan Conquest." What it came down to was essentially a myth in which fair-skinned "superior" warriors, genetically related to Europeans, invaded North India en masse and conquered an "inferior" dark-skinned population, even though the native people greatly outnumbered the Aryan invaders:

> The theory of an invasion is an invention. The invention is necessary because of a gratuitous assumption which underlies the Western theory. The . . . assumption is that the Aryans were a superior race. This theory has its origin in the belief that the Aryans are a European race and as a European race it is presumed to be superior to the Asiatic ones . . . Knowing that nothing can prove the superiority of the Aryan race better than invasion and conquest of the native races, the Western writers have proceeded to invent the story of the invasion of India by the Aryans, and the conquest by them of the Dasas and Dasyus. (Ambedkar, quoted in Bryant, 62)

According to the theory of the Aryan Conquest, the Aryans, in the form of a great conquering horde, moved eastward from the Indus Valley into the great Ganges plain of North India. Presumably they would have followed the great river courses that eventually merged in the Ganges itself. Here the scattered agricultural population would have been no match at all for the invaders. Surely they would have tried as best they could to defend their homes, but they could only hope at best to slow down the advance. The conquest of the Indian lands was a campaign spread over at least a full century. Several generations of Aryan warriors were involved before it all was over. But the broad picture is one of an invincible Aryan horde pushing relentlessly through the entire range of the Indus and Ganges valleys, plundering and conquering everything in its path.

The Aryan Conquest theory likes to picture the invaders as epic warriors. When the Aryans had to fight for possession of new land, they proved themselves to be most formidable. In a fight they had a number of advantages. They were, to begin with, a very hardy people, used to a rough and simple life. The kin group structure of Aryan society gave them a ready-made military organization and a rough-and-ready chain of command. They had the horse and could put their mobility to good advantage. The Aryan warriors harnessed the horse, sometimes two horses, to a lightweight two-wheeled chariot. Two men rode in the chariot; one was the highly skilled driver. The other—with both hands free for fighting—attacked the enemy with the deadly fire of his bow and arrows.

The Aryans loved the bow; they preferred it to the sword, the lance, or any other type of weapon. To an Aryan warrior, his bow was a close friend, and he gave it a name. Arjuna, a central figure of the *Bhagavad Gita*, referred to his miraculous bow as "Gandiva." From the *Rig Veda* comes these stirring words:

> With Bow let us win the contest and violent battles.
> The Bow ruins the enemy's pleasures;
> With Bow let us conquer all the corners of the world.
>
> She comes all the way up to your ear
> Like a woman who wishes to whisper something,
> Embracing her dear friend.
>
> Humming like a woman,
> The bowstring stretched tight on the bow
> Carries you safely across in the battle. (*RV*:6.75-2,3; p. 236)

The Aryan Conquest theory holds that the Sanskrit-speaking Aryans set themselves up as an elite class ruling over the humble native people, who were organized into an efficient hierarchy of subject castes. These conquerors, the bearers of a superior culture, went on, in time, to compose the Vedas in their own ancestral language, Sanskrit. It was like an earlier version of the story of the European conquest of South America.

The theory of the Aryan Conquest took form well before the excavations that revealed the existence of the Indus Valley Civilization. After its discovery, it would indeed be difficult to continue to maintain that the semi-barbarian "Aryans" were the bearers of a superior culture. The theory was modified by some to picture the Indus cities as old and decadent, and the Aryan invaders simply delivered the *coup de grace*, finishing them off before moving on to the completion of the conquest. Given the long popularity of this theory, is it any wonder that educated Indians have rejected it and instead support a theory of indigenous development that led to the creation of the Vedas?

Opponents of the theory argue that not only is there no solid evidence for an Aryan Conquest, there is also no logical need for it. They argue that the theory of the Aryan Conquest was born of nineteenth-century European ethnocentrism. However appealing this explanation may have been to nineteenth-century Westerners, it simply isn't true. In the words of Aurobindo Ghosh, "It is indeed coming to be doubted whether the whole story of an Aryan invasion through the Punjab is not a myth of the philologists." (Aurobindo, 11)

So, where *is* the truth? Well, this field of research is still a work in progress. But, as mentioned before, in recent decades, something of a consensus has taken shape among non-Indian scholars that bears up pretty well. The modern synthesis, if I may call it that, holds that although the general picture of the "Aryan Conquest" is a gross exaggeration, some aspects of it are in fact historically accurate.

Linguistic descendants of the proto-Indo-European parent stock did indeed migrate to places distant from the source place (whether that was the region north of the Caucasus or someplace else). Based on evidence of strong similarity of language, it is surmised that a large part of this migration branched into an Iranian group and an Afghan group. Out of the Afghan group, some Indo-European speakers, now referred to as Indo-Aryans, continued to move farther eastward, entering the northwestern part of the Indian subcontinent near the beginning of the second millennium B.C.E., perhaps as early as 1900 B.C.E. But, far from being an organized military horde bent on conquest, these Indo-Aryans, for the most part, would have been pastoral folk in search of nothing more than a better place to live. This is not to say that they were entirely pacifist, not at all; the Indo-Aryans were presumably as capable as anyone of putting up a good fight when that was called for. They had the horse and formidable weapons. The important point, though, is that they were not there in order to fight and conquer, but simply to take advantage of whatever opportunities might exist in their search for a better place to live:

> The more acceptable theory is that groups of Indo-Aryan speakers gradually migrated from the Indo-Iranian borderlands and Afghanistan to northern India, where they introduced the language. The impetus to migrate was a search for better pastures, for arable land and some advantage from an exchange of goods. The migrations were generally not disruptive of settlements and cultures. (Thapar, 105–106)

One thing, though, is clear. These migrating Indo-Aryans were in no way bearers of a "superior" culture, as implied in the original Aryan Conquest theory. The indigenous people, far from being uncivilized "lesser" beings, had created one of the world's earliest urban cultures, as we have seen. Excavations at Mohenjo-Daro and other sites in the Indus Valley reveal that this Indus Civilization, evidence of which stretches back to at least 3000 B.C.E., was the equal of early civilizations in Mesopotamia and Egypt. Quite obviously, the native ability to create the works of civilization was present in the Indian people themselves.

But, significantly, the Indo-Aryans would have serendipitously happened upon the scene at a time very auspicious for themselves. North India would have been deeply into the final decline of the Indus Valley Civilization at this time. One can easily imagine that it was a time of troubles for North India, much like western Europe experienced in the last days of the Roman Empire. And, continuing with this comparison, the Indo-Aryans might well have played a role similar to that of the Germanic barbarian tribes that overran much of what had recently been Roman provinces in the fifth century C.E. In better days, they would never have been able to get away with it. The bottom line is that these migrants did manage, one way or another, to insinuate themselves throughout much of North India, and, given the disorder of the time, they were able (like the Germanic barbarian tribes in Europe) to achieve a position of dominance over the indigenous people in many places.

To sum up, the modern synthesis holds that the motive force behind the emergence of the Vedic Age, and the creators of the Vedas, was a nonindigenous population of Sanskrit-speaking Indo-Aryans whose not-so-distant ancestors had migrated into North India during the early part of the second millennium B.C.E. and who, over a period of several centuries, had gained a dominant social position throughout much of North India.

Like so many topics in history and philosophy, this one is rich with controversy. The modern synthesis, though accepted as highly plausible by the great majority of scholars in the field, is not *proven* to be correct, and possibly it never will be. Will the mystery ever be resolved? *Can* it be resolved? Possibly it can. There is one thing that could pretty well settle the debate—the still undeciphered script of the Indus Valley Civilization. What kind of language, if any, do those strange looking signs represent? The answer to that question could bring closure to the argument once and for all. If the language spoken by the Harappans was an Indo-European one (an early form of Sanskrit, for example), the exponents of Indigenous Aryanism would appear to have carried the day. But, if that language turns out to be a non-Indo-European one, as the great majority of scholars worldwide expect it to be, the theory of Indigenous Aryanism would seem to have been fully and finally refuted. In the words of the Indologist Edwin Bryant: "If it turns out to be a non-Indo-European language, then the Indigenous Aryan critique simply becomes another curious but closed chapter in the history of the Indo-European homeland problem." (301) . . . Stay tuned.

I hope that this brief examination of the controversy has given you an idea of the importance of the background of the Vedas, and how much is still to be learned about that background. Whatever the case may be, some things seem to be beyond controversy. Following the decline of the Indus Valley cities, Indian culture underwent profound changes. And out of these changes, including the rise of the Sanskrit language, the historical social order took form. Varna, the caste system, would become its most defining element.

VARNA: THE CASTE SYSTEM

India is famous for its caste system. Legally, though, it is now a thing of the past. After being the defining element of Indian social life for at least three millennia, the caste system was formally renounced in the Indian constitution of 1949. Discrimination due to caste is now against the law in India. The old ways die slowly, though; outside the cities, life goes on more or less as it has for ages. During the Vedic Age, Indian society came to be divided into four great "castes." The word *caste* is something of a misnomer; "classes" would be a more accurate way of putting it. And this process is certainly not unique in history; virtually all evolving societies develop a class system, and in the early days it's pretty similar from one society to another.

At the top is the aristocratic class, the warrior nobility who control the land, the weapons, and most of the wealth. In India, this class, or "caste," was known as the *Kshatriya*. Presumably it emerged out of the tribal leaders among the original groups that had migrated into the subcontinent and established themselves, in northern India at least, as the dominant population.

Sharing top honors with the Kshatriyas, in fact enjoying an even higher status, was the *Brahmana* caste; these were the priests, the Brahmins, a caste unto themselves.* Above the Kshatriyas were the Brahmins; below the Kshatriyas were the *Vaishyas*. This was the caste of the commoners, the artisans and tradesmen. The Vaishyas, also presumed to be descended from the original Indo-Aryans, were very numerous, and over time they came to be divided into a huge number of subcastes arranged in a hierarchy of its own. A "sub-caste" is known as a *jati*, which is a community of related families sharing a common type of work. In the West, the word *caste* is often used when jati would be more appropriate. It would seem that every conceivable kind of work, no matter how specialized, came to be a jati unto itself. And the members of that jati, wherever they lived, inherited an exclusive monopoly in that area of work. This is somewhat similar to the guild system of medieval Europe, but in India the system was much more inflexible. Over time, many non-Indo-Aryans were incorporated into the Vaishya caste for practical reasons.

---

* The Brahmins were members of the *Brahmana* caste. Either "Brahmin" or "Brahman" is correct spelling. In this work, I will use "Brahmin" so as not to cause confusion with the name "Brahman," which will be used in a different context.

These three classes ("castes," if you will)—the Brahmana, the Kshatriya, and the Vaishya—together constituted a privileged elite known as the *arya-varna*. Members of the arya-varna referred to themselves as *dvija*, "twice born," meaning that young men underwent a "coming of age" ceremony by which they were initiated into manhood and full participation in the spiritual life of their caste. The symbol of this "second birth" was the "sacred thread," worn over the shoulder and upper part of the body, somewhat like a tiny sash. In modern times, it's usually easy to identify members of the Brahmin caste because they proudly wear the thread, often in full view. Originally, though, the Kshatriyas and the Vaishyas also received and wore the thread. For Kshatriyas, it was a bow string; for Vaishyas, a simple hemp string. It is presumed that the arya-varna were the immediate descendants of the Indo-Aryans, who had migrated into India and success-fully established themselves in the upper echelons of the social order.

This is where the similarity to other class systems, such as that of medieval Europe, begins to break down. The reason for this is that below the arya-varna, far below, were the members of a fourth great caste, the *Shudra*. The Shudra caste was more technically known as the *dasyu-varna*, which leads to the speculation that the Shudras, vast in numbers, were the descendants of the survivors of the indigenous population, reduced to the status of a lowly servant class, working for the Indo-Aryan upper castes who now controlled the land and the means of production. These were the folks engaged in tilling the land; they were essentially reduced to a class of landless serfs. Theirs was a life of never-ending toil in the heat and dust of land that belonged to feudal overlords. The Shudras were referred to as the "once born," meaning simply that they were not entitled to a ritual "second birth" and were thus forbidden to have any part in the Aryan religious sacrifice. Shudras were not allowed to study the Vedas. In fact, if a Shudra were even to overhear the chanting of Vedic hymns, the penalty could be death. The Shudras enjoyed little in the way of rights; members of the arya-varna castes could even kill a Shudra without penalty under law:

> The classic threefold Indo-European tribal division into priests, warriors, and commons quickly proved inadequate. While those three classes became the "twice born" brahmana, kshatriya, and vaishya varnas, the conquered Harappans were included quite early into the system as only once-born shudras. Or at least so we assume, for the origins of the shudras remain obscure and can only be inferred from their second-class legal status and from the fact that they were defined by the brahmans as "servants" of the twice-born who could be "exiled at will" or " slain at will." Shudras were not permitted to hear or study the Vedic hymns, which were considered potent magic and reserved for twice-born ears only; indeed, later legal texts prescribed "pouring molten lead" into the ears of any shudra caught secretly listening to Vedic mantras. (Thapar, 41–42)

Another reason for concluding that the Shudra caste was made up of the indigenous population is that the Sanskrit word *varna*, by which name the caste system was known, bears the meaning of "color" (among other things). This leads to the speculation that the caste system was based on skin color—the relatively light-skinned Indo-Aryans at the top and the brown-skinned Shudras at the bottom. The Shudras, though, were not exactly at the bottom of the system. Below the Shudras was a class of people known as the *candalas*, the so-called "untouchables," or "pariahs." These unfortunates, possibly made up of the very dark-skinned descendants of the most ancient inhabitants of the subcontinent, were so despised that they were permitted only to engage in what were considered to be the most filthy and degrading occupations, such as dealing with dead animals and the tanning of leather. As a rule, they were required to live outside the villages so as not to "pollute" the inhabitants. In many places, they were only allowed outside their hovels during the night-time so that they cast no shadows. It was believed that even encountering the shadow of a candala caused defilement, and the victim of this horrible experience must immediately undergo an elaborate purification ritual. (Can it get any worse than that?) The lowly candalas were so far down the hierarchy that they were not even accepted in the caste system at all. They were "outcastes," regarded as being barely even human:

> As more and different tribal peoples were absorbed within the spreading boundaries of Aryan society, however, it soon became necessary to add still a lower class, one whose habits or occupations were so strange or "unclean" that shudras did not wish to "touch" them. Hence the emergence of those beyond the pale of the four-varna system: the untouchables, also called "fifths" (panchamas), or outcastes. (Thapar, 41–42)

It's hard to imagine being more dehumanized than the candalas. Even though the prohibitions against the candalas have been outlawed in modern times, life is not especially kind to this large part of the population. Ghandi felt great pity for the candalas (generally referred to as *dalits* in modern times). He called them his "little angels," and tried hard to improve their lot in life and change public attitudes regarding them.

To recap, varna (the caste system) consists of four great classes: the privileged *arya-varna*, which includes the Brahmins, the Kshatriyas, and the Vaishyas. And far below the arya-varna is the *dasyu-varna*, made up of the great toiling Shudra caste. And still much farther below, the *candala*, the much-abused "untouchables," allowed to do only the most loathsome kinds of work. Within each caste, especially among the Vaishyas, were myriad subcastes (known as *jatis*), which were based on extended family relationships.

The caste was much more than just an economic thing, an area of work. The caste was economic, religious, political, social; it was a little world unto itself. One's whole life was bound up in the caste (or to be more precise, one's *jati*). All marriages were arranged by the family and only among other families within one's caste. The men performed the work of the caste and no other; there was no such thing as social mobility. The concept of "bettering oneself" was unknown and would have seemed absurd. In times following the Vedic Age, it was believed that the only way to move to a higher jati was to die and be reborn in it. And that was believed to be guaranteed to those who accepted the present life and did the best they could.

Varna, the caste system, certainly encouraged a stagnant and inflexible social order, but there are some positive things to be said about it. For one thing, it guaranteed a very stable social order. The individual, though presumably lacking the excitement of a more independent life, was at least spared its anxieties. No one had to worry about the future; the future was all laid out for a person from the time he or she was born. There was no anxiety about finding the right job, or the right spouse, or the right kind of home. The caste system sank deep roots in India. In some fundamental way, in fact, the caste system probably grew from very ancient Dravidian roots. There is some evidence that the candala class had already existed in their suppressed state in pre-Vedic times.

In the caste hierarchy, one part of the population was special, very special. This group of families was the highest of all of the castes, higher even than the Kshatriyas. These were the Brahmins, and no one except the gods were above them. The reason for their lofty status was that the Brahmins were the priests. They were man's link to the gods, and the entire society depended on them.

THE BRAHMIN CASTE

The consolidation of Brahmana, the Brahmin caste, is an example of the kind of development that takes form within virtually every early human culture. A special group of individuals, call them priests or shamans, become the custodians of the sacred rites and traditions of the community. Seen through coldly practical modern eyes, these individuals might seem to be rather like parasites; they are not fighters or producers. And yet the priests, or shamans, are held in the highest esteem. In all cultures they have been supported, protected, and honored. Why? What is it that makes this special class so special? What do they do for the community that the others can't do perfectly well for themselves? Let's take a moment to look at this question.

The men and women of an early society—such as the early Hindu society—would be acutely aware of the play of the forces of nature in their daily lives. By necessity they lived "close to nature." Unlike those of us who enjoy the way of life of modern times, they would indeed have been aware of how much they were at the mercy of the natural environment. (And we in modern times may be in for some hard lessons in that regard ourselves!) Sometimes things went well—the weather was fair and the food supply abundant—and sometimes things did not go well at all.

Perhaps it was the very fact that men and women of earlier times possessed a technology that gave them some small control which made them aware of how much more they did *not* control. But—and here is the critically important point—they would inevitably conclude that *somebody* did! Why make this assumption? Well, consider how the forces of nature operate; seen from the grand view, they are not chaotic and unpredictable. On the large scale, nature operates with great order and regularity. Patterns are the rule, not the exception, and from this comes the predictability without which there could be no science. The sun always rises in the east and moves with certain predictability throughout the daily cycle. So too for the moon, the tides, the seasons, and the life cycle of all things. Deer produce baby deer, and ducks produce baby ducks. A deer never gives birth to a baby duck, and the sun never rises in the west.

The point is that the regularity and predictability of the operations of the forces of nature can be seen to imply a grand order that simply cannot be explained by the working of blind chance. Modern science may take a different view, but to the minds of thinking men and women of the distant past, order in nature implied, of necessity, an order-giver. And thus out of the fertile human imagination were born the gods.

In this view, a god is simply a being who, by common consent, is the one responsible for the operation of any one or more of the forces of nature. There will be a god for rain, a god for wind, a god for the sun, a god for the moon, a god for birth, a god for death, and so on. In a fully developed pantheon, there must be some god for every one of the myriad forces of nature. The "person" of the god need not be conceived in human form. Very often the god was imagined in the form of some animal, whose character in some way suggested the particular power of the god—a hawk, for example, to guide a celestial body, or a snake, whose ability to molt suggested renewed life. But of course many of the gods, especially the most powerful, were created in the image and likeness of man.

So, in the worldview of ancient India, nature was organized into a vast hierarchy. At the bottom of the order was the world of brute animals. These had a hierarchy within themselves, ranging from the simplest creatures to the greatest, such as cattle and monkeys. Next came the world of human beings. The caste system with its myriad gradations was the reflection of the natural hierarchy among humankind. At the top of the worldly pyramid were the gods. These too were organized into greater and lesser. The very greatest of the gods were synonymous with the tip of the pyramid. In later times, this "pyramid" would take the form of the mythical Mount Meru, an idealized golden mountain at the center of the universe, whose summit was the abode of the gods. Mount Meru was (and is) an analogue par excellence for the hierarchical order of nature: the gods at the top, humankind at the base, and the roots of the mountain representing the gradations of the animal kingdom—everything in its assigned place.

The immortal gods ruled their individual domains, each one manipulating that aspect of the natural order over which he or she held power. What they did they did for their own reasons; they were incomparably greater than the miserable creatures beneath them, from which they remained serenely aloof. At least this would seem to be the logical state of affairs in the early part of the story.

The difference between gods and humans was as great as the difference between insects and human beings. Consider, for example, the relationship between ants and ourselves. It is not that we despise ants, nor do we want them to suffer. It's just that we regard ants to be so far below us that we tend to ignore them; we're unconcerned about the affairs of their daily lives. But we may assume that the affairs of their daily life are as important to them as ours are to us. We may assume that they do not feel indifferent when a great rainstorm threatens to flood their nest. At the risk of sounding a bit silly, I would like to continue this analogy in order to make the point.

If it were somehow possible for the ant colony to make contact with you—suppose that a certain few had learned how to send a message in Morse code—would you continue to remain aloof and uninterested in their affairs? Not likely. Most likely, you would be glad to use your powers to help them out in a time of need, especially if they were very nice about the way they asked for help. Presumably they could persuade you to go out and cover their nest during a downpour. People, like ants, were by and large at the mercy of the forces of nature. The gods controlled the forces of nature, and all too often seemed to be unconcerned about the effects on the lives of human communities. If only there were a way; *if only* there were a way to somehow make contact with the gods and persuade them to use their powers over the forces of nature in ways that would be beneficial to mankind—or, at the very least, to exercise their powers to prevent the worst disasters. If only this were possible, human beings could be free at last from the tyranny of fear. But how? Enter the priests.

The Brahmins were the priests. It was their job to make contact with the gods. So long as they succeeded in making that contact, and reasonably often getting the desired results, it is easy to see why they would be held in such high esteem. Their importance was second to none. And, of course, the great majority of their contemporaries did not question that the Brahmins were in fact able to establish contact with the gods. It is what the people *believed* that counts; belief, not necessarily truth, is what inspires action. So how did the Brahmins make contact? What did the people see them do that accounts for this great faith in their abilities?

As in virtually all early societies, the performance of sacrifice was seen to be the reasonable way of attracting the attention of the gods. An offering was made to the gods, consumed by fire so that the smoke could carry the gift to the heavens. Surrounding the performance of the sacrifice would be a rite of some kind, which in time would become enshrined in tradition. Over the centuries, the Brahmins, too, evolved a great body of such tradition. There were appropriate rituals for everything imaginable.

Ritual, therefore, correctly performed, became the operative tool by means of which the Brahmins would make the all important contact with the gods, and, if correctly performed, persuade the gods (and even in some cases *compel* the gods) to exercise their powers on the community's behalf. It's no wonder that the performance of sacrificial ritual came to be a matter of obsessive interest among these people.

But what gave real power—real, sacred power—to the ritual ceremony were the prayers spoken by the Brahmin priests. Throughout the entire ceremony, the priests would loudly and passionately call upon the gods to witness and accept the sacrifice, to hear their prayers. Such prayers were designed to be sung, or chanted, in a long and repetitive fashion. These sacred chants constituted the real lifeblood of the ritual.

Over the centuries, the most beloved of these sacred chants were preserved in great collections that were committed to memory by the Brahmins and passed on from generation to generation. These collections came to be known as the Vedas. The Vedas laid out the prescription for correct performance of ritual and also the correct way of addressing the gods. The Brahmins created the Vedas, and they used the Vedas to establish their all-important connection with the gods.

Officiating at sacred ceremonies (which we shall look at shortly) was the most visible and active role of the Brahmin priests, but there was much more to the responsibilities of this caste as well. For one thing, kingship depended for its legitimacy on the Brahmin priesthood. Only the Brahmins, through the appropriate religious rites, could bestow divine right on the king. Also, in a much subtler way, it was the religious power and authority of the Brahmins that gave religious sanction to the institution of varna and its divisions. It was in dealing with the gods, though, that the Brahmin priesthood really earned its honored place at the top of the hierarchy.

Study Questions

1. In general terms, describe of the geography of the Indian subcontinent.
2. Who were the Dravidians?
3. What gives historical significance to Mohenjo-Daro and Harappa?
4. How is it that Sanskrit links the languages of Europe and India?
5. In general terms, describe the nature of the Indo-Aryan Migration Theory. Why were the Aryans so successful?
6. Why do many Indian scholars prefer the theory of Indigenous Aryanism to that of the Indo-Aryan Migration Theory?
7. Describe the general nature of the caste system. What were its positive and negative features?
8. What was (and is) the Brahmin caste? Why were the Brahmins held in such high esteem?
9. How did the Brahmins make contact with the gods?
10. What is the point of the story about ants and humans?

CHAPTER 2

Veda and the Vedas

As mentioned in Chapter 1, the word *Veda* is derived from the Sanskrit root *vid*, which means "to know." In the present context, it refers to knowledge of the highest sort, made available to all through the revelations of ancient seers. Ordinary truth emerges from the practical experience of the community, the stuff of daily life. It is added to by everyone over time. Veda, on the other hand, concerns matters of great moral and religious importance—the meaning of life and death, for example, and the proper relationship between gods and humans. Veda is sacred knowledge. By way of a rough analogy, we could say that in a Jewish or Christian community, knowledge about weather forecasting would be ordinary truth, but the Bible would be Veda.

Although it is probable that the roots of what would become the Vedas stretch far back into the distant past, the Vedas took on their mature form during the earliest historical period following the spread of the Sanskrit language in India, roughly between the years 1500 and 1000 B.C.E. This historical era is called the *Vedic Age*. With very few exceptions, the Vedas were produced by members of the Brahmin class and, in particular, by an elite group of scholars referred to as *rishis*. A rishi is a seer, an especially learned person who has become the teacher of others. Members of the Brahmin caste were the sole guardians and interpreters of the Vedas. Brahmins alone managed the great events at which the Vedas were chanted—events that were intended to result in a coming together of gods and humans.

The Vedas were organized into four great collections. There is much similarity among them, but each of the four has its own general emphasis. The earliest, and by far the most significant, is the *Rig Veda*. The *Rig Veda* is a long and loosely organized collection of hymns and chants associated with sacrifices to the various gods Composition of the *Rig Veda* probably began as early as 1500 B.C.E., but it's unlikely that it was organized into a comprehensive work until close to 1200 B.C.E.

The *Rig Veda* and the others that followed it were not meant to be literary works in the sense of epic books. It is an aggregation of *suktas* (hymns), each of which was a long collection of verses chanted aloud by Brahmin priests at sacrificial rites. When completed, the *Rig Veda* consisted of 1,028 separate suktas. These were in turn organized into ten megasections called *mandalas*. This kind of organization was an aid to memorizing, much needed before the advent of writing.

The groundwork for the great sacrificial rituals was laid down in the *Rig Veda*, but it was followed in time by other Vedas. Two other Vedas closely associated with the *Rig Veda* were the *Sama Veda* and the *Yajur Veda*. In the *Sama Veda,* certain verses of the *Rig Veda* were arranged for chanting in the form of song. The *Yajur Veda* was essentially a collection of formulas and instructions concerned with the correct arrangement of the ritual. It was essential that everything be done absolutely correctly.

The fourth of the Vedas is the *Atharva Veda*. It stands apart from the other three and was composed considerably later than the others. The *Atharva Veda* is mainly concerned with shamanistic formulas, spells, and mystical incantations. It is widely believed that pre-Aryan Dravidian traditions are "peeking through" in the *Atharva Veda*. Nonetheless, this too came to be part of the great sacrifice rituals, and a priest called the *Atharvan* had the role of incorporating the appropriate chants from this Veda.

Thus the Vedas—*Rig, Sama, Yajur,* and *Atharva*—provided the Brahmin priests with all the sacred verses they needed to properly conduct the great rituals of *yajna*, the Vedic sacrifice. The Vedas were their link to the gods. And, in the Vedas, the gods are endlessly praised, invoked, flattered; it sometimes gets a bit monotonous to the modern reader. But behind all the praise, of course, is the real point of it all—the request.

Let's not lose sight of what this grand ritual was all about; the gods had something the people wanted—power over the forces of nature. And the Vedic rituals were their way of persuading the gods to use that power in the "right" way. But we must not assume that men and women of the Vedic Age were a dismal lot living in a state of constant worry. On the contrary, they seem to have been an optimistic, energetic people. They worshipped the gods in order to maximize the good things of life. True, they knew the weight of fear, and they prayed for freedom from illness and drought. But most of the time they were beseeching the gods for long life, success in battle, lots of healthy children, abundant food and drink—that sort of thing. The overall impression is of a people who enjoyed life and wanted to get the most out of it.

For the most part, the Vedas are not concerned with what we would call philosophical matters; they are clearly religious works—but not *entirely* religious. Threaded throughout the Vedas are questions and speculations that are like the seeds from which the lush garden of Hindu thought will later grow. In other words, the Vedas are "square one."

YAJNA: THE VEDIC SACRIFICE

Our modern way of life is so scrubbed clean of ritual that it is difficult for us to imagine what life was like in earlier times when practically everything involved some sort of ritual. Vedic society, like most ancient cultures, was seemingly obsessed with ritual. There were ritual-laden ceremonies for virtually everything of significance in life: for coming of age, for marriage, for death, for planting the crops, for going to war, for preparing food, and on and on. Ritual touched just about everything in life. The head of the family might officiate at minor rituals, but really important rituals were reserved for the Brahmin priests.

For sheer drama and excitement, nothing could have surpassed the great ceremony *yajna*, the Vedic sacrifice. In a time of crisis, or perhaps on the occasion of some special celebration—when one or more of the gods was to be approached directly—the Brahmin priests could put together a very moving event. A sacred fire was the central element of these ceremonies, and therefore it is customary to refer to such an event as a Vedic Fire Sacrifice.

The place where the sacrifice was to occur was holy ground, a special piece of land presumably set apart from the living area of the community. In those early days, it was always an outdoor event; the familiar Hindu temple was still a thing of the distant future. It all began with the construction of a low platform made of mud bricks. This was the altar where the sacred fire would be located. Near the platform-altar, a great wooden stake was driven into the ground. The *Rig Veda* informs us that this sacred object would then be anointed and adorned with colorful ornaments. There is some evidence that this stake then became the fulcrum for a large circle etched in the ground, which was then highlighted with colored sand. The circle defined the sacred space, within which only the Brahmin priests were allowed to enter.

When all was ready, the ceremony would begin with the kindling of the sacred fire and the sounding of large conch shell horns. The fire was the heart of the sacrifice. It was believed to be the living presence of the god Agni. The offering of the sacrifice would be given into the center of the fire, the "mouth" of Agni, to be consumed in the flames and carried as smoke to the gods. The fire might be small, but more likely it was a roaring bonfire. In the *Rig Veda*, we find references to the fire as the "bellowing" of Agni.

The priests were dressed in their ceremonial robes, possibly including headdresses of antler or bull's horns. The Brahmin who conducted the sacrifice was called the *Hotri*. He was the high priest and was assisted by priests of lesser rank, including the *Udgatri*, who chanted verses from the *Sama Veda* and whose special function was to summon the gods to the celebration with the hypnotic beauty of his song. The Brahmins believed that certain musical tones held magical qualities. The *Udgatri* was skilled in droning for a very long time in these tones. Another priest, the *Adhvaryu*, held the responsibility for overseeing the whole production. In a sense, he was the stage manager, and as he went about his work, he chanted aloud verses from the *Yajur Veda*.

Yet another Brahmin, highly knowledgeable in the details of ritual procedure, actually presided over the ceremony, though he took no active part in it. He sat to the side and carefully observed everything, making sure that every detail was performed correctly. Correct performance was believed to be absolutely essential if the sacrifice was to be successful.

Before the fire, the victim of the sacrifice would be ritually sacrificed and some part of it given to the flames so that the spirit of the victim could be carried to the gods. The rest would be consumed by the participants. There is some evidence that human sacrifice was practiced in the early days, but it would seem that it was not the usual form. Noblemen of the Vedic Age were horse-breeding people and cattle-raisers. In their eyes, no sacrificial offering could be more valuable than a fine stallion or a bull. The ritual offering of a fine horse was known as *ashvamedha*. Given the great love that the Indo-Aryans felt for the horse, to sacrifice one would almost be on a par with human sacrifice. Only a king, successful in battle, was entitled to sponsor the ashvamedha. An excellent white stallion would be let loose to wander wherever it wanted for one year. It was followed by a group of warriors who made a note of where it traveled, for the king had a right to claim all of the land included in its wanderings. When the year was over, the horse was driven back to the place of sacrifice, where it was ritually killed and cut up in preparation for the ashvamedha. As a part of the ceremony, the king's wife would join the just-killed horse under a cover and simulate sexual intercourse with it.

This was high drama—the great mandala marked out on the sacred ground, the roaring fire at its center, the Brahmin priests in their spectacular costumes, the endless droning of the chants summoning the gods to the celebration. What a spectacle it must have been! And that, of course, is what it was all about: elevating consciousness from the mundane to the transcendental so as to make contact with the gods. It was the gods who held power over the forces of nature. Men lacked that power, but needed it. It was the job of the Brahmins to make contact with the gods and influence their use of power. Ritual sacrifice, prescribed in the Vedas, was the way to make that contact.

Soma

One more element in these rituals remains to be considered. The modern reader might find it somewhat surprising, but to the Vedic priests it was the all-important ingredient. It played a major part in many of their sacred rituals. They called it *soma*.

Soma was a drug, a very powerful drug that produced states of ecstasy and of wildly expanded consciousness. We don't know for sure what it was. There are some clues in the Vedas, but nothing that pins it down for sure. Soma went out of use after the Vedic Age, and the source plant may have become extinct. Among still-existing possibilities, modern research has focused on a variety of the fly agaric mushroom as the best candidate. This fungus, although potentially very poisonous, produces a compound similar to psilocybin and could very well have produced the states described in the Vedas.

Whatever it was, the Brahmin priests loved it—and so too, according to them, did the gods. There was great ritual in its preparation as well as in its consumption, all of it lovingly detailed in the *Rig Veda* and the *Sama Veda*. The Brahmins alone were entitled to use soma, though some of the precious liquid was shared with the gods, presumably by being dripped into the fire.

Use of the soma plant probably predates the Aryans in India. Soma was not a domesticated plant; it grew wild in hilly or mountainous country. Apparently, it was gathered only at night and, according to some, only by the light of the full moon. The Indologist A. L. Herman describes the method of its preparation:

> The plant was brought to the place where the soma ritual was to be carried out, and there it was washed and cleaned. Then the stalks of the plant were crushed in a stone mortar by a wooden pestle, and the bruised and crushed remains were laid between stones and pressed. As the pressing stones, or wooden boards, were brought together, the juices trickled out onto a cleansing sieve, usually lamb's wool. Next the juice was strained and, finally, consumed by the priest or priests. The priestly celebrants chanted exuberant hymns to the soma to accompany both the crushing and the pressing ceremonies, hymns which invited Indra to come to the sacrifice and partake of the sacred soma juice, and which ecstatically anticipated the drinking of the juice. (42)

Naturally the soma plant was considered sacred, and the name was applied not only to the plant, but also to the god, Soma, who was the personification of the spirit of the plant. After drinking the juice of the plant, the spirit temporarily inhabited a person and took over his consciousness. The Brahmin priests were convinced that soma was a vehicle—*the* vehicle—that could take them spiritually to the place where contact with the gods was possible. In the incredible ecstasy of soma, they were themselves like gods; soma made it possible for them to share in the divine mode of being—or so they believed. Thus it was that soma became the heart of the ritual, the vital link between gods and humans. Consider these verses from the *Rig Veda*:

> Drink thou of this (soma) . . . for power and rapture.
> The men, the pressing stones, the cows, the waters
> Have made this soma ready for thy drinking.
> We have drunk soma . . .
> And in the wild raptures of the juice . . .
> We have become immortal;
> We have attained the light and discovered the Gods. (Herman, 43)

Apparently it was not always an unmixed blessing. The bad trip was ever a worrisome possibility. The *Rig Veda* even seems to suggest the possibility of heart failure:

> Be kind and merciful to us, Soma;
> Be good to our heart, without confusing our powers in your whirlwind.
> King Soma, do not enrage us; do not terrify us;
> Do not wound our heart with your dazzling light. (*RV*: 8.79-7,8; p. 121)*

Soma became the *sine qua non* of the Vedic fire sacrifice. It produced ecstasy, and in this state of mind, the Brahmin priest truly believed that he had achieved freedom from the mundane plane and had ascended temporarily to the realm of the gods:

> These glorious drops that give me freedom have I drunk.
> Closely they knit my joints as straps secure a chariot.
> The soma brings wild delight . . .
> In the wild joy of soma the Gods wrought their glorious deeds. (Herman, 43)

The verses quoted above are but a small sampling of the almost endless paeans to the delights of soma found in the *Rig Veda* and the *Sama Veda*. So what are we to make of all of this? What was really going on at these gatherings of Brahmins?

One thing, I believe, is unarguable: the Brahmins did not take soma merely for the fun of it. No doubt they enjoyed it immensely, but to them it was a religious experience, not a social event. They were amazed beyond understanding that such an effect could be produced by consuming the juice of a simple little plant that grew wild in the hills. They reasonably concluded that the gods had infused the plant with a sacred nature, a spirit, and that that spirit could enter into them if they consumed the juice of the plant. They treated it with the greatest respect and limited its use solely to the sacred ceremony. In this they were much like other cultures, such as the Native Americans of the Southwest who use peyote for certain ritual purposes. The Brahmin priests believed that the state

---

*Unless otherwise noted, all excerpts from the *Rig Veda* are taken from O'Flaherty. The page number at the end of the citation refers to the page in the O'Flaherty book.

of mind produced by the soma was a sort of god-consciousness in which they could commune directly with the gods. After all, that was their job.

After the Vedic Age, the use of soma declined and eventually died out altogether in India. Men became interested in other ways of achieving transcendent consciousness. Whether or not the Vedic priests really spoke to the gods is not the point. They believed they did, and in connection with that belief, they created a vast corpus of ritual prayer that was passed on from generation to generation. They called it Veda, sacred knowledge, and it is the solid foundation stone from which the tradition of Indian thought would develop.

All of this drama was designed to attract the attention of the gods and make contact with them. So who were these gods that were such important characters in the lives of men and women of Vedic times? This would be the appropriate place for us to turn to a brief consideration of the major deities addressed in the Vedas.

THE VEDIC PANTHEON

Hindu mythology is an incredibly complex subject. There are a vast number of gods and goddesses, and their many stories are convoluted almost beyond imagining. But that fascinating story is not the subject of this study. My goal here is simply to introduce you to some of the major deities, ones that are prominently mentioned in the Vedas, and to include a sampling of pertinent verses from the *Rig Veda*.

In the Beginning

As you might expect, the creation story in Hinduism is wonderfully complex and allows for many variations. In its simplest form we can say that: In the beginning was the One, the Ultimate Reality, which took the form of a golden cosmic egg, or embryo. The embryo became the earth and the sky, the most fundamental dual aspects of the one reality. The earth was personified as Prithivi, the mother of all, and the broad and luminous sky was personified as Dyaus, the male counterpart of Prithivi. From Dyaus and Prithivi were born the principal gods and, indirectly, all other things.

So we see that at this most fundamental level the dual character of nature, male and female, is honored in the personifications of earth and sky. They were not regarded as being distinct. The earth and sky were said to be like two hemispheres that were joined at the horizon to become one whole. The underlying unity of the two was often expressed by joining the two names together into one name, Dyavaprithivi.

Principal Gods of the Vedic Pantheon

Over time, a vast number of gods and goddesses came to populate the Hindu pantheon. Fortunately, only a few of these were prominent enough to be mentioned in the Vedas. But even among the prominent ones, the roles are a little blurry. Each of the Greek and Roman gods seemed to have fairly precise responsibilities. But the Indian deities are more casual about who does what. Among the chief gods it almost seems that everybody does everything. One sometimes gets the feeling that the people of India were more concerned with the *personality* of the god than with his or her actual "job description."

AGNI   Agni, a son of Dyaus and Prithivi, is the god of fire. In fact, he is the personification of fire. As such, Agni is very special to humankind. You could even say that of all the gods,

Agni is the *most* special because his bright, warm presence is the center of every home and every ritual sacrifice. Whether he be a little candle flame or a roaring bonfire, Agni, the god of the long flowing red hair, is the friend and constant companion of men and women. It is fitting that the first of the ten "books" of the *Rig Veda* is dedicated to him.

Consider the importance of fire in the development of human society. At one time, our distant ancestors lived pretty much like other wild animals. The taming of fire changed all that. Fire—the mystifying and beautiful flame that gave warmth, and protection and light to the fearsome dark of night—opened the door to a new way of life, a *human* way of life. We can easily imagine that it was while grouped around the communal fire that our ancient relatives developed the arts of language, and shared their first thoughts about the mighty forces of nature. The mysterious essence of fire might well have been the first of nature's powers to be thought of as divine.

Agni was associated with the sun, the ultimate life-giving fire, and descends to the earth in the form of lightning, the most awesome and terrifying of nature's acts. Blazes started by lightning strikes—which the *Rig Veda* says "descends on trees like an angry bull"—were probably our distant ancestors' first encounters with living fire. What courage it must have taken to approach the fire and overcome the natural fear of it! From that time forward, it became a friend and a powerful helpmate.

The Brahmins felt especially close to Agni, for he was the priest of the gods, as well as the messenger. It was Agni that carried the oblation to the heavens. Agni was said to be always young because his spirit was renewed each time a fire was created. The kindling of the sacrificial fire was an elaborate ritual involving the rubbing together of two wooden sticks (no matches in those days).

Sometimes the fire was small, and sometimes it was not small at all; it was a huge roaring blaze. The sound alone must have been awesome. And Agni, the god of fire, was often symbolized as a great horned bull, roaring his message to the gods. The sacrifice would be consumed in the fire and taken in the rising smoke to the gods for which it was intended:

> To you, Agni, who shines upon darkness,
> We come, day after day, bringing our thoughts and homage.
> To you, the king of sacrifices, the shining guardian of Order,
> Be easy for us to reach, like a father to his son.
> Abide with us, Agni, for our happiness. (*RV*: 1.1. 7-9; p. 99)
> Now get dressed in your robes (of fire),
> Lord of powers and master of the sacrificial foods,
> And offer this sacrifice for us. (*RV*: 1.26. 1; p. 100)

Agni loved soma. Some would have been poured into the fire at the appropriate time in the ceremony:

> Let Agni's bellowings reach to heaven
> As piercing weapons to destroy the demons.
> His angry glare breaks forth in the ecstasy of Soma.
> The obstacles of the godless cannot hold him back. (*RV*: 5.2. 10; p. 103)

Agni's presence in the fire of ritual sacrifice was the most dramatic of his visitations, but certainly not the only one. Agni was, and still is, ubiquitous in Hindu culture. As the domestic fire, he is an honored guest in every home, and the funeral pyre at the time of cremation is a man or woman's final oblation to Agni.

INDRA   Indra, also a son of Dyaus and Prithivi, held the title of first among the gods, though he was certainly not a king or ruler over the other gods. Indra was an awesome god, much like Zeus in the Greek pantheon. He was identified with great strength and sexual prowess, and thus he was often associated symbolically with the stallion and the bull. Indra carried the *vajra* with him as the symbol of his power. This has often been identified as a thunderbolt, but in fact a vajra is a short metal rod with a stylized trident head at both ends. Whether or not this was meant to be seen as a thunderbolt is debatable. Perhaps this assumption is due to the resemblance of Indra to Zeus. According to some accounts, Indra killed his father, Dyaus, taking over his place, including his identification with the bull and stallion, and even making a consort of his own mother, Prithivi.

Indra's origins go far back into the tribal past. He was regarded as a great warrior god and remained the favorite deity of the Kshatriya warriors, who sought to be, like Indra, strong and courageous in battle:

> Ever young, Indra embodies all the virtues of youth: heroism, generosity, exuberance. He stands for action and service but also for the need of force which leads to power, to victory, and booty . . . [and what's more] Indra has numerous love affairs. Many instances are recorded of his lasciviousness, and his example is often referred to as an excuse for adultery. He sends celestial nymphs to disturb holy men and bring an end to the penances that give them a power which he fears. (Daniélou, 107–108)

Indra was tremendously generous if you found him in the right mood. Many were the sacrifices performed to Indra beseeching him to grant numerous sons and to increase material welfare. Perhaps most important of all was the need for Indra's help in time of drought. India is a land that has always known terrible recurring droughts. In times of such crisis, the sacrificial fires would light the sky. It was Indra who had destroyed the power of Vritra, the demon who caused drought by welling up the river waters in the mountains. It was Indra who brought the monsoon rains on which everything in life depended. No wonder he was chief among the gods. In the *Rig Veda*, appeals to Indra are more numerous than to any other of the gods. Consider this sample:

> Indra is sovereign lord of earth and heaven;
> Indra is lord of waters and mountains.
> Indra is master of those who prosper and the wise;
> Indra must be invoked at work and at rest.
> Greater than days and nights;
> The Giver of all is greater than the earth and the ocean's waters,
> Greater than the limit of the earth and the wind's expanse,
> Greater than all rivers and all our lands;
> Greater than all of these is Lord Indra. (*RV*: VI.40.1,2,4) (Herman, 34)

Indra, like the other gods, was no stranger to the delights of soma. It would seem that he especially was fond of the experience:

> They are pressing out the impetuous, exhilarating Soma juices
> For you, Indra. Drink them!

They are cooking bulls for you; you will eat them, generous Indra,
When they summon you with food. (*RV*: 10.28.2,3; p. 146)
Wildly excited like a bull, Indra took the Soma for himself
And drank the extract from the three bowls in the three day Soma ceremony.
(*RV*: 1.32.3; p. 149)

VARUNA   Varuna was much like Indra; they were equally ancient, and their powers were almost indistinguishable. But where Indra was more responsible for warring and "making things happen," Varuna's job was more a matter of "maintaining," especially maintaining the great Order of Nature.

It was believed that everything in nature behaved in accordance with an inner natural law known as *rita*. Varuna was responsible for maintaining rita, and as such, he was present everywhere, pervading everything. When applied to human behavior, rita becomes the inner moral law that properly guides all action. Thus, Varuna was the supreme maintainer of all law, natural and moral. Varuna watched over the affairs of men and punished those who violated the sacred law of rita:

> Keep fear away from me, Varuna,
> And hold fast to me, O emperor of Order [rita].
> Set me free from anguish
> As one would free a calf from a rope.
> I cannot bear to live apart from you,
> Not even for the blink of an eye. (*RV*: 2.28.6; p. 218)

SURYA   Naturally the sun, ultimately the most important of all of the elements of nature, would be personified as a god. The reason that Surya, the sun god, is not chief among the gods is that it is not the sun itself, but *power over* the sun that was seen to be most important. Power is held by such as Indra, Varuna, and Agni. But Surya, who guides the sun in its daily path, is still a highly significant god, and verses directed to him are among the most beautiful and poetic in the *Rig Veda*:

> His brilliant banners draw upwards the god who knows all creatures,
> So that everyone may see the sun.
> The Constellations, along with night, steal away like thieves,
> Making way for the sun who gazes on everyone.
> The rays that are his banners have become visible from the distance,
> Shining over mankind like blazing fires.
> Crossing space, you are the maker of light, seen by everyone, O Surya;
> You illumine the whole wide realm of space. (*RV*: 1.50.1-4; p. 189)

USHAS   Ushas, the goddess of dawn, is one of the few female deities of high status in Vedic times. The Indo-Aryans, whose influence is so much to be seen in the Indian pantheon, were originally a nomadic, warrior society. Like their distant cousins who settled in Greece, they were a male-dominated people, and this was reflected in their gods. All of the male gods did, however, have wives, which are generally referred to as "consorts." Sometimes these consorts were influential, but all in all, the Vedic goddesses get pretty short shrift in the Vedas. Nevertheless, Ushas is much beloved, and verses dedicated to her in the *Rig Veda* go beyond even those praising Surya in poetic beauty. The Indologist V. M. Aptel puts it this way: "In the case of Usas, the goddess of dawn, the personification is light, the poet never losing sight of the beautiful physical phenomena behind the deity."

> Gaily attired like a dancer with a garment of light, she rises in the east and exhibits her graces. She is ever-youthful, being born again and again. Her association with the sun is naturally very close, He is her lover, but as she precedes him, she is also said to be his mother. She is the sister of the night. (in Majumdar, 372)

In the *Rig Veda,* it is put this way:

> Like a dancing girl, Usas puts on bright ornaments;
> She uncovers her breasts as a cow reveals her swollen udder.
> Creating light for the whole Universe,
> Dawn has opened up the darkness as cows break out from their pen.
> Her brilliant flame has become visible once more:
> She spreads herself out, driving back the formless black abyss.
> As one sets up the stake in the sacrifice,
> Anointing and adorning it with colored ornaments,
> So the daughter of the sky sets up her many-colored light. (*RV*: 1.92.4,5; p. 179)

RUDRA Almost the extreme opposite of Ushas was the god Rudra. Whereas Ushas was light and delicate and very feminine, Rudra was dark and fearsome and stormy-tempered. Like Indra, Rudra was a god associated with the storm clouds that brought the life-giving monsoon rains. The reason for this duplication is that Rudra was presumably a major Dravidian god of very ancient origins who was simply incorporated into the emerging pantheon of gods with Sanskrit names. We know that the Dravidians had worshipped a god of storms who carried the thunderbolt and was known as the "Red God," and the Sanskrit root of Rudra is *rud*, which means red. A rain-giver would be too important to pass up, so he may have been taken into the family and merely given a new Sanskrit name. But he was definitely not one of the group. Rudra had few, if any, friends among the gods or men. He lived away from the others; the mountains of the north were his haunt.

Rudra was the only member of the divine pantheon who could sometimes show a malevolent streak. True, Rudra could bring the life-giving rain, but sometimes, for no apparent reason at all, he would send the rain as fierce storms that indiscriminately devastated the countryside. The raging typhoons and floods of India were blamed on the unpredictable ferocity of Rudra's temperament. The people of Bangladesh know Rudra all too well. Rain, the very thing that made life possible, was also the thing that sometimes devastated life. Rudra, the personification of this dichotomy, united within himself both the beneficent and the dangerous aspects of nature. To Vedic man, Rudra represented the unconquered and unpredictable character of raw nature.

Rudra was a fearsome god, dark and unpredictable; he was the embodiment of wildness in the male nature. Rudra was something of a misfit among the Vedic deities. He wore his black hair long and tied in braids. Rudra got around in a splendid chariot, but one gets the feeling that if Rudra were alive today, his vehicle of choice would be a Harley.

Everyone's life has its share of calamities—seemingly unexpected and unde-served blows. Rudra took the blame for every kind of disaster. Even the other gods feared his anger. Invocations to Rudra are most often directed simply at keeping his anger at bay:

> Praise him, the famous young god who sits on the high seat,
> The fierce one who attacks like a ferocious wild beast.
> O Rudra, have mercy on the singer, now that you have been praised.
> Let your armies strike down someone other than us.
> Let the weapon of Rudra veer from us;
> Let the great malevolence of the dreaded god go past us.
> O tawny and amazing bull;
> O God, do not become incensed or kill us.
> Be here for us, Rudra, and hear our call. (*RV*: 2.33.12,14,15; p. 222)

Rudra of the Vedic Age would become identified with the great god Shiva in later times. Although Shiva retains much of the character of Rudra, his nature becomes vastly expanded and includes much in addition to the fearsomeness of Rudra. The worship of Shiva is, therefore, a direct link with the Dravidian, pre-Aryan past of India.

YAMA   Unlike the gods, men and women are mortals and must eventually know death. But the Vedas gave assurances of an afterlife, and Yama was the king of this afterworld. Yama was not exactly a god; he was the first mortal to die. The gods had granted him near-divine status and allowed him to find his way to the realm of the afterworld, over which he would preside until the end of time. His task was to conduct the dead to the realm of their ancestors:

> Yama was the first to find the way for us,
> This pasture that shall not be taken away.
> Where our ancient fathers passed beyond,
> There everyone who is born follows, each on his own path. (*RV*: 10.14.2; p. 43)

Although Yama was the personification of death and the afterlife, he was not imagined as negative and morbid. Yama's role was an important part of the total scheme of reality. Something of the notion of heaven and hell entered into the picture. Those who were faithful to the moral order of rita in their lives could expect a happy place in Yama's kingdom; the lot of those who had been unfaithful to rita was darkness and suffering.

It was not Yama, but the gods—particularly Varuna, the maintainer of rita—who decided what a person's fate would be. Yama merely carried out the judgment of the gods. But even if it should turn out to be a joyous afterlife, it was still death, and like people in all times, the men and women of the Vedic Age were terrified by death and begged their gods to help them:

> Go away, death, by another path that is your own,
> Different from the road of the gods.
> I say to you who have eyes, who have ears;
> Do not injure our children or our men. (*RV*: 10.18.1; p. 52)
> Let me not go to the house of clay [the grave], O King Varuna, not yet.
> Have mercy, great ruler; be merciful. (*RV*: 7.89.1; p. 216)

The good will of Yama was understandably very important to men and women of the Vedic Age. At the time of death, he could intercede for one with the gods, particularly

Varuna. Perhaps for that reason, the Brahmin priests were especially generous with their soma where Yama was concerned:

> For Yama press the Soma; to Yama offer the oblation;
> To Yama goes the well prepared sacrifice,
> With Agni as its messenger.
> Offer to Yama this oblation rich in butter, and go forth,
> So may he intercede for us among the gods,
> So that we may live out a long lifespan. (*RV*: 10.14.13,14; p. 44)

AN OVERVIEW OF VEDIC COSMOLOGY

The men and women of early Vedic times were fundamentally no different from people in any other time. They yearned for security and meaning in a world that is often violent and unpredictable. The awesome forces of nature dominated their lives. But the forces of nature, uncontrollable though they may be, were seen to operate in orderly ways. This could be the key to finding an underlying meaning to the great drama of life.

In response to this very human need for meaning, the religious leaders of the society created the gods, the controlling personifications of the forces of nature that shaped the destiny of human life. Along with identifying the gods there were, of course, appropriate rituals of worship and sacrifice designed to entice the gods into using their powers in beneficial ways.

Over time, an elaborate body of religious tradition grew, until it spread into every nook and cranny of life. Presiding over this scene were the Brahmins, the elite priest class of Vedic society. They were the custodians and preservers of the religious tradition, the essence of which was consolidated into a body of inspired knowledge known simply as Veda. Veda was given verbal expression in the sacred hymns, or chants, of the Brahmins—chants which we know as the Vedas.

Giving order and meaning to life is no casual concern. Veda proclaimed the truth with an authoritarian voice born of the belief in its divine source. And the truth proclaimed by Veda described a world organized into a rigid hierarchy of ascending levels of perfection. Humankind was in the middle, brute animals below, and the gods above. And in each of these there was further classification by rank. In human life, the caste system was seen as the natural order of society that conformed to essential differences of perfection among the member families that made up the larger community. Each had its place, guaranteed for all time, and appropriate responsibilities that went with that place. (Meaning and security has its price!) The highest place, of course, was occupied by the Brahmana caste. They alone spoke to the gods—but they did so on behalf of everyone.

The pantheon of the gods was a splendid creation of the human imagination. The Hindu pantheon represents man's poetic and mystical imagination at its best. In no way is this statement meant to imply that this was a foolish or erroneous pursuit. If Veda was to supply the much-desired order and meaning, the pantheon was its necessary capstone. And given the nature of human society at that time, it was both inevitable and reasonable.

The Vedas—practically our only source of information about the time—describe a society that was rigidly controlled by its own belief in a divinely inspired order. Altogether, life was seen to be like a great elaborate wheel slowly turning round and round. Everything and everyone, including the gods, had its proper place on that wheel, and its appropriate responsibilities corresponding to its place.

A person's sacred duty was to live his life in harmony with the customs and responsibilities of his caste and to faithfully worship the gods in the ways prescribed by tradition. If one did this (and nurtured a generous supply of the virtue of acceptance), his or her hunger for order and meaning would be satisfied (probably) and from that would grow the all-important sense of security. Such a person was not a helpless twig tossed about in the chaotic stream of life, but rather a dignified and meaningful part of the whole. And that person's destiny, assuming that he faithfully played the part expected of him, or her, was a happy afterlife in the kingdom of Yama. Death must inevitably come, but even this was no cause for terror or despair.

To the people of Vedic times, the gods were as real and as present as were other men and women. The stories of their adventures, and their involvement in human affairs, were endless. Invoking the favor of the gods—and staying the malevolence of demons—was the warp and woof of daily life in Vedic times. There were numberless rituals addressed to a rich variety of gods. India, then as now, was a land passionately devoted to the worship of its many deities. We may safely assume that sacred shrines and images were an important part of every village. Celebrations, festivals, and ritual sacrifice were the highlights of an otherwise very mundane existence. Religion, richly laced with magic and superstition, was what gave daily life a special meaning and excitement.

What we have here is a relatively unsophisticated agricultural society that in Vedic times was really not significantly different from other early cultures. The above description would apply to many other human societies in historical times. Traditional forms of belief and worship were the stuff of life for the vast majority of Indian men and women in Vedic times. And it must be stressed that this situation has not substantially changed for the population at large even down to the present day.

Our concern in these pages, however, is not primarily with the religious beliefs of the common people. Rather it is with the contribution of a tiny minority of men and women who struck off on a different path. They hungered for something that could not be satisfied with the customary menu. Out of their search came new answers to old questions. Had the evolution of Indian thought ended with the Vedas, one could argue that the philosophical side of the Hindu tradition would not have come to occupy the especially important place in the history of human thought that it does. But it did not end there; the Vedas were just the beginning. Much, much more was to be built on this Vedic foundation.

Some argue that, although the tradition of Indian philosophical thought did indeed begin in the Vedas, there was far more in the Vedic foundation that ordinarily meets the eye. The common modern view of the Vedas is inaccurate, they argue, and is based largely on the writings of the thirteenth-century Indian scholar Sayana, which holds that the Vedas were " . . . the sacrificial compositions of a primitive and still barbarous race written around a system of ceremonial and propitiatory rites, addressed to personified Powers of Nature and replete with a confused mass of half-formed myth" (as described in Aurobindo, 1)

There is another interpretation, though, which holds that the hymns of the Vedas can be interpreted along two quite different tracks. The straightforward, obvious, literal meaning was for the uneducated common people. The other much less obvious track, something of a symbolic "secret teaching," was intended for the spiritually aware *cognoscenti* among the Brahmins. This is the view expressed incisively by the modern Indian philosopher Sri Aurobindo Ghose. Let's let him speak for himself:

> One of the leading principles of the mystics was the sacredness and secrecy of self-knowledge and the true knowledge of the Gods. This wisdom was, they thought, unfit, perhaps even dangerous to the ordinary human mind or in any case liable to perversion and misuse and loss of virtue if revealed to vulgar and unpurified spirits. Hence they favoured the existence of an outer worship, effective but imperfect, for the profane, and inner discipline for the initiate, and clothed their language in words and images which had, equally, a spiritual sense for the elect, a concrete sense for the mass of ordinary worshippers. The Vedic hymns were conceived and constructed on this principle. Their formulas and ceremonies are, overtly, the details of an outward ritual devised for the Pantheistic Nature-Worship which was then the common religion, covertly the sacred words, the effective symbols of a spiritual experience and knowledge and a psychological discipline of self-culture which were then the highest achievement of the human race. (6)

That's quite a proposition! The argument is intriguing, isn't it? Whether or not the Vedas were constructed in a hidden symbolism is a matter of dispute. What is not in dispute at all, though, is that these largely religious works did indeed sometimes step into the realm of genuinely philosophical speculation. Threaded throughout the Vedas are questions and speculations that are like the seeds from which later Hindu thought will develop. One of the most striking examples is to be found in the final book of the *Rig Veda*. The writer confesses his hopeless ignorance regarding the real nature of Creation and suggests that everything has emerged from nothingness:

> Then even nothingness was not, nor existence.
> There was no air then, nor the heavens beyond it.
> Who covered it? Where was it? In whose keeping?
> Was there then cosmic water, in depths unfathomed? . . .
> But, after all, who knows, and who can say,
> Whence it all came, and how creation happened?
> The gods themselves are later than creation,
> So who knows truly whence it has arisen? (*RV*: X.129.1-7) (Thapar, 131)

Woven through all of the much-repeated proclamations and entreaties of the Vedas are some subtle philosophical themes that appear to evolve and become more important with the passage of time. Chief among these is the yearning for something that stands behind the myriad things of life—something that underlies it all and gives order and unity to existence. *Unity* is the key word here. A sense of underlying unity is the hallmark of so much of Eastern thought. Like seeds just beginning to sprout, this theme appears in the Vedas, but will not grow to maturity until a later age. Nevertheless, the interest is there and shows up in different ways.

We see in the Vedas that there was a developing awareness that the One was fundamentally more real than the Many. The universe began as the One and eventually would return to the primal state from which it had emerged. Between this alpha and omega, the One would propagate itself as the myriad creatures that temporarily make up the great hierarchy of being. This point of view is certainly not prominent in the Vedas, but here and there in the *Rig Veda* we find tantalizing little nuggets such as, "To what is One, sages give many a title." Or, in the same vein of thought, "that One wherein abide all things existing."

The Doctrine of Rita is another case in point. Many came to believe that there is a law, a natural law, that is immanent throughout all of creation. Even the gods do not exercise their powers capriciously. The gods, like all other creatures, must act in accord with the universal order of rita. The rising and setting of the sun was seen to be an example of rita; the changing of the seasons was rita; birth and death were the workings of rita. Applied to human behavior, the grand order of rita became moral law. Whatever one's caste, the proper goal of life was to live that life in accord with rita. Rita assures harmony and wholeness, the orderly evolution of life. Rita is the grand unifying order of Nature. In the concept of rita, the rishis gave form to the idea of a rational order that underlies and unifies all of Nature.

Again, I want to stress that, for the most part, the Vedas were not concerned with such philosophical matters. But still, there were stirrings—hints of what was to come. Undoubtedly, in the Vedas some were toying with the concept that the multiplicity of creation is really a secondary, ephemeral sort of reality. This is what we see with our unenlightened eyes, but at a more transcendent level of consciousness it is possible to see that fundamentally all of reality is One. This opened the door to a vastly richer meaning of Veda. In the age that followed, there were some who could not resist the maddening temptation to give up everything and dedicate their lives to the search for this higher truth.

Study Questions

1. How do you distinguish between *Veda* and the *Vedas*? Considering that there are four Vedas in all, why do you suppose that, in modern times at least, the *Rig Veda* receives by far the most attention?

2. How would you describe the Vedic fire sacrifice? Why do you suppose they went to so much trouble, so much spectacle and drama in the creation of a great sacrifice?

3. Why was soma so enormously important? Did they really need it? Suppose that soma had never existed: How would this have affected the religious functioning of the Brahmins?

4. How did the gods feel about the use of soma?

5. What does the term *Dyavaprithi* refer to? What is its significance?

6. How did the Hindu pantheon of gods come into existence? Why do you suppose that they were almost all male gods in Vedic times?

7. What do you make of Rudra? He seems like such a misfit among the Hindu gods—or was he?

8. Why is it argued that, beneath all the superficialities, the Brahmin rishis were deeply interested in finding a principle of unity standing behind the manifold experiences of daily life?

9. How does rita tie it all together—or does it?

CHAPTER 3

Introduction to the Upanishads

The Upanishads are an outstanding addition to humanity's search for meaning and beauty in life—and in death. The Upanishads have been a rich source of inspiration throughout the ages and seem to speak with special eloquence to men and women of modern times.

The word *upanishad* is a combination of three Sanskrit root words, *upa-ni-shad*, which literally means "sit down close to [a teacher]"—that is to say, to be part of a group that "sits at the feet" of a master to learn from him (or her). For the most part, what we call the Upanishads were "secret teachings" in the early days. They were passed along orally within the groups that created them. It was a personal transmission not meant for the ears of others.

This is a reasonable interpretation of "upanishad" and is by far the most commonly accepted. There is, however, another possibility. The word *upanishad* can also be understood to mean the final, clarifying step in a series of disclosures—the secret revelation at the end, as it were, that gives meaning to the whole. This interpretation, perhaps, makes even better sense.

In any case, the Upanishads, like the Vedas, are a part of that great body of sacred knowledge known as *shruti*. The word *shruti* originally meant "stream" in Sanskrit, but came to also carry the meaning of "revelation" (not necessarily, though, in the Judeo-Christian sense of a "God-given" revelation). Shruti, this "stream of revelation," begins with the Vedas, the seminal works concerned mainly with invocations to the gods and guidance for proper ritual action. The Vedas were followed by the *Brahmanas*, commentaries concerning matters of ritual brought up in the Vedas. The stream continued with the *Aranyakas. Aranya* means forest, or wilderness, in Sanskrit. The Aranyakas, like the Brahmanas, were concerned with proper ritual action (generally meaning sacrifice), but focused more on secret ritual. The forest was the likely place for such ritual acts or at least the teaching of them. The Aranyakas link the Vedas/Brahmanas with the Upanishads. In fact, there is a rather seamless flow. The later Aranyakas and the earliest Upanishads are almost indistinguishable.

The Upanishads form the final part of shruti. They were composed over a very long period of time, stretching from about 1000 B.C.E. to 200 B.C.E. Strictly speaking, the Upanishads are yet further commentaries on the Vedas, but the philosophical and mystical depth of the Upanishads goes far beyond anything that is presented in the Vedas. We could say—if I may be forgiven for using this analogy one last time—that the Vedas contain the seeds, but the flower comes to full bloom in the Upanishads. What had begun in ritual honoring of the gods culminated in a lofty inquiry into the true nature of reality. Whereas the Vedas were primarily concerned with success in this life, the Upanishads focus on knowledge of the ultimate nature of reality and the self.

Collectively, the Upanishads are known by the term *Vedanta*, which means "end of Veda" or "culmination of Veda." There's a bit of a problem, though, with the word *Vedanta*. Let me explain. Each Upanishad was the product of the spiritual and philosophical tradition of a distinct group. Consequently, the Upanishads taken as a whole do not present a systematic, coherent philosophy. Differing schools of thought are represented in the various Upanishads. Over time, these would crystalize into distinct philosophies, known as *darshanas*. The Hindu tradition recognizes six "orthodox" darshanas, including the darshanas of Samkya, Yoga, Nyaya, *and* the darshana of Vedanta. (We will look at these separately in Chapter 5.) Each of these darshanas is a philosophical system that attempts, each in its own way, to correctly interpret the truth of Veda. Thus "Vedanta," in addition to being the term for the Upanishads as a whole, became the name of one of the six darshanas, albeit the foremost among them, and absorbed much of the teachings of the others into itself. In other words, the teachings of the darshana of Vedanta are expressed broadly throughout the Upanishads, but not exclusively. There are also contributions from other darshanas, such as Samkya and Yoga. This will not create a problem for us.

In the following pages, our examination of the Upanishads will be based largely on the interpretation of Upanishadic thought as elucidated in the teaching of Vedanta. Certain specific contributions of other darshanas will be noted where appropriate. In this way, we can construct a coherent exposition of Upanishadic thought, and it is an exposition that conforms to what is broadly accepted as the orthodox interpretation of the Upanishads.

THE SANNYASIN TRADITION

It is safe to say that during the Vedic Age the only ones devoted to the search for transcendent knowledge were the rishis, almost all of whom were members of the Brahmana class. This search was defined pretty narrowly by tradition; it consisted for the most part in studying the Vedas and participating in ritual sacrifice. The rishi was not a rebel; he was a functioning member of the social system. Not only was he shaped by tradition, he was also the *upholder* of that tradition. Undoubtedly this situation was perfectly satisfactory for many, but definitely not for all.

During the late Vedic Age, evidence of a dramatic new movement began to emerge. The thirst for transcendent knowledge, engendered in the Vedas, began to take a new turn. Some few men were willing to give up everything and totally dedicate their lives to a search for spiritual enlightenment. Such men are known as *sadhus*, or by the English word "renunciates," because they were willing to renounce everything—all material wealth, family, even their caste status—and go off into the wilderness, living like hermits

FIGURE 3.1   Sadhus leaving a temple in Nepal. (P. Bresnan)

in order to dedicate their lives to this all-consuming search.* The wilderness was essential
for such men because they had voluntarily become "outcasts," and also because they
wanted to get far away from the lures and distractions of ordinary life. Many sadhus took
the vow of *sanyas* and were thus known more specifically as *sannyasins*. A sannyasin is
a disciple of a particular guru.

Who were these renunciates? Where did they come from in the social order of the
time? Some were Brahmins; many, though, were of the Kshatriya class. (Shakyamuni
Buddha, the most famous of all renunciates, came from a Kshatriya family, but he would
not appear on the scene until long after the tradition had matured.) The deepest
roots of the movement, though, would seem to be in the traditional culture of the long-
suppressed Dravidian people. Though suppressed, Dravidian culture was far from extinguished, and in the declining years of the Vedic Age, there is a detectable resurgence of
Dravidian beliefs and customs. What we see is a gradual fusing of the two cultures.
The growth of the sannyasin movement may well be to a large degree the reemergence
of a long-buried tradition among the Dravidian people.

The sannyasin, then as now, gave up ordinary life in order to search for transcendent
spiritual knowledge—self-realization or "enlightenment." His was a very hard life; few
could endure it. Much of the renunciate's time was given to spiritual study, prayer, and
most important of all, meditation. He might give many hours of each day to the practice of

---

*To be technically accurate with regard to spelling, "renunciant" would be preferred over "renunciate."
However, "renunciate" is so widely used that it has become the customary spelling and is the one I shall use in
this book.

meditation. All renunciates lived a life of severe self-denial, and many included rigorous ascetic practices as well, such as long fasting, or going about in the coldest weather with little or no clothing. All of this was intended to burn out the deep longing for comfort and ego-satisfaction that stood in the way of spiritual growth.*

As you might expect, some renunciates were (and are) more successful in this way of life than others. Some are so remarkable, and their spiritual growth appears to be so impressive, that they acquire a reputation. Other renunciates seek them out, if only to gain something from simply being in their presence. A holy man who attracts a following of disciples is called by them a *guru*. A guru is the leader of a spiritual community. He is their guide and teacher. The title is conferred out of respect by the disciples, never by the man himself.

The disciples of the guru are called *sishyas*. The relationship between the guru and sishya is one of mutual acceptance and love; it has to be like the relationship between a loving father and son. The sishya gives himself entirely to the guru; the guru's will becomes his will—absolute, uncompromising trust is essential. And given this kind of relationship, it is just as obvious that only a genuinely enlightened master is appropriate for the role of guru. Anything less could lead to disaster.*

Together the guru and his disciples form a tight-knit community. This kind of spiritual community is called *ashrama*. We refer to it as an "ashram." Originally, the term *ashram* meant only the community itself. It was a small community that was usually on the move. The ashram wandered about in the mountains or forest, acquiring their meager needs from the bounty of nature, or occasionally from begging. Begging was perfectly respectable. It was considered meritorious to share one's food with the holy men.

During the rainy season, the community would have to settle down in one place. India's myriad rivers, swollen by monsoon rains, made travel virtually impossible. Over time, many of these communities acquired donations of land, and gradually gave up their wandering ways. Thus, in time, the word *ashrama* came to refer to the place, the "hermitage," of a particular guru and his disciples. Once established, an ashram might continue to exist for many generations, even centuries. The disciples cycled in and out as new ones replaced those who died, and the guru typically would appoint a successor. Continuity was thus assured.

But much more than mere temporal continuity was at stake here. It was the spiritual tradition of an ashram that was its real enduring soul. The reason such communities existed at all was that the individual members believed that such an arrangement was the best way to further their quest for spiritual enlightenment. Sharing life with other searchers in a close relationship with a guru was considered to be a much richer life than the way of the solitary hermit. And what energized the community, in a spiritual sense, was its tradition of sacred teachings passed down from one generation to the next. This tradition was the community's treasure, and it was jealously guarded. It was a "secret teaching" in the sense that they believed that only those initiated into the community and guided by its guru were capable of really understanding the truth contained in it. But that truth—contained in the teachings— was the key that could unlock the gates of paradise.

---

*In ancient times, women did not become renunciates—they simply did not have the opportunity—but that has changed dramatically in modern times.

*In India, where this tradition is ancient and deeply engrained in the culture, safeguards have evolved to protect against the possibility of an imposter guru. But in the Western world, where the tradition is new, no such safeguards exist, and the naive have sometimes been exploited—to put it mildly.

Most of the Upanishads began life as just such secret teachings, enshrined in the tradition of various spiritual communities and handed down over many generations. Eventually they were committed to writing, and today they are available to all of us.

KEY ELEMENTS OF THE UPANISHADS

The purpose of this study will best be served by treating the Upanishads as a group, rather than examining the principal ones individually. Taken as a group, the Upanishads give expression to a complete system of thought, one that addresses virtually all of the basic questions of life. Using appropriate selections from various Upanishads, I will attempt to identify the key themes of the Upanishads and show how they join together into one comprehensive whole. (Please remember that the following exposition is fundamentally based on the darshana of Vedanta, but contributions from other darshanas will be included, and noted, where appropriate.)

The place to begin such a study is right where you are. Consider the world around you. There's always a world around you, and as far as your own perception is concerned, you're always right at its center. It doesn't matter what the condition of the world around you is at the moment; any condition will do. This "world around us" is what we ordinarily call reality. What can we say about this reality simply by observing it? What basic observations always seem to be true about this world around us?

The first thing to be said about reality is that there is a lot of it. We are surrounded by a seemingly infinite number of "things." Anything you can put a name on is a thing (at least as far as our brains are concerned), anything that can be a noun: a chair, for example, or a tree, or a garbage can, a guitar, a dog, a telephone, a handwoven panama hat, and so on ad infinitum. All of these myriad things are constantly interacting. And one of these things—the most important one by far—is myself. I am a thing among other things, interacting with them and changing with them as we all go along together in the flow of time.

Change is the key understanding here. Reality, as we perceive it, is constantly changing. *Everything is in a state of change, all of the time!* It is a never ending flux, and nothing in the universe is exempt from it. With some things, clouds of smoke for example, the process of constant change is obvious. With other things, such as granite boulders, it's not so obvious. But we know it's going on anyway; it's just that it's slow to show the effects. If we could see a time-lapse film of that granite boulder over some long span of geologic time, it would appear to be liquid (actually it is; everything is), or if it were possible for us right now to peek in at the atomic level of that boulder, we would see a whirlwind of movement and change. The appearance of unchanging solidity is only that: a superficial appearance.

This matter of constant change has a long history of troubling philosophers. If everything is always changing, always becoming something else, how can we say anything really definite about anything? How can we have a dependable science if nothing sits still for even an instant? The Greek philosopher Heraclitus complained that you can't put your foot into the same river twice (because the flowing body of water is constantly changing its form, it's really a new "river" every instant)—quite a problem for someone who wants to be able to make definite, enduring statements about reality. As if that's not bad enough, it gets even worse. You can't even put your foot into the same river *once* (because the flow pattern is changing even as you put your foot into the water)!

So, we live in a world made up of things that are in a state of constant change. And, these things are constantly *inter*-changing; everything is constantly becoming something else. Here again, this is sometimes easy to see, such as when a fire changes wood to smoke, and sometimes not so obvious, as when the surf changes a rock into sand. But here too it is simply a matter of time. Given enough time, everything decays, and out of that, new things take form. The tree dies and becomes the soil. Out of the soil grows a blade of grass. The grass becomes the worm that eats it, and the worm becomes the bird that eats it. The bird dies and decays into the soil becoming one with it. Out of the soil grows a tree, and so on.

That brings us to a third point about change. Change is not capricious and meaningless (though it may sometimes seem that way). Change is always orderly, always reasonable. What I mean by this is that change always conforms to the laws of nature. Change is always bound up in the process of cause and effect, wherein the effect is necessarily a logical outcome of the cause. Deer do not give birth to baby ducks, and falling apples do not fall upward.*

The important point is that everything—every*thing*—is the result of some prior thing that caused it. Everything is the *doing* of something else. An apple is what an apple tree *does*; an apple tree *apples*. Apples are an *appling* of the apple tree, and the apple tree itself is a *treeing* of the soil, and so on. Looked at in this way, there really are no such things as nouns. Nouns imply a static, set reality. But in truth everything is in movement, constantly in a state of becoming. The late Alan Watts used to suggest, tongue in cheek, that we should replace all nouns with verbs: "The horsing ate an appling from the treeing." Interesting idea, but I suspect it's not likely to happen.

Our concern here is with the fact that everything is the doing of something else. You are the doing of your parents, and they are the doing of their parents, and so on. The apple is the doing of the tree; the tree is the doing of planet Earth; the Earth is the doing of the galaxy, and on we go back in time. No matter what you start with, you can—in fact you must—trace the chain of cause and effect back to the starting point of the universe. Everything ultimately goes back to the Big Bang. (And maybe before long, science will reveal that the Big Bang itself was the *doing* of something that preceded it.)

Everything is the doing of something that preceded it in an unbroken chain of cause and effect back to the beginning of the universe. So, the ultimate question is, What's *doing* the universe? If everything in the universe is the doing of something else, what is doing the universe? (Notice that the question is not, what *did* the universe; what *started* the universe? Whether or not the universe really began in the Big Bang is not our present concern. It's an interesting question, but it's not the right question.)

Given the fact that the universe exists—given the fact that all of this "stuff" around us exists—there is a perfectly reasonable explanation for why it has all evolved in the way it has; the laws of nature explain it fully. Given the fact that the universe exists in a particular condition at Moment-A, and again in a certain condition at Moment-B, Moment-B is a perfectly logical outcome of Moment-A. But that requires a "given the fact," and why should we be willing to do that? Everything, including the universe itself, has to have a reasonable explanation. So again, the ultimate, bottom-line question is,

---

*The universality of the "law" of causality is challenged, of course, by modern quantum physics. Our purpose, though, is to understand the reasoning of thinkers who lived long ago, before a time when such considerations were even conceivable.

What's *doing* the universe?! In other words, why does anything exist at all? What is it that holds the universe in existence? Why is it that the universe continues to exist at all from Moment-A to Moment-B? *What is it that is doing the universe?* Every cosmology must answer this question. In Vedanta, the answer to this all-important question can be summed up in a single word—*Brahman*.

Brahman

In the lexicon of Hinduism there is no more important term than "Brahman." Brahman is the beginning and the end of everything. The concepts that we shall be discussing in this chapter weave around the meaning of Brahman, constantly returning to it. The meaning of "Brahman" cannot be neatly captured in words. The best we can do is to say that Brahman is the underlying reality and root cause of all that is. Brahman—derived from the Sanskrit root *brih*, which means "to grow"—is the ultimate root of existence from which the entire universe "grows" and continues to exist.

It is very important to resist the temptation to let the imagination cast the word *Brahman* in the form of some personal being, especially a god-like being. Brahman is not a god; Brahman is not a "he"; Brahman is not any *thing* at all that can be identified and separated out from all other things. We could say that, fundamentally, Brahman is the Fact of Existence—pure and simple. Brahman is the *reason* things exist. Brahman is the ultimate inner essence of all things that exist. In the *Mundaka Upanishad*, Brahman is described as being invisible, ungraspable, eternal, and without any qualities whatsoever. Brahman is the imperishable source of all things.

In the Upanishads, Brahman is often referred to as "the Self," with a capital "S," meaning the innermost Self of all that exists. From the *Katha Upanishad*,

> The supreme Self is beyond name and form,
> Beyond the senses, inexhaustible,
> Without beginning, without end,
> Beyond time and space, and causality, eternal, immutable. (*Katha Up*: 10.3.15; p. 89)*

The above quote reveals the frustration in trying to define Brahman in words. By definition, Brahman transcends everything that can be a matter of experience, and that's what words are all about. Perhaps the best verbal definition of all is given in the *Mundaka Upanishad*. A sage being questioned about the nature of Brahman keeps answering, "Neti, neti, neti" (not that; not that; not that). In other words, we can only identify Brahman by negating every possible thing that we can imagine. What's left is Brahman. What *is* left? Well, that's why the sages call it "ungraspable." The most that we can say in words is that what's left is pure, undifferentiated existence itself—not some *thing* that exists:

> Him our eyes cannot see, nor words express;
> He cannot be grasped even by the mind.
> We do not know, we cannot understand,

---

*Unless otherwise noted, all excerpts from the Upanishads are taken from Easwaren. The page number at the end of the citation refers to the page in the Easwaren book.

Because he is different from the known
And he is different from the unknown.
Thus have we heard from the illumined ones. (*Kena Up*: 1.3,4; p. 68)

Don't let the use of the masculine pronouns in this passage confuse you. Writers of the Upanishads were fairly casual about that sort of thing. Brahman clearly transcends gender; there's no question about that. But "it," nonetheless, is often referred to as "he" in the Upanishads.

In trying to describe the admittedly indescribable, sages use many words—pure spirit, eternal, infinite, immutable, uncreated, unchanging, and so on. So far as they go, all of these are good words. But words are like "fingers pointing at the moon": fine, if they direct your attention to the moon; just don't mistake the finger *for* the moon.

Maya

Suffice it to say, in the imperfect way of words, that Brahman is pure existence. Pure existence is infinitely passive and undifferentiated. But the world of our experience is not passive at all; it is highly active. As emphasized above, a vast multitude of things is constantly coming into existence and passing out of existence. But if Brahman is all that exists, and is infinitely passive and undifferentiated, how can this be? In Vedanta philosophy (*Advaita Vedanta*), existence is definitely seen to be one, but the reality of Brahman is conceptualized in two ways. Fundamentally, the term *Brahman* refers to pure existence, eternal, unmoving, passive. But there is seen to be within this fundamental "Brahman" a *potential* for an expression of itself. The cosmos—moving, changing, active—is this "expression" of Brahman.

In its pure, unmoving, essential suchness Brahman is known as *nirguna* Brahman (without attributes), absolutely perfect and absolutely passive (at least conceptually speaking). As the active "creative" source of the cosmos, though, Brahman is known as *saguna* Brahman (with attributes). It is saguna Brahman that creates the universe—in the beginning, and for every continuing moment—as an expression, a *manifestation* of itself. In this way, Brahman, the ultimate source of all that is, *does* the universe.

This is not just a sly way of preserving belief in the unity of being; it is actually an entirely reasonable solution. Consider this very rough analogy (and I stress the word *very*): Imagine yourself lying peacefully in some serene place, perhaps a quiet, grassy spot on a warm summer day. Your eyes are closed and you're not really thinking about much of anything, just enjoying the moment, enjoying your fact of existence. Suddenly and spontaneously you break out in song. After a while the song dies out, and you drift back into simply enjoying the moment. In this analogy (and I said it was rough) the quiet, passive you is like *nirguna* Brahman; the song is like *saguna* Brahman. The question is, Are you and the song two *different* things, or are they two *aspects* of one reality, you? When you sing a song, is the act of singing you, or is it something separate from you? Is not your behavior—what you do—a fundamental part of what it is that defines *you*? Singing is a modified form of breathing; it's a way of expressing yourself. In the same way, the universe could be said to be the "song" of Brahman. Seen in this way there is no separation. All is One; all is Brahman:

As the web issues out of the spider, and is withdrawn;
As plants sprout from the earth,
As hair grows from the body,

> Even so, the sages say,
> This universe springs from the deathless Self,
> The source of life. (*Mundaka Up*: Pt.I;1.7; p. 110)

Thus Brahman-in-act (saguna Brahman) accounts for the existence of the cosmos, which means all those myriad ever-changing, ever-evolving "things" that all together make up what we call the cosmos. The totality of all these "things" (or should I say "thing-ings") is known by the name *maya*. The word *maya* is derived from the very basic Sanskrit word, *ma*, which provided the root for words meaning "matter" and "measure." The English word *magic* is derived from the same root, and magic was an early Sanskrit meaning of maya. In Vedic times, maya referred to the magical powers of the gods. But in the Upanishads, maya has come to refer to the (seemingly) magical power of Brahman to evoke the appearance of the many out of the One. The word *maya* thus refers both to the creative power of Brahman and to what it is that appears to be created:

> From his divine power comes forth
> All this magical show of name and form;
> Of you and me,
> Which casts the spell of pain and pleasure.
> Only when we pierce through this magic veil
> Do we see the One who appears as many. (*Shvetashvatara Up*: IV.5; p. 225)

> Know him to be the supreme magician
> Who has become boy and girl, bird and beast. (*Shvetashvatara Up*: IV.11; p. 226)

Maya is the totality of everything that makes up the universe, the cosmos. But all of these things are constantly changing, constantly evolving, constantly becoming. So, what is it that's changing? If, for example, the earth becomes grass and the grass becomes the animal that eats it, then all of these things are really *forms* temporarily assumed by something more basic. In fact, that is the essential character of maya. All of the things of *maya* are forms, expressions of that which is fundamental to all. That sentence bears repeating: *All of the things of maya are forms, expressions of that which is fundamental to all.* So what are the forms of "maya" *forms of?* This absolutely most basic essence, out of which arise all the displays of maya is known as *prakriti*.*

Prakriti (pronounced prah-KREE-tee) may be thought of as being ultimately the most simple state of matter and energy, or simply the power that generates materiality in its primal state. The Upanishads are not precise about this point, nor does it really seem to matter. In any case, we can say that in giving birth to what we perceive as the material universe—whatever the ultimate nature of that may be—Brahman's act can be described as the *expression* of *prakriti*. And from the very first moment of time, prakriti became involved in the process of movement and change which we envision as the evolution of the universe.

One of the amazing things about Vedanta is the harmony that exists between the insights of this ancient philosophy and those of modern science. Contemporary physics is enchanted by the quest for the primal, fundamental components of materiality. In a sense, we could say that modern science is trying to get as close as is humanly possible

---

*The concepts of *prakriti* and *purusha* are elucidated in the darshana of Samkya.

to an understanding of the fundamental nature of prakriti. From the modern point of view, we could say that prakriti took the form of primal energy that "froze out" into the elementary particles of nature. A quark is a form of prakriti, and so is a photon. (So, in fact, are the alleged "strings" of string theory.) This view does no violence at all to the original meaning of prakriti. In fact, it seems to develop the original concept and make it even more meaningful.

So, could you go to the pharmacy and purchase a small bottle of prakriti? Sure you could; anything in the bottle would be prakriti, and the bottle itself too. But could you purchase a bottle of "pure" prakriti? Sorry, that's not possible. Prakriti is always in the form of something, no matter how elemental that something may be. You can no more have prakriti all by itself than you can have the color blue all by itself. It has to be a blue something.

From the point of view of the upanishads, no matter how finely you slice it, you're still dealing with "forms." Perhaps the "ultimate substance" is unknowable to the senses; we can only know its effects. But, from the point of view of Vedanta, it *has* to exist. "Forms" have to be *forms of* something. And this necessary ultimate substance is what we refer to as *prakriti.*

Prakriti is not static. It constantly responds to the forces of nature, and out of this dynamic come all of the forms which we recognize as the world around us. The fundamental forces of nature—the threefold aspects of prakriti—are referred to as the *gunas.* The three gunas, elucidated in the Samkya tradition, are: *tamas,* the character of inertia, passivity; *rajas,* the character of energy, activity, dynamism; and *sattva,* the character of equilibrium, balance and harmony. Everything that exists is said to be a result of the interaction of these three forces, though one will always dominate and it will establish the nature of the particular thing.* In a seed, tamas dominates, but when it sprouts, rajas takes command. A healthy, mature tree exhibits sattva. The guna forces are always and everywhere in movement and interaction shaping the character of the forms that prakriti assumes. In modern terms, we might think of energy as rajas, and gravity, or the urge toward increasing entropy, as tamas.

Insofar as the material order is concerned, prakriti is all that exists. The things that we can see and name are forms that prakriti has taken. Like a slowly drifting smoke cloud, prakriti is constantly assuming myriad forms—forms that take shape and then dissolve into other forms. For billions of years, the cosmic dust cloud produced by the Big Bang has been slowly evolving new and ever more complex forms. We put names on these forms and call them galaxies, stars, planets, trees, kittens, microchips, handwoven panama hats, and so on. But all of them remain at root that original cosmic dust, which has simply been good at evolving more complicated molecular forms over time. Everything that exists is simply a temporary form of prakriti. And that brings us back to maya. Maya is the world of changing forms; prakriti, so to speak, is what the forms are made of.

An analogy will help. Imagine a potter at work. The first thing that the potter needs is a tub of clay. Then he or she will shape that clay into various artifacts. If one is for holding flowers, it will be called a vase. Another meant to hold soup will be called a bowl. I say "will be called" because, strictly speaking, there is no such thing as a vase or a bowl. Those words are just agreed-upon practical descriptions of what essentially is

---

*Perhaps you see the similarity between the *gunas* in Hinduism and the concept of *yin and yang* in Chinese Daoism.

still clay. The clay hasn't changed; only its form has changed. Now some of it has become clay *in the form* of a vase, or clay *in the form* of a bowl. The names refer to the forms. If we break the vase, only the form has been destroyed. All of the clay is still there, though now it is in the form of shards.

In the above analogy, the clay, of course, represents prakriti, and the forms that the clay temporarily assumes are maya. When we give names to forms, we seem to confer on them a sort of reality that goes beyond the character of transient forms. It is the name that creates the illusion. Our mistake is to confer on the things of our experience a kind of reality unto themselves, rather than see them as the fleeting expressions of a deeper reality.

One more analogy: Let's go back to that summer day when you were lying on the grass, only this time we'll have you watching a big puffy cloud drifting slowly overhead. It doesn't take much imagination to pick out all kinds of familiar shapes. A chicken slowly turns into an alligator; a face becomes a chair. In the terms of the analogy, the cloud is prakriti; the forms it takes are maya. The forms are real; you are not hallucinating. But their reality consists in being forms of the cloud, not in being substanding things with their own separate reality. If you thought that it really was a chicken or an alligator, you would then be a victim of illusion. But it would be your own illusion, not inherently the fault of the maya. Vedanta maintains that this is a mistake that we often make.

Through the act of Brahman (saguna Brahman), the universe comes into existence and unfolds through time. What is unfolding are the myriad forms of nature; the countless, ever-changing *things* that make up the world around us. This is maya, our perception of the totality of the myriad *forms* (things) that make up the constantly changing character of nature. It is the particular way in which Brahman manifests itself. The *Shvetashvatara Upanishad* puts it this way:

> [Brahman] is fire and the sun, and the moon, and the stars.
> He is the air and the sea.
> Brahman is the Creator, Prajapati.
> He is this boy, he is that girl.
> He is this man, he is that woman,
> And he is this old man, too, tottering on his staff.
> His face is everywhere. (*Shvetashvatara Up*: IV.2; p. 225)

The same point is made in the *Katha Upanishad*:

> The Self is the sun shining in the sky,
> The wind blowing in space;
> He is the fire at the altar and in the home the guest;
> He dwells in human beings, in gods, in truth,
> And in the vast firmament;
> He is the fish born in water, the plant growing in the earth,
> The river flowing down from the mountain.
> For this Self is supreme. (*Katha Up*: II.2.2; p. 93)

There is an excellent Sanskrit word, *lila* (LEE-la), which means "play," as in "to play a musical instrument." The act of Brahman is often referred to as *lila*. Rather than say that Brahman *creates* the universe, many sages prefer to say that Brahman *plays* the universe. (It sounds so much more appealing when put that way.) After all, *why* does Brahman do the universe? There really can't be any purpose outside itself; nothing exists outside itself. Is it going too far to say that when you come right down to it, Brahman *plays* the universe for the fun of it? I don't mean to sound facetious; nor on the other hand, do I wish to pretend that this is all heavy and serious business. It is what it is, and what it is— what everything is—is the lila of Brahman.

> Brahman, pure existence, manifests itself as the universe.
> Everything that exists is the lila of Brahman.
> Brahman, attributeless Reality . . .
> Casts his net of appearance over the cosmos
> And rules it from within through his divine power. (*Shvetashvatara Up*:
> III.1; p. 222)

The above selection (repeated here) points out the difference of meaning regarding "creation" in the Hindu and the Christian traditions. In the Judeo-Christian tradition, God is separate from His creation; He creates the world out of nothing. In the Hindu tradition, Brahman "creates" the cosmos out of itself (that is, out of Brahman). Brahman and the "creation" (play) are one.

Brahman "rules" the universe. By "rule" is simply meant that the lila of Brahman is not whimsical, not erratic. From the beginning of time, the universe has been unfolding in a grand and orderly fashion. This orderly evolution of the universe, the lila of Brahman, is what is meant by the word *Dharma, Brahman-Dharma*.

Dharma—derived from the Sanskrit *dhar*, which means "to hold"—is the inner law which upholds the Order of Nature. We see it around us as the expression of Natural Law, and over time it is expressed as the awesome unfolding of the evolution of the cosmos. Brahman projects the universe from itself, but does so in accordance with the order of Dharma.

Brahman, then, is pure existence, the source of all that is. Maya is the creative act of Brahman expressed as the evolution of the universe. And Dharma is the inner law of Brahman that causes the evolution of the universe to unfold in an orderly and harmonious way. Dharma is what gives unity and harmony to all of nature. To be in accord with Dharma is the proper state of all things.

Until human beings appeared on the scene, there was no problem concerning Dharma; everything in nature automatically acted in accord with Dharma. The apple falling from the tree is Dharma; the Earth turning on its axis is Dharma; the lion pouncing on the antelope is Dharma. The balance of nature is Dharma. But human nature has the capacity for self-reflection, and, therefore, the capacity to frustrate Dharma by willfully substituting personal desire in place of desire for the good of the whole. As a result, the "balance of nature" can become very *un*-balanced (to say the least!). Thus it becomes the moral responsibility of men and women to transcend selfish desire and deliberately choose to live their lives in accord with Dharma. The word *Dharma*, therefore, refers to transcendent Natural Law and also to moral law. The concept of Dharma is in many ways an outgrowth of the Vedic concept of rita. Both are concerned with the inner order of reality.

In the grand view of the Hindu tradition, philosophical speculation is given a wonderful metaphorical expression in mythology. Sometimes this is the best way to intuitively grasp the meaning of that which admittedly is inexpressible. In Hindu mythology, the creator-god is known as Brahma (not to be confused with Brahman). Brahma brings forth from out of the depths of his own being a goddess (*Devi*) who personifies maya. The goddess is not a separate being: She is Brahma in the sense that she is the *shakti*, the female element that is intrinsically a part of the whole that is Brahma. The Hindu tradition holds that the passive and the active principles are fundamental in existence. The passive is represented by the male nature and the active by the female. Thus it is logical that the goddess, the *shakti* of Brahma, would represent maya and be responsible for the entrancing play that maya unfolds:

> *Maya* is the continuous self-manifestation and self-disguise of Brahman—its self-revelation, yet its multi-colored concealing veil. Hence the dignity of all perishable things, on all levels. That is why their sum total is worshipped as the Highest Goddess, Mother and Life-Energy of Gods and Creatures, under the formula, Maya-shakti-Devi. (Zimmer, *Myth* 151)

Brahman-Atman

We have now reached the appropriate place to take up the doctrine of Brahman-Atman, the quintessential feature of Vedanta. Given its great importance, we need to first step back a little in order to see the larger picture out of which it logically emerges.

As we have seen, prakriti, through the ceaseless play of the gunas, produced, and continues to produce, all of the maya forms of the universe. Each of us finds one of these forms, one of these entities, to be of very special interest. That particular form is, of course, "myself." I am a physical being, a part of the world of maya, just like all other physical beings. But in an important way, I am unlike most of the other "things" of my experience. I am a *conscious* being, a "sentient" being. Among the myriad forms of maya, there can be seen to exist two distinctly different kinds. There are those that exhibit consciousness, and there are those that do not exhibit consciousness. Those that do exhibit the potential for consciousness are called sentient beings (an animal, for example). Those that do not exhibit consciousness are called insentient beings (a rock, for example). This difference is, to say the least, momentous.

Consider the importance of consciousness—the absolute, unequalled importance of consciousness. Compared to it, nothing else really matters at all. And it's so completely amazing! Why does it exist at all? What causes it? How in the world can godly consciousness be "caused" by a bunch of insentient molecules which happen to be arranged in the form of certain neurons in the brain? It would seem as though the effect is infinitely greater than its cause. The Upanishadic tradition answers this question by saying simply: It can't. Prakriti can't cause consciousness. Consciousness, godly consciousness, is of the nature of Brahman itself. Brahman is pure spirit. In this view, pure spirit and pure consciousness are one and the same. Pure consciousness is not to be confused with ordinary thinking or feeling. It is in itself totally inactive. The word for this is *purusha*.

Purusha is a tricky word to nail down. (Aren't they all!) The meaning of the word changed enormously from Vedic times to the age of the Upanishads. In the Vedas, purusha refers to a mythic primal male whose body enveloped the entire cosmos. From the various parts of this body were derived the different castes. Obviously the meaning changed a lot, but the connotation of maleness was not entirely lost. In their more poetic moments, the authors of the Upanishads refer to the male/female dichotomy of nature by representing purusha as the male aspect and prakriti as the female.

Brahman is pure consciousness, purusha, and as such is aware of its own lila. Purusha is perfect and undivided; that is to say, purusha is universal, one and the same as

Brahman itself (nirguna Brahman)—it is not divided into discrete parts. Prakriti, in the myriad evanescent forms of maya, is perceived as a manifold, but purusha is the purely spiritual reality of Brahman itself and is One. Thus it follows that my physical self is prakriti—an aspect of the play of maya—and subject to all the conditions of nonconscious prakriti. But the conscious self is not prakriti. We customarily recognize the importance of this distinction by spelling the purusha "Self" with a capital "S."

The Self—the indwelling conscious core of every sentient being—is *Atman*. The word *Atman* is derived from an early root word which means "to breathe." In many ancient cultures, the principle of life, the soul, was associated with the breath. This is understandable; a baby *seems* to come to life when it takes its first breath and remains vital and warm throughout life so long as breathing continues. Breath is also the meaning of the Latin *spiritus*, from which is derived our word "spirit."

Atman, then, *is* Brahman! The Dharma-evolution of the universe is the *play* of Brahman, the manifestation of Brahman. This cannot be stressed too strongly. The Atman is not a part of Brahman; Brahman is pure spirit and cannot be divided into parts. Atman is not a role of Brahman. Atman *is* Brahman:

> This Self who gives rise to all works,
> To all desires, all odors, all tastes,
> Who pervades the universe,
> Who is beyond words,
> Who is joy abiding,
> Who is ever present in my heart,
> Is Brahman indeed. (*Chandogya Up*: III.14.4; p. 178)

Thus, in a manner of speaking, there are two important aspects to the nature of my being. The conscious core of my being (and of all sentient beings) is the Brahman-Atman. This is the Self, which, participating in the nature of purusha, is pure spirit, eternal, nonacting. The much more familiar self, though, is the ego, the maya-role that is identified with what I do. This is the prakriti-self, active, constantly changing, ephemeral, and not in itself conscious.

It is the Atman (purusha) that is the conscious *subject* of all that the ego (prakriti) does and experiences. The Atman is the "hear-*er*" of what is heard, "see-*er*" of what is seen, "think-*er*" of what is thought:

> The Imperishable is the seer, though unseen;
> The hearer, though unheard;
> The thinker, though unthought;
> The knower, though unknown.
> Nothing other than the Imperishable can see, hear, think, or know.
> It is in the Imperishable that space is woven, warp and woof. (*Brihadaranyaka Up*: I.11; p. 41)
> That which makes the tongue speak, but cannot be spoken by the tongue,
> Know that as the Self.
> This Self is not someone other than you. (*Kena Up*: I.5; p. 68)

"The *Self* is not someone other than you." Profound indeed, but unfortunately far from apparent to us. In the normal course of development, the Atman (pure consciousness) becomes entranced, as it were, with the ego-role of which it is the conscious subject. So entranced, so enchanted, that it becomes absorbed in the game, going so far as to falsely identify with the ego-role that it observes. This is the understandable but fatal mistake that we all make early in the game. By way of a very loose analogy, I would compare the relationship of Atman and ego to the viewing of a film, in which the camera gives you the impression that you are seeing the action through the eyes of the main character. If you get very absorbed in the action, you might forget that you are a separated observer and temporarily think that you really are that actor, that role. (Little children easily do this.) If the character in the film faces danger, you would feel that it was *you* who were in danger. In your entrancement, you have identified with the experience. In like manner, when Atman falsely identifies its being with that of ego, all of the troubles of the world are the result. To reveal this error, and to correct it, is the central thrust of Vedanta philosophy:

> Like two golden birds perched on the selfsame tree,
> Intimate friends, the ego and the Self, dwell in the same body.
> The former eats the sweet and sour fruits of the tree of life,
> While the latter looks on in detachment. (*Mundaka Up*: III.I.1; p. 115)

To sum things up: This philosophy holds that at the core of your being—and at the core of every other sentient being—is Atman. Atman is not maya; Atman is not a creation of Brahman; Atman *is* Brahman. The Brahman-Atman, though individualized in each sentient being, is Brahman. Atman is the true inner Self of each sentient being. Hence the powerful verse from the *Chandogya Upanishad* which ends with the Sanskrit words *Tat tsvam asi*! ("You are That!") The word "That" refers to the ultimate, unspeakable reality of Brahman:

> In the beginning was only Being,
> One without a second.
> Out of himself he brought forth the cosmos
> And entered into everything in it.
> There is nothing that does not come from him.
> Of everything he is the inmost Self.
> He is the truth; he is the Self supreme.
> And you are that, Shvetaketu; you are that. (*Chandogya Up*: VI.2.2,3; p. 183)

You are That! You are Brahman! You are not a creature *of* Brahman; *you-are-Brahman*! To really know this, to discover and know the Atman within oneself, is the ultimate goal of life. Nothing else compares in significance.

There are some *very* profound implications in all of this, in this assertion of Vedanta that the real me is Brahman. For one thing, there is ultimately no essential difference between me and all other sentient beings. We are all Brahman—the one, indivisible Brahman. We are simply different expressions of Brahman being manifest at the same time. You and I are one! The terrible feeling of separateness is only an illusion. At root, all is One.

Also, death has no reality; there can be no such thing as death. Brahman cannot die; Brahman is eternal. And Atman is Brahman. Therefore, the real enduring me cannot die. Only the role—the ego—can "die" (die out). The Atman does not die:

> We were never born, we will never die;
> We have never undergone change, we can never undergo change;
> Unborn, eternal, immutable, immemorial,
> We do not die when the body dies. (*BG*: II.20; Easwaren, p. 63)

Avidya

We say that everyone is a unique individual. And it's true; no two persons are exactly alike. But what we see, what we identify as a person, is in fact the "persona," the personality, which is the ego-role that that individual plays. Through practice, we get so good at playing the role that it becomes second nature. It's easy to see why people would identify with their roles and fail to see that they really are roles. But, according to Vedanta, this is exactly what we're doing; we're all actors going about our business, totally wrapped up in the roles we play. "All the world's a stage," said Shakespeare, "and the men and women are players on it."

The stage play analogy is excellent. An actor on stage is clearly an "actor," but we don't want him or her to *appear* to be an actor. An actor gives a good performance to the extent that he really gets into the role. Wouldn't it spoil the role, though (as the late Alan Watts used to say), if the actor was continually looking over his shoulder and winking at the audience? We want the actor to get into his role, but definitely not to the extent that he starts believing that he really *is* that role. That is going too far; it would take the fun out of the play. And it might be dangerous; there could be genuine mayhem on stage.

If an actor comes to believe that he really is the role that he plays, and adopts that personality as his own, we would judge that he had lost his mind. Such a person would be committed to a mental hospital for his own safety—and ours. Well, should we not all be committed then? Are we not all doing exactly the same thing? Typically, we all identify totally with the ego-roles that we play and believe with all our hearts that this-is-what-I-am (not something I do). If we fall for our own act, are we not just as insane as the stage actor who falls for his act?

In Vedanta, this great illusion about the nature of self is called *avidya*. The word is derived from the Sanskrit root *vid*, which means "to know." This was the same root that gave us Veda. Another derivative is *vidya*, which means "knowledge"—knowledge of the highest sort. Veda is Truth, and vidya is knowledge of the Truth. In Sanskrit, the prefix "a" has the effect of negating the word (often the case in English too, as in "moral" and "amoral"). Thus, avidya comes to mean "ignorance," ignorance of the truth that the real Self is Brahman.

Avidya is the common condition of mankind; it is *the* "human problem." Avidya, the Upanishads contend, is responsible for all suffering. Note that the contention is not that avidya is responsible for much suffering, nor even for most suffering; the Upanishads proclaim that avidya is responsible for *all of the suffering of mankind*. What a statement!

We can sum up the matter of avidya in the following manner: To identify my being with the maya-role is fundamental ignorance. It is called *avidya*. Avidya is the powerful illusion that my reality consists in the "person," the role that I play. This ego-identification results inevitably in a sense of personal separation, personal insecurity, angst regarding the unavoidability of personal death. Avidya, the common condition of mankind is responsible for all suffering.

To see through the illusion of the separate self and to come to know the real Self, the Brahman-Atman is the proper goal of life. This is true Knowledge. This is *vidya*:

> The Self is indeed Brahman.
> But through ignorance people identify it with
> Intellect, mind, senses, passions,

> And the elements of earth, water, air, space, and fire.
> This is why the Self is said to consist of this and that,
> And appears to be everything. (*Bhih. Up*: III.[4].5; p. 48)

The Self is the "eye of the eye." The eye (i.e., the body) may die, but the eye of the eye cannot die. It is Atman; it goes on forever.

Samsara

The Vedas held that death is followed by an afterlife, a sort of heaven or hell, but the Upanishads proclaim that the Atman will be reborn over and over until finally it bursts through avidya and awakens perfectly to its own Brahman identity. This may take eons of time and countless rebirths. It is Brahman's way of playing hide-and-seek with itself, so to speak, and time is of no consequence:

> The world is the wheel of God,
> Turning round and round with all living creatures upon its rim.
> The world is the river of God,
> Flowing from him and flowing back to him.
> On this ever-revolving wheel of being
> The individual self goes round and round through life after life.
> Believing itself to be a separate creature,
> Until it sees its identity with the Self,
> And attains immortality in the indivisible whole. (*Shvetashvatara Up*: I.4; p. 217)

Atman begins the odyssey of *samsara* at the absolute lowest level of sentient life, whatever that might be. Whatever it is, that minute speck of consciousness is the first step in the Atman's long journey. In accord with the unfolding of Dharma, the Atman will ascend one lifetime at a time through the vast hierarchy of sentient life-forms. As the "wheel of life" turns round and round, the Atman will have been the conscious core of many a sentient being by the time it first comes to life in a human womb.

The particular kind of each rebirth is determined by *karma*, which has been accumulated by the Atman in its previous lives. Karma must not be confused with a system of reward and punishment. Vedanta does not hold that some sort of celestial police force is watching us ready to pass out negative karma citations for our selfish acts. Karma is the natural outcome of the play of Dharma. It is purely and simply a matter of cause and effect. If I consume more calories than I burn, I will inevitably gain weight. It has nothing to do with morality; I'm not being punished. It's simply the natural play of cause and effect. At the time of ego-death, the state of one's karma is carried over into the next life and determines the character of the next rebirth.

Progression upward is natural and, as it were, "automatic" until the Atman reaches the level of human life. The hierarchy continues, of course, through the various castes. But now there is a difference. The human animal, unlike all previous species, is capable of fouling the machinery of Dharma. This is because the human life-form provides the Atman for the first time with a maya-form that is capable of self-reflection. And as we have seen, therein lies all the trouble. The ego can choose to stand in conflict with Dharma by putting its own selfish desires in place of the good of the whole. Depending on its severity, this mode of behavior creates "negative" karma, which must inevitably influence the nature of that Atman's rebirth.

Sufficient negative karma at the time of ego-death can even result in an Atman falling backward and being reborn at a lower level of sentient life. Given this belief, it was inevitable, I suppose, that someone would attempt to work out what kind of rebirth would result from certain types of negative karma. It was widely believed that an unfaithful wife, for example, would be reborn as a scorpion. (There was no mention, so far as I know, of what would happen to an unfaithful husband.)

We can summarize the doctrine of samsara thus: It is obvious that sentient beings on Earth exist in a multitude of different kinds, a vast hierarchy stretching from the lowest forms of animal life to mankind. Throughout all of this hierarchy, there is a constant cycling of death and birth. The body, being maya and material, dies. But the Atman, being Brahman and spirit, is eternal and can never die. Each Brahman-Atman is reborn over and over in successive bodies. This is the ever-turning wheel of samsara.

The doctrine of samsara is beautifully stated in several of the Upanishads. Consider this excellent example from the *Brihadaranyaka Upanishad*:

> As a caterpillar, having come to the end of one blade of grass,
> Draws itself together and reaches out for the next,
> As the skin of a snake is sloughed onto an anthill,
> And reaches out from the old body to a new,
> So does the mortal body fall.
> But the Self, freed from the body
> And dispelled of all ignorance,
> merges in Brahman; infinite life, eternal light. (*Brih. Up*: III.[4].3,7; p. 47, 49)

Moksha

> Brahman-Atman, the All in all of us, surpasses human reason, cannot be conceived of by the human imagination, and cannot be described; yet it can be experienced as the very Life within us (*atman*), or intuited as the Life of the cosmos (Brahman). (Zimmer, *Myth* 142)

In the grand unfolding of Dharma, samsara is the slow progression of the Brahman-Atman to ever higher levels of consciousness through the procession of successive rebirths. Each rebirth presents the Atman with the potential for a new and higher level of consciousness, of gradually dawning Self-awareness. Samsara is Brahman's long quest for ultimately perfect rediscovery of Self:

> As long as we think we are the ego
> We feel attached and fall into sorrow.
> But realize that you are the Self,
> And you will be freed from sorrow.
> When you realize that you are the Self,
> Supreme source of light, supreme source of love,
> You transcend the duality of life
> And enter into the Unitive State. (*Mundaka Up*: III.[1]2,3; p. 115)

"Enter into the Unitive State"; "be freed from sorrow." To be freed from the turning wheel of samsara—that's what it's all about. The Upanishads proclaim that the unquenchable yearning for perfect bliss can finally be satisfied fully and completely. The only thing that stands in the way is ego: the grip of the illusion of ego. It is like a dream that holds us in the bondage of fear, and fear is the essence of suffering:

> When one realizes the Self,
> In whom all life is one, changeless, nameless, formless,
> Then one fears no more.
> Until we realize the unity of life, we live in fear.
> His separateness becomes fear itself. (*Taittiriya Up*: II.7.1; p. 144)

But it is possible to awaken from the dream of ego. Moksha is awakening. In moksha, the ego—the illusion of the separate self—dissolves into the sea of peace that is Brahman:

> As a lump of salt thrown in water dissolves
> And cannot be taken out again,
> Though wherever we taste the water it is salty,
> Even so, beloved, the separate self dissolves
> In the sea of pure consciousness, infinite and immortal. (*Brih. Up*: II.4.12; p. 38)

The awakened man or woman—the person in whom the Atman has awakened to the experience of moksha—lives daily life in a state of perfect peace, free from fear and suffering. Such a one is free to "see himself in all, and all in himself."

In the time of the Upanishads, there was some variety of opinion regarding the exact nature of moksha and how it was achieved. Many believed, for example, that the working out of samsara denied the possibility of moksha to all but high-caste Hindu males. Some would even go so far as to say that only the elite among the Brahmin caste were capable. It might be necessary to be reborn many times, even in spiritually perfected families, before the Atman was cleansed entirely of negative karma and thus ready to make the final step. All agreed though—or so it seems—that liberating oneself entirely from all selfish desires was the essential precondition of moksha. Hence the emphasis on the life of the renunciate for those who sought this highest of all goals.

The attainment of moksha means release from the great wheel of samsara, from the cycling of birth, and death, and rebirth. In moksha, the Atman awakens fully to its Brahman nature. Like a river returning to the sea, the Atman—liberated from avidya—awakens perfectly to its Brahman identity:

> He is the eternal Reality, sing the scriptures,
> And the ground of existence.
> Those who perceive him in every creature merge in him,
> And are released from the wheel of birth and death. (*Shvetashvatara Up*: I.7; p. 218)

AN OVERVIEW OF VEDANTA COSMOLOGY

The Upanishads came into being as the "secret teachings" of various forest communities, living in remote parts of India as long as 3,000 years ago. They were part of the private heritage of those ashrams, lovingly preserved and handed down orally for generations. How amazed those spiritual seekers would have been if they could have foreseen the present-day legacy of their teachings. We can read and ponder their thoughts as if it were we who were "sitting down close to" the guru.

And why *are* we still reading and pondering the thoughts of such an ancient tradition? What is it that connects us so vitally with the genius of ancient India? We certainly don't share a similar way of life; it would seem that ours and theirs couldn't be more different. Superficially, that is obviously true; but at a deeper level, it's not true at all. Men and women in all times and all cultures are alike with respect to the basic needs of life. We all face the same questions with regard to the meaning of life, and the nature of death. People in every age—at least *some* people in every age—have yearned to get beyond the confusing complexity of ordinary life and find out what it's really all about. This is exactly what the Upanishads attempt to do, and they are as alive and provocative today as they ever have been in the past.

The Upanishads are a major contribution to the fund of human wisdom. Technically speaking, they were composed as commentaries on the Vedas. But they go far beyond the Vedas. The Upanishads, taken as a whole, present a complete synthesis of insight regarding the true character of human life. Allow me to attempt a brief summary of this synthesis.

We began by raising this question: Why does anything exist at all; what's *doing* the universe? The Upanishads answer that it is Brahman, the root cause of all that is, the Fact of Existence. Brahman is perfect and complete unto itself; there is no need for Brahman to act. Then why *does* Brahman begin to act; for what reason does Brahman "do" the universe? There is no purpose outside itself; there can't be. Brahman does the universe purely for its own sake. It is the "play," the *lila*, of Brahman.

The play of Brahman is not a haphazard affair. The universe unfolds in a rational and orderly fashion. This is due to the working of Natural Law which is inherent in the lila of Brahman. We call this *Dharma*. It is Brahman-Dharma that accounts for the orderly evolution of the universe. It is Brahman-Dharma that accounts for the harmony and balance which we observe in nature from one day to the next.

The Dharma-evolution of the world that we know (the universe) began in a state of undifferentiated potentiality. Whatever that may be, it was, and always remains, the fundamental substrate of all material reality. We know it as *prakriti*. Prakriti, responding to the ever-present influence of the basic forces of nature (the gunas) has evolved, and continues to evolve, all of the myriad forms ("things") that make up the constantly changing character of Nature.

The totality of all of these "things" of the material world is what we know as *maya*. Maya is reality in that, through the Dharma-evolution of prakriti, it is the manifestation of Brahman. Maya is illusory only to the extent that the *forms* of maya (things) may be mistaken for having a reality of their own, rather than being the expression of a deeper reality. An analogy is often made to the dream state. The elements of a dream are clearly illusory, but at the time, the dreamer believes the dream to be real.

Among the myriad forms of maya, there can be seen to exist two distinctly different kinds: those that exhibit consciousness (sentient beings) and those that do not exhibit consciousness (insentient beings). Consciousness is fundamentally different from materiality, though it can be *affected* by materiality, as, for example, in the case of thought and feeling. But consciousness itself is nonmaterial, hence spiritual, reality. Pure consciousness is the nature of Brahman.

Pure consciousness, the nature of Brahman, is known as *purusha*. Purusha relates to prakriti in a way that is somewhat analogous to you singing a song. Just as the song is an emanation of you, the material universe (maya) is an emanation of Brahman. In a manner of speaking, the song has its own reality, but fundamentally, it is you. In a similar way, the material universe has its own reality, but at a more fundamental level, being an act of Brahman, an emanation of Brahman, it *is* Brahman. Brahman (purusha) is conscious of the play of maya, just as you are conscious of the song.

Brahman, indwelling in a sentient being, is called *Atman*, Brahman-Atman. The Brahman-Atman, though individualized in each sentient being, *is* Brahman. The Atman is Brahman, not a "role" of Brahman, or a "creature" of Brahman. Atman is the true inner Self of each sentient being. Atman is the conscious core of the ego-role of each individual. The role is everything that makes up that distinct person, body as well as behavior. Role includes the "personality," the ego. Ego is the role; Atman is the conscious *subject* of the role.

To mistake the ego-role for the Atman is fundamental ignorance. It is called *avidya*. Avidya is the powerful illusion that my reality consists in the "person," the *role*. This ego-identification results inevitably in a sense of personal separation and personal insecurity. It is responsible for the universal dread of personal death. Avidya, the common condition of mankind, is responsible for *all* suffering! To see through the illusion of the separate self and to come to know the real Self, the Brahman-Atman is the proper goal of life. This is true Knowledge. This is *vidya*.

It is obvious that sentient beings on Earth exist in a multitude of different kinds, a vast hierarchy stretching from the lowest forms of animal life to mankind. Throughout all of this hierarchy, there is a constant cycling of death and birth. The body, being maya and thus material, dies. But the Atman, being Brahman and thus spirit, is eternal and can never die.

The Brahman-Atman is reborn over and over in successive bodies. This progression of rebirths, this turning of the wheel, is known as *samsara*. In the grand unfolding of Dharma, samsara is the slow progression of Brahman-Atman to ever higher levels of consciousness through the procession of successive rebirths. Each rebirth presents the Atman with the potential for a new and higher level of consciousness, of gradually dawning Self-awareness. Samsara is Brahman's long quest for ultimately perfect rediscovery of Self.

The great wheel of samsara—of birth, death, and rebirth—culminates finally in the Atman awakening fully to the knowledge of its Brahman nature. Perfect, final awakening is referred to as *moksha*. Like a river returning to the sea, moksha is the state wherein the Atman is liberated from avidya, awakening perfectly to its Brahman identity. Maya is likened to a veil that hides Brahman. In the words of a common Vedanta truism: "To see the universe as universe is illusion, *avidya*. To see the universe as Brahman is truth, *vidya*." In the final end of Dharma, all of Atman will be "re-absorbed" in Brahman, and the play of *lila* will come to an end. Thus does Brahman, by "playing the universe," evolve eventually to perfect knowledge of Self.

At this point, the only question remaining is this: How does one achieve the awakening of moksha? What does one do? How does one live in order to prepare oneself for the experience? And the answer is simply this: One practices *yoga*. In a sense, it's accurate to say that Vedanta presents the "what," and yoga presents the "how." The discipline of yoga offers the indispensable path which can lead one from the darkness of avidya to the light of moksha. In reality, the practice of yoga calls for a total transformation of life. The great *Bhagavad Gita*, a work which draws together the teachings of the Upanishads, focuses on the comprehensive nature of yoga. And that will be our next area of study.

I would like to end this chapter by returning briefly to the *Chandogya Upanishad*. In this work, a young man named Shvetaketu has returned to his father's home after formally studying the Vedas for twelve years. Uddalaka, his father, observes that Shvetaketu seems very proud of all this learning. "But," Uddalaka asks his son, "Did you ask your teacher for that special wisdom which enables you to hear the unheard, think the unthought, and know the unknown?" A surprised Shvetaketu replies that he did not. "What is that wisdom, father?" he asks. Uddalaka then uses several magnificent analogies to describe to his son the nature of the Self, the Atman within. Each of these ends with the stirring words, *Tat tsvam asi*! (You are That!)

> As the rivers flowing east and west
> Merge in the sea and become one with it,
> Forgetting they were ever separate rivers,
> So do all creatures lose their separateness
> When they merge at last into pure Being.
> There is nothing that does not come from him.
> Of everything he is the inmost Self.
> He is the truth; he is the Self supreme.
> And you are that, Shevetaketu; you are that. (*Chandogya Up*: VI.10.1–3;
> p. 184–185)

Study Questions

1. What is the meaning of the word *Vedanta*?
2. What is an ashram? What critical role did it play in the origin of the Upanishads?
3. "Deer do not give birth to baby ducks, and falling apples do not fall upward." What is the significance of this seemingly obvious statement?
4. Why is it so endlessly frustrating to try to define Brahman in words? How far are words capable of going in defining the meaning of Brahman?
5. What is the relationship between prakriti and maya?
6. Distinguish between prakriti and purusha.
7. "The doctrine of Brahman-Atman is the quintessential feature of Vedanta." What does this mean?
8. What is the all-important relationship between Atman and ego?
9. "Avidya is responsible for all suffering!" What in the world does that mean?
10. Why is it that the grip of the illusion of ego is the only thing that stands in the way of ultimate and perfect moksha?

CHAPTER 4

The *Bhagavad Gita*

The *Bhagavad Gita* opens on a field of battle where a most decisive engagement is about to begin. Two great armies have assembled to decide once and for all who will rule the North Indian kingdom of Bharata. Will it be the Pandavas or their kinsmen, the Kauravas? After much bloodshed on both sides, the noble-hearted Pandavas will eventually prevail over the evil-hearted Kauravas, but that is far in the future, and as the first battle is about to begin, the excitement is building.

The preparations for battle have been nearly completed. The sacrifices have been made, the amour has been strapped on, the battle trumpets are sounding, drums are pounding, the warriors on both sides are shouting and getting themselves emotionally keyed up for battle. At this point, Arjuna, the leader of the Pandavas, asks his charioteer to wheel him out into the no-man's-land between the armies so that he can get one last good look at the enemy's forces:

> O Krishna, drive my chariot between the two armies. I want to see those who desire to fight with me. With whom will this battle be fought? I want to see those assembled to fight for Duryodhana, those who seek to please the evil-minded son of Dhritarashtra by engaging in war. (*BG*: I.21–23; p. 54)*

The driver of the chariot is none other than Krishna, an incarnation of the divine Vishnu. When they reach the center of the battlefield, Arjuna, shielding his eyes from the sun, peers over at the army that he will soon attack. It suddenly dawns upon him that he is about to order the slaughter of old friends, former teachers, kinsmen. The realization

---

*Unless otherwise noted, all excerpts from the *Bhagavad Gita* (*BG*) are taken from Easwaren. The page number at the end of the citation refers to the page in the Easwaren book.

hits him like a bolt of lightning, and he totally loses his nerve. Numbed with sorrow, he actually sits down on the floor of his lightweight war chariot and refuses to fight:

> "This is a great sin! We are prepared to kill our own relations out of greed for the pleasures of a kingdom." Overwhelmed by sorrow, Arjuna spoke these words. And casting away his bow and arrows, he sat down in his chariot in the middle of the battlefield. With the words, "I will not fight," he fell silent. (*BG*: I.45; II.9; p. 56, 62)

To say the least, it's a dramatic moment. Krishna, ever wise and calm, must think of something to get Arjuna back into the fight; leading the army is Arjuna's duty. And he'd better come up with something fast! What follows is a dialogue between Krishna and Arjuna that makes up all of the remainder of the *Bhagavad Gita*. In the course of this dialogue, Krishna accepts Arjuna as his disciple and explains to him the teachings of Yoga. Naturally, a conversation of this sort—particularly one that rambles on for eighteen "books" (i.e., chapters)—would not ordinarily take place in the middle of a battlefield. But this story is being told in the epic style, and in an epic anything can happen.

The name *Bhagavad Gita* literally means "Song of the Lord." The Lord in this case refers to Krishna who, as mentioned above, was the mythical incarnation of the great god Vishnu. Krishna, a compassionate and loving god, is a favorite among the Hindus. The word *song* might better be translated as "discourse", or "chant." The *Bhagavad Gita* (often referred to simply as the *Gita*) was composed in verse form and was probably intended to be chanted aloud. In this respect, the *Gita* was much like the epics of other ancient cultures. Homer's *Iliad*, for example, was originally composed in verse form and was meant to be chanted, at least in part. And like the *Iliad*, the *Gita* was handed down in the oral tradition for many generations before it was eventually committed to writing.

The *Bhagavad Gita* represents the grand climax of the richly creative period that saw the creation of the principal Upanishads. In a way, the *Gita* is a synthesis of the philosophy of the Upanishads. The *Gita*, though, is not classified as an Upanishad, although it seems very much like one. The Upanishads, generally speaking, were concerned with elucidating the difference between *vidya* (awareness of truth) and *avidya* (ignorance). The *Gita*, while reaffirming the truths of the Upanishads, goes beyond this and attempts to describe the way in which one actually makes the ascent to awakening. This is the way of Yoga; the *Bhagavad Gita* is in effect an exposition of Yoga.

The *Bhagavad Gita* was not composed as an isolated work. It is a part—actually a very small part—of a much larger work known as the *Mahabharata*. The *Mahabharata* and the *Ramayana* are the two great epics of Hindu culture. They were to early Indian culture what the *Iliad* and the *Odyssey* were to the culture of ancient Greece. The *Mahabharata*, and thus the *Bhagavad Gita*, although not part of the *shruti* tradition, do belong to the *smriti* tradition, which also contributed to the development of Vedanta. Unlike shruti, which is authorless and deals with infallible truth, the term *smriti* refers to an immense body of secondary works that are much loved and respected, but are not held to be infallible. The *Puranas*, popular stories dealing with the exploits of various deities, are the most widely known.

THE *BHAGAVAD GITA* AND THE *MAHABHARATA*

The *Mahabharata* is a vast work; it seems that everything that makes up the culture of India is somehow included in it. The struggle between the Pandavas and the Kauravas is the central theme of the story, but woven in with that theme are a great many other substories. In the words of Sri Aurobindo:

> [The *Mahabharata* is] not only the story of the Bharatas, the epic of an early event which had become a national tradition, but on a vast scale the epic of the soul and religious and ethical mind and social and political ideals and culture and life of India. It is said popularly of it and with a certain measure of truth that whatever is in India is in the *Mahabharata*. (quoted in Feuerstein, 47)

History has virtually nothing to say about the composition of the *Mahabharata*; what we know is more a matter of legend than history. Presumably there was a single author of the epic, but we know nothing of the life of that person. According to legend, though, the *Mahabharata* was written by a famous sage named Vyasa. He composed the entire work in only three years, and dictated it to the popular elephant-headed god Ganesha, who was the only one with a quick enough mind to follow the swiftness of Vyasa's thoughts. Ganesha even broke off one of his own tusks to use as a writing instrument. (Some believe, incidentally, that Vyasa never died. He lives to this day, so they say, in a secret hermitage somewhere back among the high ranges of the Himalayas.)

For our purposes, the name *Vyasa* will do as well as any. A literary genius named Vyasa, it shall be agreed, was the author of the *Mahabharata*, just as it is agreed that Homer was the author of the *Iliad*. Determining when the *Mahabharata* was created is also a tricky problem. Like Homer, the author of the *Mahabharata* undoubtedly pulled together many traditional legends and stories, some of which had been in existence for centuries. We can reasonably conclude, though, that this was done sometime between the fifth and second centuries B.C.E., because it seems very likely that this was the time when the *Bhagavad Gita* was composed. And the *Bhagavad Gita* was included within the *Mahabharata*. The overall tenor of the *Gita* suggests strongly that it was composed as a response to certain spiritual movements, including early Buddhism, that had come into existence at that time in Indian history.

The *Bhagavad Gita*, then, is a small but key part of a much larger work, the *Mahabharata*. Writers on the subject almost invariably use the expression that the *Gita* is set like a precious jewel in the midst of the *Mahabharata*. Some have speculated that this jewel was not always there, that the *Gita* began life as an independent Upanishad and was appropriated by the author of the *Mahabharata*. It's a beautiful addition, they say, but extraneous to the story of the epic. Most scholars today feel that this is highly unlikely. The integrity of the style of the *Mahabharata* continues more or less evenly through the *Gita*. And, far from being a brilliant departure from the main theme of the *Mahabharata*, the dialogue that makes up the *Bhagavad Gita* provides the critical element necessary for making sense of the symbolism inherent in the story of this epic conflict.

Nevertheless, the principal reason why some believe that the *Gita* might have been a later addition to the *Mahabharata* is that it can stand so well on its own. Except for that small part which we call the *Bhagavad Gita*, the *Mahabharata* does not play a crucial role in our understanding of the evolution of philosophical thought in India during the post-Vedic age. We can lift the *Gita* out of the *Mahabharata* and ignore the rest, and that is essentially what I intend to do. However, the setting of the *Gita* is intimately connected to the larger story, and I feel that it would be helpful to take a few moments here to outline the character of the story up to the opening of the *Gita*. (And, it's an excellent story.)

Vyasa, the legendary author of the *Mahabharata*, assigns himself an important role in the story. It all started one day when his father Parasara, a renowned Indian sage, hired the services of a ferryboat girl to carry him across a river. The girl, Satyavati, was so maddeningly lovely that Parasara found himself consumed with lust. She politely spurned his heated advances. But Parasara was quite a charmer, and Satyavati finally yielded to him when he promised her that she would not lose her virginity. He magically conjured a fog by the riverbank, and they made love hidden from view by the dense mist. Later that same day Satyavati gave birth to a son, and all of this without losing her virginity. (Quite a day!)

The son, of course, was Vyasa. Like his father, he became a highly respected sage. Concerned about the deteriorating state of human life, Vyasa resolved to dedicate his own life to collecting and explaining the spiritual lore of the Indian tradition. Meanwhile, his mother, Satyavati, became the wife of Santanu, ruler of the Kuru kingdom. Since Satyavati was committed to lifelong virginity, Santanu was depending on his only son by a previous marriage to produce sons of his own and continue the family line. Unfortunately, the son died young, leaving two childless wives. Satyavati, feeling compassion for her grieving husband, summoned her own son, Vyasa, and begged him to help out. Vyasa reluctantly (or so we're told) agreed to sleep with both of the beautiful young widows. Both of the girls conceived, and in the course of time, each gave birth to a son.

Vyasa was living the life of a forest ascetic—unwashed, with long matted hair—and, under the circumstances, was said to be strikingly ugly. As he approached the first of the young widows, she was so revolted by the sight of him that she turned her face away and closed her eyes. This infuriated Vyasa, and he responded by putting a curse on the girl. (Apparently, though, he was not so angry that he declined to sleep with her.) As a result of the curse, the first girl's son, Dhritarashtra, was born blind. The other girl, being kind and noble-hearted, did not look away. Her son, Pandu, born shortly after Dhritarashtra, was perfectly healthy.

Because Dhritarashtra was the first to be born, he would have been the successor to the throne. However, his blindness disqualified him, and the rightful line of succession went to Pandu and his descendents. From an early age, it was obvious that Pandu was uncommonly good and noble, whereas Dhritarashtra was a more average sort of person— that is to say, scheming and self-centered. With his two wives, Kunti and Madri, Pandu had five sons, the Pandavas, who like him were strong and courageous young men. Dhritarashtra, demonstrating that blindness was his only infirmity, produced one hundred sons. These hundred are referred to as the Kauravas, "The sons of Kuru," Kuru being the name of a kingdom. Dhritarashtra's sons, especially the eldest, Durodhana, were mean-spirited and selfish young men. But the kingdom was secure. After all, it was Pandu and his sons who would inherit the crown. But that wouldn't make a very good story.

Pandu unexpectedly and tragically died young. It should be pointed out here that Pandu was actually not the biological father of any of the five Pandu brothers. All of them were divinely conceived. Here's how it happened. Pandu was out hunting one day with his bow and arrows. He came upon two deer that were mating, but they ran away when he appeared on the scene. He managed to kill the male, but then discovered that it was a Brahmin disguised as a deer. It was a horrible sin to kill a Brahmin, but, of course, he didn't know. Nevertheless, the dying Brahmin laid a curse on Pandu, saying that he too would die in the pleasure of sexual intercourse. To prevent the curse from being fulfilled, Pandu vowed never again to engage in sex. His two young wives, Kunti and Madri, accepted that, but wanted sons. The gods were magnanimously willing to help out. Yudhishthira, Bhima, and Arjuna, all sons of Kunti, were the result of their divine generosity. But Madri also wanted a son, and with the help of the twin Ashvini gods, she herself gave birth to twins, Nakula and Sahadeva. Somewhat later, while out in the woods with Madri looking for ripe fruits, Pandu became overwhelmed with feelings of intense desire for Madri. Intoxicated by her loveliness, Pandu couldn't resist. As they were making love, Pandu was struck dead, thus fulfilling the curse.

At the time of Pandu's early death, his five sons were still only boys. The eldest, Yudhishthira, was the rightful heir to the crown, but he couldn't wear it until he became a man. In the meantime, his uncle, the blind Dhritarashtra, seized the throne and ruled as regent. This might have been technically unlawful, but all things considered, it could be argued that it was a reasonable move at the time. He merged the two households, raising the five Pandu boys along with his own hundred sons.

The court of Dhritarashtra was a large and active one. The courtly education of so many boys called for many teachers. In addition, there were seers, court officials, military men, and countless relatives. It wasn't long before everyone was aware that the five Pandu boys stood out from the rest. They were excellent young men; the comparison was stark and embarrassing, especially to Dhritarashtra.

Dhritarashtra had hoped that in the course of time his own claim to the throne would be legitimized, and that *his* firstborn son, Duryodhana, would be accepted as the next king. To forestall this, the leaders of the court pushed through a proclamation recognizing the young Yudhishthira as the rightful heir apparent. Now the sons of Dhritarashtra were consumed with jealous hatred. They decided privately to solve their problem by killing their five Pandu cousins. This set in motion a spectacular and complicated plot designed to do away with their rivals.

We need not go into the details here. Suffice it to say that at one point, pretending to want to bury the hatchet, they presented the Pandava brothers with a splendid palace in a nearby city. The modest-minded brothers really didn't want something so extravagant, but to be polite, they accepted the peace offering. The palace was designed to be very beautiful, and also very flammable. Having been tipped off, the brothers themselves set fire to the building during the dark of night, and, with their mother, escaped by way of a secret tunnel that led into the nearby forest. Unknown to the brothers, a traveling woman and her five sons were asleep in the palace when it burned to the ground. It was assumed by everyone that the charred bodies were those of the Pandava brothers and their mother, Kunti. The Pandava brothers had survived, but to stay alive they would have to remain in the forest disguised as holy men.

Here, too, the story might have ended, but again a dramatic event came to the rescue of the story line of the epic. Drupada, the ruler of the neighboring Panchalas, sent out the word that all of the nobles of North India were invited to a great festival whereat he would select a husband for his beautiful young daughter, Draupadi. The Pandava brothers heard about it and decided to go disguised as Brahmin ascetics. Everyone who was anyone was there, including the divine Krishna, who was there as the leader of a powerful Yadava clan.

In the spirit of a good Robin Hood story, Drupada designed an archery contest for the would-be suitors. The winner, using a monster bow fashioned by Drupada himself, would have to hit a moving target, shooting through a revolving ring that was mounted high off the ground. As you might guess, it was a Pandava who won the prize. In fact, it was the noble Arjuna, destined to be one of the two central characters of the *Bhagavad Gita*. Soon Arjuna and the lovely Draupadi were married. In fact, at Arjuna's insistence, the lovely Draupadi became the wife of all five of the brothers!

As a result of Arjuna's victory, and the consequent alliance of the Pandavas with the Kingdom of the Panchalas—and, of course, their new friendship with Krishna and the Yadavas—the Kaurava brothers were more or less forced to sit down and settle their differences with their cousins. They reached a compromise settlement: The kingdom of the Kurus would be divided into two parts. The Kaurava brothers would keep the largest and best part along the Ganges River, and the Pandavas would receive an inferior piece of land along the tributary Jumna River.

Before long, trouble was brewing again. The industrious Pandavas developed their poor parcel, transforming it into a rich and attractive land, thus arousing the greed of their Kaurava cousins. Enter the wily Sakuni, an uncle of Duryodhana. He knew that the noble Yudhishthira had one weakness—one which he shared with noblemen throughout history: He was a reckless and passionate gambler. Sakuni enticed Yudhishthira into a game of dice wherein he skillfully cheated him out of everything. Yudhishthira lost his entire kingdom and all of the possessions of his brothers as well. And, as if that weren't horrible enough, Yudhisthira also lost Draupadi! At Duryodhana's orders, she was literally dragged, weeping, into the throne room and humiliated before the rage-filled eyes of her five husbands. There she would have been stripped naked but for some divine intervention that caused her sari to unwind endlessly. This unthinkable insult sealed the fate of the evil Duryodhana, but revenge would have to wait. Dhritarashtra finally intervened, and at least Draupadi was returned to the Pandava brothers, but, penniless and vulnerable, they had to retreat back into the wilderness again, forced into exile for thirteen long years.

The Pandava brothers accepted the terms of the loss without complaint, but at the end of the thirteen years, they demanded the restoration of their kingdom. Naturally, the Kauravas rejected the demand. Krishna interceded on behalf of the Pandavas, but got nowhere. Ultimately, it became apparent that the conflict could have only one resolution: war. The sons of Pandu did not want war for the sake of their own personal gain. They would have been willing to accept exile and poverty for the rest of their lives rather than visit the horror and suffering of war on their kinsmen. However, much more than personal satisfaction was at stake. This was a conflict between justice and injustice, good and evil. It was their duty as members of the warrior class to uphold the honor of their family and the good of the social order. For this reason, they sadly agreed to shoulder the awesome responsibility of war; Arjuna would be their war leader.

Both sides began the long and arduous preparations for battle. And both sides petitioned Krishna for his help. Krishna declared that he would not fight, but that he would offer instead the services of his splendid army, or his own personal counsel. Duryodhana greedily chose the army. With the help of Krishna's fighting men, he reasoned, his army would be invincible in battle. As a result of this, Krishna offered his personal service as charioteer to Arjuna. And that is how the two men, Krishna and Arjuna, happened to be together in the war chariot in the middle of the battlefield at the opening of the *Bhagavad Gita*.

As noted much earlier in these pages, the Aryan warriors of ancient India loved the bow and arrow, and the horse-drawn war chariot. The chariot was a lightweight two-wheeled vehicle, probably made of wicker and leather. Pulled by one or two well-trained horses, it was a deadly weapon. The chariot carried two men. One was the fighting man with both hands free to rain the killing fire of his arrows on the enemy. The other was the driver of the chariot. This man was no servant; he was a highly skilled and highly respected warrior. One false move could mean instant death for both men.

There is profound symbolism in the fact that Krishna was a charioteer in this story. Krishna's role in the *Bhagavad Gita* will be to instruct Arjuna in the ancient teachings of yoga. The word *yoga* is derived from the Sanskrit root *yuj*, which originally meant "to bind things together." The English word "yoke," as in "to yoke oxen," is a cognate of yoga. One who seriously practices yoga is called a *yogi*, or *yogin*. (*Yogini* is the female form.) There is some speculation that in its original meaning, a yogi was the man who trained the semiwild horses and harnessed them (yoked them) to the war chariot that he himself would drive into battle. In other words, he was a charioteer. This profession became a powerful symbol for yoga, which demands that the yogi harness the wild horses of his own nature and drive the chariot of his own person into the battle against self-will and ignorance.

THE OPENING SCENE

Thus we come to the gathering of the forces at the great battlefield of Kurukshetra, field of the Kurus. The army of the Pandavas is on one side, led by Arjuna. Facing them is the powerful army of the Kauravas, led by the eldest brother, Duryodhana. Dhritharashtra, now old as well as blind, does not travel to Kurekshetra. The battle, however, will be described to him by Sanjaya, his personal driver. Sanjaya will be Dhritarashtra's eyes and ears; he will describe for him all that occurs on the battlefield. For the occasion, Sanjaya has acquired magical powers of perception—he can hear everything that is said, even though the speakers be far away. The author of the *Mahabharata* uses this device to make Sanjaya the narrator of the entire dialogue that is about to take place between Krishna and Arjuna. Sanjaya is relating the conversation to Dhritarashtra. It is for this reason that the opening line of the *Bhagavad Gita*, delivered by Dhritarashtra, reads thus:

> O Sanjaya, tell me what happened at Kurukshetra, the field of dharma, where
> my family and the Pandavas gathered to fight. (*BG*: II.1; p. 52)

As we saw at the beginning of this chapter, Arjuna asks Krishna to take him out to the center of the battlefield where he can get one last look at the enemy before ordering the attack. What he saw, of course, were "grandfathers, teachers, uncles, sons-in-law, grandsons-in-law, and friends." Arjuna was overcome by sorrow. Despairing, he spoke these words:

> O Krishna, I see my own relations here anxious to fight, and my limbs grow
> weak; my mouth is dry, my body shakes, and my hair is standing on end. My
> skin burns, and the bow Gandiva has slipped from my hand. I am unable to
> stand; my mind seems to be whirling.

O Krishna, what satisfaction could we find in killing Dhritarashtra's sons? We would become sinners by slaying these men, even though they are evil. The sons of Dhritarashtra are related to us; therefore, we should not kill them. How can we gain happiness by killing members of our own family? Though they are overpowered by greed and see no evil in destroying families or injuring friends, we see these evils. Why shouldn't we turn away from this sin? (*BG*: I.28–31; p. 52) (*BG*: I.36–39; p. 59)

Paralyzed with sorrow and confusion, Arjuna slumps to the floor of his chariot, utterly unable to stand and lead his men into battle. "I will not fight," he says. In the heavy silence that follows this declaration, the attention turns to Krishna. Krishna now must find a way to get Arjuna back into the fight. He must persuade Arjuna to do his duty, which is to lead his men into battle against the enemy.

To put it mildly, Arjuna is a conflicted man! He is experiencing a hopeless conflict of dharmas. On the one hand, he knows that it is his sacred duty as a warrior to stand and fight in a just war. On the other hand, it is his sacred duty to protect his family, certainly not to kill them, and being that some of them stand in the enemy ranks, that is exactly what he must do. No wonder he's sitting on the floor of his war chariot!

THE *BHAGAVAD GITA* AS METAPHOR

This is an appropriate place to consider a most significant question regarding the *Mahabharata* in general and the *Bhagavad Gita* in particular. Was it the intent of the author of the *Mahabharata* that the story of this war be understood literally, or is the battlefield of Kurukshetra meant to be seen as a metaphor for a very different kind of conflict? Is Krishna, as his words clearly seem to indicate, encouraging Arjuna to really join battle with his Kaurava kinsmen and visit slaughter on them? Or do these words hold a different meaning, a metaphorical meaning, and the battle that Krishna has in mind is of a totally different sort from what is being literally described?

These questions have no easy answers. From the historical perspective, it is probably true that the battle described in the *Mahabharata* is based on an actual event that occurred in northern India sometime around the tenth century B.C.E. We know very little about this great conflict, but it became enshrined in folk legends and would eventually become the unifying theme around which the *Mahabharata* was composed. In this way, it was very much like the Trojan War, an actual historical event, which became the basis for Homer's *Iliad*. But the *Iliad* was not a documentary retelling of the Trojan War, and neither was the *Mahabharata* a retelling of its Indian war. Both epics used a dramatic event popularized in the traditional legends to provide a highly charged setting for a story about human strength and weakness.

Throughout the centuries, some scholars have argued that the *Mahabharata* is meant to be understood in a literal sense—that the battle imagery is just that and nothing else and that Krishna is indeed urging Arjuna to fight and kill the enemy. This is not glorification of war, nor even a resigned acceptance of its inevitability. It is a story about honor and duty; it is the duty of Arjuna as a member of the Kshatriya class to behave as a warrior should, courageously accepting the responsibility of war when it is destined to be. To do otherwise would be to shirk his duty, to upset the working of Dharma, and thus to bring dishonor and evil to his family and to the entire social order.

It is difficult for many modern readers of the *Bhagavad Gita* to accept the point of view expressed above. A far more compelling interpretation is to see the *Gita* as metaphorical. But what is the metaphor? Eknath Easwaren puts it this way:

> Scholars can debate the point forever, but when the [teachings of the *Gita* are put into practice] I think it becomes clear that the struggle the *Gita* is concerned with is the struggle for self-mastery. It was Vyasa's genius to take the whole great *Mahabharata* epic and see it as metaphor for the perennial war between the forces of light and the forces of darkness in every human heart.
>
> Arjuna and Krishna are then no longer merely characters in a literary masterpiece. Arjuna becomes Everyman, asking the Lord himself, Sri Krishna, the perennial questions about life and death—not as a philosopher, but as the quintessential man of action. Thus read, the *Gita* is not an external dialogue but an internal one: between the ordinary human personality, full of questions about the meaning of life, and our deepest Self, which is divine. (7)

Seen in this way, the real battlefield is right inside every man and woman ever born. It is the battlefield where the struggle between the higher nature and the lower nature is waged every day. Or to put it in the language of the Upanishads, the conflict is between avidya and vidya. Arjuna represents the ordinary, unenlightened man or woman. He is bound up in his ego-attachments and the fear and suffering generated by this state of mind. Arjuna is the self with a small "s"; Krishna represents the Atman, the Self with a capital "S." Krishna represents our innermost Self. In the terms of this metaphor, Krishna is lovingly urging Arjuna to do battle against his own infatuation with his ego-attachments. He must attack and "kill" them, as it were. His reluctance is perfectly understandable, but it is the only way that he can liberate himself from the grip of delusion and hope to awaken to knowledge of the Self. The way of liberation is yoga, and Krishna will teach Arjuna yoga.

Eknath Easwaren tells the personal story of his journey by train one time in northern India. The train stopped at Kurukshetra, the legendary site of the great battle, and everyone got off the train in excitement to see this famous place. Everyone that is but Easwaren. He didn't have to get off the train to see the battlefield; it traveled with him wherever he went, and the same is true for everyone else. The battlefield of the *Bhagavad Gita* is to be found in our hearts and minds, not in the soil of North India.

Seen in the terms of this striking metaphor, the *Bhagavad Gita* becomes a personal message to all of mankind. It is universal, and it is relevant to everyone's life in every age and every culture. The metaphorical interpretation of the *Gita* elevates the entire *Mahabharata* to the level of sublime literature. It transforms the *Mahabharata* from being simply the action-packed adventure story of one noble Indian family to becoming the story of every person's odyssey from darkness to light.

THE AWAKENED PERSON

At the end of Book One, we leave Arjuna, his will paralyzed, actually sitting down in his small war chariot, refusing to fight. To say the least, it's a dramatic moment. The spotlight turns to Krishna. He'd better think of something to get Arjuna back into the fight, and he'd better do it fast! The battle is about to begin, and the leader of the Pandavas is out in the middle of the battlefield sitting down on the floor of his chariot. Not flustered in the least by the situation, Krishna smiles at Arjuna and speaks to him in a calm, friendly tone of voice. "This despair and weakness in a time of crisis are mean and unworthy of you, Arjuna . . . It does not become you to yield to this weakness. Arise with a brave heart and destroy the enemy." Arjuna repeats his determination not to kill his kinsmen and former friends. It's a horrifying thought; he would rather be dead himself. Krishna responds by taking aim at the very heart of Arjuna's dilemma, the problem of death:

> You speak sincerely, but your sorrow has no cause. The wise grieve neither for
> the living nor for the dead. There has never been a time when you and I, and
> the kings gathered here have not existed, nor will there be a time when we will
> cease to exist. As the same person inhabits the body through childhood, youth,
> and old age, so too at the time of death he attains another body. The wise are
> not deluded by these changes. (*BG*: II.11–13; p. 62)

Clearly, the author of the *Gita* is using the character of Krishna to solidly affirm the traditional, orthodox doctrines of Atman and samsara. At the very beginning of the dialogue between Krishna and Arjuna, this all-important matter is nailed down in a clear and distinct fashion. It is the cornerstone of the Vedanta philosophy that the *Bhagavad Gita* is giving practical expression to, and the author of the *Gita* wants no doubts to exist in the mind of the listener.

Why is it so important to affirm the reality of Atman right at the beginning? We can only speculate. One possibility is that it was simply a reasonable place to begin. If the *Bhagavad Gita* is a summation of Upanishadic teaching and a practical guide for applying that teaching, then why not begin with the most fundamental principles? After all, Arjuna is grievously worried about the imminent death of many warriors, as if death were a real and final end of life. This is not an unreasonable interpretation. Another possibility exists, however. At the time the *Gita* was composed, the traditional teachings were being actively challenged by many reform movements. Some, such as the Buddhists, were even going so far as to deny the reality of Atman, the spiritual bedrock of the whole orthodox tradition. It may well be that the *Bhagavad Gita* came into existence as an inspired counteroffensive against the self-styled reform movements. The author of the *Gita*, while accepting the need for some reforms, would not throw out the baby with the bathwater. In summing up the essential teachings of the Vedanta tradition, he would answer the reformers, especially the Buddhists, by revealing the great practical truths of the orthodox tradition, and he would begin by strongly proclaiming the fundamental correctness of the doctrine of Atman.

Whatever the case may be, Krishna does indeed begin with a clear statement about the reality of Atman and samsara. Proclaiming it is one thing; knowing its truth is quite another. And Krishna's task is to lead Arjuna to an awakening in which he sees that truth. In so doing, Arjuna will see through the illusion which is responsible for his present state of confusion and suffering, and then he will be able and willing to stand up and fight. To achieve this end, Krishna declares that he will teach Arjuna yoga. "You have heard the intellectual explanation of Samkya, Arjuna; now listen to the principles of yoga." A little earlier, while expressing his feelings of despair, Arjuna had asked Krishna to accept him as a disciple. It was important for the author of the *Gita* to insert this, because in the Hindu tradition it is imperative that a person request the privilege of being another's disciple; a genuinely enlightened teacher never *recruits* disciples. Thus, it is now legitimate for Krishna to begin the teaching, and this is what the *Bhagavad Gita* is really all about. Above all else, it is a practical guide showing the listener (or reader) how to apply the teachings of the Upanishads in one's daily life. Krishna says that he will teach Arjuna yoga because, in its general sense, yoga refers to any path that can lead from ignorance to awakening.

One almost gets the feeling that Krishna is a little unsure about how to begin. His initial comments about yoga are very lofty generalizations. He tells Arjuna that "Yoga is perfect evenness of mind" and that "Yoga is skill in action." Arjuna, however, is a man of action, a very down-to-earth kind of person. He's not interested in theoretical discussions. Arjuna wants practical advice with concrete examples. After listening for a little while, Arjuna interrupts Krishna with a question. You can almost sense his frustration, but at the same time, his growing interest. Before getting into these more generalized matters, Arjuna wants to know, up front, what the person skilled in yoga is actually like; in other words, how does he recognize the real McCoy. Lots of people claim to be enlightened, but when you look closely, it invariably turns out to be only a pose. So, before getting into a discussion of principles, Arjuna wants Krishna to describe for him what the really awakened person is like. How does he walk? How does he talk? How does he behave in ordinary, everyday situations? Arjuna needs to know this so that he will have something concrete in mind that he can relate Krishna's teaching to.

Krishna apparently sees the wisdom in Arjuna's question and responds in a short monologue at the end of Book Two that is one of the most beautiful sections of the entire *Bhagavad Gita*. Gandhi felt that if this eighteen-verse section were all that had survived of the *Gita*, we would still have all of its essential wisdom. Krishna answers Arjuna's question; he describes for him the essential features of the truly awakened man or woman. Before we get to that, though, this would be a good place to look briefly at Krishna's description of the kind of person who is *not* a genuinely awakened individual. This is a very important matter to Krishna because the world is so obviously full of fakes. Many people are deluded by counterfeit wise men, and Krishna wants to be sure that Arjuna will not be one of them.

It seems that Krishna is most concerned about what he regards to be the false message of those who claim to be spiritually aware as a result of extremely ascetic lifestyles. Indian culture has always included a number of individuals who drop out of ordinary life to become itinerant renunciates—the "holy men," the sadhus. Generally speaking, they are respected by the common people, who believe that they have achieved a higher state of spiritual awareness as a result of their austerities. There have always been some who are willing to go to great extremes of asceticism. The thinking behind this, usually, is that a higher truth can only be known when the distractions of maya are completely transcended. The ultimate goal becomes total inaction, because all action is rooted in maya. Krishna declares this to be a false path. Those who follow it are deluding themselves, as well as those who hold them in high respect:

> He who shirks action does not attain freedom; no one can gain perfection by abstaining from work. Indeed, there is no one who rests for even an instant; every creature is driven to action by his own nature. (*BG*: III.4,5; p. 75)*

---

*It's quite possible that the author of the *Gita* was specifically fixing the Jains in his sights. Jainism was one of the reform movements that the *Gita* seems to be reacting to, and the Jains, especially in their early days, sought release from all worldly attachments through extreme ascetic practices.

In a way, though, Krishna's strongest censure is for those more ordinary kinds of people who proclaim, through their lifestyle, that fulfillment is to be found in a selfish and materialistic pursuit of pleasure. This way of life is far more universal than the way of the ascetic monk and is therefore much more pernicious. Often dressed in a seductively appealing form, it is the false path that Arjuna, and everyone else, has to deal with all of the time. Krishna first turns on this erroneous way in the early part of his discourse:

> There are ignorant people who speak flowery words and take delight in the letter of the law, saying that there is nothing else. Their hearts are full of selfish desires, Arjuna. Their idea of heaven is their own enjoyment, and the aim of all their activities is pleasure and power. The fruit of their actions is continual rebirth. (*BG*: II.42,43; p. 65)

Krishna returns to this theme much later in the *Gita* and makes his point in very strong words. The relevance of these words would be recognized by men and women in any age:

> "There is no God," they say, "no truth, no spiritual law, no moral order. The basis of life is sex; what else can it be?" Holding such distorted views, possessing scant discrimination, they become enemies of the world, causing suffering and destruction.
>
> Hypocritical, proud, and arrogant, living in delusion and clinging to deluded ideas, insatiable in their desires, they pursue their unclean ends. Although burdened with fears that end only with death, they still maintain with complete assurance, "Gratification of lust is the highest that life can offer."
>
> Bound on all sides by scheming and anxiety, driven by anger and greed, they amass by any means they can a hoard of money for the satisfaction of their cravings . . . "I have destroyed my enemies. I shall destroy others too! Am I not like God? I enjoy what I want. I am successful. I am powerful. I am happy. I am rich and well-born. Who is equal to me? I will perform sacrifices and give gifts, and rejoice in my own generosity" . . . Self-important, obstinate, swept away by the pride of wealth, they ostentatiously perform sacrifices without any regard for their purpose. Egotistical, violent, arrogant, lustful, angry, envious of everyone, they abuse my presence within their own bodies and in the bodies of others.
>
> Life after life I cast those who are malicious, hateful, cruel, and degraded into the wombs of those with similar demonic natures. Degraded in this way, Arjuna, they fail to reach me and fall lower still. (*BG*: XVI.8–20; p. 191–192)

That's quite a description, isn't it? Parts of it, at least, are painfully familiar to any person with human blood in his (or her) veins. So, having identified the principal enemies of the right path, let us return to Krishna's response to Arjuna's question. Arjuna had asked Krishna to describe for him, at least in general terms, the character of the person who truly is an awakened man or woman. "Tell me of those who live established in wisdom, ever aware of the Self, O Krishna. How do they talk? How sit? How move about"?

Krishna only begins his response to Arjuna's question in the section at the end of Book Two. It's a theme that he returns to often throughout the *Gita*. The essential points can be summed up as follows:

> They live in wisdom who see themselves in all, and all in them; who have renounced every selfish desire and sense craving tormenting the heart. Neither agitated by grief, nor hankering after pleasure, they live free from lust and fear and anger. (*BG*: II.52; p. 67)

> Free from self-will, aggressiveness, arrogance, anger, and the lust to possess people or things, he is at peace with himself and others and enters into the Unitive State. United with Brahman, ever joyful, beyond the reach of desire and sorrow, he has equal regard for every living creature and attains supreme devotion to me. (*BG*: XVIII.53–54; p. 210)

In these beautiful passages, Krishna is emphasizing that the genuinely awakened person is one who has come to see the underlying unity of all being, and who thus feels deep love and compassion for every being that exists. Such a person is a true "renunciate," not in the sense of renouncing the world, which Krishna insists is a false path, but rather in the sense of renouncing "every selfish desire and sense craving tormenting the heart." Thus it follows that the genuinely awakened person does not denounce sense pleasure as such (a common misunderstanding), but only *attachment to* sense pleasure. It is the nature of life to often be pleasurable; this is natural and good; the problem develops only when the pleasures of life become objects of desire, the stuff of attachment. The awakened person is said to be free from attachment and its inevitable companion, aversion. The awakened person is kind, good-natured, and above all, reveals in his or her daily life a compassion for all other beings.

Krishna wants Arjuna to understand (and remember, Arjuna represents all men and women) that the awakened person is most definitely not some rare saintly being, far beyond the reach of ordinary mortals. The awakened person is the truly real, down-to-earth human being and dwells in the heart of every man and woman, waiting only to be "awakened" by that genuinely rich way of life that Krishna wants Arjuna to see as the right path, the path of yoga.

The remainder of the *Gita* amounts to a close examination of the way of yoga. Krishna will focus on three: Raja Yoga, Karma Yoga, and Bhakti Yoga. The author of the *Gita* chooses not to include Jnana Yoga, the way of special mystical and philosophical knowledge. Perhaps this is because it would obviously not be a suitable path for the not-very-philosophical Arjuna, as would be true for most people. Also, Hatha Yoga is never mentioned by name. In fact, the word *Hatha*, referring to a specific school of yoga, dealing with a highly specialized system of bodily exercises (*asanas*) and breathing exercises (*pranayama*), did not come into existence until much later. At the time of the composition of the *Gita*, such asanas and pranayama as were practiced were seen as being entirely a companion of the yoga of meditation, and it was assumed that the student would learn these skills under the personal supervision of a master. It simply was not the sort of subject to be discussed in a work such as the *Gita*.

In the organization of the *Gita* as it has come down to us, the subject of Karma Yoga is taken up first; it is the theme of Book Three. Book Six deals specifically with Raja

Yoga, the yoga of meditation. The remaining twelve books touch on many subjects, but are largely concerned with Bhakti Yoga, the yoga of devotion. The *Bhagavad Gita* is not neatly organized, the way a modern text would likely be. To get the sense of the whole, it is necessary to read the entire work, slowly and thoughtfully. And that's exactly what I hope you will do. These pages are in no way a substitute for reading the *Gita* itself. Ideally, I hope that what you read here will inspire you to want to read the book itself and that you will be able to understand it a little better for having studied this first.

KARMA YOGA

The word *karma* is derived from the Sanskrit word *kri* ("to do"), and in its most basic sense, karma simply means "action." This basic sense of the word, though, would come to have a variety of meanings in the evolution of Eastern thought. Speaking very broadly, karma is usually associated with the principle of cause and effect: Actions one performs will inevitably have consequences. It's best, though, to pin down the specific meaning of karma for each philosophical system individually. The word *karma*, along with so much else from the "mysterious East," became enormously popular with some in the West during the 1950s and 1960s. Not too surprisingly, its meaning suffered a bit in translation from ancient Hindu culture to the modern counterculture.

Karma Yoga is the "path of right action." It deals with the kind of behavior—that is, lifestyle—that is appropriate for one who seeks to become a liberated man or woman. Having established that a life of action is natural and necessary, Krishna turns to the real question: What is *right* action? We are presented with two alternatives: action directed to the goal of personal profit and action directed to the welfare of all. It should come as no surprise that the author of the *Gita* chooses the welfare of all as the correct answer:

> Selfish action imprisons the world. Act selflessly, without any thought of personal profit. (*BG*: III.9; p. 76)

> The ignorant work for their own profit, Arjuna; the wise work for the welfare of the world, without thought for themselves. (*BG*: III.25; p. 77)

> You have the right to work, but never to the fruit of work. You should never engage in action for the sake of reward, nor should you long for inaction. (*BG*: II.47; p. 66)

Pretty startling suggestions, aren't they? Is Krishna really saying that I have no right to the fruit of my own work; that I should never engage in action for the sake of reward? How can this be? Is he suggesting that I would be a better person if I refused my paycheck? These passages seem to fly in the face of common sense. Obviously, some careful interpretation is needed here.

In the view of the author of the *Gita,* the proper goal of life is to become an awakened person; everything takes its value in relation to that all-important goal. He would agree wholeheartedly with the line from the gospel: "What does it profit a man if he gains the entire world, and suffers the loss of his immortal soul?" (Matthew; 6: 26). If the essence of enlightenment is knowing the unity of all being, then the enemy of enlightenment is the private ego and its endless selfish cravings.

The path of Karma Yoga is directed at one thing: it seeks to overcome the obsessive attachment to the welfare of the private self. It accomplishes this by redirecting the purpose of action to that which, by its very nature, is not ego-self—that is, the welfare of the larger community of which the individual is but a part. What it comes down to is a redefining of "self," a coming to see that the private ego-self is an illusion and that the real self is the entire community, ultimately all of humankind. When one identifies with the whole community, he can be entirely "selfish," so to speak, and the welfare of all will be served. In this view, we have the very interesting contention that in the long run, one's personal interests are best served by not focusing on the desires of the private self, but rather by deliberately acting in what one perceives to be the best interests of the whole community. In other words, work for the good of the whole, and your own interests will be best served. That may sound a little crazy at first, but the *Gita* insists that it is true, and that understanding it is the key to a genuinely successful life.

Karma Yoga is sometimes referred to as the yoga of Selfless Service. Selfless service does not mean "good deeds"—helping someone across the street, for example, or picking up a hitchhiker. Good deeds are wonderful, of course, but that's not the point; selfless service means something else. The "service" in "selfless service" refers simply to action that in some way is of real value to the community. This could be just about anything. "Selfless" means simply that the action is not ego-bound. We all know such self-less moments. In fact, any time that one is totally absorbed in a task, the ego-consciousness is temporarily suspended. This is what happens naturally when you work at something you love to do. An artist absorbed in a painting, a scientist focused on a research project, or even a farmer plowing a field—all of these are examples of potentially self-less action. The key point is that one forgets himself, temporarily transcends his ego-self, by becoming absorbed in a loved activity.

Now let's put them together. "selfless service" refers to any kind of action in which one loses oneself, so long as that action is beneficial to the community. Thus, the path of Karma Yoga is open to everyone! Anyone who works in a field that he or she loves, and which work is of value to the larger community, is, in fact, a Karma yogi. The farmer, the scientist, the teacher, the homemaker, the sculptor, the student, the garbage collector (yes, definitely), the delivery person, even an insurance salesman (Why not?)—almost every kind of work can be a fertile field for Karma Yoga. The only requirement is that it be of some genuine value to the community, and that, all in all, the person loves the work. This is essential because it is only love that dissolves the grip of ego. If one does not love the work, it then becomes merely a means to an end. What this usually means is that the work becomes a means to making money, which can then be used to satisfy the desires of the ego.

This separation between action and its reward is precisely what Karma Yoga seeks to overcome. So long as there is separation, the ego is in control. This is why Krishna wants Arjuna to see that it is essential that the reward be *in the doing*, not separated from it. If we work for the sake of "profit," we are separating the reward from the work itself, something which would never happen, *could* never happen, if the action was something loved in itself. Does a mother caring for her baby have to be "paid" for it? Of course not; the joy is in the doing, just as it is with the artist. It is truly said that there is no such thing as a poor artist. The bottom line is that *everyone* is an artist, potentially at least; everyone can be a Karma yogi. This is why Krishna says, "The ignorant work for their own profit, Arjuna; the wise work for the welfare of the world, without thought for themselves."

Karma Yoga is often misunderstood as meaning little more than being a giving sort of person, someone who practices good deeds. Seen in its proper light, Karma Yoga amounts to a total reshaping of the goal of action in life. It is a renunciation of the belief that selfishly serving the desires of the ego is the way to fulfillment in life. Krishna sums it up well:

> True renunciation is giving up all desire for personal reward. Those who are attached to personal reward will reap the consequences of their actions; some pleasant, some unpleasant, some mixed. But those who renounce every desire for personal reward go beyond the reach of karma. (*BG*: XVIII.11,12; p. 206)

RAJA YOGA

> In the still mind, in the depths of meditation, the Self reveals itself.

Book Six of the *Bhagavad Gita* focuses on Raja Yoga, the yoga of meditation. *Raj* means "royal" or "rule" in Sanskrit, thus Raja Yoga is the "King of Yogas." Raja rules over the others in the sense that it is most central; it is the interface between ordinary consciousness and knowledge of the Absolute. It is through the practice of meditation that the aspirant learns to control the mind, strip down the layers of ego, and ultimately achieve the state of consciousness known as *samadhi*. (We will have much more to say on this subject in other parts of this study.)

In the practice of Raja Yoga, one turns inward, deeply inward, shedding all of the layers of the private self and its restless mind. The objective is nothing less than the core of consciousness, in which state perfect peace reigns. Raja Yoga is thus the companion and the necessary opposing complement to Karma Yoga, whose nature is action. The out-going of Karma finds balance in the inward-turning of Raja. Together they are a complementary whole.

These two great yogas, Karma and Raja, are found in all spiritual traditions, though, of course, they are known by many names. In Hinduism, they became highly developed traditions. Shakyamuni Buddha, for example, who was himself a Hindu renunciate for many years, loved the practices of Raja Yoga. Although he would part company with many of the cherished beliefs of the Hindu tradition, he never abandoned the practice of meditation.

Up to this point in the discourse between Krishna and Arjuna, Krishna has wanted Arjuna to understand that through the practice of Karma Yoga he can refashion himself into the kind of unselfish man that is receptive to higher knowledge. Now, in Book Six, Krishna reveals that the actual awakening of higher knowledge is an interior experience born in the consciousness of one who has learned to control the restless mind. Hence the need for Raja as well as Karma Yoga. But Arjuna, a very normal human being, is dismayed by the thought of ever being able to control something so fitful as the thinking mind:

> O Krishna, the stillness of divine union which you describe is beyond my comprehension. How can the mind, which is so restless, attain lasting peace? The mind is restless, turbulent, powerful, violent; trying to control it is like trying to tame the wind. (*BG*: VI.33,34; p. 107)

How right Arjuna is! Controlling the thinking mind *really is* like trying to tame the wind. In India, a land where monkeys abound, the ordinary mind is called the "monkey-mind"; sometimes it is compared to a drunken monkey or even to a drunken monkey that's been stung by a scorpion (quite an image, but not far off the mark). Nevertheless, the experience of countless men and women over the ages proves that controlling the mind is possible. With dedication, and patience, the practices of Raja Yoga can lead one to mastery of meditation, wherein "the mind is unwavering like the flame of a lamp in a windless place."

In a much-loved section of the *Gita*, Krishna even gives Arjuna some practical advice about the way to practice meditation. These verses suggest that the author of the *Gita* must have assumed that his work would have a wide audience; ordinarily, this kind of teaching would be a private matter between guru and disciple. Krishna's suggestion about using a deerskin and "kusha" grass should not be taken literally; he was merely referring to what was traditional at the time among some yogins:

> Select a clean spot, neither too high nor too low, and seat yourself firmly on a cloth, a deerskin, and kusha grass. Then, once seated, strive to still your thoughts. Make your mind one-pointed in meditation, and your heart will be purified. Hold your body, head, and neck firmly in a straight line, and keep your eyes from wandering. With all fears dissolved in the peace of the Self and all desires dedicated to Brahman, controlling the mind and fixing it on me, sit in meditation with me as your only goal. With senses and mind constantly controlled through meditation, united with the Self within, an aspirant attains nirvana, the state of abiding joy and peace in me. (*BG*: VI.11–15; p. 105–106)

BHAKTI YOGA

Fill your mind with me; love me; serve me; worship me always.
Seeking me in your heart, you will at last be united with me.

With these powerful words, Krishna gives expression to what is ultimately the great goal of the *Bhagavad Gita*, leading Arjuna from the ignorance of the separate self to awakening to his union with the Divine. The *Gita* is an exposition of yoga. All paths of yoga are excellent and important, and they are clearly interrelated. But, as the *Gita* develops, it becomes more and more apparent that the author of the *Gita*, through the words of Sri Krishna, is proclaiming that Bhakti Yoga, the way of devotion, is the greatest yoga of all, greater even than Karma and kingly Raja. Loving devotion and service to a personal savior are what distinguishes Bhakti. Krishna—the incarnation of Vishnu, one with the Ultimate Ground of Being—presents himself to Arjuna as the personal, compassionate manifestation of the Godhead, and, as such, a savior who can be worshipped as an approachable, loving friend of humanity.

Just to be sure that there is no misunderstanding in this matter, the author of the *Gita* has Krishna spell it out in lucid terms. Arjuna wants to know which is better; the way of the head or the way of the heart. "Of those steadfast devotees who love you, and those who seek you as the eternal formless Reality, who are the more established in yoga"? Krishna's reply leaves no doubt as to where the author of the *Gita* stands.

"Those who set their hearts on me and worship me with unfailing devotion and faith are more established in yoga." (*BG*: XII.1,2; p. 162)

In no way is this meant to imply that there is some sort of fundamental conflict between the various paths of yoga. Nothing could be further from the truth. The various paths of yoga are complementary. Although a given individual may be disposed to emphasize this one or that one, *all* must be expressed in the life of a true aspirant. And, Krishna proclaims, the life of yoga comes together in the act of devotion, Bhakti Yoga. This is true not only for the sort of person for whom Bhakti means the customary forms of religious worship, but also for the philosophically minded person. "They worship me with a one-pointed mind, having realized that I am the eternal source of all . . . Full of devotion, they sing of my divine glory." (*BG*: IX.13,14; p. 133)

The opening up of unrestrained selfless love is what it all ultimately comes down to. This is the essence of Krishna's teaching. The various paths of yoga are ways of breaking down the love of an illusory ego-self and nourishing in its place a love of that which alone is real. Karma Yoga generates the love that transcends the private self, and Raja Yoga returns it to the source, nourishing love of the real Self. Finally, in the love of a personal representation of the Godhead, one achieves the perfection of yoga. Krishna sums it up beautifully:

> I am that supreme Self, praised by the scriptures as beyond the changing and the changeless. Those who see in me that supreme Self see truly. They have found the source of all wisdom, Arjuna, and they worship me with all their heart. (*BG*: XV.18,19; p. 186)

Lord Krishna, having given all of the teaching to his disciple Arjuna, brings the great discourse to a close. There is nothing more to say. And now Krishna wants to know if he has succeeded. Has Arjuna awakened to a higher truth? Will he now stand up and lead his men into battle? Krishna asks Arjuna if he has listened with understanding. Is he now free from doubt and confusion? Arjuna, a changed man now, answers with firmness: "You have dispelled my doubts and delusions, and I understand through your grace. My faith is firm now; I will do your will." (*BG*: XVIII.73; p. 52212)

Study Questions

1. What is the relationship of the *Bhagavad Gita* to the *Mahabharata*? Why do some believe that the *Gita* was not originally part of the *Mahabharata*?
2. How is the story line of the *Mahabharata* structured in such a way as to lead inevitably to war between the Pandavas and the Kauravas?
3. Dhritharashtra was born before his brother, Pandu. How did it come to pass, then, that his firstborn, Duryodhana, was to be denied rightful succession to the throne?
4. The five sons of Pandu were not really *his* sons. What's that all about?
5. Why is it stated that "There is profound symbolism in the fact that Krishna was a charioteer in the story"?
6. Is the *Bhagavad Gita* meant to be understood literally or metaphorically? If metaphorically, what would you say are the advantages of this approach?
7. If one interprets the *Gita* metaphorically, what is the metaphor? In your judgment, what are the terms of the metaphor, and what does each represent?
8. Why does Krishna begin his teaching with a strong affirmation of the doctrines of Atman and samsara?

9. In the final eighteen verses of Chapter Two, Krishna describes his vision of the fully awakened person. How would you sum it up? Why do you suppose that Gandhi said that even if all of the *Gita* but these eighteen verses had been lost, the entire wisdom of the *Gita* would still have been preserved?

10. Eknath Easwaren refers to Karma Yoga as "selfless service." What *is* selfless service; is it the same as what we mean by "good deeds"? What makes Karma Yoga a yoga?

11. Correctly understood, what is the relationship between Karma Yoga and Raja Yoga? Can either one stand alone? Can any yoga stand alone?

12. Loosely translated, "Raja Yoga" means King of Yoga. What makes Raja the king? Does this seem reasonable to you?

13. Even though Raja may be kingly, the assertion is made that the author of the *Gita* regards Bhakti Yoga to be the greatest of all yoga paths. How do you feel about this? In what way could it be said to be true?

14. How do the various paths of yoga come together to form a unitive whole?

15. How do you interpret the teaching of the *Bhagavad Gita*? What is the quintessential message of the *Gita*?

CHAPTER 5

Darshana

Thus far in this study, we have mostly been examining the unfolding of *shruti*, the Sanskrit name for the corpus of sacred teachings that took form in ancient India over a time span of more than a thousand years. Beginning with the Vedas, and culminating in the Upanishads, it is, to say the least, a very impressive achievement of the human mind.

The cornerstone of the orthodox view, so beautifully expressed in the Upanishads, is that the ultimate object of life is the attainment of moksha. But the Upanishads in no way attempt a carefully reasoned critique of what the experience of moksha is, nor of how it is to be attained. Clearly that was not the point of the Upanishads; for the most part they are poetic in style, emphasizing the importance of mystical intuition. Knowledge of Brahman is presented as intuitive knowledge that completely transcends ordinary knowledge. Put simply, the composers of the Upanishads had no interest in presenting critical philosophy. Their message was inspirational, intended for the ears of those who were already committed to the basic beliefs of the Upanishadic tradition.

The conservative true believers, however, were not destined to hold the field entirely to themselves. Around the middle of the first millenium B.C.E., various alternative philosophies began to develop into popular movements, often styled as "reform" movements. Buddhism and Jainism are two of the better known reform movements that developed during this time. These, and others, expressed a skeptical attitude toward the Upanishadic tradition. They criticized it for being too mystical, too dependent on intuitive knowledge. The philosophy of the Upanishads was criticized for lacking a foundation of reasonableness. However beautiful and inspiring it might be to some, it was argued, Vedanta was not a true philosophy because it could not be rationally defended. The perception of its truth depended ultimately not on reasoned argument, but on a highly personal mystical experience. In other words, this might be fine for the poet and the mystic, but it offered mighty slim pickings for the true philosopher.

Over time, both of these camps developed into a number of distinct philosophical systems. As discussed in the Introduction to Chapter 3, these systems are known as *darshanas*. Those which accepted the infallible authority of the Vedas are the orthodox darshanas, and those which rejected the infallible authority of the Vedas are the heterodox darshanas. The orthodox darshanas, six in number, supported and defended the truth of the *shruti* tradition. The heterodox darshanas offered new, and in some cases, radically new alternatives. We will examine the principle darshanas in both the orthodox and the heterodox groups.

THE ORTHODOX DARSHANAS

Over time, the Hindu tradition came to recognize six orthodox darshanas. By custom, these are arranged in three pairs: Vedanta and Purva Mimamsa, Samkhya and Yoga, and Nyaya and Vaisheshika. By far the most influential among these was, and continues to be, Vedanta. We will briefly examine the nature of each of these.

Purva Mimamsa

We begin with *Purva Mimamsa* because it is the most solidly fundamentalist of the orthodox group. It is linked with Vedanta because both systems were originally known by the name "mimamsa," which refers to the solving of a problem—in this case, the liberation from samsara—through critically examining the nature of the problem. Purva (meaning "early") Mimamsa focused strictly on the Vedas and sought the solution there. *Uttara Mimamsa* (meaning "later," or also "higher"), which would come to be known as Vedanta, focused more on the Upanishads, as we have seen.

The Purva Mimamsa darshana is associated with Jaimini, the name of a little-known fourth-century Brahmin alleged to be the author of the *Mimamsa Sutra*. In this work, Jaimini sets forth an enormous code of rules for the correct interpretation and performance of Vedic rituals. It was his belief, as well as that of many others, that the right life—that is to say, the way of life that would lead to moksha—was the life that was lived in proper accord with Dharma. Such proper behavior could not possibly be determined infallibly through perception or reason; these frail human instruments are far too imperfect. The only sure path is to faithfully follow the injunctions contained in the sacred Vedas. And it became Jaimini's self-assigned task to interpret and clarify the ritual injunctions of the Vedas so that all could follow. Clearly, this darshana is solidly fundamentalist. The words of the Vedas contain all truth, and that truth is self-evident. Their injunctions are to be followed literally and without question. This is the one and only path to salvation.

Although the unyielding position of Mimamsa was attractive to some, many wished to anchor the orthodox tradition in the teachings of the Upanishads as well as the Vedas. The great *Bhagavad Gita* was a powerful atttempt to cast such an anchor. As discussed in Chapter 4, it's quite possible that the *Bhagavad Gita* was composed at least in part as a response to the challenge presented by what the traditionalists viewed as the "heretical" darshanas. The author of the *Gita* presented a strong and uncompromising declaration of the truth of the doctrines of Atman and samsara. Beautifully presented though it may be, the *Gita* is indeed a declaration, a statement, not really a defense in the philosophically understood sense of the word. That important task would fall initially to a second century B.C.E. philosopher named Akshapada Gautama, the founder of the *Nyaya* darshana and author of the *Nyaya Sutra*. The tradition begun by Gautama was subsequently enriched and in some sense completed by Vatsyayana, a philosopher of the fifth century C.E. (Incidentally, Akshapada Gautama was not related to Siddhartha Gautama, "the Buddha," who lived more than six centuries earlier.)

Nyaya and Vaisheshika

Gautama's goal was not to prove the correctness of the assertions of the Upanishads; rather his goal was to demonstrate that there was no inevitable conflict between reason and these teachings. One could be a person of intellectual curiosity and reason *and* be a follower of the teachings of the Upanishads. They were not mutually exclusive.

The problem that Gautama faced is very similar to the situation that Thomas Aquinas found himself in. Aquinas lived in thirteenth-century Europe, a time when the traditional Christian faith was being assailed by a "new learning" that held that all religious belief is, at best, mystical intuition and often nothing more than childish nonsense. No intelligent, philosophically minded person would choose to waste his time on a pack of religious fairy tales. Aquinas, a Dominican monk and a brilliant thinker, rose to the challenge. His was a truly heroic response, resulting in a lifetime of writings that went far to establish the real possibility of being a man or woman in tune with the new learning without having to abandon the traditional teachings of the Church. Aquinas is famous for his five "proofs" for the existence of God. Actually, these are not so much "proofs," as they are reasoned arguments that seek to demonstrate that there need be no conflict between reason and belief in the Christian concept of God.

What makes the example of Aquinas peculiarly interesting in our present context is that he leaned strongly on the rational philosophy of the Greek philosopher, Aristotle. Aristotle was the first among the Greeks to work out the rules of logic and rational thinking in general. One can't help but wonder if Gautama too was influenced by the writings of Aristotle. There is no evidence at all for this, but the possibility cannot be ignored. During the century before Gautama's career, Aristotle's famous student, Alexander the Great, had, through conquest, carried Greek armies and culture as far as the region known as Gandhara, which is in the northwest part of the Indian subcontinent. Greek culture, including philosophical ideas, sank roots in Gandhara and from there influenced other parts of the Hindu world for a time.

Gautama based his defense of the Upanishadic tradition on a carefully reasoned epistemology. His goal was not to examine reality per se, but rather one's *knowledge of reality*. How does one know that his knowledge is accurate? How can one ever be certain? Perception can obviously mislead, as in the popular example of the snake in the road, which turns out to be merely a coiled rope. And reason too, as we all know only too well, is not infallible. Gautama sought to show that reason could be reliable, so long as proper rules of thinking were followed. Much of his argument was presented in the form of syllogisms (a very Aristotelian method, incidentally). He then applied this rational process to an examination of the postulates of the Upanishadic teachings and proved to the satisfaction of many that the tradition was not in conflict with reason.

Gautama was not, however, denying the reality and the importance of mystical intuition; that was not his purpose. He, in fact, agreed that moksha, knowledge of Brahman, was intuitive knowledge of the highest order. But, he would argue, a reasoned "revelation" of the true nature of reality could *lead to* the mystical experience of moksha.

The rational dialectic of Nyaya could be said to begin with a very down-to-earth proposition. For a moment, become aware of your own body; become *directly conscious* of your body. Now, are these not two different things: the body, and your consciousness of it? Certainly they are. And, of the two, the body is clearly material. Is that which is conscious of the body also material? Clearly it is not. In the view of Nyaya, that would be impossible. Nyaya argues that consciousness is not material because, among other things, consciousness is not a solid occupier of space, nor is it available to the physical senses, nor is consciousness a property of a dead body.

If the body is material, and consciousness is not material, then they must necessarily be two entirely different kinds of being. Nyaya employs the word *substance* in this regard. A "substance" is something that is an absolutely fundamental, irreducible kind of reality. When reducing something to the parts out of which it is made, "substance" is the last stop; one can go no further. For this ultimate level of irreducibility, Nyaya—taking its lead from its partner darshana, Vaisheshika—uses the term *atom*. The atom, invisibly small, is the ultimate, individual unit out of which all complex things are composed. Nyaya holds that reality, at root, consists of the atoms of different kinds of substances. (The "atom" of Nyaya, of course, is not to be confused with the atom of modern physics.)

In the Nyaya view, material reality is composed of only five possible substances.* Like the Greeks, Nyaya includes water, earth, air, and fire—and adds one of its own, sound. Each of these, at root, consists of its own specific kind of atoms. These atoms, in aggregate, present what we normally think of as water, etc. Although each substance is unique, they are able to interact, and in so doing, join together in various ways to produce the ordinary "things" of our experience. Also, in aggregate, substances can take on qualities (also referred to as "quales") such as the perceived sensory qualities of color, smell, etc. These quales are not themselves substances, rather they are the temporary properties exhibited by substances. The substance itself, though, being absolutely simple and irreducible is not temporary, nor can a substance be subject to change. The quales may change, but the substance remains the same forever. A substance, being not made up of parts, cannot be destroyed, nor can it be created. Therefore, a substance is necessarily eternal—no beginning, no end.

In addition to material substances, Nyaya recognizes nonmaterial substances as well. Among these are space and time. By far the most significant, though, is the Self (Atman). The Self, according to Nyaya, is a spiritual (i.e., nonmaterial) substance. Like any other substance, the Self is absolutely simple, unchangeable, and eternal. And, like other substances, the Self is capable of having "quales." Being that Nyaya is a proper orthodox Hindu darshana, establishing the reality and the eternal nature of the Self is, of course, what the Nyaya system is ultimately all about.

Getting back to the matter of being conscious of the body, we see that the body, being material, is made up entirely of the various material substances. But consciousness is not material. Is consciousness, therefore, a nonmaterial substance? Not exactly. In the Nyaya view, consciousness is a *quale* of the Self, which *is* a nonmaterial substance. Because consciousness comes and goes, it cannot be a substance unto itself, but it is unarguably a very significant feature (quality) of the Self. Here's how it works out.

The Self (Atman) is in contact with the body. In fact, the Self "inhabits" the body. Nyaya refers to this as "conjunction." The Self inhabits the body and *interacts* with it. Since the time of Descartes, the question of how a nonmaterial Self (or mind) can interact with a material body has posed a most serious problem for Western philosophy, but Nyaya sees no problem with it at all. Different substances, such as earth and air, clearly

---

*Isn't it interesting that modern science also proclaims a handful of "elementary particles"? The five of Nyaya become four in modern science (twelve if you include all of their variants).

interact. True, both of these are material substances, but, in the Nyaya view of the Self, though not material and therefore not solid, it is infinitely extended in space, and thus can interact with substances that occupy space.

The interaction of the body and the Self is *initiated* by the nonconscious body; it is the receptacle of all sensory experience. In its fundamental state, consciousness is clear and undisturbed. Sensory experience, though, disturbs that equanimity, causing a "ripple" (*vritti*), as it were, in consciousness. Consciousness, however, is not something unto itself; it is a quale of the Self, and it is the Self—*through its quality of consciousness*—that is actually aware of all experiences. The Self is the "substratum" of consciousness. The Self, though, is not of necessity *always* conscious. As we all know, consciousness comes and goes. But the Self endures always. Therefore consciousness is a *quale* of the Self, but it is a necessary quale if the Self is to be aware of the experiences of the body. In other words— no body, no consciousness. When one enjoys an experience—let's say lovemaking, for instance—it is the Self that is the conscious "enjoyer," but the Self must be in conjunction with a body if this is to occur (obviously).

The Self, the conscious subject of all experiences, is what gives life and continuity to a "person." Without the enduring Self, Nyaya contends, the faculty of memory would be inexplicable. And so would life itself. A body may continue from one moment to the next to be made up of all the same material substances, but if the Self is missing, that body is a dead body. But the Self, being a substance, cannot die, though it may temporarily lack the quality of consciousness, for which conjunction with a body (the receptacle of sensory experience) is necessary. The Self, therefore, can inhabit many bodies over time; there need be no limit to how many.

Thus does Nyaya assert, in terms of a rational argument, that the Self (Atman) is real, and so also is reincarnation (samsara). It's a very interesting argument. Understandably, though, the assertions of the Nyaya school were not favorably received by their philosophical opponents.

The strict materialists, such as the followers of *Charvaka*, argued against the Nyaya position, claiming that consciousness is a quale of the body, not of some eternal, spiritual "substance," the so-called Self. Consciousness is only associated with an animal body, *never* with anything else. The nature of the body is sufficient to explain consciousness. There's no logical need to go further. The alleged "Self" is only an inference.

Nyaya's answer to the materialists was that if consciousness were due solely to a particular arrangement of physical elements in the body, then surely a dead body should be at least capable of consciousness. The moment of death is followed by some period of time during which the physical elements of the body remain essentially the same as they were before the moment of death. Why, then, do we *never* see the expression of consciousness in a dead body? Further, the recognized qualities of the body—such as motion, color, etc.—all have physical causes. Consciousness, though, does not have any available physical source (according to Nyaya). Therefore, consciousness cannot be a quale of the body. Further, Nyaya would agree that knowledge of the reality of the Self is not a direct object of perception, but the Self is a *necessary* inference.

The most telling objection, though, came from the Buddhists and focused on the ever-baffling matter of memory. According to Buddhist teaching, there is no Self, no Atman. The concept of the Self is only that, a concept—much loved, much enshrined, much clung to, but nonetheless only a concept with no corresponding reality. Instead, the Buddhists maintain that a given person is a "flowing stream," a moment-to-moment succession of fleeting atttributes (*skandas*). The stream, however, maintains an identifiable *pattern* over time, like a wave that crosses a wheatfield on a breezy day. The pattern, being a moment-to-moment concatenation of cause and effect events, changes very slowly, thus exhibiting a recognizable identity over time. In other words: There is change, but no *one* who changes.

Therefore, the Buddhists would argue, memory—remembrance of a prior experience—is due to the causal connection of the impression. An experience of a blow to the head, for example, causes an "impression" within the nature of the stream (to say nothing of the skull) that will be carried forward within the character of the links that make up the stream and can thus be "recalled" at a later time when the conditions are right. In other words, that impression has become an unconscious part of the nature of the stream, passed along from link to link, and thus able to be expressed in consciousness when the conditions are right:

> Because of the relation of cause and effect from previous cognitions later cognitions are generated in accordance with the power of the previous cognitions . . . . Hence, although the cognitions are many, there is synthesis through the cause-effect relation as in the case of a seed, etc. Just as rice saplings . . . produce rice seeds in accordance with their power and not barley seeds, so also from the cognitions belonging to the same stream there is synthesis based on the relation of cause and effect and not from cognitions belonging to a diffferent stream, the latter not being preceded by that (the original experience). (quoted in Chakrabarti, p. 60)

Nyaya was not without an answer to this. If that original impression (the blow to the head) were all that was remembered, that would be one thing. *But*, that's not all! The remember also remembers that it was *he* who had the experience of the impression. He remembers the event, and, that it was he, the one who remembers now, who was also the one who experienced the event at that time in the past. This is a common experience, and it can only be accounted for by recognizing that it is the same "person" (rememberer) who was present at the original event *and* at the later recalling of that event. This, Nyaya argues, could only be possible given the existence of an enduring entity—that is to say, a conscious Self; the Buddhist "stream theory" just won't do it. The causally connected moments that make up the stream could possibly account for the preservation of an impression and its subsequent reappearance in memory, but such a stream, as the Buddhists proclaim, cannot account for the conscious sense of identity that goes with the memory. The botom line, according to Nyaya, is that memory requires a rememberer, a being that was present at the time of the original event and also at the time of the recalling. And that, of course, is the Self, Atman.*

Actually, the real bottom line is that Nyaya was not trying to win a debate, or to *prove* that its position was true and all others false. The goal of Nyaya was to establish the

---

*This debate raises intriguing questions that the ancients could never have even dreamed. A computer has memory, lots of it, and it "remembers" very well. If our amazing technology should eventually produce a "conscious" computer, will it know that it is conscious; will it know that it is remembering? Must a conscious computer have a "self"?

orthodox Upanishadic tradition on a rational foundation. Whether one agreed or disagreed with the teaching was not the point. If I may repeat a paragraph from the beginning of this section,

> Gautama's goal was not to prove the correctness of the assertions of the Upanishads; rather his goal was to demonstrate that there was no inevitable conflict between reason and these teachings. One could be a person of intellectual curiosity and reason, and be a follower of the teachings of the Upanishads. They were not mutually exclusive.

Vaisheshika

The *Vaisheshika* darshana is so closely bound up with Nyaya that it has become customary to treat the two as one. There is some distinction, though, and the Hindu tradition has consistently regarded Vaisheshika in its own right as one of the orthodox darshanas.

The Vaisheshika darshana was formulated by an unusual thinker named Kanada, a somewhat younger contemporary of Gautama, the founder of Nyaya. Kanada, in the *Vaisheshika Sutras*, used the rational, realistic approach of Gautama to elucidate the underlying nature of reality. In other words, Gautama would clarify how it is that true knowledge is attained; Kanada would use that clarification to explain the true nature of the reality that right knowledge comprehends. Both schools of thought were in agreement that a true perception of reality, rationally attained, could open the door to the higher intuitive knowledge of Brahman.

Kanada, something of a mystic philosopher himself, practiced long hours of meditation by day and then went out in the cool of the night searching for knowledge. By examining experience in the light of Nyaya epistemology, Kanada reached an "atomic" interpretation of Nature. (Again, one has to wonder if there might have been a Greek influence at work here.) Kanada concluded that reality is made up of certain irreducible substances. Like some of the Greek philosophers, he listed earth, water, air, and fire as basic substances. To these he added ether, light, space, time, mind, and Atman. The particular entries in the list are not what's most important; rather, it was the rational way in which Kanada went about determining the nature of reality that gives significance to his contribution. The Nyaya–Vaisheshika response was intellectually powerful in its time, but the impact of these darshanas gradually declined, and much of their contribution was absorbed into the evolving character of Vedanta.

Samkhya

Both *Samkhya* and *Yoga* darshanas are closely associated with Vedanta, and over time, many elements of both became integrated into the broader nature of Vedanta. The elucidation of the Samkhya darshana is attributed to an Indian philosopher named Kapila, who authored the *Samkhya Karika* in the seventh century B.C.E.

There's a wonderful story about Kapila, who was said to have an amazing power of intensity in meditation. It so happened that King Sagaran was performing *ashvamedha* (the horse sacrifice) nearby, but Indra, for reasons of his own, spirited the horse away and deposited it near to where Kapila was sitting, deep in meditation. Sagaran's 60,000 sons (!) went searching for the horse, and when they found it assumed that Kapila had stolen it. As they were about to attack Kapila, he opened his eyes and stared at them with such heated intensity that all 60,000 of them immediately burst into flames and were reduced to ashes. I'd love to tell the whole story, but this isn't the place for it. Suffice it to say that all finally turned out well. King Sagaran got his horse back, as well as his 60,000 sons, alive and healthy.

Back to reality: It was Kapila who enunciated the dual nature of *prakriti* and *purusha*. Prakriti, as we have seen, is said to be the fundamental progenitor of matter, the natural world, always changing and evolving through the operation of the three *gunas*. Prakriti is not matter as such, nor is it mind as such, though both emerge from it. Prakriti is the ultimate source of all objects of cognition, and of cognition as well. Prakriti is manifested in the interplay of the gunas, and this interplay is responsible for *everything* that happens. *Tamas*, dark and quiet, is suggested by inertia and passivity. *Rajas*, active and changing, is suggested by energy. And *sattva*, light and harmonious, is suggested by balance and "wholeness." Altogether, the interplay of the gunas accounts for the constantly changing fabric woven by prakriti.

Purusha, on the other hand, is pure spirit, pure consciousness; it is the nature of Brahman and thus of Atman. According to Samkhya, prakriti acts; it is responsible for all of the forms of *maya* and all of the role-playing that goes on within it. Purusha (pure consciousness) is a witness only; it does not act. The distinction is described well in the *Mundaka Upanishad*:

> Like two golden birds perched on the selfsame tree,
> Intimate friends, the ego and the Self dwell in the same body.
> The former eats the sweet and sour fruits of the tree of life,
> While the latter looks on in detachment. (*Mundaka Up*: III.I.1; p. 115)

In the life of any given individual, purusha can become literally entranced by the play of prakriti and fall into the fatal error of identifying its being with prakriti. This, of course, is avidya, the illusion that the maya-self is the real self. Such ignorance is said to be responsible for all suffering and for the endless turning of the wheel of samsara. But there is hope. Difficult though it may be, it is at least possible for purusha to see through the illusion initiated by prakriti and come to the realization of its own distinct nature. This is moksha: perfect Self-realization and the end of samsara.

It would be incorrect to conclude that Samkhya holds that the distinction between prakriti and purusha is the difference between good and evil. Prakriti is not evil in any sense at all. In fact, the evolution of prakriti is the necessary condition within which purusha works out its own rediscovery. Samkhya presents the philosophical explanation. How the work is actually accomplished is the province of Yoga.

Vedanta

Let me again point out that the term *Vedanta* refers both to the teachings of the Upanishads in general and to one of the specific orthodox darshanas. Vedanta, the darshana, draws its inspiration from the Upanishads, the *Bhagavad Gita*, and from certain philosophical compositions known as *sutras*. The first of these is the *Brahma Sutra* (also known as the *Vedanta Sutra*), composed by a scholar named Badarayana, who was active in or near the second century B.C.E. It all came together, though, in the writings of one of the giants of Indian philosophy, Adi Shankara.

The Vedanta darshana is first and foremost connected with the name of Shankara, a South Indian philosopher born in 788 C.E. Despite a short life of only thirty-two years, Shankara stands out as one of the greatest figures of the Hindu philosophical tradition. It was Shankara who pulled together the diffuse, often mystical strands of the Upanishads, and wove them into a coherent philosophical system—a darshana. Thanks in no small part to Shankara, Vedanta has consistently occupied the central place among the orthodox Hindu systems. Other darshanas are best understood in relation to Vedanta and, to a large degree, have been absorbed into it over time.

Shankara was an active, restless sort of person—a deep thinker, a prolific writer, and a much-traveled teacher. He was born into an upper-caste family in Kerala in South India, and, according to the story, astrologers predicted that he would become a great scholar. They prophesied that in his destruction of false doctrine, he would be like a rampaging elephant let loose in a banana grove.

Shankara was a very precocious child, and while still a boy, he wanted to become a Shaivite monk (one dedicated to Lord Shiva) so that he could devote all of his energies to study and the spiritual life. His widowed mother, though, refused to grant permission. One day, while bathing in a river, the young Shankara was attacked by a crocodile, or so we are told. It grabbed him by the leg and would soon have pulled him under. Shankara remembered the saying that if one vowed to become a monk when facing death, the gods might spare that person's life. He called out to his mother to give him permission, fast. Horrified by what she was watching, she shouted back, "Yes, yes; anything!" The struggling Shankara managed to raise his hands and call out, "Sanyasoham!" Immediately the crocodile let go of his leg, and a shaken, but still alive, Shankara climbed up on dry land. With tears flowing his mother embraced him and confirmed her promise, saying that it was the will of the gods.

And so the young Shankara received *sanyas,* and entered upon the life of a celibate, itinerant monk. He was far more interested in scholarship than asceticism, though, and soon had become something of a guru in his own right. With his small band of disciples, Shankara traveled all over India, engaging in open debate with other religious scholars. Shankara's knowledge and his skill in debate were so impressive that while still young, he came to be called *acharya* (great religious scholar). For this reason, he is often referred to as Shankaracharya.

A delightful story is told about one of these debates. In the town of Mahismati, Shankara took on a famous scholar named Mandana Mishra. The fame of both men attracted a huge crowd. Bharati, Mishra's beautiful wife, was asked to be the judge. She placed a garland of fresh flowers around the neck of each man, and announced to the crowd that at the end of the debate the one with the least withered flowers would be the winner. The loser must become a disciple of the winner. Shankara argued eloquently that the real purpose of the Vedas is to teach that Brahman alone is real. Mishra, who had never been defeated in debate, stuck with his main theme that the Vedas teach one how to accumulate merit through the correct performance of religious ritual. The debate wore on for eighteen days! When it was finally over, Bharati, sizing up the two garlands, was forced to admit that Shankara was the winner.

But Bharati wasn't about to lose her husband that easily; she had a trick up her sleeve. Announcing that through marriage a husband and wife become one, she declared that she was really a part of the life of Mishra, and that therefore Shankara would have to defeat her too in debate. Until then, she said, his victory would not be complete.

Surprised, but intrigued, Shankara said that he accepted her challenge. Turning then to the delighted crowd, she addressed them, saying, in effect, that she could not accept Shankara as a learned master until he had demonstrated that he had knowledge of *all* important matters. He must, she declared, prove that he had deep understanding of the arts of lovemaking. Could he prove that he was knowledgeable about the various forms of seduction, the ways of pleasing a woman in bed, the variety of sexual positions, and the relative merits of each? Could he speak intelligently about the sensual effects of different love potions and the influence of the full moon on the sexual urge of a woman? Turning back to Shankara, Bharati shouted, "Until you can answer these questions you are not a master of all learning!"

Well, being that Shankara was a sixteen-year-old celibate monk, this could present something of a problem. But Shankara too was not without a trick up his sleeve. He asked for, and received, a forty-day delay, saying that he needed time to think the matter over. During this time, so we are told, Shankara used his skill in yogic powers to leave his own body and enter instead into the body of a raja known for his extremely voluptuous lifestyle. For forty days (and nights), while his own body rested in a deep trance, Shankara used the virile king's body to explore every sexual experience the mind can imagine. There was *nothing* that he didn't know by the time the forty days were up. At the appointed time, he returned, in his own body, to continue the debate. To say the least, it was an astonished Bharati that soon confessed that Shankara was indeed a master of all learning, and was the rightful winner.

In the course of his travels, Shankara established four *mathas*: one in the north of India, one in the south, one in the west, and one in the east. A matha is a monastery that, at the same time, is something like a college. In addition to the usual monastic disciplines, there is strong emphasis on scholarly pursuits. In a sense, all of the mathas founded by Shankara are still functioning to this day and are living sources of Shankara's teaching.

Most of all, though, Shankara's philosophy is found in his writings, the most influential of which is the *Naishkarmya-siddhi*, a lengthy commentary on the *Brahma Sutra* of Badarayana, composed several centuries earlier. In this work, Shankara lays out the essential features of the Vedanta darshana. Brahman alone is Absolute Truth; Brahman alone is real. This uncompromising monism at the heart of Shankara's teaching is the reason for his system being labeled *Advaita Vedanta*. *Advaita* means nondual (*a-dvi*, not two). This is an important distinction, philosophically speaking, because some schools within the general Vedanta tradition, notably that of Mahdva, taught the reality of a dualism in which both spirit and the material world are separate, but real.

Drawing his inspiration directly from the Upanishads, Shankara held that the Atman *is* Brahman and that the ultimate goal of life is realization of the identity of the Atman and Brahman. What stands in the way is maya, the veil of illusion that seduces us into falsely believing that the world is real. The ego, itself a part of the world of maya, tumbles between pleasure and pain in a hopeless quest for self-centered happiness. This, of course, is the condition of *avidya*. The only hope for salvation is to accept the fact that the world of *maya* is a figment of the mind and to disengage oneself entirely from its enticing attachments. Only through renouncing *attachment* to maya can a person ascend to the knowledge of Brahman. In Shankara's view, the reality of the ordinary waking state is likened to the reality of the dream state. It all seems totally real while in the dream state, but its illusory nature becomes obvious upon waking up. In like manner, the worldly "reality" of daily life seems unarguably real, but upon awakening to a higher state of knowledge, the reality of daily life is seen to be no less a phantasmagoria than the supposed reality of a dream.

Shankara argued that through the disciplined pursuit of knowledge, a dedicated seeker can eventually transcend *ordinary* knowledge, rising to that state of higher, *perfect* knowledge. This is the path of Jnana Yoga. Shankara, though, was far from being purely intellectual. Although a highly rational man, who could not accept any doctrine that was clearly in conflict with reason, he had a mystical side as well. Shankara taught that the path of knowledge was the one best suited to elevate a philosophically minded person to the state of *samadhi*, within which state the mystical experience of knowledge-of-Brahman could occur.

Knowledge of Brahman, then, is in no way to be thought of as conceptual, or "philosophical," in the usual sense of the word. Knowledge of Brahman is a completely transcendental experience, which can be *approached* through the way of philosophical knowledge. The Brahman of Shankara may not be a personal god—that is true—but neither did Shankara choose to describe Brahman as nothing more than an impersonal abstraction. In talking about Brahman, Shankara would wisely drop into the poetic style of Bhakti. He would even sometimes refer to Brahman as a "friend." Shankara composed a number of rather mystical verses dedicated to Govinda, one of the names of Krishna; these are thus known as the *Bhaja Govindam*. It is fascinating to reflect on the fact that these words are being uttered by the man whose name is foremost among the rational philosophers of his time. Let me conclude this section with an excerpt from one:

> Worship Govinda. Worship Govinda.
> Oh you fools and rascals,
> Just worship Govinda.
> Your rules of grammar and word jugglery
> Will not help you at the time of death.
> Just worship Govinda.

Yoga

The darshana of *Yoga* is in something of a class by itself. Whereas the other darshanas are mostly concerned with philosophical explication, answering the question "what," yoga focuses on the "how." Strictly speaking, the word *yoga* refers to any path of action that is intended to lead ultimately to enlightenment. We saw a similar relationship between the Upanishads in general and the *Bhagavad Gita*.

The nature of yoga is widely misunderstood in the West, where it is often thought of as dealing exclusively with unusual body postures and breathing exercises. These are the province of Hatha Yoga, an important aspect of yoga, but far from being the whole story. The roots of yoga are widely believed to reach far back into the pre-Vedic past. Artistic representations from Mohenjo-Daro and Harappa are strongly suggestive of yogic meditation practices. Undoubtedly, Dravidian practices greatly influenced the evolution of yoga. The word, though, is derived from *yuj*, an early Sanskrit word meaning to join or "yoke." As mentioned in the previous chapter, in early Aryan times, the *yogin* was, presumably, the person whose daunting job it was to tame wild horses and harness them (yoke them) to the war chariot. The yogin was the battle charioteer. Metaphorically, this came to symbolize the challenge of taming the wild impulses of the body and "yoking" mind and body for the purpose of self-discovery. It is no accident that Lord Krishna, the divine yogin, was presented as Arjuna's charioteer in the *Bhagavad Gita*.

By the time the *Bhagavad Gita* was composed, certain yoga paths had become preeminent in Indian society. The *Gita* examines three of these: Raja Yoga, the yoga of meditation; Karma Yoga, the yoga of compassionate service; and Bhakti Yoga, the path of devotion to a personal god. Jnana Yoga, the way of philosophical inquiry, is mentioned, but not discussed in the *Gita*, and Hatha Yoga is not mentioned by name at all.

The development of yoga into one of the classical darshanas was largely the work of a man named Patanjali, who lived in the second century B.C.E. Little is known about him personally, but he is the putative author of the *Yoga Sutras*, a work of major importance in the history of Hinduism. In the *Yoga Sutras,* Patanjali draws together what he regards to be the essential elements of the yoga tradition and presents a program of action which the dedicated seeker can follow in the ascent from ignorance to the fullness of awakening.

The theme of the work is clearly presented in the first stanza of the *Yoga Sutras. Yoga nirodha chittam vritti.* Loosely translated, this reads: "Yoga is the cessation of the thought waves of the mind." What this means is that, in its most perfect sense, yoga is a state of consciousness, a state wherein all of the distractions of thought and ego have become quiet. The Self alone is all that remains, pure and simple. This state of conscious-ness is called *samadhi.* The attainment of the state of samadhi is the ultimate goal of the practice of yoga. But samadhi is to be won only at the summit of a long and arduous climb, a journey that only the truly dedicated can hope to complete.

In the *Yoga Sutras*, Patanjali presents a description of an eight-tiered ascent to the great goal of samadhi. In modern translations, these are often referred to as the "eight limbs" of yoga. Patanjali gives much attention to each of these; the following is only the briefest of descriptions.

1. Yama This is usually translated as "restraint." It refers to various practices aimed at replacing ego-attachments with self-restraint and compassion. These include *Ahimsa* (nonviolence); *Satya* (nonlying—that is, being truthful in all things); *Asteya* (nonstealing); *Aparigraha* (literally, nongrasping, which is to say, overcoming the impulse of greed); and, *Brahmacharya* (renouncing sexual lust. Patanjali expected the truly dedicated yogin to be totally celibate).

2. Niyama Usually translated as "observances," the *Niyama* are habits of mind to be cultivated by the yogin. Both Yama and Niyama refer to habits of mind; the Yama emphasize removing impediments to growth, while the Niyama focus on building positive ones in their place. The Niyama include purity and cleanliness of mind and body; an attitude of content-ment and acceptance; and the rigorous practice of ascetic disciplines, study, and devotion.

3. Asanas The word *asana* (AH-sa-na) refers to a bodily posture. By Patanjali's time, the tradition of yoga had worked out a large number of classical asanas, which, along with associated breathing exercises, were believed to constitute an excellent discipline for bringing the body under control and keeping it in the healthiest possible condition. Since mental states are greatly affected by the condition of the body, a strong and healthy body was seen to be essential to progress in the art of meditation.

4. Pranayama *Pranayama* (prah-na YAH-ma), referring to skillful breathing exercises, is closely linked to the practice of asanas. Whereas the asanas focus more directly on the condition of the body, pranayama builds on the asanas to increase vital energy, which can be turned inward for the task of increasing the energy of consciousness. The Sanskrit word *pranayama* refers to the disciplined practice of breathing with full attention given to its threefold character: *puraka* (inbreath), *rechaka* (holding the full breath), and *kumbhaka* (releasing the breath). The Yogic practices of asanas and pranayama had become highly evolved by Patanjali's time. They were the jealously guarded province of ascetic communities. Only a true master was seen to be fit to initiate and teach another. These two together form the basis of Hatha Yoga. Important as it may be unto itself, the tradition of yoga has always seen Hatha Yoga as the servant of Raja Yoga, the yoga of meditation. Hatha prepares the individual for the richest possible experience in meditation. A popular image compares these two to a tree. The crown of the tree, closest to the sun, is Raja Yoga. But the sturdy trunk, which holds up the crown, is Hatha. Without Hatha there can be no Raja.

5. Pratyahara Usually translated as "control of the senses," *pratyahara* is concerned with developing total mastery over the physical body and all of its desires and distractions. This is a matter of the higher nature coming to totally control the lower. Pratyahara does not mean renunciation; it means control. There is an excellent description of pratyahara in Book Two of the *Bhagavad Gita*. "Even as a tortoise draws in its limbs, the wise can draw in their senses at will."

6. Dharana *Dharana* is often simply called "concentration." Perhaps this is too simple, and thus misleading. Dharana is an ongoing condition of consciousness in which the restless activity of the thinking mind has been brought under control, and the person is free to be totally aware of the present moment as it unfolds. This is closely associated with *ekagrata*, which means "one-pointedness," a habit of focusing of consciousness on the reality of the moment. Many practices were developed to help one develop skill in Dharana. In modern times, this practice is often referred to as mindfulness.

7. Dhyana This is a supremely important word in the evolution of Eastern thought. We will see later in this study that it is the parent of the Chinese word *Chan*, which in turn was the parent of the Japanese word *Zen*. In itself it refers to the practice of meditation and to the state of mind of one who practices meditation. Patanjali described four stages of *dhyana* (dJAH-na), the fourth being synonymous with samadhi.

8. Samadhi In the state of *samadhi*, consciousness has shed all traces of ego-identification; the thinking mind is still, and consciousness is free to know its identification with the Brahman-Atman. Such words may be accurate, technically speaking, but, in truth, no words are capable of describing the experience of samadhi; it transcends all words, all thoughts. Samadhi is the ultimate goal of the practice of yoga.

THE HETERODOX DARSHANAS

In addition to the six "orthodox" darshanas, the Hindu tradition recognizes various "heterodox" darshanas as well. The defining element of the heterodox schools is that they did not accept the infallibility of the Vedas. The three principal heterodox darshanas are Buddhism, Jainism, and Charvaka. In addition to these, we must include Tantra, which is difficult to fit into any category.

Charvaka

We will look into the nature of *Charvaka* first because, under a variety of names, it is a philosophy of life that is found widely among us humans throughout history and is arguably the prevalent philosophy of modern times (though few would be willing to admit it).

Charvaka is the polar opposite of the way of life of the renunciate. Far from withdrawing from the world and embracing the privations of an ascetic life, the followers of Charvaka held that the present enjoyment of life is the only real value that exists. Charvaka is a thoroughgoing materialist philosophy of life. Nothing else exists. Sense perception alone is real. The wise person is the one who knows this and devotes his energies to the pursuit of pleasurable situations and the avoidance of painful situations.

It's quite possible that Charvaka grew out of a growing skepticism concerning the infallibility of the Vedas, but it probably doesn't matter what the specific cause might be. It seems that every fully developed society includes a Charvaka, by one name or another. Among the Greeks, it was Epicureanism and hedonism. Certainly no one can deny that the spirit of Charvaka is alive and well, perhaps even dominant, in the modern world. The "Playboy Philosophy" could be said to be Charvaka in modern dress.

The word *Charvaka* is derived from the name of the alleged author of the *Barhaspatya Sutras* (also known as the *Lokayatas*), were composed around 600 B.C.E. No part of this body of work has survived to modern times, and next to nothing is known about its supposed author. Our only sources of knowledge about Charvaka come from Hindu, Buddhist, and Jain writers, all of whom were deeply critical of the Charvaka school. It's hardly likely, therefore, that we're getting a fully objective view of this school, especially since followers of Charvaka openly attacked the others. They argued that religion was nothing but foolishness, or worse, a mental disease, and that so-called virtue is nothing but illusion. They aimed their strongest attacks at the Brahmin priests, whom they accused of being vipers, tricksters, and purveyors of superstition. It's no wonder that Charvaka was not exactly admired by the others. But because of this, it may be that Charvaka is getting a bad rap. Speaking about Charvaka, the modern Hindu scholar Radhakrishnan has said that "a philosophy professed seriously for centuries could not have been of the coarse nature that it is made out to be."

As best we can determine, the teachings of the *Barhaspatya Sutras* held that only material reality exists and that the "soul," so central to the teachings of the Upanishads, is only an illusion. Consciousness is not evidence of an indwelling spirit; it is simply a product of the material structure of the body, and when the body dies, consciousness disintegrates with it. And the death of the body is final; for any given person, this present life is the only one that will ever exist.

Given this state of affairs, what constitutes the "good life"? Charvaka held, very simply, that the good life is to be found in the pursuit of happiness and the avoidance of suffering. Presumably, this was not meant to be interpreted as pursuit of gluttonous self-indulgence; Charvaka was more Epicurean than hedonist. Good actions, born of compassion, conduce to happiness; bad actions, born of selfishness, result in unhappiness. In other words, learn from experience to do what works. Charvaka was very pragmatic.

Modern commentators often suggest that, apart from whatever value this philosophy might have unto itself, Charvaka may have played a valuable role within the evolution of Hindu society as a whole. The stinging attacks from the followers of Charvaka may have helped to awaken the Hindu tradition from its conservative dogmatic slumber. The sixth century B.C.E. was, philosophically speaking, a restless and revolutionary time in the history of Hinduism. It was a time that saw the emergence of many active reform movements, Buddhism and Jainism being only two. Charvaka would have appeared on the scene at right about the beginning of this eventful century. Perhaps it did play a role.

Jaina

Jaina is the polar opposite of Charvaka. The story of the development of the Jain sect is an intriguing subject, much misunderstood in the West. Like Buddhism, Jaina developed as a reaction to what some perceived as intolerable flaws in traditional Hinduism. Also, Jaina appeared on the historical scene at about the same time as Buddhism, and it too began as a very small dissident sect. Jaina would not, however, experience anything like the explosive growth of Buddhism. The Jain tradition, though, has survived down to the present day in its homeland. It is estimated that there are about two million Jains living in modern-day India.

Historically speaking, the rise of Jainism is associated with the name of Mahavira, an ascetic monk who was born during the first half of the sixth century B.C.E. and lived to be about seventy years old. It is believed that he was probably a contemporary of Buddha. Mahavira (whose birth name was Nataputta Vardhamana) was, to say the least, an ascetic's ascetic. During his years as a solitary sadhu, there were seemingly no austerities that were too extreme for him, going so far (we are told) as to pull his hair out by the roots and to go about totally naked in all types of weather. He was determined to free himself from every vestige of attachment to worldly concerns. According to the story, Mahavira (like Buddha) eventually experienced enlightenment, a profound mystical insight into what he believed to be the nature of ultimate truth. Thereafter, Mahavira became guru to a small group of disciples who joined the master in his ascetic ways, also going about naked and hairless. (Presumably, though, they chose to simply *shave* their heads.) Mahavira called his disciples *jinas*—that is, "victors" in the battle against worldly attachments. The word *Jain* is derived from this name.*

Mahavira did not claim to be the originator of the Jain sect, far from it. The Jain sect had presumably been in existence for centuries by the time of Mahavira, but it had been only one of many small communities of ascetic monks, drawing little public attention. The leader of the Jains was known as the *Tirthankara* (literally, one who finds the way across the river). Mahavira claimed to be the twenty-fourth of this unbroken line. According to the Jain tradition, the first Tirtankara was a heroic figure named Rishaba, who, among many other great accomplishments, was said to have lived for 8,400,000 years. Whatever the case may be, Mahavira was the one who brought the Jains out into the open; the historical record really begins with him.

So, you may be wondering, what is the point of all this extreme asceticism? Why were Jain monks so dedicated to starving and otherwise mortifying their poor bodies? Well, it certainly wasn't an end in itself; they weren't masochists. It all makes perfectly good sense in the context of Jain philosophy. In accord with the Hindu world that it emerged from and lived within, Jaina accepted the reality of moksha and samsara. But

---

*There is an attractive small park in New Delhi dedicated to the Enlightenment of Mahavira. It's an interesting irony that this park is located directly across the street from the opulent Maurya Sheraton Hotel. From their comfortable, air-conditioned rooms, guests can enjoy the view of a park honoring the memory of one of the most extreme ascetics of India's history.

that's about as far as the accord went. Jaina is a solidly dualist system of thought. Reality is twofold: *jiva* (spirit) and *ajiva* (nonspirit, or, in other words, the world). Jains reject the concept of maya; the world is not illusion, it is real. Both jiva and ajiva are real, irreducible, and eternal. Being eternal, there is no need for a creator-god, and none is proposed, for which reason Jaina is sometimes said to be atheistic.

The material world is said to be in a state of constant change, but it is not meaningless, haphazard change. The change that we see is part of a vast, eternal cycling—each individual cycle lasting for eons of time. Toward the end of a cycle, everything begins to deteriorate into chaos, but order will restore itself in the next turn of the wheel. The present age is a deteriorating stage, which explains the disorder and suffering present in the world. The reason for this is as follows. Ideally, jiva and ajiva are completely separate; this is as it should be. But in the deteriorating stage of a cycle, jiva comes into contact with ajiva (the material world), and therein lay trouble and suffering. Specifically, the individual jiva (spirit), already conjoined with a body, takes on a burden of karma as a result of worldly actions. In Jaina, karma is defined as a material substance, albeit an extremely rarified substance. As a vapor blurs a mirror, all actions tarnish jiva with karma. It may be heavy karma, such as willfully selfish actions incur, or it may be relatively light karma, such as results from selfless actions. But all actions result in furthering the burden of karma, necessitating rebirth (samsara). The character of the rebirth will be determined by the character of the karma at the time of death, but rebirth it will be; the wheel of samsara keeps turning over and over, dooming the individual jiva to successive rebirths into this world of endless suffering. Each individual person is jiva trapped in ajiva, and karma keeps the wheel turning.

But there's hope. Moksha, the ultimate goal, is possible. It is possible for a jiva to free itself from the wheel, free itself from all karma, and thus achieve the perfect bliss natural to it, but impossible so long as it remains bound up with ajiva. This perfected condition is known as *siddhashila*.

This is where the rationale for ascetic practices comes into the picture. Only a life of complete withdrawal and asceticism, the more extreme the better, will have any hope of success in burning out the burden of karma and avoiding the creation of new karma. Some went so far as to remain completely motionless for very long periods of time. A popular image in Jainism is a picture or statue of a standing monk with twining vines growing up his unmoving legs.

A Jain monk, especially in ancient times, was willing to abandon all of the pleasures and comforts of life and to take on the lifestyle of a naked ascetic because he was convinced that he was on the brink of moksha—that this lifetime would be the last, and when it finally ended, his jiva would at last be free to enter into the state of siddhashila. And speaking of the end of life, the perfect end would be religious suicide, the absolutely final and ultimate act of self-abnegation. It could not be a violent suicide, though; violence of all kinds was strictly forbidden. It would have to be a nonviolent end, such as fasting until one died. This is how Mahavira is said to have ended his own life. Other acceptable methods included walking out into the ocean until one's body was swept away, or, if an ocean was not available, walking out into the wilderness until one expired.

The lifestyle of the Jain monk, then, was structured in such a way as to completely eliminate the taint of karma. Ascetic practices played a large part, of course, but this was not the whole picture. Asceticism was something of an ongoing background. The affairs of daily life, in order to minimize the effect of karma as much as possible, were shaped by the Five Great Vows that every Jain monk committed himself to. I'm sure that you'll recognize these; they are exactly the same five rules included in *Yama*, the first of Patanjali's eight limbs of yoga. Actually, both Jaina and Patanjali's Yoga were drawing on the widely recognized basic rules of ascetic life already ancient in Indian culture. These Five Vows are: *Ahimsa* (nonviolence), *Satya* (nonlying), *Asteya* (nonstealing), *Aparigraha* (abstinence from greed), and *Brahmacharya* (celibacy).

Ahimsa is an especially interesting vow in the context of Jaina. Apparently in Mahavira's time, ahimsa did not yet include the meaning of compassion; it meant nonviolence, pure and simple. Since all living beings were believed to be possessed of jiva, any violence toward a living being, especially killing, would result in a terrible burden of karma. For this reason, Jain monks went to great lengths to avoid killing anything, even accidentally killing a bug. It was not uncommon for a Jain to sweep the path before him so as not to step on a single insect, or to drink water through a piece of gauze so as to strain out any tiny critters that might be in the water. Naturally, all Jains were strict vegetarians. To some extent, these practices still exist among modern-day Jains. Jains are known for their benevolence to animals. They maintain animal hospitals and refuse to use or wear leather.

Over time, the Jain sect evolved and changed. For one thing, the order of monks split into two camps. One group adopted the practice of wearing a simple white robe; they were known as the *Svetambaras* (white-clothed). Others continued to live by the strict rule of nakedness. They were the *Digambaras* (sky-clothed). After all, if the monk was to disavow all ownership, even ownership of simple clothing, nakedness was unavoidable. Eventually the two groups merged, however, and almost all Jain monks became robed ascetics.

The biggest change was in the expansion of Jaina to include a large population of lay men and women. Although laypeople lived more normal lives than monks, the belief was (and is) that following some measure of the Jain lifestyle will bring that person (that jiva) closer to the time when, as a monk, he can make the final dedicated effort. Despite the fact that the greatest part of the Indian population has always been engaged in farming, a farmer could not really become a Jain because the work of farming inevitably involves the killing of pests. As a result, most lay Jains came from the merchant castes. And as a result of this, the Jains are relatively wealthier and better-educated than is typically the case in India. This is evident in Jain temples, which tend to be elaborate and richly decorated. You won't find images of Hindu gods in Jain temples, though. No idolatry! Instead, there are pictures of Mahavira and other of the legendary Tirthankaras. Temples play an important part in the life of Jains, but their use is almost exclusively for the lay population, not the monks.

Jaina is a puzzling phenomenon—at least to the outsider. On the one hand is the underlying philosophy, which seems so life-negating. Jaina turned its back on the Vedas, which were so life-affirming. Whereas the Vedas sought fulfillment in the human condition, Jaina seeks only release from it; whereas the Vedas encouraged ritual participation in the great events of life, Jaina chose instead the way of extreme asceticism and withdrawal. It would seem that Jaina holds human life in disdain, sees no value in it, and yearns only for complete escape from it. But, on the other hand, we have before our eyes the lifestyle of modern-day Jain men and women. They are not in the least somber or withdrawn. The typical Jain is an attractive and engaging person—hard-working, peaceloving, law-abiding, clean-living. The ancient way of Jaina has survived through many ages and many persecutions. Perhaps this philosophy of life, so diametrically opposed to the way of modern materialism, will find a new surge of life among those who seek a meaningful alternative.

Buddhism

Buddhism is by far the best known and the most successful of the heterodox darshanas. Since the larger part of what remains in this study will be given over to a careful examination of the nature and evolution of Buddhism, I will only define it briefly at this point. Buddhism grew out of the teachings of Siddhartha Gautama Shakyamuni, who would later become known as the Buddha, "the Awakened One." Buddha was an itinerant guru of the sixth century B.C.E. who experienced a profound mystical intuition of truth (his "awakening") while in his thirties and dedicated the rest of his life to traveling about North India teaching his way of liberation to as many as would listen. What began as one of many reform movements within the body of Hinduism eventually became a heretical sect denying the validity of such traditional values as caste, the infallibility of the Vedas, and even the reality of Atman.

Buddhism would flourish for a while in India, but eventually it would all but die out in its homeland. The real success of Buddhism, though, was destined to be found in virtually all parts of eastern Asia, outside of India, to which Buddha's teaching migrated after his death. In its new homes, Buddhism would continue to grow and evolve into many widely differing forms. The history of Buddhism is a magnificent story and one that's still going strong today. We will take up the study of Buddhism in Part II.

Tantra

Tantra is a fascinating and much misunderstood subject. Throughout its long history, opponents have condemned it as fraudulent, hedonistic, lewd, and even outright insane. Properly understood, though, it is none of these things. Tantra is a tradition that has enormously influenced the evolution of both Hinduism and Buddhism.

Strictly speaking, Tantra is not classified as a "heterodox darshana." It's difficult to classify Tantra at all; it's something of a world unto itself. Actually, the beginnings of Tantra as a definable tradition can be traced to Buddhist communities of northern India in the sixth century C.E. This assertion conflicts with the long-held belief that Tantra began within the Hindu world and spread from there into Buddhism. Most scholars are now in agreement that, in fact, Tantra first appeared among the Buddhists and would coalesce into the school of Buddhism known as Vajrayana.

In any case, Tantra took form in both traditions at roughly the same time, historically speaking, and was heavily influenced by the orthodox doctrines and practices of both traditions. But, influenced though it may have been, Tantra definitely was a radical counter-movement in both Hinduism and Buddhism. Tantra may have retained much of the old, and even shows strong evidence of roots that go back to pre-Vedic times, but what was new was such a departure from the orthodox that Tantra was vigorously condemned by the traditionalists in both Hinduism and Buddhism.

A major misunderstanding about Tantra, at least among people in the West, is that Tantra is a distinct "school" within Hinduism, a darshana unto itself. This is not true. Tantra was more of a "movement" whose influence was felt within all of Hindusim, more strongly in some regions than in others. The northwest and the northeast of India felt the influence of Tantra most strongly of all. By way of a very loose analogy, I would compare the *expression* of Tantra to the expression of the evangelical movement in Christian America. Not that the teaching and practices of these two are similar; they couldn't be more totally different. But their role within the larger whole of their respective traditions is very similar.

FIGURE 5.1   A beautiful sculptured example of a *yab–yum*, perhaps ninth-century Tibet. (P. Bresnan)

The influence of evangelicism, like that of Tantra, is diffused generally within the Christian establishment, some feeling it more than others. But evangelicism, like Tantra, is not a specific "church" within the Christian family; it is a movement that has a life of its own, being expressed strongly in some congregations and not at all in others. That's the way it was with Tantra also.

The term *tantra* refers to the varius texts which formed the scriptural base of the movement. This Sanskrit word, taken originally from the weaving craft, refers literally to the weft—the horizontal strands that weave the yarn into a unified whole, a fabric. Tantra texts did the same sort of thing; they wove the various strands of the tradition into a unified whole, a philosophical system. The reliance on texts would become far more important in *Vajrayana* ("Tibetan Buddhism") than among Hindu Tantrists, whose approach was much more informal, emphasizing the relationship between guru and disciple, as well as spiritual practices tailored to meet the individual needs of each disciple, known as a *sadhaka*. It was these tantric practices that drew the condemnation of traditionalists, who denounced Tantra as being criminally lewd and misleading.

The earliest of the Tantric texts appeared in the fifth or sixth century B.C.E., and by the eigth and ninth centuries, the movement was flourishing. This period was something of a golden age in the history of Hinduism. It seems that beautiful Hindu temples were rising just about everywhere, many of these showing strong Tantric influence. But, alas, it was not to last. The Muslim conquest, beginning in the eleventh century, brought the curtain down on the golden age. Muslim armies zealously crushed what they perceived to be the work of idol-worshippers, and in their eyes Tantric influence was seen to be especially depraved. On the whole, only temples in remote places escaped destruction. Those that remain—such as the temples at Khajuraho and at Konarak—give us a wistful glimpse of how glorious the era must have been.

In Tantra, as in orthodox Hinduism, the ultimate goal is the same: full awakening, freedom from the suffering of attachment. In more practical terms, we might say that the ultimate goal is the creation of that state of consciousness within which awakening can arise. In traditional Hinduism, this state of consciousness is known as samadhi. To the Tantrists, this amounted to something much too passive, too body rejecting, too withdrawn from the fullness of human life.

Like orthodox Hindus, Tantrists too wanted to climb to the summit of Mount Meru (the mythical mountain, whose summit, the abode of the gods, was symbolic of the state of perfect enlightenment). But Tantra would offer a different means; Tantra would offer a "fast track" to the summit. Tantric teaching took the position that if one is going to attempt to climb the mountain, he (or she) must start the climb from where he is, which means, of course, at the base of the mountain. You can't just spirit yourself to a higher level; you have to make the climb one step at a time, and square one (step one) starts at the base. In the metaphor of Mount Meru, the base is associated with the animal roots of human nature. This is where happiness is equated with the pleasures of the flesh—eating, drinking, copulation, that sort of thing. There's nothing wrong with that; it's neither moral nor immoral; it's just the way things are at root. Where human consciousness is concerned, happiness is potentially capable of ascending to much higher states, but this is where it starts; ask any baby. (The point is illustrated graphically in the ground level friezes of some Tantric-influenced temples, which portray vividly sensuous scenes of orgies that include just about everything you can imagine.)

What gave Tantra its special character was its effort to involve the whole person in the adventure of spiritual growth. In place of the more traditional approach of asceticism and transcendence of desire, Tantra developed a host of ritual practices that *embraced* the body, desires and all, and saw it as a wonderful vehicle that could be used to carry one to higher states of knowledge. Rather than regarding the pleasure-craving body as an impediment to growth, rather than renouncing desire, Tantra sought to harness the energy of desire and use it to generate higher states of awareness. Of course, such an unorthodox approach could only hope to succeed if directed by a highly skilled master. Consequently, in the spirit of the ashram tradition of India, Tantra originally took the form of small groups of disciples tightly bound to a guru.

The guru–sadhaka relationship is everything in Tantra. Almost always this would take form within the context of an ashram. The guru trains the sadhaka, who, necessarily, is already a highly self-disciplined person. In no way at all is it reasonable to suspect that the disciple is actually a self-serving hedonist using the practices of Tantra as a front to disguise his appetite for sensual pleasure. Far from it! In an imperfect world, it may be true that a fraud slips through from time to time, but this would be very infrequent. For one thing, if a person was interested only in sensual pleasures, there would be far easier ways of satisfying these desires, even in India at any time in the past.

Tantra was something of a reaction to the extreme conservatism of classical yoga. Tantra, though, really went all the way. Far from renouncing the world and the body, the attitude of Tantra was to love the world, and love the body—cherish it, embrace it. As the vehicle of liberation, the body, all of it, was to be respected and *used*, not rejected! What we seem to have here is the strong re-emergence of pre-Vedic (Dravidian) traditions that had been suppressed, though certainly not eliminated, for a thousand years.

If we stand back and try to see the Big Picture, what we find, first of all, is a rich Dravidian culture that created the Indus Civilization in the third millenium B.C.E.; the second millenium was largely dominated by the Aryan invaders, who created the Vedic Age and the caste system, thereby suppressing the native Dravidian population (at least in the North). In the first millenium B.C.E., things changed dramatically. The Vedic Age was history; Dravidian culture, never extinguished, was free to come forth once again. A gradual process of amalgamation occurred. The result was "Hindu Civilization," a marriage of the Aryan and the Dravidian ways. In this marriage, the Dravidian partner would no longer play a subservient role. In many ways, the old Dravidian traditions became dominant once again. The rise of Tantra is only one example of this, although a most significant one.

Revival of the ancient Dravidian ways are prominent in Tantra. Most important is *shakti* worship, the mother-goddess. Closely tied to that is the greatly elevated position of women, even going so far as to believe in the equality of the sexes. The caste system was condemned (a fairly predictable expectation from the Dravidian part of the population). And, diametrically opposed to the teaching of classical yoga, the world was seen as fundamentally good. This followed naturally from shakti worship because, after all, it is the shakti of Brahman whose role it is to "play" the universe. If the world is good, then everything in it is good and that includes, significantly, the human body. Tantra teaches love of the body; it is the vehicle of liberation. In the Tantra view, the body rejecting attitude of classical yoga was nothing short of pathological. There were to be no taboos in Tantra; everything is the play of shakti; everything is sacred.

The influence of Tantra was pervasive (much like Zen in Japanese culture), but the actual *practice* of Tantra, life in the Tantric ashram was limited to a relative few. What sort of person would choose to join a Tantric ashram, and what kind of life could he or she look forward to?

It's a rare person that fits the bill; definitely it's not for everyone. If an unsuitable person took up the tantric way of life, it would lead to disaster. And certainly an authentic guru would weed out the unfit early on. The guru is in control of the entire process; the disciple must be willing to totally surrender to the will of the guru. Without his (or her) guidance, the seeker would quickly become lost in the woods.

The long path to the summit begins with *diksha*, the ancient ceremony of initiation. This establishes an intimate, personal relationship between guru and sadhaka. The most important element of diksha concerns the *mantra*. A mantra is a spiritually powerful word of syllable, or string of words or syllables, that a person repeats (often chants) in order to forge a strong psychic connection between himself and the force or deity that the mantra represents. The guru intuitively selects the appropriate mantra for his new disciple and gives it to him privately, perhaps by whispering in his ear. The sadhaka repeats the mantra to be certain that he has it right, then buries it in his heart, from where it will be repeated endlessly in the days and years to come. Disciples do not reveal their mantra to others, not because it's a secret, but rather because it is very personal. The importance of the mantra cannot be overstated. It is widely believed among adherents of Tantra that to reveal one's mantra would cause it to lose its power.

The actual work involved in climbing the mountain consists in a variety of psychoexperimental meditation exercises called *sadhana*. It is through the execution of sadhana that the guru steers the development of the sadhaka. Sadhana come in many varieties, but all are grounded on traditional yogic exercises, especially Kundalini Yoga, and all are designed to prepare the sadhaka for the experience of powerful psychic states. The sadhaka is skillfully guided (hopefully) to discover the real nature of his mind by exploring all possible psychic states. Needless to say, nothing less than a fully enlightened guru is even thinkable in this kind of relationship. Does the guru employ the use of psychoactive drugs? Yes, sometimes drugs are used, but definitely not as a matter of course. As you might guess, this has always been one of the major objections to Tantric practices, but it can easily be exaggerated. Much more common, and equally reprehensible to the traditionalists, is the possible presence of sexual intercourse in Tantric sadhana.

That needs to be explained. Tantra maintains that reality is One. The key to enlightenment is to see, to intuit, the unity behind the apparent polarities of life. Tantra uses a great deal of symbolism to express the unity of polarity. Chief among the symbols is that of male and female, representing the active and the passive principles of existence. In Tantra, as in Hindusim generally, the male, representing Brahman as *purusha*, is the passive, and the female, representing the *shakti* of Brahman, is the active (just the reverse of what one might expect in the West). The mating of the active and the passive, wonderfully symbolized in the act of sexual intercourse—or more specifically in the ecstasy of orgasm—became the central icon of Tantra. In Vajrayana Buddhism, this icon took the form of the *yab–yum*, a sculpture or painting depicting a male and his female consort joined sexually in the moment of ecstasy. (See illustration on p. 91.) This depiction did not become popular in Hindu Tantra, but the act itself did. Called the *maithuna*, it became the climax (so to speak) of a long and elaborate tantric meditation exercise known, appropriately, as the Maithuna Meditation.

Tantrists took the position (and still do) that the sublime joy of sexual orgasm is a powerful way of achieving self-transcendence, and, is available to all. Everyone knows that the sex drive is an extremely powerful force. How absurd it is to shy away from such a potent force, even trying to suppress it! It should be embraced, developed, celebrated, used to the full in the quest of spiritual transcendence.

This is best exemplified in the Maithuna Meditation exercise. Although intensely physical—involving the body, the emotions, and the mind—this was not at all meant to be an erotic experience, in the sense that sex normally is, but rather a very powerful vehicle involving the whole person, that, used properly, could transport the sadhaka into a transcendent state of consciousness in which he or she could experience—or better still, *become*—the unity, the oneness behind the illusion of polarities.

The Maithuna Meditation involved a great deal of ritual; it could easily take up the better part of a whole day. On the appointed day, the sadhaka would rise early to bathe and perform a variety of other ritual observances and offerings, including much chanting of prescribed verses. At the proper time, the sadhaka imbibed a liquid concoction of

Indicus cannabis (a very potent variety of hemp, which is to say, marijuana), known as *vijaya*. Following this, the sadhaka would use rice powder to trace a mandala on the ground, within which he would perform further offerings and chants. In the final part of the exercise, the sadhaka would ritually approach the "Five M's": *madya* (liquor), *mamsa* (meat), *matsya* (fish), *mudra* (roasted grain), and *maithuna* (sexual intercourse). The significance of this group is that they were specifically forbidden to the disciple in the orthodox Hindu tradition. So, you might say, that by indulging in these, the sadhaka was flaunting his rejection of the traditional way. In another way, though, these things represent some of the most basic and natural elements of life. Why shouldn't they be celebrated? Also, it was believed that the first four of these were aphrodisiacs and would thus be very helpful to the sadhaka when he joined with his female partner (the *shakti*). The sexual finale might last for a very long time, during which time it would be necessary for him to maintain an erection. It's interesting to the modern student of the subject that, with the possible exception of wine, the first four M's have no aphrodisiac properties at all, but the *vijaya* could indeed have this effect.

The grand finale of the Maithuna Meditation was the maithuna itself. Again, I want to emphasize that this was not intended to be erotic in the usual sense of the word. The prescribed posture for maithuna was the yogic position pictured in the yab–yum. The male sadhaka would sit, back upright with legs crossed, and the female, his shakti, would take her position in his lap, with her legs and arms folded around him. (See illustration on p. 91.) Interestingly, in this position, the male is capable of almost no movement at all, but the woman is capable of a great range of movements. It is she, in fact, who generates all of the action. This is in keeping with the symbolism, in which the male represents the passive principle and the female the active.

In the Hindu Tantric tradition, discharge of semen was expected to occur. It was the ultimate perfection of the whole long procedure. In the Vajrayana tradition, however, discharge was most definitely not supposed to occur. (Avoiding this would obviously require great self-discipline on the part of the sadhaka.) It was believed that this would squander the vital energy of the sadhaka just at the time he needed every bit of it to break through to transcendental awareness. Retention of the semen (*bija*) became the *sine qua non* of perfection in the performance of this sadhana.

In the historical evolution of Tantra, two schools of practice developed. In one school, called "right-handed Tantra," the sex act and other physical elements came to be represented only symbolically in sadhana exercises. This became especially true in Buddhist Tantra. The other school, the so-called "left-handed Tantra," continued to include actual physical experiences in sadhana. Whether one or the other is right, or more right, is, of course, a question that can never be answered definitively. In modern times, though, it would seem that right-handed Tantra pretty much has the field to itself—but not entirely.

Tantra is world affirming, body affirming. However, that being said—and it needs to be said—it is nonetheless true that the ultimate goal of Tantra meditation, as with all schools of yoga meditation, is to achieve transcendence of the physical nature in perfect union with the Absolute. This is not because at root the body is seen as sinful or corrupt, not in the least, but rather because the body, being a part of the world of maya, is imperfect and impermanent. The body is loved and respected, but *the body is used to transcend the body.* By way of analogy, we might compare the body to childhood. Childhood is wonderful, but in the natural order of things it is meant to be transcended by the fullness of maturity.

Study Questions

1. How would you sum up the essential teaching of Shankara? Why is his system referred to as "Advaita" Vedanta?

2. Why do you suppose that Samkya and Yoga are traditionally paired among the six orthodox darshanas? Do you think that the three pairings make sense?

3. What are the traditional "schools" of yoga? Are these yogas separate and distinct, or are they somehow related into one comprehensive whole? Which of the schools of yoga appeals most to you? Why?

4. "Yoga nirodha chittam vritti." What does this mean? Why do you suppose Patanjali chose it to be an opening line in the *Yoga Sutras*?

5. What do you make of Patanjali's "eight limbs" of Yoga? How does the practice of Hatha Yoga fit into the whole unified fabric of yoga?

6. How are the darshanas of Nyaya and Vaisheshika related? Do you think that it's going too far to suggest that the teaching of Aristotle may have had some influence in these darshanas?

7. With regard to Jainism, the question is asked, What is the point of all this extreme asceticism? Well, what *is* the point? Does it make sense to you?

8. Why is it suggested that Jainism and Charvaka are polar opposites? Are they *really* polar opposites?

9. Can you see any socially redeeming value to Charvaka? Do you agree with the suggestion that the school of Charvaka, more than any of the other darshanas, is most like the prevailing philosophy of life in modern times?

10. Why in the world, throughout its long history, have opponents of Tantra "condemned it as fraudulent, hedonistic, lewd, and even outright insane." Do you share this opinion?

11. Tantra is the real maverick among the traditional darshanas. Do you think it's this way just to be different, or is there a "method in their madness"?

12. What does Tantra mean by a "fast track"? Is such a thing possible? Do the methods of Tantra seem reasonable to you? Can you see yourself being a follower of Tantra?

13. Why is sexual symbolism so strong in Tantra? Is it genuinely reasonable to say that sexual symbolism is not meant to be erotic in the ordinary sense of the word?

14. Of all the darshanas, orthodox and heterodox, which one appeals most to you? Why?

CHAPTER 6

The Devotional Movement

As we have seen in Chapter 4, the *Bhagavad Gita* emphatically declares the primary importance of Bhakti Yoga, the way of devotion to a personal god, one who is a loving savior of humankind. In doing this, the *Gita* was reflecting a current within Indian society that was growing very strong. It is known as the *devotional movement.*

The philosophical systems, the darshanas, were, for the most part, of interest to specialized communities. In other words, only a minority of the people would have been personally involved as followers of a particular darshana. It would be going too far to say that they were of interest only to scholars, but it would definitely not be going too far to say that the great majority of the people were concerned with other things in their daily lives. As in all times and places, what mattered to most people were the *devotional* aspects of the spiritual life. Temples, idols, processions, prayers, bells, candles, gongs, incense, singing, and so on—this was the stuff of religious life for most. In other words, *Bhakti.*

The popular traditions of Bhakti grew from roots that reach far back into pre-Vedic times. These roots nourished, and continue to nourish, a strong and broadly based religious life among the population at large. As always, only a small minority favored a more philosophical approach to the mysteries of life.

At the same time that the principal darshanas were being formulated, a great surge of devotional movements took form. In part this was fueled by the appearance of the *Puranas,* popular compositions that brought the teachings of the Vedas and Upanishads to the people at large in the form of mythical stories that often included the wondrous doings of the various Hindu gods. Also of importance in this regard were the great popular epics, the *Ramayana* and the *Mahabharata.* And, in the *Bhagavad Gita,* as we have seen, Krishna proclaimed Bhakti to be the foremost of all Yogas.

Popular cults developed for all of the gods, but most of all for the worship of Vishnu and Shiva, the right and left hands of what would come to be known as the *Trimurti.* The worship of Vishnu and/or Shiva spread throughout the land. Temples were going up everywhere. It must have been an exciting time. This vigorous devotional movement came to establish the general character of Indian life, and it would continue to define the broad nature of Hinduism down to the present time.

THE TRIMURTI

Trimurti is a Sanskrit word that means "threefold expression"—in other words, trinity. The Hindu Trimurti is the closely bound trinity of three gods—Brahma, Vishnu, and Shiva—that came to occupy the place of paramount importance in the Indian pantheon during the post-Vedic Age. In its most simplified presentation, the Trimurti offers a straightforward role for each of its three members: Brahma is the creator, Vishnu is the preserver, and Shiva is the destroyer. However, as cult followings for Vishnu and Shiva grew over time, devotees of each of these deities came to see their own patron deity, by himself, representing all three aspects of the Trimurti. This did not happen with Brahma, though, who slowly sank into a role of less importance. In fact, in all of India there is only one temple dedicated to Brahma.* The worship of Vishnu and Shiva, though, spread throughout the land. To understand what all this means we have to back up a bit.

The gods were brought forth in the first place to give meaning to the forces of nature. Someone with rational intelligence and superhuman power, it was believed, was in control of the forces of nature and deliberately manipulated them in such a way as to account for the natural phenomena of daily life. The gods were created out of the human imagination to play this role, and they personified the forces of nature that they controlled. In early Vedic times the gods were imagined, much like the Olympians of Greece, as a very humanlike family of individual characters, and tales of their adventures, like those of their Olympian counterparts, make an engrossing story.

But from the very beginning, there was believed to be more to the story than simply the ongoing exploits of the gods; there lay behind the doings of the individual gods a sense of the grand uniformity, the oneness, of nature. The many had come out of the One and eventually would return to the One. There was an emerging view among the more thoughtful that, just as nature operates in cycles in the short run, over the long haul of time, worldly existence goes through enormously long cycles as well—cycles of generation, destruction, and regeneration. Existence alone endures forever, but the *things of existence*, gods as well as human beings, would emerge and eventually dissolve. And then the process of generation would begin all over again; and so on forever.

This more sophisticated view of reality called for a more sophisticated view of the gods. After all, the underlying purpose of the gods was not *really* to control the forces of nature, but rather to provide men with an intelligible symbol, or personification, of all those awesome aspects of nature that make up reality.

It would seem that, with the passage of time, what the forces of nature had in common became more important than how they differed. More and more it was the unity of nature that interested thinking men and women. But the unity of nature expresses itself in grand dualities: male and female, light and dark, land and sea, youth and age, and so on. The most fundamental duality of all was seen to be the interplay between the process of generation and the process of dissolution—creation and destruction. The gods associated with these great processes gradually became more and more important.

---

*In a technically accurate sense, there is indeed only one temple in India dedicated to Brahma. It is on the banks of a sacred lake in the city of Pushkar. There are, however, other places in India where Brahma is venerated, if not actually the deity of a specific temple.

FIGURE 6.1 The Kandariya Mahadeva (Shiva Temple), Khajuraho. (P. Bresnan)

As we have seen, in the Upanishads the movement toward greater unity ultimately came together in the name of Brahman—the ultimate ground of being, the source and end of all that is, the Fact of Existence:

> The supreme Self is beyond name and form,
> Beyond the senses, inexhaustible,
> Without beginning, without end,
> Beyond time and space, and causality, Eternal, immutable. (*Katha Up*: 10.3.15; p. 89)

Clearly, the concept of Brahman is a metaphysical abstraction of the highest order. In fact, it's too abstract for all but the most philosophically inclined. As a result, the reality of Brahman came to be personified by an anthropomorphic image that the human mind could more easily deal with. Brahma, an anthropomorphic creator-god was introduced in the post-Vedic Puranas, those popular myths regarding the Hindu gods. "Brahma," the creator-god, though, was not derived from "Brahman," despite the similarity of the names. It was not the intention of the composers of the Puranas to be deliberately substituting the mythological Brahma for the metaphysical Brahman. It would seem that Brahma was derived from the Vedic god Prajapati, in much the same way that Shiva can be identified with the Vedic Rudra. Nevertheless, Brahma, as the creator-god, can't help but be seen as playing the role of a sort of anthropomorphic Brahman.

Brahma is always depicted with four heads, corresponding to the four directions of the compass. This enables Brahma to see all things at once, appropriate for a creator-god. Each face is said to be reciting one of the four Vedas. According to the story, Brahma originally had but one head, just like everyone else. Here's what happened: Brahma engendered the great goddess Saraswati out of his own being. She was so incredibly beautiful that he couldn't take his eyes off her. Saraswati modestly tried to step away from his lustful gaze, but each time she moved he grew a new head, so that his eyes could follow her everywhere. That accounts for the four heads, but there was also a fifth one in the center above the others looking upward. Shiva, the great ascetic, was angered that Brahma would show such feelings for Saraswati, whom Shiva regarded to be Brahma's daughter. In a rage, he drew his sword and cut off the topmost of Brahma's heads. And that's how Brahma came to be a god of creation with four heads.

Creation, though obviously of fundamental importance, was not seen to be, by itself, the whole story. Creation is an ongoing, unfolding event that involves within itself the continuing play of the forces of generation and dissolution. If the *things* of creation were not always changing and impermanent, creation would be static and, ultimately, meaningless. Therefore, it became desirable to personify the inexpressable Brahman not as one god, a creator, but as three gods: a creator, a preserver, and a destroyer. And thus was born the Trimurti: Brahma, the Creator; Vishnu, the Preserver; and Shiva, the Destroyer.

It must be remembered that, philosophically speaking at least, the Trimurti is an allegorical representation of Brahman. The three gods *personify* the three basic aspects of the manifestation of Brahman. (In some interesting ways, this parallels the concept of the Christian Trinity, which is said to be three "persons" in one divine "nature," thus not really violating belief in one God.) This philosophical interpretation, though, is definitely not for everyone. Many Hindus accept a personal objective reality for each of the three gods.

Originally, Brahma, as Creator, was the foremost partner in the Trimurti. His preeminence, though, began to fade as devotion to Vishnu and Shiva grew. Eventually Brahma was eclipsed by the other two, but he was never erased altogether. The concept of the Trimurti survived, but it changed in a dramatic way. Devotees of Vishnu came to see him, by himself, as embodying all three aspects of the Trimurti. And in like manner, devotees of Shiva came to see him too embodying all three aspects of the Trimurti. For various reasons, Brahma never attracted a similar cult following and that's why he faded into the background.

Each of the three members of the Trimurti was (and is) associated with a female counterpart. This needs to be explained. In the Hindu view, Nature—and hence all of the things of Nature—is a ceaseless interplay of elemental forces, the most fundamental of all being the interlinked processes of generation and dissolution, which can also be described as the interplay of the active and the passive (similar to the Daoist concept of *yin* and *yang*). The passive force is represented by the male nature and the active force by the female nature. You can't have one without the other; they are the two sides of one coin. Thus, any given person is really a composite of the two. The female force is called *shakta*; it is what enlivens and energizes every being. Thus, when Brahma brought forth Saraswati, his *shakti* (personalized *shakta*), he didn't really "create" her; she was there all the time as a fundamental part of his being. Brahma simply *made manifest* his shakti, and it was manifest, understandably, in the form of a beautiful woman. And, according to the story, it is therefore the Brahma-shakti (the active aspect of Brahma) that does the actual work (or "play") of creation.

The same, of course, would be true of Vishnu and Shiva. Each is associated with his shakti, which is personified in the form of a goddess: Lakshmi in the case of Vishnu and Parvati (among others) in the case of Shiva. Lakshmi and Parvati are often referred to as "wives" or "consorts," but these terms are misleading. They are not separate from, and certainly not inferior to, the god they are associated with. Lakshmi is the shakti-essence of that which is called Vishnu, and Parvati is the shakti-essence of that which is called Shiva.

Over time, devotion to the shakti—that is to say, the "goddess"—grew enormously. This gradual elevation of the importance of the divine female seems to be concomitant with the maturing of civilization in cultures throughout the world. Eventually, worship of *Devi* (the "goddess") became equal to that of Vishnu and Shiva. Devi might be personified for some as the goddess Lakshmi, or as Parvati, or Durga, or as Brahma's shakti, Saraswati. (Saraswati is a wonderful goddess. As the goddess of art, music, and literature, she should certainly be the patron deity of the Humanities.)

Although the original conception of the Trimurti changed drastically, in a manner of speaking, a new sort of Trimurti took its place: *Vaishnava*, the worship of Vishnu; *Shaiva*, the worship of Shiva; and *Shakta*, the worship of Devi.

So, Vishnu and Shiva each came to represent the fullness of the Trimurti to their followers. You might understandably wonder why Indian society would need or want this duplication. Wouldn't one all-embracing god be enough? The answer probably lies in the fact that there were really two "Indias"—the North and the South. The North, more strongly influenced by Aryan culture than the South, favored Vishnu. The South, where Aryan influence had only marginally affected the indigenous Dravidian culture, preferred Shiva, whose roots are assumed to be pre-Aryan. In fact, as mentioned earlier, carved seals found in excavations at Indus Valley sites displays a figure seated in a yogic position that most scholars believe to be a depiction of a proto-Rudra/Shiva. It should be kept in mind, though, that this division of India into a North and a South is true in only a very general way. Some Shiva temples are to be found in the North, and some Vishnu temples are to be found in the South. The Srirangam Vishnu Temple, for example, the home temple of Ramanuja, a prominent Vaishnavite philosopher, is located in the southern city of Tiruchirappalli. Speaking generally, though, the division into North and South holds true.

Vishnu Worship

Vishnu is presumed to have originally been some sort of solar deity, but is only occasionally mentioned in the Vedas. In the post-Vedic era, though, Vishnu, the preserver of the world, became enormously popular in all parts of India, but more so in the northerly parts. Vishnu was pictured as an approachable, compassionate, loving god—someone you could pray to and he would really *hear* your prayers and care. To put it simply, Vishnu was a friend of humankind.

The name Vishnu is derived from the Sanskrit *vish*, which means "to pervade." As a member of the Trimurti, Vishnu's role was that of preserver of the world (the world initially created by Brahma), and in doing this work, he must, understandably, pervade all. However, as mentioned above, Vishnu, like Shiva, came to be seen by his followers as embodying all three aspects of the Trimurti. In this capacity, Vishnu became the Great God, a complete personification of Brahman unto himself.

Vaishnava mythology conceives of Vishnu recumbent on the coiled serpent Ananta, which itself rests on the dark surface of the cosmic milky ocean. Vishnu alternates between vastly long periods of deep sleep and dream sleep. (These periods are known as *kalpas* and are said to be four billion, three hundred and twenty years long.) When Vishnu dreams, his dream becomes the world of *maya*. From its creation to its ultimate dissolution, the evolution of the cosmos is the "dream" of Vishnu. At the end of the dream, all is withdrawn again into Vishnu, who then enters a kalpa-long period of deep sleep before the cycle begins again. It's a wonderfully

FIGURE 6.2 Sculptured panel from the exterior of the Kandariya Mahadeva. (P. Bresnan)

allegorical myth. That's what myth is all about, and the creative Indian imagination excels at the art. In the words of Heinrich Zimmer, "In the myths of India we are brought the intuitive, collective wisdom of an ageless, anonymous, and many-sided civilization" (*Myths*, 41).

There are many depictions of Vishnu asleep on the coiled Ananta. Perhaps the greatest of them all is to be found at Budhinakantha, a Vishnu shrine just outside Kathmandu in Nepal. It's a large beautiful representation, enclosed within a quiet pond. The only sounds are the occasional ringing of bells and the soft cooing of doves. This beautiful sculpture was lost and forgotten until it was discovered by accident in the nineteenth century. According to popular belief, the king of Nepal must never visit this site. Since he is regarded by his subjects to be an incarnation of Vishnu, were he to gaze on his own Vishnu-likeness, the spell would be broken, and he would immediately die. (Now that the king has been deposed, it seems reasonable to conclude that certainly not everyone in Nepal believes that he is the incarnation of Vishnu.)

It is the various incarnations of Vishnu that receive the most popular attention. In some ways, Vishnu was like the Greek god Apollo, or better still, a Christ figure for the Hindu world. Not only was he a loving friend, but he was also a *savior*. As proclaimed in the *Bhagavad Gita*, the compassionate Vishnu would incarnate himself on Earth to rescue a troubled humankind in times of dire need:

> Whenever dharma declines and the purpose of life is forgotten, I manifest myself on Earth. I am born in every age to protect the good, to destroy evil, and to re-establish dharma. (Easwaren, *Gita*, 86)

These incarnations of Vishnu are called *avataras*, and according to traditional belief, Vishnu is destined to play this all-important role ten times over the ages. Some of the incarnations were as animals—in fact, the very first one was as a fish named Matya. It seems that Manu, the first human, rescued little Matya who was about to be eaten by a larger fish. Manu took Matya to his home and kept him in an earthen jar. In time, Matya got too big for the jar, so Manu made a pond for him, but eventually Matya outgrew this too. So, Manu returned Matya, now big enough to defend himself, to the ocean. Out of gratitude, Matya spoke to Manu and warned him that a great flood was coming that would cover the world and destroy all living things. Manu must build a boat, and, in the spirit of Noah, he was to take representatives of the many plants and animals with him until the flood had passed. Manu did as instructed, and Matya pulled the boat to the only mountain whose peak rose above the waters. Manu tethered the boat there and waited. When the flood receded, Manu, thanks to the beneficence of Vishnu incarnated as Matya, was able to repopulate the world.

The most important avatars, though, were as men, and the most important of all was, of course, Sri Krishna, Arjuna's charioteer in the *Bhagavad Gita*. Vishnu, as Krishna, became a highly popular deity in India (and still is). Indian spiritual literature reaches a great height in Book Eleven of the *Bhagavad Gita,* wherein Krishna allows Arjuna a brief glimpse of his sublime Vishnu-nature. It had to be brief: Without Krishna's help a mortal would be completely overwhelmed by such a vision:

(*Arjuna speaks*)
Just as you have described your infinite glory, O Lord, now I long to see it. I want to see you as the supreme ruler of creation. O Lord, master of yoga, if you think me strong enough to behold it, show me your immortal Self.

(*Krishna responds to Arjuna's request*)
He appeared with an infinite number of faces, ornamented by heavenly jewels, displaying unending miracles and the countless weapons of his power. Clothed in celestial garments and covered with garlands, sweet-smelling with heavenly fragrances, he showed himself as the infinite Lord, the source of all wonders, whose face is everywhere. If a thousand suns were to rise in the heavens at the same time, the blaze of their light would only resemble the splendor of that supreme spirit. There, within the body of the God of gods, Arjuna saw all the manifold forms of the universe united as one. Filled with amazement, his hair standing on end in ecstasy, he bowed before the Lord.*
(*BG*: XI.3, 10–14; p. 150–151)

Strictly speaking, only nine of the ten avatars have thus far appeared among us. The tenth avatar, Kalki, is yet to come. He is pictured as a great warrior riding to humanity's rescue on a white horse (naturally). On the other hand, many Hindus believe that Vishnu is not limited only to these ten avatars, but that he has performed this loving service far

---

*Arjuna's vision of Vishnu has a most interesting parallel in the Christian tradition. As told in the gospel of Matthew, shortly before his death, Jesus took some of his disciples to a remote place in the mountains where he allowed them to see the sublime radiance of his divine nature. The experience was similarly overwhelming. (Matthew, 17:1)

more often. Many believe, for example, that Jesus and Mohammed were avatars of Vishnu. Some Hindus even attempted to swallow Buddhism by declaring Shakyamuni Buddha to be the ninth avatar.

Vishnu is an interesting god. The most popular depiction of Vishnu shows him colored dark blue, with four arms, and Lakshmi at his side. The four hands hold a conch shell (whose spiral shape is a symbol of the origin and evolution of existence), a discus (which may have originally been a symbol of the sun), a club, and a lotus blossom (or sometimes a bow). Statues of Vishnu are found in the many temples dedicated to him. My favorite is one that greets visitors near the entrance to Angkor Wat in Cambodia. It's beautifully done and is thought to have stood in the temple's sacred center when it was a Hindu place of worship. After Angkor Wat was converted to a Buddhist shrine, though, Vishnu was demoted (but not expelled) and moved out to the entrance to serve as a greeter.

Shiva Worship

Entering the world of Shiva worship is to enter the world of India at its most awesomely mysterious and bewildering, at least for the non-Indian. In Shiva worship, the Indian creative imagination erupts in a never-ending multiplicity of gods and demons, occult rituals, and stunning sexual symbolism. The devotees of Shiva account for many of the odd stereotypes that exist in the Western mind regarding Indian spiritual life.

Like Vishnu, Shiva in various forms came to represent all three aspects of the Trimurti: creator, preserver, and, ultimately, destroyer. In the enchanting role of Shiva Nataraja, a four-armed Shiva is pictured performing the dance of the cosmic cycle. The beginning is slow, bringing the world into being; then it becomes a dance that maintains the cosmos. The wild finale, the dance of fire, represents the final destruction of the world. Then, after a time, it will all begin again.

Shiva as Destroyer has roots that go back to Vedic and even pre-Vedic times, when he was identified with the god Rudra. Shiva is pictured as the archetypical ascetic yogin, and as such, he became widely popular as the patron of India's myriad ascetic sadhus, who do the best they can to imitate the appearance of Shiva. This god of the untamed and brooding nature was said to spend most of his time in seclusion on Mount Kailash, far back among the Himalayan peaks in Tibet. He let his black hair grow wild and long, tying it in a topknot from which he let the mighty Ganges rush forth. He practiced severe austerities, going about totally naked, but covering his body with ashes from the cremation grounds and wearing only a necklace of human skulls. As Destroyer, Shiva's symbol is the trident, which he carries with him everywhere.

Shaivite monks honor their patron by wearing various symbolic adornments, including a small trident on a string around the neck. Typically, they also wear little or nothing, let their hair grow long, and smear ashes into it daily. The ash comes, not from the cremation grounds, but from the little sacred fire, the *dhuni*, (or *yajna*), which is lovingly set up and ringed by flowers every day. Ash is also used to make the *tilaka*, three horizontal stripes on the forehead and on various parts of the body. Shaivite monks are wanderers but usually not hermits. There is a loose organization among them, and from time to time they gather for religious festivals. Great numbers congregate at Allahabad on the Ganges for the *Khumba Mela* festival held at twelve-year intervals.

The itinerant, ascetic Shaivite monks are a fascinating part of Hindu culture, but they account for only a tiny proportion of Shiva's worshippers. Among the people at large, it is

FIGURE 6.3 Shiva and Parvati from an exterior panel of the Kandariya Mahadeva, Khajuraho, India. (P. Bresnan)

Shiva as Preserver that is most honored. In this role, Shiva is the patron deity of many temples throughout India, especially in the South. The symbol of Shiva the Preserver is the *linga*. A linga is a simple upright shaft, rounded at the top, which represents the erect phallus, the male sex organ. The linga is found and venerated *everywhere* within the world of Shiva worship. It is found in temples, shrines, home altars; in earlier times, it was even worn around the neck by married women. Its voluptuous ubiquity was, to say the least, shocking to Westerners who first came into contact with Hindu culture*.

The roots of linga veneration are very ancient in India. There is reasonable evidence that these roots stretch far back into pre-Vedic times. There are some references to indigenous "phallus-worshippers" in the *Rig Veda*—and why not? It is a natural symbol for fertility, for procreative power, which is exactly what made Shiva the Preserver an all-important god. Ritual veneration of the linga was, and to some extent still is, the central act of worship in Shiva temples. Actually, the linga is virtually always found in association with a *yoni*, a round base (sometimes square), made of wood or stone, into whose center the linga is inserted. The yoni represents the female sex organ; together they form a complete symbolic representation of the dual male—female character of nature. The linga represents Shiva; the yoni represents his shakti—that is to say, the female aspect of the Shiva-nature. Though represented in the arts as a separate being, the shakti is not a separate being at all. As discussed earlier, the

---

*Among other things, the Sanskrit word *linga* means "distinguishing feature." Given that the fullness of the Shiva-nature is the Shiva–Shakti relationship, it does seem reasonable that the "distinguishing feature" of the male part of this duality would be his sex organ.

shakti is the active, creative "female" aspect of the whole. The matter of "the whole" extends necessarily to Brahman. Because the concept of shakti is of the essence of Brahman, it is of the essence of everything. There can be nothing that lacks this twofold nature, *characterized* as male and female. In mythological terms, all of the male gods had female shaktis, described as "consorts," but in reality, both were the manifest aspects of one unitary being.

The traditional manner of linga–yoni veneration can seem pretty startling to most Westerners. In a typical ritual, Shaivite priests pour any combination of milk, oil, honey, and perfume onto the linga, which are then most gently kneaded into the surface of the sculpture. In some cases, a vessel is hung directly above the linga, onto which it continuously drips a sacred oil. Candles and garlands of fresh flowers decorate the scene. Clearly, this is a highly sensual form of worship. And, to the devotees of Shiva, therein lies its special beauty.*

Linga–yoni veneration was not the whole of it. Sexual symbolism in general plays a huge role in Shiva worship. Some of the sculpture associated with Shiva temples is often very frankly sexual. Young women, known as *devadasi*, were commonly connected with Shiva temples and participated in the rituals—sometimes only in a symbolic fashion, sometimes not.

As mentioned, Shiva is very often depicted in association with his shakti. Shiva, in union with his shakti, forms a cosmic wholeness. Shiva's shakti is personified in the goddess Parvati, who, in addition to her primary identity, is able to take on various other forms, the principal ones being Uma, Durga, and Kali. They are, to put it mildly, a foursome that would be hard to ignore.

Parvati, the subject of many mythic stories, is presented as Shiva's favorite. Parvati is maddeningly beautiful and intensely erotic; she and Shiva are often portrayed in passionate sexual intercourse. One time, to hide her nudity, Parvati playfully put her hands over Shiva's eyes. He immediately created a third eye at the center of the forehead, thus supposedly giving rise to the concept of the third eye in yoga. On another occasion, when Shiva had been away for a long time, she created a baby from her own saffron bathing paste and named him Ganesha. Then she put the child nearby to guard her privacy while she bathed outdoors. Not recognizing Shiva, Ganesha ordered his "father" away. Shiva wasn't exactly used to being so treated, and he promptly decapitated Ganesha. When she discovered this, Parvati was furious. To make a long story short, Shiva ordered his men to go out and bring back the first head they found. One of the men came upon a baby white elephant, cut off its head, and brought it back to Shiva, who joined it to Ganesha's body. And thus was the origin of one of Hinduism's most popular gods: the fun-loving, snack-eating, good-luck-bringing, wisdom enhancing, elephant-headed Ganesha.

Uma's roots probably go back to the time when she was a Dravidian mother-goddess. She is associated with domesticity and the abundance of the earth. Durga, too, probably evolved from a prehistoric mother-goddess. But unlike Uma, Durga could be fierce and bloodthirsty. Durga was the one who craved blood sacrifice, including human

---

*Linga veneration, as described above, is not something that existed only in the distant past, nor is it limited only to exotic temples found in India. Devotees of Shiva see it as an entirely respectable form of religious worship, and it has traveled with them to many parts of the world. In Livermore, California, for example, right in the middle of a typically American tract of suburban homes, there stands a Hindu temple dedicated to both Vishnu and Shiva. The temple maintains a staff of priests from India who perform traditional rituals daily. Far from being bizarre, it's really quite beautiful.

FIGURE 6.4 Linga and Yoni; South India. (P. Bresnan)

sacrifice. Kali is by far the most fearsome of the lot. She gives life, but she more often destroys it. Shaivite artists used a lot of imagination in portraying Kali. She is pictured as wild and hideously ugly, with fangs for teeth and a naked withered body. She carries a severed head in one hand and in the other a staff topped with a human skull. There's much more, but you get the picture. Kali is associated with death and destruction, but out of that arises the potential for renewal. Her most renowned temple was the Kalighat, near the British colonial city of Calcutta (which has been restored to its original native Indian name, Kolkata).

RAMANUJA

The devotional movement reached a summit in the person of Ramanuja, resident scholar (*acharya*) of the Sri Ranganathaswamy Temple at Srirangam in South India in the eleventh century c.e. Like Shankara, Ramanuja was a Vedantist and a brilliant thinker, but unlike Shankara, Ramanuja was fully rooted in the Bhakti tradition. Ramanuja's name is inevitably linked with Shankara, whose abstract, intellectual philosophy he opposed. Ramanuja was a scholar, able to meet Shankara on his own ground, and thus gave a respectable defense to Bhakti, all too often dismissed as naive and unphilosophical by educated Hindus. Ramanuja sought to establish Bhakti as a fully intelligent alternative to the intellectual philosophy of Shankara.

Ramanuja agreed with the Vedanta position of Shankara that reality is One, but strongly disagreed as to the real nature of the One. Ramanuja argued that the empirical world is real, not the illusory maya of Shankara, but this does not amount to a dualistic interpretation because the world is not separate from Brahman; it is the direct *manifestation* of Brahman. The One manifests itself in pluralities. He used the familiar analogy of the body to explain this point. Each part of the body is real and distinct unto itself, but altogether the parts form an organic whole, a "self," that is real, whose reality transcends that of the parts, and upon which each of the parts is wholly dependent. You could say that the individual beings of the world are the manifested parts of the "body" of Brahman. But just as your own self is infinitely more than merely the sum of the parts, so too is Brahman, the ultimate "Self," the final one reality that defines everything.

The great importance of this interpretation is that it opens up the possibility of sin, and redemption. If the individual self is real (even though that individuality is subsumed in the organic wholeness of Brahman), then the individual self is capable of independent action, including sin. This is not the same as the avidya of the Brahman-Atman that results in suffering. Ramanuja is talking about real, free-will sin.

Human beings are capable of sin, but redemption is possible. Being that each of us is only a part of the organic wholeness of Brahman and that therefore none of us is in any way capable of independent existence, the solution is to fully accept that fact—loving Brahman with complete self-surrender. Loving Brahman is not loving some lifeless abstraction, the "Absolute," for example. Since the whole is greater than the parts, and the parts (us, at least) are personally conscious beings, it must follow that Brahman too is *at least* as real and personal a being as we are. (Interesting concept, isn't it?)

Ramanuja was encouraging men and women to love Brahman in the form of a personal god, a compassionate savior. And for Ramanuja none fit the bill better than Vishnu, the much-loved deity who represented the Brahman nature. The way to do this, of course, is through Bhakti. The customary practices of Bhakti—temple worship, festivals, prayer, etc.—are the means par excellence for one to generate the saving grace (*prasada*) which brings redemption from sin. And the highest form of Bhakti, in Ramanuja's view, is the worshipful repetition of the name of God. Ramanuja urged his followers to pray constantly, lovingly repeating God's name. Thus did Ramanuja attempt to put the way of Bhakti on a par with the more intellectual darshanas.

Ramanuja's lifetime coincided with the golden age of temple building in India. Can there be any doubt that his devotional teaching influenced the movement in subtle but powerful ways?

THE HINDU TEMPLE

The Hindu temple is one of the truly great architectural conceptions in the history of human civilization. But it is much more than an architectural masterpiece. It is, in fact, an exposition of Hindu philosophy writ in stone. Unfortunately, though, in the West the Hindu temple is little known and hence little appreciated. Understanding the Hindu temple requires a new way of seeing for the Western eye, a new way of knowing for the Western mind.

Unlike a church or a mosque, the Hindu temple is not designed to have a spacious interior wherein a congregation can gather for religious service. The Hindu temple is a sacred structure in which a representative image of a god can be preserved and venerated. The community that the temple serves is represented by priests who tend to the needs of the temple, and perform, in the name of the whole community, the ongoing religious rituals associated with the deity enshrined within. Devotees visit the temple, either individually or in small groups, to pay homage to the deity, and to experience *darshan*, the profound joy of being spiritually close to the divine, an experience which the temple is wonderfully designed to promote.

There are times, religious festivals for example, when the entire community may gather in the vicinity of the temple, but these are outdoor events. The temple interior, by its intended plan, is a relatively small space, dimly lit by candle flame, quiet and conducive to contemplation. (The words *contemplate* and *temple*, incidentally, are derived from the same root.)

Let's stand back and look at the temple as a whole. What do you see? (The photo of the Kandariya Mahadeva on page 102 will help with this.) We can see that the temple, as a structure, is a unified complex of many parts, that rests on a large flat platform (known as a "plinth"). There are several towers, one taller than the others, and a great adornment of sculptured images on the walls. There is a horizontal as well as a vertical sense to it all. Perhaps we can see that the temple itself is the centerpiece of a larger area, a "sacred precinct." There's a lot for the eye to take in. But what is the meaning of it all? That is not obvious. To begin to answer this question, we must look deep into the past. The temple that we see before us represents the maturity of a long, historical evolution.

There were no temples, as such, in the Vedic Age. But there was, of course, much active worship of the gods, such as the great fire sacrifice discussed previously. The earliest roots of the Hindu temple may possibly be traced to the brick altar constructed for the sacrifice. Building the altar was done according to an elaborate ritual process. It began with the laying out of a spiritually potent mandala on the ground. The altar was then built up most carefully in accord with the diagram of the mandala. The Hindu temple begins in exactly the same way. A great mandala (the *Vastupurusha*) prescribes the manner of construction. Whereas the Vedic altar that rose from its foundation was out in the open, the "center" of the later Hindu temple would be entirely enclosed, deliberately made to be like a cave.

In Vedic times, the gods could be summoned to the sacrificial altar, but left to themselves, the gods were said to be attracted to mountains and caves. Shiva's much loved home, for example, was the summit of Mount Kailash, deep in the highlands of Tibet. And the mythical Mount Meru was believed to be the abode of all the gods. People, too, are attracted to mountains and caves (maybe that's why the gods are). There's something so awesome and mysterious and beautiful about them. One thinks of our distant ancestors who created the amazing paintings deep in the caves of western Europe. Clearly they had some sort of spiritual or magical purpose, and their cave location must have intensified this effect.

Consequently, we may reasonably surmise that some of the earliest "temples" in India were natural caves that were selected to be protected places where an icon representing a god could be venerated by devotees of that deity. A little shaping and cleaning would be all that was necessary. Such remote cave sites could easily have been associated with places where renunciate "forest dwellers" congregated in post-Vedic times.

The next step would have been to intentionally *create* temple-caves in suitable places. This would become one of the most fascinating features of temple building in India. In some places—such as Mamallapuram, Elephanta, and Ellora—caves were hewn out of solid rock and then carved into breathtakingly beautiful temples. At Ellora, for example, the rock was hewn not face on, but *from above*, and one of the most beautiful temples in all of India was the result.

Ultimately, the temple plan of choice became the freestanding structure, constructed of stone, capable of being built almost anywhere. But the form of the cave was preserved. The cavelike heart of the temple would remain its all-important feature. Here, in the inner womb of the temple, would reside the physical symbol of the god.

The earliest freestanding stone temples date all the way back to the fifth century c.e., but they were almost certainly preceded by structures made of timber and thatch, and later of brick. This parentage is revealed in the design of some early stone temples, such as the sixth-century Parvati Temple at Nancha. (It's interesting to note that the development of the Greek temple followed the same evolution.) The early temples were understandably small and simple compared to their later descendants, but already, the beginnings of a Northern style and a Southern style could be detected.

The construction of the temple begins with the selection and preparation of the site. As you might expect, a great deal of ritual is involved. The site must be both auspicious and suitable for aligning the opening of the temple to the east, the direction of the rising sun. Then the great mandala (the *Vastupurusha*) is etched out on the ground. The Vastupurusha is so-named because the outline of the "cosmic man" (the *purusha*) is folded within the square that holds the mandala. Among the rishis of India, the square was held to be the perfect earthly form, whereas the circle was the perfect heavenly form. The temple would rise, layer by layer, from the mandala, the temple itself becoming a mandala in three dimensions. Presumably, when the temple was finished, all of the outer surfaces would be plastered and painted, much as one still sees today in some temples that are in regular use. Typically, the plinth (the raised platform) that the temple proper stands on would be large and extend out on all sides from the base of the temple. Sometimes, small structures such as shrines would be built at the four corners of this terrace. Directly in line with the opening of the temple would be a grand stairway, which is where the devotee begins his or her ascent to the higher state of consciousness represented by the temple as a whole.

Devotees actually begin their visit at ground level. It is common to commence *pradakshina* ("circumambulation," always in a clockwise direction) around the base of the plinth, contemplating the imagery carved thereon. Typically, the imagery on the plinth is very earthy (as befits that part closest to the earth) and sometimes surprisingly erotic. Sexual imagery is thought to be auspicious and sometimes decorates the walls, particularly near the entrance. This is especially true of temples influenced by Tantra.

Then proceeds the ascent up to the terrace level of the plinth. Pradakshina continues, this time contemplating imagery of a more refined sort, typically showing themes related to the deity whose idol is within. And finally, up the stairs to reach the entrance to the temple interior, a stylized cave of three chambers. (All visitors, by the way, are expected to enter the temple with bare feet, but exceptions are sometimes made for non-Hindus.)

In India, the word *mandap* is used for a sort of canopy that is put up outdoors for many uses: weddings, for example. The word is applied to parts of a temple, where the overhead "canopy" is made of stone. The first of the chambers, the *mandapa*, is like a porch, usually with some openings in the side walls. It is airy and light, similar to the entrance to a cave. The mandapa may give way to a *mahamandapa* (a "great" *mandapa*), which is much darker and more cavelike. Both the inner and outer walls of the mandapa and the mahamandapa are likely to be decorated with sculpture. The mahamandapa is the anteroom to the holy of holies, the *garbhagriha*. This is the *sanctum sanctorum*, the heart of the temple wherein the idol of the god is displayed on a pedestal. This may be a statue, or an abstract symbol, such as the linga–yoni, which is found in the garbhagriha of all temples dedicated to Shiva. The idol is at the center of the chamber so that pradakshina may continue in this most sacred place. The god is said to sometimes actually reside within the idol, and it is in contemplation of this image—lighted dimly by flickering candles or oil lamps—that the devotee hopes to achieve a transcendent religious experience, which, after all is said and done, is the real purpose of the temple. *Garbhagriha* means "womb chamber"—a very apt name, for the devotee hopes to emerge from the temple, as from the womb, reborn in a spiritual sense.

The highest tower of the temple rises directly above the garbhagriha. The finial at its summit represents moksha, the attainment of perfect awakening. The vertical plane thus majestically represents, stage by stage, the long journey from base ignorance (avidya) to ultimate moksha. The image of the god within is at the exact intersection of the horizontal and vertical planes of the temple. When you stand outside and take it all in, it's easy to see why the Hindu temple is described as the essence of Hindu philosophy writ in stone.

In the Northern style, the tower is called a *sikkhara*, and its finial is typically shaped like a collar of discs surmounted by a plain stone sphere. In the Southern style, the tower is called a *vimana*, and its finial is more in the shape of a dome. These finials can be huge and weigh many tons. The finial of the Brihadishwara Temple in Tanjore (Tanjavur), for example, weighs 80 tons and required a temporary earthen ramp more than 4 miles long to raise it to its intended place 216 feet above ground level. The Brihadishwara vimana, though, is an exception among temples of the South. Generally in southern temples, the vimana is relatively small, greatly exceeded in height by the *gopurams*, those dazzling truncated pyramids, covered with sculpture, that rise above the gateway entrances to the temple area. Temples of the South are more likely to have a sacred pool ("tank," as the British call it) associated with the temple. And, the great majority of the temples of the South are dedicated to Shiva, whereas in the North, Vishnu is often the one being honored.

The golden age of temple building in India was the tenth and eleventh centuries c.e., the same time that the earliest of the great cathedrals were being erected in far-off Europe. Sadly, though, this golden age was not destined to last. Soon the Islamic conquest of India was about to commence, and before it was over, much was destroyed. The temples that we see today are only a remnant that survived that very difficult time. Many have been lovingly restored in recent times and are once again serving the faithful.

It should be pointed out that Hindu temples are not only to be found in India. In its more expansive days, Hinduism spread far throughout Southeast Asia; the remains of temples can be found in many places. Angkor Wat in Cambodia began as a Hindu temple and was only later transformed into a Buddhist temple. Very impressive temples are to be found in central Viet Nam and in Java, which also was Hindu before becoming Buddhist (and then Muslim). The beautiful little island of Bali is the only place outside of India where Hinduism sank its roots and remained permanently. There are many striking Hindu temples in Bali, but with the exception of a few very early ones, the Balinese have developed their own style, and the temples, though beautiful, do not have the same appearance as those of India. And, of course, Hindu communities all over the world have, in modern times, constructed their own temples, often in the traditional style. As mentioned before, in Livermore, California (of all places!), a Hindu temple dedicated to both Vishnu and Shiva rises from the center of a typical suburban housing tract. Oddly enough, it seems to fit right in.

I'd like to end this section with an excellent quote from a work by the Indologist, George Michell:

> The temple functions as a symbol of ultimate enlightenment: it is the house of the gods among men, the place where the gods may be approached and divine knowledge discovered. As the centre of religious and cultural activities, the temple is the focus of all aspects of the life of the community it serves. But the temple is also the product of a desire to transcend the world of man—the principles of its construction, the forms of its architecture and decoration, as well as the rituals that take place within its walls, are all aimed at ultimate liberation. (49)

Study Questions

1. What does the term *devotional movement* refer to? Was it unique to the Hindu world? Do you see any modern-day parallels?

2. What accounts for the great popularity of the god Vishnu? Why has he chosen to be incarnated multiple times throughout history? What is Krishna's relationship to Vishnu?

3. How do you account for the great popularity of the god Shiva, particularly in the south of India? Why, in fact, does Hindu society venerate both Vishnu and Shiva? Don't they seem to serve the same religious function within Hinduism?

4. What do you make of linga veneration in association with Shiva? Do you feel that this is a profound religious expression? Perhaps you feel that it is out of place in modern times?

5. How do you explain the growing importance of the deified female, "the goddess"? Over the millennia, the place of the goddess has moved from relative obscurity to preeminence. What accounts for this?

6. Everyone, it seems, loves Ganesha. Why?

7. In what significant ways does the teaching of Ramanuja differ from that of Shankara? Why is it claimed that "the great importance of this interpretation [Ramanuja's] is that it opens up the possibility of sin and redemption"?

8. Do you agree that Ramanuja put the way of Bhakti on a par with the more intellectual darshanas?

9. The architectural difference between the Taj Mahal (illustration on page 114) and the Kandariya Mahadeva (illustration on page 102) is striking, to say the least. What does this comparison suggest to you about fundamental differences between the two cultures? Do you have a preference?

10. "The Hindu temple is a statement of Hindu philosophy stated in stone." Do you feel that you understand the intended meaning of this assertion? Does the "statement" succeed?

CHAPTER 7

A Millennium of Strife

THE MUSLIM ERA

The fortunes of civilization have risen and fallen for millennia in India. Empires have come and gone, and so too have invaders. Foreign invasion is as old as the story of history in the Indian subcontinent. But always, it seems, the would-be conquerors were themselves the conquered as the great ocean of Hindu culture ultimately swallowed up the invaders, assimilating them into the multifaceted world of Indian peoples. The Muslim conquest of India was a different story. This time the invaders came, not only to stay, but to remain an aloof and unassimilated class of conquerors.

The Muslim conquest of India began a thousand years ago. Wave after wave of invaders poured in out of the Persian-Afghan west. Native Indian resistance was strong and passionately determined, but all to no avail. Muslim armies ultimately succeeded in conquering and establishing rule over almost all of the subcontinent. Only parts of the South escaped incorporation. Muslim rule would prevail in India until the nineteenth century, when it was finally replaced by another foreign power, the British. The presence of Muslim rule is finally over, but the bitter legacy is far from being a thing of the past: Modern democratic India continues to be wracked by problems born of ancient hatreds.

Actually, the very first Muslim incursion into the subcontinent occurred all the way back in 711 C.E. That was less than a century after the founding of Islam in far-off Arabia. After the death of Mohammed, crusading Islamic armies swept out of Arabia, and in less than a generation, had created an empire that stretched from Gibraltar to Persia. One of the principal centers of this empire was the Caliphate of Damascus, and it was from here that a small invading army was dispatched to India. They succeeded in establishing control over a region in the lower Indus Valley, but it really never went beyond there, and effective rule lasted for less than a century. It was a harbinger, though, of things to come.

The conquest began in earnest in the year 1001 C.E., when Mahmud of Ghazni, ruler of a small Afghan kingdom, launched the first of seventeen invasions into northwestern India. Between 1001 and 1026 C.E., Mahmud's fierce horse armies plundered and devastated huge portions of northern India. His favorite targets were the temples, where so much of the

FIGURE 7.1 Taj Mahal. (P. Bresnan)

wealth of the land was concentrated. So many temples were pillaged and desecrated that Mahmud is known in Indian history as "the Idol Breaker."

Mahmud's conquest might have been turned back at the start, and conceivably centuries of Muslim rule in India averted, had one particular day in history gone differently, or even if one little incident on that day had not happened. It was on a hot summer day in the year 1008 C.E.; the place was a broad dusty field near Peshawar in northwestern part of the subcontinent. Mahmud's army, mainly an Afghan cavalry 15,000 strong, had been dug in for more than a month. They were facing the much larger army of Anandpal, the maharaja of the Punjab. Anandpal's father had lost an earlier battle with Mahmud, leaving 15,000 dead on the battlefield, and Anandpal vowed that such would never happen again.* Many of the rajas of North India had contributed forces to the army. The women had sold their jewels to raise funds. A force of several hundred war elephants had been collected. And now the moment of truth was at hand. Anandpal ordered an attack. Perhaps that was a mistake, although all went well at first. Mahmud was about to call for a retreat when, for some unexplainable reason, Anandpal's elephant panicked and charged away from the battle. In the confusion, the Indian army believed that their leaders were fleeing, and all began retreating in disarray. The battle turned into a rout; Mahmud's forces slaughtered thousands. Never again was he seriously challenged in India. Who can imagine how differently all of Indian history might have been if only Anandpal's elephant had stayed the course on that fateful day? But that's not the way it happened.

---

*Anandpal's father, incidentally, driven mad by his anguish over the defeat, is said to have committed suicide by throwing himself on a kinsman's funeral pyre.

Following the invasions, vast quantities of loot were hauled back to Mahmud's Ghazni, originally the capital of a rather small and humble Afghan kingdom. But thanks to his conquests, both east into India and west into Persia, Ghazni for a time became a rich and splendid city, second only to Baghdad in the Islamic world. Mahmud's court attracted artists and thinkers from all over the Islamic world, and presumably some of this cultural influence would be felt in India. But the people of the conquered regions were not yet thinking of that; they knew only death and devastation. Their people were slaughtered, their villages burned, and their beautiful temples broken and ransacked. Some of their finest "heathen" idols were hauled back to Ghazni, where they could be publicly desecrated and crushed under the hooves of the army's horses.

Successive waves of Muslim invaders followed Mahmud, extending Muslim rule throughout most of North India. But it was a patchwork affair, not a unified state by any means. One of these invaders was to have special significance for the future. Timur, generally known in the West as Tamerlane, led his incredibly ferocious horse army into northwestern India in the year 1398. Timur was in the process of forging a huge central Asian empire, and it was a process that knew no limit to violence and mayhem. It is said that parts of his army competed among themselves to see how large a pyramid of skulls could be built in the remains of devastated cities that lay in their path. North India felt his destructive violence, but fortunately for India, Timur had not come to stay. He did, however, lay claim to conquered regions in the northwest.

It was to claim Timur's legacy that another central Asian warlord entered India about a century after Timur had departed the scene. Babur, the founder of the Mughal Raj, invaded India out of his base in Afghanistan in 1525 C.E. Being descended from Timur on his father's side and from Ghengiz Khan on his mother's side, Babur certainly had the blood of conquerors in his veins. And conquest was what it was all about. Nominally Babur, like Timur before him, was Muslim, but spreading the faith was not his real goal; his real goal was the creation of empire, and at that task, he was very good. Babur welded together virtually all of the regions of North India, creating a unified state ruled from the Sultanate of Delhi and Agra. This empire, known in history as the Mughal Raj, would endure for more than three centuries, until finally it would be absorbed into the growing British Empire during the nineteenth century.

It does not serve our purpose in this study to go into detail about the political side of the story. Let me simply identify the principal successors of Babur so as to provide a temporal framework that we can refer to. One of his successors, Akbar, deserves more than passing mention.

- Babur (1525–1530) A fierce central Asian warlord, descended from Timur, who swept into India from Afghanistan in 1526, and succeeded in establishing the empire that would come to be known as the Mughal Raj.
- Humayun (1530–1556) Babur's rather inept son and successor. An opium addict, he lacked the zeal to extend the empire, but managed to hold on to most of Babur's conquests. His principal contribution was in being the father of Akbar.
- Akbar (1556–1605) Clearly the greatest of the Mughal line. His contribution could have changed the course of history, but his successors, unfortunately, did not choose to continue the work that he had begun.
- Jahangir (1605–1627) Something of a nonentity, Jahangir was in power during the time when the Europeans made their first important inroads into India.

- Shahjahan (1627–1658) Best remembered as the builder of the incredibly beautiful Taj Mahal. Constructed on the south bank of the Jamuna River in Agra, it was finished in the year 1654 C.E. The Taj is not a mosque; it was built to be a mausoleum for Shahjahan's much-loved wife, Queen Mumtaz, who died young. There is some evidence that workers began clearing a spot on the farther bank of the Jamuna, where an identical copy of the Taj was to be constructed, but this one would be all black marble instead of white. It was to be Shah Jahan's own final resting place, and the two were to be linked by an oval bridge of intermixed white and black marble. (Quite an awesome thought, isn't it!) Before building could begin, though, his sons, worried about the cost, declared Shah to be mentally unwell and removed him from power. He spent the rest of his days confined to a splendid suite in the family palace a short distance upriver from the Taj, which he could gaze at from his window. His sarcophagus finally joined that of Mumtaz in the Taj.
- Aurangzeb (1658–1666) All of the great promise of Akbar's reign of tolerance was finally crushed out of existence by Aurangzeb. Apparently, he was a fundamentalist of an almost fanatical frame of mind, who waged a nonstop holy war against his own Hindu subjects. Understandably, Aurangzeb was hated by the Hindus. All hopes of achieving Akbar's dream of some sort of cultural synthesis died on the vine. Aurangzeb's reign was the beginning of the end for the Mughal Raj. He was followed by a series of inept rulers who allowed the empire to fragment, making it much easier work for the Europeans (especially the British) to increase their influence until it reached the point of outright rule.

Aurangzeb fully scuttled any lingering possibility in the dream of his famous great grandfather, Akbar, that a bridge might be built between the Muslim and Hindu cultures. Akbar, though, was not the first to hope for this cultural bridge. Two other important names in this respect are Kabir and Nanak, both of whom were native Indians who made their mark decades before Akbar came to power. Before we learn more about the great Mughal, Akbar, and his dream of synthesis of religion and culture, we will look briefly at the lives of these two ordinary men whose impact on Indian thought was great.

Kabir

Kabir was a poet, a writer of religious verse. He was a deeply sensitive and compassionate man whom many regard as one of the finest thinkers in all of India's history. Kabir was born in (or close to) 1398 C.E. into a family of weavers in Varanasi, the holiest of India's holy cities. He would live until the mid-fifteenth century, some say until the end of the century. If the latter is accurate, Kabir would have been a close contemporary of two famous Italians: Christopher Columbus and Leonardo da Vinci. It's very doubtful, though, that he would ever have heard of either one of them. He was not concerned with the Europeans—nor was anyone else at that time; his mind was totally absorbed in the problem of the great gulf which separated the Hindu and Muslim peoples. Not long after Kabir's death, another famous European—the Portuguese, Vasco da Gama—was the first European to reach the shores of India. This event, which was to have such far-reaching significance for all of India, occurred in the fall of 1498. News of such a seemingly trivial event, though, happening far to the south, would not likely have attracted much attention at that time.

Although Kabir's people were of the native stock, they were not Hindus. At an earlier time, the entire weavers' caste of Varanasi had converted to the Islamic faith. There were obvious advantages in doing this, and some of the other craft castes had done the same thing. As a result, Kabir was raised in a Muslim family and was educated in Muslim schools. Nonetheless, he did not become an ardent Muslim. He was, however, a lover of the Sufi way, that maverick sect within Islam that attaches so much importance to devotional practices and mystical intuition. But Kabir was also a lover of much that he found in the Hindu Bhakti tradition. He felt no love whatsoever, though, for the Brahmin priesthood, which he attacked as perpetrators of superstition:

> Kabir detested the fundamentalist spirit amongst the Brahmins and Ulemas alike. He opposed the superstitions perpetrated by them. He cast doubts on the authority of the Vedas, opposed idolatry and rejected the doctrine of incarnation. He also criticized asceticism, fasting, pilgrimage, ceremonial ablutions and denounced all forms of dogmatism. (Verma, 168)

So what did Kabir *not* reject? On what would he anchor the bridge that he hoped to build? Kabir concluded that Islam and Hinduism—indeed *all* religious philosophies—attempt to accomplish the same thing: They all attempt to break down the barrier that separates man from God. And it is the *same God* that all are addressing, whatever the many different names that are used. All men and women are brothers and sisters, and whether they realize it or not, they are all striving to find union with the one God that is reflected in their many different religions. Muslims and Hindus must not quarrel; they should be united in love, knowing that they both seek the same God, only using different words to address Him.

Much influenced by Muslim Sufi and Hindu Bhakti, and perhaps most powerfully of all by the teachings of Ramanuja, Kabir urged people of all faiths to find salvation in total surrender to God. This alone is the true path, and one walks the path by lovingly repeating the name of God. Any name will do; they all address the same loving God. Kabir's message is best expressed in his own emotional poetry:

> O servant, where dost thou seek me?
> Lo! I am beside thee.
> I am neither in temple nor in mosque.
> I am neither in Kaaba nor in Kailash.
> Neither am I in rites and ceremonies,
> Nor in yoga and renunciation.
> If thou art a true seeker,
> Thou shalt at once see me.
> Thou shalt meet me in a moment of time.
> Kabir says, "O Sadhu!
> God is the breath of all." (quoted in Verma, 167)

Guru Nanak

Nanak was the founder of the Sikh religion, followers of which are those dignified, turbaned Indians one sees in seemingly all parts of the world. The Sikhs are known for a highly militant history, but it didn't start out that way.

Nanak was born in 1469 in a small village near Lahore, in what is today Pakistan. His family was Hindu, but his education was in Muslim schools where he learned to read Persian and Arabic. As a result, he grew up with a foot in each world, and throughout his whole life longed to find a way to bring harmony between the two cultures. Understandably, Kabir's poetry much influenced his thought and his teaching. Nanak too composed religious poetry as a young man.

While still in his student years, Nanak became something of a leader of a group of philosophically minded young men who made a practice of bathing together every morning before dawn in a nearby river. In the evening, they would gather to discuss philosophy, often listening to the newly composed devotional poetry of Nanak. The group included both Muslims and Hindus, and they continued to meet for a number of years. One morning, when he was about thirty, Nanak went off to bathe alone, but he didn't return home at the usual time. His clothes were found near the river, and everyone was horribly afraid that he had drowned. Three days later Nanak reappeared, but he seemed as if he were in some kind of trance. He would not talk, except to repeat: "There is neither a Hindu path nor a Muslim path. So how shall I know the right path? I will follow God's path, for God is neither a Muslim nor a Hindu."

Eventually Nanak began to communicate again, and he told his friends about an experience he had had on the morning when he was at the river alone. According to the story, Nanak was all of a sudden overwhelmed by a powerful vision of God, who spoke to him and told Nanak that He wanted him to be His messenger. God told him, "Go, and repeat my name, and encourage others to repeat my name." Spiritually transformed by this mystical experience, Nanak vowed to become a guru and devote his life to spreading the true devotion to the One God. The very first thing he did was to express in writing the essence of what he had intuited in his vision:

> God is only One.
> His name is True.
> He is the Creator,
> He is without fear.
> He is inimical to none.
> He never dies.
> He is beyond births and deaths.
> He is self-illuminated.
> He is realized by the kindness of the True.
> Repeat His Name.

The above prayer became the opening words of the *Adi Granth*, a book composed of the collected teachings of Guru Nanak. Technically speaking, Adi Granth means "original book," but it is generally referred to as the "Holy Book." It is the "Bible" of the Sikh religion and part of the prayers that make up the daily devotion of every Sikh. A beautifully bound copy of the *Adi Granth* is displayed at the heart of every Sikh temple.

The beauty of Nanak's spiritual philosophy is in its straightforward simplicity. In this regard, the influence of Islam can be clearly seen. But Hindu influences are also evident. His overriding goal was to reveal an underlying harmony between the Muslim and Hindu ways. He sought to get down to the roots: discard all of the externals. Nanak rejected all dogma, all scriptures; he rejected the caste system and everything even suggestive of idolatry. After his thorough house-cleaning of both traditions, there wasn't much left. But what was left was the all-important core.

Nanak declared that there is One God. ("Beside God there is no other.") Salvation consists in the soul's escape from samsara, the cycle of birth and death. This is accomplished by the total destruction of self-love, and this is accomplished through total submission to the will of God. The perfect, and universally available, way to achieve total submission is through *naam jaap*, the constant repetition of the Divine Name. Naam jaap will slowly but steadily clear away all of the impurities of self-love. Naam jaap, daily prayer, and service to the community—these three rules were the common core of worship that Nanak distilled from the teachings of Islam and Hinduism. Both groups respected the man and his work, and when Nanak died in 1539 at the age of seventy, both Hindu and Muslim groups claimed the body so as to honor it with their own ritual services.

Over time, a devoted group of disciples had collected around Guru Nanak. He called his followers *sikhas*, which is a Hindi word meaning "disciples." The community remained small and peaceful during Nanak's lifetime. Before he died, however, Nanak appointed a successor, who would also bear the title of Guru. Thus did the Sikhs become a sect—one that would continue over time and preserve the teachings of the founder.

The history of the Sikhs was peaceful at first. The sect was supported by the tolerant Akbar, who even gave the community a grant of land in the city of Amritsar. This became the site of the splendid Golden Temple (the Harmandir Sahib), the earthly center of the Sikh faith. The Golden Temple, so named because of its golden dome, is situated at the center of a small artificial lake and is approached by a narrow causeway. Pilgrims can enter the temple through large doorways on each of its four sides. These signify the four major divisions of the castes, which is to say, everyone is welcome.

The good times came to an abrupt end during the reign of Emperor Aurangzeb, the great-grandson of Akbar. Unlike his liberal-minded great-grandfather, Aurangzeb was a religious fundamentalist who launched a brutal persecution of all "nonbelievers." The Sikhs seemed especially to arouse his puritanical ire. He demanded that Guru Arjian remove some objectionable passages from the *Adi Granth*; when Guru Arjian, of course, refused, Aurangzeb ordered that the he be tortured and put to death.

It was in direct response to the persecution of Aurangzeb that the tenth Guru, Gobind Singh, in 1606 established the *Khalsa*, a quasi-military group within the Sikh community whose function was to protect the Sikh faith from persecution. The Khalsa was open to anyone, men or women, who were totally dedicated and fully willing to shed blood or even give their lives for the cause. Induction into the Khalsa followed an elaborate military-style ceremony which included acceptance of the "Five K's": *kesh* (uncut hair), *kanga* (the hair comb), *kara* (an iron bangle), *kacha* (special knee-length trousers), and *kirpan* (a sword) or its substitute, *khanda* (a dagger). The long hair is typically tied in a topknot and hidden under a turban.

Thanks to the ferocious resistance of the Khalsa, the Sikhs fought back effectively against their would-be persecutors, even going so far as to carve out an autonomous realm in the Punjab, which they hoped to make into an independent Sikh state. This was to have problematic consequences for the future. Fighting against the declining power of the Mughals was one thing, but taking on their well-armed British successors was quite another. After the British forcibly annexed the Sikh realm into their own growing Indian empire, the Sikhs perhaps saw the handwriting on the wall. From being violent opponents of the British, the Sikhs became loyal supporters. Many joined the British army, no small number of them serving in colonial security forces all over the Empire. Maybe they believed that, all things considered, this would be the most promising path toward eventual independence. Unfortunately, that was not to be. When independence came to India in 1947, the Punjab, to the bitter disappointment of the Sikhs, was divided between a Muslim Pakistan and a Hindu India. To escape horrible brutalities, the Sikh (and Hindu) families of the soon-to-be Pakistan had to uproot themselves and relocate to the eastern part of the Punjab included in Hindu-ruled India.

Even though the democratic constitution of India fully protected Sikhs, and many of them have risen to the highest offices in India, including president of the republic, some of the more fundamentalist Sikhs continued to yearn for their own Sikh state. The Sikh independence movement continued in the new India, sometimes indulging in what the government labeled terrorist activities. Things came to a head in 1984 when Jarnail Singh Bhindranwale, the leader of a "rebel" group, and several hundred of his followers sought sanctuary inside the Golden Temple. After a brief siege, prime minister Indira Gandhi ordered her troops to storm the temple. It was a terrible scene: the sacred temple was partially destroyed, and hundreds of Sikh defenders were killed. Shortly after this bloody event, two Sikh members of Mrs. Gandhi's security guard assassinated her in the garden of her residence. And so it goes. What the future holds is impossible even to guess. There are approximately seventeen million Sikhs in the world today, many of them living outside of India. It is reasonable to assume that this large and vital population will contribute in as yet unimagined ways to the progress of Indian and world civilization.

Akbar

Akbar is known in history as Akbar "the Great"; he certainly deserves that qualifier. Akbar was an enlightened ruler, a true visionary, in the same mold as Charlemagne, or Frederick the Great, or perhaps the best fit of all, that other great Indian ruler, Ashoka (whom we will meet in Chapter 10).

Akbar inherited an already large empire. Conquest was not the order of the day (although he did engage in some of that). Unification and consolidation were what was needed. Akbar took up the challenge with intelligence and passion. He wanted to be perceived as a just ruler of *all* the people. To achieve this, he instituted a policy of conciliation toward his formerly downtrodden Hindu subjects. The days of persecution were to be over forever. The special tax on the Hindu population, the *jizya*, was abolished (to the outrage of his Muslim advisers). Hindu religious rights were respected, but the abhorrent practice of *sati* was outlawed. (Sati was the widely hated custom of requiring a widow to immolate herself on her husband's funeral pyre.) Akbar sought out famous Hindu holy men and listened respectfully to their teachings. Many high-ranking Hindus were admitted to court, where they enjoyed the same opportunities as Muslim noblemen.

What began simply enough as a policy of conciliation evolved into something bigger, much bigger. Akbar allowed himself to dream the impossible dream, genuine cultural synthesis. Why not use his great power and influence to override the entrenched hostility between the two cultures, Muslim and Hindu? And it went even further than that: Why not add to this marriage the best of other great cultures as well, the Christian, the Buddhist, the Jain, and the Zoroastrian? Akbar envisioned nothing less than a cultural synthesis that would bring together the finest elements of all of the world's great civilizations. And he got the ball rolling himself, shocking his traditionalist courtiers by marrying four wives: a Muslim, a Buddhist, a Christian, and a Hindu. In fact, it was the Hindu wife, a princess from nearby Jaipur, who bore him the son who was to become his heir and successor.

Under Akbar's leadership the gentle war went well—for a while. He built a splendid new palace and town at nearby Fatehpur-Sikri, a visible model of the policy of cultural fusion. At Fatehpur-Sikri, he created a wholly new architectural style, combining elements of both the Muslim and Hindu traditions. Akbar encouraged the arts and invited artists and learned men from all over the Eurasian world to come to his court and join in the great work. To Akbar, by far the most exciting part of his dream was what came to be called *Din-i-Ilahi*, known in English by the name "Divine Faith." Akbar hoped to create nothing less than a wholly new religion, one that would incorporate the best elements of all of the world's great religions. It was to be a religious syncretism of the highest order, and no doubt he dreamed that its obvious appeal would sweep the world and usher in a new and greater age. Akbar created a special forum for religious debate; Muslim theologians were there, so were Buddhist scholars, and Hindu Brahmins, and even Jesuits from Goa on the west coast of India where the Portuguese had established a trading center.

Life was certainly exciting in those early days at Fatehpur-Sikri, but this little Golden Age of tolerance and cultural exchange was destined to be short-lived. Perhaps Akbar was not sufficiently pragmatic; he failed to create a situation in which it would be to the personal advantage of his Muslim privileged class to want to continue the great policy of cultural synthesis. Human nature being what it is, it was thus only a matter of time before the tide would turn. When Akbar died at sixty three in the year 1605 C.E., the tide turned.*

Despite the heroic efforts of the likes of Akbar, no real amalgamation ever occurred. There was a measure of artistic influence, and indeed there was some resonance between Sufi mysticism and Hindu Bhakti, but the great goal of cultural fusion died. Perhaps it was doomed from the beginning, but the intolerant policies of those who came after Akbar guaranteed that his dream of uniting the two peoples and the two faiths would remain only that—a dream. After Akbar, Hinduism in India seemed to turn in on itself, forsaking the often-hostile world and stressing the devotional side of the spiritual life.

THE MODERN ERA

In 1858, Queen Victoria of England signed the bill that officially transferred political control of the Indian states from the British East India Company to the Crown. For almost another century, India would be the "Jewel in the Crown" of the British Empire. But Queen Victoria's signature was only the capstone to a process of British colonial involvement in India that had been developing since 1600, the very year in which the first Queen Elizabeth granted a charter to eighty London merchants who had come together to form the British East India Company. What began as an opportunistic trading venture turned into a truly incredible adventure in which a private trading company, step by stumbling step, wrested

---

*It was Akbar's dream that Fatehpur-Sikri would be the fountainhead of a great new culture for ages to come, but in little more than twenty years, it was abandoned and forgotten. It is widely suspected that a shortage of water doomed the place. Today it is a popular tourist attraction—the exciting hope of the world when it was constructed, but now quiet and deserted.

control of an empire from the Mughal overlords. Muslim rulers had been increasing their control over the subcontinent of India since the invasions of Mahmud of Ghazni that began back in 1001 C.E.

The bottom line of this story is that Hindu India changed masters; the British Raj replaced the Mughal Raj. But there was far more to this than simply a change of overlords. This time, the foreign power was really *foreign*. The British had absolutely no interest at all in invading India, taking up permanent residence, and ruling as conquerors. Within the British Empire, India was simply one jewel in the globe-circling necklace of colonial dependencies. History reveals that such empires have limited life expectancies, and therein lay the incredible possibility that after so many centuries of foreign rule, Hindu India might hope to once again become free and independent. British rule in India accomplished two historically significant things: It served as a means for assimilating India into the modern world, and, despite itself, it provided a matrix within which Indian leadership could evolve the means for becoming a modern independent state. This is not in any way to excuse the abuses of colonialism; India suffered greatly under the exploitation that is an inevitable part of colonial rule. But, despite that, the nature of the British Raj included within it opportunities that were never available during the long centuries of the Mughal Raj.

Hindsight, of course, is 20/20. In the early days of European encroachment in India, no one could see what lay ahead in the distant future. The only thing apparent was that a new age was dawning in which the progressive civilization of the West had put the conservative Mughal rule on the defensive. To some Hindu thinkers, it became more and more apparent that a spirit of accommodation meant accommodation with the West, not accommodation with the Muslims. The first to tread out on this slippery new ground was Raja Ram Mohan Roy.

Raja Ram Mohan Roy

"The first modern man of India"—that is how Raja Ram Mohan Roy is often described. He was the first to see the wisdom of integrating India's ancient cultural tradition with modern currents of thought being generated by the West. Kabir and Nanak had sought integration with Muslim culture, and their efforts had ended in nearly total failure. That avenue was no longer open; it was time for something entirely new.

Roy was born into a Brahmin family of Bengal in 1772. As was generally the case in those days, Muslim schools offered the only opportunities for education, so, like Kabir and Nanak before him, Roy was educated in the classic curriculum of Persian and Arabic. But by the late eighteenth century, British influence had become strong in Bengal. Calcutta, a fundamentally new city created by the British, was becoming a center of Western ideas and learning. The young Roy became captivated by Western ideas and chose to turn his back entirely on the Muslim alternative. He became a convert to Western ideology, but not a captive of it. To the mind of the young Raja Ram Mohan Roy, Western ideas could be *used* to rejuvenate a seemingly moribund Hindu culture. The seductive technology and philosophy of the West was just what the doctor ordered. Western ideas could *revive* the ancient Hindu tradition, not *replace* it.

In 1828, by which time Roy was fifty-six years old, he founded the Brahmo Samaj, the "Society of the Devotees of Brahma." The program of the society was a blend of Upanishadic monotheism and liberal modern ideology. The essential heart of Hinduism was to be saved by cleaning out all of the accumulated evils that were now being denounced by Western critics. Roy condemned idolatry, sati, female infanticide, child marriage, and, of course, caste privilege. He argued that more than anything else it was the caste system that kept Indian society disunited and thus unable to stand strong against foreign oppressors. What tied it all together was worship of the one true God worshipped by all people, but called by many names.

In some ways, the Brahmo Samaj was like an early form of Unitarianism, a nonreligious religion. The movement was popular with middle-class intellectuals in India, but never caught on with the population at large. The real significance of the Brahmo Samaj, though, was to be found outside the realm of the religious and philosophical. It was an early voice in the Indian "national movement."

Swami Dayananda

Swami Dayananda, a puzzling religious figure from Gujarat, was the founder of another home-grown organization, the Arya Samaj. The name means "Aryan Society," but in this case the word *Aryan* is meant to refer to all native Indians; its use is meant to distinguish Indian from non-Indian. This distinction was very important to Dayananda because he aimed at nothing less than cleansing India of *all* foreign influences, Muslim and European alike. He dreamed of returning India to its pure Hindu roots, and by roots he really meant roots: In his very fundamentalist view, the Vedas alone were the depository of truth and thus the only suitable foundation for life and culture. Dayananda's teachings are presented in his influential book, *Satyartha Prakash*, "The Light of Truth," published in 1874, at which time he was fifty years old.

It might seem that the Arya Samaj was the direct antithesis of the Brahmo Samaj, and at the superficial level it was, but at a deeper level they shared much in common. Both helped to shape the early character and goals of the Indian national movement, and both were strongly influenced by Western ideals. Dayananda would never have admitted that; in fact, he would have argued that it was the other way around. He held that the Vedas contained all Truth and all knowledge, that *everything* of value in human history had grown from the teachings of the Vedas. In his convoluted logic, Dyananda could even "prove" that the principle of the steam engine, for example, had been known in Vedic times and only re-discovered by the modern West.

It's one thing for Dayananda to teach, and to personally believe, that a return to the wisdom of the Vedas would be the salvation of India. To the student of this subject, though, what is important, and interesting, is the character of the teachings that he inferred from his reading of the Vedas. His program has a familiar ring to it: It's very much in the spirit of all of the other reformers of relatively modern times. He proclaimed the existence of one God, one *personal* God, worshipped by many names. He condemned the hereditary caste system and "idolatry." Dayananda liked to tell the story about how. as a boy. he had come to see the light regarding the foolishness of stone idols. One time he had watched a mouse crawling around disrespectfully on the face of a stone god. It occurred to him that if the god lacked the power even to remove a little mouse from its face, how could it possibly be powerful enough to affect the affairs of people's lives?* Another element of Dayananda's teaching was indeed significant. His was an early voice

---

*That story has always puzzled me. Wouldn't it be just as logical to conclude that the god, being a god, couldn't care less if a little mouse was scampering around on its stone face?

calling for respectful treatment of women. This reform, certainly inspired in part by Western ideals, was perhaps the most important of all.

Both the Brahmo Samaj and the Arya Samaj enjoyed moderate success in their day, and in fact both still exist in India, although their membership is not large now. They, however, played an important role in shaping the early character of the movement that would ultimately lead to the modernization and independence of India.

Ramakrishna Paramahansa

If Mahavira was an ascetic's ascetic, Ramakrishna was a mystic's mystic. Or another way of putting it: "If Raja Ram Mohan Roy was the mind, and Dayananda was the physical arms, Ramakrishna was the soul of the new India." (John Spear, quoted in Verma, 236)

Ramakrishna was born in 1836 and grew up in the vicinity of Kolkata (still known by its British name, Calcutta, in those days). He spent most of his life associated with the Temple of Kali at nearby Dakshineshwar. Ramakrishna was totally devoted to Kali, the Divine Mother. This passionate love relation with Kali began with an incident that occurred when he was a young man. His father had died, and the young Ramakrishna was so filled with grief that he was almost suicidal. He went to the temple of Kali and begged her to help him. In the awful silence that followed his prayer, he took a ceremonial sword from one of the statues intending to kill himself. His own blood would be his offering to Kali. Just as he was about to do the deed, Ramakrishna tells us, a radiant vision of the goddess appeared before him. She embraced him lovingly, and he entered into a state of indescribable ecstasy. This experience transformed Ramakrishna; he became a teacher and devoted the rest of his long life to promoting the worship of Kali.

Ramakrishna experienced many more ecstatic visions; his reputation spread, and he became widely known as a saintly mystic. Not all of his visions were of Kali; some, we are told, were of Jesus and Mohammed. These visions convinced Ramakrishna that all religions worship the same God. The God of the Hindus, the God of the Christians, the God of Islam—it is all the same One Supreme Being. There are many paths—and that is good—but they all lead to discovery of the One God:

> Man is like a pillow-case. The color of one may be red, another blue, another black, but all contain the same cotton. So it is with man—one is beautiful, one is black, another is holy, a fourth wicked, but the Divine dwells in them all. (Ramakrishna, quoted in Verma, 238)

Clearly, the teaching of Ramakrishna was not unique or revolutionary. What made him important was the saintly power of his person. He attracted people to him and inspired them. Perhaps what was most important of all about Ramakrishna was that he was responsible for the career of Vivekananda, his foremost disciple.

Vivekananda

During the twentieth century, the Western world has been visited by countless Eastern gurus, teachers, seers, and more than a few charlatans. Many of them have attracted huge followings in the West. This globalization of once-remote Eastern philosophies is a major feature of modern culture. The dissemination of Hindu teachings began with Vivekananda, the great disciple of Ramakrishna.

At the urging of Ramakrishna, Vivekananda traveled to Chicago in September of 1893 to address the World Parliament of Religions, a rather unusual feature of that year's Chicago World's Fair. It was the first time that a Hindu had carried the message of Hinduism to the people of the world. Vivekananda's message, and his eloquence, stunned the gathering. One of the listeners summed it up beautifully: "That man; a heathen! And we send missionaries to his people. It would be more fitting that they should send missionaries to us!"

And send they did! Once Vivekananda opened the door, many would pass through. Yogananda, Satchidananda, Krishnamurti, Maharishi Mahesh Yogi, A. C. Bhaktivedanta, Eknath Easwaren, Bhagwan Sri Rajneesh—these are only a few of the better known names from a long list. They range the gamut from exotic mystics, such as Yogananda, to the modern eclectics, such as Easwaren; and from the highly conservative, such as Krishnamurti, to the highly controversial such as Rajneesh. It is a fabulous parade of ancient India's modern sons; the West has gained enormously from the experience.

Narendra Nath Datta, better known as Vivekananda, was born in Kolkata (Calcutta) in 1863. Unlike Ramakrishna, Vivekananda's family was part of the English-educated elite of Calcutta. (By this time, the sons of well-to-do Hindu families were being educated in English, not Persian.) Vivekananda met Ramakrishna in 1881, when he was only eighteen, and immediately became one of his disciples. Soon he was the most prominent disciple and was widely regarded as Ramakrishna's successor. From the beginning, Vivekananda was more concerned with the broad teachings of Vedanta than he was with Kali worship. He especially loved the spirit of compassion that he found in Vedanta, and came to believe that it offered the best possible philosophy of life for all people. Vivekananda ardently believed that a rejuvenated Vedanta could be the inspiration that would restore India to its former glory.

Following the explosive success of his talk in Chicago, Vivekananda launched a world mission, taking the message of Vedanta to many countries, where it was always warmly received. In 1892, he founded the Ramakrishna Mission, an organization dedicated to spreading the teaching of Ramakrishna in particular and the philosophy of Vedanta in general. Chapters of the Ramakrishna Mission can still be found in cities throughout the world.

Aurobindo Ghose

Like Vivekananda, Aurobindo also hailed from Kolkata and received a Western education. He too loved the teachings of Vedanta, but whereas Vivekananda sought to carry the essential message of Vedanta to the world, Aurobindo sought to refashion that message in modern dress. In the process, Aurobindo constructed a truly fascinating body of teachings, presented in his work, *The Life Divine*. It is a wonder that Aurobindo is not more widely known and read in modern times.

Aurobindo anchored his teaching on the reality of Brahman, the Absolute. The ultimate goal of all is identity with Brahman. The wheel of birth and death, samsara, whose seemingly endless turning is generated by karma, is the process through which ultimate reunion in Brahman is worked out. So far so good. This is basic, traditional Vedanta. Aurobindo's contribution was to explain the working of samsara in the context of modern evolution theory. The dreary, ages-long turning became a whole new ballgame when interpreted in the light of evolution theory.

Aurobindo argued that the entire universe is always in a state of evolution, struggling to change from a lower state of perfection to a higher state of perfection, which is to say, nearness to the Brahman-nature. For any given part, the struggle is sometimes successful, and sometimes it is not, but the general character of the whole is forward movement. Humanity is, of course, a part of this general evolution. Our challenge is to go beyond "mind," in the ordinary sense of the word, to "supermind," as Aurobindo called it. In other words, our challenge is to transcend ordinary, worldly based ego-consciousness, achieving in its place knowledge of the pure spirit-nature that is the substratum of ego. Thus can we open the way to identity with the Absolute (Brahman). Aurobindo saw evolution as proceeding through stages. Humankind is a stage advanced over what came before, but it is the destiny of humanity (or at least some part of it) to ascend to the next stage of perfection, which Aurobindo called a Kingdom of Heaven on Earth:

> The evolution of the universe as a whole and of particular species within the universe is seen as the returning of the manifested powers of Brahman to their source. As these powers move toward their source, evolution moves to higher and higher forms of life and consciousness. (Koller, 127)*

Individual men and women have some control over the direction of their own evolution. (After all, at root we *are* Brahman.) In *The Life Divine,* Aurobindo laid out the program that could elevate personal existence to the point where it would become "life divine." He called it Integral Yoga. This is a program, or lifestyle, that "integrates" all of the aspects of traditional yoga in a way that is suited to the way of life of a modern lay man or woman. Aurobindo's teaching was to find its physical and spiritual center in the world-famous model ashram, Auroville, located near Pondicherry, not far from Chennai (formerly known as Madras) in southern India.

Mahatma Gandhi

Mohandas Karamchand Gandhi is known to the world as Mahatma Gandhi, the "great souled" one. He was not a prolific writer—Gandhi wrote only the *Autobiography* and a translation of the *Bhagavad Gita*. He was not a founder of a religious or philosophical sect; he was not a political leader in the usual sense; but Mahatma Gandhi is universally regarded as one of the truly great figures in India's long and rich history. Albert Einstein put it well: "Generations to come, it may be, will scarcely believe that such a one as this in flesh and blood walked upon this earth."

Gandhi made his mark on history as the leader of the Indian National Congress, an organization that worked tirelessly to achieve India's independence. Struggling against incredible obstacles, Gandhi achieved his goal in 1947, only to be cut down at his moment of triumph by an assassin's bullets. With his dying breath he whispered his lifelong mantra: "Hare Rama; Hare Rama."

Gandhi's real greatness is not to be found in the fact that he led India to independence, but in the way that he did it. His was not the way of violent confrontation; Gandhi's

---

*Doesn't this sound an awful lot like the evolutionary theory of Teilhard de Chardin, expressed in his book, *The Phenomenon of Man*? Chardin saw physical nature evolving through stages into spiritual nature, all directed toward an ultimate "omega point" at which time all would be reabsorbed back into the nature of the Creator.

infinitely more powerful way was the way of love, of compassion, of patience, and humor. In the process, Gandhi became a living model for humankind.

So where did this great power in Gandhi come from? It certainly was not obvious from the beginning. His was a rather unremarkable youth, growing up in a middle-class Hindu family in Gujarat. His family was able to send him to England to study law. Curiously, it was in England that he began to discover the richness of his roots in the Hindu tradition. After law school he returned to India, but soon he was off to South Africa where his personal experiences with racial discrimination set in motion a process that would change his life. Returning again to India in 1914, Gandhi threw himself into the independence movement, summoning a great spiritual energy generated by his love for the teachings of the ancient Hindu scriptures. Founding his daily life on the teachings of the Upanishads and the *Bhagavad Gita*, Gandhi succeeded in transforming himself from a very ordinary man into a giant of spiritual strength and compassion. *That* is where Gandhi said his power came from.

Gandhi's philosophy is associated with two closely related key terms: *satyagraha* and *ahimsa*. These are usually translated as "passive resistance" and "nonviolence." As such, they do describe the visible character of Gandhi's struggle against British rule. His followers were unrelenting in their opposition, accepting physical brutality and imprisonment, but never striking back in violence. Ultimately, they wore down the British, and even won over some British leaders to the cause of independence for India. But, at a deeper level, these terms refer to something much greater than passive resistance and nonviolence. These are more an *effect* of what the words are really all about.

Satyagraha means "holding fast to the truth"—embracing the truth and not letting go for any reason. Gandhi used to say that "Truth is God." To know the truth is to know God; naturally such knowledge cannot be compromised. But how does one know that one's knowledge is truth? Doesn't everyone believe that his own knowledge is correct? Gandhi was not interested in epistemology; he believed that truth was expressed clearly and distinctly in the Upanishads and the *Bhagavad Gita*. Herein one could find a beautiful expression of truth and could easily check it out in his daily life. The teachings of the Upanishads and the *Gita*, brought to life in one's ordinary daily affairs, amounted to a clear affirmation of their truth. Gandhi had experienced this personally; he had transformed himself. The example of his life was all the evidence one needed.*

The cornerstone of Gandhi's personal life was summed up in the opening line of the *Isha Upanishad*: "The Lord is enshrined in the hearts of all." His special love, though, was the *Bhagavad Gita*, and most of all that sublime section of eighteen verses at the end of Book Two. In these verses, Arjuna wants to know what an awakened person is really like. How does he recognize the real McCoy? Krishna's reply beautifully sums up the essential spirit of what the *Gita* is trying to teach. He begins with the words, "He lives in wisdom who see himself in all, and all in him." Gandhi said that even if all of the *Gita* had been lost except those eighteen verses, we would still have in essence the entire truth of the *Bhagavad Gita*.

Ahimsa, a great word that we have encountered before, was for Gandhi the way of putting knowledge of Truth into action. The two ideas are intimately related. Ahimsa may

---

*Gandhi acknowledged that his program of passive resistance was in part inspired by reading Thoreau's tract *Civil Disobedience*. This is interesting, considering that Thoreau's personal philosophy was much influenced by his reading of the Upanishads and the *Bhagavad Gita*.

mean nonviolence in the literal sense, but nonviolence refers not to controlling an urge to violence, but to the compassionate heart from which violence of any sort would be unthinkable. One who truly sees "the Lord enshrined in the hearts of all" is not capable of hatred or violence. For such a person, opposition to evil is to oppose the evil act, but love the evil-doer. This is exactly what Gandhi did, and it explains the great power of his program of passive resistance. He proved that evil can be conquered by love.

In the long run Gandhi's most important gift, and the basis for his greatness, is the way he showed by the example of his own life how every man and woman on Earth can transform themselves, as he did, and thus be able to solve the problem of evil in the world, not by the usual path of greater violence, but by the infinitely superior path of greater compassion.

Study Questions

1. Why do you suppose that this chapter is titled "A Millennium of Strife"? Is "strife" an accurate way of describing it? Can you think of a more apt title?

2. Why did almost all of the Indian subcontinent fall under the rule of Muslim overlords? Do you believe that this was inevitable? Do you see any similarity between the Muslim Conquest and the so-called Aryan Conquest?

3. Kabir wanted to be a "bridge builder." What sort of bridge did he want to build? Do you feel that his approach had any chance of success?

4. Why did both Muslims and Hindus feel deep respect for Nanak? What was the essence of his teaching?

5. What do you imagine life was like at Fatehpur-Sikri? Was Akbar's dream of cultural synthesis a reasonable one, or was it doomed from the start?

6. How would you define the "Indian national movement"? What did Raja Ram Mohan Roy have to do with it? Why is he called "the first modern man of India"?

7. Why is it claimed that the Brahmo Samaj and the Aryo Samaj are only superficially different? What is it that they share at a deeper level?

8. Why do you suppose that Dayananda had a sort of religious awakening in reverse when he saw a mouse crawling around the face of a stone god?

9. Why is it said that Ramakrishna was "a mystic's mystic"? What does this mean?

10. Why did Vivekananda make such a powerful impression at the Chicago World's Fair? What do you suppose was the gist of the speech he delivered there?

11. What did Aurobindo mean by "supermind"? In what way did Aurobindo seek to "modernize" the teaching of Vedanta? What is your reaction to his approach?

12. Albert Einstein put it well: "Generations to come, it may be, will scarcely believe that such a one as this in flesh and blood walked upon this earth." Do you agree?

13. Gandhi claimed that his power came from a love of truth as revealed in the Upanishads and the *Bhagavad Gita*. Does this make sense to you? How was it revealed in Gandhi's life?

14. At the turn of the millennium, the names of many candidates were offered for "person of the century." Gandhi appeared to be the favorite. Can you think of a better candidate?

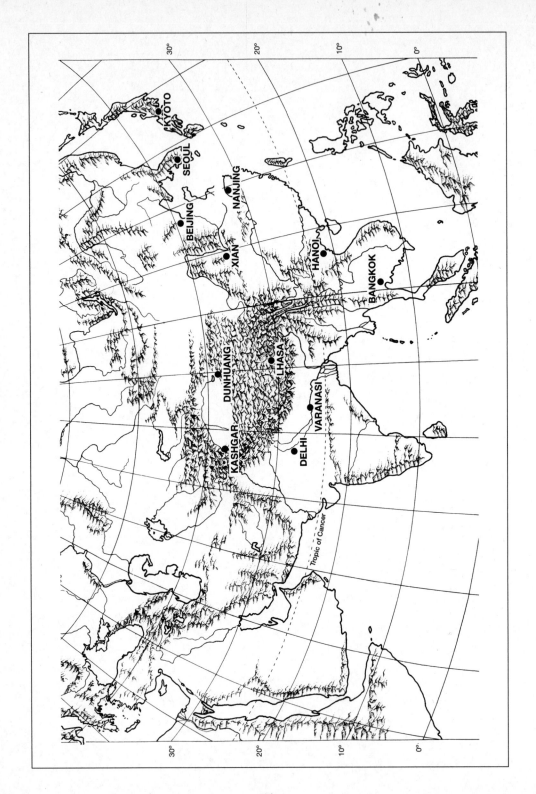

Asia

PART TWO

Shakyamuni Buddha
and the early Development
of Buddhism

Buddhism is a subject vast in scope. It is compared to a wheel with many spokes, each one representing a distinct tradition. Taken altogether, the spokes represent a complete circle of possibilities. Buddhism can be very religious or very secular, very mystical or very philosophical. It can be comfortably at home with the supernatural and esoteric as well as with the purely rational and scientific.

In Part II, we will follow the evolution of this great tradition, beginning with the life and teaching of the founder, Shakyamuni Buddha. We will then examine the early development of the tradition that bears his name, focusing on the formation of Theravada and the Mahayana. Most of this development remained still within the subcontinent of South Asia.

CHAPTER **8**

The Life of Shakyamuni Buddha

The man we know as Buddha (or, more properly, Shakyamuni Buddha) was not a mythic figure. He was a flesh-and-blood human being—of that we can be certain. He was born in North India sometime around 563 B.C.E. and presumably lived a long life, perhaps being about eighty years old when he died.

Buddha, of course, was not his name. The word *Buddha* is derived from the Sanskrit *budh*, which means "to wake up." Buddha was "the awakened one," one who had awakened to the ultimate truth of the nature of reality. Followers of this man, out of deep respect and love for him, conferred the title *Buddha* on him. And so he has been known ever since.

Unfortunately, very little is known about Shakyamuni Buddha that we could call historical fact. Historical record keeping was not much practiced in those days, and his followers were far more concerned about preserving his teaching than with the details of his life—and, of course, that's what really matters. Still, there has always been an inevitable curiosity about the life of this great man, and as a result, a body of legends has taken shape over time. I want to emphasize this point: Commonly repeated stories about the life of Buddha are the stuff of legend, not history. It is not unreasonable to believe that the seeds of such stories were originally founded on real events and circumstances, but over time they were richly embellished and given a mythic character. The legend was fashioned to fit the man.

Buddha was certainly one of the most influential persons ever to have walked the earth. His teaching blossomed into a tradition that has profoundly shaped the course of human history, and continues to shape it. Buddha gave us not so much a religion as a philosophy of life, and that philosophy is as vital today as it ever has been. The greatest impact of Buddha's teaching may still lie before us.

The critical event in Buddha's life—in fact a critical event in the history of the human race—was the moment of his "awakening." This occurred in his thirty-sixth year. The remainder of his life was devoted to teaching. Buddha, in the company of a small band of disciples, wandered the northern plain of India, teaching as many as could hear his words how they too might awaken to the truth. The essence of that teaching is what most concerns us here. But the years that led up to his awakening are also of interest and relevance. These years divide into two parts. The first part includes Buddha's youth and young-adult years. During these years, young Buddha was a prince being groomed to become a great king. Far from becoming a king, Buddha renounced this legacy and chose instead to become a forest-dweller living the life of a renunciate. Those six years as a renunciate, a *sadhu*, form the second part of his life and lead directly to his awakening.

Various ancient sources give us information about the life of Buddha. The oldest and most important of these is the Pali Canon. Committed to writing in the first century B.C.E., the Pali Canon is a carefully assembled collection of the then-existing scriptural works and traditions regarding Buddha. (We will have much more to say about the Pali Canon in Chapter 10.) The accounts in the Pali Canon, however, are really nothing more than two short, terse commentaries that deal with two different parts of Buddha's life. They give us nothing more than some very basic facts. The first complete biography of the Buddha was written in the first century C.E. by the philosopher and poet, Ashvaghosha. This work, known as the *Buddhacarita* ("The Acts of the Buddha"), is unreservedly mythical; the author was not interested in historical veracity. Many of the legends about Shakyamuni Buddha's life are derived from the *Buddhacarita*.

Although the story of Buddha's life is much more the stuff of legends than of history, it is nonetheless well worth surveying, however briefly. As you might expect, there are numerous variations to these legends. My goal here is to present the story in its generally accepted form. The importance of the story of Buddha's life is simply to provide an understandable background for his teaching. The legend of Buddha's life is carefully structured, as you will see. It is the story of an evolution that leads dramatically and almost inevitably to the great moment of his awakening.

THE PALACE YOUTH

Before becoming "the Buddha," he was known by his regular family name. *Siddhartha* was his proper name and *Gautama* the family name. And even without becoming "the awakened one" Siddhartha Gautama was far from being a nobody. He was a prince, the only son of Shuddhodana Gautama, the leader (king, if you will) of the great Shakya clan, one of the many large clans that dominated the land of northern India. After Siddhartha gained fame as a great sage, a "muni," yet another part was added to his name, "Shakya-muni," the sage of the Shakya clan. Putting it all together, he was, Siddhartha Gautama Shakyamuni, the "Buddha." To distinguish him from other buddhas, recognized by some sects, he is often referred to simply as Shakyamuni Buddha.

The Shakya "kingdom" was an irregular-shaped patch of land in the far north, bordering on the foothills of the Himalayas. Its capital city was Kapilavastu, and it was at a nearby place called Lumbini that young Siddhartha came into this world. His mother's name was *Maya*. To give you an idea of the kind of legend that has become woven into the story of Buddha's life, it is widely told that he selected his own mother before birth and that she conceived during her sleep when she dreamed that "a white lord of elephants entered her body." Ten months after this "immaculate conception," Siddhartha was born from the side of his mother's body to the accompaniment of flowers blooming out of season and all the world knowing a brief period of peace and joy. Immediately upon being born, Siddhartha "walked seven steps, firmly and with long strides . . . and spoke these words full of meaning for the future: 'For enlightenment I was born, for the good of all that lives'" (Conze, 36). Seven days later, Maya died peacefully, so as not to defile her sacred body by giving birth again. Siddhartha would be raised by an aunt, Maya's sister, who loved the boy as if he were her own son.

The legend informs us that on the day of Siddhartha's birth, a great sage named Asita learned of it from the gods, who told him that a person of exceptional spiritual power had assumed human form near the city of Kapilavastu. Asita went there immediately, and as he held the baby in his arms, he recognized the signs that foretold a glorious future, including webbing between the fingers and a tuft of hair between his eyebrows.

The court astrologers had prophesied that this boy would grow up to be a great leader. But, it wasn't clear which kind of leader he would be. Either he would be a great worldly leader, a king of kings, or, he would be a great spiritual leader, a sage of sages. The stars left the question open; only the passage of time would reveal the answer. Asita, though, was certain that the boy would one day choose to leave his home and follow the path of a sage. After announcing this news, Asita broke down in tears. He was an old man, and he wept because he knew in his heart that he could not possibly live long enough to know this little baby as a man and to hear his teaching with his own ears.*

Reinforcing Asita's prediction, the astrologers declared that if and when Siddhartha were to encounter a sick man, an old man, and a dead man, he would thereupon choose to follow the life of a renunciate. Shuddhodana could not be indifferent to these words. Spiritual leaders were fine and good, but this was his son, his *only* son, the heir to the throne, and the future hope of his family and his people. In Shuddhodana's mind, Siddhartha was destined to be a great king. That's how the stars were to be read, and there was to be no doubt about it.

From the day of Siddhartha's birth, Shuddhodana put into play a carefully thought-out plan. The boy was to be groomed to be a lover of the things of this world. This is not to say that he would be allowed to become a spoiled self-centered hedonist serving only his sensual appetites. Far from it, he would learn discipline and self-restraint befitting a princely heir to the throne, but only to more perfectly refine his enjoyment of the good things of life. He would become a connoisseur of all things: a lover of fine music, food, poetry, rhetoric. He would, in a phrase, become a first-rate man of the world. It was his father's hope that in this way Siddhartha would become so firmly attached to the worldly life that he would naturally seek his own happiness in the finest possibilities that a worldly life has to offer. And thus his destiny as a great king would be fulfilled.

Thus did Shuddhodana order that the young prince was to know nothing but the rich and beautiful possibilities of this world. During the character-forming years of childhood, he was not to see, hear, or in any way experience the violent and ugly side of life. Within the confining walls of the palace grounds, all was to be perfect. His personal apartments in the highest part of the palace were to be as much like a heaven as possible. Even the palace gardens were to be kept always in a state of perfection. Every evening, just after sunset, an army of servants would comb through the gardens removing every leaf that had died, every flower petal that had wilted. Such was the world that the young Siddhartha would grow up in. Inside the walls of the palace, his gilded cage, he would know nothing of death and corruption, of ugliness and failure, of imperfection. He would be a stranger to suffering.

---

*The story of Asita is amazingly similar to that of Simeon told in the gospel of Luke. There are many interesting comparisons to be found in the accounts of the lives of Buddha and Jesus.

Years later, when chatting with some of his disciples, Buddha commented on the extreme luxury of his youth:

> Monks, I was delicately nurtured, exceedingly delicately nurtured. For instance, in my father's house, lotus pools were made thus, one of blue lotuses, one of red, another of white lotuses, just for my benefit. No sandalwood powder did I use that was not of Kasi; of Kasi cloth was my turban made; of Kasi cloth was my jacket, my tunic, and my cloak. By night and day a white canopy was held over me. (Ch'en, 19)

The legends of Buddha's life include many wondrous and supernatural happenings, appropriate, of course, for someone of his special importance. For example, we are told that when Siddhartha was still a little boy he was taken by his family to the annual plowing festival. His father, the king, presided over the ceremonies and even plowed the first furrow. They made a comfortable spot for little Siddhartha in the shade of a large tree, thinking he would fall asleep. Some hours later, they found him seated serenely upright in the posture of meditation, and though the shade of all the other trees had moved considerably, nature had bowed before the future Buddha, and the shade of his tree had remained exactly in place.

As he grew older, Siddhartha was tutored by the finest teachers in all of the arts and sciences. He learned to ride like a champion, and his skill in archery was the talk of the kingdom. He became the model of a prince—handsome, gracious, refined, skilled in everything. And he was a wonderfully happy young man, exuberantly enjoying the best that life has to offer. He lacked only an appropriate mate who would be his future queen and a befitting mother of the next heir to the throne. Here too the father's wishes were not to be foiled.

Yashodhara was to become the wife of Siddhartha. And as you might have guessed, she was the most beautiful young woman in all the kingdom. Her father, one of the most powerful nobles, arranged an archery contest to test the skill of her many suitors (shades of the story of Arjuna in the *Mahabharata*). Siddhartha's principal rival struck the target in the center of the bull's-eye. But the cool and steady Siddhartha did him one better, splitting that arrow down the center, thus winning the hand of Yashodhara. They were madly in love and soon produced the much-desired son. They named him Rahula, and he was, of course, everything parents could want in a child.

I'm sure you get the picture. The legend is carefully and deliberately setting up a situation in which everything is as perfect as it can possibly be. If Siddhartha is going to turn his back on his princely life, as, of course, he will, it is very important that there be nothing lacking at all. The life that he rejects must be the most perfect situation that a worldly life can offer. If the lifestyle of the young Siddhartha cannot deliver complete happiness, then it is the worldly lifestyle itself that is lacking in some fundamental way. This understanding is crucial to the development of the story.

Eventually, as one might have predicted, Siddhartha reached a time when he became aware that the pleasures of life had come to lose some of their former excitement. He was feeling restless without knowing why. For the first time in his life, he found himself bothered by age-old questions: Is this all there is? Is the good life simply a round of pleasures? Has life no purpose? The snake was in the garden now. The father's carefully laid plan, which had worked so beautifully, was now in trouble. Siddhartha was no longer satisfied with his gilded cage. He was curious about the real world beyond his walls, and he made up his mind that he was going to go exploring.

At this point in the story, as told in the *Buddhacarita*, Siddhartha went to his father and asked permission to visit the city beyond the palace walls. Shuddhodana felt a pang of anxiety as he recalled a prophesy that his son would renounce the world when he saw a sick man, an old man, and a corpse. However, he could not keep his son forever within the safety of the palace walls. Thus, Shuddhodana reluctantly agreed, then quietly gave orders that Siddhartha's route through the town was to be scrupulously cleaned of all vile sights. Maybe, he thought, Siddhartha would see only "acceptable" sights.

Siddhartha finally breaks out of his artificial worldly paradise and comes face to face with the larger realities of life, most of all the reality of suffering. Siddhartha goes through the gate, actually and symbolically, and once through the gate, he would certainly have experienced profound culture shock. The serene and perfect world of the palace grounds was suddenly replaced with all of the noise and disorder and hubbub of the crowded city. Street vendors, animals, beggars, shouting people, shoving people, every imaginable smell and sight—what a scene it must have been to his eyes! Siddhartha moved slowly through the crowded streets, taking it all in.

Predictably, one thing in particular shocked him to the core. It was the sight of a badly diseased and crippled man. We can imagine it being a beggar horribly deformed by a disease like leprosy. Siddhartha had never seen a truly sick person before. He had never seen real suffering before. "What is that!?" he would have shouted. "That is a very sick man, master," Chandaka, his driver, would have answered. "Disease is a part of life. And it is no respecter of rank. You too could become like that some day."

It was a changed Siddhartha who returned to the palace that night. His uneasy curiosity had now become shock and dismay. The stark imperfections of life could no longer be hidden from him. His former pleasures no longer satisfied. He yearned only to go back and see more. Again Chandaka wheeled him out into the city, and again the wild scene greeted his eyes. This time his attention focused on a very old man. He was ancient and feeble, bald and toothless, bent far forward, and he was able to hobble only slowly and painfully with the help of a stick. This too was a new sight for the pampered eyes of Siddhartha. He gazed in stunned silence, especially when Chandaka explained that Siddhartha too might become like that some day.

On their third excursion, they ventured into the city by way of the western gate, the direction of the setting sun. By now Siddhartha was becoming used to some of the sights. But nothing could prepare him for what he was about to see. It was a corpse, the stiff dead body wrapped in funeral linens, being carried by weeping mourners to the place of crema-tion, where the wood for the fire was being assembled. When Chandaka explained it to him, Siddhartha was stunned. This was his first encounter with the reality of death. His dread turned to horror when Chandaka said, "You may escape the agony of disease and of old age, but no person ever born escapes the fate of death. One day you too will become a corpse, and your loved ones, filled with suffering, will carry your body to the place of cremation."

Now Siddhartha could know no joy at all. His former happiness was gone. All he could think about was what he had seen in the world beyond the palace walls. How can anyone enjoy the present? It is only a fleeting moment, ready at any time to change into suffering, and eventually into the awesome nightmare of death. Nothing of value endures. Does anything matter? Is life ultimately just a meaningless bad joke? Awareness of the inevitability of death made all temporal pleasures disturbingly imperfect. Siddhartha was brooding and depressed. What more could there be? Can anything be worse than death? "What rational being would stand or sit or lie at ease, still less laugh, when he knows of old age, disease and death." (*BC*, p. 53)

In the telling of the legend, this is the all-important crisis of Buddha's life. Siddhartha is experiencing, poignantly, the hopelessness, the despair, the fear of meaninglessness that lurks in the shadows of consciousness in all human beings. Given the inescapable reality of death, how can our brief lives have any meaning or joy at all? Aren't we all like innocent persons awaiting certain execution? In the agony of Siddhartha, the legend is holding our faces to the fire too and making us feel the heat. Virtually everyone wants to break free and flee into the comfort of denial; it takes many forms: religion, partying, etc. But Shakyamuni can't escape. His eyes have been opened to what appears to be the ugly reality of meaninglessness. Deep in this feeling of despair, he directed Chandaka to return to the palace. Chandaka, though, had been ordered by the king to take Siddhartha instead to an unusual "surprise party" at the Padmashanda Pleasure Garden. There, in the hope of reminding Siddhartha of the wonderful attractions of the opposite sex, his father had arranged a gathering of beautiful young women. Their assignment was to rouse his now dormant feelings of sexual desire and bring him back to his senses. Siddhartha descended from his splendid chariot, hardly noticing the young women gathered around him:

> And as they approached him, their eyes opened wide in wonder and they welcomed him respectfully with hands folded like lotus-buds. And they stood around him, their minds absorbed in love, and seemed to drink him in with eyes that were moveless and blossomed wide in ecstasy. Enthralled by his beauty, they writhed suppressedly, and smiting each other with their glances, softly sighed. (Johnston, 44)

But soon the young lovelies were reminded of their assignment and began to turn on the charm:

> As if somewhat frightened, the women made gestures designed to cause rapture with brows, looks, and blandishments, with laughter, frolicking and movements. Then surrounded by the women, the prince wandered through the garden, like an elephant through the Himalayan forest, accompanied by a herd of females . . . Some of the young women there, pretending to be under the influence of intoxication, touch him with their firm, rounded, close-set, charming breasts . . . Another repeatedly let her blue garments slip down under the pretext of intoxication . . . Some walked up and down so as to make their golden zones tinkle and displayed to him their hips veiled by diaphanous robes. (Johnston, 47–49)

But, alas, try as they might, the young ladies were unable to excite Siddhartha, who, in his present mood, was not about to be moved at all by the pleasures of the flesh:

> It is not that I despise the objects of sense, and I know that the world is devoted to them; but my mind does not delight in them, because I hold them to be transitory. If the triad of old age, disease and death did not exist, I too should take my pleasure in the ravishing objects of sense. (Johnston, 57)

Taking his leave of the pleasure garden, Siddhartha found his horse, Kanthaka, and made off to the nearby forest where he found a solitary spot and allowed himself to sink into deep contemplation about the transitory nature of life. While Siddhartha was thus absorbed, the gods arranged that a holy renunciate, a mendicant, came up to him and spoke.

> Since the world is subject to destruction, I desire salvation and seek the
> blessed incorruptible stage, I look with equal mind on kinsmen and stranger,
> and longing for and hatred of the objects of sense have passed from me.
> I dwell wherever I happen to be, at the root of a tree or in a deserted temple,
> on a hill or in the forest, and I wander without ties or expectations in the
> search of the highest good, accepting any alms I may receive. (Johnston, 65)

Having said these words, the mendicant ascended into the sky and disappeared. Siddhartha was thunderstruck. Those words cleared his mind and his heart. In that moment, Siddhartha saw the truth of Dharma, and resolved to follow the path of the renunciate. He would leave the palace and make the forest his home. His troubled mind now knew peace. His life would never be the same again.

Siddhartha reluctantly returned to the palace, but only to meet with his father and tell him of his decision. Now it was Suddhodhana's turn to be thunderstruck. He and all the ministers of the palace begged Siddhartha to change his mind. They tried everything, but Siddhartha was steadfast. To his father's emotional appeal he replied,

> I will refrain from entering the penance grove [the forest], O king, if you will
> be my surety on four points. My life is not to be subject to death. Disease is
> not to injure my health. Old age is not to impair my youth. Disaster is not to
> take away this my worldly fortune. (Johnston, 68)

Siddhartha would spend his last night in his splendid apartments, and depart forever in the morning. The ladies of the palace made one last effort to lure his heart back to them. He was treated to the very finest of music and dancing, worldly beauty at its best. By the wee hours of the morning, though, the beautiful people weren't so beautiful anymore. Most were drunk and sleeping; their partially clothed bodies sprawled around in an assortment of indelicate poses. Some had been vomiting, many were snoring loudly; it was quite a scene. As he surveyed the spectacle, deep disgust welled up within Siddhartha. He saw clearly that the life he was used to would never bring him true inner happiness. In that moment, Siddhartha confirmed his resolution. He would abandon his princely life, turn his back on it forever, and become a sadhu.

A word of explanation is appropriate here. As mentioned before, the legend of Buddha's life has a logical structure to it. His experience of awakening at the age of thirty-five is the great watershed of his life. From that experience will issue his teaching years, during which time he will establish the foundation of the Buddhist tradition. But the years before his awakening are significant, too; these years are divided into two parts, and the character of these two parts is deliberately described as being different in the extreme. Until the age of twenty-nine, Buddha was living a life of luxury and ease in his father's palace. Then he does a complete reversal, and for the next six years, he withdraws to the wilderness to live as a renunciate. He gives himself completely to both lifestyles and finds that neither path leads to the freedom he yearns for. His awakening emerges out of the desperation that follows. To better understand the nature of Buddha's awakening, we must look carefully at both of these parts of his life that led up to it.

What do we see when we stand back and look at the first part of his life, the palace years? We find Prince Siddhartha, a young man of intelligence and character, who wants passionately to make himself into the finest person he is capable of becoming. He wants to please his father, and he wants to fulfill his own destiny, which presumably means becoming a great king. In the process, he works out his father's plan, immersing himself in the life of worldly experiences, desiring only the best, and steadily increasing his sophistication. He becomes a connoisseur of the finest things in life.

Siddhartha finds great pleasure in this lifestyle, great self-satisfaction, but the perfect happiness that he yearns for always eludes him, and eventually his happiness is shattered completely when he comes face to face with the realization that happiness based on the satisfaction of desires inevitably includes the company of suffering. Try as his father might, they cannot be kept separate. The greater the pleasure, the greater the pain; they go together like the two sides of a coin.

Why should it be that pleasure and pain go together like the two sides of a coin? We aren't masochists; we all seek to be happy; we all seek to avoid suffering. To many, happiness can be defined simply as the pleasing state of mind that accompanies the enjoyment of pleasurable experiences, and suffering can be identified with the more or less unpleasant state of mind that is the companion of painful experiences. We desire to possess the one and to avoid the other. Therefore, according to this line of thinking, the good life, the happy life, is to be equated with satisfying our desires. To the degree that we are successful in satisfying our desires, both positively and negatively, we will be happy. And if we can succeed in *perfectly* satisfying our desires, we will be *perfectly* happy. That's the theory. (Does it sound familiar?)

It *should* sound familiar, very familiar. It is a dominant theme of modern culture (and probably all others throughout time). This value is pitched at us in a million ways from cradle to grave. Look at the advertising that surrounds us. Do you want to be happy? Why aren't you? Is it because you desire a certain kind of car, and you don't have it? Then get it, and you'll be happy. And the right clothes, or house, or job promotion, or that beautiful hand-woven Panama hat, and on and on and on. And, of course, for a while it does make us happy—even elated—to satisfy our desire. The problem is, as we all know, that it doesn't last. It is of the nature of desire that it can never be fully satisfying; desire always begets further desire.

At a deeper level, the problem with desire is that it begets attachment (or call it longing). The word *attachment* occupies a very important place in the philosophy of Buddha. *Attachment* means *craving*—the kind of desire that has grown so strong that one believes that he or she cannot possibly be happy without the object of desire. It could be a thing, another person, or even a way of life. Desires easily grow into attachments, and once they do we are trapped, prisoners of our own desires. That, at least, is the argument, and that's why it is argued that pleasure and pain go together like the two sides of a coin.

Buddha, or should I say the young Siddhartha, had been totally absorbed in this way of life. He yearned passionately to know the joy of self-fulfillment. But as he stood surveying the ugly scene that was the aftermath of the party, he experienced a profound realization, the first in a series of realizations that led to his awakening. It can be stated simply: *There is no self-fulfillment through self-indulgence.*

The young Siddhartha had done the best job that anyone could ever hope to do in trying to achieve lasting inner happiness through indulging his own ego desires, and he had discovered that this path simply doesn't work. In this he was a model for all humanity. But that would come later; his quest for the right path still had a long way to go. If the worldly way of self-indulgence was not the answer, then Siddhartha would reject it altogether. Compromise was out of the question; settling for a life that was only second best was equally out of the question.

Siddhartha had not been able to forget the sadhu, the mendicant, that he had seen at the edge of the forest on his last venture out of the palace. The words of the man haunted him. To go on living the opulent life of the palace was out of the question. Why take any half measures? Why not go for broke? Adopt the life of the sadhu, give it one hundred percent, just as he had given one hundred percent to his life up to now. He would find out for himself if this was the path to perfect happiness.

Hindu society then, as in all times, has held great respect for those rare few who were strong enough to give up everything and take on the harsh life of the renunciate, dedicating themselves to the search for a transcendent truth, the truth of Atman. Such a person, it was believed, paid a high price, but the reward was a perfect inner peace that passed beyond pleasure and pain. The sadhu escaped from the net of suffering and knew "the joy of perfect freedom."

Desire and its inevitable companion suffering were believed to be the result of attachment to the ego-role. And such attachment was the almost inevitable result of being human. It is the character of the role; the only hope is to stop playing the role, completely. Only then can one discover the Atman within. And the only way to stop playing the role is to drop out of ordinary life completely, practice ascetic disciplines that will slowly burn out every desire for worldly comforts, peel back the layers of ego one by one until ultimately there is nothing left but the pure undifferentiated consciousness of Atman. Here and here alone can one come to knowledge of transcendent abiding happiness.

And so Siddhartha, at the age of twenty-nine, decided to go from one extreme to the other, from the luxurious life of the prince to the utter poverty of the sadhu. According to the legend, he acted on his decision immediately. In the middle of the night, he roused the sleeping Chandaka, and together they rode off to the edge of the forest where he had first seen the sadhu. Siddhartha scavenged some saffron-colored rags from the burial place of executed criminals. With these he fashioned a simple robe; that and a humble begging bowl were all he would call his own. His own elegant clothes were folded and handed to Chandaka. Also he cut off his beautiful long hair, and placed it atop the clothing. "Give these to my father," he is supposed to have said. "He will understand."

The bewildered Chandaka was stricken with sorrow. He begged Siddhartha to allow him to go with him. But this was a journey that Siddhartha intended to make alone. Chandaka returned to the palace in tears. And in the days that followed, his tears were joined by those of many others.

THE SADHU YEARS

Thus did Siddhartha embark upon the second great part of his life. For the next six years he would live the life of a forest-dweller, a *sadhu*. He would study with the finest gurus of his time, and he would become a master himself. His fame would spread far, and many other sadhus would seek him out to gain from his wisdom and the power of his example.

No one practiced the yoga of renunciation with greater zeal or with greater success. After long and hard ascetic practices, Siddhartha burned away every last vestige of desire for comfort and sense pleasure. Cold or heat, wet or dry, a bed of soft grass or a bed of thistles—it did not matter. He totally freed himself from the worldly attachments that had fettered him in his palace days.

Toward the end of his sadhu years, Siddhartha, along with a small group of other renunciates, moved on to practicing the most extreme forms of asceticism, intensifying his effort to discover the Atman. He fasted continuously, ultimately reducing his intake of food to but one sesame seed and one grain of rice per day. Siddhartha's body came to look like a walking skeleton, and he rejoiced in this evidence of his progress. He practiced meditation for hours at a time and then for days at a time without interruption. He became, indeed, a great master of the life of the renunciate.

Here again, the legend deliberately sets up an extreme situation. It is essential to the story that Siddhartha explore this path to its absolute fullest. He must be the perfect master; anything less than this won't do. If he is ultimately going to reject this life, and of course he will, it is necessary that he know that there is nothing in this way of life that he has not personally experienced.

Again, the goal of the sadhu's hard way of life is to slough off the ego, the role, layer by layer until eventually all that is left is Atman. In the course of this quest, as his skills sharpened, Siddhartha had many a mind-boggling experience. His consciousness expanded; in states of ecstasy he saw things his mind had never imagined; he transcended the earthly plane. But, try as he might, he had to admit the awful truth: He never experienced the glory of Atman. Slowly, he was moving toward the terrible conclusion that this way of life, although capable of producing new and ecstatic experiences, was really no more capable than his old way of life of achieving true self-fulfillment. The ego was just as strong as it had ever been. In fact, in insidious ways, it was stronger; he was proud of the self-discipline that separated him out from ordinary men. Siddhartha was on the verge of despair. He did not know what to do. Going back to his old life was out of the question, but continuing with the present way was coming to be equally unthinkable. What else was there?

It was while he was in this state of mind that Siddhartha reached his second great realization. The legends offer a variety of accounts of how it happened. In the *Buddhacarita* account, Siddhartha is walking alone beside a stream. He is deep in this inner quandary when he sees a young milkmaid. She has just milked a cow and is returning home with the warm milk in a wooden bowl. Without thinking, Siddhartha splashes across the stream and walks up to her, saying not a word. The milkmaid looks at his emaciated body, seeing that he is weak and sick at heart. Taking pity on him, or perhaps thinking he is some sort of demi-god, she offers him the bowl of milk, and he hungrily gulps it all down. As the fresh milk reaches his stomach Siddhartha is transformed. He feels strength returning to his body and to his mind. In that instant, he suddenly sees clearly the truth that he had not been willing to face. *There is no self-fulfillment through self-denial!*

Earlier, he had discovered that self-fulfillment is impossible through self-indulgence. So he had tried the opposite tack. And there too he had ultimately come up against a dead end. No self-fulfillment through self-indulgence, *and*, no self-fulfillment through self-denial either. What to do?

At this time, Siddhartha had been traveling with five companions who felt great respect and admiration for him. When they caught up with him and heard what he had done, they were horrified. Siddhartha had just broken two of the most basic rules of the life of the sadhu: He had taken milk, and he had consorted with a woman. They backed away from him in shock, but Siddhartha didn't care. His strength had returned, he could see clearly again, and he was through with this way of life. He continued on alone for a while, not knowing what to do.

Another variation of the legend holds that in a place where Siddhartha and his companions were temporarily staying, a pregnant young woman from a nearby village sought him out. She had heard of his great spiritual powers, and being somewhat superstitious, she thought he might be the incarnation of a god. The woman desperately wanted her baby to be a son, and hoped that praying in Siddhartha's presence might produce the desired result.

The baby turned out to be a boy, and in thanksgiving, the grateful mother prepared an assortment of delicacies, which she laid out before the ever-fasting Siddhartha. To the dismay of his companions, he accepted the offering, eating all of it. The nourishing food restored his strength and clarity of mind. It was this event that triggered his realization that there can be no self-fulfillment through self-denial.

According to the story, Siddhartha then fashioned a makeshift oil lamp out of a large leaf, some oil from the food he had been given, and a piece of cloth from his robe which he made into a wick. He lit the wick and set the lamp afloat in the nearby stream. "If I am never to find the truth I seek, let this lamp drift downstream with the current," he said. With all eyes watching, the little lamp eddied around a bit at first, then moved slowly upstream, seeming to drift against the current.

THE AWAKENING

Siddhartha continued on alone for a while. He didn't know what to do. On the banks of the Niranjana River, near the town of Gaya, in a personal sense he reached the end of the line. There was no point in going on any farther. The one and only thing that mattered to Siddhartha was breaking through his own wall of ignorance, *avidya*, and discovering the truth. What is the truth of the reality of life and death? What *really is* this thing we call "life," and this thing we call "death"? What *is* the reality of Atman? Unless he could find his way to this truth, life itself was not worth living.

One element from the sadhu way of life was not to be discarded. All else might go, but Siddhartha held the deepest respect for the power of meditation. Meditation was his last hope. Meditation had become his real friend and teacher. Now he would ask everything of it; there was no other way.

Siddhartha found a roomy spot beneath the spreading branches of a large tree. He prepared a place on the ground for meditation, and taking his posture with the legs crossed and the spine straight, he turned inward. The legend would have him thinking something like this: "I have mastered the art of meditation. Now I will call upon that mastery to turn deep within myself, and I will not leave this spot, come what may, until I have uncovered the truth that I seek. The truth I seek is the ultimate truth of all things; I will find it within myself; I will be a lamp unto myself." Eknath Easwaren puts it very nicely:

Near the city of Gaya he found a tranquil spot under a sacred fig tree and carpeted a place with fresh, fragrant grass. Folding his legs beneath him, he drew himself straight for meditation and took a solemn vow: "Come what may—let my body rot, let my bones be reduced to ashes—I will not get up from here until I have found the way beyond decay and death." It was dusk, and the moon was rising, the first full moon of the first month of spring. Thus determined, full of peace, Siddhartha passed into deep meditation, when the senses close down and concentration flows undisturbed by awareness of the outside world. (Easwaren, *Dhammapada*, 26)

The time Siddhartha spent in meditation near the town of Gaya is the pivotal point in the story of the life of Buddha. Some accounts say it was for one full night, others say it was for seven days and seven nights; it doesn't matter. For Siddhartha, time stood still. He withdrew completely from the world around him, and in the great depth of his own inner being, he worked through the layers of ignorance that had held him back from seeing the truth. When he returned from his withdrawal, he was a new man; he had found what he was looking for. He was awakened.

Early on in his meditation, the legend tells us that the Hindu god Mara came to visit Siddhartha. Mara, when he chooses to reveal himself completely, is described as the fearsome embodiment of death itself. No one had ever seen perfectly into the mystery of life and death before, and Mara was worried. Knowing the great strength and the great resolve of Siddhartha, Mara was worried that Siddhartha might discover the truth that could liberate humankind from the fear of death. He sat down beside Siddhartha and was silent for some time. When he finally spoke, in a soft and appealing fashion, it was to tempt Siddhartha. He was hoping to derail Siddhartha from his intended destination. Perhaps he could persuade Siddhartha to give up, to see his task as hopeless, and to choose instead some other path.

Of course, the presence of Mara need not be interpreted literally. It is a poetic way of telling the story. Mara can be seen as an aspect of Siddhartha himself. The demons that

FIGURE 8.1 Shakyamuni Buddha with right hand in the posture of bhumishparsha (earth touching). (P. Bresnan)

Mara sent against Siddhartha were the demons of his own inner struggle. There was a war going on within him. Siddhartha had to struggle against what remained of his own doubt, his own weakness, and worldly desires. In overcoming the temptations of Mara, Siddhartha's higher nature was victorious over his lower nature. This is the real meaning of his awakening: Siddhartha became Buddha by rising above all that was base and fearful in himself. Deep in meditation he conquered his own fear, and saw the truth.

The temptations of Mara resemble the hierarchy of Mount Meru, or the structure of a Hindu temple. There is a progression upward from the very simple to the very refined. After testing Siddhartha with visions of terrifying demons, Mara reversed the scene, attempting instead to tempt Siddhartha with his daughters, young women of maddening sexual beauty. "Give up this nonsense, Siddhartha, and enjoy the company of these women. Anything you want is yours. Enjoy yourself. You deserve it; you have denied yourself the pleasures of the flesh for too long."

Sexual pleasure makes a good symbol for all kinds of pleasure. This is where happiness starts, close to the earth. Siddhartha was tempted, but his strong self-discipline made it relatively easy for him to get past that one. Before his eyes, the beauty turned into ugliness. Deeper he sank within himself. We can easily imagine Mara then moving on to a more subtle plane. "Siddhartha, the time has come to return home. Get up from this ridiculous quest and return to the embrace of your wife and son. How happy your father will be; he will receive you with open arms. Do you not owe him that before he dies? You've seen both sides now. You can take your father's place when the time comes, and rule with wisdom and compassion. It is your destiny to be a king, not a 'holy man,' and the experience of your years as a sadhu will make you that much greater. Get on with it, Siddhartha, go back home, now."

Such thoughts must have arisen in Siddhartha's mind, and he would have been moved by them, but his resolve did not break. Calling upon great interior strength, he moved deeper into meditation. He would not allow himself to be swayed by temptation. Mara hurled his entire arsenal against Siddhartha; he tried everything available to him, but nothing would move Siddhartha. Finally, in anger, Mara appeared personally before Siddhartha; Mara, the undisguised, stark reality of death revealed himself to Siddhartha, and demanded to know by what authority Siddhartha dared to challenge this ultimate mystery of life. Siddhartha silently answered by touching the earth with his right hand. The earth itself, from which all comes and to which all returns, would be his witness and his authority. At that Mara retreated, leaving Siddhartha completely alone. He had weathered the storm of Mara's temptations. Now the farther shore was in view. Some say that when Siddhartha opened his eyes the first thing he saw was Venus, the morning star, and the vision of it dissolved the last veil of ignorance:

> The dark waters of the unconscious closed over Siddhartha, and he slipped into that profound stillness in which thought stops and the distinctions of a separate personality dissolve. In this profound state he remained immersed throughout the night. When dawn came the tree under which he sat burst into bloom, and a fragrant spring breeze showered him with blossoms. He was no longer Siddhartha, the finite personality that had been born in Kapilavastu. He was the Buddha, "he who is awake." He had found the way to that realm of being which decay and death can never touch: *nirvana*. (Easwaren, *Dhammapada*, 27)

So what is this *nirvana* that Buddha experienced? Naturally, the experience is ineffable—that is, it cannot be expressed in words. Each person must experience it personally; no one can *tell* another what it is. The word *nirvana* literally means "to blow out," as to blow out the flame of a candle. What Buddha blew out was the last vestige of the ego-illusion, and with it the last remnant of ego-craving. And in that moment, all illusions having gone, he saw perfectly the truth of his own nature: that his being was one with all Being. He saw the truth of life and death. He saw that human fear arises from a nightmare of illusion. But he was now awake, and the nightmare was gone forever.

According to the story, Buddha was overwhelmed by the rapture of his vision of truth. He remained in meditation for a long time, absorbed in the joy of it. Once again, Mara came to him. Now Mara had good reason to be worried. Again he sat down beside Buddha and remained silent for a long time. At last he spoke, "Well Buddha, you have done what no other person has done. You have seen what no other person has seen. You are free even from the tyranny of the fear of death. Congratulations, Buddha; I salute you. What is there left for you? Surely you can no longer expect to keep the company of other men. No one could understand or share your experience. You would be treated as a fool if you tried to talk about that which no one else can fathom. What is there for you now but to withdraw to a private place for the remainder of your mortal days, there to enjoy the perfect bliss of your enlightenment?"

Mara was in fact putting Buddha to a test; in a way it was the "last temptation of Buddha." If Buddha had agreed with this eminently sensible suggestion, Mara would have known that Buddha's awakening was not perfect awakening. But Buddha's awakening *was* perfect awakening, and he did not take the bait. However tempting it might be to go off alone and enjoy the bliss of his discovery in splendid solitude, Buddha would not even consider such a thing. The greatest thing about Buddha was his compassion, compassion for all of the suffering men and women of the world. He had discovered a path that led to the release from suffering, and all that he cared about was sharing this discovery with others. He himself could not be perfectly happy until all others were too. This act of total compassion is taken to be conclusive evidence of the fact that Buddha's enlightenment was perfect.

To Mara's objection that no one would be able to comprehend his message, Buddha answered with the analogy of the lotus pond, a familiar sight to the people of Buddha's time. Then as now, it was a part of the natural landscape in many parts of India. The lotus plant begins as a seedling buried deep in the muck at the dark bottom of the pond. From there the stalk grows to the surface of the pond, where the tightly wrapped flower bud, in the full light of the sun, opens into a beautiful symmetrical blossom. Few things in nature seem more fully open than does a lotus blossom in full bloom. This whole process from seed to flower makes a wonderful symbol for the path that leads to awakening.

Buddha said that everyone can be compared to some stage in the growth of the lotus plant. Many people are still at the seedling stage, immersed in darkness. Others have begun to sprout and are making their way toward the light. Some have broken through the surface but are still holding back; the bud is well formed but still tightly wrapped. And there are those few who are already beginning to open and simply need the full light of the sun to blossom completely. Buddha's teaching would be that sunlight. "Everyone," he said, "can benefit from it to some degree. No matter where he or she may be, every person can make some progress toward the light. And some can be moved to awaken completely." For this reason, Buddha concluded, his mission was to bring the light of his teaching to as many as could hear his words. He would dedicate the rest of his life to spreading the good word of his awakening.

THE TEACHING YEARS

And that's exactly what he did. Buddha was said to be thirty-five years old at the time of his awakening. He lived for about another forty-five years. For all of this time, he lived as an itinerant teacher, walking the length and breadth of the great Ganges plain, spreading his message to the crowds that would gather wherever he stopped. He became famous in his own time. Buddha treated all people with equal compassion and respect; there was no caste system of privilege in his eyes. He accepted equally the hospitality of kings and poor farmers.

According to the story of Buddha's life, the first discourse after awakening occurred at a place called the Deer Park, near the town of Sarnath, which is not far from the holy city of Varanasi. The spot would naturally become a place of pilgrimage for followers of Buddha and still today attracts great numbers of visitors. In time, a large shrine was erected there to commemorate the event.*

When Siddhartha went off alone to meditate, his dismayed companions lost track of him. But soon they missed him deeply and went looking for him. They caught up with him at Sarnath, and it was to this small group of companions that Buddha delivered his first discourse. They were shocked at the sight of their friend and the great change that had come over him. When Siddhartha, now properly referred to as Buddha, told them that he had seen through to the truth of life and death, they at first chided him and challenged him to share his vision with them. And thus did the teaching career of Buddha begin. We will examine the substance of this discourse in the next chapter.

The original group of five companions eventually grew to ten. Buddha referred to them as the *sangha*. The sangha would become a permanent and basic element of Buddhist life. The communal group, living closely together under the direction of a spiritual leader, and helping one another along the path, was seen from the earliest times to be a powerful help in the quest of awakening. It's easy to see that the sangha was very much like an ashram. The word *sangha* originally referred to a representative body of nobles that consulted with a king. There was something of a democratic element in a sangha. Perhaps Buddha chose this word because he encouraged a more individual democratic spirit in his group and thus wanted to distinguish his ashram from the more traditional type. Although Buddha retained much of the Hindu tradition, he was in a fundamental way making a break with the past.

In addition to the small group of close companions that traveled with Buddha, many others who heard his words were deeply moved and wished to dedicate themselves completely to this new way of life. Thus did communities of monks, to use the common English term, take form in many places. Buddha referred to these men as the Order. For a time, he resisted the suggestion that women be allowed to join the Order; he feared that the distractions and temptations would be too great for human nature in a community of

---

*There are four "holy sites" associated with the life of Buddha: Lumbini, where he was born; Bodh Gaya, where he experienced awakening; Sarnath, the site of his first discourse; and Kusinara, where according to traditional belief Buddha died.

men and women living closely together. Eventually, though, he relented and organized a separate Order of women.* This is not to suggest that ordinary householders were left out of the picture. The sunlight of Buddha's teaching was to fall on everyone. But some felt the heat more intensely and were eager to dedicate themselves wholeheartedly to the quest. For these zealous ones, the communal life of the Order was the logical path.

Buddha and his immediate group of disciples lived the itinerant lifestyle, calling no place home. It is said, though, that in his later years he accepted a small piece of land near the town of Sarvatthi which the group could use as a home base. It was a gift from a wealthy landowner and would have been a real benefit during the rainy season. Most of the time, though, they would have been out on the dusty road. Buddha wanted to share his teaching with as many as possible. In this, Buddha was far from being a unique figure. The itinerant guru has always been a part of life in India, and in the turbulent time of Buddha's life, there must have been more gurus than usual. Undoubtedly, Buddha and his teaching attracted especially great attention. Still, he was only one of many teachers, and we might never have heard of him had it not been for the work of his disciples. Buddha never wrote any books; all that we know of his teaching was preserved in memory by his disciples and handed down for several centuries in the oral tradition.

There were many disciples in Buddha's sangha; tradition has it that ten of these were especially close to him. Tradition also has it that one of these ten was his own son, Rahula. There is a legendary story about Buddha returning to his home city, Kapilavastu. By this time, he was a famous man. During his stay in Kapilavastu, Buddha made peace with his father and with his wife, Yashodhara, who joined the Order of women. It was at that time, according to the story, that Rahula became one of the Ten. This story is clearly one of the later embellishments; whether or not anything like this ever actually happened is impossible to say.

In any case, even if Rahula did become a disciple, he is not described as Buddha's favorite. The "one that Buddha loved most," according to the legend, was the young Ananda (whose name means "bliss" in Sanskrit). Ananda probably joined the group as a boy. He is described as youthful and charming and something of an innocent. We can imagine him being totally devoted to Buddha and always ready to help out with any chore. He is often pictured sitting close to Buddha. (How similar this is to the story of Jesus's relationship with his young disciple, John.)

Almost the opposite of Ananda in personality was the disciple named Malunkyaputra. Here was a man who dearly loved to think deeply and rationally about the problems of life. In a way, it's odd that he became a disciple at all; Buddha was nothing like that. In no way at all were Buddha's "discourses" rational expositions. He taught by example and by parable. In Buddha's opinion, metaphysical questions were a

---

*Buddha's commitment to equality, including gender equality, was undoubtedly very far ahead of the general attitude of his time. Nonetheless, his stand regarding the place of woman has drawn criticism in modern times. Kate Wheeler, herself a practicing Buddhist for seventeen years, takes up this matter in an article which she wrote for the Buddhist periodical, *Tricycle*. She points out that Buddha was indeed very reluctant to organize a women's Order and only agreed to it on the condition that the women accept many additional rules, the total effect of which was to assure that the women would live in subjugation to men. The very first of these rules concerned bowing. Male monks bowed to all senior male monks, but Buddha decreed that a woman monk, "even of a hundred years standing," shall bow before all male monks, even if he has been a monk for only one day. Ms. Wheeler concludes her article with the interesting and intentionally provocative challenge, "In the case of women, the Buddha was wrong—and we have to have the courage to say so."

waste of time; they did not get at real truth. Such discussions come down to nothing more than intellectual game-playing. When such questions were raised, Buddha's typical response was to smile and remain silent. This must have been very perplexing to Malunkyaputra. Apparently, he tried endlessly to draw Buddha into a discussion of metaphysical matters, especially the nature of nirvana, but Buddha always deflected the discussion to other subjects. Finally, in desperation, Malunkyaputra went to Buddha and put the matter right on the line. His mind was in turmoil regarding certain vexing questions, and if Buddha refused to answer them, he had decided that he was going to leave the Order and go back to his home:

> Blessed One, there are theories which you have left unexplained and set aside unanswered: whether the world is eternal or not eternal; whether it is finite or infinite; whether the soul and body are the same or different; whether a person who has attained nirvana exists after death or does not, or whether perhaps he both exists and does not exist, or neither exists nor does not. The fact that the Blessed One has not explained these matters neither pleases me nor suits me. If the Blessed One will not explain this to me, I will give up spiritual disciplines and return to the life of a layman. (Easwaren, *Dhammapada*, 40)

It's easy to picture Buddha sighing deeply when Malunkyaputra had finished. "Malunkyaputra," he might have said, "when you took up the spiritual life did I ever promise you I would answer these questions?" Poor Malunkyaputra; he must have known right then that he wasn't going to get his answers—not in the way he wanted, anyway. But Buddha did give him a reply. He asked Malunkyaputra to imagine a warrior being wounded in the leg by a poison-tipped arrow. The wound was severe, and the man was in imminent danger of death. What he needed above everything else was to have that arrow removed, immediately! Would he tell the surgeon to wait until he knew more about the man who shot him? Before having the arrow removed, would he demand to know the archer's caste, his family background, the kind of wood his bow was made from, the name of the fletcher who made the arrow? Of course not! Malunkyaputra had to agree that only a fool would raise such questions; he'd be dead long before they were answered. "Well, Malunkyaputra," Buddha would have said, "I don't teach whether the world is finite or eternal. I teach how to remove the arrow."

The disciple named Kasyapa fell somewhere between the extremes of Ananda and Malunkyaputra. He was devoted, loyal, compassionate, and very intelligent. One gets the feeling that if the group had been the crew of a ship, Kasyapa would have been the first mate. It was to Kasyapa, we are told, that the Buddha entrusted his only possessions—his robe and begging bowl—when he knew that the end was near. These two items would later be interpreted as the "insignia" of the rightful claim to be the spiritual successor of Shakyamuni Buddha, and thus the leader of the sangha.

Buddha was about eighty years old when he died. He had spent the last forty-five years of his life traveling through much of North India, and his teaching had an enormous impact wherever he had gone. But like all things in life, the teaching career of Buddha must finally reach its end. The Pali Canon gives us a fairly detailed record of Buddha's last days. The final three months are summed up in a short work known as the *Discourse on the Great Decease*. It was fitting that death would come to Buddha while he and his closest disciples were on the road. They were on their way to the city of Kusinara (also spelled Kushinagara; modern Kasia) when the end came.

It was the custom of the sangha to spend the night wherever they happened to be at nightfall. They would gratefully accept whatever hospitality might be offered to them. Buddha had become famous and much loved; it was a great honor to give him and his disciples shelter for the night. At one place where they stopped, a humble village on the road to Kusinara, the excited owner of a blacksmith shop did his best to make them comfortable. The smith, a man named Cunda, prepared a dinner for Buddha and his companions. It would be Buddha's last meal:

> The Master and his group were invited to a meal for the following day by the smith Cunda. In order to put something special before the venerable guest, Cunda had, among other dishes, prepared *sukara-maddava* [literally, the "soft food of pigs"]. What exactly this was still remains uncertain. Some writers think it was pork, others think of tender bamboo-shoots such as grow near a pigsty, others again some kind of fungus, possibly truffles. But, whatever it may have been, the Buddha viewed this food with suspicion, and asked Cunda not to offer it to the other monks. He himself, however, partook of it, in order not to disappoint the well-meaning smith. (Shumann, 247)

Buddha became very sick and suffered extreme pain. Nevertheless, the next day the group moved on. They stopped to rest in a fruit orchard near the town of Kusinara. It was springtime and the trees were in bloom. Buddha's disciples made a comfortable place for him to rest, but it was soon clear to everyone that the end was near.

That which they dreaded was now close at hand. What would happen to them without their beloved leader? Who would lead the sangha? Indeed, who *would* lead the sangha? This has been an important question in the history of Buddhism. Did Buddha appoint a successor, and if he did, what would have been the basis for making such a profoundly important choice? The tradition of Zen Buddhism teaches that Buddha chose the brilliant monk, Kasyapa, to be his successor, and he in time chose another, and so on in a long unbroken succession down to the time of the founding of Zen.

From the writings of the Pali Canon, we get a different view. When the disciple Ananda, whom Buddha loved greatly, approached the master and tried to discreetly raise the subject of a succession, Buddha gave him this answer:

> Ananda, you should live as islands unto yourselves, being your own refuge, seeking no other refuge; with the Dharma as an island, with the Dharma as your refuge, seeking no other refuge . . . Those monks who in my time or afterwards live thus, seeking an island and a refuge in themselves and in the Dharma and nowhere else, these zealous ones are truly my monks and will overcome the darkness. (*Digha-Nikaya*, quoted in Shumann, 246)

In other words, at least according to this version, Buddha chose not to name a particular person to stand in his place. His teaching (the Dharma) would be their leader, and the Dharma would stand on its own as the guide for all time to come. Buddha made a strong point of insisting that followers of his teaching be "islands unto yourselves."

Elsewhere he declared, "Be lamps unto yourselves. Be a refuge to yourselves." This is not to say that the sangha, the community of monks helping one another was not important; it was seen to be *very* important. Ultimately though, each person must discover the truth within himself. There is to be no blind dependence on an outside authority.

On the afternoon of his last day, Buddha wanted to be sure that there were no strings left untied. He gathered his disciples around him and asked if anyone had any last questions. Was there anything at all that they had perhaps been reluctant to raise? "It may be that one of you has doubts or uncertainty about the Buddha, the Dharma, or the sangha, or about the practice. Ask, if you do, lest afterward you feel remorse." Everyone was silent. A short time later, Buddha uttered his last words: "Now, monks, I declare to you: all things that come into being are subject to decay. Strive on untiringly!" After saying this, Buddha slipped into a coma, and during the night, he died.

To say the least, his disciples were stricken with grief. They were now orphans. But Buddha had been with them a long time and had instructed them carefully. They would take the time to lovingly perform the rites of cremation, and then get on with the work. Buddha had entrusted them, and all who would come after them, with the task of spreading the Dharma, the word of his teaching, of not ceasing to work with compassion until every man and woman on earth had achieved the freedom of awakening. In time, the followers of the way of Buddha would find refuge in what came to be called "The Three Jewels": Buddha himself, the Dharma, and the Sangha. And it is to an examination of this wonderful philosophy of life, the teaching of Buddha, that we shall now turn.

Study Questions

1. How did Shakyamuni come to be called "the Buddha"?
2. Why is it important to the story of Buddha's life that both his youth in the palace and his years as a sadhu be perfect examples of these two kinds of lifestyle?
3. What did Siddhartha encounter each of the four times he left the palace, and what is the symbolic significance of each?
4. What led Siddhartha to conclude that self-fulfillment cannot be attained through self-indulgence, nor through self-denial?
5. What was the essential character of Buddha's "awakening"?
6. What was the role of the god Mara in Buddha's struggle to become awakened? How is Mara's role to be interpreted?
7. What is the meaning of the "analogy of the lotus pond"?
8. In responding to Malunkyaputra's effort to lure him into a discussion of metaphysical questions, Buddha tells the story about the man wounded by a poison-tipped arrow. What point is Buddha trying to make?
9. What final advice did Buddha give to the sangha? How do you interpret its meaning?

CHAPTER 9

Basic Teaching of Shakyamuni Buddha

Buddha taught by word of mouth and by personal example. So far as we know, he didn't commit anything to writing. Thus, all that we know of Buddha's teaching has come down to us from others. From the very beginning, though, an oral tradition existed, and eventually a written tradition developed as well. Approximately four centuries after Buddha's death, the first great effort was made to gather together the existing sources and determine, insofar as was possible, the true record of Buddha's life and teaching. This scholarly and thorough-going work came to be known as the Pali Canon. We shall examine it in detail in the next chapter. The Pali Canon is the scriptural core of the first great organized movement in the evolution of Buddhism. For our purposes, that can be equated with the tradition known as *Theravada*.

Historically speaking, there are two great traditions in the evolution of Buddhism. The earlier of these is what is here referred to as *Theravada*, the "teachings (or doctrines) of the elders." Strictly speaking, the name *Theravada* (pronounced: tair-a-VAH-da) refers to only one school, albeit the dominant school, within the closely related parts of the early development of Buddhism. In the course of time, Theravada Buddhism would be joined, and even overshadowed, by the second of the great traditions. For the most part, these later developments are joined together under the name *Mahayana Buddhism*. The Mahayanists referred to the older orthodox tradition as "Hinayana," which was something of a derogatory term and implied an inferior status. Due to the great influence of Mahayana (mah-ha-YAH-na), the terms *Mahayana* and *Hinayana* are used by many even to this day to distinguish between the two great Buddhist traditions. In modern times, however, there is a growing preference for the term *Theravada* in place of *Hinayana*. For one thing, Theravada is the only part of the original tradition to survive into modern times. For all practical purposes, the terms *Theravada* and *Hinayana* mean the same thing. In this work, I shall use the term *Theravada*. We shall thoroughly examine both Theravada and Mahayana in the appropriate place.

Naturally, the presentation of Buddha's teaching, and the emphasis given to various themes, would evolve and change over time. Mahayana differs from Theravada in many important respects. Fundamentally, though, all of Buddhism emerges from the same original core. In this chapter, we shall examine the initial core teaching, essentially as it is given in the Pali Canon. This is the logical place to start. The far-flung evolution of the teaching, as we find it in the history of Mahayana, will be presented as we investigate the historical development of Buddhism.

It is a common mistake to think of Buddha as a spiritual leader, the deliberate founder of one of the world's great religions. He did not see himself as a religious leader at all. If anything, Buddha was a teacher. Following his awakening, he dedicated his life to teaching others how to live in such a way that they too could do what he had done—that is, find the way to freedom from fear and suffering.

Another common mistake is to assume that Shakyamuni Buddha spoke the final word on the subject of awakening, as if he delivered a dogmatic sort of "truth," and since that time, all followers of the Buddhist way have agreed that nothing further needs to be said. Shakyamuni Buddha was the founder of a tradition, not a religion. His teaching, which grew out of personal experience, laid the foundation for a tradition that has continued to grow and mature from Buddha's own time down to the present. As Buddha was the founder, his teaching—and most important of all, his experience of awakening—has been the core of that tradition. But much has been added over the centuries.

Buddha was not interested in dogma. He did not wish to tell people what is right and what is wrong. He made no appeal to a higher authority of any kind. What Buddha taught was a philosophy of life, a way of living. That way of life could lead to freedom—that is, to awakening—for any man or woman willing to follow it. Neither sex, nor age, nor wealth, nor rank in society would make any difference at all. Any person, in any place or time, willing to take on this way of life and follow the path, was assured of making progress toward liberation. And throughout the ages, countless men and women have taken up the challenge and have found their own lives revolutionized by the teaching of this man who lived so long ago.

Various schools of Buddhism have evolved over the past two-and-a-half millennia, especially within Mahayana. And there is quite a range to the character of these traditions—everything from the very secular to the decidedly religious. Each, of course, claims to be faithful to the original spirit of Buddha's teaching. Our present task is to attempt to determine the essential teaching that is fundamental to all of Buddhism, Buddha's own foundation, so to speak, from which so much has grown.

The place to begin is Buddha's awakening. It is because of the awakening that we call him by the name *Buddha*. As mentioned in the previous chapter, the term *Buddha* is derived from the Sanskrit *budh*, which means to wake up. In a moment of supreme insight, Buddha "awakened" to a clear vision of the truth of his real nature. There was no way that he, nor anyone else, could describe this experience in words. Buddha couldn't share this great experience with others simply by telling them what it was. But, through his teaching, he could show others how to achieve the same experience of awakening in their own lives.

When talking about Buddha's awakening, we tend to fall back on metaphor. The word *awakening* is itself a metaphor. Buddha compared our ordinary state of consciousness to a dream state. While sleeping, we don't know that we're dreaming; at the time, it all seems very real and often very frightening. But when we wake up, we know right away that it was just a dream, an illusion, that there was really nothing at all to be afraid of. Buddha would say that even when we wake up from what we ordinarily call dreams, we still remain in something of a dream state. Of course, we don't recognize that; we assume that our everyday state of consciousness is fully awake. But is it? Buddha would say that it is not—that we remain prisoners of our illusions and fears. It is possible to awaken from this state in the same way that we awaken from dreams.

Buddha's awakening is sometimes referred to as his "Enlightenment" or "Liberation." Whatever word we use, we are talking about an experience that was the great watershed moment of his life. When Buddha (or rather Siddhartha) withdrew into meditation, it was as though he died, and then in the moment of awakening, he came forth reborn, a "new man." He "awakened" to a sudden and clear vision of the truth of his real nature. But what does this mean? Is metaphor the only way we can approach this tantalizing subject?

Granted, the subject of Buddha's awakening is not something that can be neatly captured in words. Words can go only so far, but they can help to point the way to understanding truth. Our common sense perception is that reality is not one at all, but rather is made up of myriad separate and discrete things, "myself" being one of them. Buddha saw beyond this illusion and beheld a more fundamental reality, in which all the seemingly separate realities are but manifestations. Thus it is that by seeing into the essential reality of his own nature, he beheld the reality of all nature. Penetrating to the core of *any* expression of reality is penetrating to the core of *all* reality.

The Upanishads had, of course, proclaimed the fundamental unity of Being: all is Brahman. Some argue that for Buddha to penetrate to a deep vision of this truth would not put him in conflict with the Hindu tradition of his time. In fact, his awakening would be a dramatic affirmation of the Vedanta tradition. It is argued by some that this is the correct way to interpret the awakening of Buddha. His great insight was not basically in conflict with the traditional teaching of Hindu spirituality. Buddha did not use the term *Brahman* in his teaching, but in a section of the Pali Canon known as the *Udana*, he is said to have referred to "the unborn, the unformed, the unbecome." Some would see this as carrying essentially the same meaning as the concept of Brahman. Interpreted in this way, Buddha's awakening was a reaffirmation of the essential truth of the Hindu tradition; he simply saw more deeply and clearly and thus was able to give new life and meaning to the age-old wisdom. He was not so much a revolutionary as he was a reformer.

There is another, quite different interpretation. Some maintain that what Buddha discovered in that moment of perfect insight was in stark contradiction to the fundamentals of the traditional teaching. It was a new departure, and it was the moment of birth of a revolution in human thought. This interpretation can be summed up in what is generally referred to as the Doctrine of Anatman. (Writers on this subject often use the Pali word *anatta*, but we shall stay with the Sanskrit term, *anatman*.)

Buddhism is not a dogmatic system of thought. There is no such thing as an institutional hierarchy to make final decisions about the truth. Ultimately, each person must make these decisions for himself or herself. Buddha himself set the tone for this in his famous words, "Be a lamp unto yourself." The matter of anatman is no exception; the student of Buddhist philosophy must evaluate it personally. It is a fascinating subject and well worth our time to examine it carefully. What follows is an exposition of the Doctrine of Anatman. Please bear in mind that what follows is not an attempt in any way to present "the truth" in a convenient package; it is simply an effort to clarify what is meant by the Doctrine of Anatman and its possible implications for the teaching of Buddha. The Doctrine of Anatman, it should be pointed out, is the philosophical centerpiece of several closely related principles that concern the nature of reality. We shall focus on anatman but bring into the discussion other matters as they become appropriate.

THE DOCTRINE OF ANATMAN

In Sanskrit, the prefix *a* or *an* is a negative; it negates the noun. Therefore, the word *anatman* technically means "no Atman," "no Self." Before we go into this, it would be helpful to briefly review the meaning of Atman. Belief in Atman was the cornerstone of traditional Vedanta teaching.

According to this teaching, all is Brahman, the source and upholder of the universe. Brahman, as Atman, is the core, the soul, of every sentient being. The Brahman-Atman is the core consciousness; ego is the role. Our own role-playing enthralls us and blinds us to the deeper truth. It is the ignorance (avidya) of ego-identity and the hopeless effort to satisfy the cravings of ego that burden us with all of life's suffering. The Upanishadic tradition taught that the way to freedom from suffering is to break out of the cage of ego-delusion and discover the real Self, the Atman. Such discovery is called *moksha*. It might take many lifetimes, but eventually all would climb to the summit of the mountain, and Brahman would perfectly rediscover itself.

During his sadhu years, Buddha (then Siddhartha) gave himself over completely to freeing himself from the shackles of ego, the role, and to discovering in the depths of meditation the pure experience of Atman. He put forth as fine an effort as any human being possibly could. But, as we know, it didn't happen. Thus came about what we may call his second great realization: *There is no self-fulfillment through self-denial.* The second great realization goes hand in hand with the first. Seemingly, they are the two sides of one coin. First Buddha discovered that he couldn't find self-fulfillment in self-indulgence; then he found that its opposite, self-denial, didn't work either. What else is there!?

In desperation Buddha withdrew into deep meditation, determined not to leave the spot until he penetrated through his ignorance and discovered the real truth of the Self. What set the stage for the great moment of his awakening was what we might refer to as a third and final insight regarding self-fulfillment. Buddha saw that his first two insights, though truthful in themselves, were founded on a fundamental error. And now he could see what that error was. We may put it in the following way.

In his first great realization, Buddha concluded that there is no self-fulfillment through self-indulgence. In the second great realization, he concluded that there is no self-fulfillment through self-denial. His third great realization was the sudden awareness that there is no self-fulfillment at all—no *self-fulfillment, period*. There can *be* no self-fulfillment because *there is no self to be fulfilled!*

His heroic quest had been an impossible one from the beginning because there is no Atman to be discovered (an-Atman, no-Atman). It's a shocking thought; let me repeat it. His quest had been an impossible one from the beginning, because *there is no Atman to be discovered!* There is no *Atman-Self* to be fulfilled. The whole notion of Atman, the cornerstone of Vedanta philosophy, was simply a fantastic error. However appealing, however enticing, however reasonable, however enshrined in tradition, Buddha saw in a flash of insight that it is all a construction of the human mind and has no objective reality at all.

The concept of Atman had developed as a logical necessity. I am a conscious being. What I am conscious of (aware of) are my own experiences. I am aware of what I see, what I taste, what I think. In other words, I am the conscious subject of my own experiences— that seems self-evident and undeniable. My sight cannot be aware of itself; "I" am aware of what I see! According to the Vedanta view, the "I" that is aware is Atman. Atman is the con- scious core, the subject of all conscious experiences: the hearer of sounds, the see-er of sights, the feeler of feelings, the thinker of thoughts. The ego-role is part of the world of *maya*; it "dances" before Atman, so entrancing it that Atman is hypnotized into falsely identifying with it. Thus evolved yoga, whose goal it became to shed the layers of ego until nothing remained to hide Atman, the reality at the core of one's being. In the words of the *Bhagavad Gita*,

> The body is mortal, but he who dwells in the body is immortal and immeasurable.
>
> As a man abandons worn-out clothes and acquires new ones,
>
> So when the body is worn out a new one is acquired by the Self, who lives within. (Easwaren, *BG*: II.18, 22; p. 63)

A similar line of thinking developed in modern Western philosophy. The British empiricist John Locke (much influenced by Aristotle) introduced the concept of what he called primary qualities and secondary qualities. Secondary qualities are the things that we perceive with the senses: color, texture, smell, etc. We never directly perceive the primary qualities, such things as extension in space, but they are what "hold," or express, the secondary qualities, which we do perceive. Someone once asked Locke how he could be sure that the primary qualities really did exist if we never perceive them directly. His answer was classic: "My God, man, they have to!"

Well, given Locke's system of reasoning, they do have to exist. But that doesn't mean they really do. The same could be said with regard to the concept of Atman. Buddha, like virtually everyone else of his culture, had accepted the reality of Atman without question because it seemed so reasonable and necessary. The only problem was that it was nowhere to be found. Buddha (as Siddhartha) had become a master of all the disciplines of yoga, yet, try as he might, he never experienced any state of consciousness that he could honestly identify as the Atman. Buddha concluded that there is no such thing as Atman. There is no subject of the role; there is only the role. And that insight finally freed him from all ignorance. Suddenly, the dreamlike state that is ordinary consciousness dissolved, and Buddha saw clearly the true nature of his being.

Buddha saw that there is no substanding self of any kind (that is to say, no substantive enduring reality "standing beneath" and supporting the changing appearances). There is movement; there is change; there is development over time. But there is nothing that is *doing* all of this. There is no need for Brahman; there is just the process itself, no do-er thereof. Reality, you might say, is a constant flow of patterns of energy. But there is nothing that is *doing* it; there is just the flow. All substanding "things," including the notion of Atman, are concepts only, illusions of the imagination. Buddha is supposed to have said, "There is liberation; but no *one* who is liberated."

According to the Doctrine of Anatman, Buddha was saying, in effect, that not only does the concept of self lack substantial reality, but *everything* lacks substantial reality. Anything you can think of is, at bottom, a fleeting process of change. Nothing can really stand on its own as a permanent, self-explaining entity. This teaching is expressed in two principles: the Doctrine of Anitya, which holds that impermanence is a characteristic of all existence, and the Doctrine of Dependent Origination, which explains that the intelligibility of anything is dependent on a variety of causes and conditions outside itself. In other words, nothing can explain itself. Whether it's a house, a horse, or a star or whatever, the existence of every single thing can only be understood in terms of other things that define it and cause it to be. These two matters then—impermanence and dependency—are said to be of the fundamental character of existence. They explain the nonsubstantiality of everything, including, therefore, the concept of Atman.

The concept of anatman can sometimes seem to stand common sense on its head. And it does! But sometimes common sense can mislead us. The discoveries of modern physics make that abundantly clear. Let's examine this subject in an orderly way, and I think that most (if not all) of the confusion will disappear. Please remember, the most important thing is that you *understand* the concept of anatman, not necessarily that you agree or disagree with it. What follows is an attempt to explain how the all-important sense of a separate substanding self develops. The Doctrine of Anatman holds that this error—all but universal among us humans—is the root cause of suffering.

Virtually every normal person has a strong sense of "myself"—a strong sense of "I am." And the "I" here refers to a substanding entity with which the person identifies. It is the conscious "me" that is the subject of all personal experience, of all memories; it is the feeler of feelings and the thinker of thoughts. It is the underlying "me" that remains constant through time from birth to death and perhaps beyond death as well. It is the ego, the "me," that makes decisions and hence gives me a sense of control and direction in life. When I make a fist, "I" make a fist; when I walk across the room, "I" walk across the room.

We are conditioned from infancy to see ourselves in this way. A baby receives a distinct name right on his or her birth certificate and is encouraged in myriad ways to identify with it. One of the first words a child learns to say, usually loudly, is "mine." The language is full of such subtle conditionings. "Let yourself go." "Be yourself!" "Collect yourself!" And then there's always "self-esteem," "self-pity," and even "self-loathing."

Everywhere we turn, the culture supports our unquestioned conviction that the sense of self—a substanding, enduring self—is real and beyond question; it is "self-evident." This fixed belief was given the seal of authority by the French philosopher, René Descartes, who laid the cornerstone of modern Western philosophy with his famous dictum, *cogito, ergo sum*: "I think, therefore I am."

Personal experience also comes into play in support of the reality of the ego-self. It has to do with the experience that we call "self-consciousness." Rather than attempting merely to talk about it, let me ask you to take a few minutes to perform a simple meditation exercise. It won't matter whether or not you have experience in meditation practice. Just sit quietly in a comfortable position, close your eyes, and turn your attention inward. Become aware of the chatter that's going on in your thinking mind. Try to let the thoughts drop away so that as far as possible you're not *doing* anything mentally; you're simply aware of your fact of existence, your act of being.

This exercise in self-consciousness can lead to a dramatic experience, and the deeper you're able to go the more dramatic it will become. As the activity, the play of the mind, settles down, you will become aware of yourself as a watcher, an observer, of what's going on mentally. This subtle sense of self, usually lost in the background of our active daily life, can become very profound when the activity is turned off and the awareness is turned inward. It is as though the real me, down at the core, is some silent, unblinking, wise being observing and managing all this ego-role-playing that I endlessly engage in. Thus, the sense of the underlying, enduring self is supported not only conceptually, but experientially as well.

Buddha was a master of meditation. He plumbed the depths of his own inner being, convinced originally that the silent self at the center was Atman, and he would not rest until he saw it perfectly, until he was fully and consciously one with it. But, as we know, all his efforts came to nothing. In this, the most important goal of life, he came up empty. Buddha concluded that the whole concept of Atman was only that—a concept. He didn't find the Atman because there was no Atman to be found. Those who claimed otherwise were simply deluding themselves. Atman is just another trick of the thinking human mind. It is nothing more than a subtle way of conceptualizing the self-image, the ego.

We can easily speculate that our distant human ancestors, out of yearning for permanence, invented the idea of an eternal spirit ("soul"), which inhabits the all-too-obviously nonpermanent body and is the *real me*. It's a comforting notion held tenaciously by the vast majority of men and women. But is it true? Buddha's answer is a resounding NO! Not only is this belief not true, but clinging to it is in fact responsible for *all* of the suffering in the world. What a thought!

Ego, the concept of one's substanding self, is at the heart of the problem. Buddha believed that attachment to ego is what the cause of human suffering is all about. It is the core attachment; all others relate to it because ultimately all cravings seek to satisfy the wants of the ego, and most fervently of all is the ego's yearning to be immortal. Awakening depends on liberating oneself from the bondage of attachments. Most of all, this means liberation from the prison that is the delusion of the ego-self. There is no substanding "me" at all. We are urged to awaken from the dreamlike delusion that we take to be real and cling to desperately. (It is important to note that Buddhism does not seek the annihilation of "ego" per se, which is impossible; ego as a behavioral model is a natural expression of human life. What Buddhism seeks to annihilate is the *illusion* of ego—that is, the false identification of one's very being with the ego-self.)

Of course, the authors of the Upanishads had also taught that liberation means liberation from the delusion of the ego-role. Both Buddha and the Upanishads taught that the road to ruin lay in man's hunger to identify with the ego and the effort to satisfy its insatiable desires. Attachment to ego is fundamental avidya for the Upanishads and for Buddha. The great difference, though, is to be found in the matter of Atman. The Upanishads proclaimed that one broke through the illusion of ego by discovering the real Self, the conscious subject, the Atman. Buddha proclaimed that this is an impossible dream. There is no Atman! Faith in its existence only perpetuates the delusion of a substanding self. Faith in the existence of Atman tragically increases one's attachment to ego. In smashing the idol of Atman, Buddha was breaking with the most cherished belief of the past and stepping out onto entirely new ground. This matter of the revolutionary nature of the Doctrine of Anatman is summed up very nicely by the Buddhist scholar Rahula Walpola:

> What in general is suggested by Soul, Self, Ego, or to use the Sanskrit expression *atman*, is that in man there is a permanent, everlasting and absolute entity, which is the unchanging substance behind the changing phenomenal world. According to some religions, each individual has such a separate soul which is created by God, and which, finally after death, lives eternally either in hell or heaven, its destiny depending on the judgment of its creator. According to others, it goes through many lives till it is completely purified and becomes finally united with God or Brahman, Universal Soul or *atman*, from which it originally emanated. This soul or self in man is the thinker of thoughts, feeler of

sensations, and receiver of rewards and punishments for all its actions good and bad. Such a conception is called the idea of self.

Buddhism stands unique in the history of human thought in denying the existence of such a Soul, Self, or *atman*. According to the teaching of Buddha, the idea of self is an imaginary, false belief which has no corresponding reality, and it produces harmful thoughts of "me" and "mine", selfish desire, craving, attachment, hatred, ill-will, conceit, pride, egoism, and other defilements, impurities and problems. It is the source of all the troubles in the world from personal conflicts to wars between nations. In short, to this false view can be traced all the evil in the world. (51)

"To this false view can be traced all the evil in the world." That's quite a statement! It certainly emphasizes why the Doctrine of Anatman is regarded by many as a key to understanding the teaching of Buddha. He urges us, as did those before him, to seek liberation through discovering the truth about our real nature. And the first order of business is to proclaim that the traditional path is a false path: There is no Atman; it is just an idea created by the human imagination.

To say that there is no Atman is tantamount to declaring that there is no "soul," no enduring, eternal, spiritual entity, inhabiting the body and giving it life. That's a pretty powerful statement; people have been burned at the stake for less. To say the least, belief in the existence of a soul is widespread and always has been. And it's easy to see why: In the past, how else could one explain such things as consciousness, and memory, and decision making. Don't decisions require a decision maker? To say that the nature of the human brain—that warm three-pound tofulike, blood-soaked sponge—made these things possible would have seemed totally ludicrous before modern times. Even the great Aristotle, one of the finest thinkers of all time, investigated the brain and concluded that its function was simply to cool the blood (not a bad guess, though).

There is a wonderful line in the movie *Total Recall*. A very bewildered Arnold Schwarzenegger asks, "If I'm not me, then who the hell am I?" That question expresses the frustration that one often feels at first in trying to comprehend this whole matter of anatman. You may well be asking the same sort of question: If there is no me, then who am I? If I am being asked to believe that I am deluding myself by believing that I, at the core, am a substanding being, a "soul," then *who* is it that is doing the deluding? And *who* is it that is being deluded? Who is it that decides to walk across the room? Who is it that remembers events from the past and makes plans for the future? Who or what am I really? If I'm not me, then who the hell am I!? Is Buddha saying that I don't *really* exist?

Certainly not. It's not that "you don't exist"; obviously, you do exist. It's that you *as a substanding entity* do not exist. According to this interpretation, you are the "doing" itself, not someone doing-the-doing. Another way of putting it is to say that there is no "you"; there is a "you-ing." Words at best are awkward in trying to capture the meaning of this. One needs to get a feeling for it, as well as an intellectual definition.

Consider the word *whirlpool*. It's a noun, a fixed idea. But when we look closely at it we see that there really is no such *thing* as a whirlpool; it's always a whirlpool-*ing*. In fact, there is really no such thing as a whirlpool that *is whirlpooling*; the whirlpooling *is* the whirlpool. Everything is like that, including you and I. According to this interpretation, all of the "things" of experience are patterns of movement (or should I say pattern-ings). Patternings often give the illusion of substantiality, as for example a wave crossing a wheatfield on a breezy day. It is obvious that the wave is not a *thing* that crosses the field; the wave is really a wave-ing.

This is obvious in such perceptions as a whirlpool, or a circle of flame made by a fast-spinning torch. It's just as true, though perhaps not as immediately obvious, in the case of your own being. The real you is a pattern of energy flowing through the "wheatfield" of time. The concept of self-identity is rooted in the continuity of the movement of the pattern, exactly as we perceive continuity in the wave that the breeze creates in the wheatfield, or the sustained spiral form of wind in a hurricane. A hurricane is an excellent metaphor. It's obvious that a hurricane is really nothing more than a constantly moving, changing pattern of energy, something that the atmosphere is doing. We even give them names! "Andrew turned his fury on south Florida today." (Can there be any doubt that the indigenous people of what we call Florida in ancient times believed that their "Andrews" were hurricanes inhabited by malevolent spirits?)

As mentioned earlier, Buddha is said to have proclaimed, "There is liberation, but no one who is liberated." He might also have said, "There is birth, but no one who is born. There is death, but no one who dies." Buddha wanted to wake us up to the illusory nature of the separate self that we cling to. He probably would have smiled at Descartes' dictum: I think, therefore I am. What a preposterous unquestioned assumption is inherent in that statement! How would Buddha have finished Descartes' declaration? "I think, therefore . . . (therefore what?)" Buddha might have said, "I think, therefore there is thinking."

Still, that unquestioned assumption, the belief that your *idea of self* represents a real substanding being, albeit a spiritual being, that is the real you, doesn't easily roll over and die. This feeling is unquestionably very strong. But, as Buddha would surely point out, it never actually goes beyond feeling, never goes beyond an *idea* of self. Ultimately, it comes down to being only an inference, a mental image, a concept. We never, never directly confront the reality of this being whom we tenaciously assert to be the real me, the thinker of my thoughts, the controller of my actions. What we do experience—and all that we ever experience—is a never-ending succession of discrete mental and sensory events. From these, we *infer* the necessary existence of a substanding me that is the subject of these events. But again, that is only an inference.

In reflecting on this succession of discrete mental and sensory events, Buddha described them collectively as the Five Skandhas, or as it is often put in English, the Five Aggregates. Put simply, the Five Aggregates are such things as sensations, perceptions, feelings, memories, and volitions. They are the ever-fleeting bits and pieces of consciousness, and they are all that we ever know and experience directly:

> [Buddha said that he] found only a conglomeration of the five skandhas or aggregates, material body, feelings, perception, predispositions, and consciousness. At any one moment, according to him, we are but a temporary composition of the five aggregates, and as these change every moment, so does the composition. Therefore all that we are is but a continuous living entity which does not remain the same for any two consecutive moments, but which comes into being and disappears as soon as it arises. Why then should we attach so much importance to this transitory entity, in which there is no permanent self or soul? Once we accept this truth of the nonexistence of a permanent self, when we see that what we call the self is nothing but a stream of perishing physical and psychical phenomena, then we destroy our selfish

desires and self-interests, and instead of suffering from anxieties and disappointments, we will enjoy peace of mind and tranquility. (Ch'en, 44–45)*

The Doctrine of Anatman is not simply a theoretical curiosity, something merely to amuse scholars, but not really concerned with matters of practical importance. The implications of anatman are profoundly important. Perhaps the most important implication of all concerns the matter of the reality of spirit. Some (but definitely not all) maintain that by denying the reality of Atman, Buddha was implicitly denying the fundamental reality of spirit. This is a matter of tremendous significance, both in Buddha's time and in all times. Men and women of virtually all human societies in all times of history have been terribly burdened by their belief in, and fear of, the world of spirits. Typically, the spirit world has been believed to be more real, and much more powerful, than the perceived world of everyday experience.

Buddha, it is argued, by denying the reality of Atman pulled the rug out from under the rationale for belief in spirits. To believe that I am, at the core, a spirit gives credence to the proposition that reality comes in two kinds, matter and spirit. The Brahmin scholars may have limited spiritual reality to the concept of Brahman, but to the masses of the people, as you would expect, spiritual reality meant a vast and dazzling population of gods and demons and departed souls. By sweeping this away like the goblins of a nightmare, Buddha, in his great compassion, sought to set his people free from this tyranny of fear.

An extremely important liberation was involved in this attitude regarding the reality of spirits. The foundation of the caste system was belief in the reality of Atman, and more specifically, belief in reincarnation (samsara). It was accepted belief that a person was born into a given caste because his Atman, due to past karma, had ascended (or descended) to that particular level and no other. For any individual to attempt to defy his destiny was a grievous sin and would generate a devastating burden of negative karma. The rigid hierarchy of the caste system was governed by this dogma. Buddha saw the caste system as a great evil. The elite few took advantage of this belief to suppress and exploit the suffering masses. In Buddha's eyes, there were no caste distinctions. Every man and woman was equally a glorious part of the one seamless whole of humanity. He yearned to liberate his people from this evil. But so long as the hypnotic spell of Atman endured, there would be no hope for change.

According to this interpretation, then, the Doctrine of Anatman denies the reality of a substanding self, and, by implication, denies also the reality of spirit. And there is more. In sweeping away the reality of a spirit world, the Doctrine of Anatman has special significance with regard to the awesome matter of death. Death, the frightening mystery, the great nightmare—what's it all about? What a horrible thought—that I, this infinitely wonderful being, this personal center of the universe, could eventually just stop existing! Reflecting on it leads to a feeling of despair. Buddha himself had felt despair keenly before his awakening. How hopeless and meaningless it all ultimately is if, at some point, I simply go out of existence forever. Shakespeare's *Macbeth* captures the feeling perfectly:

> Life is but a walking shadow, a poor player who struts and frets his hour upon the stage, and then is heard no more. It's a tale told by an idiot, full of sound and fury, signifying nothing. (*Macbeth*, Act 5, Scene 5)

---

*Much the same approach is expressed in the "bundle theory" of contemporary science of the mind: "According to the bundle theory, there is no single and permanent self that persists through time; the self is rather a bundle of constantly changing and psychologically continuous experiences or mental episodes." (Thompson, xi)

The Upanishads stood up to the challenge of death and denied its reality. The real you is Atman, and Atman is Brahman; it never dies. Krishna expresses it succinctly in the *Bhagavad Gita*:

> There has never been a time when you and I and the kings gathered here have not existed, nor will there be a time when we will cease to exist. As the same person inhabits the body through childhood, youth, and old age, so too at the time of death he attains another body. The wise are not deluded by these changes. (*BG*: XII.12,13; p. 62)

The Atman, unfolding through the path of samsara, is reborn over and over until finally achieving perfect reabsorbtion in Brahman. The ego "dies," but that is only a role. Atman, the real you, never dies.

What then, if there really is no Atman? Has our victory over the horror of death been only another dream? Buddha would answer that our fear has no basis; death has no real meaning. There is nothing to die—no *thing* that can come to an end and be annihilated. "There is death, but no *one* who dies." Worry about death is based on attachment to our idea of the substanding self, the "me" that exists for a time and then may be annihilated in death. But to those who have seen through the illusion of the separate self, death is nothing more than the cessation of a particular flowing pattern of energy. The wave across the wheatfield comes to an end, but nothing has "died"; nothing has been destroyed.

Stated more precisely, the pattern of energy "runs out," but nothing has been annihilated the energy is simply transferred into a new form, a new pattern. Consider, for example, the great tsunami that devastated much of coastal South Asia in late 2004. Latent energy in the earth's crust became active in the earthquake, which lasted only a minute or so, just long enough to unleash a massive underwater landslide. This energy was transferred to the surrounding water in the form of a powerful wave. When that wave, the tsunami, reached the shore it died out, but in the process transferred its energy to the onshore environment (with horrific results for many). And so it goes.

The concept of anatman places the unreality of death on a new plane. No one dies, not really, because there is no *one* to die. Death is the cessation of a doing, not the annihilation of a being. It is the running out of a pattern of energy, as when we say the music "died" out.

Thus do we have the Doctrine of Anatman. Again, let me point out that this particular interpretation of Buddha's teaching is speculative. Indeed, there are those who contend that it does not accurately represent his thinking. Many people in this world who call themselves Buddhists do not personally accept the Doctrine of Anatman as explained here. Instead, they consider reincarnation to be real and consequently accept the reality of an individual spirit which is reincarnated. Others, including some who do accept the Doctrine of Anatman, choose to see a real and continuing presence in the succession of generations. Death can be interpreted as a sort of transfer of karmic energy. A personal, individual soul may not migrate from one life to the next, but the great pattern of energy that is any given personal life continues on in one way or another and continues to influence the condition of succeeding lives. There is thus a sense in which "rebirth" is real. (Much more about this later.)

Also, there are those who argue that we do not know enough to have any idea what Buddha's stand would be on this subject. But in the long tradition of Buddhist scholarship, there have always been many who take the position that the Doctrine of Anatman provides the conceptual key to making sense of the teaching of Buddha. Thus, if for no other reason, it is essential that the student of Buddhist philosophy have a clear understanding of this matter of "no self" and its profound implications.

What it comes down to is simply this: Either Buddha was an exponent of traditional Upanishadic philosophy, fundamentally in agreement with its teaching, or he was a revolutionary, a man who parted with the past and struck out on a new path. It all comes down to the character of his awakening. If his awakening was a powerful reaffirmation of what was traditionally regarded to be truth, the life and teaching of Buddha can be seen as a flowering of the Hindu tradition. On the other hand, if the essence of Buddha's awakening is that he saw a whole new meaning in the ultimate truth of self, then his life and teaching can be seen as the beginning of a new path to Liberation.*

Did Buddha affirm Atman or did he deny Atman? Or, is there another possibility? An interpretation that has gained favor in recent times is that he neither affirmed nor denied Atman. Rather, Buddha took the position that it is all completely irrelevant. One could never know Atman even if it were to exist, no more than your eye can see itself. Since Atman would be completely unknowable, even if it were to be real, the only sensible thing for us to do is to ignore the whole subject and get on with our lives.

Wouldn't it be wonderful if Buddha himself could enter the room and sit down among us? What would he say if we could ask him about these things? Very probably he would say nothing at all; he would just smile and remain silent. We are told that this was his customary response to metaphysical questions. (Remember Malunkyaputra?) Buddha was concerned with teaching a way of living that would lead men and women to liberation from suffering. But we are students of the teaching of Buddha, and we seek a meaningful philosophical interpretation of it. The nature of Buddha's awakening is the proper place to begin and that's what we have done. That was the seed from which all else would grow. Let us now turn to that growing.

THE FOUR NOBLE TRUTHS

Let's begin with a riddle: What is it that everyone wants to avoid at all costs—in fact will do virtually anything to avoid—and yet wants to be able to say that he or she has experienced more of it than anyone else? And the answer is—suffering.

There's more than a little truth in that suggestion. Some indeed may wish to claim that they have known suffering in the past, but no one looks forward to the likelihood of suffering in the future. Indeed we will do almost anything to avoid it. If it were not for suffering, life would be paradise. But life, of course, is a mixed bag. There are bound to be good times and bad times. Not all of life is suffering, at least not in the usual sense of the word. Certainly life can have its bitter times. But it can also be sweet. We all know the joy of living sometimes, maybe even most of the time.

Nevertheless, misery and suffering never fail to claim their share. A survey of human society at any time and place reveals the same dreary story of widespread violence and agony. We humans have a long history of exploiting and torturing and slaughtering one another. Suffering, and the threat of it, is a very real fact of life. Not only do we wreak our hatred and violence on one another, we even devastate the natural environment on which we depend. By the time of the present age, human society has managed to totally

---

*Both views are alive and well. The Hindu world eventually made a place for Buddha, declaring him to be one of the incarnations of Vishnu.

disconnect itself from its original harmony within the natural order. Incredible though it may seem, we are actually in danger not only of destroying ourselves, but of taking the entire natural order of life on Earth with us. Something has gone terribly wrong!

Buddha was very sensitive to the problem of human nature. He was passionately aware of the ubiquity of suffering in human life. It was personal suffering that propelled him step by step to his own awakening. And once he realized that liberation was possible, it was the suffering of others that moved Buddha, in a spirit of compassion, to return to the world of everyday life. He would devote his life to trying to help others find their own path to liberation.

Shortly after Buddha's awakening, his five sadhu companions caught up with him and were startled by the change that had come over him. They questioned Buddha's claim to have discovered the truth and challenged him to share it with them. And so, according to the story, the freshly awakened Buddha delivered his first teaching discourse. This great event occurred at a place called the Deer Grove, not far from the town of Sarnath, close by the holy city of Varanasi. To his five companions Buddha laid out what would become the essence of his teaching.

Arya-satya is the Sanskrit term that identifies this foundation piece of Buddha's teaching. It translates literally into English as "noble truth," and since there are four facets to its presentation, it has come to be known as the Four Noble Truths. Perhaps you recognize the Sanskrit word *arya* in there. That was the Aryan's name for themselves, the "noble ones." Hence it is technically accurate to say the Four "Noble" Truths. Some, though, find the word *noble* misleading in modern English, believing that it wrongly implies a kind of aristocratic meaning and prefer to say the Four Great Truths. There is some logic in this, but in the present work, I will stay with the traditional usage, the Four Noble Truths.

In the Four Noble Truths, Buddha succinctly laid out the problem of human life and what can be done about it. He goes right to the heart of the problem: human suffering. Suffering, as everyone ever born knows, is the spoiler of life. And yet, Buddha assures us, suffering is not inevitable; it is not inherent in the nature of life. Physical *pain* may be natural and sometimes inevitable, but the mental pain that we call suffering is definitely not inevitable. Suffering can be overcome and left behind forever. This is the promise of awakening: freedom from suffering.

The First Noble Truth deals with the reality of suffering. It is universal, and it is the essence of the human problem. In the Second Noble Truth, Buddha identifies the cause of suffering. He then goes on in the Third Noble Truth to assure us that release from suffering is possible, that every man and woman is capable of awakening to the truth that brings freedom from suffering. The Fourth Noble Truth lays out the way of life that can lead one to awakening. This way of life is referred to as the Noble Eightfold Path.

The character of the Four Noble Truths reveals why it has been popular through the ages to compare Buddha to a doctor. (There is no evidence, however, that Buddha used this analogy himself.) He has a patient—humanity. The patient is suffering. He examines the patient and determines the nature of the illness and its cause. Then he makes a prognosis; a cure is possible, even though it may not be certain. Finally, he prescribes a course of treatment, which if followed with dedication has a very good chance of resulting in a full recovery. Like a genuinely good and compassionate doctor, Buddha does not depend on drugs; his treatment encourages the working of the patient's own natural healing power. Buddha can't *make* us get well, but the "curative power" of his teaching can certainly help us to heal ourselves.

Maybe it all sounds too simple when reduced to these terse everyday words. But simple it's not. Correct understanding of these concepts calls for much pondering. It is important that we enter into this subject carefully. The Four Noble Truths are separate, but closely related facets of one subject—suffering—and how to overcome it. As this inquiry unfolds, I hope you will see why we first took the time to fully analyze the meaning of anatman. Many believe that understanding the Doctrine of Anatman is the key to understanding the Four Noble Truths.

The First Noble Truth: *Sarvam Duhkha*

Sarvam Duhkha is a Sanskrit term that is generally translated, "All is suffering." This is square one in Buddha's philosophy of life, the recognition of the fact of human suffering. Every culture creates a myth of Paradise. Usually you have to die first, but then, if you're lucky, you can go on to a place of unending peace and joy. But real life, of course, is different, very different. Suffering is a universal reality. Liberation from suffering is the endless quest of all human beings.

Because of this fundamental emphasis on the universality of suffering, Buddhism is sometimes said to be a pessimistic philosophy, as if Buddha had taught that life is *nothing but* suffering and pain. Nothing could be further from the truth. Such an accusation rests on a misunderstanding of Buddha's characterization of suffering. It is an undeniable fact that suffering plays, and always has played, a major role in the lives of human beings. But it's also an obvious fact that not all of life is suffering, not in the usual sense of the word anyway. Life is a mixed bag; it is an interplay of the sweet and the bitter. And, of course, Buddha did not say, "All is suffering"; he didn't speak English. What he said was that all is *duhkha*.*

Sarvam carries the meaning of universality, but *duhkha* (DOO-ka) is not quite so precise. In addition to meaning suffering, duhkha can also imply incompleteness, impermanence, and dissatisfaction. It is the antonym of the Sanskrit word *subkha* which means "happiness" in the sense of joy or being well-satisfied. In his very first discourse, the famous "Turning of the Wheel of Dharma" discourse, Buddha had this to say about the nature of duhkha: "Birth is duhkha; aging is duhkha; sickness is duhkha; dying is duhkha; care, distress, pain, affliction, and despair are duhkha; the nonattainment of what one desires is duhkha."

That statement reveals that Buddha was getting at something far more profound than simply the states of anguish that we customarily call suffering. Duhkha certainly refers to states of terrible pain and grief, but it refers as well to other kinds of experiences, even including ones that we ordinarily call happy. In other words, duhkha is a feature of human consciousness that pervades *all* of our experiences, not simply the painful ones that we want to escape from.

The final statement in the above quote provides the key: "Duhkha (suffering) is the nonattainment of what one desires." There is always a *gap* between the world as we want it to be and the world as it actually is. In our yearning for happiness, we wish for the world to be a certain way—every item on my personal wish list checked off—and then to remain that way. Nothing less than perfect happiness will fully satisfy us, but perfect happiness

---

*Actually, Buddha didn't speak Sanskrit either, so he wouldn't have used the term *duhkha*, but it was close. We don't know for sure what language Buddha spoke, but many scholars believe that it was the Sanskrit derivative, Pali, or something close to it. The Pali word is almost the same as the Sanskrit; we spell it *dukkha*.

must be beyond all that threatens it. This, of course, is impossible in the real world. Even if we were somehow able to arrange all of the things of life exactly as we wanted them, it would still be imperfect because they simply wouldn't stay put for very long. All things are impermanent; all of life is in a constant state of flux. No state of life can be held permanently; life itself is transient. Thus the gap can never be closed. The gap itself is duhkha. When it is manifest as some terrible agony, such as the death of a loved one, duhkha is clearly suffering in the usual sense of the word. But even when it is manifest as a happy experience, such as pleasure in the company of a loved one, it is still duhkha, because rumbling underneath the temporary experience of pleasure is the disquieting knowledge that it *is* temporary; its continuation is always uncertain, and its loss—over which I ultimately have no control—would be devastating. The Buddhologist John Koller puts it nicely:

> But there is a deeper level of suffering, where suffering is equated with change. At this level even the pleasant and joyous moments of life are a form of suffering, for hidden in them is the poison of temporariness. Every moment of love or joy will pass away. Not only does their passing bring suffering, but even the presence of these happy moments is tinged by the sorrow, fear, and anxiety that the underlying awareness of their temporariness produces. Frequently we are successful in pushing this awareness into the deeper recesses of consciousness that we call the subconscious or unconscious. But still it works its way, creating unconscious fears and anxieties that dominate our lives to a much greater extent than most of us realize. (139)

At the deepest level, duhkha is the inescapable awareness that everything is transitory and always in flux. This applies even to the perception of my own being. I yearn for reality—especially my *own* reality—to be permanent and perfect, but the undisguised fact of impermanence stares me in the face. This is duhkha, and in the attempt to flee from it, I try to find happiness (*suhkha*) in myriad distractions. Talking, including thinking, becomes a wonderful form of escape. Music, partying, and television can work well for a while, and of course sex, as well as the now-ubiquitous cell phone. And when all else fails, there are always drugs and alcohol. But ultimately nothing can work perfectly. The unblinking fact of impermanence—especially my *own* impermanence!—swallows even the happiest moments.*

Thus, at root, duhkha permeates all of ego-life. It is a pervasive negative anxiety. It is the irrepressible dissatisfaction that arises from the ever-present gap that exists between the world as it is and the world as we wish it to be. It is a worrisome fear that I will not acquire—or if acquired, will not sustain—what it is that I deem necessary for my happiness. Duhkha is a mental conditioning, and it is present in all of our experiences from the most sorrowful to the most joyful.

The Second Noble Truth: *Trishna*

In its original Sanskrit usage, *trishna* (*tanha* in Pali) meant "thirst." By Buddha's time, though, it had come to have the derived meaning of "desire." Trishna does not mean desire in the everyday sense, such as a desire for a sunny day or even a desire for world peace.

---

*This whole discussion reminds me of a depressing bumper sticker that was popular some years back: "Life sucks . . . . then you die."

More specifically, trishna refers to strong selfish desire. "Craving" would be the best English equivalent. It is craving, selfish craving, that is the cause of suffering. (In some cases, the word *longing* seems to be the best fit.)

Each of us has personal knowledge of suffering; we experience it in our own lives. If this is what Buddha is referring to, how can he possibly speak of eliminating this? Is not suffering an inevitable part of the great duality of nature, like youth and age, winter and summer, night and day—joy and suffering? Is freedom from suffering really possible?

To answer this question, let's briefly examine the way in which the problem develops. As we know all too well by now, the human mind—and presumably *only* the human mind—is very good at creating an idea of itself, the ego, with which it identifies tenaciously. In doing this, I have separated "myself" out from everything else. And once I have fashioned this "myself," this ego, and placed it upon its throne at the center of the universe, I naturally yearn for it to be happy—in fact, to be perfectly happy. Memories of past experiences record that when I wanted something, I was happy (temporarily, at least) if I satisfied that desire. It might be a desire to *get* something, like food or sex, or it might be a desire to *avoid* something, like hunger or loneliness. If satisfying some of my desires makes me partially happy, then isn't it reasonable to conclude that satisfying all of my desires would make me perfectly happy? It seems logical enough: The way to banish suffering from my life is simply to satisfy all of my desires and to do this consistently. Thus do we happiness-seekers embark on the quest of the perfectly "good life" by attempting to satisfy all of the desires of the ego by checking off every item on my "wish list."

There's only one problem: it's impossible to be completely successful in this. I might get close, but never all the way there. In order to be successful, I need control. But it is painfully obvious that to a very large degree, I lack control over that world out there. If I am a reasonably normal human being, I will therefore work hard at fashioning a mini-universe where I *do* have imperial control. (Money is such a universally popular item because it seems to give one a certain amount of that precious control.) But even the most successful effort is doomed to fall far short of perfection. I want to control everything, but I can't even come close.

The real problem, again, is not with ordinary desire, *but*, ordinary desire can grow to become craving. The difference is profound; it's not simply a matter of degree. I might, for example, desire to spend my vacation in Hawaii. That's a simple desire, and I can remain happy even if it is not fulfilled (well, maybe). Craving, on the other hand, guarantees suffering. Craving breeds attachment, which can be defined as a state of mind in which a particular craving has grown so strong that one is convinced that he or she cannot possibly be happy unless that which is desired is also possessed. For example, let's say that I have experienced pleasure in some of the expensive things of life and can easily imagine that a rich lifestyle would make me wonderfully happy all of the time (a common enough example). I desire wealth with which to live this rich lifestyle. Even if I am largely successful in this pursuit, it will never be enough. Desire begets desire and grows to craving. Craving breeds attachment, which takes possession of my will. The desire for more, and the desire for permanence, are doomed to be something less than perfectly satisfied (to say the least). And in that frustration of desire is suffering, duhkha. It may be very great—especially if I should lose my wealth and know the agony of desire to recover it—or it may be relatively less dramatic. But so long as attachment is present, the anguish of unsatisfied craving is inevitable.

There are many species of attachment; attachment to wealth is only one of the most visible. There can also be attachment to youth, for example, or to one's home or job; one can become attached to physical comfort, to drugs, to a loved one, to fame, or even to some object, such as an excellent handwoven Panama hat.* The greatest attachment of all, though, is attachment to oneself—to one's *self*—that is to say, attachment to the much-beloved ego-identity and the consequent horror in the face of the knowledge of the inevitability of death. Whatever the form it takes, attachment guarantees suffering. And selfish desire that grows to craving guarantees that attachment will follow. To the extent that we are successful in satisfying our desires, a state of partial and temporary happiness will result. It will never be perfect though, because this gap of desire can never be perfectly closed.

Desire creates a dislocation in the human mind. On the one hand, we have the world as it is perceived to be—reality the-way-it-is, in other words. On the other hand, we have an imaginary view of the world the-way-it-is-desired-to-be. The desired world and the real world are not the same world; there is a gap between them. The driving power of desire seeks ceaselessly to close this gap. But it can never be done. One can become a control *freak*, but no matter how much money one piles up, no matter how much control one succeeds in acquiring it will never be perfect control. Many things—old age and death, for example—are beyond our power to control. Therefore, so long as desire rules, the gap will persist. And it is in this gap that the problem of human suffering is to be found. To close the gap, I need control. I want to control everything, but I can't even come close. So what happens? What happens can be nicely summed up in the phrase "a sense of pervasive negative anxiety." Let me explain.

It seems that nature loves a state of stasis, a state wherein everything is in balance, harmony, the "balance of nature." Not that everything stays nicely put all the time—far from it. The harmony is regularly upset: earthquakes, volcanoes, tsunamis, wildfires, asteroid impacts, rock slides, you name it. But it isn't long before any of these runs its course and things get back to normal—stasis. Those sliding rocks and asteroids, though, are not conscious; they simply respond naturally to the laws of physics. With conscious beings, things are similar but different. Among conscious beings, upset of stasis generates anxiety. This too is perfectly natural. The feeling of anxiety is unwanted; it stimulates that creature to some sort of action that will hopefully solve the problem, thus ending the anxiety and getting things back to stasis. The meerkats spot a hawk in the sky. That produces anxiety, lots of it, and as a result they scurry about to get the babies, and themselves, into their burrows. Problem solved, end of anxiety; now they can relax again. All of this is perfectly natural and it works fine. However, one species of animal is different. *Homo sapiens* has evolved with all of the standard anxiety equipment, but, to say the least, it has gone terribly awry. Unlike the meerkats, humans face a problem that seemingly can't be resolved. And the reason for this lies in the difference between humans and all other animals: humans form concepts.

Once we have created the concept of the ego-self, and identified with it, a deeply felt sense of insecurity is inevitable. This is at the core of the human problem: a pervasive anxiety, a sense of insecurity. Sometimes it is felt very strongly, sometimes it lurks in the background, but it is always present in human thought. At least, it is always present

*My father used to tell the story, a fable really, about a man who lived in Scotland who seemed to have everything: wealth, good health, a beautiful wife, esteem in his community. But something was wrong; he was a down deep unhappy man. The truth finally came out. It seems that there was a man in a neighboring town who owned a necktie that our wealthy man coveted. But nothing could induce the tie-owner to give it up. Without that necktie, life just could never satisfy.

in the mental states of humans who are held in the grip of ego. The ego perceives certain needs in order to be happy. The gap mentioned above opens up. The ego tries to gain control over its own little universe in order to close that gap and assure that these needs are satisfied. But it is at the mercy of forces that it can't possibly control. Life is threatening. A sense of negative anxiety is the result.

This anxiety breeds fear. The ego yearns for lasting happiness, but happiness is conditional, its continuation is uncertain. Thus the anxiety of insecurity and impermanence expresses itself in the dreadful feeling of fear. It may be very great, as in the fear of death or the loss of a loved one. Or it may be less dramatic, as in the fear of loneliness or failure. It may even be relatively insignificant, as in the fear that the dinner will be overcooked. But the common element throughout is a disquieting anxiety born of the fear that what we want in order to satisfy the ego will not or might not be attained. The gap may never be closed.

Fear—or call it worry if you prefer—is at the heart of suffering. Look at it closely. Examine your own experiences with suffering. There may, on rare occasions, be suffering resulting from some terrible physical torment, but I think you will find that by far the greatest part of the anguish is the mental state of fear, worry. Thinking about that which we fear is what suffering is. (Check it out for yourself.) And the continuing fear, the continuing worry, is that I, this ego-person, will not achieve and preserve what is thought to be necessary for happiness. And beyond that, the most terrifying fear of all, lurking always in the shadows of life, is the nightmarish fear of death. It's a ghastly thought that I, this magnificent being, should eventually, maybe even without any warning, simply cease to exist.

The key point here is that fear, worry, is a form of thought, a creation of the thinking mind. It arises from the deeply felt concern that the cravings of the ego will not be satisfied—that the gap will not be closed. But, the concept of ego is also a product of the thinking mind. My sense of self, and my worry about it, are both but forms of thought! In seeing this, the way to a solution of the problem may reveal itself.

The Third Noble Truth: *Nirvana*

The Third Noble Truth concerns the cessation of suffering, the complete liberation from suffering. Buddha's awakening was the model for such liberation, and the whole point of his teaching was to reveal to others a way of life that could lead to a similar awakening. His term of choice was *nirvana* (*nibbana* in Pali). Nirvana is such a slippery word. But then it would have to be, wouldn't it? By definition, nirvana is inexpressible, ineffable, can't be conceptualized. The renowned Capella Sanskrit Dictionary offers a long list of possible English translations: blown out, extinguished, highest bliss or beatitude, causing extinction of all sense of individuality. The one I like best is "bathing of an elephant." However, they neglect to say whether it applies to the *bather* or the *bathee*.

For our purposes, nirvana means "extinction" or "extinguishment," as in the extinguishing or blowing out of a candle flame or the dying out of a fire. In nirvana, what is to be "blown out" is the last trace of the illusion of the separate self, the lordly ego which holds us in its grip, and thus the "dying out" of the bonfire of craving and anger.

Buddha would not attempt to describe the nature of nirvana. It is a reality that is inexpressible, beyond the power of thought and words. Nirvana cannot be captured by the imagination. Nevertheless, although we cannot describe the nature of nirvana, we can, by way of indirect abstraction, say some meaningful things about the subject. To begin with, we can say that nirvana is awareness of the genuine truth of reality. One thing meant by "truth" is that all illusion of fundamental separateness is overcome, and in its place there is an awareness of the essential oneness of existence, the "unitive state." Nirvana is the final and perfect expression of the unitive state. This can only be apprehended by the awakening of an intuitive wisdom that transcends ordinary human consciousness. Such intuitive wisdom is known as *prajna* (PRAHG-na, not PRAZH-na). The power of *prajna* is latent in everyone, but only when it is awakened is the truth of nirvana revealed.

The full realization of the Buddha-nature is likened in Buddhism to a river returning to the sea. There are many individual rivers, but their separateness is something of an illusion. They are really all expressions of one great system which begins in the sea and is destined ultimately to return to the sea. Perhaps for this reason, many in the West have wrongly assumed that nirvana refers to the extinguishment or annihilation of the person altogether, a sort of melting away into nothingness. This is certainly a false view. Once again, what ceases to exist is attachment to the separate self, born of ignorance that fuels the arising of duhkha.

So long as the grip of the ego-illusion persists, one will necessarily center his or her quest for happiness on satisfying the cravings of the ego. But as we have seen, this will inevitably create a gap that no amount of manipulation can close. The self, though—the sense of a separate enduring self—is an illusion. Buddha saw the truth of this perfectly at the time of his awakening. There is no enduring self—no ego, no ego-player, no Atman—of any kind. Thus there is no *objective self to be* satisfied. The attempt to satisfy the cravings of the ego can never be successful because fundamentally there is no ego-self to be satisfied. It's all a great hoax that we perpetrate on ourselves. Once this illusion is unmasked—which is essentially what nirvana entails—the cravings associated with attachment must necessarily melt away like waking from a dream. The flame of selfish craving is "blown out" with the ego-illusion.

But, if the substanding self does not exist—and is ultimately seen to be illusion— who or what is it then who does this seeing? Who is it who *experiences* nirvana? This is a very good question. It might seem that the concept of nirvana *affirms* the ultimate reality of the individual self. Such a conclusion is a misunderstanding of the Buddhist view. Strictly speaking, nirvana is not an experience; there is indeed no *one* to experience it. Nirvana is simply the final and natural expression of the process that, in its developmental stages, is manifest as what we call individual life. The analogy of the river returning to the sea makes the point very well. The process is not complete—and thus will continue to cycle on—so long as ego-based desire continues to generate unresolved effects.

Referring to the process "continuing to cycle on" brings up a matter that is worth considering briefly at this point. You will sometimes read that nirvana is defined as the cessation of samsara, which is to say, the cycle of rebirth. But—at least according to the Doctrine of Anatman—didn't Buddha deny the reality of Atman? How can there be rebirth if there is no permanent self to be reborn? It all comes down to how you define "rebirth." Unlike Hinduism, Buddhism does indeed deny the reality of a permanent self, but the process of change that we identify with individual life does nonetheless generate karma, both positive and negative, as a result of all volitional acts. The consequences of this karma will be played out over time, affecting the character of successive "rebirths." What is reborn is the *process itself*, not an Atman that endures through time. Life is "reborn" every moment. Each of us is "reborn," in a sense, every morning when we wake up. Shakespeare referred to sleep as a "little death." Looked at another way, one life-process is "reborn" in another through the continuation of the karmic influence one person's life has on another. It is like one candle flame lighting the wick of another. In the case of human beings, desire creates karma, and karma keeps the "wheel of samsara" turning. Only with the end of desire—nirvana, in other words—does the wheel come to a stop, and we can speak of the "cessation of samsara."

Does Buddhism maintain that a genuinely awakened person never experiences suffering? Indeed it does—but, in the sense that "suffering" is equated with duhkha, which is a pervasive, anxiety-generated sense of fear. Physical pain and even grief, for example, are totally natural occurrences and are not *of themselves* examples of duhkha. Pleasure and pain are part of the natural course of things. (Ask any mother.) Grief too is a natural, cathartic response to certain situations. It is only when the mental state of desire-born fear is introduced that they become duhkha.

Buddhism asks us to be accepting of life, not always trying to control it. Every life is an integral part of the grand unfolding of Nature. Nature, as a whole, is what it is, and it is unfolding just fine. Embracing it, loving it, celebrating it—rather than the anxious effort to control it—results in great abiding joy, whatever the ups and downs may be (and there will be downs just as surely as there will be ups). Labelling some things "good" and other things "bad" is a huge mistake. It inevitably results in an unhealthy grasping after the "good" and aversion toward the "bad." Generation and dissolution will go on whether we like it or not; they are simply different aspects of one reality. Why fight it?

Thus to sum up, nirvana is not the extinguishing of personal existence, it is the realization of perfect freedom, perfect unending joy. Nirvana is the "blowing out" of the ego-illusion and hence the "dying out" of desire (craving). With the end of attachment comes the end of fear, the end of suffering. How that is to be achieved is the subject of the Fourth Noble Truth.

The Fourth Noble Truth: *Madhyamarga*

It is of the essence of Buddha's awakening that he saw through the illusory nature of the separated self. He proved that it is possible for human consciousness to see through the illusory reality of the thinking mind and to awaken fully to awareness of the "unitive state"; it is the state of consciousness in which one perceives clearly and directly the essential seamless unity of all being. In the unitive state, one is forever free from the chains of fear. The Buddhist tradition, although denying that any substantial being (such as Brahman) is responsible for the underlying unity, would continue at its heart to hold to the indivisible oneness of reality. This would come to be called the Buddha-nature. (Much more about this in the discussion of *Dharmakaya* in Chapter 11.) To be fully aware of the Buddha-nature is, in fact, to be in the "unitive state." The illusory character of the separate ego is clearly beheld. It is like waking from a dream, a nightmare, and the terrors of the dream melt away in the sun of this higher knowledge. How can one worry about satisfying the needs of an ego that has no real existence?

Buddha freed himself, but how does someone who is not Buddha achieve this? To begin with, it is inherent in the meaning of the Buddha-nature that we are all One; at the deepest level we *are* Buddha. The Buddha-nature is universal. We have only to clear away the cobwebs of ignorance to see what already exists. This is precisely what Shakyamuni did, and he then dedicated all of his vital energy to showing all others how to do it as well.

Siddhartha Gautama Shakyamuni, the Buddha, had already fully explored the two extreme paths—the path of self-indulgence and the path of self-denial—and found them to be dead ends. It is not essential that we repeat that experience; he has done it for us. Buddha proposes instead a path between the extremes, a Middle Path. In Sanskrit, this is known as *madhyamarga*. Walking this path will not lead into a dead end; it will take one all the way to liberation. But it is not an easy path to follow. In the words of Buddha, the Middle Path is likened to "the razor's edge."

To guide the dedicated seeker, Buddha described certain standards of behavior. These came to be known as the Noble Eightfold Path. Taken altogether, the elements of the Noble Eightfold Path constitute a total lifestyle. It is the lifestyle, crafted by Buddha himself, which is designed to safely carry a man or woman across the river from the bank of ignorance to the bank of enlightenment.

In the First Noble Truth, Buddha nailed down the universality of suffering. In the Second Noble Truth, he identified selfish craving as the cause of suffering. Then, in the Third Noble Truth, Buddha affirmed that liberation from suffering is possible. Liberation does not depend on a power outside oneself; it arises from the personal realization of nirvana. Nirvana is rare, and the way to it is difficult, but liberation is, nonetheless, at least potentially available to every man and woman. Buddha's teaching, the Dharma, will show the way. The "Eightfold Path" does not refer to eight successive "steps," so to speak, but rather to the eight fundamental elements of the lifestyle of one who seeks to walk the Middle Way.

Buddha's image of the "razor's edge" refers to the difficulty of the Middle Way between the false ways of self-indulgence and self-denial. And he should know, having devoted many years of his life to a full exploration of both extremes. It is very important to see that the life of self-indulgence can never lead to lasting happiness. It is important for the simple reason that the vast majority of men and women fool themselves into believing that this really will work—if only it's done right. This is clearly the prevailing philosophy of our own age, and probably all other ages too. But Buddha would insist that so long as the quest for happiness is founded on the satisfaction of desires, it is ultimately a hopeless quest.

In like manner, the quest for transcendent happiness through a life of self-denial is also doomed to failure. The very effort to expunge the self by ascetic self-disciplines only increases its psychological strength. Here too the basic problem lies in the cultivation of self-centered desires. In an interesting way, the desire to *destroy* the self is every bit as much an ego-centered desire as the desire to *please* the self. So what's left?

It must be remembered that nirvana does not depend on changing what we fundamentally already are. All that is necessary is for us to get out of our own way, to allow the arising of our own natural endowment of intuitive wisdom, *prajna*. It is *prajna* that sees through the clouds of ignorance and beholds the Buddha-nature. To guide us along the Middle Path to the place where the "eye of *prajna*" may open, Buddha gives us the guidelines of the Noble Eightfold Path.

THE NOBLE EIGHTFOLD PATH

In Sanskrit, it is *arya-astangika-marga*; we know it as the Noble Eightfold Path. Taken altogether, it constitutes the basic elements of the total way of life of one who seeks to follow Buddha's Middle Way to enlightenment. These are not eight separate activities, nor are they eight steps to be followed consecutively. They are the interwoven aspects of the daily life of one who seeks to awaken intuitive wisdom.

Students new to the subject of Buddhism are often surprised, even disappointed, by their first reading of the Noble Eightfold Path. One might expect that Buddha's own core teaching regarding the path to liberation would be highly dramatic and exciting. But in reading over the Noble Eightfold Path—as it is customarily presented—one can't help but wonder what all the fuss is about. As usually presented, the Noble Eightfold Path seems to be surprisingly mundane stuff, more like a list of common platitudes than great spiritual insights. This is due partly to the fact that the elements of the Noble Eightfold Path actually *are* concerned with rather common, down-to-earth behavior. Perfecting these behaviors, though—fully integrating them into one's life—is not common at all. It is also important, and often overlooked, to see these eight elements in the context of the whole. They are the facets of one reality, one total life, which is greater than the sum of its parts. Seeing the Eightfold Path in relation to the larger reality gives meaning to the individual parts.

Let me first present the breakdown of the Noble Eightfold Path in the way that one usually encounters it.* These eight principles are:

1. Right Understanding
2. Right Resolve
3. Right Speech
4. Right Action
5. Right Livelihood
6. Right Effort
7. Right Mindfulness
8. Right Concentration

Perhaps you, too, find it difficult to see how these principles can be the basic elements of a revolutionary lifestyle, one that can transform an ordinary man or woman into an awakened buddha. Once again, please remember that this is not a secret recipe for enlightenment; this is merely a group of words that identify behavioral categories of the lifestyle of a person who is working to transform himself or herself into one who is free from the attachments of ego. The greatness is to be found in the doing, not in the words. Let's look at these eight principles separately.

Right Understanding (often referred to as Right Views) is square one. It means seeing things as they are, understanding reality as it really is. Clearly, Buddha's awakening was not a rational sort of experience, an "understanding" in the usual sense of the word. Rational understanding by itself could never result in awakening; it is, in fact, the rational mind which must be transcended. Nevertheless, it is an appropriate place from which to begin. Right Understanding is square one in the Eightfold Path because, if a person is going to address the problem of human suffering, he or she must address the real problem, not some imaginary problem. Thus, "seeing things as they really are" is what is meant by Right Understanding.

In Buddha's age, as in all ages, human suffering was typically blamed on a host of external causes. It could be due to the working of demons, for example, or to a cruel fate, or even to divine punishment. Buddha would say that efforts to solve the problem based on these views are doomed to failure. Buddha wanted men and women to see—to *understand*—that we ourselves are the cause of the problem. The root cause of suffering (duhkha) originates in our own minds, not somewhere outside of us as we tend to believe. Therefore, the solution to the problem also lies inside of us.

---

*The Sanskrit word for each of these is *samyak* (*samma* in Pali). Translating this as "right" can be misleading because it suggests the duality of right and wrong. An alternative translation is "perfect," in the sense of complete. Various writers prefer this translation, including the well-known Buddhist scholar, Lama Govinda. However, because the word *right* has come to be so widely used and recognized, I will continue this more familiar usage in the present work.

Consider a man who has discovered that he has the dreaded lung disease emphysema. More than anything, he wants to be well again. But how? He may conclude that the emphysema is divine punishment for a lifetime of dishonest business dealings. He decides to confess his sin and give back as much as he can. He even sells his home and gives the money to the poor. Fine, but none of that will cure the emphysema. Not until he understands that the real cause of the disease is his addiction to smoking cigarettes will he have any hope of dealing successfully with the problem.

What it boils down to is this: Buddha wants us to see reality as it really is—that is, as a unified process of constant change, constant flux, in which there simply are no separate, permanent essences of any kind. The mind's yearning to see reality as made up of separate, permanent essences is a self-generated illusion born of ignorance and insecurity. This illusory view of reality—particularly as it applies to the concept of the separate self, the ego—is what gives life to the web of desire, and hence to the inevitable companion of desire, suffering. To see this is to have "right understanding." To see it perfectly is, in fact, to be liberated.

It should be pointed out that the fullness of this understanding is not some sort of prerequisite to living a genuinely Buddhist lifestyle. All of the elements that make up the Eightfold Path are interrelated; they can mature together. But the development of Right Understanding is very fundamental, and that's why it is presented first.

In Sanskrit, the second principle is known as *samyak-samkalpa* (*samma-samkappa* in Pali). *Samkalpa* allows for many different translations in English. Consequently—unlike the other members of the Eightfold Path, for which there is broad agreement in translation—you will encounter a variety of terms that identify this one. In addition to Right Resolve, authors on this subject will use such terms as *resolution, intention, purpose, motive, mental attitude*, and *thought*. What do all of these terms have in common?

We may say that samyak-samkalpa deals with a particular kind of thought or mental attitude, one that could be described as a firm resolution to live in a certain way. Generally, that certain way is described as a sincere renunciation of the mental patterns that, through right understanding, one has come to see as being the underlying source of the problem of suffering. Prime among such negative mental patterns are selfish desire, hatred, and violence. Not only does one resolve to renounce negative mental attitudes, but, of course, to nourish positive ones in their place. A follower of Buddha's teaching resolves that mental attitudes that serve to strengthen the illusion of the separate self will be replaced by mental attitudes that promote growth toward the unitive state, such as compassion, goodwill, and nonviolence.

The all-embracing mental attitude that one seeks to develop can be summed up in the word *ahimsa*. This is one of the most important words in the Sanskrit lexicon. Gandhi loved the term and seemed to feel that it summed up the essence of all virtuous action. "Nonviolence" is the customary English translation of ahimsa, but it is something of a weak choice because ahimsa means far more than merely refraining from violent behavior. Ahimsa is a very positive concept, not a negative one. What should not be *violated* are the rights, the natural rights, of all beings. This is accomplished, not by the negative process of avoidance, but by the very positive effort to love and identify with all other beings. Consequently, ahimsa is compassion in action. Seen in this way, ahimsa identifies the very essence of the spirit of action that Buddha is promoting in the Eightfold Path.

Right Resolve must be understood as a total dedication to the task of changing one's mental attitude. It calls for a kind of rebirth; nothing short of total dedication is sufficient. Following the path of Buddha must be the most important thing in one's life. In fact, if it is truly *right* or *perfect* resolve, one must be willing to completely renounce his or her previous way of living in whatever way is judged to be necessary. Right Resolve is the attitude of a man or woman who is like a starving person who will do *anything* to find food. In this case, the food of life is the Dharma, the teaching of Buddha.

Right Speech simply means applying the principle of ahimsa to all the utterances of the mind, whether these be spoken aloud to another or quietly to oneself (which is what we ordinarily call "thinking"). Unflagging honesty and goodwill are the defining characteristics of Right Speech. Buddha specifically warned his followers to be on guard against the temptation to lie, to speak ill of others, and to engage in idle gossip.

Right Action (often referred to as Right Conduct) is also a matter of applying the principle of ahimsa to what one does. The scope is broader than speech, though, extending out to embrace one's relationships with all other beings. In the way we relate with other beings, we can either break down or build up the existing sense of separation. Action that breaks down the sense of separation, such as behavior that is respectful and compassionate, is in the spirit of ahimsa. Contrary actions, including such obvious examples as stealing, wounding, and killing, are clearly to be renounced. Some things are not quite so obvious. Buddha denounced "immoral sexual activity." This is a subject that probably needs to be defined anew by the men and women of each new age.

Right Action applies not only to a person's dealings with other people and not only to his or her dealings with other sentient beings; it concerns a person's relations to the entire universe of being. Ahimsa means respect and compassion for *all* of the environment. The unity of being is seamless; an enlightened person knows his or her identity with *all* of existence.

Right Livelihood is also an application of the principle of ahimsa. If one is to follow the path of Buddha with total dedication, it's pretty clear that he or she will have to structure the ongoing work of daily life in a way that is in harmony with the spirit of Buddha's teaching, specifically with the Noble Eightfold Path. Any kind of work that is in conflict with the spirit of goodwill toward the environment and other sentient beings will obviously not do at all. Buddha pointedly denounced such professions as trading in weapons, or drugs, or poisons; procuring others for prostitution; or working at a trade that involves the killing of animals. These, of course, are only a few of myriad possible examples, the point being that *any* kind of work that potentially hurts others or deliberately causes suffering is in conflict with the teaching of Buddha and will sidetrack one from the path that leads to liberation.

In Buddha's age, the work that a person did was largely a family matter and was tied up with one's birth and place in society. It was the defining centerpiece of a whole way of life. Clearly, that's not the case in today's world. Therefore, it might make more sense for us to speak of "Right Lifestyle" instead of the narrower term "Right Livelihood." What's really at stake here is a person's entire way of life, which certainly includes one's profession, but involves much more than just that. In an important way, the choices one makes about a home, a neighborhood, even the car one drives are all tied together with the work one does; it's all one package. And, of course, "work" is not necessarily limited to a job. For many, work may mean being a student; for many others, it may mean being a homemaker; for some, it may mean nothing more than being merely an interested observer of the unfolding drama of life. In other words, "livelihood" has a richer meaning within the context of Buddha's teaching if we broaden it to include all of those elements that go into making up a total "lifestyle."

Many of those who have chosen to follow the path of Buddha, especially in the early centuries, gave up everything in order to become Buddhist monks. It was widely believed that only total dedication to the disciplines of the monastic life was sufficient to the challenge of achieving nirvana. Is, therefore, the really "right" livelihood, the "right" lifestyle, that of the Buddhist monk? Not necessarily. For some, it may undoubtedly be the right choice. But clearly, Buddha did not feel that it was essential. If he had, he would have said so. The fact that he denounced certain specific kinds of livelihoods implies that he accepted others as appropriate. Without question, the way of the monk is a powerful lifestyle for one who wishes to live the Dharma, but liberation is not the exclusive prize of the monk—anyone of sincere heart and dedication can make the grade.

The sixth principle is called *samyak-vyayama* in Sanskrit. This is usually translated as Right Effort. Buddha's meaning of Right Effort is not easy to pin down neatly. The Buddhist scholar Walpola Rahula (and others who have followed his lead) explains Right Effort as the will to get rid of existing habits of thought that give rise to evil and unwholesome states of mind and to prevent new ones from forming. Also, it involves developing existing states of mind that are good and wholesome while encouraging new states of mind that will also be good and wholesome. But what does this mean?

Right Effort is associated with the principle of *karma*, a concept that weaves through the evolution of Buddhist thought from the very beginning. Karma is the continuing influence that ethical decisions have on the course of subsequent events. Karma is not the effect itself, as many mistakenly believe; it is the *influence*, or *disposition*, that leads to certain kinds of effects. Karma greatly influences the character of a person's life at any given time. Most simply put, Right Effort refers to the determined will of a man or woman to put an end to the generation of negative karma. This is accomplished by a consistent act of the will which determines that all of one's behavior—in thought, word, and deed—will be motivated by a spirit of selfless compassion. (That, at least, is the ideal.) In this way, a person can more easily escape from the bondage of selfish attachment and thus become receptive to the experience of awakening.

The seventh principle is Right Mindfulness or, as it is sometimes called, Right Attentiveness. This is a wonderful quality of mind, much emphasized in Buddhist teaching. Right Mindfulness concerns cultivation of the habit of mind of being consciously one with the present experience—being aware of thought, feelings, and sensations as they occur—in other words, *being here now*. Living with one's awareness rooted in the present is not as easy as it may seem. Despite the fact that one never exists anywhere other than in the present moment, the typical human mind seems determined to give as little attention to it as possible. We substitute instead a fantasy world of imaginings about the past and future. This thought-based fantasy world, the home and support of the ego-illusion, becomes more real than reality itself, which is to say the continuing reality of the present moment. To locate oneself in the reality of the experience of the present moment, just as it is, is to begin to free oneself from the ignorance of the separate self.

Right Mindfulness is the companion of the final principle, which is nearly always referred to as Right Concentration. It is somewhat baffling (to me, at least) that this has come to be the widely accepted word. The Sanskrit term is *samyak-samadhi*. *Samadhi* refers, not to concentration in the usual sense of the word, but to that meditative state of consciousness wherein one dwells in the unitive state. As there is no word in the English language that carries this meaning, perhaps it would be best simply to say Right Dhyana, or Right Meditation. Nevertheless, it has become customary to refer to the eighth principle as Right Concentration. What is to be concentrated on is growth in the practice of *dhyana* (pronounced rather like dJAH-na). Dhyana very definitely involves what we ordinarily call the practice of meditation. Buddhist teaching identifies four stages in the growth of dhyana, the final one leading to and becoming one with nirvana. Dhyana is thus the culmination of the Eightfold Path; it is the way in which a dedicated Buddhist lifestyle ultimately transcends itself in nirvana.

When one looks over these eight separate principles and views them as a group, the mind seeks to see relationships among them. One traditional way of doing this is to divide the eight principles into three groups known as Mental Discipline, Moral Conduct, and Intuitive Wisdom. Through Mental Discipline—which includes Right Effort, Right Mindfulness, and Right Concentration—one becomes free of bondage to attachments. In Moral Conduct—which includes Right Speech, Right Action, and Right Livelihood—one develops compassion, which has the effect of breaking down the sense of the separate self. And finally, in Intuitive Wisdom—which includes Right Resolve and Right Understanding— one engenders *prajna* (intuitive wisdom) which ultimately issues in nirvana.

There is no one necessary way of interpreting the Eightfold Path. Each person is free to be personally creative in making sense of it. Let me suggest a way of looking at the Noble Eightfold Path in which it is seen not so much as a list of behavioral guidelines, but rather as a simple description of the overall way of life that leads to awakening. It begins and ends in Right Understanding, seeing reality as it really is. Initially, this seeing is of a rational sort—seeing that selfish attachment is the cause of suffering—but ultimately rational understanding will transcend itself in the perfect understanding of *prajna*.

Once one has Right Understanding of the problem, Right Resolve enters the picture. A true follower of Buddha must dedicate himself or herself to walking the path. Buddha's teaching involves a transformation of consciousness; Right Resolve means really *dedicating* oneself to replacing the mental attitude of separation with the mental attitude of compassion.

Understanding the problem and resolving to do something about it are preliminary matters in a way. The actual doing begins in Right Lifestyle, the reconstitution of the elements of one's way of living so that the lifestyle serves rather than hinders the goal of living in harmony with the teaching of Buddha. Right Effort involves putting that chosen lifestyle into execution on an ongoing daily basis. It is the actualization of ahimsa in all that one does—in thought, in word, and in deed. Right Speech and Right Action simply focus on the working of Right Effort in these two major aspects of human behavior.

These six principles in themselves, if lived to the full, describe a rather remarkable person. But the goal is to go beyond this, to work a transformation of consciousness through the enkindling of intuitive wisdom—to break down completely the illusion of the separate self and achieve the unitive state. Meditation is the key to this. Right Mindfulness trains the mind to live in the present reality and prepares the ground for the planting of the seeds of Right Meditation. The practice of meditation leads one through the stages of dhyana to the point where the ripening of intuitive wisdom (*prajna*) "sees reality as it really is." Thus does consciousness become nirvana.

An even more fundamental way of analyzing the Noble Eightfold Path is to boil it down to the two essential qualities that define the character of the Buddhist lifestyle—*prajna* (wisdom) and *karuna* (compassion). These are the two sides of the one coin that is the Dharma, the teaching of Buddha. Ultimately, they amount to one and the same thing, but in the ongoing affairs of daily life, we speak of them separately. Compassion is the outgoing, behavioral side of life. It seeks to "feel with," to be one with all other beings. *Prajna* is the inner side of life. It is the intuitive state of consciousness—influenced by compassion—in which one comes to see the unity of all being. They go together; one nourishes the other. Seen in its most fundamental sense, the Noble Eightfold Path is simply a description of the way of life that is ideally suited to the engendering of wisdom and compassion.

As mentioned earlier, the elucidation of the Four Noble Truths and the Noble Eightfold Path was central to the teaching of the first great organized movement in the history of Buddhism. This movement, most prominently expressed in Theravada, would be largely overshadowed, though not replaced, by another great movement known as Mahayana. We will examine each of these traditions fully. In Mahayana Buddhism, the teaching of the Noble Eightfold Path would become somewhat transformed, though never renounced. The place to begin, though, is at the beginning, and that is what we have done in this chapter. The Four Noble Truths and the Noble Eightfold Path, as presented here, constitute the core of the first great presentation of Buddha's teaching. Let us now turn to a broader consideration of the Theravada tradition from which that teaching emerged.

Study Questions

1. In what way is it true to say that the term *awakening* is itself a metaphor?

2. Why do some feel that the "doctor" analogy makes a good fit with regard to Shakyamuni Buddha? Can you think of any other good analogies?

3. What led Siddhartha to conclude that self-fulfillment cannot be attained through self-indulgence, nor through self-denial? Do you agree?

4. Siddhartha was longing for self-fulfillment. As Buddha, he came to realize (or so it is claimed by some) that self-fulfillment is impossible. Why is this?

5. "These two matters then—impermanency and dependency—are said to be the fundamental character of existence." What does this mean?

6. How might Buddha have reworded Descartes' famous dictum, "I think, therefore I am."

7. Why is the Doctrine of Anatman regarded as being a complete break with the traditional teaching of Hinduism? Do you feel that it is, or can the two be reconciled?

8. "Some maintain that by denying the reality of Atman, Buddha was implicitly denying the fundamental reality of spirit." How so?

9. Do you believe in the reality of spirits? Is the real you a spirit? Think about it. Be able to defend your position, whatever it is, with solid, logical argument.

10. What very important conclusions are implied in the Doctrine of Anatman? What do you think Shakyamuni Buddha would say about all of this?

11. "The Doctrine of Anatman holds that this error [the sense of a separate substanding self] is the root cause of all suffering." What's this all about? Do you agree that the "sense of self" is really the root cause of all suffering?

12. The Four Noble Truths can be said to be four aspects of one underlying thesis. What is that one underlying thesis? How do you personally size up the argument presented in the Four Noble Truths?

13. *Sarvam Duhkha* is usually translated "All is suffering." Why is this an imperfect translation? How do you define this elusive word *duhkha*? What are some examples of how it manifests itself?

14. "Thus does Buddha say that trishna, selfish craving, is the cause of suffering." What does this mean?

15. In your own words, explain the matter of "the gap." How does the concept of "the gap" explain the origin of suffering? How do you feel about this theory?

16. What is nirvana? What happens to a person who experiences nirvana; does he or she just melt away and die? If the "substanding self" does not exist, who or what is it that experiences nirvana? Can you think of a better word to use than *nirvana*?

17. The Noble Eightfold Path includes eight principles. Do you see an underlying theme to these eight?

18. An even more fundamental way of analyzing the Noble Eightfold Path is to boil it down to the two essential qualities that define the character of the Buddhist lifestyle—*prajna* and *karuna*. What do these two words mean, and why do they represent the essential character of the Buddhist lifestyle?

CHAPTER 10

Theravada Buddhism

In 80 B.C.E., virtually all of the leading Buddhist monks and scholars of the time gathered at Anuradhapura, the capital city of the island kingdom of Sri Lanka (formerly known as Ceylon): In addition to nourishing their own practice, they were there for the purpose of formally establishing an authentic body of Buddhist scripture. They worked long at the task, debating issues and weeding out what they believed to be questionable sources. It was their hope that they could come to agreement on a fundamental corpus of documents that faithfully preserved Buddha's teaching, including his teaching regarding the proper organization and discipline of the sangha. After many months of work, the members of this Great Council put their seal of approval on a collection of writings that has come to be known as the *Pali Canon*.

The Pali Canon constitutes the definitive core of Theravada Buddhism. *Theravada* is the name of one, albeit a prominent one, of the schools of Buddhism that took form in India during the centuries following the death of Buddha in the early fifth century B.C.E. In addition to Theravada, several other Buddhist traditions flourished, notably the Sarvastivada. Theravada, however, was not only a leading movement of the time, but was destined to be the only one of the early schools to survive into modern times. Because of this, and the fundamental similarity of the teachings of the early schools, it has become customary to focus on Theravada as the signal representative of Buddhism in the early centuries.

As mentioned earlier, the history of Buddhism is broadly divided between two great traditions, Theravada (also known as Hinayana) and Mahayana. Over time, Mahayana would become the larger and historically more influential movement. Actually, the roots of both Theravada and Mahayana can be traced back to the earliest days, but Theravada preceded Mahayana in becoming a well-defined and organized movement, and for this reason, we shall examine it first. It was the Pali Canon that defined the character of Theravada.

It is known by the name Pali Canon because scholars within the council reproduced all of the agreed-upon works in the written language of Pali. Pali, was not the original spoken language of the common people of Sri Lanka; it had come to the island with invaders from

North India. Pali was a derivative language of Sanskrit, in much the same way that Italian is a derivative of Latin, and it was widely believed by the members of the council that Pali was the language that Buddha himself had spoken.

The Pali Canon is of enormous value to the student of Buddhism. It is where the documentary history of Buddhism really begins. Almost everything before this time is speculation. But with the Pali Canon, the fundamental teachings and practices of Buddhism were written down and preserved for all time. Since they were written in Pali, this language became a sort of quasi-official language of Theravada Buddhism. This creates something of a problem. The original writings of Mahayana were typically in Sanskrit, not Pali. Thus, both Pali and Sanskrit terms will often appear in the study of Buddhism. Usually they are quite similar: *Dharma* in Sanskrit becomes *dhamma* in Pali, for instance, and *nirvana* in Sanskrit becomes *nibbana* in Pali.*

You will notice that 80 B.C.E. is a long time after the death of Shakyamuni Buddha, four hundred years to be precise. How can we be sure that the writings of the Pali Canon do in fact faithfully preserve the teaching of Buddha as Buddha meant this to be understood? We can't, of course. But there is broad consensus among modern scholars that the tradition was carefully preserved in the centuries following Buddha's life and that the scholars at the Anuradhapura council used great care in their research and textual criticism. We can be reasonably confident that the Pali Canon does indeed give us an accurate presentation of Buddha's teaching, true to the intentions of the founder.

But what was happening during those four long centuries between the death of Buddha and the establishment of the Pali Canon? In these centuries, the acorn had grown into a spreading oak, so to speak. To understand the mature character of Theravada, it is helpful to have a general knowledge of its background. Let's pick up the story, as best we can determine it, at the time of Buddha's death and see how the tradition developed. Some of our evidence for these centuries comes from the Pali Canon itself; other parts of the story, such as the reign of the emperor Ashoka, are from research in the broader fields of history and archaeology. We will look more closely at the Pali Canon in its appropriate place in this development.

THE EARLY CENTURIES

During his lifetime, Buddha himself was the strong unifying influence among his followers. But what would happen after he was gone? Would the sangha that he had worked so hard to create be able to preserve itself without him? After all, Buddha had not founded a religious organization with a priesthood and a fixed body of dogma. The followers of Buddha were a diverse lot, and they were spread over a vast area of northern India. Many were so-called forest-dwellers, individuals who pretty much went their own way, like the sadhus of the broader Hindu tradition. Others, the members of the Orders, were collected into communities, but these were widely scattered and had only limited contacts. There was a real danger that things might come apart or at least go off in a multitude of different directions.

---

*Being that Pali, the language of Sri Lanka, was therefore the spoken and written language of Theravada, references in this chapter will use the Pali spelling. Where appropriate, the Sanskrit spelling will be included in parentheses. The two languages are very similar, but this double usage does unfortunately cause some unavoidable confusion.

Aware of these problems, the leaders of the movement came together in council within a year after Buddha's death. This was the First Great Council of Buddhism, and the place they chose was the city of Rajagriha, the capital of the Magadha kingdom, which at that time was the dominant state of North India. Buddha had spent much of his teaching career in that part of India. We are told that five hundred *arhats* (awakened ones) attended the council and that it stayed in session for seven months. They had a twofold purpose: to compile a body of doctrine and to develop a monastic code that would be an authentic expression of the teaching of the master.

The First Council established the tradition on a firm foundation and prevented a kind of doctrinal centrifugal force from developing that would have splintered the movement. But after the passage of a century, the leading Buddhists were back in council again. This Second Great Council met at Vaisali. These early councils had to deal with controversies that threatened to divide the ranks. Among these was one that concerned the fundamental nature of Buddhahood. The argument came down to a simple issue: Was enlightenment something that one *acquired*, or was it *uncovered*? In other words, did one become a buddha by working hard to change oneself fundamentally, or was everyone born a buddha, but simply ignorant of this fact until awakening? It might seem like an unimportant distinction, but it had far-reaching implications. It would seem that the majority view favored *acquired* enlightenment, but the seeds of a permanent division were already in the ground.

Our source of information for these early councils is the Pali Canon, and some have wondered if they ever really occurred. Perhaps they were invented by the creators of the Pali Canon in order to give the impression that their research grew out of a solid tradition. Their own work would thus seem more credible. This is possible, but most agree that if this were the case, the Pali Canon would not have reported the deep doctrinal disagreements at these councils. Almost surely the councils did occur, and reveal to us that the tradition of Buddhism was growing and flourishing in its early centuries and struggling to preserve an integrity of doctrine.

In tracing the evolution of this tradition, we have to remind ourselves that, strictly speaking, there really was no such thing as "Buddhism." This is a subtle point, but one well worth reflecting on. These three little letters, *i-s-m*, effect a profound influence on the meaning of a word. And the use of "ism" is a modern innovation that reflects a modern way of thinking. As soon as we make an "ism" of a word—be it Marxism, feminism, voyeurism, capitalism, or Buddhism—we have mentally organized it into a distinct system of thought. We have put it in a mental box, distinct and different from other mental boxes. There is sometimes value in this, but there is also danger.

When we use the term Buddh-*ism*, we tend to picture a precisely defined movement, with its own internal organization. It would stand beside, and perhaps be in conflict with, other precisely defined movements, such as Jainism or Hinduism. This was surely not the case at all. The followers of Buddha's teaching never encountered the concept of "Buddhism." They were integrally a part of the rich and varied culture of India at that time. Buddha was one of many great leaders who had attracted a following. As the tradition developed, there was much interplay, much give-and-take between the Buddhists and others. It was a very fluid situation that might have lived and flourished for a while and then merged back into the broader culture that it was a part of. It's possible that the modern world might never have heard of Shakyamuni Buddha had it not been for one person. That person, to say the least, played a pivotal role in the development of the Buddhist tradition. His name was Ashoka.

ASHOKA

In addition to being a powerful conqueror, Ashoka was a very interesting personality. After hammering all of North India into a strong empire during the third century B.C.E., he then sought to unify that empire internally on the basis of Buddhist teachings. Under his patronage, Buddhism flourished and began its migration to the world outside India. Ashoka (a-SHOH-ka) was the grandson of the founder of the Mauryan dynasty, Chandragupta Maurya.

At the time of Shakyamuni Buddha, North India was divided into a number of relatively small competing kingdoms. But just beyond the mountains to the west, the process of making big kingdoms out of small ones had produced a huge and powerful neighbor, the Persian Empire. Then, in the fourth century B.C.E., Alexander the Great appeared on the scene. After consolidating all of Greece, he turned on the Persians, totally defeating them in one of history's most spectacular upsets. Alexander then reorganized the Persian Empire as his own. His campaigning in the conquered lands carried his army, in 326 B.C.E., all the way to the fringes of the Indian world. There were some test raids, not really an invasion, in the northwestern part of the subcontinent. Then peace returned temporarily as Alexander focused on consolidating what he had already won.

But would the insatiable Alexander return, intent on devouring all of North India? Who could possibly stop him if he did return? Well, an early death stopped Alexander and caught his whole world by surprise. But the warlords who inherited the pieces of Alexander's empire were no less of a threat. The handwriting was on the wall. It seemed that India was destined to be unified—if not from within, then from without.

It was in this climate that a powerful North Indian king, Chandragupta Maurya, began a successful series of conquests. Only five years after the departure of Alexander, Chandragupta's armies were forcibly annexing the very territories claimed by Alexander. Chandragupta created an empire of great military strength. It included much, if not all, of North India. Feeling the need for a buffer zone to the west, Chandragupta even annexed territory in the region of the Hindu Kush mountains that had technically been part of the Persian Empire. Alexander's successor in the region, Seleucus Nicator, sensing the great power of Chandragupta, chose to make peace instead of war. Chandragupta sent Seleucus five hundred elephants, and Seleucus in return sent one of his daughters to be a wife of Chandragupta (an interesting bargain). Chandragupta created what history calls the Mauryan dynasty. For a while, India would be safe from outside invaders. After a reign of twenty-three years, Chandragupta was succeeded by his son, Bindusara. He also reigned for twenty-three years, during which time India enjoyed relative peace. Bindusara was a consolidator, not a conqueror. He preferred to use his great wealth on things like building up the splendor of the royal court. The story is told that Bindusara, hearing about the fame of Greek philosophy, sought to purchase a Greek philosopher. He was told that their philosophers were not for sale. The most important thing about Bindusara is that he was the father of Ashoka. Ashoka came to the throne in 274 B.C.E. and would reign for twenty-eight years. There is a popular story that Bindusara had sixteen wives and one hundred sons. Ashoka, in order to secure the throne for himself, arranged the slaughter of all ninety-nine of his brothers. There is no historical evidence for this, but some kind of palace civil war is easy to imagine. During his youth, Ashoka apparently had no scruples about being ruthless.

Once he had the crown on his head, Ashoka lost no time in returning to the warpath. During the first part of his reign, Ashoka carried out an incredibly bloody series of campaigns, seeking to complete the total conquest of North India begun by his grandfather.

Much of the warring was in the eastern part of India in the region known as Orissa. Success was finally his; all of the Indian subcontinent except the most southern part was welded into one great empire. But India had paid a terrible price. In Orissa alone, over 100,000 men had been slain, and countless more had been uprooted and driven into slavery. The burden of suffering was enormous.

Then, supposedly, something remarkable happened that truly sets Ashoka apart from the other great empire builders of history. He had a change of heart. We are told that Ashoka, surveying the devastation and suffering that he had caused, was deeply moved by a spirit of remorse. Compassion replaced greed, and he vowed to dedicate the remainder of his years to healing the wounds that he had inflicted. He would transform the empire of gloom into the peaceable kingdom. And he would do this by promoting, in every way possible, the Buddhist way of life. Ashoka had been won over to Buddhism; he had seen the light; and now all of his energy would go into the conquest of the spirit, not of the sword.

Ashoka is sometimes compared to Saint Paul (of the Christian tradition). What Paul did for Jesus, Ashoka did for Buddha. Perhaps a better way of looking at it is Heinrich Zimmer's comparison of Ashoka to the Roman emperor Constantine. Constantine was a practical man. Instead of persecuting the Christians, who had become numerous, he adopted Christianity and made it the official religion of the empire. In this way, he unified the state and gave it a greatly renewed strength. Constantine then, under his own authority, convened a great council of all the Christian bishops at the city of Nicaea, which was close to his own new capital, Constantinople. Apparently, there was much greater advantage in *using* the Christian Church than in opposing it. In like manner, Ashoka called for a great council of Buddhist leaders. It met, under Ashoka's sponsorship, at his capital city, Pataliputra (modern Patna). Like Constantine, Ashoka understood the value of controlling a powerful spiritual organization.

This is not to say that Ashoka's conversion to Buddhsim was not sincere. Perhaps it was. According to the story, Ashoka, feeling deeply distressed as he reflected on the suffering he had caused, summoned to his court a famous and much-respected Buddhist monk. The monk's retreat was a great distance from the court, but he and a few companions obligingly made the long trek on foot. When Ashoka heard about the teaching of Buddha, his heart was won over. He and the entire court were consecrated to the Buddhist way of life, and the same day he set out on a pilgrimage to Lumbini, Buddha's birthplace.

At Lumbini, Ashoka had a memorial stone pillar erected. Inscribed on the pillar were quotes from the Buddhist *sutras* (discourses said to have been delivered by Buddha himself). This seemed like such a good idea that Ashoka repeated it hundreds of times all over the empire. A vast number of these rock pillars were commissioned; thirty-five of them still exist today. They were placed along the roadways and in the towns. On the pillars, and some-times simply on large natural rocks, were inscribed the Imperial Rock Edicts, Buddhist ethical principles which were intended to shape the lives of Ashoka's subjects.

In addition to the Rock Edicts, we are told that Ashoka funded countless Buddhist monasteries, which supported 64,000 monks. He paid for the creation of 80,000 *stupas*, shrines that honored the memory and teaching of Buddha. Ashoka traveled extensively throughout his vast empire, checking personally on the progress of his many programs. He built a first-rate system of roads, with drinking-water wells at regular distances, and along with these a series of comfortable inns for both human travelers and their animals. True to Buddhist teaching, Ashoka insisted on respectful treatment toward all living beings. He outlawed the sport of hunting and the use of animals for sacrifice. He encouraged all to adopt vegetarianism (though he himself came to it gradually). Ashoka was the benefactor of many hospitals, and they were to treat needful animals as well as human patients. In a way, Ashoka is the first important name in veterinary medicine.

So what are we to make of all this? Was Ashoka's conversion to Buddhism really sincere? Or should one adopt the cynical view that Buddhism was merely a convenient device that he could use to consolidate and pacify the empire that he had won by violence? Once there was nothing left to conquer, perhaps it had become expedient to switch horses. Or should I say, change gloves? Replace the iron-gloved fist with one of velvet; seek to pacify his potentially rebellious subjects by giving them peace, an improved standard of living, and above all, an inspiring ethical system that would justify his rule. Seen in this light, Ashoka's conversion to Buddhism could be very convenient indeed.

It can be argued that it wasn't even Buddhism, exclusively, that Ashoka was promoting. Buddha's name does not appear anywhere on the Rock Edicts, at least not on any that have survived. Although the inscriptions are Buddhist in spirit, some have speculated that Ashoka was not promoting Buddhism specifically, but rather a sort of "universal wisdom" distilled from many sources, Buddhism being only one of them. Indeed, Ashoka is quoted as saying, "The faiths of others all deserve to be honored for one reason or another. By honoring them, one exalts one's own faith and at the same time performs a service to the faith of others . . . If a man extols his own faith and disparages another because of devotion to his own and because he wants to glorify it, he seriously injures his own faith."

Perhaps Ashoka—like another great Indian emperor, Akbar, who ruled almost 2,000 years later—was hoping to create a kind of religious and philosophical syncretism, a new philosophy of life that would bring together the best of many religious and philosophical systems. This, drawn from many sources, would be the most powerful tool of all for pacifying and controlling his subjects. Ashoka's own words give us another reason for wondering just how dedicated a Buddhist he had become. He inadvertently tips his hand while praising himself for being available at any time to someone with a problem. He is quoted as saying that he is available, "whether I am dining, or in the ladies' apartments [the harem], or in my bedroom, or in my closet, or in my carriage, or in the palace gardens." This simple description of his lifestyle is hardly that of someone, even a king, who has sincerely dedicated himself to following the Eightfold Path.

Nevertheless, after all is said and done, the weight of evidence seems definitely to fall in favor of the argument that Ashoka did indeed sincerely embrace Buddhism and worked hard to spread it throughout the empire. It's possible that his motives were largely pragmatic at the beginning, but over time, he became more genuinely committed to the Buddhist lifestyle. For one thing, he gradually phased out the serving of meat at court dinners, eventually adopting the strict vegetarian rule of Buddhism. One is not likely to go that far merely for show.

By far the most significant evidence that Ashoka's Buddhism was genuine was his sponsorship of missionary activity. Not only did he promote Buddhism within the empire, but he was responsible for sending Buddhist missionaries to many other parts of the world. Ashoka was broadcasting the seeds of Buddhism, hoping they would fall on fertile ground. It is recorded that Buddhist emissaries from the court of Ashoka traveled all the way to the Mediterranean world, visiting such centers of Hellenistic culture as Alexandria in Egypt and Ephesus in Syria. These seeds did not fall on fertile ground. But closer to home it was a different story. Neighboring Myanmar (formerly known as Burma) received the teaching, and Buddhism began to sink roots there.

Of all the foreign contacts, it was in the island kingdom of Sri Lanka that Ashoka had the greatest success. In fact, it may not be going too far to say that Ashoka's claim to greatness rests on the single act of transplanting Buddhism to Sri Lanka. Considered from the long view of history, all of his other accomplishments fade into insignificance when compared with this one success. Under Ashoka's sponsorship, Buddhism in India flourished and enjoyed a brief golden age. But Buddhism was destined to decline in its homeland. However, outside of India, most notably in Sri Lanka, Buddhism would not decline, but rather would continue to grow and spread. We can thank Ashoka for this.

At the time of Ashoka, the ruler of Sri Lanka was King Tissa. There is a legendary story that Tissa, wanting to be on friendly terms with the superpower to the north, sent a valuable gift to Emperor Ashoka. It was a large, perfectly formed black pearl which had been found in the waters off Sri Lanka. "This is the most perfect thing that *I* know of in the whole world," Tissa is reported to have said. Ashoka graciously accepted the pearl and responded with a gift of his own to Tissa. "This is the most perfect thing that I know of in the whole world, the teaching of Buddha." He sent his own son, Prince Mahinda, to carry the message of Buddhism to Sri Lanka.

King Tissa and the whole court were won over by Mahinda and were consecrated to the Buddhist way. Mahinda lost no time in forming an order of monks and summoned his sister, the Princess Sanghamitta, to come to Sri Lanka and form a women's order. Sanghamitta is said to have brought with her a cutting from the Bodhi Tree, the tree that sheltered Buddha at the time of his awakening. It is claimed to this day that a pipal tree in Anuradhapura is the direct descendant of that cutting. It is also claimed that a relic in the stupa at nearby Kandy is a tooth from the mouth of Buddha himself.

The important thing, of course, is that Buddhism established strong healthy roots in Sri Lanka. It was the first place outside of India proper where this would happen. And a century and a half later, Sri Lanka would be the site of the Great Council that would lay the scriptural foundation of Buddhism. Which brings us back to the Pali Canon. I hope that this diversion into the historical background helps you to better understand the Big Picture. The Pali Canon did not emerge out of thin air; it was the end result of a long line of development, and there were good reasons why Sri Lanka was the place where it happened.

After Ashoka's death in 232 B.C.E., the Mauryan line fell into decline, and so, too, did royal sponsorship of Buddhism. It's a complicated story, and certainly it's not an overstatement to say simply that Buddhism entered into a period of decline. Ultimately, the various schools of Buddhism in India were all but annihilated by the brutal conquests of foreign invaders. Only Theravada and its sister traditions, safely ensconced on the island of Sri Lanka, managed to survive. But that's getting ahead of the story. Long before that depressing end, there were troubles enough for Buddhism in India. It's likely that Buddhists looked upon the time of Ashoka as the good old days. The old Hindu ways were making a strong comeback, challenging Buddhism. And the Buddhists themselves were separating into different schools of teaching, quarreling among themselves. In other words, it was a time of troubles for the Buddhists. Undoubtedly, there was a yearning in the hearts of many to reestablish order and orthodoxy. This was the climate out of which grew the call for the Great Council which would meet at the serenely distant site, Anuradhapura, in Sri Lanka.

THERAVADA BUDDHISM

The Great Council convened in 80 B.C.E., during the reign of King Vattagamani, and, as we know, the outcome of its work was the Pali Canon. The intention was to set the practice of Buddhism on a solid scriptural foundation, one that would permanently provide a reliable link with the life and words of Buddha himself. The result of this was that the council gave a specific character to the tradition of Buddhism in its time. The leading school of this movement, the first great organized movement within Buddhism, is known by the name *Theravada*. (As mentioned earlier, Theravada is often referred to as Hinayana. We will take up this subject in the next chapter.)

Theravada literally means "teachings (doctrine) of the elders," but in more everyday language, we could translate it simply as "the orthodox tradition." The Theravada tradition, given form in the Pali Canon, is spelled out in the scriptural writings that make up the canon. These are divided into three groups which altogether are known as the *tipitaka* (*tripitaka* in Sanskrit), which literally means "three baskets." The various books were written on palm-leaf sheets, which were carefully bound and stored in separate collections, one for each of the three great categories.

The first of these categories is the *suttas* (*sutras* in Sanskrit), sayings and discourses believed to have been handed down directly from the lips of Buddha. The suttas constitute a very extensive collection of writings. Included among the suttas is the well-known *Dhammapada* (*Dharmapadda* in Sanskrit). The second category is the *vinaya*, the rules of organization and everyday life for the members of the sangha. These too were believed, at least essentially, to have come from Buddha. The third "basket" held the *abhidhamma* (*abhidharma* in Sanskrit). The importance of the *abhidhamma* cannot be overstated. It contains the collected wisdom of several centuries of commentary. These were works of a more speculative and philosophical nature that were held in high respect. Such writings were later than Buddha, but were important interpretations of the tradition, and added to its full development.

Through his teaching, Buddha had shown humanity how to liberate itself from suffering. Theravada's reason for being was to preserve and promote that teaching. The goal of Theravada, therefore, was to provide a nourishing context within which any person who wished to make the effort could strive to become an *arhat*—that is, a fully awakened man or woman. The vinaya was the way this was worked out in daily life.

Vinaya, therefore, was the matter of most immediate practical concern. Although all men and women, indeed all living beings, were considered to be within the embrace of the Buddhist way of living, it was clearly the underlying conviction of Theravada that only the person willing to dedicate his or her life totally to following the Middle Way, in other words a Buddhist monk, had any realistic hope of achieving nirvana. The Theravadin monk, free from family entanglements and worldly concerns, was thus able to devote his life to the way of poverty, celibacy, study, and discipline.

Laypeople were not left entirely out of the picture, though. They too could generate karma that would affect their own lives in positive ways. This was done by observing certain moral rules and engaging in devotional practices. Most of all, though, laypeople gained merit by helping the Order through the giving of alms. The laity, therefore, could play a supporting role and would benefit enormously from this in their personal lives, but realistically speaking, only the monk stood a reasonable chance of reaching the farther shore. And the farther shore was attainable only to the monk who lived scrupulously by the rules of vinaya. We must not think of these rules as some kind of moral code handed down from a divine authority. These were very practical, time-tested guidelines derived from the teaching of Buddha and centuries of experience.

Buddha taught that it is ignorance that is at the root of human suffering. Ignorance leads us down the path to the bondage of attachment. The path that leads to freedom from attachment is long and difficult; it is indeed the razor's edge. Only by living every day in perfect

FIGURE 10.1 All young men in Thailand are expected to serve some time as a monastic. (P. Bresnan)

accord with the Dharma, which is to say, living in accord with the ideals of the Eightfold Path, can one hold his balance on the razor's edge and avoid falling into the fatally self-destructive impulses of "lust and hatred and confusion" (which, it is interesting to note, seem very similar to the terrible triad that Krishna introduces in Book Two of the *Bhagavad Gita*, "lust and fear and anger"). Thus, all of the rules of the Buddhist monastic orders were directed at helping each member do the best possible job he or she could in becoming a living expression of the Eightfold Path. The rules of vinaya were designed to keep the traveler on the path.

The essence of the Theravadin rules of vinaya are summed up in the "Five Dedications": no killing; no stealing; no lying; no unlawful sex; and no alcohol. This is not as arbitrary a list as it might at first seem. Though expressed in the negative, this group of dedications pretty well sums up the Theravadin monk's way of life. Although these rules were meant to guide the life of anyone who wished to follow the way of Buddha, it was primarily the monk who was expected to adopt them with dedication. Let's look at each one briefly.

1. No Killing: Buddha taught compassion and respect for all living beings. Life is one; there are no real separations. How could anyone dedicated to living according to the Dharma even think of deliberately taking the life of another living being? For this reason, Buddhists strove to develop a love not only for all men and women, but for all of life, for all of Nature.

Understandably, Theravadin monks lived according to a strictly vegetarian diet. But aren't plants living beings too? Yes, but most would follow the traditional Hindu interpretation and take living beings to mean only "sentient beings," in other words, animals. But there was really no need to *kill* plants anyway. Monks lived on an extremely simple diet. It was possible to take from the plant world what some plants naturally produce to be food, such as fruits and the fleshy part of seeds. The important thing, though, was to show love and respect for all living beings. Like Jain monks, one of the few simple possessions of a Theravadin monk was a small piece of gauze, which he would use to strain liquids before drinking. After all, there might be some tiny living beings in the liquid. (It probably resulted in a longer life for the monk too.)

2. No Stealing: This might seem like a rather odd rule for a Buddhist monk. Can't we take it for granted that a monk will not be a thief? Not necessarily. Stealing can take many forms. Greed is a form of stealing. Even envious thoughts are a kind of mental stealing. Hoarding something may be legitimate from the legal point of view, but from the moral point of view, it's really stealing if someone else is in need. In fact, do I have a right to anything more than I need if someone else is lacking what he or she needs?

Living in accord with the Dharma is living in a spirit of love and compassion for all others. We are all brothers and sisters of one family. This is the love that matters; the love of wealth and material possessions is in direct conflict with it. When one puts the love of possessions before compassion for his suffering fellow man and woman, it ultimately comes down to what is essentially stealing.

The only solution to this dilemma is to simply give up worldly wealth altogether. Become totally poor and thus drop out of the acquisitive game completely. Stealing, in thought and deed, will then have no meaning. Buddhist monks, following the example of Buddha himself, were to own nothing except the absolute basic necessities. And strictly speaking, in most cases these were really "owned" by the monastic order to which the monk belonged. A Buddhist monk was allowed these simple possessions: two robes, a pair of sandals, and a begging bowl. That's all. There were two robes so that one could be worn while the other was being cleaned. In modern times, in countries where the Theravadin tradition continues, one other item has become common, an umbrella (a practical necessity in tropical climes). By reducing his possessions to the absolute basic necessities of life, the monk was totally freed from the prison of acquiring and managing and protecting and worrying about—and lusting for—material possessions. He, or she, could give full time and energy to practicing the Dharma.

3. No Lying: Obviously this involves more than what we ordinarily mean by lying. Lying in speech is preceded by lying in thought, and that's what this precept was directed at. The Buddhist monk was expected to make every effort to be completely truthful, not only in dealings with others, but in dealing with himself as well.

4. No Unlawful Sex: *Unlawful* did not refer to the civil law of the state; it referred to what was understood to be the moral law of Dharma. If the great power of sexual desire was not to hurl one off the path, it must be controlled. For the householder or the parent, this meant one thing. But for the Theravadin monk, it meant simply this: There was no legitimate place whatsoever for sexual thoughts or sexual deeds. So long as one is a monk, one is to be entirely celibate. That, at least, is the ideal.

This is not new. In the Hindu tradition, the person who left his family home and took up the life of yoga was expected to commit himself to *brahmacharya*, which meant total abstinence from sexual behavior in thought and deed. And, of course, celibacy has always played an important part of the religious life in the Western tradition. The reason for this is fairly obvious. It's not necessarily that sex has been seen as evil or corrupting; it's just that if one is to have any hope of reaching the goal of freedom from attachment, sexual desire must be controlled. And all experience shows that, particularly among the young, the only realistic way of controlling sexual desire is to eliminate it from one's life altogether. Not to do so would be like trying daily to thread a needle in the middle of a raging forest fire. You may well be thinking that this expectation is ridiculous. Certainly it's not for everyone. But for those who are willing and able to make the sacrifice, the promised reward will be infinitely great (or so we're told). The incredible energy of the sex drive can thus be channeled into the all-consuming effort to walk the path of Dharma.

5. No Alcohol: As with all of these rules, this simple dictate is really something of a symbolic way of getting at a much larger concern. This is not to say that alcohol was not forbidden; it was strictly forbidden. But it went much further than that. Any intoxicating influence was forbidden. The purpose was not to prevent the monks from partying; it was to help each monk avoid the kinds of powerful enticements that could lure him off the path and ensnare him (or her) in the fatal briar patch of attachment. Freeing oneself from attachments was (and is) the *sine qua non* of the Buddhist way.

And there is a more subtle aspect to this rule as well. The practice of meditation is at the core of the Eightfold Path. A community of Buddhist monks would spend a good part of each day together in meditation. Meditation looks so calm from the outside. But internally, it can sometimes be a ferocious struggle. To really succeed in meditation, one must concentrate tremendous energy into the present act of consciousness. That's why all other forms of energy use are temporarily shut down. Anything that lessens the available energy is to be avoided. Long experience shows that alcohol and drugs, without necessarily being bad things in themselves, will rob the body of energy to some degree, and this will compromise the meditation experience. For this very practical reason, they can have no place in the life of one who loves meditation and is dedicated to exploring its possibilities.

These Five Dedications, taken as a whole, constitute a broad program of guidelines intended to help the monk stay true to the spirit of the Eightfold Path throughout the routine of daily life. Daily life begins early for the Theravadin monk. We can observe that routine today in the daily life of Buddhist monks, particularly in Southeast Asian countries such as Burma (Myanmar) and Thailand, where the underlying influence of Theravada has endured over the centuries.

The monks leave the monastery grounds shortly before dawn and go into the neighboring towns or city to practice mendicancy—that is to say, to beg for food. The word *beg* needs to be explained. In no way does this refer to begging in the sense of panhandling or pleading. It is a highly dignified, almost ritualistic matter. The monks in their saffron robes and carrying their bowls in both hands stride slowly about the dawn-lighted streets of the town. In many places, they will find one or more people waiting for them with a large bowl of food, usually rice. They silently bow to each other, and the layperson will scoop some rice or vegetables into the monk's bowl. They bow again and the monk moves on. This is not seen as charity; it is considered an honor to share one's food with the monks, and it is a way of increasing one's store of positive karma.

After an hour or so, the monks return to the monastery and share the food in common. They eat in silence and consume all of the food or use it in some way; nothing is wasted. Then the utensils are carefully cleaned and put away. In many monasteries, all of the day's food is taken before noon so that the rest of the day can be given completely to the practice of the Dharma. This means that the remainder of the day is given to work, study, teaching, and meditation. Monks will spend several hours of each day in communal meditation. At certain times of the year, this is increased to almost the entire day for several days in a row.

Becoming a Buddhist monk is not necessarily a lifetime commitment, as is generally the case with the monks of the religious orders in the West. In Thailand, for example, the custom has continued down to the present day that every man is expected to spend some part of his life as an active member of a Buddhist monastic order. It may be only six months or it may be for several years. This is commonly done in early adulthood, before entering upon a lifetime career. While serving as a monk, he will follow the rules of the order completely. And it makes no difference what rank in society he comes from; all are treated exactly the same in the order. Even the king of Thailand is expected to do this. It's a wonderful custom. One can't help but wonder how different the world would be if all countries followed this custom.

Theravada is generally referred to as being a religion, but this is stretching the definition of "religion" quite a lot. Indeed there is monasticism, and "monks," and "ordination," but at its core, Theravada has always been a powerful secular movement, based on the very practical teachings of Buddha, which aim solely at helping a person become an *arahant* (*arhat*), a fully awakened man or woman. As such, it is one of the truly great achievements of the human genius.

Theravada Buddhism emerged out of the common beliefs and practices of the early centuries of Buddhism and was given a solid, enduring expression in the Pali Canon. By the time of the Pali Canon, Buddhism had been growing and evolving for four centuries, and its influence had spread far beyond the Indian homeland. Sri Lanka had become a bastion of Theravada Buddhism and became a new fountainhead of missionary activity, particularly in Southeast Asia. As with Buddhism generally, in Theravada the practice of meditation remained the all-important core teaching.

As we have seen, Hinduism was the matrix within which early Buddhism developed. Much of the old was carried over to the new, the most important of which was the practice of meditation. Patanjali's *Yoga Sutras* defined a way of life built around the "Eight Limbs of Yoga" that culminated in the perfection of *samadhi*. In like manner, Buddha defined a way of life, described in the "Noble Eightfold Path," that culminated in *dhyana*. *Samadhi* and *dhyana* are both Sanskrit terms, and both are intimately related to the practice of meditation. In the case of samadhi, liberation is to be had within a state of consciousness in which perfect one-pointed stillness is achieved, and knowledge of one's identity with Atman becomes clear.

Buddha, as we know, became a master of yoga meditation in his quest for knowledge of Atman, but was forced to conclude that it was an impossible quest. He did not, however, reject the practice of meditation itself. His great insight was in seeing that it simply did not go far enough. That, at least, was the conclusion of those who followed Buddha's teaching. Buddha, they maintained, held that the yoga experience of samadhi was indeed a wonderful stillness of consciousness and could, unfortunately, be coaxed into issuing in an illusory sense of knowledge of Atman, but was not, in itself, capable of producing true liberation. For that, one had to see through the illusory nature of the self (Atman, for example) and that required a whole new plane of meditation experience: a plane *grafted to* the existing discipline of yoga meditation.

Based on their understanding of Buddha's teaching, the followers of the Theravada tradition taught that there are two kinds of meditation practice: one leading to samadhi and the other leading to right understanding of the self. These are not in conflict at all; in fact, they complement each other. The first type is called *samatha* meditation in Pali (*samadhi* in Sanskrit). It is basically traditional yoga meditation leading to a state of perfect stillness. In this practice, the meditator focuses consciousness on a single object—for example the act of breathing, or perhaps a visualization exercise. Not until the meditator has achieved a reasonable degree of mastery of samatha meditation is he or she ready to take up the second type of practice. In Pali, it is known as *vippasana* (*vipasyana* in Sanskrit).

The modern world has become acquainted with the word *vippasana*. It is the term that identifies a worldwide movement, emanating from the Southeast Asian nation of Myanmar (aka Burma) that offers training programs in "Insight Meditation." It is, in my opinion, an excellent nonprofit enterprise and has done much to bring awareness of the value of meditation to a very needful world.

Although the foundation of Theravada was codified in the Pali Canon, much development was still to come. The fifth century Theravadan philosopher, Buddhaghosa, did much to clarify the tradition and pull it all together. Buddhaghosa ("voice of Buddha") spent much of his life at the great Mahavihara monastery in Sri Lanka, at which place he composed the very influential *Visuddhimagga*, considered to be one of the great classics of the Buddhist tradition. Basically a long commentary on the Pali Canon, with special emphasis on the *abhidhamma* and the *Sattipattana Sutta*, the *Visuddhimagga* defined the character of vippasana meditation and established the Theravada position that the roots of vippasana reach back to Buddha himself.

Like so many other important figures in the history of Buddhism, Buddhaghosa was not exempt from having extraordinary adventures, at least according to the legends. We are told that the elders at the Mahavihara monastery were a bit unsure at first about this stranger from India. To test him, they asked that he write a commentary on certain of the Pali Canon suttas (sutras). The result was much more than they bargained for: Buddhaghosa wrote out the entire text of the *Visuddhimagga* for them. But, we are told, he had to do this not once but *three* times. It seems that the elder monks were able to persuade the gods to hide the completed first manuscript. Buddhaghosa wrote it all out a second time and then the gods hid the completed manuscript again! It finally worked on the third try.

Buddhaghosa taught that samatha meditation, exclusively, is appropriate for the beginner, whose mind is still chaotic and difficult to focus. But it's not only for the beginner; samatha is an excellent way to begin every meditation session; it promotes a state of clarity and equanimity, the right condition for the practice of vippasana. In samatha meditation, one confronts what Theravada refers to as the "Five Hindrances": desire for sense pleasure, hatred, anxiety, laziness, and doubt. These strong weapons of the ego are especially effective at undermining progress in meditation. In the *Visuddhimagga*, Buddhaghosa offered forty specific object-meditations, some of them dealing with one or another of the five hindrances. For example, if a meditator is bothered by recurring spontaneous sexual fantasies, the teacher might instruct him (or her) to concentrate attention on a visualization of a dead body—a rotting, stinking, ugly dead body. (That should do it!) Not all are that dramatic; the idea is to lessen the grip of a hindrance by focusing on its opposite.

When the meditator is able to enter at will into a state of reasonably tranquil consciousness, he is ready to take up the practice of "Insight" meditation (also known as "Mindfulness Meditation" in modern times). In the context of vippasana, "insight" does not refer to a flash of intuition, but rather to single-minded awareness ("seeing") of whatever is the present nature "in" one's consciousness ("seeing"-"in"; insight). In vippasana meditation, one does not focus on a single object, not at all. Rather, one totally concentrates on *whatever* is happening in consciousness at the present moment, without in any way trying to control or direct it. It is clear, completely nonjudgmental, and in no way engaged with anything that appears. It is bare awareness, nothing else. Anything at all may take form: thoughts, images, sensations, emotions, anything—or perhaps nothing at all. Whatever does take form will soon dissolve, and then something else will take form. Doing this is difficult, especially at first, but it can be mastered. Vippasana meditation holds that this is the right path of meditation, discovered by Buddha himself, and over time will clear away the ignorance of ego-attachment and result in "insight" regarding the true nature of the self.

One of the most important discoveries to be had in vippasana meditation is the way in which attachments and aversions are created. It all has to do with the way we react to certain situations. Buddhaghosa described it as a sequence of events beginning with a given sense experience in a conscious person (for example, a visual event). The visual event becomes a conscious perception—nothing more than root consciousness of some assemblage of color and form. The perception is then recognized (identified) in consciousness (a mountain lion). Recognition evokes an emotion, a "feeling" (fright) and *that* triggers a response (run like hell!—actually, that would be the worst possible reaction in this situation).

Let's imagine instead that the visual event is perceived to be a person, which you then recognize as Jean Jones, the very person who publicly called you a liar only yesterday. A wave of negative emotion flows over you, and you react by: (a) insulting Jean (b) tripping Jean (c) snubbing Jean (d) greeting Jean in a warm and friendly way. And the correct answer is: well, any choice will do; they all make the point. The problem is in the response, the ego-response. A particular kind of response easily becomes a *conditioned* response, a habit. Clearly seeing for yourself how this process unfolds—in a dispassionate, nonengaged way, which is what vippasana meditation allows—is the royal road to successfully disengaging oneself from the conditioning altogether. Theravada holds that this process of emotion and reaction is fundamental to the state of ego-attachment. Some sort of emotional feeling goes with virtually every thought and invariably sparks a reaction. The process is almost never completely neutral. Human beings have the potential ability to insert a moment of reflection between emotion and reaction. Vippasana mediatation helps a lot in the development of this important ability.

The practice of vippasana meditation developed originally in Theravada, but it was destined to play a significant role in Mahayana Buddhism as well. As we shall see further on in this study, vippasana meditation, by various names, will be important in Tiantai Buddhism and from there to Chan and Zen Buddhism. Although itself influenced by Mahayana to some extent, Theravada Buddhism has endured through the ages in Southeast Asia, where it has become one of the major schools of Buddhism in the world today. As recently as 1955, a Great Council of Theravadin scholars was held in Myanmar (Burma). The council remained in session for two years.

Meanwhile, back in North India, the homeland of Buddhism, conditions were changing rather dramatically. As mentioned before, Buddhism in India was not seen as a totally separate and distinct philosophy, a revolutionary alternative to Hinduism. Rather, it was seen as a somewhat radical movement, but still well within the vast umbrella of Hinduism. The teachings of Buddha certainly were in conflict with some of the mainline traditional views of Hinduism, but this was true of many sects. Buddha himself was a Hindu. He saw himself as a reformer, not a rebel, and he had preserved much of the Hindu tradition in his teaching. In this respect, Buddha is understandably compared to Jesus. Jesus was a part of the Jewish culture of his age and is quoted as saying, "I have come not to overthrow the Law, but to fulfill it."

Hinduism is not a religion in the Western sense of the word. There is no precisely defined doctrine in Hinduism, no Hindu pontiff to enforce conformity of belief. One of the great strengths of Hinduism was (and is) its tolerance of differences; its great variety of sects is the natural consequence of this. In its early days, Buddhism in India would undoubtedly have appeared to most observers to be one of the sects of Hinduism, albeit a radical one. Over time, various sects would rise and take form, like the waves of the ocean, and eventually decline and merge back into the sea. There was danger that this would happen to Buddhism in India.

During the time of Ashoka, Buddhism had enjoyed a splendid period of support and expansion. But the growing popularity of Buddhism reversed in the years after Ashoka, and by the time of the Pali Canon, the future of Buddhism in India was in deep trouble. By far the greatest part of the Indian population was poor and lived in the numberless rural villages. They went about life in ways that hadn't changed much over the ages. The traditional ways of Hinduism lived in the villages, then as now. Buddhism had not advanced much into this part of the population. Even though Buddha intended that his teaching be for everyone, in fact most of the Buddhists were from the better-educated upper classes. The hard-working rural people were not much attracted to a philosophy that must have seemed lofty and esoteric to them, that appeared to demand total commitment to a different way of life, and worst of all, turned its back on traditional beliefs and ceremonies. And at this time in history a reinvigorated Hinduism was giving new life to the traditional ways and beliefs.

All of this conspired to invigorate a revolutionary movement within the Buddhist community of India. A growing number of Buddhists were moved to reject the general spirit of Theravada. They were ready and eager to embrace a new interpretation of Buddhism. They called it *Mahayana*, and it would drastically change the character of Buddhism forever.

Study Questions

1. What does it mean to say that in the centuries immediately following Buddha's death, there was no such thing as "Buddhism"?

2. There were several Buddhist councils in the centuries following the death of Shakyamuni Buddha. Why? What was the purpose of these councils? Did they have any lasting effect?

3. Why is Ashoka regarded as a hero in the early history of Buddhism? What did he do for the Buddhists that they couldn't do perfectly well for themselves? Do you believe that he was a sincere Buddhist?

4. Why is it argued that the spread of Buddhism to Sri Lanka was Ashoka's single greatest contribution to the progress of Buddhism?

5. What is the meaning of the word *Theravada*?

6. The writings of the Pali Canon are divided into three major groups, the "three baskets," known as the *tipitaka*. How would you describe each of these three groups?

7. The "Five Dedications" appear to be very negative and limited in scope. Is this really true? Taken as a whole, what do you see as the point of the Five Dedications? Can you imagine yourself following this way of life?

8. What was happening to Theravada Buddhism that opened the way for a revolutionary new movement, ultimately to be known as Mahayana?

9. Distinguish between *samatha* meditation and *vippasana* meditation. Where did Buddhaghosa stand with regard to these two kinds of meditation practice?

10. What does the practice of meditation have to do with the way in which reactions occur?

CHAPTER 11

Mahayana Buddhism

To preserve and spread his teaching, Buddha formed the sangha, and in the centuries following his death, Buddha's legacy grew into a strong, unified tradition. Countless men and women came together in Buddhist communities to help one another along the path that leads to liberation. The tradition that we know as Theravada brought it all together and established a solid orthodoxy based on the scriptural foundation of the Pali Canon.

Theravada Buddhism was not a religious institution; it was a secular movement based on the teaching of Shakyamuni Buddha, within which men and women could devote their lives to the great quest for personal liberation. The sangha was preserved in the form of the monastic order, a community of monks, each one of whom was totally dedicated to becoming an *arahant* (*arhat* in Sanskrit), an enlightened person. It was the commonly shared belief that this great goal could be achieved by one who worked constantly at realizing the aims of the Noble Eightfold Path in his or her daily life. Because the experience of awakening was all that really mattered in the long run, it followed that only the select few who joined the orders and gave their lives to the discipline of the vinaya were really Buddhists in a truly meaningful sense of the word.

The doctrinal system that came to be known as Theravada represented the views of the majority in the early centuries of Buddhism. However, from the earliest times there had been a minority—an "opposition party," so to speak—whose views did not neatly conform with the majority. These were the Buddhists of a more spiritual, more mystical frame of mind. We may speculate that this minority group wished to see Buddhism more influenced by traditional Hindu beliefs and practices. The writings of the Pali Canon do not give us much information about these "dissenters," but there are allusions to their existence in references to protesting groups who "walked out" of various councils. This dissenting minority, in existence from the very beginning, provided the background out of which the Mahayana movement would grow. Although there were occasional clashes, it would appear that the two groups generally coexisted in harmony during the early centuries:

It is clear that Mahayana developed in organic connection with the whole of Buddhism, that is, that it originated directly from the early schools of

Buddhism as a result of internal division. We know from the sources that the followers of both vehicles lived peacefully for a long time side by side in the same monasteries, observing the same Vinaya discipline. (Dumoulin, 28)

The nascent Mahayana movement began to gather momentum in the century following the great council that produced the Pali Canon. Very likely, it was a response to it. Although all of northern India was affected by the stirrings of Mahayana, it was in the northwestern part of the subcontinent that the greatest activity was focused. In a way, it is true to say that the real homeland of Mahayana Buddhism was the upper Indus Valley in what is today parts of Kashmir and northern Pakistan. This is a hilly region rich in fertile valleys. A look at the map will show that the area, called Gandhara in ancient times, is tucked into a large bulge in the great mountain systems of the north. Alexander the Great had claimed Gandhara for a time, and, as a result, it became something of a distant outpost of Hellenistic culture. Greek artistic styles became established in Gandhara, and from there would spread their influence as far as China. Gandhara was a crossroads of trade routes, and hence a place where foreign ideas and religions could mix freely. It was in this climate that Mahayana, the great alternative to Theravada, would begin to mature into an entirely new tradition in Buddhism. Not all Buddhists of India were part of the Mahayana reform movement; many remained true to the traditional way. But the Mahayana was going to carry the day.

What initially fueled the rise of Mahayana was a deep dissatisfaction on the part of some with the traditional interpretation of Buddha's teaching by the dominant majority, the Theravadins. An attitude was developing among some Buddhists that the Theravada tradition had become too conservative, too rule-bound, too elitist, and too narrow in scope. It seemed that the only genuine Buddhists were the members of the monastic orders; the laity played hardly any part at all. Buddha, though, had directed his teaching at everyone, not just a select few. And within the orders, which seemed to attract members almost exclusively from the upper classes, each monk directed virtually all of his attention to his own personal goal of achieving nirvana. Theravada had become far too self-centered. How ironic this was, considering that the whole thrust of Buddha's teaching had been directed at overcoming the prison of self. Yes, it seemed to a growing number that the Theravadins had become too concerned with discipline and had lost sight of Buddha's real concern, the nurturing of compassion.

Mahayana, however, was far from being *only* an opposition party, only a protest movement. It was a positive revolutionary movement in its own right. Mahayana would reinterpret the meaning of the Dharma. During the first century C.E., the movement, somewhat diffuse up to this time, began to coalesce around a powerful new body of writings known as the *Prajnaparamita* (Prahg-na-pahr-a-MEE-ta). The *Prajnaparamita*, actually a collection of about forty separate works, was declared to be a sutra by its votaries. In essence, the *Prajnaparamita* purports to be a series of discourses between Shakyamuni Buddha and some of his closest disciples. The philosophical foundation of Mahayana is laid out in these discourses. In fact, the name *Mahayana* itself is derived from the *Prajnaparamita*. Subhuti, one of Buddha's disciples, asks Buddha, "O Lord Buddha, what is this Great Vehicle, the Mahayana? What is its point of departure? Its destination? Through what realm does it move? How can one who travels in the Great Vehicle be recognized? Who is the person courageous enough to travel this way?" Buddha begins his reply by saying that "Mahayana is synonymous with immeasurability." He then expands on this for the remainder of the dialogue, spelling out what the adherents of Mahayana regard to be a new and deeper interpretation of the meaning of his teaching.

Mahayana is a Sanskrit word; literally it means "great vehicle," as noted above. One popular interpretation of "great vehicle" is to understand it to refer to the kind of vehicle that serves as a ferryboat, in this case a "large ferryboat." Buddha compared his teaching to a raft (a *yana*) that could ferry a person across the river of ignorance. It was an apt metaphor to use. India is a land of many rivers and few bridges. The traveler, especially in ancient times, often needed the services of the ferryman. Ordinarily, ferryboats are small, being just a simple raft or dugout that carries only a few people. Such a craft was known as a *hina-yana*, a small ferryboat. The adherents of this new wave of Buddhism, the self-styled "Mahayana," labeled the traditional school of Theravada, the "Hinayana." They themselves would pilot the large ferryboat, the "maha-yana," that had room enough for everyone, while the conservative Theravadins would make do with the little ferryboat that only had room for an elite few. It was logical to use symbols that the people were familiar with. If the movement were occurring today, we might instead refer to minivans and city buses.

There is undoubtedly some appeal in this metaphorical understanding of the words *Mahayana* and *Hinayana*, seeing them as referring to larger and smaller vessels. The Hinayana only has room for the elite few, while there is room on board the Mahayana for the whole population. Perhaps, though, it is more accurate to understand Mahayana as simply meaning "greater vehicle," in the sense that the doctrine and teaching of Mahayana constitute a greater vehicle than what came before for expressing the profound and true meaning of the Dharma. In this sense, Hinayana is simply a lesser, and therefore inferior, vehicle (at least in the opinion of the Mahayanists).

> The focus of the change to the Mahayana within India can best be represented as a modification of the ideal of enlightenment. Those Buddhists who did not go along with the new Mahayana changes were labeled the Hinayana or Smaller Vehicle by their opponents. It was a pejorative term and was intended to suggest that the ideals of this more conservative group were more confined and more limited. The Mahayanists asserted that the others had become too easily satisfied with merely becoming arhats, persons whose whole goal was defined in terms of their own private and individual enlightenment. They charged that the Hinayanists were relatively unconcerned about the fate of others and what would today be called a "social conscience." The Mahayanists claimed that any enlightenment or nirvana enjoyed by an individual in and by himself would not really be enjoyable at all. In their more acerbic comments, they castigated the Hinayanist group as being, at bottom, self-absorbed and even selfish. How, they asked, can the adherents of a philosophy that states that there is no permanent "self" allow themselves to become so concerned only for their own spiritual well-being? (LaFleur, 23)

The Theravadins—insensitively referred to as Hinayanists by the self-styled Mahayanists—complained that the *Prajnaparamita* and other so-called sutras that soon followed it were not sutras at all. A sutra, by definition, is a record of the words of Buddha himself; the teaching of the master directly from his own lips. The Pali Canon, they would argue, was a careful compilation of sutras that had been gathered together shortly after the death of Buddha and lovingly preserved over the centuries. But these Mahayana "sutras" were brand-new productions. How could they be the authentic words of Buddha? They were, in fact, nothing more than the heretical imaginings of contemporary authors. Now it was the turn for outraged Theravadins to walk out of meetings in which Mahayanists insisted on recitation from the new works.

Mahayanists responded to attacks on the veracity of their sutras by arguing that the *Prajnaparamita* and other sutras were not new at all. They had been passed directly from Buddha to some specially chosen disciples, but deliberately not committed to writing. Instead, they had been most carefully preserved in memory and passed along from generation to generation in the grand oral tradition. The reason for this, the Mahayanists argued, was that they preserved the deep and esoteric heart of Buddha's teaching. Most of the world simply was not ready to receive this teaching at the time of Buddha's death. Hence, sutras of an important but less profound nature were promulgated first. This "lesser vehicle," the Hinayana, was what one found in the Pali Canon. But now, the Mahayanists would say, after five centuries of evolution, the Buddhist world was ready to hear the deeper truth; it was time to commit the secret teaching to writing and make this "greater vehicle," the Mahayana, available to all.

One may be forgiven for being a little cynical about this Mahayana explanation. It sounds like an all-too-convenient way of getting around the Theravadin objection. The majority of modern scholars agree that the Mahayana sutras were in fact composed by anonymous authors at the time of their appearance in the first and second centuries C.E. Nevertheless, there is probably more than a grain of truth in the Mahayana argument. It was not all that unusual in premodern times for scriptural works to be memorized and preserved orally. After all, the vedas and the Upanishads were passed along for centuries in the oral tradition before being written down. Many of the themes that appear in the Mahayana sutras very likely were passed along orally, a sort of secret tradition, before being finally incorporated in the *Prajnaparamita* and other sutras. But, on the whole, these compositions, however faithful they may have been to the spirit of Buddha's teaching, were essentially the product of the genius of the time when they were written.

The Mahayana sutras made their appearance in the first and, at the latest, the second century C.E. All originated in India and were written in Sanskrit. Some, however, have survived only in Chinese and Japanese translations. Taken altogether, they constitute a Mahayana canon that established the spiritual and philosophical foundation of the new tradition. The Mahayana sutras build upon and overshadow—but do not replace—the Theravada sutras of the Pali Canon. Let me identify by name the basic Mahayana sutras, and then discuss some of the general features of Mahayana which derive from the influence of these sutras.

First, in time and importance, is the great *Prajnaparamita*. *Prajna* refers to "intuitive wisdom," the wisdom that sees into the deepest truth of reality. *Paramita* literally means "attaining the farther shore." The derived meaning is "perfected," "transcendent," or "supreme." Put them together and *Prajnaparamita* becomes "the Sutra of Transcendent Wisdom." As mentioned earlier, the *Prajnaparamita* purports to be a series of discourses between Buddha and certain of his disciples. These conversations are not exercises in discursive reasoning, such as we find in the dialogues of Plato. Rather, they are discussions that provoke intuitive responses. The *Prajnaparamita* is revelation, not exposition.

With all the later additions included, the *Prajnaparamita* became vast in size, running to more than 100,000 verses. Reference to the *Prajnaparamita*, though, generally means only what many consider to be the oldest part, known simply as *The Prajnaparamita in 8,000 Verses*. Two sections that are excerpted from the *Prajnaparamita* are known as sutras in their own right and have been immensely popular over the ages. These are the *Diamond Sutra* and the very short *Heart Sutra*.

Probably second in the order of time was the *Avatamsaka Sutra* (short for *Buddhavatamsaka Sutra*, which translates as the "Garland of Buddha Sutra"). This sutra, focusing on the oneness of all being, was traditionally believed to have been delivered by Buddha only a short time after his awakening and dealt with matters too deep for most of his followers to understand at the time.

Another sutra of major importance is the *Lankavatara Sutra*. The dialogue of this sutra takes place at an imagined assembly of notables convened by the king of Sri Lanka (as the name implies). In response to various questions, Buddha enunciates the doctrine of *Tathagata-garbha*, which is to say that the Buddha-nature dwells in all sentient beings. It remains only to be uncovered. This is accomplished purely by removing the ignorance that hides its realization. As we shall see, this highly psychological sutra, along with the *Diamond Sutra*, would later have a profound influence on the development of Chan and Zen Buddhism.

And finally, the much-loved *Saddharma-pundarika Sutra*, which is popularly known as the *Lotus Sutra* (or to be more precise, the "*Sutra of the Lotus of the Good Dharma*"). Among the last of the sutras to be written down, the *Lotus Sutra* is something of a summary or compendium of the essential teachings of Mahayana Buddhism. The setting here is also an assembly of notables, both worldly and supernatural, gathered at Vulture Peak, a highly dramatic setting at Mount Gridhrakuta near the Indian city of Rajagriha. The *Lotus Sutra* would exert a powerful influence over the development of Buddhism in China and Japan. Among its many notable features, the *Lotus Sutra* emphasizes the dignity of woman and taught that enlightenment is open to women as well as men.

These four sutras—the *Prajnaparamita*, the *Avatamsaka*, the *Lankavatara*, and the *Saddharma-pundarika* (six if we include the *Diamond Sutra* and the *Heart Sutra* as sutras in their own right)—constitute the core group of Mahayana scripture. There are many other important writings that are peripheral to these; two in particular deserve to be mentioned here—the *Vimalakirti Sutra* and the *Sukhavati-vyuha Sutra*. These two sutras deal extensively with the way in which a layperson can achieve enlightenment, a subject almost totally ignored in the Theravada tradition. *Vimalakirti* was, in fact, the name of a householder, not a monk. The sutra that bears his name lays out a picture of the ideal way of life of a layperson who is devoted to following the path of Buddha and confirms very clearly that one does not have to be a monk to seek enlightenment. The *Sukhavati Sutra* is the cornerstone of Pure Land Buddhism, which is by far the most "religious" of all Buddhist sects. The *Sukhavati Sutra* proclaims the way in which all men and women, whatever their status, can achieve Buddhahood. Over the ages, Pure Land Buddhism has been enormously popular with the population at large in Buddhist countries. In modern times, it is fair to say that the great majority of people who call themselves Buddhists are members of the Pure Land sect. We will have more to say about this interesting school of Buddhism in Chapter 15.

The sutras provided the spiritual and philosophical underpinning of Mahayana. From this base, the evolution of Mahayana radiated in many directions. Different though the various sects might become over time, all of the schools that make up the Mahayana share certain essential elements. In the remainder of this chapter, we will examine six of these most fundamental aspects.

1. Diversity and Religious Elements in Mahayana
2. The Nature of Buddha
3. Madhyamaka
4. Yogacara
5. The Bodhisattva
6. Artistic Expression in Early Mahayana

DIVERSITY AND RELIGIOUS ELEMENTS IN MAHAYANA

Diversity is the most immediately apparent feature of Mahayana. Unlike Theravada, in which there was general uniformity of doctrine and practice, Mahayana opened its arms to embrace a huge variety of *upaya* (ways of practicing the Dharma). In Mahayana, there is something for everyone. Included within this new openness was the appearance of decidedly religious practices. It is in the development of Mahayana that Buddhism begins to take on a distinctly religious character.

Not only were elements of Hinduism generously incorporated into Mahayana, but also its development was influenced by systems of thought that were completely non-Indian. This was especially true in the Gandhara region, where so much of the early growth occurred. The result of this was the emergence of a broad spectrum of "schools," each proclaiming its own version of Buddhist doctrine. On the one hand, we have Theravada: conservative, traditional, essentially secular; and on the other hand, we have Mahayana: a new and revolutionary movement proliferating into a broad variety of sects. But all of these identified themselves as Buddhists. Something very fundamental was holding it all together.

The popular British Buddhologist Christmas Humphreys gives us the image of a wheel to indicate the fundamental relationships within the family of Buddhism. Theravada is the hub of the wheel—solid, essential, at the core. Mahayana is represented by the many spokes of the wheel, a full circle of variations, but all having their source in the hub. The essential teaching of Buddha was common to both Theravada and Mahayana. But the interpretation and application of Buddha's teaching allowed for some very dramatic differences. The scriptural writings of Theravada may have remained at the hub of the wheel—they were never renounced by Mahayana—but their importance was eclipsed by the new Mahayana sutras.

In the history of the growth of Mahayana, it is an obvious fact that what we ordinarily think of as "religious" elements—that is to say, devotional practices—came to have an important place in the total picture; devotional practices became one of the essential elements of Mahayana Buddhism. Undoubtedly, this is largely the result of assimilating into the Buddhist family great masses of people from the humbler classes of society to whom the relatively nonreligious character of traditional Theravada must have seemed barren and uninspiring. In its original Indian homeland, Mahayana Buddhism was responding to a resurgent Hinduism; it had to meet this challenge on its own ground. To a certain extent, the Dharma was reinterpreted in terms of the myths and religious customs of the common people.

Among the common people of the Hindu world, the practice of Bhakti Yoga—so much celebrated in the *Bhagavad Gita*—had become an important part of daily life.

Bhakti focuses on devotion to a loving and compassionate deity, with all the attendant *puja* (forms of service) and paraphernalia. Flowers, incense, bells, gongs, statues, mandalas, chants, processions, pilgrimages, prostrations, icons, etc., etc.—all of this was part of the daily fare of Bhakti. Bhakti was going to have an enormous influence on the development of Mahayana. And in addition to Hindu influences, Mahayana was being shaped by traditional beliefs and practices of non-Indian cultures as well. It seems that in the numerous Buddhist cults that germinated, everything could find a place somewhere.

And why not? Was not the teaching of Buddha supposed to be open to all? Had not Buddha compared the human family to a lotus pond? Everyone could benefit from the Buddhist way of life, but each person would have to plug into that way of life at his own level. If, for some, this meant belief in deities and the trappings of religion, so be it:

> During this prolonged period of expansion, Buddhism infiltrated many cultures and absorbed unfamiliar influences. It should, therefore, come as no surprise to encounter, in the permissive, far-wandering Mahayana, types of worship that seem unrelated to early Buddhist teaching. In various sects and schools of the Mahayana, one finds proliferation not only of Buddhas and Bodhisattvas of varying significance and with different attributes but also complicated pantheons of such minor deities as Guardians of the Four Directions, Serpent Kings, wrathful demons, assorted nature spirits and so on, each "manifestation" accompanied by the inevitable altars, rosaries, gongs, bells, incense, prayer wheels, mantras, thankas, mudras, and asanas representative of the ritual-loving and mythmaking proclivities of mankind and the resultant art of religious expression. (Ross, 49)

THE NATURE OF BUDDHA

The most striking of the religious features to be found in Mahayana is the deification of Shakyamuni Buddha himself. Whereas in the Theravada tradition (that is, in the *abhidhamma* tradition generally) Shakyamuni was a man of flesh and blood, with his feet very much on the ground, in the Mahayana Sutras he is transmuted into a godlike being whose feet are far removed from the dusty earth. The superhuman characterization of Buddha, which was to run through all of the sutras, is established at the very beginning of the *Prajnaparamita*:

> The Lord dwelt on the Vulture Peak at Rajagriha with a large gathering. He sat down cross-legged on His lion throne and entered the King Samadhi . . . His whole body became radiant. The thousand-spoked wheels on the soles of his feet shone forth sixty hundred thousand trillions of billions of light rays, as did every other part of his superhuman body. These light rays illumined and lit up our vast billion-world universe . . . And all the beings lit up and illuminated by these dazzling light rays became focused upon the unexcelled, true and perfect enlightenment. (Hixon, ix)

Further on in the *Prajnaparamita*, in another typical scene, 6,000 monks kneel reverently before Buddha. Bowing their heads, the monks begin to bring their hands together at the level of the heart. At that moment, Buddha miraculously causes their hands to fill with flowers. "With surprise and jubilation, the practitioners reverently scatter the brilliant and fragrant blossoms over the golden body of the Awakened One." Buddha (of the golden body, no less) responds with a smile, "variously colored rays of light sparkle like rainbows from the parted Buddha lips and pearl-like Buddha teeth, assuming delicate and harmonious shades of blue, yellow, red, white, crimson, crystal, silver and gold . . . This smile of light ascends to the highest paradise realm, returns again across vast distances to the shining body of the Buddha, swirls thrice around it, and vanishes, just as the beautifully formed lips meet once more." (Hixon, 187)

As if that's not impressive enough, the scene becomes even more awesome in the *Lotus Sutra*. Here the vast assembly includes every kind of sentient being, not only monks and sages and kings but even dragons and gods. After the enthroned Buddha had delivered a discourse, the multitude was "filled with joy and, pressing their palms together, gazed at Buddha with a single mind." Buddha then, "emitted a ray of light from the tuft of white hair between his eyebrows, one of his characteristic features, lighting up eighteen thousand worlds in the eastern direction. There was no place that the light did not penetrate, reaching downward as far as the Avichi hell and upward to the Akanishtha heaven." And going beyond this, he later, "extended his long broad tongue upward till it reached the Brahma heaven, and from all his pores he emitted immeasurable, countless beams of light that illuminated all the worlds in the ten directions." (Watson, 6, 273)

We could go on and on with examples like this. The Mahayana sutras are full of such marvelous doings. Over and over, Buddha is portrayed as a being of godlike power and majesty, pretty far removed from the humble daily life of the man who trekked the dusty roads of North India preaching to crowds of very ordinary people.

So what's going on here? Were the authors of the Mahayana sutras in fact attempting to deify Buddha? Did they really intend that their listeners imagine Shakyamuni Buddha to be a divine being, and that the scenes pictured in the sutras were literally accurate descriptions? Not exactly. There's no doubt that the literary style of the sutras involves a good deal of poetic license. The depiction of Buddha in heavenly splendor was deliberate and unrestrained hyperbole. But there was a purpose to all of this. Each of the sutras was a vehicle for the presentation of a new interpretation of the teaching of Buddha. And the transcendent character of the setting—even if not meant to be taken as a factually accurate description—was a very important element in the literary presentation of that new interpretation. These mind-boggling descriptions were intended to overwhelm the imagination and jolt us out of our customary ways of thinking. This is most pointedly true with regard to the new—that is, the Mahayana—understanding of the nature of Buddha.

This point needs to be stressed. It is quite different from what became common in the Western world. Traditionally, in the West, what has been presented as religious truth has tended to be very dogmatic. Buddhism, on the other hand, is not dogmatic at all. Each person, each "Buddhist" is ultimately free to interpret the Dharma in his or her own way. In this regard, there are two possible paths: the literal and the metaphorical. There have always been many, and still are, who have chosen the path of literal interpretation, but there have also been many who have preferred the path of metaphor.

The literalist, as the name implies, accepts things exactly as presented. If the sutra says that Buddha "emitted a ray of light from the tuft of white hair between his eyebrows," then that's exactly what happened, literally. The metaphorical path, however, allows for a very different interpretation. The hyperbole of the description in the sutra may be seen as a dramatic metaphor concerning the character of Buddha's perfect enlightenment. The tuft-of-white-hair business is seen as a dramatic way of emphasizing the point but certainly not meant to be understood as meaning that Buddha *really did* emit a "ray of light from a tuft of white hair between his eyebrows." The metaphorical interpretation frees one from the weight of dogma and makes possible a happy marriage between religion and philosophy, a hallmark of Eastern spiritual traditions.

The Buddha of the Theravada tradition was very much a flesh-and-blood human being. He was a compassionate and much-honored teacher of mankind. The Buddha of the Mahayana tradition remains the human teacher, but he comes to represent much, much more as well. The nub of the difference comes down to this: In Theravada, Buddha was seen to be a mortal; in Mahayana, Buddha comes to be seen as an eternal being.

Mahayana teaching regarding the nature of Buddha is summed up in the Doctrine of Trikaya, which translates literally as "three bodies." The flesh-and-blood body is referred to as the *nirmanakaya* ("body of transformation"). This was the "body" known as Shakyamuni, the man who lived and taught in North India. Shakyamuni was born just like any other man, grew old, and died. But Shakyamuni was not just an ordinary human being, albeit one with extraordinary gifts. Shakyamuni was the incarnation—the temporary, human incarnation—of a "Buddha," who on a higher plane of understanding is seen to be a transcendent being, the embodiment of wisdom and compassion.

This higher order of being is *sambhogakaya* ("body of joy"). This is the aspect of Buddha that is pictured in the Mahayana sutras and consequently explains the authors' use of superhuman descriptions. When Shakyamuni died, that nirmanakaya ceased, but sambhogakaya transcends earthly time. In sambhogakaya, Buddha is seen as a transcendent, godlike being—the embodiment of enlightenment—who does not die, but exists throughout time in a paradise (known as a "Buddha-realm," or "Buddha-field") over which he presides. *And*, there is not just one such Buddha, but a countless number of them, all presiding over their respective Buddha-realms, which are populated by vast numbers of their devoted followers, including some who are on the path to becoming future Buddhas. (In Pure Land Buddhism, the word "Buddha" does not refer to Shakyamuni Buddha at all, but rather to Amitabha Buddha, a completely different Buddha, into whose Buddha-field, the "Pure Land," his devotees yearn to be reborn.)

According to this view, from time to time over the ages, a Buddha will be moved by compassion for the suffering of mortals and choose to be born among them in the form of nirmanakaya. By means of this selfless act, he can bring the liberating truth of Dharma directly to the people in a time of special need. According to Mahayana teaching, this is how Shakyamuni came to be. It should be pointed out that this world is seen to be only one of a great many worlds. Since the beginning of time, incarnate Buddhas have been arising in this and myriad other worlds. Shakyamuni was only the most recent occurrence in this world. And, we are told, Shakyamuni will not be the last. The next Buddha—who will appear when the time is right—will be known by the name *Maitreya Buddha*.

Mahayana teaching holds that Buddha chose to incarnate himself as Shakyamuni purely out of a spirit of love and compassion for suffering humanity. Clearly, this is a theme of broad scope in human history. Can we doubt that Mahayana Buddhism, heavily influenced as it was by the traditions and beliefs of Hinduism, is here reflecting the Hindu teaching regarding Vishnu, who on several occasions became incarnate in order to be of help to a world in trouble? In fact, Hinduism's final accommodation with Buddhism was to declare that Shakyamuni himself was one of Vishnu's incarnations. Another obvious parallel is to be found in the Christian story of the incarnation of Jesus, who became man for the express purpose of bringing "salvation" to a wayward humanity. Jesus could be described as the nirmanakaya of God "the Father." The Mahayana interpretation of the incarnation of Shakyamuni Buddha is somewhat in this spirit.

To sum up, the nirmanakaya, then, is the manifestation of a sambhogakaya Buddha. This manifestation, or incarnation, appears in the world as a flesh-and-blood man for the purpose of teaching the Dharma in a time of need. The historical Shakyamuni was the nirmanakaya, who as a sambhogakaya Buddha is a transcendent being of supernatural powers that is the embodiment of the Dharma, and, like myriad other Buddhas, presides over a divine domain known as a Buddha-realm. It is Buddha in the sambhogakaya mode that is presented in the Mahayana sutras.

The apex of the Doctrine of Trikaya is *dharmakaya* (the "universal body"). Dharmakaya is one of the truly sublime terms in the lexicon of Mahayana. This is where everything—literally *everything*—comes together. Dharmakaya refers to the ultimate, metaphysical nature of all being. The ultimate nature of being—the essence of the universe—is oneness; ultimately All is One. This universal oneness is identified with Buddha, the Buddha-nature. Dharmakaya, then, refers to the essential nature of Buddha, which is identical with the indwelling oneness of all reality. Thus, all Buddhas, all mortals, all of the universe is joined in dharmakaya. In the most final sense that we can imagine, dharmakaya is the unity of Buddha within all that exists.

I'm sure you will agree that this description of dharmakaya can become very abstract, very metaphysical. The nature of the subject makes this inevitable. It's true today, and it was just as true in the formative days of Mahayana. Largely as a result of this, the concept of dharmakaya came to be represented by a symbol that the human mind can more easily take hold of. One of the more important Buddhas—Vairochana by name—came to *symbolize* the dharmakaya. This was especially helpful in artistic representations. The dharmakaya, of course, transcends all individual entities, including Buddhas, so it is important to remember that Vairochana was not *identified* with the dharmakaya; Vairochana *represents* the dharmakaya. (In much the same way, a statue of the blindfolded Justicia holding the scales is meant to represent the concept of justice.)

This description of the trikaya may bring to mind a similar teaching in Hinduism. Certain similarities do indeed exist. The dharmakaya can be likened to Brahman and the sambhogakaya to various Hindu deities—Vishnu, for example. And, the nirmanakaya suggests the kind of incarnation we find in Vishnu becoming Krishna. The most important difference, though, concerns the dharmakaya. Buddha as dharmakaya is not a being that manifests itself as the universe, such as Brahman was conceived to be. There is no "Buddha-Atman." Dharmakaya is the process itself, seen in its simplest, most universal essence.

It is this universality of the Buddha-nature that is at the heart of the Mahayana revolution. This is the Buddha of the Mahayana sutras, so different from the very human teacher of the Theravada sutras:

> [Buddha] is now conceived as a being who transcends all boundaries of time and space, an ever-abiding principle of truth and compassion that exists everywhere and within all beings. (Watson, xix)

"An ever-abiding principle of truth and compassion that exists everywhere and within all beings." This theme—the universal Buddhahood of all reality—is especially stressed in the *Avatamsaka Sutra*. In the *Avatamsaka*, we are encouraged over and over to see the Buddha-nature in everyone and everything. A love of Buddha and a love of the harmony of Nature are one and the same thing. The harmony of Nature is the larger context within which human life takes its meaning. Thus, the natural order has a certain sanctity about it and is deserving of reverence. Even the smallest thing contains the mystery of the entire universe. The author of the *Avatamsaka Sutra* uses many humble analogies to illustrate the universal indwelling of the Buddha-nature. We are assured that we can know the entire ocean in a drop of water and see all of the universe reflected in one grain of sand. This same great theme was given expression in the *Chandogya Upanishad* and also brings to mind the famous lines of William Blake:

> To know the world in a grain of sand,
> And a heaven in a wild flower;
> Hold infinity in the palm of your hand,
> And eternity in an hour. (from "Auguries of Innocence")

The teaching of dharmakaya has profound implications. It grew out of Buddha's view regarding the unity of being. The Mahayanists believed that everything and everyone possesses the Buddha-nature; or to put it more precisely, everything and everyone is an expression of the Buddha-nature. Differences and separations are only superficial. Given this view of truth, each person's underlying reality is, *by its very nature,* complete and perfect. It remains only for one to sweep away the cloud of ignorance to see it. The illusion of ego and its fierce attachments are what stand in the way of our seeing the real truth of our nature. Buddhahood is not something separate from us, hopefully to be *acquired* through long hard work; it is our very nature.

Another way of putting this is to say that everyone is "Buddha" by nature, but through ignorance and fear, our true nature, our "Buddhahood," is hidden from us, and we falsely identify with ego. The goal is to see through the stifling illusion of ego and to wake up to what we really are. Buddhahood is uncovered, not acquired. This difference of opinion had already had a long history in Buddhism. The Buddhologist Nancy Wilson Ross makes the following interesting comment on this matter:

> A modern Zen roshi has suggested a further point of comparison between the two great divisions which also warrants careful consideration. In his view, Theravada emphasizes the humanity of the Buddha; Mahayana emphasizes the Buddha-nature of humanity. Whereas Theravada stresses the following of a moral life and high-principled behavior as the road to eventual Buddhahood, Mahayana inclines more toward tapping an intuitive wisdom to achieve the realization that one already possesses the Buddha-nature; it has simply to be "recovered" or uncovered, so to speak. (44)

The reason why I maintain that this difference is of great significance is because it focuses on a very basic question: Is the human problem of suffering due to a real imperfection in our nature, albeit one that can be healed, or is it the result of a self-created illusion about what we really are? There's a great difference in these two alternatives. Mahayana takes the position that all beings possess the Buddha-nature, and it is only ignorance that stands in the way of realizing it. Overcoming this ignorance—uncovering one's Buddhahood—is what the Buddhist way of life is all about. And the Buddhist way of life, thanks to the Doctrine of Trikaya, was free in Mahayana to find almost limitless forms of expression. Trikaya was open to every imaginable kind of interpretation, everything from cult veneration to highly sophisticated philosophy—and all of it was brought together in dharmakaya.

MADHYAMAKA

Like Theravada, Mahayana is a part of the evolution of Buddhism; both traditions grew from the same fundamental core. But Mahayana doctrine moved far from the original teaching of Theravada. The foregoing discussion of the nature of Buddha should make that clear. The changes that we find are not to be explained simply by arguing that Mahayana was allowing itself to fall back into the Hindu world out of which Buddhism had emerged in the first place. Nor in similar fashion can it be argued that Mahayana Buddhism was nothing more than a religious and philosophical syncretism in which a spirit of "anything goes" became dominant. There is, in fact, a solid philosophical foundation to Mahayana; it is what unites and gives common substance to the many different spokes that make up the wheel. The Mahayana sutras create that foundation, especially the kingly *Prajnaparamita*. The basic teachings of Mahayana, though, are diffused throughout the sutras, nowhere presented in a concise form. It would become the task of various philosophical schools to establish specific interpretations of the teachings found in the sutras. One of these schools—one that was destined to have far-reaching influence—is known by the name *Madhyamaka*.

Before we take up the subject of Madhyamaka in detail, it would be helpful to survey a bit of the background. The bottom line in Buddhism, all of Buddhism, is the reality of suffering, *and* how to overcome it. Buddha's compassion embraced a concern for all kinds of suffering, but most of all that uniquely human existential anxiety (*duhkha*) that arises from our awareness of our inability to control the universality of impermanence, and especially the ultimate example of that impermanence, the grim inevitability of death. *Duhkha*, Buddha taught, was the certain result of a deep-seated conceptual ignorance regarding the true nature of the self. Buddha laid out the fundamentals of the problem and the way of life that could lead to its solution. His teaching, stemming from his awakening and the model of his life, firmly established the core character of what came to be known as "Buddhism." But Buddhism, of course, is and always has been a work in progress. Over the centuries, what Buddha started has been amplified and interpreted in countless ways. There has always been, and continues still, a never-ending effort to better understand the mystery that is the Dharma.

From its beginnings, Buddhism had held that the greatest obstacle to liberation (from suffering) is attachment to the illusion of a "self," a substantive, enduring personal self. This mistaken belief is held to be the root cause of all our woes. To overcome it, to see through the illusion, is liberation, *nirvana*. And, in the Noble Eightfold Path, Buddha had laid out the way of life that leads to nirvana. But what *is* nirvana? What is the nature of this great goal of the Buddhist quest? For some, it's enough to say that nirvana is simply a state of being free from ignorance and suffering. But to the philosophically minded, that answer is not sufficient. There had always been an effort—insofar as the discursive, thinking mind might be capable—to clarify the nature of that greatest of all goals, nirvana.

In the early days of developing Mahayana, the general approach was to posit two different kinds of reality: "ordinary reality" and "ultimate reality." Ordinary reality refers to what we commonly experience as truth. Ultimate reality, though, refers to what we do not perceive directly, but which *stands behind* ordinary reality, so to speak, and which reveals directly the fundamental unity of being. Knowledge of ordinary reality is "ordinary knowledge," conceptual, relative, ever-changing, capable of leading us into error and all of the woes of human life. But, it was maintained, a vision of ultimate reality awakens one to the absolute, underlying Truth of reality and is synonymous with liberation from suffering.

That's pretty much the way things stood when Nagarjuna appeared on the scene in the later part of the second century. Nagarjuna (pronounced na-GHAR-joo-na), one of the most important names in the history of Buddhism, was the founder of the school known as *Madhyamaka* (mah-dya-MAH-ka).* The name refers to what Nagarjuna proclaimed to be the "middle way" to the truth of reality—middle between the extreme positions of nihilism (nothing really exists, or at least, nothing can be known) and objective realism (only physical, permanent entities exist). All of this is laid out in his seminal work, the *Mulamadhyamakakarika*. (Don't let words like that intimidate you. Just break them down into their logical parts: *Mula-madhya-maka-karika*—root-middle-way-statement—a "concise statement of the root of the middle way." Isn't that easy?)

Not a whole lot is known about Nagarjuna. Some say that he was raised by serpents (*nagas*) in an undersea palace where he was initiated into the ways of the occult. While exploring some underwater caves, he discovered a cache of Buddhist scriptures that had been hidden there. Overwhelmed by their message, he left the nagas and became a passionately devoted Buddhist. Well, anything's possible, but a more humdrum version of his life presents Nagarjuna as a Brahmin priest living in North India during the century from 150 C.E. to 250 C.E. In the course of his studies, he discovered the *Prajnaparamita* and was won over to Buddhism by it. He devoted the rest of his life to elucidating the inner meaning of this great work.

The way in which the traditional systems dealt with the problem of nonself was not satisfying to the mind of Nagarjuna. He was not comfortable with the notion of an "ultimate reality." As a result, he subjected every system that presupposed the existence of an ultimate reality to a penetrating critique, known as a "dialectic." He's famous for using the method of *reductio ad absurdum*, in which he would logically trace back every claim until it reached the point of self-contradiction. In the end, he came to the conclusion that there is no such thing as an "ultimate reality." It is a concept only and has no corresponding objective existence outside the thinking mind.

It must be emphasized that Nagarjuna had no intention of creating a rival system, one that would "get it right." Nagarjuna argued that *all* systems based on discursive reasoning are doomed to failure if their goal is to reveal an "ultimate truth," an "ultimate reality." He was not offering a new epistomology, a new way to get at "ultimate reality" rather. Nagarjuna's goal was to expose the fallacy of all systems that propose to rationally uncover *ultimate* truth, and thus show that they are incapable of being authentic guides to liberation.

In the process of critiquing the various systems, Nagarjuna came to some conclusions of his own. These are summed up in what is known as the Doctrine of Shunyata, which, Nagarjuna claimed, was derived from a careful reading of the sutras, especially the

*"Madhyamaka" refers to the school; "madhyamika" (—MEE-ka) refers to a follower of that school.

Prajnaparamita. These teachings, though, are diffused throughout the sutras, nowhere presented in a concise form. It remained for Nagarjuna to pull it all together.

The word *shunyata* is derived from *shunya* (pronounced SHOON-ya), which in Sanskrit means "zero" (i.e., empty). Shunyata, often therefore translated as the "Doctrine of Emptiness," became truly fundamental to the teaching of Mahayana. When the Doctrine of Shunyata is correctly understood, the word *emptiness* is seen to be a perfectly suitable choice of words. In some ways, though, it is an unfortunate choice because it so easily leads to a huge misunderstanding. Some in the West, lacking understanding of shunyata, have misapprehended the use of the word *emptiness*, concluding that shunyata (and by association, all of Mahayana Buddhism) is fundamentally a nihilistic philosophy of life. Shunyata is not nihilistic; it is not negative at all. Properly understood, shunyata is a very positive approach to understanding the nature of Nature.

So what *is* shunyata, this all-important Doctrine of Emptiness? First of all, what it is *not*: "emptiness" definitely does not mean "nothingness" (an unfortunately common misunderstanding, and undoubtedly the source of charges that Buddhism is nihilistic). In the sense that we're using the word, "emptiness" has nothing to do with "nonexistence," nothing to do with what might be called an "ontological vacuum." Simply put, emptiness means empty of intrinsic essence. Let me explain.

In exploring this most fundamental question concerning the true nature of reality, Nagarjuna carefully observed human consciousness and concluded that indeed there *are indeed* two kinds of knowledge, two fundamentally different ways of knowing. Notice, though, this is not to say that there are two different *kinds of reality*, a contention that Nagarjuna completely rejected. Reality is reality. There can be only one reality, not two realities: "ordinary" reality and "higher" (or "ultimate") reality. The goal is not to see a "higher" reality, but to see the *truth* of the one, ordinary reality. There are, however, two different *ways of knowing* reality, but it's the same reality in both cases. There is ordinary knowledge, which is conceptual and rational, and which sees the relationships among things. This kind of knowledge is very practical and it is good at seeing relative truth. And then there is transcendent knowledge, known by its Sanskrit name, *prajna*. *Prajna* is intuitive, direct seeing into the truth of reality, whatever that may be (and what it may *not* be: two essentially distinct, irreducible *kinds* of reality—for example, matter and spirit). *Prajna* is different in kind from ordinary knowledge; it is not simply a matter of degree that separates them. The action of *prajna* is the only way of knowing the intrinsic truth of reality, that same reality which ordinary knowledge misconstrues. Though the rising of *prajna* is rare—so rare that few even know of its existence—its potential is inherent in human nature and lies dormant in the consciousness of every person, waiting only for the right conditions to bring it to life. Truly seeing for oneself the insufficiency of ordinary knowledge is just such a right condition that can clear the way for the rising of *prajna*.

Nagarjuna's critique was aimed at "ordinary knowledge." Ordinary knowledge is conceptual. We don't often think about it—and in the practical affairs of daily life it's better that we don't—but when we sit back and reflect on the nature of our knowing it's clear that all of our knowledge is, in fact, a body of concepts. Through our concepts we "objectify" the world around us, but the concepts themselves are ideas—interior, subjective states.

When I "know" something, I know it (if I know it at all) indirectly, not directly. Take that tree over there, for example. I may say that, by observing it, I know its existence. And although this is certainly true at the practical level of everyday experience, it remains nonetheless a fact that what I *know* is not the tree itself but my *idea* of the tree. The point is that what I know—and all that I ever know at the level of ordinary knowledge—is my own collection of ideas, my own concepts. This is true of all concepts, including those that seek to interpret reality.

To see how this works, imagine that you are leaning over the railing on a bridge, gazing down into the river flowing beneath you. What catches your attention is a whirlpool just below you. Your brain has no trouble isolating it out from the river as a whole in order to examine it. However, you know that the whirlpool can't *really* be separated from the river. You know that you can't lower a bucket into the whirlpool and take some of it home with you. You'd haul up a bucket of inert, ordinary river water, that's all. Why can't you remove the whirlpool from the river? Your brain can easily do that by forming a concept of the whirlpool and giving it a name. But your hands can't do it because it's obviously not really a "thing" unto itself that can be separated out. In fact, it's not really a "whirlpool" at all: it's a "whirlpool-*ing*"; it's something the river is *doing*; at this time and place the river is whirlpool-ing. The whirlpool is intrinsic to the river; it's a doing of the river, just as the "river"—"river-ing"—is a doing of its environment, and so on all the way up to the universe as a whole. We can mentally separate the whirlpool from the river and think of it as an entity by itself, but that's not the way it really is. Everything is like that! Reality is not a stable collection of separate entities; it's a vast unified field of interrelated, interconnected processes of becoming.

Why don't we see that? Why do we customarily perceive the universe as a collection of *interacting*, separate things, "myself" being one of them? Well, because that's the way the brain works. It didn't evolve for philosophical musing; it evolved to be a very practical manager that would be successful in the struggle for survival and reproduction. On the whole, animal brains work quite well at that task, but when we come to the human brain, things get a little strange. Our brains, like other animal brains, are capable of generating consciousness, but unlike other animal brains, ours are capable of forming concepts. And that's the snake in the garden.

This time, instead of a whirlpool, consider a banana. It's a nice, ripe, good looking banana resting on a table in your kitchen. Here, again you can easily focus consciousness on it, separate it out from the larger field, form a concept of it, assign it the name, banana (a "convenient designator"), and file it in memory for possible future use. The brain does that effortlessly, and it's a very practical process. Of course, that banana is no more really an entity separate unto itself that the whirlpool is. It's just not as obvious in the case of the banana. But if we stop and think about it, that banana, just like the whirlpool, is an integral part of a larger whole, without which it couldn't exist.

Whirlpools and bananas are only the beginning. We do that with *everything* we encounter, which is to say, we form concepts to represent the "things" we experience. Concepts are like snapshots: very useful in some situations but clearly only a static models of what they represent. To confuse the concept with the reality is big trouble. But that's what we humans do all the time. Our brains, being the way they are, allow us to create a mental universe of separate entities (labeled concepts). This conceptual world exists in the "mind," not in the real world; it is a substitute for the real world, which it *represents*. Thus do we imagine an "in here" (the observer) and an "out there" (the observed). In a manner of speaking, the mind concocts a *substitute* world of concepts and then persuades itself to believe that it is genuine reality. The "in here" observer becomes the concept of the "self," the separate self, which *has* a body, and by means of that body confronts all of the other entities ("things") that make up it's "out there."

This whole way of thinking—rational, discursive, conceptual thought—produces what Nagarjuna identified as "ordinary knowledge." To see that all of our knowledge, at least "ordinary knowledge," is conceptual is a tremendously important understanding, because concepts are a product of the way the mind works. In other words, what we call ordinary knowledge is determined not by objective existential reality, but rather by the character of the human brain. Mental processes have evolved to be practical, not to be instruments of philosophical speculation. In forming concepts, the human mind by its very nature seeks to find meaning in relationships. A concept has meaning *in relation to* other concepts. This is quite obvious in some cases, such as night and day, or hot and cold. But it is equally true for all concepts, though often the relationship is more subtle.

Our ordinary knowledge of what we take to be reality is *exclusively* conceptual knowledge and thus it is always *relational* knowledge. No matter what we think we know, we know it only in relation to other things. Nothing can stand entirely by itself. In this world of ceaseless flux—and the knowing mind is itself an integral part of that flux—things have meaning only in relation to other things. That is to say, concepts have meaning only in relation to other concepts. Even our concept of the entire universe—call it "being"—has meaning only in relation to the concept of nonbeing. Absolutely nothing (no-thing), Nagarjuna argues, exists purely on its own, independent and separate from all other things. Everything is interconnected. What we have here is what Buddha presented as the Doctrine of Dependent Arising.

This line of reasoning led Nagarjuna to what is summed up in the wonderful Sanskrit word *nihsvabhava* (nee-shvah-BAH-va). This means "empty of self-existence." It is the antonym of *svabhava* ("self-existence"), the acceptance of which was the underlying reason for Nagarjuna's rejection of all prior systems. Nihsvabhava is at the heart of shunyata, the "Doctrine of Emptiness." If the reality of any given thing is conditionally dependent upon its relationship to other things, then nothing can stand all by itself. It is "empty" of self-existence. Any given "thing" is the result of the causes and conditions that give it definition. Take these away and it ceases to have existence.

> The world perceived through the senses, the phenomenal world as we know it, was described in early Buddhism as "empty" because it was taught that all such phenomena arise from causes and conditions, are in a constant state of flux, and are destined to change and pass away in time. They are also held to be "empty" in the sense that they have no inherent or permanent characteristics by which they can be described, changing as they do from instant to instant. (Watson; *Lotus Sutra*, xv)

Everything—everything that we can imagine—is bound up in the conceptual relationships that give it meaning. And thus nothing is fundamentally real *unto itself*. There is no such *thing* as night—"night" is a concept only, and it has meaning solely in relation to other concepts, such as "day." This poses no problem with such concepts as night and day, but the heat gets turned up when we direct Nagarjuna's spotlight on such concepts as the Doctrine of Anatman. This, however, is a concept too, and Nagarjuna would insist that it, no less than any other, must be seen as ultimately empty of self-standing reality. For example, anatman only has meaning in relation to Atman; both are aspects of one conceptually relative reality. Is this to say, then, that Atman is real after all, or at least as real as anatman? It is not to say that Atman is real or unreal. It is what it is, a concept—and the same goes for anatman. Being concepts, both are empty of substanding reality; neither, therefore, can represent absolute truth. In fact, Nagarjuna would insist, we must abandon the very notion of an absolute truth.

Because nothing imaginable is exempt from conditional existence, ultimately all of being is reduced to a state of "emptiness." Again, though, emptiness definitely does not mean nonexistence. To say that reality is empty of permanent self-standing entities is not to say that reality does not exist. In no way was Nagarjuna a nihilist, denying the existence of reality. Nagarjuna was simply denying the ability of the conceptualizing mind to know the genuine nature of reality in itself.

> The reality to which all names refer is utterly ungraspable and inconceivable, possessing absolutely no physical or metaphysical self-existence . . . Given this irreducible fact of unthinkability—not as a frustrating limit to our understanding, but as a beautiful, blissful openness and freedom from all limits—we know that no authentic expression of Perfect Wisdom will permit us to picture or conceptualize What Is. (Hixon; 14, 35)

We cannot conceptualize *what is*; we can only experience it. And this is the experience of awakening, the "opening of the eye of *prajna*." *Prajna* is *completely* different from the working of ordinary knowledge. No amount of discursive reasoning will ever open consciousness to the fundamental truth of reality. So then, what is the point of all this philosophizing, all of this dialectic? Isn't it just a grand example of the very thing it criticizes? If the exercise were an intellectual end in itself, that would surely be true. But the real objective of the dialectic is to help free the mind from its attachment to concepts. By loosening the grip of the thinking mind a little at a time, one is moving closer to the place and time when the great light of awakening can occur. The dialectic itself becomes a form of *upaya* (skillful means).

The discursive, thinking mind is indeed a fabulous creation of the evolution of nature. Who could possibly dispute that! Our ability to conceptualize makes it possible for us to live successfully in this world of never-ending challenges. It has enabled the human species to create an awesome technology which has made a Grand Canyon of the gulf which separates *Homo sapiens* from all other species. But it's not an unmixed blessing (to say the least!). That same ability results inevitably in a conceptualization of "myself" and all the suffering (duhkha) that is consequent to that. It is the thinking mind that produces suffering, not the world with which it interacts. Coming to understand this, coming to realize that the self is a concept—not an ultimate, unchanging reality—is to understand the rising of duhkha.

Awakening to the realization that there is no "ultimate reality" is not awakening to a realization that nothing really exists (nihilism), nor is it a confirmation of the customary view that reality is a collection of discreet, fixed entities, outside of "me," but with which I must constantly contend. Rather, it is awakening to a realization that reality is a constantly flowing, changing, interrelated flux, always in a state of becoming, a *unitive* state of being—and I, the real me, am an integral part of it all. It promotes among us happiness-seekers a way of life that is no longer fixated on a private "me" whose happiness depends on satisfying endless desires, but rather a way of life that is joyfully immersed in the play of the present, *feeling* the interconnectedness of everything. For one so enlightened, the world of "samsara" *becomes* "nirvana." Nirvana is not a higher reality, separate from the world of samsara; they're one and the same. It's always been that way; we just didn't see it. That's why Nagarjuna asserted that *samsara* is *nirvana*; *nirvana* is *samsara*. Allow me to repeat a brief section from Chapter 9:

> This whole matter of the relationship of *samsara* and *nirvana*, so difficult to explain in words, is wonderfully expressed by the Chinese Chan Master, Ching Yuan:
>
>> Before I had studied Zen for thirty years, I saw mountains as mountains, and waters as waters. When I arrived at a more intimate knowledge, I came to the point where I saw that mountains are not mountains, and waters are not waters. But now that I have got its very substance I am at rest. For it's just that I see mountains once again as mountains, and waters once again as waters.

Let's now try to put it all together. Since its beginning, the universe has been grandly unfolding. What began as a single uniform reality has evolved into countless forms. These forms are constantly arising into existence and passing out of existence; they are forever changing and interchanging. The forms of the universe are real; they are not chimera. But their reality is precisely that: "forms," *aspects* of one unitary reality. But we don't see it that way.

In order for a conscious being to live successfully within its environment, nature has evolved various senses which detect information from the "outside world" and communicate it to the brain where the information is processed into an intelligible sensory experience. This is called "representationalism" because the brain *represents* the object of sense experience in a practical way. Looking back again at "that tree over there," the image in the brain—including color, smell, etc.—is very useful, but there is no reason to conclude that what is being represented is anything at all like the image that represents it. Think of a waveform pattern on your computer screen. It's a remarkable representation of the music; you can work with it. But, of course, it's nothing at all like the music itself.

Humans, just like all other sentient beings, process sensory information into brain representations, but we have the ability to go one momentous (and dangerous) step further. Our brains' insatiable hunger for order and meaning results in the formation of concepts, mental representations that are fixed and permanent, like snapshots. In redesigning reality into a body of separate, permanent, static entities, and then believing that that's the way reality actually is, we have substituted a world of fixed concepts for the dynamic, unitary, changing world of reality. This is playing right into the hands of the insecure, ever-desiring ego, the concept of which is judged to be the real "self." The life of duhkha becomes a foregone conclusion.

Ordinary "discursive" knowledge can never break out of that imprisoning world of conceptual knowledge, but the consciousness of the ordinary mind can be transcended through the practice of meditation, ultimately resulting in the "opening of the eye of *prajna*," which "sees" reality as it really is. This experience of awakening sees through the illusory nature of ordinary knowledge, which includes seeing through the illusory conceptual nature of the separate self, and like waking from a bad dream, the life of duhkha is left behind forever.

The Doctrine of Shunyata recast the philosophy of Buddhism in a very fundamental way. In varying ways it would shape the character of the many disparate "schools" of Buddhism that make up the Mahayana. We will later see that shunyata was a powerful shaping influence in Zen Buddhism. But in different ways, it is equally influential in sects far removed from the spirit of Zen. Turning again to the image of a wheel, Theravada and the Pali Canon are the hub of the wheel, and the various expressions of Mahayana are the spokes. It might be helpful in this metaphor to picture shunyata as a circle that surrounds the hub. It is physically separate from the hub, but it is closely associated with it, and like the hub it joins together the spokes.

I feel that it is important to keep reminding ourselves that "awakening" is what the teaching of Buddha is all about. Whether it be Theravada or Mahayana, it is the experience of awakening that gives meaning to the Buddhist lifestyle. Mahayana, influenced by the Doctrine of Shunyata, gave a new meaning to the quest. Freed from the strict interpretation of Theravada, freed from all conceptual interpretations, Mahayana Buddhism could follow any and every path that led to the opening of *prajna*.

The Doctrine of Shunyata established the fact that awakening consists in the opening of the "eye" of *prajna*. And *prajna* is the wisdom that sees through the illusion of the separate self. That's the bottom line. That, Madhyamaka proclaims, is the teaching of Buddha. The *Prajnaparamita* and Nagarjuna are simply expounding on it. But *prajna* by itself is not the whole story. You may recall that Buddha linked *prajna* with *karuna* (compassion). They are the two elementary facets of one reality. In seeking the opening of *prajna*, seeing the insufficiency of ordinary knowledge may be helpful, but the cultivation of compassion is essential. And that brings us to the subject of the Bodhisattva, which we will take up right after we briefly examine another influential school of Buddhist philosophy, Yogacara.

YOGACARA

The madhyamikas (students of Madhyamaka) always had to deal with the charge that shunyata (the Doctrine of Emptiness) was really a thinly disguised version of the philosophy of nihilism, the extremist view that nothing at all really exists. After all, to contend that all things are "empty" of self-standing existence does indeed seem to weaken the objective reality of that world "out there."

Given this state of affairs, it wasn't long before a new school of thought was attracting the attention of the more philosophically minded. It goes by the name *Yogacara*, which is misleading. Literally, "Yogacara" means "practice of yoga," but Yogacara had nothing to do with the Indian darshana of Yoga. Possibly it had to do with the practice of meditation (yoga meditation). There are other names for this school; Vijnanavada (Doctrine of Consciousness) is one, but Yogacara has become the commonly accepted term.

The genesis of Yogacara is attributed to a scholar-monk named *Vasubandhu*, who lived in north central India during the fourth century C.E. Apparently, he worked with his brother (half-brother, to be precise), Asanga, who deserves some of the credit. The whole story is a little murky. Some contend that there were actually two Vasubandhus, but that need not concern us here. The teaching of Yogacara is what matters.

Philosophically speaking, Yogacara is classified as "subjective idealism." What this means is that Vasubandhu denied the real, objective existence of all external things—*all* external things! Mind alone exists; ideas have absolutely no corresponding reality outside the mind. What we take to be the real world simply doesn't exist; it's an illusion, a creation of the mind. Only mind exists.

Subjective idealism is a fascinating theory (well, to philosophers anyway), but the mind understandably recoils at what seems to be the absurdity of it all. Certainly, our senses are aware of *something*! If I walk around a bend in the path and my sense of vision is suddenly stimulated by the sight of a beautiful tree, certainly *something* outside of my mind has generated the experience. Its objective reality may be nothing like what I perceive it to be, but some kind of external agent must be triggering my response. Not so, Vasubandhu would argue. When you're dreaming you experience what you take to be an external world, even though it's entirely imaginary. How do you know, for certain, that you're not dreaming right now?

Subjective idealism was not unique to Yogacara; it finds a place in the philosophical tool kit of most cultures. In the history of Western philosophy, idealism is almost synonymous with the name of the nineteenth century Irish bishop, George Berkeley. There's a wonderful story that one day the learned but very down-to-earth Samuel Johnson was out for a stroll with his friend and biographer, James Boswell. The conversation turned to Berkeley's defense of idealism. The very idea was preposterous to the level-headed Johnson. The more they talked, the angrier he got. Finally, to make his point, he strode over to a large boulder and kicked it hard. "Thus do I refute it!" he shouted. Well, it's easy to understand his feeling, but even if he had kicked Bishop Berkeley himself, he wouldn't really be refuting anything. It's a great response, though.

Vasubandhu's basic argument was simple: We are regularly conscious of sensory experiences. These perceptions take the form of ideas in the mind. Understandably, we assume that such ideas are representative of a corresponding reality in the world external to our senses. It is undoubtedly practical to make that assumption. But is it true? In fact, all we ever know directly are our ideas. We assume that they represent an external world. But we never, *ever* experience that alleged world directly. We *assume* it to be real and to be the progenitor of our sensory experiences. That, however, is an inference, an inference only. Why should we trust an inference? What solid evidence is there that the images we experience are caused by external agents? There is none; there *can be* none. We know that the mind is fooled some of the time. No one doubts that the images of dreams and hallucinations have no corresponding external reality. How can we be sure that this is not *always* the case?

There was no shortage of critics willing to take on this debate. The opponents of Yogacara responded with a variety of arguments. Chief among them were these:

- Different people can have the same experience at the same time. If I'm walking along the sidewalk, lost in thought, and suddenly I hear a loud sound like a gunshot, everyone around me responds in the same way. They all heard it too. How could you explain this coincidence unless there actually was a stimulus external to all of us?
- It may be true that my perception of a rattlesnake looks and feels the same whether I'm awake or dreaming. I may even be bitten by the snake in both situations. But there's a big difference. The one I take to be real has effects; I really do have a snakebite.
- If Yogacara were right, my sensory experiences would all be nothing but a form of imagining, like a daydream. I can control a daydream, though. For example, I could choose to imagine the snake slithering away. I can't automatically control what I take to be real experiences. I can't just make it up as I go along.

Yogacara did not choose to try to rebut the various criticisms point by point but was content rather with the "Principle of Lightness" as its defense. The Principle of Lightness is also known as "Occam's Razor," a reference to the medieval British philosopher who insisted that of two opposing theories, the simplest one, the one with the fewest assumptions, should prevail. His "mental razor" would slice out everything that was unnecessary or ambiguous. Vasubandhu argued that of the two competing theories—idealism, and the causal agency of a real external world (usually referred to as representationalism), his was the simpler. Both theories accepted the reality of mental images, but that's all that his theory required. His opponents required that one also accept the reality of an objective phenomenal world. Yogacara insists that the real existence of a phenomenal world which initiates our sensory experiences is always but an inference. No one can actually prove that it exists. Since it can't be proven, why invent it? The simpler theory is adequate to explain the nature of ideas, therefore it should be accepted.

However preposterous subjective idealism might seem, Yogacara did nevertheless become a prominent school of thought in Mahayana Buddhism. In fact, for a time, Yogacara even eclipsed the Madhyamaka school, apparently appearing to be a further development of the work begun by Nagarjuna. The Yogacarins took the Madhyamaka view that all things are empty of self-standing reality, and went beyond that to say that all "things" are empty of reality period. Only the mind has real existence.

The Yogacara approach appealed to some as offering a more reasonable solution to the great conundrum regarding the seeming continuity of a given "person." If it be accepted that a "person" is not a permanent, substantive entity which only exhibits superficial change (the near-universal opinion of humankind) but rather is a pattern of constant change, giving only the appearance of permanency because of the gradual nature of change in that pattern, then why is that pattern not a new "person" every moment? How can a constantly changing pattern have memories of past times at which time it was a different pattern? This was understandably an enormous problem for Buddhist philosophy. Vasubandhu's answer was the "store consciousness."

Lacking any of the knowledge that modern science has revealed regarding the neurology of the brain, the problem of memory was a huge obstacle to the "no-self" doctrine of Buddhism. Vasubandhu argued that a physical explanation was not necessary. The "mind" continues to exist whether it is awake (conscious) or not. Thus, it is reasonable to conclude that in addition to conscious awareness the mind also has an "unconscious" dimension, and it is there that the mind stores "seeds" (as Vasubandhu put it) of all conscious experiences. These "seeds," squirreled away in the "store consciousness," can come to life and blossom into our various conscious recollections when conditions are right for triggering this.

Was there any practical benefit to be gained by adopting the Yogacara view? Perhaps. Vasubandhu could have argued that belief in an inner and an outer world results in a duality that encourages belief in a separate self, an "inner me" that confronts the outer world, and reacts to it. The possibility of attachment to worldly things and desires becomes much greater. Thus, it could be argued that belief in subjective idealism is a helpful means of breaking down the illusion of the separate self. (Sounds like Freud was reading Vasubandhu, doesn't it?)

THE BODHISATTVA

One of the distinguishing features of Mahayana is that it offers a Buddhist way of life for the whole community, not just for the fully dedicated few. Mahayana is Buddhism for the entire lotus pond; there's something for everyone. In Theravada, it seems that the principal function of the laity was simply to provide support for the sangha. In Mahayana, it goes much, much further than that. Reflecting the broad scope of Hinduism, Mahayana Buddhism too came to include an endless variety of popular rituals and ceremonies and cults—in other words, a devotional movement. The layman and woman had access to a lifestyle that was thoroughly Buddhist, and even, as the *Lankavatara Sutra* proclaimed, the possibility of achieving enlightenment.

However rich the life of the laity might become, though, it was clear from the beginning that the order of monks remained central in importance. The monk would continue to lead the way. The Mahayana Buddhist monk was, and remains, the embodiment of the philosophy of Mahayana.

The goal of the Theravadin monk was to become an *arhat*, that is, a fully enlightened person. He sought to achieve this by following the Eightfold Path with total dedication. Mahayanists criticized the Theravadins for being self-centered; the enlightenment of an arhat was simply for oneself. The goal of a Mahayana monk, on the other hand, was to become a *bodhisattva*.* A bodhisattva may also be an enlightened person, but the meaning goes far beyond that of the arhat. For one thing, it is the intention of a bodhisattva to achieve enlightenment not for his own good alone, but for the good of all beings.

Strictly speaking, a bodhisattva is one who has achieved awakening, but the word is sometimes used to include as well those who have not yet become fully awakened but have made great progress and would seem sure to ultimately achieve it. Whereas a Theravadin monk is dedicated to the "Five Dedications," a Mahayana monk works on the "Six Perfections" (eventually increased to ten in some Mahayana sects). There is much similarity between the two. These "perfections," known as *paramitas*, are to be fully mastered by the bodhisattva-to-be in the course of his or her development. In brief, they are as follows:

1. *Dana-paramita* (becoming a giving, other-directed person)
2. *Shila-paramita* (development of correct moral disciplines)
3. *Kshanti-paramita* (cultivating patience and tolerance)
4. *Virga-paramita* (determination and perseverance)
5. *Dhyana-paramita* (skill in meditation)
6. *Prajna-paramita* (supreme wisdom that sees Reality as it is)

Each of these six paramitas nourishes all of the others, but the apex, of course, is *Prajnaparamita*, mastery of which makes the person a fully realized bodhisattva, an "awakened one." In the Mahayana tradition, it was widely understood that achieving mastery of the Six Perfections could take a very long time, many lifetimes in fact. Consequently, a fully realized bodhisattva was believed to be one who had lived through many previous lives.

The above statement may come as something of a shock to you. *"Many previous lives"*? Is this not a bold reassertion of the idea of Atman, the very heart of *avidya* that

---

*Bodhisattva is a Sanskrit word that simply means "one who has achieved the goal" (the goal being enlightenment).

Buddha had sought to liberate humankind from? Not really. For one thing, Buddha never defined doctrine; he assiduously avoided answers to metaphysical questions. He was much more interested in the right way to live. Much of what we hold to be the philosophical character of Buddha's teaching is what has been inferred by various traditions, beginning with the Theravada. The Doctrine of Shunyata had undermined the either/or approach to truth. It was no longer a question of whether atman was true or false. *All* conclusions based on conceptual thinking were ultimately irrelevant. It could go either way. Mahayana simply opened the door to a much wider spectrum of interpretations. If there are to be many paths—something for everyone—then it should come as no surprise that humanity's infatuation with the idea of reincarnation would find some place for expression in Mahayana Buddhism.

I don't want to give the impression, though, that Mahayana was philosophically indifferent on this subject. It may be true that the lack of a defined orthodoxy has resulted over the ages in many taking up a belief in personal reincarnation—but, philosophically speaking, the Mahayana tradition has always been steadfast in denying the existence of any permanent, self-standing essence that endures through time. If there is no substanding self—no substantive, spiritual entity, the real *me*, that endures through time—then, obviously, there is nothing (no-*thing*) to be reborn. So, *who or what* is it that exists for many "lifetimes"? How does one explain the "many previous lives" of a bodhisattva? Sounds like a problem, doesn't it?

Here is one way of responding to this question. It all comes down to what is meant by the term *lifetime*. Philosophically speaking, Mahayana definitely does not contradict the essential teaching of the Doctrine of Anatman. What is said to be "reborn" is not a substanding entity, a "self," but rather an identifiable process of change, which, in fact, is being reborn constantly, every moment. All of existence is being reincarnated constantly, always in a state of *becoming*.

In Mahayana, the word *samsara* refers to the cycling of existence—a great cycling process which is a continuous flow of energy. What we call human life is a part of that process. With regard to human beings, though, the particular character of the flow is generated by karma, the consequences that follow every kind of volitional act. "Rebirth" is an aspect of the process that is going on all the time, every moment in fact. The word does not refer to the "rebirth" of an Atman, a spiritual entity, though; rather it refers to the continuation of an identifiable and enduring pattern within that karma-generated process. But again, it is not some*one* who is being reborn; it is the process itself that is reborn, that is, continuously regenerating itself. The term *mindstream* is often used in this connection. A given bodhisattva (or anyone else, for that matter) is the inheritor of an evolving mindstream; or to be more precise, the bodhisattva *is* the mindstream. The rationale for a bodhisattva having many "lives" is that the process of development that leads to mastery of the Six Perfecions takes a very long time. Over time, positive karma is being generated which influences subsequent development. Eventually, karma sufficient to the genesis of awakening is accumulated. Something of an analogy is to be found in the idea of a family, which over several generations raises itself from poverty and ignorance to become distinguished for scholarship and public service. Each successive generation of that family was influenced in a positive way by the "karma" generated by those who came before.

It is the life of compassion (*karuna*) that generates the karma that leads to awakening. The importance of compassion cannot be exaggerated; the central importance of compassion is a truly distinguishing feature of Mahayana. Compassion, however, cannot be separated from *prajna*; perfect compassion is *prajna*. *Prajna* is the wisdom that sees reality as it is, which is to say, that opens in awakening. But the ultimate victory of *prajna* over the entrenched power of ignorance does not come easily. It is growth in compassion, not discipline, that little by little loosens the grip of ignorance. Thus, in seeking to extend compassion until it has no limits, the bodhisattva is dissolving all illusions of separation and daily moving closer to the point at which *karuna* and *prajna* merge in awakening.

A bodhisattva is, in fact, *defined* by the ultimate and perfect act of compassion. He or she, just like Buddha, willingly postpones entry into the perfect and permanent reality of nirvana. In fact, the Mahayana monk takes a vow not to accept the final perfection of nirvana until all other beings may also enter into it. This is done out of a spirit of pure and unlimited compassion; it would be unthinkably selfish to accept the fullness of nirvana until all other beings can do so too. This decision reflects Buddha's decision to put off the perfect solitary enjoyment of his awakening, choosing instead to return to the everyday world and dedicate his life to helping others along the path to freedom. Also, this decision is evidence that one has fully awakened to the truth of the Unitive State; there is no self apart from the whole; there really can be no other course for a genuinely awakened man or woman. We can express the difference by saying that in the Theravada tradition one seeks to become totally enlightened; in the Mahayana tradition one seeks to become totally compassionate.

Let me sum things up this point. A fully realized bodhisattva is a man or woman who, through dedication to the spirit of the Dharma, has seen through the illusion of the separate ego. The bodhisattva is a liberated person, free from fear and attachment, one who genuinely sees the underlying truth in the unity of being. Such a one could, to put it in the clumsy way of words, go on to extinguish his or her ego individuality completely, dissolving perfectly—at least at the time called death—into the universal oneness that is the underlying reality of all that is. But to allow this would be to put the interests of the self first, which is unthinkable (and impossible) to one who has truly come to realize that the separate self is an illusion. The whole is all that matters—all that is. Only the wholeness of being can enter into perfect nirvana; nothing else really exists. So, out of boundless compassion for all beings who have not yet made the discovery, the bodhisattva must choose to wait at the brink, being of service to others, until nirvana is available to all. Heinrich Zimmer describes the bodhisattva thus:

> . . . in the Mahayana tradition the term designates those sublimely indifferent, compassionate beings who remain at the threshold of nirvana for the comfort and salvation of the world. Out of perfect indifference (egolessness) and perfect compassion (which is also egolessness) the Mahayana Bodhisattva does not experience the "real or true enlightenment" (*samyak-sambodhi*) of the Buddha and then pass to final extinction (*parinirvana*), but stops at the brink—the brink of time and eternity—and thus transcends that pair of opposites: for the world will never end; the round of the cosmic eons will go on and on without ceasing. The vow of the Bodhisattva, to remain at the brink till all shall go in before him, amounts to a vow to remain as he is forever. (*Philosophies of India*, 535)

" . . . to remain at the brink till all shall go in before him, amounts to a vow to remain as he is forever." The concept of a bodhisattva as an enlightened person of infinite compassion who lovingly puts off the completed perfection of nirvana so long as any other being needs help is, I'm sure you will agree, a magnificent ideal. It would be a mistake, though, to picture the bodhisattva as a lofty, saintly being, distantly removed from the humdrum affairs of daily life. The true bodhisattva is a very down-to-earth person; a friendly, caring, compassionate man or woman. And the bodhisattva's caring extends not only to other people, but to everything in nature. It can certainly be argued that the true bodhisattva is the finest example of a human being that we can imagine.

Another important matter concerning the compassion of a bodhisattva has to do with the huge store of positive karma that he or she accumulates. According to popular belief, this is available to be shared with less enlightened folks and thus help them along the path to their own liberation. (In a sense this parallels the Christian concept of "grace," which can be dispensed among the faithful.) As a predictable result of this, certain eminent bodhisattvas have become cult figures, attracting large and devoted followings among the laity. Such revered bodhisattvas play the role of "saints" within Mahayana Buddhism. Many bodhisattvas have risen to this role in the history of Mahayana. Three of the most beloved are: Avalokiteshvara (Kannon in Japanese), the embodiment of compassion; Manjushri (Monju in Japanese), the embodiment of wisdom; and Maitreya (Miroku in Japanese), who is believed to be a bodhisattva who will eventually achieve Buddhahood and become the next earthly Buddha. Representations of these bodhisattvas (and others) have always been highly popular in the art of Buddhism.

ARTISTIC EXPRESSION IN EARLY MAHAYANA

The rise of Mahayana was accompanied by a great flowering of Buddhist art. This was true in the Indian homeland and every other place that Mahayana Buddhism migrated to. In sculpture, painting, architecture, and many other forms, much of the finest art produced in Asian cultures throughout the centuries has been inspired by Buddhist ideals. It's probably true to say that familiarity with Buddhist art is the only experience that most people in the West have with Buddhism. But that's bound to change as Buddhist influences continue to sink roots and grow in the West.

Perhaps in the not-too-distant future, the Western world will experience a whole new flowering of Buddhist art, a modern renaissance, this time inspired by a marriage of Buddhist ideals and the Western artistic tradition. It's interesting to note that this actually did happen once; it was back in the early days of Mahayana development. You will recall that Alexander the Great had extended not only his conquering armies but Greek culture as well, across the world of the Persian Empire as far as the region in northwest India known at that time as Gandhara. That cultural influence, known as Hellenistic, profoundly affected the artistic styles of early Mahayana Buddhism, especially with regard to sculpture. Hellenistic Greek influences can be seen clearly in some of the finest Buddhist sculpture of the early period in North India and central Asia. This early affair with the West was, unfortunately, destined to be short-lived. Nonetheless, some of those early renderings of Buddha and various bodhisattvas make them look positively Greek.

The Theravada tradition deliberately abstained from honoring the memory of Buddha with artistic likenesses; statues and paintings could all too easily become idols. Undoubtedly, this was, in part, a reaction to the highly sensuous religious art of Hinduism. The Theravadins were not entirely iconoclastic, though; some symbolic works of art were tolerated, such as a carved or painted footprint representing the path of

FIGURE 11.1   Too bad this Thai stupa isn't in color. The entire surface is covered in small gold tiles. (P. Bresnan)

Buddha's teaching. And, of course, that perennial trademark of Buddhism, the *stupa*, was widely distributed in the lands of Theravada Buddhism.

A *stupa* is a structure, generally made of masonry covered with painted plaster that looks something like a hand-held bell, with the handle at the top. It can be any size, but not even the largest ones are meant to be entered. The original stupas, derived from Hindu sources, were simply ceremonial monuments erected over the remains of the dead. In Buddhist hands, the stupa became a shrine to house a relic of Buddha or sometimes of a bodhisattva. As such, the stupa provided an attractive focus around which a Buddhist community could gather for the purpose of honoring the memory of Buddha and renewing their commitment to the Dharma. In no way was the stupa a sacred object meant to be a place of worship (at least that was the intention). Some Theravadin stupas were modestly ornate, but, on the whole, the artistic side of Theravada was noticeably less than exuberant.

What Theravada shunned, Mahayana welcomed with open arms. The stupa, a relatively small and humble affair in Theravada, became a splendid memorial in Mahayana Buddhsim. Each land that Mahayana migrated to evolved its own style. Although most remained small, some were built on a colossal scale. The Tibetan Buddhist stupa at Bodnath near Kathmandu, for example, is a full square block at its base, and nine stories tall. Festooned with prayer flags and large painted eyes at the summit, it is one of the most striking examples of Buddhist art to be found anywhere in the world. Some of the greater stupas became Mahayana pilgrimage sites. At Bodnath, there is a never-ending flow of pilgrims circumambulating the great stupa, endlessly turning the many prayer wheels built into all four sides of the base. It's an entrancing spectacle, full of beauty and spiritual power.

Sculpture, too, evolved in many directions as Mahayana migrated to new lands. Like the stupa, this also found expression on the grand scale. In India and China, Buddhist statuary of incredible size was carved right out of the virgin rock in some places. At Kamakura, Japan, an immense seated Buddha was until recently the largest bronze statue in the world. On a more modest scale, but no less spectacular, the Wat Trimitr temple in Bangkok is home to a larger-than-life Buddha cast in solid gold. These are just a very few examples; I could go on and on. The point is that wherever it went, Mahayana Buddhism inspired a tremendously rich and varied output in the arts.

Oddly enough, with all of this wealth of imagery, a great many people in the West continue to cling to the notion that Shakyamuni Buddha was a jolly fat man with a big belly. Nothing could be further from the truth. This mistaken idea stems from a confusion of Buddha with certain mythical characters. In fact, one of the most popular themes for images of Buddha represents him at the time of his awakening. At that time in his life, Buddha had been practicing extreme ascetic disciplines, including fasting. Such statues often show him looking almost like a skeleton, the only thing protruding being his ribs.

But far and away the favorite theme, found in all Buddhist cultures, is the seated Buddha in the posture of meditation. Serene, peaceful, blissful; this is what it's all about. What an interesting contrast this makes between the central icons of Christianity and Buddhism. The figure of Jesus is shown on the cross, writhing in the agony of a terrible death. Buddha, on the other hand, is shown as a man perfectly composed and totally at peace with himself and the universe. How is this difference to be interpreted?

So what are we to make of this "great vehicle," the self-styled Mahayana? One thing should be clear: Mahayana was a part of the same broad development that had earlier

FIGURE 11.2   Great bronze statue of Amida Buddha at Kamakura, Japan. (P. Bresnan)

produced Theravada. Mahayana is not a system that stands in opposition to Theravada, but it certainly was an opening-up of Buddhism. Everyone now had access to it. It's almost as if Buddhism turned the tables on Hinduism. Early Buddhism, in danger of being swallowed up in the vastness of Hinduism, transformed itself into something of a likeness of Hinduism. All of the various Yogas found new expression in Buddhism, including Bhakti, the devotional yoga that promotes love and veneration of a personal savior. In this way, Buddhism transcended itself, invigorating itself with great new life and launching out on a new age of expansion that is still continuing today.

The Doctrine of Shunyata, implications of which can be traced back to Buddha himself, was a logical new foundation for Mahayana. It cleared away dependence on philosophical systems of all kinds, opening the way to every conceivable kind of expression of the Dharma. Shunyata allowed the focus to be solely where it should be, on the development of wisdom and compassion. More and more, Buddha came to be referred to as "the compassionate Buddha." Compassion, not arhatship, became the guiding principle of the Buddhist monk.

An important question in this study concerns the matter of religion. Did Mahayana, as it grew to overshadow Theravada, transform Buddhism from a fundamentally secular way of life into a fundamentally religious way of life? Many believe that it did, and that therein lies its glory. Quite obviously this is the opinion of the Russian Buddhologist T. Stcherbatsky. Consider this florid comment of his on the subject (and all in one sentence at that):

> When we see an atheistic, soul-denying philosophic teaching of a path to personal Final Deliverance consisting in an absolute extinction of life, and a simple worship of the memory of its human founder, when we see it superseded by a magnificent High Church with a Supreme God, surrounded by a numerous pantheon, and a host of Saints, a religion highly devotional, highly ceremonial and clerical, with an ideal of Universal Salvation of all living creatures, a Salvation not in annihilation, but in eternal life, we are fully justified in maintaining that the history of religions has scarcely witnessed such a break between new and old within the pale of what nevertheless continued to claim common descent from the same religious founder. (quoted in Murti, 6)

Stcherbatsky nicely states the prevailing opinion of the nineteenth and early twentieth centuries. Theravada was seen as a purely secular, non-theistic system, very limited in scope, that was replaced by—and transcended by—the magnificent new spiritual system, Mahayana, which rapidly grew to become one of the world's great religions. The modern view is much less polarized. Modern study of the history of Buddhism is more interested in the common roots and shared interests of Theravada and Mahayana. Mahayana is seen not so much as a system in conflict with Theravada as it is a new direction, an opening up, in the evolution of Buddhism. Obviously, Mahayana, in its willingness to offer a meaningful interpretation of Buddha's teaching to all sectors of society, absorbed into itself some elements of practice that we ordinarily think of as religious in nature. And some of the "spokes" of the wheel of Mahayana went much more deeply into that sort of thing than did others. But we must keep in mind that part of the greatness of Buddhism is the freedom that ultimately resides with every individual man and woman to follow the Dharma in the way that is personally judged to be right. Religious elements? Definitely, for many. But a religious institution? That's a different story. Unlike the evolution of Christianity, for example, there has never developed within Buddhism an overarching institutional framework; there has never been a Buddhist "establishment" to define and enforce orthodoxy.

Undoubtedly, some within the Buddhist fold did transform the Dharma into what can generally be regarded as religion. Buddhist "churches" flourish throughout the world even today. In this, Buddhism was reflecting the general character of the world that it grew up within. Some of the spokes of the wheel, such as Pure Land Buddhism, became very religious. Others, such as Zen Buddhism, much less so. Speaking of that metaphor of the wheel—Theravada at the hub, and Mahayana being the spokes—perhaps the outer rim of the wheel, where the rubber meets the road, can be seen as representing the actual practice of the Dharma. That's what keeps the whole thing rolling.

And roll it did. Mahayana Buddhism would make its way north to central Asia and China, and then on to Viet Nam and to Korea and Japan. A look at the map might suggest that the route to China would go through Tibet, but the geography of the region worked against this. Actually, Buddhist ideas established a permanent place in China by way of the great trade route known as the Silk Road, named for that much-desired trade item that originated in China. It was an overland route that wound for over two thousand miles through the wilds of central Eurasia connecting the civilized centers of the East and the West. The Indian subcontinent was connected to the Silk Road by way of a subsidiary route that wound up through the mountain passes of the northwest. Goods—and ideas—were thus passed back and forth between India and China. The teaching of Buddha entered China proper during the time of the Han dynasty, and eventually found a welcoming new home there. Other than Marxism in the twentieth century, Buddhism is the only significant foreign philosophical system ever to be integrated into Chinese culture. Buddhism in China has a very rich history indeed, and it is to the native traditions of China, and the emergence of Buddhism alongside them, that we now turn.

Study Questions

1. What was it about the character of the Theravadin tradition that opened the way for the rise of Mahayana? Why did Mahayanists refer to the Theravada tradition as "Hinayana"?

2. How did early Mahayanists defend their contention that the Mahayana scriptures were authentic sutras?

3. Why do the various sects of Mahayana all love the *Prajnaparamita* so ardently? What is it about the *Prajnaparamita* that makes it a suitable foundation for all of these sects, which differ greatly among themselves?

4. How does Christmas Humphrey's image of the wheel attempt to tie together the many disparate elements that make up the world of Buddhism? Can you think of a better way of picturing it?

5. How does the nature of Shakyamuni Buddha change from Theravada to Mahayana? How do you make sense of that enormous transformation?

6. Explain the Doctrine of Trikaya. Why was trikaya a logical development in the growth of Mahayana? What's your personal reaction to the concept of trikaya?

7. "It is the universality of the Buddha-nature that is at the heart of the Mahayana revolution." What does this mean?

8. Why is the "Doctrine of Shunyata" sometimes referred to as the "Doctrine of Emptiness"? Do you

feel that you understand this matter of shunyata? In what way does it open the door for manifold legitimate interpretations of Buddha's teaching?

9. Nagarjuna concluded that there are fundamentally two different kinds of knowledge. What are they, and how do they differ? Do you agree with him?

10. What was Nagarjuna's goal with regard to his dialectic concerning human knowledge?

11. What does nihsvabhava mean? How does it relate to the Doctrine of Shunyata?

12. In what way does a bodhisattva differ from an arhat? Is one "better" than the other? Which holds greater appeal for you?

13. How does Mahayana explain the reality of samsara (reincarnation)? How does this differ from the Hindu interpretation? What's your personal reaction to the Mahayana interpretation?

14. In general terms, what was the difference in the role of the arts between the Mahayana tradition and the Theravada tradition? What accounts for this huge difference?

15. What do you made of the quote from the Russian Buddhologist, T. Stcherbatsky? Is Mahayana Buddhism in fact a religion in the customary sense of the word?

PART THREE

Non-Buddhist
Traditions of East Asia

In Part III, we will examine three influential non-Buddhist traditions native to East Asia. Confucianism and Daoism, which developed in China, were well-established traditions in their homeland by the time Buddhism appeared on the scene. Important in their own right, they would also interact with Buddhism in various ways, significantly influencing its development. Shinto is an indigenous tradition that developed in Japan. It too would influence the development of Buddhism. Each of these non-Buddhist traditions has maintained its integrity over time and has survived into the modern era, where they are all now showing signs of renewed vigor.

CHAPTER 12

Confucius and Confucianism

Confucius gave to Chinese civilization a grand ideal for the ordering of society. If followed perfectly, the Confucian system promised to fashion a society that would be harmonious, peaceful, prosperous, and governed by wise leaders dedicated to the welfare of all. And, the individual within this society would be a person of refinement and compassion. All of this was to be accomplished by reestablishing the harmony between human society and the natural order, which is continually threatened by unchecked selfish interests. More than other Chinese schools of thought, Confucius's vision of the right social order became a model that has inspired Chinese social thinking through the ages.

As best we can tell, Confucius lived in eastern China from 551 to 479 B.C.E., a tumultuous, but undoubtedly exciting, time to be alive in that part of the world. Due to the incessant jockeying for power among the many feudal warlords, the time is known to historians as the Period of Warring States. It is also known as the Period of a Hundred Philosophers. The insecurity of the age spawned many (if not quite a hundred) competing philosophical systems, each claiming to have the cure for the ills of the time. Confucius was the founder of one of these schools, certainly one that was destined to become most famous and influential over time. His teaching, therefore, deserves our full attention. But to fully understand the teaching of Confucius, we must see it in its larger context, both with respect to the competing philosophical systems and in the broad historical context out of which the Age of Confucius evolved.

The cultural history of a society proceeds slowly and seamlessly from the very simple to the highly complex. There tend not to be decisive moments, "cultural asteroid impacts," when one era abruptly ends and another begins. But, our human brains have a craving for order, and if it's not inherent in the things we study, we'll simply impose it on them. As a result, history is neatly divided into "Ages" and their subdivisions. Understandably, little is known for certain about the very early history of China. Nevertheless, historians and archaeologists are in general agreement that history proper in China (as opposed to its more tribal antecedents) first took form around 2100 B.C.E. This first chapter is known as the Xia dynasty. Not much is known yet about Xia, but research is actively underway. Knowledge about the dynasty that followed, though, known as Shang, is on much more solid ground. Much of the earliest historical material, including artifacts and the beginnings of a written script, has been gathered from excavations at Shang sites.

In most important respects, therefore, we can say that the formative period of Chinese civilization was the *Shang Period*, or the Shang dynasty. Its time of birth can't be dated precisely, but 1800 B.C.E is a reasonable approximation. Its end, though, was a different story; about that we can be more precise. In the year 1054 B.C.E. (or close to it), the Shang dynasty came to a violent end at the hands of its warlike neighbors—more about that later. Thus, Shang endured for some six or seven centuries, and during this formative time, Chinese civilization developed much of its basic character.

The people of Shang were conscious of their own identity and distinguished their own small world from the surrounding sea of "lesser" peoples. They were an agricultural society, living for the most part in small settled villages and exercising some measure of control over their destiny. They were united under the rule of a hereditary king, and he maintained a royal court at a capital "city," which, in essentials at least, was an embryonic urban center. And, most strongly felt of all, the men and women of Shang were united in a shared set of religious beliefs and practices.

The general animism of earlier times lived on in Xia and Shang, but became more refined. The world of spirits was presided over by a supreme being, known simply as *Shangdi* (*Shang Ti*). The heavenly realm ruled by *Shangdi* was an analogue of the earthly realm ruled by the Shang king. Generations might come and go like the leaves of the forest, but, unlike the leaves of the forest, departed ancestors were not mere dust to be lost and forgotten. Their spirits took up residence in *Tian Shangdi** and could remain an influential force in the world of living men and women. Thus, the people of Shang defined themselves, not only in terms of the space they occupied, but also as a society enduring over time. The past, the present, and the future were united as one great family in *Tian Shangdi*. It was therefore appropriate that ancestors should be respected and venerated. Eventually, everyone would become an ancestor.

No hereditary priestly class took form in China as it did in India. There were no Chinese "Brahmins," so to speak, but there were many who played the role of shaman and sorcerer. Religious ritual and sacrifice were a common part of life in the time of Shang and provide us with many of the artifacts that have survived from that distant time. Divination, the foretelling of future events through supernatural means, was apparently a widely practiced art. This commonly took the form of heating animal bones, often the sternum of an ox, in a fire. The resulting cracks were believed to hold clues about the future, clues that could be interpreted by the skilled diviner. Large numbers of these so-called "oracle bones" have been found at Shang archaeological sites. Sometimes the bones were inscribed with characters, and these give us valuable glimpses into the first stage in the evolution of Chinese writing. They also give us tidbits of information about life in the Shang dynasty.

Of one thing we can be sure: The very success of Shang became its greatest problem. This was a difficulty shared by all early centers of civilization. The sedentary way of life, based on simple farming, made possible a growing wealth in agricultural land and valuable goods.

---

*There is controversy among scholars regarding the use of the word *Tian* as far back as the Shang dynasty. For our purposes, though, it suffices to indicate the "heavenly realm" of *Shangdi*.

Such a situation would, naturally, excite the interest of predatory neighbors. The resources of Shang must have been increasingly devoted to defense, but eventually the greater size and power of the outsiders proved to be too much. In the eleventh century B.C.E., the kingdom of Shang fell to an onslaught launched by the armies of their much larger and very warlike neighbors to the west, the people of Zhou. The story of the evolution of Chinese civilization would enter a new chapter; the Shang dynasty was replaced by the Zhou dynasty. In its turn, Zhou would hold the stage for eight centuries.

Zhou conquered Shang, but did not destroy it. The lands and resources of Shang were absorbed into the kingdom of Zhou, which extended over a vastly greater area of eastern China. In fact, the new Zhou kingdom was much too large to be ruled by a centralized authority. Instead, it was divided up into approximately seventy semi-autonomous duchies, each presided over by locally powerful nobles who owed allegiance to the monarchy. Even some of the Shang nobles were allowed to continue to hold power so long as they were willing to pledge their loyalty to their new king. The Zhou kingdom was, in other words, a solidly feudal state, similar in organization to the feudal states of Europe in the Middle Ages. The power of the king was directly proportional to the amount of control, and loyalty, he held over the regional princes. In the early days of Zhou, this power was strong, but it would slowly erode.

The ancient religious beliefs and practices were retained in Zhou, but evolved toward a somewhat more humanistic outlook. Man's proper relationship to nature became a matter of growing interest. The importance of this subject would remain central in Chinese thought throughout the ages. We can also detect a growing interest in the nature of right government. The concept of the "Mandate of Heaven" took form and became a matter of major concern. The Mandate of Heaven refers to the belief that the earthly king presides as something of a steward of the gods. His rule is legitimate only so long as he fulfills the will of heaven, which is to say, to govern wisely and well, in the interest of all. If he allows selfish interest to replace concern for the common good, he will lose the Mandate of Heaven and thus the right to rule. This principle became, retroactively, a rationalization for the Zhou conquest of Shang. After all, it was rationalized, they were just doing the work of heaven, dismantling a corrupt monarchy that had forfeited its right to govern and replacing it with legitimate rule.

In the course of time, the rulers of Zhou faced the same problem they had caused for the rulers of Shang: aggressive incursions into the western parts of the kingdom launched by the more numerous tribal peoples from the lands beyond. Finally, in the year 771 B.C.E., the monarchy was forced to abandon the ancestral capital and move "lock, stock and barrel" to a new headquarters farther east at the city of Luoyang (Lo-yang). The Zhou monarchs would hold on here, at least nominally, for another five hundred years, but the power of the king over his nobles gradually deteriorated to the point where the king of Zhou ultimately became nothing more than a figurehead. He was powerless to control the regional nobles, whose relationship more and more degenerated into a condition of constant feudal warfare.

The Zhou dynasty would reach the end of its road in 255 B.C.E. The four centuries preceding its demise constitute a time of troubles known as the Period of Warring States. Feudal warfare, ravaging armies, brutal conquest, shifting boundaries, ruined crops and villages—such was the general picture. Life for the peasantry was full of insecurity and suffering. Not only did they have to deal with the predations of unruly armies, but the men were forever being torn from their families to fill the battlefield-reduced ranks of those same armies. Death and privation were the order of the day.

Given the length and chaotic nature of the Period of Warring States, it should not be surprising that many thoughtful individuals felt inspired to try to find a better way, a way that would restore the much-yearned-for peace and security. "In disorderly times men long for order," Confucius declared. And, in fact, the time of the late Zhou did see the appearance of many new social philosophies, all of them seeking to be a blueprint for the right ordering of society and government. This was a natural response to the turmoil of the times. And there was quite a range of offerings to choose from. It is for this reason that the Warring States period is also known as the Period of a Hundred Philosophers. One of the great philosophies to emerge from this time was that which we know as Daoism (Taoism).* The tradition of Daoism deserves a full examination and shall be the subject of the next chapter. The earliest of the schools, though, and the one that we shall examine in this chapter, was founded by the man we know as Confucius.

CONFUCIUS

Unfortunately, we don't have a great deal of verifiable information about the life of Confucius. The sources that do exist are pretty bare bones, and much of what is commonly reported about the man is based on legend and conjecture. The earliest known biography of Confucius is a short entry in the *Shiji*, a collection of biographies written in the first century B.C.E. by the Chinese historian Sima Qian (Ssu-ma Ch'ien). Four centuries had elapsed between the death of Confucius and the writing of this biography; Sima Qian had to rely on scanty and unreliable sources.

A much better source is to be found in the words of Confucius himself. Although Confucius never wrote an autobiography, much of his teaching has been preserved. Most of what we believe to be his words, though, are really nothing more than a collection of aphorisms written down and preserved by his disciples. These were gathered together in the *Lun Yu*, which we know in English as the *Analects of Confucius*.

Perhaps the best source of all for reliable insight into the life and character of Confucius is the *Mencius* (the *Meng Zi*), which is an exposition of the philosophy of Mencius, a devoted follower of Confucius, who added much to the total picture of what we call "Confucianism." Mencius was not a contemporary of Confucius—he lived about a century later—but he was close enough in time and association to have access to a great deal of reliable information about him. The *Mencius* is full of little insights about Confucius.

These three—the *Analects*, the *Mencius*, and the biography of Sima Qian—comprise our basic sources of information about Confucius, his life, and his teaching. Other sources

---

*There are two systems for rendering Chinese names and terms into the Roman alphabet. The newer system, the pinyin, is rapidly replacing the older system, the Wade-Giles. I have used pinyin throughout this book. However, since only recently published works employ the pinyin system, many of the quotations in this book include Wade-Giles spelling. Please keep this in mind when you encounter a difference in spelling. (Quotations appear exactly as written.) For example, Tao in Wade-Giles, becomes Dao in pinyin. And *Tao Te Ching* in Wade-Giles becomes *Dao De Jing* in pinyin. Spelling of individuals' names will also change. Lao Tzu, for example, becomes Lao Zi. This can be confusing, but it is the necessary price we must pay to convert to a much more sensible system.

exist, but their accuracy is often questionable. From these various sources, taken as a whole, we can abstract a simple but reasonably credible account of the life of Confucius.

Let's begin with his name. Confucius, of course, was not his name; it is a Latinized version of the Chinese pronunciation, a practice popular in the West when Europeans first began to take scholarly interest in cultures other than their own. (It seems pretty quaint today. Imagine, for example, referring to Mao Zedong as Madocius.) The family name was Kung, and he became known as Kung Fu Zi (K'ung Fu-tzu, in the Wade-Giles system). "Kung Fu-tzu," in the hands of nineteenth-century Europeans, became "Confucius." So, should we now revert to the more properly Chinese pronunciation? Perhaps so, but the Western world has become so used to saying "Confucius" that there seems to be little inclination to do this. Even "K'ung Fu-tzu" is a far cry from the actual Chinese. Thus, for the time being anyway, Confucius he shall remain.

Confucius was born, according to the Western calendar, in 551 B.C.E. His home region was the state of Lu, which more or less corresponds to the modern Shandong Province. This is a very populous region in northeastern China that includes the large peninsula which forms the southern gateway to the Gulf of Po Dai. Then, as now, this area was very much at the center of Chinese life and culture. Not much is known about Confucius's early life. The family was not particularly well off, and this situation was made much worse by the death of his father when Confucius was only three years old. He was raised by his widowed mother and claimed, in later life, to have known real poverty as a child. At nineteen he married, producing one son and two daughters. The family could claim some aristocratic ancestry, and this connection helped Confucius secure a government job around the time when he married. He worked within the bureaucracy of the state of Lu, first as the manager of a state granary and later as the manager of some state-owned herds of cattle and sheep. Supposedly, he did very well at both posts, but his heart was set on other things.

Undoubtedly, Confucius had a brilliant mind and also a winning personality. From an early age, he had been very interested in learning, especially the study of the already ancient history and culture of his people. While still quite young, Confucius made something of a name for himself as a scholar. At the amazingly young age of twenty-two, he gave up his bureaucratic post and opened his own school. This, of course, was not a school in the modern sense of the word; it was more a group of already educated young men from the better families who wished to associate closely with a master. It was probably much like the academies founded by such Greek philosophers as Plato and Aristotle. Confucius would draw on the traditional wisdom of China to teach his disciples about the principles of right living and right governing. He described himself as a transmitter, not an originator. Any sincere seeker was welcome, rich or poor, but presumably most of the disciples were from wealthy families, and Confucius was able to make a decent living doing what he loved most.

His career really took off when one of the leading nobles of Lu sent his own two sons to study with Confucius. This opened doors for him, and soon Confucius was associating with the movers and shakers of Lu. With his two noble students, Confucius visited the capital city and gained the respect of the Duke of Lu. What Confucius wanted most of all was to secure a government post which would make him the power behind the throne. Then he could put his ideas of right government into practice and transform Lu, or any other place willing to give him the chance, into a model of good government. "If any ruler would submit to me as his director for twelve months," he said, "I should accomplish something considerable; and in three years I should attain the realization of my hopes."

Unfortunately, Confucius never got the opportunity he longed for. This was largely due to the fact that high posts in government went only to members of the top noble families. For a few years, Confucius did occupy the office which today we might call Minister of Justice, and while serving in this post, he instituted some social reforms that attracted a fair amount of attention. However, a feud in the ruling family forced Confucius to temporarily flee the state of Lu, and he never again had an opportunity to hold high office.

Confucius would not return to his home district of Lu for twelve long years. During this time of self-imposed exile, his was the life of an itinerant philosopher, accompanied by a small band of disciples. He was generally welcomed at the courts he visited and shown high honor, but no one was willing to turn over the power of government to him. He yearned for the opportunity, though, and apparently felt rather bitter that no one recognized his genius. Commenting on the situation, his sense of frustration was sometimes obvious: "Am I a bitter gourd, fit only to hang out of the way, not good enough to eat?"

Confucius's ideas on the right ordering of society remained basically in the realm of theory. But he had started a fire that would never go out. For all time to come, his name would be highly honored, and in time, his system of values would be integrated into the very essence of Chinese social and political life. Confucius died in 479 B.C.E. at the age of seventy-three. He was buried near his native town; a shrine at the gravesite remains even to this day an important pilgrimage place among the people of China.

The suffering of the common people was the central concern of Confucius. That point deserves to be emphasized. Confucius was a very compassionate man, and the suffering that he saw everywhere among the common people moved him to action. Much like that of his great contemporary, Shakyamuni Buddha, Confucius's teaching amounted to a solution to a problem, and at the root of the problem was the ubiquitous suffering of ordinary men and women who were the victims of the turmoil of the age.

As pointed out before, Confucius lived during a very stressful time in Chinese history. He was born into the later part of the Zhou dynasty, the second of the great historical eras of Chinese civilization. The Zhou, named after the dynastic ruling family, was essentially a feudal era and would eventually give way to the Han, during which dynasty China would be welded into a great unified empire.

In Chinese history, the Han dynasty plays a role similar to that of the Roman Empire in European history. But at the time Confucius was born, all of that was still three centuries in the future. In Confucius's time, the ruling Zhou no longer held the vast realm of China together as it had in former times. The tightly knit fabric of feudalism was unraveling. Petty wars, feuds, and class conflicts had become the order of the day. From our perspective, we can see that Chinese society was evolving away from feudalism toward something new, but the transition was difficult. People of the time, not being any better than we are at seeing into the future, looked backward instead. Life in the time of the ancestors had been peaceful and orderly, but now it had become chaotic. The conclusion: the social order was sick; it was in a state of decline; and the future would be even worse.

Confucius, too, looked back to a "golden age" when the feudal system had been strong, when everything had been in its appointed place and life was peaceful and prosperous. Undoubtedly, he exaggerated the positive side of the picture somewhat, but he did study the history of the early Zhou with great thoroughness. He identified certain prominent figures of the era, "sages" as he called them, to whom he attributed almost divinely inspired wisdom. By carefully studying the lives and the works of these men, Confucius believed that he could determine the essence of their wisdom and come to understand the essential elements of right governance. He would then be a teacher to his own troubled age, a transmitter of the wisdom of the ancients, and hopefully bring about a healing reformation of the social order. He would reveal the truth of Dao, which, to Confucius, meant the right "way" for men to live.

A thoroughgoing reformation was obviously necessary. Leadership at all levels of society was in a sorry state. Government, which should be the leader and protector of the people, was often oppressive instead. Nothing was worse than living under oppressive government. To emphasize this point, Confucius told the story of a woman he happened upon one day weeping beside a gravesite. She told him that her husband had been killed by a tiger at that spot, and before that her husband's father had been killed at the same spot by the same tiger. "And now," she wept, "my only son has also been killed here by that tiger." Confucius asked her why she didn't go away from such a dangerous place. "Because," she answered, "in this place there is no oppressive government." "Remember that," said Confucius, "oppressive government is more terrible and more to be feared than a killer tiger."

To Confucius's mind, the overriding concern was order—that is, reestablishing order in society. But not just any kind of order would suffice; it must be a natural order. Confucius believed that there is a right ordering of society that is natural to it, in the same way that there is a right ordering to all of the things of nature. Human society had gotten out of harmony with the larger natural order of which it is a part. (Sound familiar?) We are part of a natural world in which all of the myriad elements, from wildflowers to stars, fit together in a perfectly ordered harmony. Everything is an expression of the working of the whole. The ancients had understood this, but their descendants, pursuing selfish interests, had strayed from the path.

Nothing in nature ever sets itself apart and operates in conflict with the universal harmony. Well, nothing, that is, until we come to the evolution of human society. And therein lies the problem. But it doesn't have to be that way. As the study of ancient society revealed to the mind of Confucius, human society properly led and properly ordered can exist in perfect harmony within the natural order. Man is a part of nature, and therefore human nature, in the judgment of Confucius, need not be in conflict with the natural order. Evil and selfish acts are a corruption of the innate tendency of man's nature to be in harmony with the universal order. Right leadership can reestablish that harmony.

So where to begin? Confucius would begin with the family. The family was seen as the basic unit of society; nothing could be more important. In the Confucian system, the importance of the family cannot be exaggerated. Individual families are the living cells which together make up the organism of society. Society is an extension of the family. In fact, the entire social order of China was regarded as being one great extended family. The ruler of the state was in effect the *paterfamilias* of this one great family. And he was expected to play the role and assume the duties appropriate to the father in this relationship.

In the Confucian system, though, the king "reigns," but he does not actually "rule." He is groomed from childhood to be a symbol—a father figure, a watchdog, in a sense— but the business of day-to-day governing was to be in the hands of carefully selected ministers. And these men, far from being the corrupt, self-serving nobles of Confucius's age, were to be a legion of "new men," chosen for their suitability and their dedication to the ideal of service. What a revolution that would be! The existing aristocracy could keep their titles and their wealth, but like the contemporary bluebloods of England, for example, they would be "relieved" of the often-onerous responsibility of governing. Confucius would do nothing less than sweep away rule by the predatory hereditary aristocracy and replace it with governance by a new nonhereditary aristocracy, one based on talent, compassion, and commitment to serving the needs of the common people. The character of this "new man" that Confucius envisioned was called *junzi* (*chun-tzu*); the achievement of *junzi* was, and still is, the heart and soul of the Confucian system.

But where in the world were such men to be found? Confucius could imagine that men of *junzi* were common in some idealized past age, but in his own troubled times, such a man was rare indeed. Confucius was well aware of this dilemma, and thus his program of reform did not call for an overnight solution. In the Confucian program, a new system of government necessitated a new system of education. In fact, there was no real system of education at all—the sons of noblemen were educated, if at all, by tutors and on-the-job training. Most of their time and energy went into mastering the arts of warfare. Confucius had no interest in this; he had a whole new plan in mind. Confucius would institute an actual system of education, an organized program of development spread out over many years. This program, based largely on study of the classics of Chinese literature, was designed to produce the new man of *junzi*. Confucius would take the malleable child, and through the right kind of education, which included the teacher as role model, he would create a man of superior humanistic learning, of refined personal manners, and the will to govern wisely and compassionately. And, most important of all, this new system of education was to be open to all! At least potentially it was to be open to all. Anyone who showed promise would be accepted, no matter what his rank in society.

Considering all of this, isn't it amazing that Confucius is sometimes criticized as being a defender of feudalism? What could in fact be more revolutionary, more nonfeudal, than the system that he proposed? The charge grows out of a misunderstanding of Confucius's admiration for what he perceived to be the condition of society in the early days of the Zhou dynasty. The social organization was undoubtedly very feudal in those days. What Confucius admired was the stability of society, the peace, the apparent respect for law and order, the harmony with nature—all of the things, in other words, that were painfully lacking in his own age. And, it must be admitted, he did accept a heirarchy of rank in society as being completely natural. He attributed the felicity of the former time to the wisdom of its rulers, "sages," as he called them. And he saw his own role as being a transmitter of this ancient wisdom; he would be the bridge that would link his own troubled age with the wisdom of the past. But, it was not so much the *form* of government that he wanted to emulate, as it was the sage-like *character* of those entrusted with the actual task of governing. In other words, Confucius believed that he saw men of *junzi* in the past and wanted to bring that ideal back to life in his own time. Of course, despite his modest denial, Confucius was far more than simply a transmitter. His system may have owed a debt to traditional values, but nothing like it had existed before. Within the body of Confucius lived a creative mind of the first order.

To sum up, the perpetual suffering of the common people had persuaded Confucius that the existing social order, founded as it was on rule by a corrupt and predatory aristocracy, was untenable. In its place, he would establish an orderly society governed by men chosen for their superior ability and dedication to service. His new system of education would mold the best from all ranks of society into men of *junzi*. They would become not only the governors, but the living models for all members of society, and in this way, health and order would be restored.

Confucius's vision of a healthy society is an inspiring creation. Let's now look more closely at the specific elements out of which this vision was constructed. And again, the place to begin is with the institution of the family. For Confucius, as for virtually all Chinese, the family is the bedrock foundation of the social order. The family is the beginning and end of all. Also, it is the model for the entire society. Perhaps more than being simply a model, Confucius viewed the whole society as actually *being* one great family. Values learned within one's own family were simply to be extended to the broader society as one matured. The family, in other words, was the learning ground where one developed (hopefully) the attitudes and behavior upon which the healthy social order depended. Chief among these social virtues was, and is, *filial piety.*

The cultivation of filial piety could be said to be the cornerstone of Confucius's social philosophy. In its simplest sense, it refers to the love and respect shared between father and son, and between older brother and younger brother. It is in these relationships that the virtue of filial piety is first cultivated, but by extension, it reaches out to embrace many other relationships that are part of the social order: ruler and subject, for example, master and apprentice, older person and younger person. Filial piety, then, refers to the proper mode of behavior between individuals in situations in which a natural relationship of superior and inferior exists. In Confucius's day, society was organized hierarchically, and many such relationships were a part of daily life. Of course, modern society has its rankings too, but perhaps not to the same degree.

Confucius's reform program, revolutionary though it was, did not aim to obliterate the hierarchical arrangement of the social order. His was not yet the "classless society." Confucius accepted class distinctions as natural and therefore good. His goal was simply to carefully define the *natural* relationships that exist in a healthy society and to establish these relationships on a foundation of virtue and respect. It was Confucius's conviction that the proper ordering of society was the logical and necessary beginning place for his program of reform and that a clear definition of social relationships was at the heart of the proper ordering of society.

To be more precise, Confucius discerned Five Cardinal Relationships within the social order: ruler and subject, husband and wife, father and son, elder brother and younger brother, and friend and friend. The first four of these—at least in the opinion of Confucius and his contemporaries—carried a relationship of superior and inferior, which was expressed as rule and submission. There were appropriate duties for each. The responsibility of the "ruling" party was to govern with righteousness and benevolence. The responsibility of the "submitting" party was to obey with righteousness and sincerity. In the "friend and friend" relationship, it was the responsibility of each to promote the growth of wisdom and virtue in the other.

I should point out that this subject can take us onto some shaky ground. There is controversy among modern scholars regarding how deeply Confucius himself actually went into the matter. It's true that in the *Analects*, when Confucius was asked by a disciple what should be the first order of business, he answered, "the rectification of names." This is taken to mean defining the social order, identifying everything in its proper place, and spelling out the proper role of each. There is some evidence, however, that this part of the

Analects was added at a later time by those who sought to use Confucius's authority to justify an authoritarian form of government. Making a virtue out of submission to the ruler would suit their purposes very well.

Confucius would never advocate blind submission to an unjust superior. But he obviously respected the role of submission, broadly speaking, in a natural relationship between superior and inferior, so long as that relationship was guided by the virtue of filial piety.

And what about the place of woman in the Confucian system? Well, it's also pretty obvious that Confucius did not believe in the equality of the sexes. We would have to search far in his age to find someone who did. Like ancient societies generally, the culture that produced Confucius believed that the female sex is innately inferior to the male sex, and therefore, the natural and proper role of woman is submission. This is not to say, however, that the role of woman was not important; it was *very* important. But that role was entirely bound up in the affairs of family life. (It would seem, in fact, that Confucius believed it was not possible for a man to achieve real excellence of character without the help and support of the women in his life. Confucius was deeply attached to his mother and mourned her death with great passion. But not a word has come down to us about her, or his wife, or either of his two daughters.)

We must keep it in mind that Confucius believed that the discord of his age was to be explained by the fact that Chinese society had lost its moorings. What was needed was to reestablish the natural order of society, such as had existed in earlier times. This could be accomplished by studying the practices of the ancestral sages and applying that wisdom to the present situation. Above all, it was necessary to rectify the fundamental relationships in society and to reestablish respect for the duties appropriate to each of these. So far, so good; but, stated in this way, the matter remains at the theoretical level. The working out of these relationships in daily life, though, is not theoretical at all; it is very real and very down to earth. Another way of putting it is to say that it's one thing to *design* a proper society, but, how do you make it work? What is it that will regulate and maintain the proper harmony in the interrelationships among the members of society? This is where *li* enters the picture.

In its original meaning, the word *li* meant sacrifice, but over time, it came to refer more broadly to an elaborate set of procedures and protocol that governed the celebration of religious rituals, including the offering of sacrifice and the honoring of ancestors. *Li* was the operative procedure that regulated intercourse between the world of men and the world of spirits. As such, *li* was seen to be extremely important to the whole society. Gradually, the formal manners of *li* had expanded from this core religious position to embrace as well the formal manners that regulated social intercourse between members of the feudal nobility. By the time of Confucius, *li* had become something similar to the ceremonial code of chivalry that later evolved within the feudal nobility of medieval Europe. It was an elaborate system of customs and manners that specified the ways in which noblemen would relate to one another in formal situations—in other words, court etiquette. This included such things as what one said, how one said it, how one dressed, how one stood or bowed, whether or not one carried a sword, everything. There was never any guesswork, never any embarrassment or offense; everything was spelled out by the formal customs of *li*.

In effect, what Confucius proposed was to extend the scope of *li* to include the *entire* social order. *Li* was not merely to regulate the relations of noblemen or persons participating in religious celebrations; *li* was to become an external way of regulating all relations. All of the elements of social intercourse—for everyone—would be structured in certain ritualized manners. Many modern readers, particularly Western readers, probably find the whole concept of *li* somewhat repugnant; it seems to make daily life so formal, and rigidly divides the social order into elitist ranks of authority and privilege. But please remember that the world of Confucius was nothing like the world of today. He was not egalitarian in any sense of the word. People of his time accepted the ranking of the social order as natural and inevitable. The important thing was not to abolish ranking in society but to bring harmony and peace to the complex interrelationships that made it up. Confucius saw the customs of *li* as a marvelous way of achieving that end.*

Li, then, in the Confucian system became a refined system of manners designed to regulate the personal interactions arising in the various social relationships. And, most important, by doing this, *li* supported and upheld this system of relationships which Confucius believed to be the essence of a healthy social structure:

> [Confucius] believed that the proper observance of *li* was essential to the development of goodness in an individual as well as in a society. *Li* for him was the restraining and refining force, creating the sense of balance and harmony in a man . . . The concept of *li* is "a kind of balance wheel of conduct," guiding a way of life that avoids extremes, and a state of mind in which human reasoning and feeling reach perfect harmony. This is exactly what Confucius said: "Among the functions of *li*, the most valuable is that it establishes harmony." (Chai and Chai, 42–43)

Perhaps *li* is not as foreign to us as it might at first seem to be. To a certain extent, all societies have customs and manners deemed appropriate for certain relationships. Isn't one likely to act in a somewhat formal way with one's employer, or with a judge in court? And in military society, these customs are not subtle at all. But the Confucian system went far beyond this sort of thing. *Li* was the superficial expression of a whole philosophy of social organization. However, Confucius would have been the first to insist that it was the *principle* of *li*—honor and respect for the dignity of the other person—that gave *li* its value. Practicing the external manifestations of *li* was worthless if it lacked a sincere heart. If it were only a matter of superficial display, Confucius had no use for it at all. "Does *li* mean no more than a display of jade and silk?" he asked.

To sum up, Confucius's vision of a healthy society was built on the foundation of order. The Five Cardinal Relationships, which he believed to be inherent in the nature of human society, were the expression of that order. And *li*, the well-regulated system of relationships among the members of society, assured that the harmonious order of society would be maintained in daily life. Together, *li* and the Five Cardinal Relationships provided the framework of a healthy social order. But separately, they are only frameworks, an orderly but basically lifeless situation. It was *junzi* that breathed life into this body. It was Confucius's vision of *junzi* that evoked excitement in the hearts and minds of his disciples. The real life of the Confucian system is *junzi*.

---

*We can get something of a feel for the character of *Li* in the "gentlemen's code" of the Victorian Age.

Loosely translated into English, *junzi* means "the Superior Man." Above all, what Confucius was after was the re-creation of the kind of man exemplified by the ancestral sages that he so much admired and loved. Such superior persons, men of *junzi*, occupying positions of leadership would be able to restore harmony and prosperity to Chinese society. Furthermore, such superior men, by the power of their example, would initiate a general spreading of the spirit of *junzi* throughout all of the parts that made up the great family of Chinese society.

So what actually is *junzi*? What is the "Superior Man"? To begin with, the Superior Man was created, not born. That is, the man of *junzi* was not some kind of inherently superior breed, such as people of noble birth liked to believe themselves to be; he could emerge from any rank of society. What made the Superior Man superior was that he had worked long and hard to cultivate within himself those virtues that distinguished the ancestral sages. Anyone willing to make the effort could make the grade. (We must again remember that traditional society excluded women from roles of public leadership. Although a woman might achieve great strength of character and be highly respected within the family, the term *junzi* in the time of Confucius could be applied only to men.)

Before all else, Confucius was a teacher by profession; he operated a school in the broad sense of the word. Understandably, he made education the foundation of the process of development that would lead to *junzi*. He was largely responsible for defining what education should consist of and that it should be available to promising men from all ranks of society. The Superior Man would be knowledgeable in the entire legacy of the past. This was not simply book learning; it was total education for life. Confucius's Superior Man, rather like the Renaissance Man of European history, was to be a well-rounded human being, conversant and skilled in all areas of life. He was to be polished, dignified, self-confident, and very well-mannered. He was to be the finest expression of his culture. The Superior Man was, in a word, a true *gentleman*. But there was more.

The Superior Man did not live to serve his own self-centered ends, no matter how refined these might be. His reason for being was to serve the common good. His goal was to make himself as fit as he possibly could be to best serve the needs of the community. If he held public office, service was the one and only reason for seeking it. After personal refinement, a deep-rooted spirit of altruism was the mark of the Superior Man.* And there was still more.

At the core of the Superior Man—in fact, the golden nugget at the absolute heart of the entire Confucian system—was *ren* (*jen*). This is a very difficult word to translate. Perhaps the best we can do in English is to call it "human-heartedness." It was not enough for a man to be refined and altruistic. Most important by far was that he be a man of *ren*; this was the real spirit of *junzi*. A Superior Man was the embodiment of *ren*. *Ren* is sincere feeling and caring for others; *ren* is gladly putting others first; *ren* is compassion; *ren* is human-heartedness.

How can such a thing be taught? Confucius would say that you can teach yourself; everyone can. There is nothing metaphysical about it; nothing supernatural. "*Ren* is a natural feeling that comes directly and spontaneously from the human heart" (Chai and Chai, 37). Every normal person, Confucius would argue, has deep-seated warm and compassionate feelings about himself (or herself). By looking deeply inward, we can

---

*Doesn't this seem similar to the concept of *noblesse oblige*?

discover this core of love and learn to gradually extend it outward to embrace others, ultimately all others. It begins with the immediate family and expands to include the greater family of the whole community.

But, you might ask, isn't this all rather naive? Loving your fellow man and practicing the Golden Rule are fine ideals, but most human beings are far too weak and selfish for such ideals to be dominant in real life. Not so, Confucius would respond; people are selfish and insensitive out of ignorance and fear. They mistakenly believe that they will be the winners and achieve happiness. But all experience shows that this is not the case. Man is basically loving by nature; we see it clearly in our feelings about ourselves. If we fail to extend it to others, it is because of fear and ignorance. We fail to perceive our underlying bonds with others. But, whenever we are moved to overcome this resistance, we experience great happiness, great joy. And that's because *it is our nature* to be loving. Confucius would never have asked anyone to take his word for this; it's something that each person can easily check out for himself or herself. The experience of dealing with others in a human-hearted way is its own reward and gives rise to the greatest happiness. One can see for oneself that the way of *ren* is *the human* way to live. (Consider how you feel when you wave another driver into a line of traffic instead of pulling up so that they have to wait. Or, consider how easily these feelings flow from you to a little child or an injured person, that is to say, one who is not a threat, one who provokes no defensive reaction. These may be a rather humble examples, but I think they make the point.)

Confucius was a wise and practical man. However much he may have believed that *ren* was available to all, he was realistic enough to know that it wasn't simply a matter of pointing this out, and everyone would shout, "Why didn't we think of that before?"—and suddenly all society would become kind and loving. But there were undoubtedly some—those who were the true men of *junzi*—who would make the discovery. They would become the embodiment of *ren*. These Superior Men, out of a spirit of service, would become the leaders of society, and *they would be the models for society as a whole.*

Confucius firmly believed that the common people are profoundly influenced by the example set for them by the leaders of society. If the leaders are greedy, everyone is greedy. But if the leaders are selfless, that same quality of selflessness will flower among the common people. This is presumably what Confucius meant by this somewhat enigmatic statement: "Not more surely does the grass bend before the wind than the masses yield to the will of those above them." The sense of it is that bad government encourages bad habits in all; good government promotes virtue in all. In an age where the leaders are selfish and greedy, the people become cynical and think that this is the way it always is. But when a society establishes procedures that allow Superior Men to become the leaders, that society will enjoy peace and harmony; it will enter a golden age.*

And that, precisely, is what Confucius proposed to do for his own age. It's true that he never got the opportunity to implement his ideas on a grand scale, but his teaching touched the hearts of many. And for the ages to come, Chinese society was profoundly shaped by the philosophy of Master Kung Fu Zi.

---

*To some small degree, this sort of thing happened in the United States when John Kennedy was president back in the 1960s. His leadership was viewed, especially by the young, as a departure from the old ways and the dawning of a new era, one with an emphasis on service and equality. Looking back on the time, one can't help but be impressed by the temporary outpouring of optimism and cooperation, the Peace Corp being only one of the better-known achievements of the age.

There are some interesting similarities between Confucius and Shakyamuni Buddha. Confucius, like Buddha, encouraged people to look inward. "Be a lamp unto yourself," as Buddha put it. Discover your true nature, and be free of ignorance and all of the human suffering that ignorance gives rise to. Surely Buddha would have liked Confucius's core concept of *ren*. "The man of *ren* is always happy; a common man is always sad," Confucius declared. Buddha's invitation was to become an "awakened" person, a person of *prajna*. Confucius's invitation was to become a "superior" person, a person of *junzi*. Leaving feeble words aside, how different really are these two?

MENCIUS

Confucius was survived by a community of disciples dedicated to preserving the teaching of the Master. As noted, this is how the *Lun Yu* (the *Analects of Confucius*) came into existence. The tradition flourished for a while, but might have become scattered and forgotten had it not been for the work of Mencius, who was born just about a century after the death of Confucius. Mencius (also a victim of the Latinizers—his Chinese name was Meng Zi) loved the teaching of Confucius. "There never has been another Confucius since man first appeared on Earth," he said. He also paid Confucius a high compliment by saying of him that "he had a child's heart." (What do you suppose he meant by that?) Broadly speaking, the evolving tradition that came to be known as "Confucianism" contains as much of the thought of Mencius as it does of Confucius himself. For this reason, Mencius is sometimes referred to as the "Second Sage."

Mencius was born in 372 B.C.E. (or close to it) and lived until 289 B.C.E., a generous life span of eighty-three years. Although not a contemporary of Confucius, his life too was situated squarely within the tumultuous Warring States period. If anything, things were even more tumultuous during Mencius's life; the warring among the Chinese states was building to a climax that would finally reach its bloody end only thirty-four years after his death.

Although Mencius was not an immediate disciple of Confucius, the two men were closely linked philosophically. One can't help but think of the relationship between Socrates and Plato. Confucius, like Socrates, was a relatively humble man with a passion for truth and devoted his whole life to an inquiry into the truth that men should live by. He wrote little, if at all, and were it not for his disciples, his teaching would have died with him. Mencius, on the other hand, was more like Plato; he was a rich man and took pleasure in elegant clothes and manners. He was far more doctrinaire than Confucius, seeming to want to preach the truth, rather than search for it. But he loved the teaching of Confucius deeply and was largely responsible for it becoming a permanent part of Chinese culture. And, also like Plato, his thinking built on the teaching of the master, developing what was only implied in it, and taking it further.

The work associated with Mencius is known by his name. (It is referred to as the *Mencius*, or the *Meng Zi*.) As was the case with Confucius, and with many other philosophers of the time, it seems most likely that the *Mencius* was not directly written by Mencius himself, but rather was the collected teachings of the master, put together by some of his disciples after his death. In many ways, the *Mencius* is similar to the *Analects*, but the *Mencius* offers us a much fuller development of the themes. Whereas the *Analects* is a rather brief collection of terse and pithy aphorisms, the *Mencius* is a collection of genuine stories; it includes far more detail and humor. The wry wit of the author comes through clearly. We don't have this kind of personal connection with the *Analects*. Reading the *Mencius*, though, throws much light on the *Analects* because the *Mencius* takes up many of the same themes. The *Mencius* has similar themes, similar goals, much the same spirit as Confucius, but by no means are the two works indistinguishable. If nothing else, times had changed too much between their lifetimes. The evolution of Chinese history was more than a century further downriver by the time of Mencius and this shows clearly in his work. If I may borrow a metaphor from Isaac Newton, Mencius may have stood on the shoulders of Confucius, but this allowed him to see farther.

Before we focus on what Mencius contributed to the Confucian tradition, let's identify what the two men shared in common. Both Confucius and Mencius were from the same general region, the state of Lu. Both were products of the Period of Warring States. Both were itinerant philosophers, who failed in their desire to hold powerful public office. Both men founded schools, attracting large numbers of disciples, and in both cases, it was the disciples who eventually put the teaching of the master into writing.

Of greatest importance was the basic agreement between them as to the truth of *Dao*, the right "way" (that is, the natural right way) of conducting one's life. Both men believed that right education could transform the wild infant into a man of *junzi*, a "Superior Man," a sage—and that achieving sagehood was the only legitimate goal of life. Mencius fully agreed with Confucius that the family is the basis of the social order and that the maturing of compassion begins within the family. Then, through right education, compassion can be directed to move outward, ultimately to encompass the universal family.

Perhaps the most salient point of difference between Mencius and Confucius concerns purpose. Confucius saw the Superior Man's reason for being in terms of government service. He would fashion men of *junzi* precisely so that they could enter the ranks of the governing class and dedicate their lives to serving wisely and being a model for all. Mencius, on the other hand, focused on right living, not right governing, as the proper goal of the Superior Man. This is not to say that Mencius was indifferent to the need for wise rulers—far from it; but this was not the *focus* of his teaching. His interest was more basic, more individualized. Identify those who are capable, and help them achieve sagehood. A society that honors this ideal in its educational system will naturally incline toward good government.

Mencius believed that everyone is at least potentially capable of becoming a sage because he believed in the inherent "goodness" of human beings. This belief is often attributed to Confucius, but, in fact, Confucius had very little to say on the subject; it was Mencius who added this element to the teaching of Confucianism. This is not to say that Confucius denied that man is good by nature. Rather, it would seem that Confucius focused more on the matter of "naturalness." Confucius believed that man is born in a state of harmony with the natural order and only falls out of harmony by choosing selfish interest that is in conflict with the common good. Mencius went beyond this to actually define human nature as being naturally inclined to that which is morally "good." Obviously, human nature can be corrupted, and often is, but, Mencius would maintain, at its root, human nature is good, and no matter how often it's wounded, the urge to goodness is always ready to grow back, like grass on the sunny side of a hill.

Anticipating the Daoists (or perhaps borrowing a metaphor from them), Mencius compared human nature to water. Human nature seeks the good in the same way that water seeks the lowest place: "Human nature is good just as water seeks low ground. There is no man who is not good; there is no water that does not flow downwards" (Lau, 160). For all practical purposes, Mencius equated goodness with compassion. We could say that goodness is the latent disposition, but the action that flows from it is compassion. To support his contention that the inclination to goodness, compassion, is inherent in all men and women, Mencius offered the example of a person, any person, who suddenly comes upon a scene in which it appears that a small child is about to fall down a well.

> My reason for saying that no man is devoid of a heart sensitive to the suffering of others is this. Suppose a man were, all of a sudden, to see a young child on the verge of falling into a well. He would certainly be moved to compassion, not because he wanted to get in the good graces of the parents, nor because he wished to win the praise of his fellow villagers or friends, nor yet because he disliked the cry of the child. (quoted in Lau, 82)

In the above example, Mencius is arguing that virtually any person would feel a spontaneous burst of compassion for the child. It's the universality and suddenness of it that makes the point. Given time to think it over, some might find selfish reasons to ignore the child or, on the other hand, find selfish reasons to go the child's rescue. But in so doing, they have allowed their natural disposition to be smothered by selfish desires and fears. What this all adds up to, at least for Mencius, is that the goal of right education must be to work with the natural inclination to goodness that lies at the heart of every person; cultivate it from the time a person is very young and don't allow self-centered fears to stunt its growth. On this path, any person can eventually become a sage.

In most respects, Mencius would agree with Confucius as to the definition of a sage. Confucius's Superior Man and Mencius's sage were similarly highly educated individuals in whom compassion ruled over selfish interest. Both admired the self-contained individual who freely chose to serve the needs of the community with no thought of reward. His reward is the abiding joy that comes from knowing that he is a contributing part of the whole. Mencius summed up his own view of the superior person in these words:

> When he achieves his ambition he shares these with the people; when he fails to do so he practices the Way alone. He cannot be led into excesses when wealthy and honored, or deflected from his purpose when poor and obscure, nor can he be made to bow before superior force. This is what I would call a great man. (quoted in Lau, 107)

But what *really* is a great man, a sage? Is it simply a matter of adding up all of these fine virtues, or is there something else, something most essential of all that truly defines the sage? Mencius's answer would be far different from that of Confucius. And here, it may well be, we come to that element of the teaching that most distinguishes Mencius from Confucius. In his heart of hearts, Mencius was a mystic; Confucius most definitely was not. For Mencius, the ultimate reward for cultivation of the self was to know the unspeakable bliss that arises only from the obliteration of that same self. The end of wisdom is to be achieved in becoming "one with Heaven," in which state all distinctions between the self and nonself are dissolved. "For a man to give full realization to his heart is for him to understand his own nature, and a man who knows his own nature will know Heaven." (Lau, 182) Perhaps in this statement Mencius added a profundity to Confucianism which was something wholly new.

OTHER VOICES FROM THE PERIOD OF A HUNDRED PHILOSOPHERS

The teaching of Confucius inspired a host of alternative systems in the Age of a Hundred Philosophers. Some, like Mencius, loved the teaching of Confucius and sought only to further develop its potential. Others disagreed fundamentally with the Confucian philosophy and sought to eclipse it with competing systems of their own. Among those who disagreed with Confucius, the Daoists would become paramount. We shall examine their contribution in the next chapter. Here, we will look briefly at three important figures from this restless time who reacted in various ways to the teaching of Confucius.

Xun Zi (Hsun-tzu)

The teaching of Confucius occupied something of a central position; others ranged out from that center in all directions. If Mencius pondered the teaching of Confucius and concluded that man is by nature good, then it was almost predictable that another would ponder the teaching of Confucius and conclude that man is by nature evil. This, in a manner of speaking, was the conclusion of Xun Zi, and it became the cornerstone of his teaching in the same way that the "goodness" of man became the cornerstone of Mencius's teaching.

It may be going too far, though, to reduce their philosophies to such simple terms as "good" and "evil." Mencius focused more on the concept of compassion, arguing that man has a natural disposition to be compassionate, which, of course, results in behavior that we normally call "good." Xun Zi, on the other hand, argued that man is selfish by nature, not compassionate. Goodness—that is, compassion—is an acquired virtue, Xun Zi would say, which develops naturally as one's inherent selfishness is overcome. So, in a way, both compassion and selfishness are inherent in human nature, but selfishness is initially the stronger and crowds out nascent compassion unless the individual, through right education, learns to deny the impulse to selfishness. In that event, the individual is free to develop into a "Superior Man."

Like Confucius and Mencius, Xun Zi regarded self-cultivation leading to sagehood to be the most important goal of life. And he agreed that right education was essential if one were to follow the Dao, in the sense that Confucius used that word. Unlike Confucius and Mencius, though, Xun Zi believed that only a very few were capable of making the grade. Theoretically, his educational system might be open to all, but it was a foregone conclusion that the great masses of the common people would be excluded for lack of potential ability. Apparently, Xun Zi thought of the common people as being little better than animals.

Perhaps we're being a bit too hard on Xun Zi. Not much is known about him for sure, not even his dates, though the best guess is that he lived from about 300 to 225 B.C.E., which would make him a much younger contemporary of Mencius. From what has survived of his teaching, we can see that he was a powerful thinker and very influential in his own day. Presumably, he was as popular as Mencius at the time. He makes a nice foil to Mencius. If Mencius's relation to Confucius was like that of Plato to Socrates, then, in some ways, Xun Zi played the role of Aristotle in this triangle. Like Aristotle, Xun Zi was a brilliant thinker and totally rational; mystic insight seemed to have no place at all in his philosophy. He, in fact, had no use for religion in any guise. To his way of thinking, religion is nothing more than a collection of ignorant superstitions—acceptable perhaps for keeping the common people in line, but not worthy of having any place whatsoever in the life of a Superior Man.

Although Xun Zi's creative mind carried the evolution of Confucian thought into rich new ground, his influence was short-lived, and his name was eventually all but forgotten. Maybe this is due to the apparent dichotomy between the teaching of Xun Zi and Mencius. Mencius's insistence on the native goodness of human nature carried the day. Or maybe it was the result of his attitude regarding the common people; Xun Zi's contempt for the masses could have been the fatal flaw in his philosophy. H.R. Creel, a noted historian of Eastern thought, argues that Xun Zi simply lacked faith in humanity. "Hsun Tzu [Xun Zi] was, without qualification, one of the most brilliant philosophers the world has ever produced. But he lacked faith in humanity. This flaw, like the fatal weakness of the hero in a Greek tragedy, went far to nullify his best efforts." (Creel, 115)

Mo Zi (Mo-tzu)

Mo Zi lived relatively close in time to Confucius, but we can't be precise about his exact dates. We can say with some confidence, though, that he lived at least most of his life in the fifth century B.C.E., and at an early age, became an ardent Confucian. However, he soon became disgusted by what he perceived to be corruption of the master's teaching among many of those who claimed to be his followers. For example, there was a movement among some Confucians to form themselves into a sort of elite class, a Confucian *literati*, distinguished by overly elegant manners and a special kind of elaborate clothing unique to themselves. Also, some Confucians encouraged the practice of costly funerals, which they would manage at no small profit to themselves. These kinds of abuses sickened Mo Zi, and he finally abandoned his association with the Confucians, going off to found his own school.

Apparently, the influence of Mo Zi's teaching was very strong in his own time. It is presented in a short book of the same name, a collection of aphorisms compiled by his disciples. He completely agreed with Confucius with regard to some basic matters. Above all, both men wanted to reform the corrupt social order of their time. They would accomplish this by persuading the rulers to turn over administrative power to virtuous men who were dedicated to serving the common good. And both men would fashion these new men through a process of education aimed at resurrecting the ways of the sage-rulers of ancient times. But that's where the similarity ended.

Mo Zi had no interest at all in the liberal humanities of the Confucian system. He felt that it simply did not get at the root of the common people's problem. Like Confucius, Mo Zi believed that restoring order to society was the overarching need of the day. And not just any system of order would do; it had to be a system that would be in full harmony with the order of nature. Such a system, once achieved, would be perfectly stable. In Mo Zi's opinion, this called for a rigidly organized hierarchy of authority, which he believed was the way of nature. At the top of this pyramid of power would be the hereditary monarch, whom Mo Zi referred to as the "Son of Heaven." The government of the Son of

Heaven would rule with an unchallenged authority, and, interestingly enough, with the total support and loyalty of the people.

Why would the people be so supportive of an authoritarian regime? Because every man and woman would be imbued with a sense of what Mo Zi referred to as "universal love." He was not talking about love in the usual sense of the word; he had something far different in mind. In fact, that's exactly where this kind of love resided—in the mind. It was to be a philosophical kind of love springing from the recognition of the natural interrelatedness of all of the parts of a society. When one grasped the organic unity of it all and saw one's own real identity in terms of that unity, a deep love and loyalty to the system would inevitably follow. (An intriguing thought!)

Mo Zi totally dismissed Confucius's emphasis on the family as being of fundamental importance. In Mo Zi's opinion, the family was a breeding ground of segregation and emotionalism; it was an obstacle, not a help, to the achievement of universal love. Everyone should love everyone, without distinction. "If everyone in the world would practice universal love . . . then the whole world would enjoy peace and good order." Education was the key. Educate every person to see, clearly and distinctly, that the way of universal love was in their own best interest. We might almost describe it as a love engendered by enlightened self-interest. The ruler-sages would be models, and their example would eventually be followed by everyone.

Mo Zi was willing to sacrifice anything and everything that might interfere with the success of his ideal society. His teaching was ruthlessly utilitarian; if it doesn't help, out it goes. One of the things to go was emotion. Strange as it may seem, Mo Zi held that emotionalism was the enemy of the state. It has no place in the natural order of things because it serves no useful purpose. Emotion feeds individual desires and uncontrolled behavior. Therefore, in Mo Zi's ideal state, all expressions of emotion were to be purged. There was to be no art, no music, nothing at all that might excite the emotions of the people. It may seem hard to believe, but that is exactly what Mo Zi advocated.

In this highly Spartan state, absolutely everything was to be subordinated to the good of the whole. The love of all for all would arise when the people discovered that such a state was the natural way for human communities to be organized and that it was the only reasonable alternative to the chaos and corruption of the times. The smooth functioning of such a state depended on the unquestioned loyalty of the subjects. That loyalty would arise out of a sense of identity, and ultimately, all must identify with the supreme ruler, the Son of Heaven. He in turn identified with Heaven itself. When this state of total integration was achieved, the system would function perfectly.

But what if it didn't function perfectly? What if something went wrong? What if someone, even conceivably the Son of Heaven himself, were to do the unthinkable and choose selfish interest ahead of the good of the whole? Such disloyalty could be disastrous, but how would you know? Mo Zi's answer to this was that wrongdoing (otherwise known as disloyalty) would be punished by Heaven. Mo Zi declared that natural calamities were the punishments of Heaven.

> Heaven sends down immoderate cold and heat and unseasonable snow, frost, rain and dew. The five grains do not ripen, and the six domestic animals do not mature. There are diseases, epidemics, and pestilence. Hurricanes and torrential downpours occur repeatedly. These are Heaven's punishments, visited on men below because they fail to identify themselves with it. (quoted in Creel, 59)

What would Confucius have said if he could have heard this? Confucius had sought to liberate the common people from their superstitious fears of the spirit world, but here was Mo Zi playing on these very fears, thus reviving what Confucius had attempted to purge.

Han Fei Zi and the Legalists

In the springtime of 1974, a farmer was digging out a well near the modern city of Xian in central China. Not far from the surface his shovel suddenly scraped against the head of a buried statue. It was a life-sized terra cotta figure of a soldier, but not like any soldier seen in a very long time. The figure hauled out of the earth had not seen the light of day in more than two thousand years. It was, in fact, the startling first look at what was to become one of the greatest archaeological finds in all of human history.

The farmer had stumbled upon the outskirts of the giant tumulus tomb of Shi Huangdi, the first emperor of China, founder of the Qin (Ch'in) dynasty. His megalomania in life was intended to continue in death, and following his earlier orders, his body was laid to rest in a burial scene of incredible splendor and size. The whole world has become fascinated with the find and is eager to see it all uncovered, but the site is being most carefully excavated, and the work remains only partially completed. It is becoming clear, though, that a full-sized replica of the entire court accompanied Shi Huangdi to the grave in 210 B.C.E.

The original tumulus was over six hundred feet high, and that man-made hill was only the centerpiece. It was constructed to guard the court, little of which has yet been excavated. Surrounding it is an immense entourage of at least seven thousand full-sized terra cotta soldiers and horses with chariots, all arranged in military formation. Each was originally painted and adorned with the appropriate provincial headdress.

All of this stupefying display of wealth and power was made possible by Shi Huangdi's successful conquests. But it hadn't always been that way. Before becoming the first emperor, Shi Huangdi had been simply the Duke of Qin, living in much humbler surroundings. But things began to change one day when he read a philosophical tract authored by one Han Fei Zi.

Han Fei Zi was the principal spokesman for a group known collectively as the Legalists. The book that bears his name was presumably written by him, not compiled by his students, and lays out in chilling detail the essentials of the Legalist philosophy. They are called the Legalists, not because they valued law as a means of protecting the rights of the people, but rather because they saw written law as a powerful instrument by means of which the ruling authority could exercise control over the whole society. The Legalists were authoritarian in the extreme. A better word might be totalitarian.

Like Confucius, Han Fei Zi aspired to reform the sick social order of his time, and he agreed with Confucius that this could not be accomplished unless hereditary rule was abolished. But he completely disagreed with Confucius about the power of virtue. To Han Fei Zi's way of thinking, virtuous, unselfish action was fleeting and unpredictable. In no way was it something to be counted on. To base the governance of a state on the presumed virtuous behavior of its ministers was, in his opinion, completely ridiculous.

Han Fei Zi was an advocate of strongly centralized rule and a thoroughly Spartan way of life. He went far beyond even Mo Zi in this regard. The entire society was to be regimented in the form of a military organization, always ready, and even eager, for war.

The law, which would be publicized and clearly known by everyone, would be like military law. Terrible punishments would be meted out for even trivial offenses. For example, if Han Fei Zi had his way, one would lose a hand for merely throwing waste ashes into the street. Han Fei Zi believed that large crimes could be prevented by dealing severely with small crimes. Above all, law and order must prevail. On the other hand, extreme punishments were to be balanced by generous rewards. Reporting a crime, for example, would earn a handsome reward. A complete listing of rewards and punishments would be spelled out in the law. *Everything* would be spelled out in the law. But again, this was not to protect people's rights; the common people had no rights, as we understand the word. People exist for the state; the will of the state must be their will. Such a system, the Legalists argued, was a strong and healthy alternative to the chaos and corruption of that time.

This extreme philosophy of statecraft, so totally contrary to the spirit of the teaching of Confucius, might have remained only an academic curiosity had it not aroused the interest of the Duke of Qin, one of the independent regions of China during the Warring States period. After reading some of Han Fei Zi's writings, the Duke wanted to meet the man behind the writing and learn more about this intriguing militaristic philosophy. Han Fei Zi accepted the invitation, traveling to the court of Qin in the year 233 B.C.E. Ironically, he died there in prison that same year, having been unjustly accused of spying. But the flame of interest was already lit, and it would soon grow to a bonfire in the state of Qin.

Inspired by the teachings of Han Fei Zi, and the Legalists generally, Qin made itself over into a one hundred percent military machine, and then went on the warpath. The various states of China had been fighting among themselves for centuries, but no one of them had been able to overwhelm all of the others. That was about to change. In a series of unbelievably bloody conquests, the state of Qin finally brought the Period of Warring States to a close by conquering all of the others and welding all of China together into its first true empire. We know it as the Qin dynasty. (Qin is spelled Ch'in in the formerly popular Wade-Giles system, and that, in fact, is why that land came to be known in the West as "China.")

The triumph of Qin was a very violent affair. A bloodbath followed the completion of the conquest. Legend has it that 400,000 troops who had surrendered were summarily executed. Many similar incidents were reported. All critics of the new government were executed, especially Confucian scholars. Han Fei Zi had written that "in the state of an intelligent ruler there are no books, but the laws serve as teachings." Consequently, a decree was issued ordering the burning of virtually all books; almost the only books to be spared were those dealing with military science and agriculture. The Spartan way of life of Qin was imposed on the whole land. The law came down with ferocity on even the smallest of offenses. It must have seemed that there was no way to avoid being labeled a criminal.

Given this general state of affairs, many gave up hope of being able to live peacefully in the new state. Great numbers of people, including many Confucians, fled into the hill country where they organized themselves into guerrilla bands. As the severity of the rule increased, the strength of the counterrevolution also grew. The government was completely unable to stamp it out. In the year 210 B.C. E., Shi Huangdi, the founding emperor of Qin, died. But he had done everything in his power to see that he would not be forgotten. The incredibly opulent burial scene discussed earlier was his parting shot. And it was certainly an appropriate sendoff for the founding emperor of a dynasty that was decreed to see ten thousand more emperors. Well, not quite—four years later, the whole Qin administration collapsed in the face of a general uprising led by a peasant soldier, Liu Bang, who would found a wholly new dynasty, the Han dynasty, on the ashes of Qin.

The extreme totalitarianism of the Legalists moved from theory to practice in the administration of Shi Huangdi, but the downfall of Qin did not permanently put an end to this philosophy; it occupies a part of the spectrum of social philosophy that is ever-present. It was the contribution of the Age of a Hundred Philosophers to enunciate systems that represent virtually all of the various possibilities of this broad spectrum.

LATER DEVELOPMENTS IN THE EVOLUTION OF CONFUCIANISM

Confucianism in the Time of Han

Broadly speaking, the Han Empire was to eastern Eurasia what the Roman Empire was to western Eurasia. Both were universal states, ruled by an authoritarian central power, which, through military conquest had welded together the disparate parts of their respective cultures. And, also broadly speaking, they existed at the same time in history. The Roman Empire came into being somewhat later than Han, and would outlive it, but both endured for approximately four centuries. Both empires brought to an end a long period of civil strife, replacing it with an enforced peace upheld by uniform law and military power. Eventually, the central authority of the Han Empire and the Roman Empire succumbed to the onslaught of tribal peoples from beyond the frontiers, having lost the vitality needed to hold them back.

The Qin Empire could conceivably have endured, and there never would have been a Han. Their own excesses of brutality and repression, however, provoked the uprising that resulted in the fall of Qin after less than half a century of rule. The founder of the new dynasty was, surprisingly, a peasant. His name was Liu Bang, but as the first emperor of Han, he became known as Han Gaozu (Han Kao-tzu). He had been the leader of a resistance group whose original power base had been in the Han River valley, and it was in honor of that special place that the new dynasty took its name.

The Han Empire came into existence in 206 B.C.E. and would hold onto power for four centuries. The boundaries would eventually include almost all of what we commonly think of as China today. To the east was the ocean, to the south and west great masses of mountains, and to the north the endless steppes of northern Asia. It was the northern frontier that was most worrisome. Here were to be found potentially predatory tribal peoples in numbers beyond counting. Their mounted armies could sweep in like the wind. It was to hold them back that the Great Wall was begun in Qin times. During Han, the wall was greatly expanded and fortified. It worked well, for a while, just as Hadrian's Wall worked well for the Romans, for a while. Eventually both walls proved insufficient to their assigned task.

Of great importance in the history of Confucianism was the reign of Emperor Wu Di (140–87 B.C.E.). He was a strong ruler who did much to consolidate the power of the central authority. Wu Di became a champion of Confucianism, and during his reign, the Confucian system of governmental administration became established as the orthodox system of the empire. With the usual ups and downs of fortune, it would remain a guiding influence in the government in China until modern times. We may question how deeply Emperor Wu Di understood or cared about the actual teaching of Confucius. Some feel that the adoption of Confucianism on his part was a purely utilitarian move. Perhaps he simply liked what he heard about the Confucian respect for the rankings of authority. Here could be a philosophy, properly adjusted to fit the needs of the empire, that could help to unify the state and provide a convenient disguise for his authoritarian rule. In any case, it was Wu Di who sponsored the implementation of the first Confucian system of governmental administration in China.

The real hero of the story, though, was a Confucian scholar by the name of Dong Zhong Shu. Dong was a man of great learning, widely respected, and known to be a little unusual. For one thing, it was his habit to deliver his lectures from behind a curtain so that the purity of his scholarship would not seem to be tainted by his personality. Unusual or not, it was to Dong Zhong Shu that Emperor Wu Di entrusted the daunting task of establishing a system that would produce the Confucian sages that would be needed to fill the ranks of administrative posts. It was Dong who created the famous Confucian system of competitive examinations, designed to single out men of proven excellence, who would thus be selected for careers in government service. This became the established system not only in China, but in other East Asian countries as well.

The examination, however, was only the capstone of the process. Dong instituted an educational system, open to any young man who showed ability. It was designed to be a long and very rigorous education, focusing on what Dong identified as the essential five classics of Chinese culture (known as the *Wu Jing*). These included study in metaphysics, politics, poetry, the social graces, and history, as well as special emphasis on the classics of Confucian teaching. Far more students were accepted than would ever finish the course of study; their numbers were winnowed by a series of examinations leading up to the final great examination, conducted over a period of days by learned Confucian scholars. Pretty formidable, to say the least, but those few who made the grade became highly honored members of society and were the privileged ones allowed to enter into careers in responsible government posts where they could spend their adult lives in service to the whole society.

The Confucian educational system, of course, took time to mature. When Dong Zhong Shu set up the first group at the court of Wu Di in 134 B.C.E., he employed only five teacher-scholars and had only a handful of students. Within ten years the number of students had grown to fifty, and within a century there were more than three thousand. The initial establishment was something of an "imperial university" located at the emperor's court. In time, it became necessary to found branch locations in strategic places. Eventually, the system created by Dong was responsible for more than a hundred men a year entering government service.

Great as the success of Confucianism was during the time of Han, by no means would it be true to say that they had the field all to themselves. By this time, the Daoists were a strong presence throughout Chinese society and in the imperial court as well. Confucians and Daoists engaged ceaselessly in a generally friendly competition for influence. (Much more about the Daoists in the next chapter.) And the Buddhists, too, were slowly but steadily growing in influence, especially by the time of late Han. The Daoists, despite themselves, were intrigued by the philosophy of Buddhism and absorbed much of it into their own way. The Confucians, however, at least initially, were repulsed by what they perceived to be a foreign religion that sought to lure promising young men into the seclusion of the monastery instead of into a life of public service. They opposed the Buddhists and would have been happy to see the whole foreign thing extinguished. But that was not to be; they were destined, in fact, to work out an interesting accommodation.

Neo-Confucianism

Officially, the Han dynasty came to an end in the year 220 C.E., but it had been unraveling for decades before this due to a host of problems, internal and external. Chinese society would not be unified again until the establishment of the Sui dynasty in 581 C.E., more than three-and-a-half centuries after the fall of Han. This long interregnum was marked by all kinds of civil strife, regional warfare, barbarian invasions, and a return to that troubling insecurity that was the hallmark of the Period of Warring States. The relative anarchy of the time was a boon to Buddhism, which flourished in China during the time after the fall of Han, but they were hard times indeed for Confucianism, which had been so closely iden- tified with the now-defunct Han establishment. By the time of the Sui reunification, Buddhism was triumphant. The Confucians had much work to do if they were to regain influence in the affairs of Chinese society.

The Sui dynasty was short-lived, existing for a total of only twenty-six years. Sui's contribution was simply the reunification of China. Tang and Song, however, the two dynasties that followed Sui, were long and brilliant. Together they dominated the scene until 1236 C.E., a six-century span of time that many regard to be the golden age of Chinese civilization. Buddhism was ascendant in China during this historical period; it certainly was the golden age of Chinese Buddhism. Chan Buddhism (which would become Zen in Japan) matured in China during the Tang and Song dynasties. The relative stability of the times was the opportunity the Confucians had been waiting for. What resulted was a Confucian revival, but with a difference. Because of that difference, the Confucian revival of Tang and Song is generally known as "neo-Confucianism." This new breed of Confucianism would persist until the early twentieth century.

Oddly enough, this new breed resulted from what started out as an effort to reform Confucianism by going back to the purity of the original sources, Confucius himself and Mencius. But there was a problem with this. Pure Confucianism, however admirable it might be as a system of social philosophy, would simply not be able to compete head to head with Buddhism. Buddhism had become a total philosophy of life; it dealt with areas—metaphysics, for example—that had never been a part of Confucian thinking. If the Confucians were to restore the primacy of Confucianism, they would have to match what Buddhism offered. This they promised to do, and more.

If they were to meet the challenge of Buddhism, the Confucians would have to *read into* the Confucian classics much that simply wasn't there. The result, of course, was an interpretation of the classics that stretched their original meaning. It came down to an effort to make over Confucianism into something of a "secular religion." The net result was a hybrid of traditional Confucian teaching, some recast elements of Buddhism, and even bits of Religious Daoism. Taking parts from here and there, they produced what was really a brand-new creature. This revamped breed of Confucianism would enjoy long life; it was to remain an important part of Chinese culture until the beginning of the twentieth century.

So, was neo-Confucianism a success? Did the Confucians reestablish their primacy? Did they succeed in matching what Buddhism had to offer, and more? Not really. Buddhism was entrenched among the masses of the common people, and that wasn't going to change one bit. Among the educated upper class of Chinese society, though, Confucianism did reestablish a place of importance. Up to the time of the Communist revolution, it was largely true to say that Buddhism was the way of the masses, but Confucianism was the way of the educated upper class.

Confucianism in the Modern Era

Following the Sui reunification in 581 C.E., China was ruled by an emperor until the collapse of the Qing dynasty (popularly known as the Manchu dynasty) in 1912. During this long span of time, Confucianism had reasserted itself, at least among the upper class. It proved its durability, adapting well to the changing of dynasties, whether these be homegrown or imposed by foreign conquest. Qing, the last of the dynasties to rule China, came to power as a result of the Manchu conquest of 1644. From the beginning of Qing, Confucians played an important role in the government. The system of competitive examinations continued right up until the end. However, as time progressed, the upper class became more and more conservative; *stagnant* might be a better word. This seems to be the destiny of all empires. The Confucian establishment was a part of this process of ossification. Far from being the reform-minded servants of the people envisaged by Confucius himself, the Confucian scholars had all too often become mere bookworms, deliberately distancing themselves from the people they were supposed to serve. They were often nothing more than "frail weaklings, laughed at by soldiers and farmers."

The winds of change began to blow, though, and they were blowing from the West. By the late nineteenth century, the windstorm had become a typhoon. The impact of the West had a powerful effect on the culture of China. While Chinese civilization had been stagnating under the Manchu emperors, European civilization had been plunging forward, creating the technological revolution that was totally changing the world. European influence—cultural, technological, and even religious—became very strong in China. While Manchu China had allowed itself to become mired in its conservative ways, these "Western barbarians" had become a force that imperial China could not control. The European powers arrogantly divided China into "spheres of influence" so as to better exploit its trade. The unthinkable had to be thought: China had become so weakened that it might possibly lose its sovereignty altogether. What to do?

What to do indeed? Predictably, some wanted only to retreat into the shell of China's vastness, and wait out the Westerners. Eventually, this time of troubles would pass; it always does. To many, that seemed to be the attitude of the imperial court. Others sought to deal with the challenge of the West by absorbing the enemy: Integrate the desirable elements of Western culture and salvage the essence of traditional Chinese culture by making concessions where the nonessentials were concerned. Then it might be possible to stand up to the Western Powers without having to become one of them.

One such person was a reformer named Kang Youwei (Kang Yu-wei), who had become much impressed by the inspirational power of the Western religious groups who were aggressively proselytizing in China. Kang believed that all of the people of China could be aroused in a similar way by a new native religion based on the teachings of Confucius, which to his mind contained the essential germ of traditional Chinese culture. He would use the methods of Western religion to create a revolutionary movement that would unite all of the Chinese people in a crusade that would carry China back to independence and greatness. His vision of a new Confucian "religion" would go even beyond that. Under Chinese leadership, it would spread around the globe, initiating a New Age of world peace and progress:

> Kang argued that Confucius was not merely a transmitter of ancient teachings
> but a prophet who, ahead of his time, cast his message in subtle language full

of hidden meanings. Confucius, according to Kang, saw history as a universal progress through three stages, each with its appropriate form of government: the Age of Disorder (rule by an absolute monarch), the Age of Approaching Peace (rule by a constitutional monarch), and the Age of Great Peace (rule by the people). Kang's Confucius was thus a seer and prophet not only for China but for the entire world. (Shirokauer, 471)

Kang's interesting vision never materialized, but that of others did. The ultimate victors were, of course, the Marxist communists, who came to power in 1949. But it almost didn't turn out that way. Thirty-seven years before the communist triumph, in February of 1912, to be precise, six-year-old Pu Yi, the last of the Chinese emperors, abdicated the throne. A system of government that had ruled China for more than two thousand years had come to an end. It seemed at the time that China was destined to become a democratic republic on the Western model. Sun Yat-sen, the "Father of the Republic," and his successor, Chiang Kai-shek, labored hard to make that dream come true. But it was not to be. The stormy conditions of the time, both within China and globally, conspired to lead China down a different path. The leader of that different path was the peasant-turned-revolutionary national leader, Mao Zedong (Mao Tse-tung), founding father of the People's Republic of China.

From the very beginning, it had been a major goal of the communist movement in China to destroy all vestiges of Confucianism, and this has certainly been the policy of the CCP, the Chinese Communist Party in modern times. The Confucian educational system, competitive examinations and all, was rooted out entirely. (It should be pointed out, though, that a start in this direction was made in the final years of the Qing dynasty.) The official position of the People's Republic of China is that the teaching of Confucius is elitist and diametrically opposed to the goals of Marxist philosophy, particularly the goal of achieving a classless society.

Considering the state of Confucianism in China in recent centuries, it is easy to understand the bitterness that any self-respecting Marxist would feel. The Confucians in China had indeed become a privileged elite class, and they jealously guarded their special position. It could easily be argued that they had become parasitic and distanced from the common people. But would not Confucius himself condemn this situation just as vehemently as the communists did? I think so. The Confucianism condemned by the Chinese Communist Party was a corrupted version of the original teaching, a version that had grown largely out of "neo-Confucian" roots. The authentic teaching of Confucius has much to say to all of those who wish to establish a just social order in which those who govern are selected for their skill and compassion. Perhaps the time has come to re-open the door a bit and re-think the teaching of Confucius.

> ... the two areas of concern of Maoism [Chinese communism] are still very much like the Confucianism of the past. One concern is for values; the other for reality. For example, in Maoism, happiness means the relatively secure possession of the minimum necessities for decent life and the absence of suffering from deprivation, oppression, exploitation and neglect. These have also been the cardinal aims of Confucianism. (Chai and Chai, 172)

No one knows what the future holds, both for China itself and for the human family as a whole. It seems at least plausible, though, that whatever the form of government may be, China in the future will move more in the direction of democracy. Should this be the case, the teaching of Confucius may be in for a resurrection. "Democracy values freedom and the individual, and denies unlimited authority to the state; so does Confucianism. The entire humanistic and liberal background out of which Western democracy grew has much in common with the best traditions of Chinese thought." (Creel, 244)

Is a renaissance of Confucian humanism coming into view on the horizon? Or is it, perhaps, still just beyond the horizon?

Study Questions

1. The chapter begins with the statement that "Confucius gave to Chinese civilization a grand ideal for the ordering of society." In general terms, what was this grand ideal? Do you agree that it was all that "grand"?

2. What did Confucius mean by saying that human society had gotten out of harmony with the larger natural order that it is a part of? Would you say that the same thing is true today? How so?

3. What do you think Confucius was like as a person? Could he be compared to any modern person? What do you think Mencius meant by saying that Confucius had a "child's heart"?

4. *Junzi* is referred to as "the heart and soul of the Confucian system." What would a man (or woman) of *junzi* really be like? Do you feel that this ideal has any application in the modern world?

5. Why was the whole matter of *Li* so important to Confucius? What would you say is probably the most common misunderstanding regarding Confucius's concept of *Li*?

6. *Ren* is defined as compassion, "human-heart-edness," and then the question is asked, "How can such a thing be taught"? Well, how *can* such a thing be taught, or is it impossible?

7. In what fundamental ways are Confucius and Mencius in agreement, and disagreement? What is your reaction to the suggestion that Mencius took the teaching further?

8. What is your reaction to Mencius's story about the child about to fall into the open well? Does it really prove anything? Are people really "good" by nature?

9. It is suggested that Mencius was a mystic at heart. What does this mean? What is the evidence for this?

10. Why do you suppose that Xun Zi "thought of the common people as being little better than animals"? How do you react to this comment of his?

11. What does it mean to say that Mo Zi revived what Confucius had purged?

12. What is neo-Confucianism? Why is it called *neo*-Confucianism? How do you think Confucius would have felt about it? Do you see any outright contradictions in neo-Confucianism with regard to the original teaching of Confucius?

13. How do you think Confucius himself would have reacted if it had been possible for him to examine the system that bore his name at the beginning of the modern era?

14. Why, apparently, do the Marxists hate the teaching of Confucius? Trying to see the matter from a Marxist point of view, do you feel that this opposition is justified?

15. The chapter ends with the question: Is a renaissance of Confucian humanism coming into view on the horizon? Or is it, perhaps, still just beyond the horizon? What is your answer?

CHAPTER 13

Daoism

We have already encountered the word *Dao* in the previous chapter. Confucius had made the intriguing assertion that "If a man hears about Dao in the morning, and dies in the evening, his life has not been wasted." For Confucius, though, the word *Dao* apparently referred only to the right *way* of conduct—the right way for a person to live. For the Daoists, it would mean much more.*

"Way" or "road" was the original meaning of Dao. With such a broad possibility of applications, it's not surprising that use of the word *Dao* became rather pervasive in Chinese culture. A very early derived meaning of Dao referred to the grand way in which the heavens appear to revolve around the earth. The central pole of this revolution, the Pole Star, was seen to be the seat of the power of Dao, from which flowed continuously the creative force that ordered not only the movements of the heavenly bodies around itself, but all of the activities of nature. Over time, the concept of Dao became more and more abstract. Dao came to be regarded as the impersonal and infinite force, cosmic in scope, that stood behind the being and the unfolding of the natural order.

There is an interesting accord here between the Chinese concept of Dao on the one hand and the Indian concept of Dharma (Brahman-Dharma) on the other. In some ways, they appear to be quite similar. It would be a valuable exercise to mentally compare the two just to see to your own satisfaction how close a fit they really are. And this is just the beginning; there are many other tantalizing parallels to be found between Chinese and Indian philosophical thought. This, as we shall see, would become especially true with regard to Buddhism. In the early days of Buddhism in China, many of its terms were translated using Daoist concepts.

The distinct philosophical system that we know as Daoism crystallized during the same historical era in which Confucius lived, that is to say, the tumultuous Warring States

---

*A reminder: There are two systems for rendering Chinese names and terms into the Roman alphabet. The newer system, the pinyin, is rapidly replacing the older system, the Wade-Giles. I have used pinyin throughout this book.

period. Daoism took form a little later than the lifetime of Confucius, and to some extent was undoubtedly a reaction to the teaching of Confucius. On the surface, at least, Daoism seems to be the very antithesis of Confucianism. You'll see what I mean by this as we go along.

Once established, the Daoist tradition, like the Confucian, would continue on to the present day. Both traditions, however, would evolve over the course of time. In neither case would it be true to say that what exists today is a completely faithful expression of the original teaching. In addition to that, the Daoist tradition is divided into two very different species: One is known as Philosophical Daoism and the other is called Religious Daoism. Our primary concern in this study will be with Philosophical Daoism, but some attention will be given to the nature of Religious Daoism as well.

The central teaching of Philosophical Daoism is to be found in two fascinating works, the *Dao De Jing* (*Tao Te Ching*) and the *Zhuang Zi* (*Chuang Tzu*). Both of these were produced during the Zhou period, and, as you might expect, there is a great deal of uncertainty regarding both of them. Modern research strongly suggests that the *Zhuang Zi* is the older of the two, but we will take up the *Dao De Jing* first. For one thing, it has become traditional to begin the study of Daoism with the *Dao De Jing*; it is a very succinct statement of Daoism thinking. Also, it would appear to be a more direct reaction to the teaching of Confucius.

THE *DAO DE JING* (*TAO TE CHING*)

The *Dao De Jing* is an awfully small work considering the great size of its influence. It consists of only 5,000 Chinese characters. These are somewhat arbitrarily arranged into eighty-one short "chapters," perhaps better described as verses, many are only a few lines long. Presumably, in its early days, the *Dao De Jing* was a growing anthology of much-loved verses collected from a variety of sources. The arrangement into eighty-one "chapters" came later and had little to do with the original composition. Nine was an auspicious number among the Chinese, and nine times nine was seen to be especially auspicious.

The word *Jing* in the title refers to the fact that it was regarded as a classic work. *Dao* and *De* refer to what the work is all about. There are, in fact, two major parts to the *Dao De Jing*, one dealing with the art of governing , the other with right virtue. The word *Dao* in the title refers to the part dealing with governing, and *De* refers to the part dealing with right values. We will look into the meaning of these extremely ambiguous words shortly. The *Dao De Jing* is also commonly known as the *Lao Zi* (*Lao Tzu*), the name of its alleged author.

I say alleged because next to nothing is known about the man, not even whether he is fact or fiction. Therefore, as you might guess, a large body of legend has grown up around his name. Lao Zi is something of a nickname that means "the old master," possibly meant to be understood in the sense of "the old philosopher." Fortunately, the name *Lao Zi* escaped the attention of the Latinizers; we might otherwise know him as *Laotius*. There is an entry for Lao Zi in the *Shih Chi*, that collection of Chinese biographies compiled in the first century B.C.E., but the author, Sima Qian, admits that he is puzzled; there is so little to go on. But that never stops the mythmakers, and a life story was crafted that many mistakenly assume to be historically accurate.

According to the most popular version of the legend, Lao Zi (Lao Tzu) was an older contemporary of Confucius. He was said to have been born around 600 B.C.E. in the part of China that is today known as Honan Province, just to the west of Confucius's home region. We are told that he worked as a minor bureaucrat in the government of Zhou, possibly as a keeper of historical records in the royal library system. This would have given him a lifelong access to the literary tradition of Chinese culture and would explain his deep knowledge of Chinese history. He was not an intellectual, though; far from it. It seems that Lao Zi felt only scorn for the *literati* of his age. He was a very humble man, living a simple life, avoiding public attention. His fame spread far, however, among those who loved the ancient traditions.

Within the Daoist tradition, there is a wonderful story about a meeting between Lao Zi and Confucius. In the context of the legend, this would have happened when Confucius was a young adult, and Lao Zi would presumably have already been an old man. According to the story, Confucius sought out Lao Zi at his modest home and spent the better part of a day with him. A few disciples traveling with Confucius waited for him at the nearby village, and when Confucius finally returned to them, they were struck by his appearance. The young Confucius was exhausted and almost shaking. His visit with Lao Zi had been a profoundly moving experience, but he wouldn't talk about it except to say, "Don't have anything to do with that man. He is a very dangerous man!"

What in the world are we to suppose that to mean? We can only guess. Perhaps we are meant to imagine that the stark, uncompromising realism of Lao Zi had been too much for the young intellectual mind of Confucius. Perhaps at that time in his life, Confucius was full of a self-confidence that was deeply shaken by Lao Zi, who held his face to the edge of the abyss of nonconceptual reality and made him look. No one knows. (And remember, it's a story.)

In the legend of Lao Zi's life, we are told that when he realized that he did not have much longer to live, he set off on foot to spend his final days in the wilderness. When he reached the frontier that led off into the barbarian lands, the warden of the gate tearfully begged him not to leave. How could they bear to live without him? His wisdom was too important to be lost forever. But Lao Zi was determined. Finally, out of compassion, he agreed to leave behind a brief written account of his understanding of the Dao. He stayed for a few days in the gatekeeper's hut, and there he wrote down the essential insights of his wisdom in eighty-one terse verses. The task completed, he said farewell and disappeared into the wild lands beyond the frontier of civilization. The work that he left behind is what we know as the *Dao De Jing*. It's purely a story, of course—one of several about how this great work came to be composed—but something like this is not entirely out of the question.

Legend aside, the actual facts about the author of the *Dao De Jing* present a much more prosaic picture. First of all, due to sharp and stylistic inconsistencies, it would seem almost certain that there was more than one author of the *Dao De Jing*. Most modern scholars agree that it is an anthology, a collection of aphorisms, some of which may have been popular for a long time before the *Dao De Jing* was committed to writing. There is general agreement that it was gathered together in the fourth century B.C.E. It is quite possible that there was one principal "gatherer," and it's not unreasonable that we should call this person Lao Zi, whatever his actual name might have been. In the pages that follow, use of the name Lao Zi will be understood to refer to the "author" of the *Dao De Jing*. In any case, the principal gatherer—let's call him Lao Zi—would probably have done his work after the time of *Zhuang Zi* and definitely could not have been a contemporary of Confucius.

Nevertheless, the *Dao De Jing* is, to a large degree, concerned with the same problem that Confucius addressed—namely, what sort of person is best suited to govern, and how should he go about doing it. Like the *Analects*, the *Dao De Jing* is largely addressed to the ruler, offering that person many sage, and often ambiguous, pieces of advice. Ambiguous is putting it mildly. Translating the *Dao De Jing* into modern languages presents an enormous problem. The Chinese character does not lend itself to a precise translation; varying interpretations are possible. As a result, the many available translations differ from one another to a degree that can only be described as dismaying.

This being the case, how is one to go about selecting a translation to read? We must understand that translating ancient Chinese into modern English is as much an art as it is a science. There are two schools of thought about how this should be done: the so-called "scholarly" and the "flowery." The "scholarly" translator strives to translate each word, each expression, in as literally accurate a way as possible. The "flowery" translator attempts to capture the overall meaning and present it in an appealing poetic way—without, of course, sacrificing the intended meaning of the text. As you might guess, there is little love lost between these two camps. It seems to me that there is a legitimate place for both of these approaches, assuming, of course, that the so-called "flowery" translation is indeed fundamentally accurate.

In a book of this sort, I believe, the only reasonable course is to present the reader with both styles of translation. And that is what you will find in the following passages quoted from the *Dao De Jing*. For the more scholarly offerings, I have selected the Robert Henricks translation, first completed in 1983, and updated recently as a result of very ancient texts unearthed in 1993 at the Goudian site in China. For the more poetic sort of translation, I feel that we can do no better than the work of Stephen Mitchell, published in 1988.

My hope is that the discussion of the *Dao De Jing* in this chapter will stimulate your interest and that you will be moved to go to the source itself. The best way to begin your study of this intriguing subject that we call Daoism is to read carefully through the *Dao De Jing*. I strongly encourage you to do this. The following section can serve as an introduction. I have attempted to give you a brief overview of the essential components of the work and have selected some lines from the *Dao De Jing* to illustrate the points being made. But again, this attempts to be nothing more than an introduction to the most enjoyable task of reading the entire work. Let's begin with the word itself, *Dao*.

To attempt to define the meaning of Dao is a daunting task because it is another of those concepts, like Brahman, which *by its very nature* cannot be put into words. The very first of Lao Zi's statements on the subject declares, "The Dao that can be spoken is not the eternal Dao." But we've been in this spot before, and a little matter like ineffability won't stop us. We must simply remember that "words are like fingers pointing at the moon." Words can be very helpful if we avoid confusing them with the reality of that which we seek to understand. Rather, we should allow words to nudge our consciousness toward the light of understanding:

> There was something formed out of chaos,
> That was born before Heaven and Earth.
> Quiet and still! Pure and deep!
> It stands on its own and does not change.
> It can be regarded as the mother of Heaven and Earth.
> I do not yet know its name:
> I style it "the Way." (Henricks, 80)

The same passage (Chapter 25) in the Stephen Mitchell translation reads thus:

> There was something formless and perfect
> Before the universe was born.
> It is serene; empty; solitary; unchanging; infinite; eternally present.
> It is the mother of the universe.
> For lack of a better name, I call it the Tao. (#25)

"For lack of a better name, I call it the Tao." (Sounds like he could have said, "For lack of a better name, I call it Brahman," doesn't it?) Lao Zi is here alluding to the underlying reality that gives meaning to all that is. Never perceived directly, it is known in its workings, and everything that happens is the working of Dao. Above all, though, the play of Dao is seen to be spontaneous and harmonious. To be in accord with Dao is to be one with it, like the wind and the waving of the wheatfield. Consider these verses:

> *(Mitchell, #34)*
> The great Tao flows everywhere.
> All things are born from it, yet it doesn't create them.
> It pours itself into its work, yet it makes no claim.
> It nourishes infinite worlds, yet it doesn't hold onto them.

And the same passage from Henricks (89):

> The Way floats and drifts;
> It can go left or right.
> It accomplishes its tasks and completes its affairs,
> And yet for this it is not given a name.
> The ten thousand things [all things] entrust their lives to it,
> And yet it does not act as their master.

> *(Mitchell, #23)*
> If you open yourself to the Tao, you are at one with the Tao
> And you can embody it completely.

> *(Henricks, 79)*
> Therefore, one who devotes himself to the Way is one with the Way.

Daoism is founded on a deep love of nature, a love of the harmony and organic wholeness of nature. Mankind—that is, human society—is seen to be an integral part of the natural order, and as such, human life is potentially a perfect expression of the play of Dao. The currents of human life are one with the currents of the sea, the flight of birds, the growth of grass and trees. From the movements of the stars to the movements of the tides all is one awesome harmony—at least potentially. Humans, unfortunately, have the ability to get out of sync with the harmony of Dao. And then all hell breaks loose. All of the suffering and tribulations of human life are the consequence of human society straying from the "way," the Dao. To the Daoist, restoring humanity's proper harmony within the natural order thus becomes the only matter of real importance. As with a person who has become gravely ill, restoring health is all that matters.

Thus, in the broad sense, Confucius was in agreement with the fundamental view of Daoism. He accepted without question that human society is one of the things that nature does and that a healthy human society is one that lives in perfect harmony with the natural order of which it is a part. Confucius would create a system for the proper ordering of society, assuring that only enlightened selfless men would come to power. In this way, he would reinstitute the harmony that had been lost.

The problem, in the eyes of the Daoists, was the nature of the remedy that Confucius proposed for reestablishing the harmony that had been lost. The Confucian "system" aroused the ire of the Daoists because, basically, they felt that not only did it fail to restore man to his natural state, it actually made things worse! The simple, natural life that the Daoists cherished was seen to be smothered in the complex, highly formalized way of the Confucian system. But, back to the *Dao De Jing*. As mentioned, the *Dao De Jing* opens with the cryptic statement, "The Dao that can be spoken is not the eternal Dao." The entire first verse reads thus:

> *(Mitchell, #1)*
> The Tao that can be spoken is not the eternal Tao.
> The name that can be named is not the eternal Name.
> The unnamable is the eternally real.
> Naming is the origin of all particular things.
> Free from desire, you realize the mystery.
> Caught in desire, you see only the manifestations.

> *(Henricks, 55)*
> As for the Way, the Way that can be spoken of is not the constant Way;
> As for names, the name that can be named is not the constant name.
> The nameless is the beginning of the ten thousand things;
> The named is the mother of the ten thousand things.
> Therefore, those constantly without desires,
> by this means will perceive its subtlety.
> Those constantly with desires,
> by this means will see only that which they yearn for and seek.

Dao is not a something in itself. Though its working is in everything, Dao can't be separated out and examined:

> *(Mitchell, #35)*
> When you look for it, there is nothing to see.
> When you listen for it, there is nothing to hear.
> When you use it, it is inexhaustible.

> *(Henricks, 90)*
> When you look at it, it's not sufficient to be seen;
> When you listen to it, it's not sufficient to be heard;
> Yet when you use it, it can't be used up.

Dao, the beginning and the end of everything, is strikingly similar to the concept of Brahman. Consider these verses (from Mitchell):

> In the beginning was the Tao.
> All things issue from it; all things return to it. (#52)

> All things end in the Tao, as rivers flow into the sea. (#32)
> The Tao is like a well: used but never used up.
> It is like the eternal void: filled with infinite possibilities. (#4)

Every being in the universe is an expression of the Tao.
It springs into existence, unconscious, perfect, free;
takes on a physical body, lets circumstances complete it.
That is why every being spontaneously honors the Tao. (#51)

We can go on and on saying profound-sounding things about the Dao—it is the metaphysical first principle; it embodies and underlies all Being—but we can never say precisely what it is. The meaning of Dao lies beyond the power of language to describe; it is ineffable. We can only suggest, allude, imply. One must learn to sense the presence of Dao, to grasp it intuitively. Once we grasp the intuitive sense of Dao, we can spontaneously move in harmony with it. To a Daoist, this is what life is all about—moving in harmony with Dao, not in conflict with it.

Dao itself is the first principle. The ongoing *expression* of Dao is called *wu wei* (pronounced woo-way). This wonderful Daoist word refers to the way nature acts—perfectly, spontaneously, not forcing or trying to control. In the words of John Blofeld, it is "the spontaneous, mindless activity with which nature succeeds most admirably in accomplishing her ends." The way grass grows is *wu wei*, so is the flowing of a river, the blowing of the wind, or even the crying of a baby.

Literally, *wu wei* means "nonaction" in the sense of "not forcing," but in the more everyday sense, it suggests flowing freely, going with the current. The natural patternings of nature are examples of *wu wei*, such as the grain in wood, or the movement of clouds in the sky. This is not a strictly passive concept; actually, it expresses a lively interplay. "Going with the flow" means far more than simply floating. Dead fish go with the flow; live fish swim against the flow, but they *use* the current to do it. *Wu wei* is using the current to get where you're going, whether this be in the river or in the marketplace.

Consider a person in a motorboat and a person in a sailboat. Each wishes to get from Point A to Point B. The motorboat roars its way to Point B, overpowering everything in its path and probably gets there faster. But in the process, it has created a general disruption of noise and pollution. The sailboat also reaches Point B, but without disrupting anything. It is designed to fit into the natural order of the environment, going with, not going against, the forces of nature. By skillful handling, the sailor, like the fish, uses the natural currents to get where he wants to go. This example is a good metaphor for the basic difference between the modern lifestyle and the Daoist lifestyle. The Daoists would say that sometimes we should stop and ask ourselves if "getting there faster" is really all that important.

Wu wei is the way of living of a man or woman who is in harmony with Dao—accepting, yielding, always flexible, more like bamboo than an oak, more like water than a rock. The oak and the rock may seem to be much stronger, but in the long run, bamboo and water will win out every time; they can yield and spring back.

> To describe this mindless, purposeless mode of life, Chuang Tzu [Zhuang Zi] turns most often to the analogy of the artist or craftsman. The skilled woodcarver, the skilled butcher, the skilled swimmer does not ponder or ratiocinate on the course of action he should take; his skill has become so much a part of him that he merely acts instinctively and spontaneously and, without knowing why, achieves success. (Watson, 6)

The man or woman whose life is perfectly in harmony with Dao, whose life is an embodiment of *wu wei*, who cares nothing about fame and fortune—such is the one whom the Daoists consider to be a Superior Person. The word that describes such a person is *De*, the second word in the title *Dao De Jing*. *De* is a subtle word that refers to the power of expression of Dao. *Wu wei* has to do with the *flow* of Dao; *de* refers to what that flow *produces*. For example, the way grass grows, naturally and spontaneously, is a wonderful expression of *wu wei* in action, but the power of the earth and the seeds to germinate and grow as grass is *de*.

Robert Henricks offers an account of a popular analogy that does a very good job of clarifying the meaning of *de*. It is known as the "Analogy of the Uncultivated Field."

> In that analogy the Tao resembles an untended and uncared-for ("uncultivated") field, and the varieties of the wildflowers that grow in such a field represent the "ten thousand things." Were you to go to such a field in the winter, you would see only brown soil or white snow. The field appears to be one in essence, undifferentiated, and "empty" of all forms of life. Nonetheless, should you return to that field in May or June, you would discover that a marvelous transformation had occurred, the field now being filled with all kinds of wildflowers. There are, as it were, "ten thousand" different varieties of flowers . . . And you now know that what had appeared to be devoid of life in the winter was in fact a very fecund womb, containing within itself in its oneness the seeds and roots of all different things.
>
> Moreover, the work of the field does not end with the springtime creation. For the field continues throughout the summer to care for and nourish its "children," supplying them with the water and nutrients that are vital for life. And in this nurturing work, the field cares for all of the flowers without discrimination, and it takes no credit for all that it does. The brown soil is always in the background and "unseen," our eyes being dazzled by the colors and forms of the flowers. Finally, the field accomplishes all that it does "without taking any action" (wu wei) that is to say, we never see the soil actively doing anything; all that happens seems to happen on its own "by nature." (xxv–xxvi)

The meaning of *de* becomes especially important with regard to human activities. Certainly the Daoist wishes to live in the spirit of *wu wei*, but how shall that be expressed in the work of daily life? So much that we humans do seems to be in stark conflict with *wu wei*, totally out of harmony with Dao. In Lao Zi's view, it is not technology and civilization per se that are at fault, it is the exaggeration of these that leads us astray. The simple life of the craftsperson can be an excellent expression of *de*. The special faculties of human intelligence are not an aberration of nature; human society doesn't have to be in conflict with Dao. The woodworker, the farmer, the childrearer—each working naturally and spontaneously at his or her craft—are fully in harmony with Dao, at least potentially.

> Te [*de*] refers to the fact that all things contain an inherent power or strength that comes from their own essential being or true inner nature. This power derives from the fact that our true self is an expression of the Tao, because it is intrinsically connected with the power of the Universe. However, the idea of te is that of power exercised without the use of force and without inappropriate interference in the existing order of things.

Like the Confucians, the Daoists believed that the solution depended on the fashioning of a "new person," a person of *de*. But the Daoist new person was a far cry from the

"Superior Man" of Confucius. The Daoists would fashion a "new person" whose lifestyle would be the embodiment of the Daoist philosophy of life. (The "new person" is really an "old person," because Daoists believed that originally man lived in a state of nature in which human society was perfectly harmonious. This had been lost in the progress of civilization and needed only to be restored.)

So how do we recognize the truly Daoist man or woman? In the *Dao De Jing*, Lao Zi offers many observations on the subject, but always stated in an oblique sort of way. The most foolish mistake of all would be to assume that such an important matter could be reduced to a few words on paper. In fact, it is Lao Zi himself who informs us that "Those who know, don't speak. Those who speak, don't know." That is to say, those who truly understand the Dao exhibit it in the way they live; such a person would never attempt to explain it. But, as we have noted many times, words can be useful if they act to stimulate thought and awaken insight. It is in this sense that Lao Zi's observations must be understood.

In the *Dao De Jing*, the truly Daoist person is often referred to as a "sage," or "master," not to be understood in the sense of master and servant, but rather as the master of an art. And the greatest art of all is the art of living. The true "life master" in the Daoist sense is a very modest person. A modest, cheerful person living an absolutely simple lifestyle—that seems to be fundamental to the Daoist view of right living:

> The Master has no possessions.
> The more he does for others, the happier he is.
> The more he gives to others, the wealthier he is. (Mitchell, #81)

The master may in fact have some possessions—even Lao Zi had his small house and garden (or so we're told)—but they would be only the essentials of life, and most important, he would not be *attached* to material possessions. Attachment, of course, is the key; the Daoist man or woman is free from that kind of bondage.

Simplicity in the form of the lifestyle is fundamental, but so, too, is the way the Daoist master behaves in going about daily life. The Daoist master is completely natural, completely spontaneous; he goes with the flow of life without excessively trying to control it.

Lao Zi clearly preferred a society that was simple and that lived close to the earth. Only in this way could humans avoid the excesses of civilization. But even a very simple society needs some kind of governing leadership, however humble it may be. Government, too, is a craft. It is an especially important craft because of its broad influence. Only a true master, only a man or woman fully in harmony with Dao, is fit to be a leader. Many of the offerings in the *Dao De Jing* concern the subject of right government. This may be in part a response to the teaching of Confucius. Or perhaps more likely, both the teaching of Confucius and the teaching of Lao Zi arose mutually as a response to the discord of the age in which they lived.

Lao Zi was in total disagreement with the Confucian ideal in which the leaders of society constituted an elite class of "superior" men, highly educated and highly refined in their manners. He would have found Thomas Jefferson's views more to his liking. Both men seemed to think of government as at best a necessary evil. Both men would have agreed that "That government is best which governs least." Both idealized the agricultural and craft way of life based on small, largely self-sufficient communities. Jefferson strongly disliked and mistrusted the crowded city, the factory, and especially the machinations of high finance. No doubt Lao Zi would have smiled and nodded in agreement.

Lao Zi's classic comment on the subject of government is found in Verse 60 of the *Dao De Jing*: "Governing a country is like frying a small fish." In other words, leave it alone as much as possible. Too much poking will wreck it. The Daoist leader helps, largely by example, to keep things in their natural channels. He or she does not attempt to control and shape. The very last words of the *Dao De Jing* sum it up: "By not dominating, the Master leads."

(Mitchell, #81)

The Master has no possessions.
The more he does for others, the happier he is.
The more he gives to others, the wealthier he is.
The Tao nourishes by not forcing.
By not dominating, the Master leads.

(Henricks, 164)

The Sage accumulates nothing.
Having used what he had for others,
He has even more.
Having given what he had to others,
What he has is even greater.
Therefore, the Way of Heaven is to benefit and not cause any harm;
The Way of Man is to act on behalf of others and not to compete with them.

Lao Zi was well aware of the powerful temptation to use power in order to control, but how disastrous this turns out to be:

(Mitchell, #58)

When the will to power is in charge,
the higher the ideals, the lower the results.
Try to make people happy,
and you lay the groundwork for misery.
Try to make people moral,
and you lay the groundwork for vice.

The secret of success is self-restraint, yielding control, going with the Dao.

(Mitchell, #57)

If you want to be a great leader,
you must learn to follow the Tao.
Stop trying to control.
Let go of fixed plans and concepts,
and the world will govern itself.

(Henricks, 142)

Therefore, the words of the Sage say:
I do nothing, and the people of themselves are transformed;
I love tranquility, and the people of themselves are upright;
I'm unconcerned with affairs, and the people of themselves become rich;
I desire not to desire,
And the people of themselves are genuine and simple, like uncarved wood.

The true Daoist master "reigns" but doesn't "rule." He is a model of the virtue of *de*:

(Mitchell, #30)

The Master does his job and then stops.
He understands that the universe is forever out of control,
And that trying to dominate events goes against the current of the Tao.

Lao Zi and the Daoists believed that the world could be restored to health and harmony and that the sickness of greed, violence, and human suffering could largely be healed. It all depended on returning to the simple life that is natural to mankind. And the role of the leader was to gently assist this process of reform:

(Mitchell, #32)

If powerful men and women could remain centered in the Tao,
All things would be in harmony.
The world would become a paradise.
All people would be at peace,
And the law would be written in their hearts.

What if the Daoists were to be successful? What would this Daoist "paradise" really be like? Surprisingly, in the next to last verse of the *Dao De Jing*, Lao Zi gives us a most interesting description of that ideal village community, the building block of a healthy social order:

(Mitchell, #80)

If a country is governed wisely, its inhabitants will be content.
They enjoy the labor of their hands
and don't waste time inventing labor-saving machines.
Since they dearly love their homes, they aren't interested in travel.
There may be a few wagons and boats, but they don't go anywhere.
There may be an arsenal of weapons, but nobody ever uses them.
People enjoy their food,
take pleasure in being with their families,
spend weekends working in their gardens,
delight in the doings of the neighborhood.
And even though the next country is so close
that people can hear its roosters crowing and its dogs barking,
they are content to die of old age without ever having gone to see it.

(Henricks, 37)

Let the states be small and people few—
Bring it about that there are weapons for "tens" and "hundreds,"
yet let no one use them;
Have the people regard death gravely and put migrating far from their minds.
Though they might have boats and carriages, no one will ride them;
Have the people return to knotting cords and using them.
They will relish their food,
Regard their clothing as beautiful,
Delight in their customs,
And feel safe and secure in their homes.

> Neighboring states might overlook one another,
> And the sounds of chickens and dogs might be overheard,
> Yet the people will arrive at old age and death with no comings and goings
> between them.

Did Lao Zi really intend that his readers take that passage literally? Perhaps he did, but most likely he did not. It's difficult to believe that a man so profoundly wise and full of worldly experience would propose a social solution that, at least on the face of it, is so naive. He is asking nothing less than that mankind abandon practically everything that we consider to be the "advancements" of civilization and return to the very elementary social life of the small agricultural community. The attractions are great, but the disadvantages are also great. Is there to be no light after dark, no books, no travel? One wonders if Lao Zi didn't have a twinkle in his eye as he penned the line about never in one's life caring to travel even as far as the next village, though "the people can hear its roosters crowing, and its dogs barking." (Actually, not a bad reason to stay home when you think about it.)

That line may provide the key to understanding the whole passage. Perhaps the author of that passage deliberately overstated it—in a way that his contemporaries would find amusing—in order to emphasize his point. The problem he was addressing results from the overcomplexity of civilized life. The author may be highlighting this insight in the reader's mind by dramatically oversimplifying the proposed solution. At least it serves to emphasize how far civilized society has traveled from its original roots, at which time, no doubt, human society had much less difficulty living in harmony with Dao.

Leaving aside specific suggestions, the general tenor of the Daoist philosophy of life comes through loud and clear in the *Dao De Jing*. The "good life" for every man and woman is the perfectly natural life—that is to say, becoming one with the Dao. Such a person does not try to forcibly control his environment and to pile up worldly wealth and honor. These are ignorant delusions that lead inevitably to unhappiness, and, all too often, to violence as well. Instead of trying to become great rocks, we are encouraged to become like water—accepting, yielding, moving spontaneously with the currents of nature, "seeking the lowest place." The *Dao De Jing* tells us in many ways that the simple life is the secret of happiness—the simpler the better. To own nothing is to own everything.

The genuine Daoist man or woman is a very modest person, unrecognized by most people as anything special. He or she asks nothing of life and is content with what life gives. This kind of acceptance of life, this childlike spontaneity, frees the person from the customary anxiety that stifles cheerfulness. It's impossible to imagine Lao Zi, for example, as a somber sort of person. One gets the feeling from reading the *Dao De Jing* that he was often laughing (or at least chuckling). Confucius and Buddha might possibly have been serious types, but Lao Zi?—not likely.

ZHUANG ZI (CHUANG TZU)

Zhuang Zi is a name that is linked closely with that of Lao Zi. Historically speaking, we're on more solid ground with Zhuang Zi than with Lao Zi, but not much. The traditional view, which accepted both men as real, placed Zhuang Zi about a century later than Lao Zi. It is now widely believed, however, that the work we know as the *Zhuang Zi* was actually produced a little before the *Dao De Jing*. Both works, though, were probably produced in the fourth century B.C.E.

The majority view among scholars today is that the *Zhuang Zi*, like the *Lao Zi*, was not the work of a single author. Rather, it, too, was a collection of various teachings, presumably collected into a single work by an individual whom we shall call Zhuang Zi.

Unlike the *Dao De Jing*, which is very terse and cryptic, the *Zhuang Zi* presents a much fuller exposition of Daoist themes. It is composed in a down-to-earth prose style that reads like a conversation. The *Zhuang Zi* is enjoyable reading, often amusing and full of anecdotes. The focus of the *Zhuang Zi* is squarely on the nature of right living. Unlike the *Lao Zi* and the *Analects of Confucius*, the *Zhuang Zi* deals hardly at all with the matter of right government; it doesn't seem to be of much interest; the right way of living is the theme. Taken as a whole, the *Zhuang Zi* presents a fully developed philosophy of life.

Both *Zhuang Zi* and Confucius addressed the same question: How can a person find fulfillment and happiness in a world that is often meaningless, ugly, violent, and full of suffering? Zhuang Zi agreed with Confucius that the common response—which is to say, self-indulgence—will not succeed, not even if it is highly refined self-indulgence. To seek to create a little miniuniverse of family and friends where one can tastefully go about satisfying one's desires, safely out of view of the ugly realities of the larger world, is nothing more than a cultivated hedonism; it cannot succeed. Zhuang Zi disagreed, though, with the solution offered by Confucius—that is, the cultivation of *junzi*.

The idea of *junzi*, the "Superior Man," was at the heart of Zhuang Zi's complaint with Confucius. The Confucians envisioned a new ruling elite, based not on birth and wealth but on demonstrated knowledge and compassion. These modest men would be the selfless leaders of society, cultivating by their example the native goodness that dwells in the hearts of all men and women. To the Daoists, this vision was preposterous, and they held it up to ridicule. Man is by nature neither good nor evil, they would argue. Both "good" and "evil" are but concepts. If man is naturally good, then he must also be naturally evil. The two concepts are intimately bound together. You can't have one without the other; they are the two sides of one conceptual coin. To the Daoist, the very defining of a "good" man necessarily gives rise to the "evil" man; they arise mutually: "When people see some things as good, other things become bad."

This is a very subtle point, but it is an essential element of the Daoist philosophy of life. It strikes at the human tendency to conceptualize the realities that we encounter in daily life and then substitute the concept for the reality it represents. For example, happiness is a state of mind that we experience from time to time; it is an integral part of certain situations, such as being with a friend or eating a good dinner. To mentally abstract this condition of happiness, as if it were a something in itself, and then make it an object of desire is a fatal mistake. But that's what we humans do all the time. "Happiness" thus becomes an external object, as it were—something to be attained—just as "unhappiness" is a thing to be avoided. The same can be said for "good" and "evil" and so on. In Zhuang Zi's view, this was the problem with Confucius's concept of *junzi*; it was a *concept*. In other words, the problem with seeking to be a man of *junzi* was in the very seeking itself. One can only truly seek that which is external to oneself. Confucius, admittedly with the best of intentions, had mistakenly conceptualized the notion of a Superior Man, thus making it an external object which could never be realized. At best, Zhuang Zi would argue, the man of *junzi* would be only a well behaved, intellectually cultivated person, but never a man of real fulfillment. He would see only the *effects* of Dao, but not its *essence*.

The central point of Zhuang Zi's teaching, and indeed of Daoism generally, is that fulfillment in life is not to be found by seeking it, which in everyday terms comes down to trying to grasp it. This inevitably results in an ongoing effort to control one's environment, and that effort is ultimately doomed to failure. The effort to grasp and control life creates a kind of bondage to one's concepts of what "the good" is, and the desire to achieve it. Fulfillment is to be found, not through seeking it, but through *not-seeking*, through letting go of the self altogether. Only by letting go of our precious, but phony, conceptual world do we discover real freedom. Awakening to the nature of freedom is the key to understanding the teaching of Zhuang Zi.

All of us acquire a set of values as we grow up. Ordinarily, these are the "conventional values" of the society in which we live, values that were first taught to us when we were children. Having such values seems to be an important part of a successful life; our values shape our goals. But Zhuang Zi would have us unceremoniously discard the entire baggage of conventional values. These are concepts only; they have no corresponding reality in Nature. "Ills are only ills because we recognize them as such." In other words, something is "bad" and therefore makes us unhappy not because it really is bad in some objective sense, but rather because we have *decided* that it is bad. If, at some deep level, we decide that having lots of money is good, then it must follow that having very little money is bad. Of course, neither one is objectively good or bad. But once the decision is made and the concept is formed, it follows that we will seek to achieve the conceptual reality that we have defined as "the good" and thus, hopefully, be happy. Zhuang Zi maintains that freedom results from completely letting go of the struggle to *achieve* these conceptual goals:

> It is this baggage of conventional values that man must first of all discard before he can be free. Chuang Tzu saw the same human sufferings that Confucius, Mo Tzu, and Mencius saw. He saw the man-made ills of war, poverty, and injustice. He saw the natural ills of disease and death. But he believed that they were ills only because man recognized them as such. If man would once forsake his habit of labeling things good or bad, desirable or undesirable, then the man-made ills, which are the product of man's purposeful and value-ridden actions, would disappear and the natural ills that remain would no longer be seen as ills, but as an inevitable part of the course of life. Thus, in Chuang Tzu's eyes, man is the author of his own suffering and bondage, and all his fears spring from the web of values created by himself alone. (Watson, 4)

The bottom line is simply this: When the struggle ceases, one is free to be in harmony with Dao. And not until then. This is the natural state of all things, including humans. When the struggle ceases, one is free to become an embodiment of *wu wei*—not intent on results, not calculating, not making value judgments about everything, not attempting to control one's little world; one can relax and allow himself or herself to be a free and spontaneous expression of the movement of the natural world. In doing this, one will intuitively come to see the magnificent unity of nature. "Things" have no independent existence or meaning, including myself.

Very much at odds with the traditional Western attitude, Zhuang Zi saw no special *relationship* at all between man and nature, or to be more precise, between the human mind and nature. But far from belittling human nature, the teaching of Zhuang Zi liberates humanity from the self-imposed isolation and loneliness of being some kind of godlike visitor in the universe, surrounded by the natural world, but essentially not a part of it. For Zhuang Zi, humankind is very much a part of it—wholly, integrally, voluptuously! And for that reason, there is nothing to be gained by mentally setting ourselves apart. It's ridiculous. The genuine Daoist does not have to prove to himself that he is a godlike being or that he can conquer nature; he doesn't have to prove anything. He is free to live simply and modestly. He has nothing more to prove than does the grass, and each is splendid just as it is.

Far from seeking to be at the center of things (controlling, governing—even governing righteously, as would the Confucian Superior Man), the genuine Daoist values solitude, sometimes to the point of being a recluse. Above all, the Daoist inclines to a lifestyle that permits the contemplation of nature not just nature in the sense of "woods and wildlife," but that grand order of Nature that encompasses all, including the self. The joy derived from this awareness banishes all fear and suffering. Cosmic awareness reduces the trivial problems of life to the point of being meaningless. Even the once monstrous fear of death dissolves in the contemplation of the natural order. It is seen to be, like everything else, a perfectly natural event.

In the *Zhuang Zi*, Daoism is elevated to the level of nature mysticism. John Blofeld, a modern Daoist philosopher, puts it nicely: "I do not see how anyone who has studied his works can doubt that he was well acquainted with states of mystical rapture lying well beyond the frontier of quietist accord with nature." (46) Perhaps this is what Zhuang Zi was referring to when he complained that Confucius did not go far enough—that he saw the *effects* of Dao, but never Dao *itself*.

Inspired by his vision of the unity of nature, the Daoist is thus free to live as a natural man, a natural woman—an embodiment of *wu wei*. This does not mean that the Daoist chooses a life of inaction, of torpor. This is a misunderstanding of *wu wei*. He is like the grass or drifting clouds only in the sense that the energy of Dao *plays through* him naturally, without forcing or trying to control. Nature is so beautifully regulated, that once in accord with it, one doesn't have to *do* anything, in the sense of pushing it around. Just go with it, like the grass grows. Of course, the nature of grass is very different from the nature of man, and therefore *wu wei* is expressed differently in a human being.

The true Daoist is a skilled artist. His or her instrument might be the keyboard of a piano or the keyboard of a computer, the brush of a painter, or the knife of a butcher. It could be anything; the art is in the effortless way that the person becomes one with the work: this is *wu wei*. Zhuang Zi tells the story of an old butcher who was so deft at slicing up a carcass that even though he had been doing it for years, he had never needed to sharpen his knife. In a similar vein is the venerable old aikido master who looks so frail, and never seems to expend any effort, but no attacker can ever lay a hand on him. This is *wu wei* in action. The ultimate art is life itself. When one's daily life becomes an expression of *wu wei*, the perfection of Daoism is achieved.

Like Lao Zi, Zhuang Zi loved the nature of water. It is so all-encompassing, so primal, so beautiful, so strong—yet yielding. The movement of water perfectly reveals the way of nature. Water is powerful—as a glacier or a tsunami it can crush anything in its path, yet it is also the most yielding thing in nature; it always seeks the lowest place. Water is a wonderful example of *wu wei* in action and thus is a favorite metaphor for the Daoist lifestyle. Bamboo is another popular image in Daoism, for the same reason. Like water, bamboo is very strong, but it never tries to force itself—bamboo yields and then springs back.

Yielding is the key, not in the sense of resignation, but rather in the sense of going with the flow. Bamboo yields to the wind and thus does not break. A sailboat too "yields" to the wind and thus reaches its destination. One of the great sailing crafts of modern times was the *Kon Tiki*. It was an embodiment of *wu wei* in action. In building the *Kon Tiki* and learning how to sail it, Thor Heyerdahl learned much about the meaning of *wu wei*. Commenting on that great adventure he said, "Among primitive races the golden rule was: Don't resist nature, but yield to her command, and accommodate."

There is a popular story in the *Zhuang Zi* that makes the point beautifully. It's known as "three in the morning." A man acquired a small group of monkeys, and he planned to give them four measures of chestnuts in the morning and three measures of chestnuts in the evening. The monkeys, however, complained loudly when they heard about this, so he changed his plan and gave them three measures in the morning and four measures in the evening. Now everyone was satisfied. So, what's the moral of the story? It has nothing to do with the irrationality of the monkeys or the cleverness of their keeper. The point is that he was wise enough to see that stubbornly insisting that the monkeys were being unreasonable would solve nothing; he would only become unreasonable himself. Since his goal was to provide the monkeys with adequate nourishment, he was willing to yield with regard to the means for achieving it. He became like water seeking the lowest place. So long as he reached the lowest place, he was perfectly willing to yield to the boulder in his path and go around it. The teaching of Zhuang Zi consistently follows the principle of "three in the morning."

RELIGIOUS DAOISM

To be human is to be able to think about the future, and thus to be able to worry about it— and thus to yearn for some measure of control over it. We humans have always done that; the evolution of technology, which gives us that measure of control, has been the result. In modern times, the high priests of society are the ones who understand and operate our amazing technology. But what about life in the early days? Who did you turn to in times of sickness and death, and drought, and all those other worries that cause sleepless nights. Enter the shamans. By one name or another, all human cultures have produced men, and women, to play the role of shamans. In early societies, the shamans were believed to have special powers that enabled them to make contact with the spirit world. Since it was customary to ascribe virtually all crises to the activities of spirits, the shaman held the power to potentially influence the course of events. This was especially true with regard to illness, the most common and immediate of problems, but their powers could also be brought to bear in other important situations.

The tradition of shamanism evolved in China from the earliest times. We can assume that in China, as in other cultures, the roots of shamanism stretch far back before the beginnings of recorded history. They would have served the general population in many ways: contacting the spirit world, foretelling the will of the gods, interpreting omens, interpreting dreams, rainmaking, and, of course, healing the sick. It was probably as healers that they most often served the common people, but the aristocrats could afford to focus on other things as well. They were, for example, especially interested in divination and longevity. By *divination* is meant the foretelling of future events through the interpretation of omens and oracles. This became a highly refined art in early China. Archaeological sites are rich in the tools of the craft, especially what are referred to as "oracle bones." Cracks formed in the heated bone, often the breast bone of an ox, would suggest a pattern which the diviner could allegedly interpret and thereby gain knowledge of a future course of events. The rationale for this rested on the belief that everything in the cosmos is interconnected. Everything that happens has an effect on everything else that happens, although that effect is usually too subtle to be seen. The special gift of the shaman, however, enables him, or her, to detect its traces.

The other special interest of the aristocracy was longevity. Because, among other things, the shaman was a healer whose powers hopefully resulted in prolonging life temporarily, it was a reasonable step to want to extend those powers to prolong life indefinitely. In response to the longing for immortality that lives in all human hearts, a "science" of longevity developed. This included many elements that would seem pretty strange to us today and probably seemed pretty strange to a great many in those days as well. There were special diets, potions, charms, breathing exercises, and even unusual sexual exercises. Only members of the privileged class had the necessary wealth and leisure time to pursue this sort of thing, and, apparently, many did. By the time of the late Zhou dynasty, a secret cult of immortality had developed.

The general picture, then, is of a large complex society, mostly agricultural, which included a heterogeneous population of shamans. This was a perfectly normal situation; it was the responsibility of the shamans to deal with all those mysterious problems and worries which might somehow have a connection with the spirit world. In a way, they served a religious function. That was an essential part of early Chinese society, and there are those who play this role even to this day. Most of the things the shamans did were pretty mundane—healing, fortune-telling, etc. But some of their arts, especially those dealing with the quest for immortality, were more specialized.

So what does all of this have to do with Daoism? Well, it's not exactly clear how it happened, but somehow the lexicon of Daoism was adopted by the shamanistic "religious" element within Chinese society, giving the impression that the two were really one tradition. Undoubtedly, there were some common points, but the Daoism of Lao Zi and Zhuang Zi was clearly distinct from the shamanistic tradition and the cult of immortality. Some would argue that they were hijacked in order to lend respectability to the more decidedly religious tradition. In any case, during the time of the early Han dynasty, as the shamanistic tradition coalesced into something of a native Chinese religion, the terminology of Daoism became widely used. These new "Daoists"—referred to in modern times as Religious Daoists, or Magical Daoists—even went so far as to claim spiritual descent from Lao Zi and Zhuang Zi, both of whom were deified. (What would Zhuang Zi have said about that!) Thus, the history of Daoism divides into two quite different traditions: Philosophical Daoism (*Dao Jia*), and Religious Daoism (*Dao Jiao*).

The Han emperors were strongly supportive of Dao Jiao (Religious Daoism), being especially interested in the possibility of personal immortality. They turned their imperial backs on the old-fashioned court shamans, looking instead for guidance from a new group of itinerant "philosophers" known as the *Fang Shi*. These men were far more sophisticated than ordinary country shamans and were specialists in the more occult arts, particularly those associated with the quest for immortality. But they had a problem. In the opinion of many people, all those connected with the immortality cult were nothing but a bunch of charlatans. And it's not hard to see why—some of the practices were, to say the least, bizarre. H. G. Creel reports, for example, that it was suggested by some that a man seeking immortality should have sexual intercourse with 1,200 girls sixteen or seventeen years of age. (Seems like it would have the opposite effect, doesn't it?) The Fang Shi above all needed to bring a little respectability to their profession and were the ones most responsible for trying to cover themselves with the mantle of Philosophical Daoism.

On the other hand, I don't want to leave the impression that these men were nothing more than a group of schemers who contrived to steal the name and reputation of others. It's quite possible that they honestly perceived some essential relationship between their teaching and that of Lao Zi and Zhuang Zi. Let's remember that the word *Dao* had wide application in Chinese culture; it was not coined by the Philosophical Daoists. Confucius had focused on the term before the Daoists. In fact, those who objected to the Confucian system, Lao Zi and Zhuang Zi in particular, emphasized the word *Dao* in order to get it right. You might say that they regarded their teaching as *true* "Daoism," whereas other systems taught a *false* "Daoism." The Dao of the Religious Daoists was close in meaning to that of the Philosophical Daoists and was the foundation of their theoretical system. It is the ineffable ground of being and the source of all that is. "From the Tao all the myriad objects derive their being, their illusory separateness being wrought by the interplay of *yin & yang*." (quoted in Blofield, 1)

Many mistakenly believe that the concept of *yin and yang* was a feature of Philosophical Daoism. The spirit of *yin and yang* is implied in the writings of Lao Zi and Zhuang Zi, but the principle was actually enunciated in Religious Daoism. And let's give credit where it is deserved—the principle of *yin and yang* has profoundly influenced the development of Chinese philosophical thought and enjoys wide popularity in modern times.

All of nature exhibits a wonderful harmony. The harmony results from the interworking of the basic forces of nature, which the Daoists refer to as *yin and yang*. The movement of Dao is manifest in the interplay of *yin and yang*. Derived originally from the Chinese words for moon and sun, *yin and yang* stand symbolically for the dual forces of nature that are the most elementary of all. *Yin*, the passive force, associated with the feminine principle, is the force that maintains and regulates. *Yang*, the active force, associated with the male principle, is the force that initiates action. One could say that a modern expression of *yin and yang* is energy and entropy. One can't exist without the other, nor is anything ever purely an expression of one as opposed to the other. Even male and female are a mixture of the two, in which one is merely dominant. The play of *yin and yang* is always a mix, a dance as it were. *Yang* thrusts a volcanic eruption out of the earth. But at the same moment, *yin* goes to work, confining the explosion, and giving definition to the new mountain. And over the course of time, patient *yin*, in the form of erosive forces, will gradually wear that mountain back to the level plain from whence it all began.

Everything is like that; you and I are like that. *Yang* keeps trying out new forms of being, and *yin* is always there to gradually dismantle them. Thus does the unfolding of nature progress through time. Eventually, we are told, the force of *yin* will return the entire universe to the state of amorphous dust from which it began. But this is not an ultimate victory of *yin* over *yang*, because *yang* is ever there ready when the time is right to start the game all over again with a new Big Bang. (I'm sure you see the similarity between the Daoist concept of *yin and yang* and the Hindu concept of the *gunas*. Some things are universal. However, here we have the opposite of Hinduism, in which the passive force is associated with the male and the active with the female.)

Daoists do not see *yin* as being in conflict with *yang*; it's not *yin* versus *yang*. It is very important to understand this. In the West, we're accustomed to seeing life in terms of great dichotomies—good versus evil, man against nature. The superior force must win out over the inferior. This is not the Daoist view at all. *Yin and yang complement* each other. They are more like positive and negative than good and evil. The goal is to achieve balance, harmony, not to have one defeat the other. Thus, to the Daoist, the goal of human life is not to conquer the natural world and bend it to our purposes, but rather to go with the natural world, finding the "way" that achieves harmony with the whole. What a world of difference there is in these two attitudes!

The ceaseless play of *yin and yang* is the subject of the *Yi Jing* (*I Ching*), one of the most intriguing works to come down to us from the civilization of ancient China. The *Yi Jing* (literally, the "Book of Changes") probably evolved out of what was originally a manual of prophecy. It would develop into a guidebook which anyone could use to tap into the traditional wisdom of the culture and thereby acquire a kind of guidance for harmonizing one's life with the movement of Dao.

The *Yi Jing* consists of sixty-four sections, each of which has a name—such as "Following," or "Deliverance"—and a short commentary dealing with the subject of that name. (It is traditional to ascribe many of the commentaries to Confucius, but it is almost certain that they were produced several centuries after his life.) The commentary is written in the form of personal advice, though it is usually cryptic, and requires skillful interpretation. One approaches the *Yi Jing* as one would a sage or an oracle, to receive its guidance. This advice may be in the form of an answer to a specific question, or, more likely, general guidance relevant to harmonizing one's life with Dao.

There is a precise, time-honored method for consulting the *Yi Jing*. A simplified method involves the use of three coins, but the classic method employs a bunch of fifty yarrow stalks, (lightweight strawlike sticks). These are cast onto the ground, and from the random arrangement that forms, a precise pattern of lines can be derived. Lines are either solid or broken (— or - -). Solid lines represent *yang*, the male principle; broken lines represent *yin*, the female principle. Three of these lines, stacked one above the other, is called a trigram. A pair of trigrams forms a hexagram. Given the various combinations of broken and unbroken lines, sixty-four different hexagrams are possible. Thus it is that each hexagram corresponds to one of the sixty-four sections of the *Yi Jing*. It then remains only to look up the appropriate section and apply its commentary to the stated question. The process gets a bit more complicated than that, but in essence, that's all there is to it. The art, of course, is in the interpretation. That calls for real wisdom.

Defenders of the *Yi Jing* argue that it is in no way to be confused with fortune-telling or fortune cookies; it is not magic, not a Chinese version of the ouija board. The *Yi Jing*, they maintain, evolved out of the same worldview that produced the "oracle bones" in ancient times; it is a conviction that the entire cosmos is one interconnected whole. One part affects all parts. The human mind is an internal state that reflects the external state of the universe. The sagely advice of the *Yi Jing* prods the mind to bring forth out of itself solutions to the seeming dilemmas of daily life. The hexagram is something like a Rorschach Inkblot; it is the individual's own struggle for meaning, together with the ancient wisdom contained in the text, that creates the guidance.

Through studying the changing lines and developing ourselves accordingly, we are able to make our lives complete. The I Ching, therefore, is a lantern through the hidden world that underlies our everyday lives. In counseling us it does not take over our self-direction, it leaves us entirely on our own. It does not spell out right and wrong as a religion does; instead, it draws on our inner knowledge of what is good and reinforces this. (Anthony, xix)

In addition to Dao and *yin and yang*, there is a third fundamental element in the theoretical basis of Religious Daoism; it is the concept of *qi* (*ch'i*). The Daoist *qi* (pronounced chee) is very similar to the Hindu concept of *prana*; both refer to a vital energy that permeates all of space and is responsible for life. Like *prana*, the amount, or fullness, of *qi* can vary in a given individual. The greater the fullness of *qi*, the stronger the health and vitality of that person; depletion of *qi* was believed to result in sickness, and, ultimately, death. Given this belief, it's easy to see why followers of Religious Daoism gave much attention to practices that were designed to increase and retain healthy levels of *qi*. In the context of Religious Daoism, *qi* was believed to result from the interplay of *yin and yang*, at least under the right conditions. Therefore, a study of the operation of *yin and yang* could lead to an understanding of how to generate and control *qi*. Here, too, there is an interesting similarity to Hindu practices, particularly Hatha and Tantric Yoga.

This brings us back to that most important and fascinating aspect of Religious Daoism, the quest for immortality. Given that vital energy is synonymous with *qi*, and *qi* could be controlled (or so they believed) through an application of perfect understanding of the operation of *yin and yang*, it was predictable, to say the least, that certain of the Fang Shih would seek to become experts in the art of extending life. What began as an interest in simply extending life became an all out effort to find the secret of immortality.

There seemed to be no question about the real possibility of immortality. It was widely accepted that some humans did, in fact, achieve the state of immortality and that these lucky ones lived an Elysian sort of life, forever young and happy, in places distant from the hurly-burly of ordinary life in China. Some lived atop mountains far to the west, but the most fortunate of all dwelt in the "Isles of the Blessed," enchanting mountainous islands located somewhere in the eastern sea:

> During the reigns of Kings Wei and Hsuan of Ch'i, and King Chao of Yen, the practice began of sending men out to sea in search of the three sacred mountains, . . . reportedly not very far away from men. Unfortunately, just as the men are about to reach the shores, the boats are swept back and away by the wind. In earlier times, some people actually managed to reach them: there, the Blessed and the drug that prevents death can be found; there, all things, birds, and four-footed animals are white, and the palaces are made of gold and silver. When these people were just short of the mountains, they could see them from afar like a cloud. When they arrived, the three sacred mountains were washed away by the waves. In short, no one has ever been able to land there. There is not one of the rulers who would not like to have gone there. (quoted in Kaltenmark, 118)

Three important elements are included in the above passage: There is a matter-of-fact statement regarding the reality of these islands of the immortals; several Chinese emperors sponsored searches for them; and there is reference to "the drug that prevents death." Immortality could be had by ingesting a drug! What wonderful news that must have been. The only problem was, though—what drug? Was it a naturally growing plant, like soma? Was it common or rare? In that day—as would certainly be the case in this day too—the belief that immortality could be had through basically chemical means stimulated a passionate interest in identifying or creating the wonderful substance. The emperors may not have been any more passionate about it than anyone else, but they had the means to sponsor what promised to be a difficult research. And thus was born the fascinating field of Chinese alchemy.

The pseudoscience of alchemy has a very interesting history, and there is much misinformation about the subject. It became a highly developed field in European civilization as well as in China. European alchemists are best remembered for their tireless effort to find the "philosopher's stone," the secret substance that would enable them to transmute common elements, such as lead, into gold. Chinese alchemists focused more on discovering the secret concoction that would forever banish the waning of *qi*.

Modern scholars divide the historical focus of Chinese alchemy into two great parts: "external" alchemy and "internal" alchemy. Internal alchemy developed later, and, in some ways, amounted to an almost metaphorical application of the procedures of external alchemy. (We will get to that in just a bit.) The original alchemists, the external alchemists, were so named because they put their faith in a substance, external to the body, which possessed properties that, when ingested, would confer immortality. The search for this elixir of life resulted in some pretty amazing concoctions. One of these concoctions led to the serendipitous discovery of gunpowder. An alchemist, having mixed some honey with sulphur and saltpeter (potassium nitrate), accidentally touched a flame to it. In the dazzling display that followed, the first example of fireworks was born. It worked even better when powdered charcoal was substituted for honey. For a long time, this amazing invention was used only for pyrotechnic displays. Later, particularly in the West, its potential for a much deadlier use was realized. Isn't it ironic that a recipe intended to confer immortality should end up conferring so much mayhem and death?

The principal alchemical text, the *Zandonji (Tsan-tung-chi)*, listed a large number of substances that were thought to hold promise. Among these were lead, mercury, sulfur, zinc, nickel, gold, silver, and cinnabar (they especially loved cinnabar, an old-fashioned name for mercuric oxide). These, and other chemicals, were carefully mixed and tried out on the eager subjects. One can only imagine the effect such a witch's brew would have on the poor victim. Needless to say, there were many deaths. Lacking a supply of laboratory rats, these elixirs were sometimes tested on condemned criminals. (There is no record of any having achieved immortality.)

The embarrassing paucity of success, and the equally embarrassing ampleness of failure, led to a growing lack of confidence in alchemy. By the time of late Han, alchemy had all but died out. But it would experience a strong revival during the Tang dynasty. A new development generated a lot of interest, especially among the Tang emperors, who were eager to fund a new program of research. What had them so excited was "the pill." It was believed that, under the right conditions, a small pellet would form naturally in certain rocks, and that this pellet was in fact the long-sought-for "immortality pill." The only problem was that this natural process was extremely rare. It occurred only in stones that had absorbed *yin and yang* vapors in the form of exactly the right amounts of sunshine and moonlight. And, it was a process that took 4,320 years to complete. During this time, there was a slow transformation of lead and mercury into cinnabar. The outcome was the crystallization of a tiny golden-colored nugget, the Pill!

Understandably, given the complexity of the process and the time it required, Mother Nature wasn't likely to produce much in the way of immortality pills. But not to despair; alchemy could rise to the challenge and synthesize it under "laboratory" conditions. All that would be necessary was to simulate natural conditions in the laboratory, and, of course, to significantly speed up the process. The heart of the procedure was a special cauldron, which had to be designed in such a way that it could function both as a furnace and a cooling chamber. It was necessary to duplicate the *yang* heat of the sun and the *yin* cooling of moonlight. Fire and water represent the activities of the sun and moon; these would be used alternately in a carefully balanced fashion. And, all of this had to be precisely timed in accord with a very complex schedule that simulated the movements of the sun and moon and stars. Further, it was essential that the ingredients be mixed with great precision. Even a tiny mistake here could ruin the whole batch, to say nothing of what it did to the body of the hopeful imbiber. Mistakes did occur, but even if they didn't, the result was a poisonous mixture whose effects were far more likely to confer death than immortality. "Many poisonings did occur. People who swallowed the pills of immortality suffered slow poisoning that led to the failure of the liver and spleen. Other fatal effects included breakdown of the nervous system and various forms of mental disorder. After three hundred years of failure in research and experimentation, external alchemy declined." (Wong, 75)

After many deaths, including those of some Tang emperors, and no successes at all, faith in the power of alchemy definitely began to wane. But the desire for long life, and possibly even immortality, did not wane at all. It merely looked for a new way to achieve its goals. During the Song dynasty, which followed the Tang, a whole new approach to alchemy began to take form. We call it "internal" alchemy to distinguish it from the older, discredited "external" alchemy. Instead of relying on something derived from outside the body—the pill, for example—internal alchemy worked with the naturally occurring internal condition of the body. Specifically, these new alchemists focused their interest on the body's store of *qi*, vital energy.

There was a range of opinion regarding a person's endowment of *qi*. Some believed that people are born with their full supply of *qi*, like a car starting out with a full tank of gasoline. Death results when the tank runs out, so the longer one can make it last, the longer life will be. Those who followed this belief recommended "stillness" as the greatest of virtues. Since any kind of activity, even sensory activity, depleted *qi*, it was in the interest of long life to avoid as much as possible all kinds of activity: physical, mental, even sensory. Some emperors went so far as to wear an unusual headdress with a fringe of tiny pearls covering the ears and eyes. This reduced sensory involvement and thus, or so they believed, added years to their lives.

More common was the belief that it was possible to actually replenish *qi*, although this was certainly not an easy thing to do. Activity did indeed reduce the original supply, and some *qi* could simply leak away through bad mental and physical habits, but special steps could be taken to restore it and thus achieve longer life, and maybe—just maybe—it was still possible for the really dedicated to achieve immortality. (The hope, at least, never dies.) Followers of this approach developed a body of practices designed not only to maximize the body's store of *qi*, but also to facilitate its optimum distribution and use by the body and mind. Religious Daoism's earlier interest in yogic techniques experienced a strong revival. Diet, for example, became a matter of prime importance, as did various breathing exercises. And so, too, did a variety of Tantriclike exercises in sexual yoga. It was believed, for example, that sexual arousal increased *qi*, but, at least for the male, that increase was more than dissipated in the act of ejaculation. Therefore, as in Tantra, a veritable science developed around techniques for generating arousal but retaining semen. Some practices, such as the last mentioned, would appear to be outlandish in the eyes of modern health science, but much of what they practiced did undoubtedly contribute to better health and, therefore, to longer life.

The techniques of external alchemy were not entirely forgotten. In a way, they were transposed metaphorically into the practices of internal alchemy. The body itself became the alchemist's cauldron. The *yin and yang* of fire and water became the interplay of body heat and perspiration. As in the cauldron, the process carefully burned away the impure dross, leaving only the "golden elixir" of pure *qi*.

Over time, the scope of Religious Daoism broadened as it evolved into something more like a genuine religion. The heavy emphasis on shamanistic practices continued, but there was room for other things as well. To some degree, the teachings of Philosophical Daoism, emphasizing man's relationship to the natural world, were integrated in fact as well as in name.

Religious Daoism borrowed heavily from Buddhism, its rival, but it gave as much as it took. Daoism was destined to exert a tremendous influence on the development of Buddhism in China. The easy naturalness of Daoism would help to bring Buddhism "down to earth," to ground Buddhism more deeply in a love of nature and, especially, in a love for the need of a healthy human society to live in harmony with the natural order. Daoism helped to soften some of the still-too-sacred and ritualistic edges of Indian Buddhism; in other words, it made Buddhism more "human." This would become especially obvious in the tradition we know as Chan Buddhism, the Chinese predecessor of Zen Buddhism.

Buddhism was not the only beneficiary of Daoist influence; practically everything in Chinese culture has been touched by it. We see its influence strongly in the traditional art of China. The love of nature, and the harmonious relationship of man and nature, has been a major theme in Chinese art over the ages and that love has been extended to other cultures of East Asia.

The influence of Daoism can be seen in the modern world as well. The environmental movement has been strongly touched by the values of Philosophical Daoism (or Nature Daoism, if you prefer). The interest in Feng Shui is an outgrowth of Daoism. And there is more than a little of the programs of Religious Daoism to be found in the New Age movement, including the obsessive interest in exercises and elixirs that promise long and healthy life (to say nothing of the popularity of that rather odd practice of preserving frozen bodies, or even just heads).

And what of the search for immortality? Did it finally just die out? Not really; but it is truly said that "The only thing immortal about the search for immortality is the search itself." That search finally tired of magical elixirs and pills. At least for some, immortality came to have more of a metaphysical meaning:

> An immortal is one who, by employing to the full all his endowments of body and mind, by shedding passion and eradicating all but the simplest and most harmless desires, has attained to free, spontaneous existence. . . . He has undergone a spiritual rebirth, broken free from the shackles of illusory selfhood and come face to face with his "true self," aware that it is not his personal possession, being no other than the sublime undifferentiated Dao! . . . Death, when it comes, will be for him no more than the casting off of a worn out robe. He has won to eternal life and is ready to plunge back into the limitless ocean of pure being! (quoted in Blofield, 16)

The above words are quoted from *Zhuang Zi*. It is interesting and fitting that he should have the final word on the meaning of immortality. In the final analysis, the true "immortal" turned out to be Zhuang Zi's sage.

Study Questions

1. Why do you think the Daoists were so passionately opposed to the Confucian system? What especially did they dislike about it?

2. Why do you suppose that Confucius (at least according to legend) said of Lao Zi, "Don't have anything to do with that man. He is a very dangerous man!"

3. How does the Daoist Superior Person differ from the Confucian Superior Man? Do they have anything at all in common? Which one do you find more appealing? Why?

4. The very first line of the *Dao De Jing* declares that "The Dao that can be spoken is not the true Dao." What does this mean?

5. Why is it suggested that the motorboat-versus-sailboat story is a good example of the Daoist way? Can you think of another good example?

6. What really is *wu wei*? How do you distinguish between *wu wei* and *de*? What's the best example you can think of that reveals the working of these two?

7. The Daoists were very fond of the use of water as a symbol, a metaphor. A symbol of what? What else might they have used?

8. What in the world do you suppose Lao Zi meant by saying that governing a country is like cooking a small fish?

9. How do you size up Lao Zi's description of the ideal village community? Do you think he meant his description to be understood literally? What, in essence, is he saying here?

10. Would you say that the relationship between Zhuang Zi and Lao Zi was similar to that of Mencius to Confucius? Were there any important differences? In your opinion, what was the essence of Zhuang Zi's teaching?

11. "Three in the Morning" is considered by many to be an excellent example of the Daoist way of life. How so? What point is the story making, and in what way is this Daoist?

12. Why did Zhuang Zi not see anything special about the relationship between man and nature? How do you feel about it?

13. Is Religious Daoism a natural outgrowth of Philosophical Daoism? Why do we make this distinction between "Religious" and "Philosophical" Daoism? Which appeals more to you?

14. What is *yin and yang* all about? Why do you suppose that many feel that this concept is one of the most important contributions of Chinese philosophical thought?

15. How would you explain the difference between "internal" and "external" Daoist alchemy? What do you make of this whole subject of Daoist alchemy? Does it deserve to be called "Daoist"?

16. Why is it ironic that the Daoist tradition ultimately came down to a focus on the search for the secret of immortality?

17. In a nutshell, how would you sum up the philosophy of life that we call "Daoism"?

CHAPTER 14

Shinto

A vast crescent of islands extends along the northern and western rim of the Pacific Ocean. It stretches all the way from the Aleutian Islands to Australia. The archipelago of Japan, a complex of more than 3,000 islands, lies roughly in the center section of this crescent. Most of the islands of Japan are quite small; the four largest ones make up almost all of what we normally think of as Japan. By far the largest of the four main islands is Honshu. Tokyo, the modern capital of Japan, and Kyoto, the historic capital, are located on Honshu. South of Honshu lie the islands of Kyushu and Shikoku. Together with Honshu, they partially enclose an area of ocean known as the Inland Sea. Throughout much of Japan's history, the Inland Sea area has been a center of economic and cultural life.

Geologically speaking, Japan is new land. It and many of the other island groups exist because of the subduction of ocean plates in the western Pacific. The resultant volcanic activity slowly but steadily creates new real estate. For this reason, Japan is a very mountainous country, including many volcanic mountains, such as Mount Fuji, the symmetrically beautiful symbol of Japan. It is also the reason for Japan being earthquake country. The mountains, being relatively young, tend to be steep, with deeply cut valleys and fast-rushing streams. Such country can be very beautiful, and provide excellent locations for Zen monasteries that like to be tucked away in the wilderness, but it presents a real challenge to a farming population. Only about 15 percent of Japan is flat enough to be good land for agriculture.

Long before our human ancestors became interested in agriculture, though, some of them were already living in the islands we know as Japan. Evidence of human occupation extends far back into prehistory. Perhaps the earliest migrants arrived in Japan on foot. From time to time in the geologic past, during ages of glaciation, the ocean level has been low enough to expose dry land between the Korean peninsula and southern Japan. For the most part, though, the modern Japanese are descended from a mainland people who migrated to the southern part of Japan in a series of waves beginning in the third century B.C.E. This sporadic migration continued for about four centuries. The newcomers had to do battle with a relatively primitive people already in possession of the land. We know these original dwellers as the Ainu. Little by little the Ainu were pushed back, but never entirely exterminated. Today, a small remnant of the descendants of the Ainu can be found on the northern island of Hokkaido. The newcomers, though, took possession of all of the good land of the south, and by the beginning of the fourth century C.E., they had pretty much settled down to the task of building a new culture.

And build they did. The modern culture of Japan is the direct descendent of what was begun more than two millennia ago. All modern cultures have roots that extend back into ancient times, but unlike most others, Japanese culture still has a living link with that ancient past; it is the tradition known as Shinto.

Western travelers are often surprised to discover how strong a role Shinto plays in the life of modern Japan. Far from being a quaint old tradition, largely forgotten, the visible presence of Shinto is ubiquitous. There are many thousands of Shinto shrines in Japan, and these play an ongoing role in the lives of the local communities that they serve. In addition, the Japanese people celebrate numerous annual festivals which are basically Shinto in nature. The imperial family, the absolute center of Japanese culture, derives its very meaning from the tradition of Shinto. Shinto is the core of Japanese culture; it unifies and defines the Japanese nation. But saying what it actually is, is no easy task.

One of the first Europeans to write about Japan was the German traveler Engelbert Kaempfer, who visited the islands of Japan in the late seventeenth century and was greatly impressed by most of what he found there. Shinto, though, didn't much interest him at all. He brushed it off as "the old religion of idol worship." Our knowledge of the Shinto tradition has come a long way since Engelbert's time. No one today would describe it as mere "idol worship," but most would agree that, broadly speaking, Shinto is a native Japanese religion. I say *broadly speaking*, though, because Shinto is far from being a perfect fit in our customary definition of "religion." Consider the following list of exceptions. Shinto has no distinct founder. There are no special scriptures, no revelation, not even a special religious philosophy or moral code. And, perhaps most important of all, in Shinto there is no worship of a supreme godhead.

So, on what basis can Shinto be defined as a religion? Let's begin with the word itself. The "shin" of *Shinto* is derived from an old word which carried the meaning of deity, or god. And the "to" of *Shinto* is a descendent of the Chinese *dao*, meaning "way." Thus, in its simplest form, Shinto means "way of the gods." This takes some explaining, though, because among the Japanese people of ancient times, the concept of divinity was definitely not limited to celestial gods and goddesses of superhuman powers. Indeed there were some of these, many in fact, but a great many divine beings were not of humanlike form at all. Trees, mountains, and rivers could be divine beings, and so too could natural happenings, such as thunderstorms and earthquakes. Many animals too were seen as divine. In fact, anything at all that held the power to inspire a sense of awe and mystery was easily seen as possessed of a divine nature. The spirits of such things, whether earthly objects or heavenly beings, were known as *kami*. "It may be said that 'kami' is essentially an expression used by early Japanese people to classify experiences that evoked sentiments of caution and mystery in the presence of the manifestation of the strange and marvelous." (Holton, 24)

It should be pointed out that it was not the thing itself that was the kami; kami refers to the spirit of the thing, that which gives it its awe-inspiring character. The kami, as spirit, resides within the place or thing, but is capable of moving about freely. Aspects of an earlier animism peek through clearly in developing Shinto. Veneration of the kami, through ritual and sacrifice, was an important part of life among the early people of

Japan. Thus, we might more properly define Shinto as "the way of the kami," recognizing that "way" here refers to the proper observance of ritual veneration.

Due to the close association of kami with natural phenomena, Shinto is sometimes described as a "nature religion." There's more than a little truth in this suggestion. The Japanese have always felt a profound love for the beauties of nature. And it's no wonder that they would; they inhabit an island world of magnificent natural beauty. It is almost inevitable that they would develop a sense of religious awe for the wonders of nature and a feeling of closeness to it all.

THE SHINTO CREATION STORY

But where did it all come from in the first place? Like people in all parts of the world, the Japanese of early times developed stories to explain the act of creation and the origin of their race. These mythic accounts are the foundation stones of Shinto; it is well worth our time to look at them closely. Naturally, there is frustratingly little in the way of dependable historical records about those early times. But we do have some, and they are sufficient to give us a reasonably well-rounded picture.

Our earliest glimpses come from excavations of third-century burial tumuli. Here we find some artifacts, but not much that is useful to the historian; no written records at all. The earliest written records derive from about the same time, but come from China, not Japan. The chronicler Wei Zhi made reference to the Land of Wa, an island kingdom located "in the middle of the ocean." He said that it was then ruled by a female shaman named Himiko, who occasionally sent tribute-bearing envoys to China. Further, he stated that the people of Wa engaged in the cultivation of rice and made fine linen and silk. It's not a lot of information, but it's a start. Much more helpful are the earliest Japanese

FIGURE 14.1   The famous Torii Gate at Miajima on the Inland Sea, Japan. (P. Bresnan)

sources, the *Kojiki*, written in 712 C.E., and the *Nihon Shoki*, from about 720 C.E. Both of these were chronicles that recorded the historical narrative beginning in the fifth century and also the important events of the mythic "history" before that time. From these sources, we can put together, in broad outline at least, the mythic foundation upon which Shinto was built.

The universe came into existence as a result of the mating of the kami representing the basic forces of nature, a sort of Japanese version of *yin and yang*. This also resulted in the creation of the twelve primary kami, who resided in a heavenly realm. The last to be created of this twelvesome were Izanagi, who would become the Sky Father, and Izanami, who was something of an Earth Mother. Before there was any land, the heavenly realm drifted serenely above a vast dark ocean. One day, Izanagi and Izanami strolled out from the heavens onto what is described as a "floating bridge," possibly a rainbow, from which they could peer down into the deep waters below. Izanagi plunged his bejeweled spear into the ocean, and each time he pulled it back, drops of brine would fall onto the water where they would coalesce into beautiful islands. In this way, the islands of Japan were said to form. Enchanted by what they had done, Izanagi and Izanami descended to their new island creations, where in the privacy of the forested mountains, they passionately made love. As a result of their lovemaking, more islands formed and also more kami were born.

The last of the kami to be born was Fire. It was a terribly difficult and painful birth, and Izanami died as a result. Izanagi was overwhelmed with grief, and like Orpheus, he wandered off to the underworld in search of his lost love. He eventually found Izanami, but was ordered not to look at her, as by this time the decay of death had become grotesque. Izanagi could not control his excitement; he disobeyed the order and was horrified by what he saw. In the next moment, furious kami drove him from the underworld. Izanagi fled to a nearby river, where he did two important things. First, he renounced his connection with Izanami, symbolically confirming the essential separation between the world of the living and that of the dead. The second thing he did was to wash himself thoroughly in the river water, symbolically purifying himself after being defiled in the underworld. This is regarded as the beginning of a rich tradition of purification rituals in Japanese culture. As Izanagi stood in the river, three more kami were created from his act of washing. These were the kami of the stars, of the moon, and of the sun.

The kami of the sun, the "sun goddess," was named Amaterasu, and would become the most important of all the celestial deities in Japanese culture. Izanagi and Izanami played the role of first parents, but it is Amaterasu that the Japanese people most revere. It was Ninigi-no-Mikoto, the grandson of Amaterasu, who descended to Earth and introduced the all-important cultivation of rice, the physical foundation of Japanese civilization. Ninigi-no-Mikoto was also the direct ancestor of Jimmu Tenno, the legendary first emperor of Japan, thus establishing the imperial family's claim to divinity. The emperor is not the only divine offspring, though. We are told in the *Shinsen Shojiroku*, the Record of Surnames compiled in the eighth century, that the founders of 402 clans also trace their lineage to Ninigi. Thus could virtually all of the Japanese clans claim some measure of divine descent. In an interesting way, it is fundamental to Japanese belief that humanity (or at least the Japanese part of it) is *descended from* the gods, not *created by* them.

It was this origin myth that provided the Japanese people with the story of their own beginning. It established a logical explanation for order coming out of the primeval chaos and also established a divine connection for the nation. That divine connection would continue forever in the special relationship between the people of Japan and the various kami of the land and sea. Shinto developed specifically to honor and perpetuate this tradition.

THE SHINTO SHRINE AND FESTIVAL

The most visible expression of Shinto is the shrine, *jinja* in Japanese. The shrine is the sacred place where the kami dwells. Here, it can be directly approached and venerated. In the earliest days, the kami shrine was simplicity itself. Typically, it would have been a natural place of some sort, a great tree perhaps, or a waterfall, which the local people believed to be a source of spiritual power. Often such kami-places were located far back in the mountains; a remote spot was favored, mysterious and full of natural beauty. Such early shrines would be marked off with nothing more than a pile of rocks or sometimes an ornamental rope to which strips of cloth would be tied. Here, the community would gather from time to time in order to venerate the kami with ritual and sacrifice. Its good will was understandably a matter of high importance.

The spread of agriculture changed all that. Now, instead of the people going to the kami, the kami had to come to the people. More specifically, it was important for the kami to journey to the rice fields, especially at certain critical times, such as the time of the harvest. It thus became customary to build some sort of simple, temporary abode for the kami to dwell in while it was in attendance. This custom spread throughout all of Japan and is the background out of which the national system of Shinto shrines grew. Today, there are some 18,000 Shinto shrines in Japan, tended by approximately 22,000 Shinto priests. Most of these shrines are relatively modest affairs; only about 2,000 would be classified as major sites.

The most major of all is the great shrine at Ise, on the seacoast of southern Honshu. In an odd sort of way, Ise is one of the oldest, and newest, of Japan's many great shrines. It was constructed more than thirteen centuries ago, but it is completely torn down and rebuilt every twenty years. The plan, though, is meticulously copied each time, so that the Ise that stands today is very faithful in appearance to the original. The next rebuilding will be in the year 2013 C.E. Ise is the official shrine of the imperial family. By long-standing custom, the emperor announces important matters of state to the gods at Ise. New prime ministers are introduced to the gods at Ise. Even high-ranking sumo wrestlers dedicate themselves at this great shrine.

Although some evolution was inevitable, there has been a conscious effort through the ages to keep the nature of the Shinto shrine as much as possible like it was in the early days, and herein lies its special beauty. There is variety—sixteen subtly different styles of architecture are recognized—but the basics are common to all shrines, great and modest. For one thing, only natural materials may be used. For the wooden structures this means cypress logs, shaped only with the use of hand tools. No metal parts or nails are used; these were not available in the early days. The carpentry is an amazing art; complex joinings not only hold the parts together, but are able to slide against one another in the event of earthquake.

The fully developed Shinto shrine consists, first of all, of a fenced enclosure, usually rectangular, within which are one or more wooden buildings. This is a sacred precinct, and the visitor is reminded of that right at the entryway, which, not uncommonly, is flanked by two guardian stone lions. These fierce-looking beings, introduced from China in the ninth century, examine all who enter. Almost immediately, the path passes under the *torii*, the crossbar gateway that has almost become an icon of Japanese culture. Often painted red, the two upright posts are joined by one or two crossbars. We are accustomed to seeing a gentle curve in the upper piece. This too is a Chinese introduction and would not have been found in the early days. As with so much else, we can only guess at the original intention. Quite possibly the earliest torii were roosts for sacred birds and were meant to keep evil spirits away.

If means permit, the shrine will support two buildings, the *haiden* and the *honden*. In smaller shrines, the functions of the two will be combined in one building. The haiden is the more public of the two. This building, referred to as the "worship sanctuary," usually has an open front which the worshipper can approach for prayer and for making offerings. To get the attention of the kami, he will clap his hands and ring a bell by pulling on an ornate rope. He or she will then bow deeply and offer the prayer. The haiden is also the place where the Shinto priest conducts ordinary ceremonies.

The honden is more hidden from public view. Within it is the "holy of holies," the place where the kami dwells. Only priests are allowed inside the honden and then only to tend the *shintai*. The shintai is the *sanctum sanctorum*, the kernel at the center, the actual object within which the kami takes up residence. This will be a symbolic representation of that particular deity. It may be a stone, a scroll, or perhaps a sword. Bronze mirrors often serve the purpose. The shintai is always elaborately wrapped, usually in silk and linen. It is so sacred that not even the Shinto priest may gaze upon it without permission. The shintai is the soul of the Shinto shrine.

There are other less essential items that are likely to be found on the grounds of most shrines. One of these is the *chouzubachi,* a "sacred font," often a natural stone basin filled with clear water intended for a simple purification ritual. The visitor uses a bamboo dipper to pour water over the hands before approaching the haiden. Purification is a major theme in Shinto. Another very popular feature of the Shinto shrine is the *ema-den*. An ema is a small wooden tablet on which the visitor writes out a short prayer, usually a request or a thank you, and then ties it to a standing wooden frame. In earlier times, members of the aristocracy often donated a horse to the shrine in thanks for an answer to a prayer. The common people, being unable to afford a horse, adopted the custom of donating instead an ema, a picture of a horse painted on wood. A large shrine may have hundreds of these on display at any given time. The sight is both picturesque and touching. (Nowadays, the "ema" is sometimes in the shape of a little car. Horses aren't so popular as they used to be.) Another common feature of the Shinto shrine is the *toro*, the familiar Japanese stone lantern resting on a stone pedestal. These may line pathways or be placed anywhere on the grounds. As a rule, the lanterns were acquired as gifts.

The Shinto shrine's most basic reason for being is simply to provide a sacred place for the kami to reside and thus a place where the local people can commune with the resident kami. The typical shrine, though, serves other important functions as well. It serves as a center for the performance of certain sacred rituals, such as festivals, rites honoring the major stages of life, and ritual purifications. This last is an extremely important function.

Oharai is the Japanese name for the ceremony whose purpose is to please and soothe the kami. Hopefully, a benign kami will extend its power to make things right. This is especially important in any situation where there is danger of defilement. And defilement results from contact with any kind of polluting influence, such as death and disease, or even plain old bad luck. Thus, "purification" is a good choice of words. It's not a matter of driving out evil; rather it is the removal of *tsumi* (impurity). The priest beseeches the kami to correct the defilement, restoring natural order and harmony.

There are myriad examples of situations that call for oharai—everything from the profound to the profane. Oharai may be performed at the shrine, or the priest may travel to the place where it is needed. In Japan, it is common to call in the Shinto priest to perform oharai before occupying a new home, an office building, a shop, or even a new car.* On July 16, 1969, an oharai ceremony was conducted at the United Nations headquarters on behalf of the Apollo 11 mission, when the first humans landed on the surface of the moon.

The ancient ceremony of oharai is conducted by the Shinto priest, dressed in his sacramental vestments. Typically, as he chants aloud, the priest waves the *onusa* over the person or thing to be purified. The onusa is a sort of stick, or wand, that blossoms into a large spray of white paper strips at one end. The procedure will probably call for ritual washing as well. As anyone who has traveled in Japan knows well, the Japanese are a scrupulously clean people; everyone and everything gets scrubbed thoroughly and often. Undoubtedly, this national passion has roots in the purification ceremonies of Shinto.

Salt plays an important part in oharai. Salt is the symbol of purity. In ancient times, it was believed that salt water was a more efficacious purifier than drinking water. The Shinto priest will sprinkle salt over the thing to be purified, probably several times. Westerners may be familiar with this practice from watching sumo matches on television. Sumo has its roots in Shinto. The ring used in sumo is actually meant to be a replica of a Shinto shrine building. In modern times, the uprights have been removed for the benefit of television cameras, but the roof is traditional Shinto and is suspended from above. When entering the ring, the sumo wrestler sprinkles some salt, a traditional Shinto purification gesture. He is, in effect, dedicating the match to the kami, just as Greek athletes in ancient times dedicated their games to their gods.

The traditional use of salt as a spiritual purifier has made its way into many aspects of Japanese life. People attending a funeral are customarily given a small bag of salt to sprinkle around the doorway of their home before entering so as not to carry the defilement of death into the home. Restaurant owners, after diligently washing their section of sidewalk, sometimes put little mounds of salt on either side of the entryway—thus no defilement is carried inside. The Shinto scholar Stuart Picken reports even having seen salt sprinkled in the dugout of a Japanese baseball team that was in a prolonged slump.

The festival is another important feature of Shinto. Festivals are a very big part of life in Japan. Some are huge productions and go on for several days. It seems that everyone gets involved. There is feasting, partying, and endless decorations. The parade, or rather, the religious procession, is the big event. To the accompaniment of much drumming and cheering, the elaborately decorated floats are hauled down the crowded streets by throngs of boisterous young men. Since most of these festivals are Shinto in origin, one of the floats is very special. When included, it comes at the end and carries the kami. A delegation had gone to meet it at a designated spot and are now exuberantly escorting the deity to its home shrine. The kami rides in splendor, hidden deep within its lavishly

---

*There aren't many Shinto shrines outside Japan, but there is a fully functioning one in Stockton, California (of all places!). I went there once just to see if it was really true. Indeed it is, in the house and backyard of an ordinary tract home. The priests were very friendly and even offered to do a purification ceremony for my old car. I've always regretted that I didn't take them up on it. Think about it: a genuine Shinto shrine in a tract neighborhood of Stockton and a genuine Hindu temple (including the architecture) in a tract neighborhood of nearby Livermore. (Only in California?)

decorated wagon. It's quite a spectacle. No wonder the traditions of Shinto occupy a special place in the Japanese heart!

The general word for festival is *matsuri* in Japanese. The tradition is deeply rooted in Shinto. Some matsuri are personal, being family celebrations marking the important events in a person's life. The big ones, though, involve the whole community and celebrate the important events in the annual calendar. Most festivals have ancient roots and were originally related to the agricultural cycle, especially the spring planting of rice and the fall harvest. The imperial family has always played a major role in these festivals. Traditionally, the emperor plants the first rice seedlings and also harvests the first grains. These are then offered to Amaterasu at Ise.

The greatest festival of the year is *Niiname*, the autumn harvest festival. It is the central event of the Shinto annual cycle, much as Easter is in the Christian calendar. The Niiname festival is essentially a wedding feast, celebrating the marriage of heaven and Earth. The heavenly being represents the male, who descends to Earth to join with the female in order to renew the life that is now being celebrated in the harvest. A tremendous banquet precedes the wedding night "nuptials," for which a new wedding hut has been constructed. Typically, there is much singing and dancing, and drinking.

But things aren't intended to go entirely smoothly. In the traditional Niiname celebration, a "disruptive force" enters the picture. This intruding male, derived out of the Shinto myths, appears on the scene and tries to prevent the marriage from being consummated, obviously so that he can have the bride for himself. He, of course, is eventually defeated, but his intrusion provides all kinds of exciting opportunities for drama. Apparently, at least in ancient times, the village people were much more than mere spectators. The Shinto scholar Robert Ellwood gives us an interesting glimpse into early Niiname customs. He begins with a verse which was intended to be spoken by one of the participants:

> Though it be the night when I make offerings of the early rice of Katsushika,
> I will not keep you, darling, standing outside the house.
> Away, you who rattle at my door on this sacred night of new rice-offering.
> When I've sent my man out and worship in the house alone.

Ellwood goes on to say, "These poems suggest that on the night of Niiname, the husbands left their houses and went out, leaving their wives within to make offerings of new rice. Later, 'mysterious visitors' arrived and banged violently on the doors. Of course these were the menfolk, perhaps disguised as gods and perhaps not at their proper home. No doubt in time they won admittance by proving they were gods, and renewed the seasons with feasting and orgy." (72–73) (Ellwood neglects to speculate on how these menfolk "proved that they were gods.")

HISTORICAL DEVELOPMENT OF SHINTO

The history of Shinto, like that of Japanese culture in general, is divided into three broad eras: ancient, medieval, and modern. The time that we call ancient was the formative period of Japanese culture. Our knowledge of that time must depend more on legend and myth than on solid history. During ancient times, Shinto was the religion of all the people; it had no rivals.

An enormous change came over the land in the eighth century. For one thing, the influence of Chinese civilization began to be felt strongly in Japan. In the year 710 C.E., an imperial capital, based on the Chinese model, was established at the new city of Nara. In 794 C.E., the court relocated to nearby Kyoto, and there it would remain for more than a thousand years. This long period of time, characterized by a feudal organization of society, is known as the medieval period.

During the medieval era, Shinto had to cope with a vigorous new rival, Buddhism. Buddhism arrived from China by way of Korea. It first appeared in Nara right at the beginning of the era and became very popular with the aristocracy. For a long time, interest in Buddhism was limited only to the feudal aristocracy; the religion of the common people continued to be traditional Shinto. But gradually, the influence of Buddhism spread to all classes of society. Interestingly, there was no war between the two ways; it was a friendly rivalry. Buddhism in Japan absorbed much from Shinto. (One of Buddhism's great strengths has always been its adaptability.) For one thing, it was not uncommon for Shinto shrines to be included on the grounds of Buddhist temples. Shinto, however, was not greatly changed by its contact with Buddhism. It pretty much continued to go along as before, preserving the ancient ways. Buddhism gained a permanent place in Japanese society *alongside* Shinto; each has its own sphere of interest, and they coexist peacefully.

Technically speaking, the modern era began with the promulgation of the Meiji Constitution in the year 1889. More realistically, perhaps, the modern era could be said to have begun for Japan in the summer of 1853. In that year, the uninvited Commodore Matthew C. Perry of the United States Navy, in command of a small fleet of eleven warships, sailed into Tokyo Bay and demanded that the Japanese government grant certain trade concessions to his country. To be more precise, he "requested" these concessions, then departed saying that he would be back in one year to receive their reply. Considering the fact that, at that time, the Japanese were hopelessly far behind the Western powers in military technology, Perry's not so subtle show of force was in effect "making them an offer they couldn't refuse." Nor did they. A small package of trade agreements was signed which was the initial wedge in prying Japan out of its long self-imposed isolation. Commodore Perry's visit to the waters of Tokyo Bay opened an era in Japanese history that would not come to its end until another uninvited visitor from the American military appeared in the sky over Hiroshima slightly less than a century later.

Perry's visit was the catalyst that started the juices flowing again after centuries of relative stagnation in Japan. The entire society was seized with a passionate determination to remake the culture of Japan in the Western image, at least to the degree that was necessary in order to catch up and be able to compete as an equal with the highly aggressive Western powers of the nineteenth century. The rapid absorption of Western technology, and Western culture generally, was a truly amazing phenomenon. It can only be compared to the similarly ravenous appetite for all things Chinese that had occurred in Japan back in the Nara Period of the eighth century. The initial preoccupation understandably focused on military technology. Underdeveloped Japan was in a terribly precarious situation; the imperialist-minded Western powers, hungry for colonial possessions, had gobbled up nearly the entire globe. Other than Thailand, which was a special case, Japan was the only Asian nation to have escaped the colonial net of the Western powers.* And, after Perry's rude interruption, it was obvious that time was running out.

Japan's response to Perry's visit began as an effort to modernize and acquire only the means of national self-defense. But the Japanese industrial revolution proved to be so successful that by the end of the nineteenth century, Japan had achieved parity with the Western powers and actually became one of their club, creating its own dream of imperial conquest in Asia. Shinto, like it or not, was destined to play an important role in this frightening adventure.

The Meiji Constitution officially brought an end to the long feudal age and established a constitutional monarch on the model of the German Empire. The emperor, in all his divine glory, would preside over this new government. The Meiji Constitution, though, did not emerge out of thin air; it was an outgrowth of what is called the Meiji Restoration of 1868, which itself was an outgrowth of the turmoil set loose by Perry's "opening of Japan" only fifteen years before. What was being restored in the Meiji Restoration was the authority of the emperor as the de facto head of the government, as he had been in ancient times. For many centuries, the Japanese emperor had been nothing more than a pampered figurehead, a symbol of the Japanese nation, holding court at his palace at Kyoto. The real power, though, rested with the *shogun*, a military warlord who ruled over the feudal nobility from his own palace at Edo. One of the effects of the Meiji Restoration was to abolish the shogunate, installing the emperor in his place at Edo, which became the new national capital and was promptly renamed Tokyo.

The powerful clique responsible for the Meiji Restoration was primarily concerned with three goals: the total dismantling of feudalism, the rapid Westernization of the Japanese state, and the centralization of authority in the national government presided over by the emperor. The highly intoxicating spirit of nationalism swept over Japan. Those in power saw the ancient tradition of Shinto as a potentially very useful tool for promoting the nationalist spirit and achieving a strong national unity under the emperor. In fact, Shinto was a natural; it already was a source of national identity, and the central fact of Shinto was the divinity of the emperor. Thus, it was that Shinto came to be pressed into the service of those who dreamed of transforming Japan into a strong and aggressive imperialist Asian power. The person of the emperor was to be at the center of it all, and his special importance was to be emphasized by stressing his divinity. Consider these lines from the opening section of the Meiji Constitution. Article One states that "The Empire of Japan shall be reigned over and governed by a line of Emperors unbroken for ages eternal." And in Article Three, it continues, "The Emperor is sacred and inviolable." The sacredness of the emperor was stressed in every way possible, even getting into the schoolbooks of little children. A national reader for primary grades contained this verse:

> Great Japan! Great Japan
> Our seventy million citizens
> Look up to the Emperor even as to God
> And love and serve him as a parent.

---

*Strictly speaking, China was never a de facto *colony* of a Western power; that is, China's sovereignty was never surrendered to outright rule by a foreign power. However, the government of China was very weak at this crucial time in history, and the very aggressive Western powers (including the United States) exercised a high level of control within China, even going so far as to establish what they referred to as "spheres of influence," a way of splitting up China into regions where each of the Western powers would have an exclusive right to trade, and to exploit, within their respective spheres.

This kind of thing was right up Shinto's alley, so to speak. But not just any old kind of Shinto would do. The government promoted a particular Shinto sect known as *Fukko Shinto*, referred to in the West as "Pure Shinto." This highly nationalistic sect advocated a return to the "pure" roots of ancient Shinto. They would purge it of all foreign contaminations, such as Chinese influences in general and Buddhist influences in particular. The Fukko idealized a golden age in the past, before Japanese civilization had been vitiated by the cultural influences of "lesser" peoples, most of all the Chinese, and more recently the "Western barbarians." They would make Japan strong again by returning the country to its original source of strength, pure Shinto, centered on a divine emperor, the living voice of the will of Amaterasu, the goddess of the sun.

The most influential spokesman for Fukko Shinto was the nineteenth-century writer Motoori Norinaga. Reaching out from the central fact of the divinity of the emperor, he became unabashedly messianic:

> From the central truth that the Mikado [emperor] is the direct descendant of the gods, the tenet that Japan ranks far above all other countries is a natural consequence. No other nation is entitled to equality with her, and all are bound to do homage to the Japanese sovereign and pay tribute to him. . . . It relies on a rationalization of history in order to develop the two-fold thesis of a *jure divino* sovereign in an Imperial Line unbroken from divine ages and destined to rule Japan eternally and a divine Japanese race which, by virtue of the directness of its genealogical connections with the kami, is braver, more virtuous and more intelligent than all other races of mankind. The god-descended Japanese Emperor is divinely destined to extend his sway over the entire earth. (quoted in Holton, 49, 51)

The world watched with awe as the industrial and military strength of Japan mushroomed into greatness, but few outsiders could see that an also-mushrooming nationalism was a less visible part of the same picture. When the warlords gained control of the government during the crisis of the Great Depression, it was only a matter of time before the Empire of Japan would attempt to make the dream come true. As the European colonial powers, newly intent on slaughtering one another in the second of the century's World Wars, began to loosen their grip on their Asian possessions, Japanese leadership saw its chance and began to move into the power vacuum. Japan, fulfilling what they believed to be the obvious will of the gods, would create its own imperialist empire in East Asia. It was an exciting vision, to say the least. There was only one problem. One of those Western powers, the United States of America, had similar designs. And, unlike the European nations, the United States was most definitely not a declining power. In one of the most horrendous miscalculations in all of human history, the Empire of Japan made war on the United States in the vain hope of removing that country as a threat to their own imperialist designs. Four years later, a completely devastated and broken Japan was forced to face a very different future from the one that the warlords had dreamed about.

Emperor Hirohito, if he was to keep his throne, was required to face the nation and publicly deny his claim to divinity. This dramatic disclaimer was to be the first step in a program aimed at dismantling the nationalistic infrastructure of pre-war Japan. Under the direction of the occupation military government, a new constitution was promulgated in

1947, this time on the more liberal and democratic model of Britain and the United States. Included in the constitution was a clause specifically prohibiting public support of the Shinto religion. Never again could Shinto be the publicly funded tool of a nationalistic-minded government. The victorious allies naively expected that, forced to rely on local private funding, the whole institution of Shinto would simply dry up and blow away.

Well, not quite. Under the organizational leadership of the *Jinja Honcho* (The Association of Shinto Shrines), far from dying out, Shinto is now stronger than ever. Free from the shackles of government support and control, Shinto has become the inspiration for a healthy national unity in modern times. It's a truly amazing tradition. As before, Shinto shrugs off efforts to change it. Shinto has in its time weathered the assaults of Chinese culture, of Buddhism, of Western influence, and of totalitarianism. Shinto continues to live among the Japanese people, as it always has, preserving a living link with the ancient past.

Study Questions

1. On what basis can Shinto be defined as a religion? In what important ways does Shinto differ from the generally accepted definition of "religion"?

2. Describe the creation myth that Shinto employs to explain the beginnings of the Japanese people. Do you think that it is meant to be understood literally or metaphorically? What is the relationship of the imperial family to this myth?

3. Historically speaking, what has been the relationship between Shinto and Buddhism in Japan?

Why is it suggested that the borrowing has been only a one-way street?

4. How in the world did Shinto get tangled up in the affairs that led to World War II? Was Fukko Shinto a reasonably characteristic expression of the tradition of Shinto?

5. How do you size up Shinto? Is it a "living fossil"—an archaic but still dangerous form of nationalism—an inspiring tradition? What is it?

PART FOUR

Buddhism
in China and Japan

Part IV focuses on the rise and mature development of Buddhism in East Asia, primarily within China, where early Buddhism branched into several significant schools. Among these are Tiantai, Pure Land Buddhism, Vajrayana, and Chan Buddhism. All of these schools of Buddhism traveled to the lands neighboring China where the traditions continued to flourish, but with a new character shaped by their new homelands. This is especially interesting with regard to Chinese Chan Buddhism, which became Zen Buddhism in Japan.

The ups and downs of the history of Buddhism in Asia make a fascinating story. Buddhism has entered the twenty-first century not as some archaic "living fossil," but rather as a vital and creative force that is playing, and undoubtedly will continue to play, a significant role in shaping the evolving character of modern global civilization.

CHAPTER 15

Early Buddhism in China

The source of the Mahayana revolution was that now-familiar region in the northwestern part of the Indian subcontinent, the region known as Ghandara in ancient times. In the early centuries of the common era, Mahayana Buddhism radiated out from there, ultimately traveling great distances. (In fact, it's still traveling.) Much of North India was influenced by Mahayana, but Buddhism's days were numbered in its Indian homeland. Over the next several centuries, Buddhism in India would slowly fade into near insignificance. Those Buddhist communities that did endure were ultimately all but destroyed by foreign invaders, first the Huns in the fifth century C.E. and finally the Turkish Mughals, whose brutal conquest of India began in the eleventh century. By this time, though, Buddhism—especially Mahayana Buddhism—was alive and well in many places outside of India.

Geographically close to India is Tibet, and Mahayana, or more specifically Vajrayana Buddhism, would eventually travel up into the high country where it was to become solidly established. Before that, though, Buddhism traveled far afield, hitching a ride on that fascinating highway of trade that we know as the "Silk Road." The Silk Road was an extremely long caravan route that connected China with the other parts of the Eurasian continent. Much more than silk was traded, though; everything imaginable made its way back and forth between East and West, and thanks to a subsidiary route, south into India as well. Buddhist ideas, Buddhist books, even Buddhist monks entered the flow and moved with it wherever the Silk Road might take them. The lands to the west were not particularly receptive, however. During the late Roman times, the institutional monolith of the Christian Church presented a bulwark of resistance, and beginning in the late seventh century, this was superseded by the even more intransigent resistance posed by the rise of Islam.

Toward the east, though, it was a different story. Mahayana Buddhism would eventually make its way into China and become thoroughly integrated into that culture. But there was a very interesting intermediate step that most people in the modern world have never heard about.

BUDDHISM IN THE TARIM BASIN

Near the center of the map of Eurasia is a well-defined oval depression named the Tarim Basin. Within the Tarim Basin is the Takla Makan, today one of the world's most formidable deserts; it ranks with the Sahara in heat and lifeless aridity. It is a nearly thousand-mile-wide sea of nothing but scrub and shifting sand dunes. But, it wasn't always that way. Tens of thousands of years ago, the Takla Makan was a lake, and the sand we see today was then the lake bottom. That was when much of the Northern Hemisphere was covered with ice. Then about 10,000 years ago, the ice began to retreat. By the time Mahayana appeared on the scene, the lake was gone and the desert was well established. But there was still a good deal of residual glaciation in the higher elevations of the mountains that surround the Takla Makan. Continual glacial melt fed numerous rivers that plunged out of the mountains and into the desert, where they eventually petered out and disappeared. But along the fringes of the desert, at the base of the mountains, there was a margin of well-watered and fertile land. Here were to be found many towns, some of them quite large, that grew rich on the trade passing through the Takla Makan region.

When it reached the desert of the Takla Makan, the Silk Road necessarily split into a northern route and a southern route. In the extreme western part of the Takla Makan, caravans traveling west converged again at the cosmopolitan city of Kashgar, a welcome stopping place before heading off into the treacherous passes of the Pamir Range. Kashgar is still there, but today's city is only a tiny hint of what it used to be. Kashgar was a major trade center, and transfer place, for the caravans traveling the Silk Road. At its height, the exotic bazaars of Kashgar rivaled those of Istanbul. Everything in the world was available in Kashgar, for the right price.

Kashgar was not a Chinese city, but near the eastern end of the Tarim Basin the routes converged on Dunhuang (Tun-huang), the farthest western outpost of Chinese civilization. Dunhuang was a lot like Kashgar, but it was decidedly Chinese. A section of the Great Wall—the farthest west it would go—was constructed to the area of Dunhuang.

The justly famous Mugao Grottoes, one of the most splendid of all the remains from that distant time, are located near Dunhuang. The grottoes, actually a series of hand-chiseled caves, line the face of a cliff that fronts on a now-dried-up watercourse. The walls and ceilings of the caves are decorated with very beautiful paintings of Buddhist themes from the earliest period of Buddhism in China. Many of the paintings are pure enchantment. Viewing these treasures is not a problem; the government of China has fixed up the site and opened it to the public. The problem is getting there. To say that Dunhunag is remote is very much an understatement. From Dunhuang it was another thousand-mile journey to the great city of Changan, the imperial capital of China in those days.

Changan, now known as Xian,* is a capital city no longer, and the original character of Dunhuang has disappeared entirely. So too have the glaciers and the rich life of the towns and cities they nourished around the perimeter of the Takla Makan. But in the days when the water poured from the mountains, and the trade goods moved on the caravan routes, Buddhism became established in this area and flourished for several centuries.

---

*It was near Xian that the amazing army of full-size terra cotta figures was discovered in 1974. The site is still being excavated.

It was a mini-"golden age" that history has largely forgotten. Numerous Buddhist monasteries were established in the area, some of them actually out in parts of the desert where water was still available at that time.

These monasteries were surprisingly rich treasure houses of Buddhist art and scholarship. Some of them were home to hundreds of monks. And then—as is the fate of all things eventually—this happy age came to an end. The drying-up of the highlands was only a part of the story, though undoubtedly a big part. Nature was assisted by a series of invasions: Mongol tribesmen from the north and later the conquest of Islam. One by one the monasteries were destroyed or abandoned. In time, the sands covered their remains and they were forgotten. By the end of the eighth century, nothing much remained of the region's once-great Buddhist culture.

Thus did the remains of this great historical legacy lie unnoticed beneath the desert sands for more than a millennium. Interest was revived in nineteenth-century Europe as the study of history and archaeology began to take its modern form. Unfortunately, it wasn't quite modern enough yet. With no strong government to control research in the area, freebooting self-styled "archaeologists" in the late nineteenth and early twentieth centuries ransacked the region, plundering everything they could find. Their "excavations" more often looked like battlefields than careful research sites. Monastery libraries were looted of their manuscripts, well-preserved in the dry desert conditions. Much artwork, too, was stolen, some of it chiseled directly from the walls of monastery rooms, and shipped back to museums in Europe and America that were willing to pay top dollar for these treasures. Finally, in 1920, the Chinese government moved to halt the plunder, and today what is left is being properly studied and exhibited. Enough remains to dazzle the eye and convince the world of Buddhist studies that in the region of the now-desolate Takla Makan Buddhism once flourished, and it was from there that Buddhism launched the beginning of its gentle conquest of China.

The earliest Chinese Buddhist document that is widely accepted as being historically verifiable comes to us from the middle of the second century C.E. It is a fragment of the Pali Canon translated into Chinese by a scholar named An Shigao (An Shih-kao). There is reason to believe, however, that Buddhist monks had been spreading the good word in China for a full century before this. Thus, Buddhism first encountered Chinese culture during the time of the Han Empire, a time when China was unified and the governing class was strong. The Han Empire was to the far eastern parts of Eurasia what the Roman Empire was to the far western parts. They coexisted during the first and second centuries C.E.

During the time of Han, there was some resistance to Buddhism from Confucians, who, as a group, held virtually all important government posts. Buddhist roots grew slowly at first. But the Han Empire, like the Roman Empire, was destined to fall. The Great Wall had kept the barbarous hordes of the north at bay for five centuries, but in the third century C.E., they finally broke through, overwhelming China and plunging much of the land into an era of tumult and division. (It's a fascinating story; two centuries later descendents of these invaders, known to history as the Huns, would wreak the same kind of havoc on Roman Europe.) In the aftermath of the fall of Han, Buddhism in China grew rapidly. So, in sum, we can say that Buddhism entered China during the first century C.E., grew relatively slowly for its first couple of centuries, and then began to spread rapidly.

Like so many other countries, the land of China is divided into a "north" and a "south." Speaking very broadly, North China centers on the basin of the Yellow River (the Huanghe), and the south centers on the great Yangtse, one of the longest and mightiest rivers in all of Eurasia. The invaders overran only the northern parts of China. Many people, especially from the upper classes, fled to the south, where the traditional culture, if not the empire form of government, was preserved. Life was far from peaceful, though. For three centuries, all parts of China would be convulsed by constant warfare and shifting borders. Slowly, very slowly, the Chinese people would win back the land of the north, but it would not be until the year 589 C.E. that all of China would be reunited again. In that year, the Sui dynasty was established, and the bad old days were over, at least for a while.

Buddhism became solidly established in China during the turbulent three centuries that separate the fall of Han and the rise of Sui. There were a number of reasons for this, the most obvious being that Confucian officials lost their position of power with the fall of Han and thus were not able to offer effective resistance to this "foreign" influence. In North China, the very foreignness of Buddhism worked to its advantage. The conquering warlords of the north were attracted to the fact that Buddhism was not a native Chinese system. In the south, though, where Confucian and Daoist scholarship continued to flourish, Buddhism succeeded *despite* its still-evident foreign character.

Little by little, the original hostility changed to curiosity and finally to warmth. But why? Why did Buddhism eventually experience a friendly reception in China? What was the appeal? What did this exotic philosophy have to offer to a people who already possessed a rich and ancient civilization? This is a very interesting question, especially when one stops to consider that, with the exception of Marxism, Buddhism is the *only* foreign philosophy of life ever to be integrated into the culture of China. (And the jury is still out with regard to the enduring effect of Marxism.)

For one thing, the essentials of Buddhism did not really stand in conflict with the teachings of Daoism and Confucius. There was a resonance among them, especially between the philosophies of Buddhism and Daoism. Apparently, the Buddhist emphasis on disciplined meditation was a strong part of its initial appeal. Meditation, in the broad sense of the word, was a part of the Daoist way of life, but it was ill-defined. Buddhist meditation would give a new and dynamic form to this latent potential of Daoism. One cannot help but think of a similar situation that exists in the modern Western world, where we have seen a succession of Indian gurus promoting various schools of meditation. Huge numbers of Westerners have been excited by this "new blood" from old India. Perhaps something like this was part of Buddhism's early days in China.

This "resonance," though, went much deeper than simply a shared interest in meditation. Buddhism did not work a revolution in China; rather it helped to bring out and give clearer form to attitudes that were already inherent in Chinese philosophy. As Heinrich Dumoulin points out, "Buddhists were especially impressed by the Chinese rejection of the duality between being and non-being, and by their emphasis on the ineffability of reality." (66)

Before long, the entire vast world of Buddhist scripture was being translated into Chinese. What an undertaking that must have been! In some places, government-sponsored "Translation Bureaus" were established. The languages, like the cultures, were very different. Finding appropriate words in Chinese was no easy task. Since Daoism seemed to have the closest philosophical affinity to Buddhism, Daoist terms were widely used in the work of translation. Just as the Christians are sometimes accused of "baptizing" Aristotle in translating his works into Latin, the Chinese to some extent "Daoicized" Buddha. It was the beginning of a process of development that would eventually result in a thoroughly Chinese Buddhism.

We can't overstate the scope or the importance of the work of translating the vast literature, especially the Buddhist sutras, into Chinese. In this connection, one name stands out with singular greatness. We know him as Kumarajiva (koo-mar-a-JEE-va). Born in 344 C.E., Kumarajiva studied for many years at a Theravadin monastery in Kashmir, that fertile ground of Buddhism up in the northwestern part of India. He started out as a Theravadin, but the exciting new ways of Mahayana were in the air and, in time, got into his blood. Finally, he relocated from Kashmir over the mountains to Kashgar, where, before long, he began to make a name for himself in the work of translation. His fame spread to China, and, at long last, he took up residence in the great city of Changan.

Kumarajiva headed a large Translation Bureau in Changan, focusing mainly on translating the Mahayana sutras into Chinese. Kumarajiva's most important work was the meticulous translation of the *Prajnaparamita* and the related works of Nagarjuna into Chinese. These works had tremendous impact on the developing character of Chinese Buddhism. Given the fundamental importance of the *Prajnaparamita* in Chinese Buddhism, it's no exaggeration to say that Kumarajiva was largely responsible for the ultimate ascendancy of Mahayana in China. "That the Chinese showed a preference for Mahayana over Hinayana is due principally to the wisdom teachings of the *Prajnaparamita* sutras, which they found to resonate deeply with their own spiritual heritage." (Dumoulin, 66)

Kumarajiva died at the age of sixty-three in 409 C.E. By this time, Buddhism—more particularly Mahayana Buddhism—was well on the way to becoming an established part of the culture in all parts of China. The Mahayana sutras, newly translated from Sanskrit into the Chinese language, provided a base from which many different "schools" of Buddhism would grow. Not all of these schools emerged immediately—some would not take final form until the sixth or even the seventh centuries—but the net effect was a broad proliferation of Buddhist sects in China. All, however, shared common roots in the Mahayana sutras. Let me mention just a few of the better-known ones; they are representative of the wide variety of possibilities.

TIANTAI BUDDHISM

Tiantai takes its name from Mount Tiantai, located in the hilly province of Zhejiang in southeastern China. It was there in the sixth century C.E. that a monk named Zhiyi (Chih-i) founded Gouqing monastery and initiated the teaching of "Tiantai" Buddhism, the first truly Chinese school of Buddhism. It would be transplanted to Japan in the ninth century, where it would become known as Tendai Buddhism. Although Zhiyi is recognized as the founder of Tiantai, he was (as is so often the case) largely responsible for pulling together and giving a coherent form to currents that had been developing for centuries before his time. Zhiyi played the role of a peacemaker, a compromise-maker, who brought together the disparate and often feuding members of the family of Buddhist teaching in China. Tiantai Buddhism became something of a syncretistic school in which all of the elements of Buddhist teaching could live in harmony.

As the vast storehouse of Buddhist scripture became translated into Chinese, many were puzzled by the seeming inconsistencies and even contradictions. How could Buddha have been so inconsistent in his teaching? This was especially problematic with regard to the doctrinal disputes between Mahayana and Theravada. How was one to ferret out of all this the true teaching?

Zhiyi solved the problem by proclaiming that all of it was true teaching. Differences were to be explained—certainly not as contradictions, but as having originated in different levels or periods in Buddha's teaching career. According to Tiantai, the total message of Buddha's teaching unfolded in five distinct periods following his awakening. The first of these lasted for only three weeks. This was the time, immediately after his awakening, when Buddha gave the teachings to be found in the *Avatamsaka Sutra*, which deals with the mystifying subject of the interfusion of all things. To his surprise, Buddha found that this teaching was too deep for his disciples; they were not yet ready to understand its message. He therefore changed gears, and for twelve years taught the very fundamental doctrine to be found in the Theravada sutras. In this, the second period, he introduced such matters as the Four Noble Truths and the Noble Eightfold Path. In the third period, which lasted for eight years, he gave his disciples the elementary Mahayana sutras, stressing the superior worth of the bodhisattva over that of the arhat. Then, for a full twenty-two years, he gave the "wisdom teachings" to be found in the *Prajnaparamita Sutra*. It took this long time to fully work out the Doctrine of Emptiness and its implications. Finally, in the fifth period, the final eight years of his life, Buddha proclaimed the teachings of the *Lotus Sutra*. The *Lotus Sutra* brought it all together, resolving all dichotomies, revealing the absolute identity of all contrasts.

It's a wonderful approach (whether or not it is historically accurate). Tiantai dissolves all conflicts within the Buddhist fold, most notably that between Theravada and Mahayana. Theravadins might not have appreciated being relegated to the most immature ground floor, but there weren't really many Theravadins in China anyway; Mahayana had succeeded in claiming the field almost entirely for itself. The problem was not one of resolving difficulties with Theravadin groups, but with Theravadin sutras, the basic sutras of the Pali Canon. The Tiantai approach was an excellent solution to this problem. All of the sutras had an important place, but in the most cherished place of all was the lordly *Lotus Sutra*. This became the bible of Tiantai Buddhism.

Of course, organizing and harmonizing the teachings, excellent though that may have been, was not meant to be an end in itself; the real task was to *live* the teaching in one's daily life and thus to achieve awakening. Zhiyi was the master of a monastery; the ongoing routine of his community of monks was his chief concern. What gave overarching structure to the daily life of the monk was the practice of the monastic precepts (*paramitas*). Certainly this would hold true in all Buddhist monasteries, but Zhiyi gave special importance to the third precept, "acceptance." Indeed it is a great virtue, and one that is especially hard for us humans to nurture. The mortal enemy of acceptance is hatred. The strength of hatred (and its fellow traveler, anger) is a perfect gauge of the strength of ego. And the ego, the illusion of a private self, is what Buddha held to be the greatest obstacle to liberation. It was for this reason that Zhiyi emphasized the nurturing of compassion in all things. Compassion and hatred cannot dwell together under the same roof. Hatred is rooted out by compassion. Here's how Zhiyi put it:

> To root out hatred brings happiness,
> And gives freedom from anxiety.
> Hatred is poison's root,
> To destroy it brings moral excellence.

As in virtually all monasteries, meditation claimed a large part of every day. In this regard, Zhiyi was surprisingly open-minded. He emphasized sitting meditation, but was open to other styles—whatever works. He was also open-minded as to the method the meditator chose to employ. In this regard, Zhiyi became something of a forefather of the future of Buddhism in China. Indeed, widely divergent sects, such as Pure Land and Chan (Zen), regarded Zhiyi as one of their patriarchs.

The old dispute regarding "gradual" versus "sudden" enlightenment was alive and well at Gouqing. The "gradual" approach (*shih*), emphasizing object meditation and visualization, was generally encouraged. But the "sudden" school, insight meditation (*li*), although relatively rare, also had a place in Zhiyi's community.

These two came together in a powerful method called One Practice Samadhi, during which the meditator would sit alone in a small bare cell for ninety days! He might circumambulate the room from time to time, but most of that long time was spent sitting. He was to stay focused on the purity of mind, the simple fact of existence. He was also encouraged to practice *nien-fo*, the ceaselessly repeated invocation of the Buddha's name. Out of this practice might come a breakthrough, a sudden insight into the nature of truth.

Tiantai held that *all* is the Buddha-nature, and therefore enlightenment is not something to be *acquired*, rather it is to be *uncovered* by removing the impediments (attachments) that prevent one from knowing it. Easier said than done. But that's what the monastic life was all about. And Tiantai—under the guiding hand of its founder, Zhiyi—was destined to be a strong influence on all that followed.

HUAYAN BUDDHISM (HUA-YEN)

Like Tiantai, Huayan Buddhism began to take on a coherent form in sixth-century China. Huayan Buddhism had much in common with Tiantai Buddhism. Both held that Buddha's teaching unfolded in five distinct periods, although the two schools differed somewhat with regard to the particulars of these five periods. Also, the doctrine of both schools centered on one of the sutras. But whereas Tiantai focused on the *Lotus Sutra*, alleged to be the last of Buddha's sutras, Huayan based its teaching on the *Avatamsaka Sutra*, regarded by most in Mahayana to be the first of Buddha's sutras. The name *Huayan*, in fact, is the Chinese translation of the Sanskrit *Avatamsaka*. In both languages, it has the literal meaning of "flower garland."

Like Tiantai, Huayan was concerned with the nature of absolute reality, but unlike Tiantai, the focus of Huayan was much more directed to the relationships within the world of phenomenal reality. The message of the *Avatamsaka*, and hence the thrust of the teaching of Huayan, is the inherent mutual interrelationship of all things. Everything is related *inherently* to everything else. The Buddha-nature is universal; everything is an expression of the Buddha-nature—that is to say, *everything* is a perfect manifestation of the Absolute. Reality is one seamless unity. The unity manifests itself as the many. All "particulars" are thus equal and interdependent. Everything, even a grain of sand, manifests the perfection of the Absolute. "To see the universe in a grain of sand" is to discover the Buddha-nature in all things.

The Buddhologist Kenneth Ch'en tells the story of a Huayan master who illustrated the principle of universal interpenetration in an interesting way. He assembled ten large mirrors in such a way that eight of them formed the walls of an octagon, like the eight points of the compass. He then placed one mirror above the octagon and one below it. Finally, he used strings to hang a small statue of Buddha right in the center of this arrangement. When he illuminated the whole thing with torchlight, the effect was enchanting. Not only was the Buddha image directly reflected in the ten mirrors, but each reflection was re-reflected *ad infinitum* in all of the other mirrors. Well, it was supposed to make the point that every single thing in the universe reflects the being of all other things. The unity of being is absolute. All is the Buddha-nature.

PURE LAND BUDDHISM

Pure Land Buddhism warrants our special attention. Pure Land, also referred to as Amitabha Buddhism, grew directly out of the broader world of Mahayana, but its doctrine is arguably the farthest removed from the original teaching. Despite this, in sheer numbers alone, Pure Land has consistently been by far the largest of all Buddhist sects.

We have seen that in the broad system of Mahayana belief, Shakyamuni Buddha is regarded as only one of many Buddhas, each presiding over his own celestial Buddha-realm. A Buddha-realm is also known as a "Pure Land" (*Jingtu* in Chinese; *Jodo* in Japanese). The Pure Lands are identified with the directions of the compass. One of these in the south, for example, is the Pure Land of Buddha Ratnaketu, in the north, Buddha Dundubhishvara, and in the east is Buddha Akshobhya. Most popular by far, though, was (and is) the Pure Land of the west, presided over by Buddha Amitabha (*Amida* in Japanese). This "western paradise," an unimaginably great distance from Earth, is known as *Sukhavati*.

Philosophically minded Buddhists have in all ages interpreted this matter of Pure Lands in a metaphorical way. The different Pure Lands represent the various aspects of enlightenment. This approach has been popular in Buddhist art, particularly in the use of mandalas to represent the totality of the Dharma. The mandala becomes like a great compass with the many Buddhas appropriately located. Generally, the central position is occupied by Buddha Vairochana, who represents the *dharmakaya*. Those not so philosophically minded, however, have tended to interpret the concept of Pure Land, and the possibility of personal rebirth in a Pure Land, in a literal way. This range of interpretations is characteristic of Mahayana; everyone plugs in at their own level. Buddha's teaching is for the *whole* lotus pond. It was in response to the active role of the common people in Mahayana, and their interest in the possibility of rebirth in a Buddhist paradise, that Pure Land Buddhism took form.

The deepest roots of Pure Land Buddhism are lost in the obscurity of the early centuries of Mahayana. No such school ever took definite form in India, but it is quite possible that the tradition germinated in the spiritually fertile region of northwest India that was the original source-place of Mahayana. One of the many non-Indian religious systems active in that region as Zoroastrianism, which originated among the Persians. Some scholars feel that Pure Land Buddhism exhibits some parallels with Zoroastrianism and was influenced by it. In any case, the first systematic organization of Pure Land doctrine was accomplished by a Chinese monk named Hui Yuan, who founded a Buddhist organization named the "White Lotus Society" in the year 402 c.e. The purpose of this organization was to form a community of people—monks and laypersons—who were dedicated to being reborn in Sukhavati, the western Pure Land of Buddha Amitabha. The doctrine of the White Lotus Society was based on the teaching of various sutras, the most important of which was the *Sukhavati-vyuha*. (Actually it is two sutras, a larger and a smaller.)

All Buddhist sutras address the matter of enlightenment; achieving enlightenment is the bottom line in Buddhism. The *Sukhavati-vyuha* also deals with the path to enlightenment, but in a very special way. It holds out the possibility of awakening for *everyone*—not in some distant future after many rebirths as a monk—but here and now, at the end of this lifetime, and it matters not in the least how great a sinner a person may have been. The prevailing view was that the road to enlightenment is long and difficult; one has to slowly overcome the enormous burden of negative karma that has accumulated over time. But Hui Yuan and those who followed him taught that there is another way, a faster and easier way. Incredible though it may seem, it is possible, even for the worst of sinners, to be rescued from the ignorance and depravity of this life, and at the time of death be reborn in the Pure Land of Buddha Amitabha, where the fullness of enlightenment is assured. Thus did reverence of Buddha Amitabha become the central concern of Pure Land Buddhism. Note that in Pure Land, the word "Buddha" by itself refers not to Shakyamuni Buddha, but to Buddha Amitabha. Shakyamuni's importance is limited to his role as deliverer of the sutras upon which the Pure Land doctrine is based.

According to the teaching of the sutras, Amitabha began his career toward Buddhahood immeasurable ages ago when he lived on Earth as a king. He lived during the time of an earlier Buddha, Lokesvara-raja, and after hearing one of this Buddha's sermons, he gave up everything and became a monk, taking the name Dharmakara. Dharmakara became a genuine bodhisattva and was reborn countless times before finally achieving perfect enlightenment, at which time he became more properly known as Buddha Amitabha (the Buddha of "infinite light"). Amitabha's Buddha-realm is Sukhavati, the Pure Land of the west, where he has presided over a vast number of followers ever since.

The story gets interesting, though, when it is revealed that Dharmakara had taken a special vow. Every bodhisattva declares many vows, and Dharmakara was no exception. One of these vows, though, (the eighteenth, to be exact) stated that he would not become enlightened unless he were to make good on a promise to welcome into his Buddha-realm all beings who trusted themselves to him with sincere devotion. "If all beings in the ten quarters, when I have attained Buddhahood, should believe in me with all sincerity of heart, desiring to be born in my country, and should, say ten times, think of me, and if they should not be reborn there, may I not obtain enlightenment."

But how is this to be accomplished? How in the world could an ordinary human being, full of greed, and,anger, and depravity, possibly make himself deserving of rebirth in the Pure Land of Sukhavati? The answer was simple; he couldn't. No one could do such a thing on his own—but Buddha Amitabha could! By compassionately sharing his infinite store of merit, built up over eons of time, Buddha Amitabha could wipe out the negative karma of anyone and transform that person into a being suitable for entry into his Buddha-realm, where enlightenment was assured. And, he had vowed to do exactly that for any person who came to him with a sincere heart. It's a can't-lose situation. No wonder this school of Buddhism grew rapidly among the population at large.

This approach to enlightenment might seem to involve a very basic change in the teaching of Buddhism, perhaps even a contradiction. From the beginning, Buddhism had taught that one is capable of transforming himself or herself on the road to enlightenment; no outside supernatural help is necessary. Shakyamuni himself had said, "Be lamps unto yourselves; be a refuge to yourselves; betake yourselves to no external refuge." But now, advocates of Pure Land Buddhism were proclaiming that no amount of self-directed effort can ever be sufficient. There will always be an inescapable taint of ego in everything we do. Many people continue for a long time to have confidence that they can do it on their own. But Pure Land Buddhism holds that they are fooling themselves. Eventually, each person will reach the point, like someone who is drowning, where he will realize that one's own efforts are simply not enough. When that point is reached, the person will finally be willing to give up the struggle and appeal to the compassionate Buddha for help. Buddha—and Buddha alone—can save us. Buddha can, and will, pluck us out of the water—but we have to ask for help. We have to have *faith* in Buddha.

It's no wonder that Pure Land Buddhism has often been compared to the teaching of the early Protestants in the history of Christianity. Martin Luther was proclaiming very much the same sort of thing. Luther concluded that man is by nature sinful, and therefore no amount of "good works" can ever *earn* salvation. The finite can never add up to the infinite. Salvation cannot be earned, but it can be had nonetheless as a loving gift of God. Luther taught that the infinite merit (grace) created by Jesus in his death on the cross is available to everyone. All that is required is *faith*, a loving faith in God.

How similar this is to the teaching of Pure Land Buddhism. One cannot achieve "salvation"—that is, awakening—through self-power (*jiriki*), but one can achieve salvation through "other-power" (*tariki*). All that is required is faith—a loving faith in the goodness and infinite compassion of Buddha Amitabha. He has vowed to bring salvation to every person sincerely devoted to him.

Devotion to Buddha Amitabha is demonstrated in many ways, but one is of crucial importance. It is generally identified by its Japanese name, *nembutsu* (*nien-fo* in Chinese). Nembutsu is the distinguishing feature of Pure Land Buddhism—so much so, in fact, that some simply refer to Pure Land as Nembutsu Buddhism. Nembutsu involves the repetition of the name of Amitabha (Amida in Japanese). Nembutsu is the operative agent in bringing about salvation in the Pure Land. Here is how the modern Japanese Buddhist scholar D.T. Suzuki puts it:

> When Amida [Amitabha] attained the Supreme Enlightenment, he compressed all the merit he had acquired through the spiritual discipline of innumerable kalpas into this one phrase, na-mu-a-mi-da-bu-tsu (Namu Amida Butsu). For this reason when this one phrase . . . is recited with singleness of purpose and with all the intensity of feeling, all the merit contained in it is miraculously transferred into the soul of the devotee, and he is at once embraced into the light of Amida. The miraculous power thus lying latent in the name of Amida belongs to the unfathomability of the Buddha-wisdom, and the only thing we ignorant mortals can do or have to do for our own salvation is to believe the wisdom and invoke the name just for once; for the "other-power" achieves the rest for us. In one sense, "Amida" is a kind of mystic "Om," a spiritual "sesame," or a mantra which unlocks the secrets of life. (*Collected Writings on Shin Buddhism*, 4)

It would be inaccurate to think of nembutsu as some sort of magical device; it's not really a spiritual "sesame." Nembutsu is an external manifestation of what comes from within, the power of *faith*. A sincere loving faith is what it's all about. But nembutsu, the external expression of that faith, plays an important role. Another valuable external in Pure Land is "visualization." It is believed by the faithful that the practice of nembutsu becomes especially powerful if one is trying to visualize Buddha Amitabha or the Pure Land of Buddha Amitabha. Visualization helps to deepen the devotion, and thus the bond between oneself and Buddha Amitabha. If a person experiences a spontaneous vision of Amitabha, it is taken as evidence that that person is certain to be free of terror at the time of death and will be reborn in Sukhavati. According to traditional belief, when death occurs, Amitabha's companion, the much-loved bodhisattva Avalokiteshvara, will come to ward off fear and guide the spirit of the deceased to its splendid rebirth in the Pure Land.

And what of this Pure Land? What's it like to be reborn there? As you might suspect, the wishful thinking of the folks has greatly influenced the traditional picture. In general terms, the Pure Land is a place of blissful happiness; there is no suffering of any kind. It's basically a paradise, and, therefore, an ever-popular subject in the temple art of Buddhism. Perhaps the designation "paradise" would depend on whom you're talking to. This may come as a surprise, but there are *no women* in the Pure Land! This doesn't mean that women are barred from entry; what it means is that an earthly female is "reborn" as a male. Strictly speaking, that's not entirely true. In the Pure Land, all beings are transcendent beings (referred to as "golden-bodied"). They have risen above the practical considerations of gender; there is no need for sexual difference. Everyone is a perfected being in every way, including the physical. Given the prevailing attitude of that day, a perfected being would naturally exhibit male characteristics if there's a choice between male and female. This probably seemed perfectly reasonable in the early days of Pure Land. But it has caused problems through the ages, and you can imagine the problem it causes today! (This preference appears in many spiritual traditions throughout history.)

It must be remembered that the overriding value of being reborn in the Pure Land is that in this way one can achieve enlightenment. The object of being reborn in the Pure Land is to be brought to enlightenment; that's ultimately what it's all about. When a person admits to himself that he cannot do it on his own (or her own), that person surrenders voluntarily to the infinite power of the compassionate Buddha Amitabha. Amitabha has vowed to share his enlightenment with all those who have faith in him. Not only would a person be brought to enlightenment in the Pure Land, but then might expect to return to Earth as a compassionate bodhisattva in order to help others. This being the case, the "heavenly body" that transcends gender makes perfectly good sense. However accurate this interpretation of the Pure Land may be, though, it must be admitted that in the minds of most people, achieving enlightenment has not necessarily been the prime concern. Throughout the ages, most have seen this "western paradise" as a permanent abode, a sort of heaven where one will be reunited with ancestors and deceased family members and live together blissfully until the end of time in the loving company of Buddha Amitabha.

So, is Pure Land Buddhism nothing more than another variation on the theme of "die and go to heaven"? Do the followers of this school believe in the literal truth of these teachings? Some do, a great many do; that's the nature of Mahayana. But there is another way of interpreting all of this that needs to be recognized. The great popularity of Pure Land may indeed have been anchored in the common folk from the beginning, but there are also followers of Pure Land who in no way would be described as naive. In a somewhat surprising way, it's true to say that Pure Land has always had strong appeal for some of the most sophisticated among Buddhists. Pure Land is not likely to attract the strongly rational and philosophically minded, but it is pure enchantment for the person of a more mystical frame of mind. Pure Land represents the more emotional, artistic, "spiritual" side of Buddhism. More than any other sect, Pure Land is the *bhakti* of Buddhism.

The teachings of Pure Land Buddhism can be seen as a grand metaphor for that which can never be reduced to understandable words and concepts. Suzuki expresses this point of view very well:

> Those who are told . . . to seek rebirth in Amida's kingdom are not really seeking after a Western world lying so many thousands of kotis of miles from this earth of ours, but an inner illumination which has a miraculous power to transform or rather transfigure every object it touches into that of the Pure Land . . . Wherever its historical development may be traced, the Pure Land is not a world existing in space-time but an idealistic world of enlightenment, or, to use the phraseology of the Pure Land sutras, a world illumined by the eternal light of Amida and subsisting in it. In one sense, it has nothing to do with this world of dualistic limitations and defilements, but in another sense it is right here with us and has reality as we read in the *Vimalakirti Nirdesa Sutra* that "Wherever your hearts are pure there is a Pure Land." (*Collected Writings on Shin Buddhism*, 5)

PERSECUTION AND RECOVERY

Of the many Buddhist sects that flourished in China, two were destined to dominate the scene in the long run. One of these was Pure Land Buddhism. The other, which developed in China under the name *Chan Buddhism*, is known to most people in the modern world as Zen Buddhism. The word *Zen* is simply the Japanese rendering of *Chan*. Zen is the product of a tradition that matured in China and then continued to develop in Japan. In modern times, it has spread out of Japan and taken root in many parts of the world. The evolution of the Chan–Zen tradition is an interesting and very important part of the total history of Buddhism. That story shall be the subject of the final two chapters of this book.

The spread of Buddhism in China was a great success story in the centuries following the fall of Han. Buddhism gained acceptance with all classes of society and prospered in both the north and the south. A variety of sects flourished, and by the mid-fifth century, Buddhist monasteries had proliferated throughout many parts of China. The monasteries were often well-endowed and attracted large numbers of men (and some women) to the monastic way of life. More than a few of these monastic communities became quite wealthy, especially in land. In general, it was quite a rosy picture for Buddhism. However, there was a dark side too, and this would become painfully evident in the year 445 C.E.

To say the least, not everyone was delighted with the growth of Buddhism in China. There were those among the Confucians and Daoists who feared and hated the intrusion of this powerful new institution. In their eyes, Buddhist monasteries were responsible for the disharmony of the age. They saw Buddhist monasteries as seditious institutions that were undermining the stability of the society. These monastic communities even went so far as to set themselves up as independent entities, refusing to recognize the overlordship of imperial governments. They paid no taxes, they offered no military service, and they even adopted their own insignia and calendar. Worst of all, Buddhist monasteries threatened the stability of the Chinese family, luring away increasing numbers of sons and daughters to the parasitic and celibate life of the monk.

Things came to a head in the state of Northern Wei, which had grown to include almost all of northern China. In 445 C.E., the emperor of Northern Wei was persuaded to order an attack on the monasteries that was clearly intended to be a total annihilation. All monks were to be slaughtered, and all traces of Buddhism erased from the soil of Wei. Hopefully, the movement would spread from there to the rest of China. Thus commenced the first great persecution of Buddhism in China. There would be others in the future, and as we know only too well, the modern era has not been exempt.

The extremely violent nature of the program provoked revulsion in all classes of society, and as a result the persecution was short-lived. After only three years, a change of leadership not only put an end to the persecution, but did a complete about-face. For the time being, the enemies of Buddhism were defeated. The friends of Buddhism wished to repair the damage that had been done and reestablish Buddhism in China on a new and higher level than ever before. In the state of Northern Wei, the imperial government, far from being an adversary of Buddhism, would become its protector and benefactor. New monasteries were sponsored, new Translation Bureaus were established, interchange between China and India was encouraged, and Buddhist works of art were commissioned for public places.

Among the art projects, one was especially impressive. In a hilly region, at sites known as Longmen (Lung-men) and Yungang (Yun-kang), work began in the late fifth century on a series of rock carvings, many of them inside natural and man-made caves, that over time would become truly unbelievable in scope. Altogether, the statues and images of various Buddhas would grow to number more than 100,000!* Five of the Buddhas are gigantic, the tallest, a beautiful sculpture representing Vairocana Buddha, reaches fifty-six feet (17 meters). There are more than 2,000 caves in this complex, all of them filled with artwork. Outside the caves are forty pagodas chiseled from the native rock. Only sites like Dunhuang in the far west of China and Ellora in India can boast of anything close to the colossal scope of Longmen and Yungang. Surviving inscriptions show that in addition to generous contributions from the imperial family, works were commissioned by people from all ranks of society. Why had this interest in Buddhist sculpture become so strong? Undoubtedly, the persecution of 445 C.E. had something to do with it. Perhaps it was seen that books and bodies can rather easily be destroyed, but enormous stonework is likely to endure. Longmen was a statement that Buddhism was here to stay.†

In 589 C.E., China was finally reunited in the Sui dynasty. Shortly after this, an interesting event occurred that gives further evidence of the triumph of Buddhism. It is known as the "Enshrinement of the Relics of Buddha." The new emperor wished to symbolize the unity of the country—not only politically but spiritually as well. In his possession in the imperial treasury were thirty relics of Shakyamuni Buddha (or at least that's what they were said to be). Step One of the plan was to order the construction of stupas in thirty different regional capitals. Step Two was to commission thirty separate

---

*The figure is correct, but it should be pointed out that most of that number consists of caves "wallpapered" with thousands of tiny bas-relief carved images of Buddha.
†As recent history in Afghanistan sadly reveals, even very large works of sculpture can be destroyed when extremist passions run high. The standing Buddha at Bamiyan was not, however, the world's largest. Topping out at 233 feet, that honor continues to belong to the rock carving of Maitreya Buddha at Le Shan in western China. It was created in the eighth century C.E. and would seem to be secure in its title for some time to come.

Buddhist delegations to carry the relics to these various cities. Then on the same day— in fact, on the fifteenth day of the tenth month of the year 601 C.E.—with great ceremony, the relics were enshrined in the waiting stupas. At exactly the same time a similar ceremony was being conducted at the imperial palace. By royal edict, the day was declared a national holiday so that everyone could take part in the celebration. Thus, with the full support of the imperial government, Buddhism would be the ideological system that gave unity to the people of China.

The official actions of the new government of Sui more or less put the capstone on a process of Buddhist growth that had been developing all through the previous three centuries. As mentioned earlier, one of the elements of the new policy of openness that followed the persecution of 445 C.E. was the encouragement of Buddhist contacts between China and India. In those days, Indian and central Asian Buddhists of all kinds were traveling and teaching in various parts of China. Of these Indian meditation-masters, one in particular was going to have an especially significant impact. His visit would initiate a new and profoundly important tradition in the history of Mahayana Buddhism. His name was Bodhidharma.

Before we turn to that story, though, we will detour slightly into the high plateau of Tibet where Mahayana would evolve into one of the most fascinating species of Buddhism to be found anywhere on Earth. In the isolation of their Himalayan world, the people of Tibet created Tibetan Buddhism, otherwise known as Vajrayana.

Study Questions

1. How did it come to pass that the remote Tarim Basin was temporarily home to a flourishing Buddhist culture? What was the relationship between Buddhism in the Tarim Basin and the development of Buddhism in China?

2. Given the original hostility, why was it that Buddhism eventually experienced a friendly reception in China? What changed?

3. Who was Kumarajiva? What was special about his role in the historical development of Buddhism in China?

4. How did Tiantai Buddhism attempt to solve the seeming inconsistencies of the early Buddhist tradition? Do you feel that it's a reasonable solution, or is it too contrived?

5. How would you explain the purpose, and use, of the contraption that the Huayan master constructed using several large mirrors?

6. In Pure Land Buddhism, "Buddha" refers to Amitabha Buddha, not Shakyamuni Buddha. Why is this? Does Pure Land Buddhism reject Shakyamuni Buddha as a genuine buddha?

7. What would it be like to visit the Pure Land of Sukhavati? What would you find there? Why do you suppose that it's the ardent desire of Pure Land Buddhists to be reborn in Sukhavati?

8. Pure Land Buddhism's approach to enlightenment "might seem to involve a very basic change in the teaching of Buddhism, perhaps even a contradiction." What does this mean?

9. Explain in your own words the gist of D. T. Suzuki's point of view regarding the Pure Land of Sukhavati.

10. "The teaching of Pure Land Buddhism can be seen as a grand metaphor for that which can never be reduced to understandable words and concepts." What does this mean?

11. The first great persecution of Buddhism in China commenced in the year 445 C.E. Why? Why in the world would anyone want to exterminate such a peaceful, compassionate way of life?

12. What was the "Enshrinement of the Relics of Buddha" all about? What do you think was *really* behind the whole thing? Was there a hidden agenda?

CHAPTER 16

Tibetan Buddhism

California is a land of many unusual things. Few, though, are more unusual than one that is to be found in a secluded spot along the northern coast. Its brilliant copper roof gleams golden in the sunlight and is often used as a location reference by passing ships. This amazing place, tucked away in the coastal redwood forest, is in fact a Tibetan Buddhist monastery known by the name *Odiyan*.

Named after the region in India that was the home of the founder of Tibet's first Buddhist monastery, Odiyan defies description. Surrounded by two-hundred acres of rolling wooded hills, the main structure of the monastery is a vision of rare beauty. A great copper roof surmounts a temple constructed in the style of a pagoda. It rises eighty feet above the central courtyard of a large square structure. This complex is the heart of the monastery and houses, among other things, the library and residence hall. Each of the four sides is pierced at the center by an entry that is itself overarched by a large pagoda-style roof. Surrounding the whole is a broad moat whose still water reflects the beauty of the whole.*

From any perspective, it is an enchanting sight. A thousand prayer wheels turn endlessly at Odiyan. Despite all this size and splendor, not many people even know of Odiyan's existence; publicity is shunned, and except for rare public events, the grounds are closed to all would-be visitors. The community at Odiyan goes about its work in peaceful seclusion.

Odiyan was founded by Tarthang Tulku, a refugee Tibetan lama of the Nyingma sect, the most ancient of the Tibetan Buddhist sects. In addition to being a potential haven for other refugee scholar-monks, the Odiyan community has assimilated into itself a number of Western men and women. Working together, they are dedicated to creating a safe refuge for the living tradition of Tibetan Buddhism, which they believe faces the real possibility of extinction in its homeland. Above all, the residents at Odiyan are laboring to translate and preserve the vast literary tradition of Tibetan Buddhism.

But much more is at stake here than merely preserving the scriptures of Tibetan Buddhism, important though that may be. Just as the founder, Tarthang Tulku, is regarded

---

*The Odiyan Web site features information about Odiyan, as well as pictures.

as being a reincarnate lama, Odiyan itself may be seen as the reincarnation of the spiritual essence of Samye Gompa, the very first Buddhist monastery of Tibet. (*Gompa* is the Tibetan word for "monastery.") Samye Gompa was founded in the eighth century and remained a fountainhead of Tibetan Buddhist culture until its desecration at the hands of anti-Buddhist zealots in the late 1960s. Just a decade later, Odiyan was founded. With its consecration in 1979, Odiyan became a genuine Tibetan Buddhist monastery, a "reincarnation," in a sense, of the spirit of Samye Gompa.* The ancient tradition, though threatened with annihilation in its homeland, has sunk roots in new places and is determined to cling to life and even to flourish.

Odiyan is not the only Tibetan Buddhist monastery to be found outside the Himalayan world. Since the scattering of refugee monks following the Chinese assimilation of Tibet in 1959, Tibetan Buddhist communities have taken form in many parts of the world. But in some ways Odiyan is the most remarkable, and its ties are closest to the ancient core of the tradition. How Odiyan happens to be there, peeking out from among the redwood trees of northern California, is a complex and fascinating story. It begins "a long, long time ago in a faraway land across the sea."

Tibet is the high ground of Eurasia, very high ground. A look at the map of Eurasia (p. 130) shows the great oval plateau of Tibet dominating the geography of the eastern part of the continent. Everything seems to flow from it in all directions. But it wasn't always that way. Many millions of years ago, what we know as the plateau of Tibet was basically a low coastal plain occupying the southern flank of the Asian continent. It probably looked much like the Gulf Coast of the United States. Approximately sixty million years ago, this all began to change, slowly but dramatically. The Indian plate collided with the southern boundary of the Asian plate, slowly crumpling up the land. Over eons of time, the southern portion of the Asian continental mass rose higher and higher, creating in the process the great plateau of Tibet and its many associated mountain ranges and river systems. We can find a similar geographic phenomenon in western North America. The high mountainous plateau of Nevada and Utah is much like Tibet, but significantly smaller in scale. The Tibetan plateau is five times the size of the Nevada plateau and averages twice the altitude.

The entire complex of the plateau of Tibet forms a huge oval, approximately fifteen hundred miles from west to east and seven hundred miles from north to south at the widest part. The southern flank of the plateau is formed by the mighty Himalayas, the greatest mountain chain on Earth. Many Himalayan peaks are over 24,000 feet; Everest, the greatest mountain on Earth, tops off at just under 30,000 feet. The northern boundary of the oval is formed in large part by another great mountain system, the Kunlun Shan. North of this range, the plateau descends steeply into the vast desert of the Takla Makan, home to the Buddhist monasteries discussed in the previous chapter. Between the Himalayas and the Kunlun Shan lies a high and arid world of alternating ranges and valleys. Many of these valleys support icy blue lakes of varying sizes. It is a stark and beautiful landscape, appearing (to me, anyway) much like the semi-desert geography of Nevada, though much higher. The average altitude of the plateau is around 15,000 feet; few of the valleys are below 10,000 feet. The valley that is home to Lhasa, the capital of Tibet, is 12,000 feet above sea level. (Compare that to Denver, the "mile high city," which

---

*Since there is not yet an actual population of ordained monks at Odiyan, in a strictly technical sense it is not yet a monastery. Presumably, this will change in the future.

is a mere 5,300 feet. Even thin-aired Mexico City does not quite reach 8,000 feet. Imagine the Olympic Games being held at Lhasa!)

The high ground of Tibet is in the western part of the plateau. The mass of mountains in the western region is home to the sources of some of the world's greatest rivers. The Indus begins its way westward, creating a maze of deep valleys that connect Tibet with Kashmir and other parts of northwestern India. Flowing southward are the tributaries that will join to form the great Ganges River. And traveling in an eastward direction is Tibet's own great river. It is called the Zangbo ("Tsang-po" in Wade-Giles) in Tibet and China, but most of the world knows it by its Indian name, the *Brahmaputra*. The Zangbo travels from west to east across the whole breadth of the Tibetan plateau. It parallels the Himalayan range, running approximately a hundred miles north of the crestline. The Zangbo forms the main artery of Tibet's geography; most of the population is to be found along its course and the tributary valleys that feed into it.

In the east the plateau falls off sharply, forming a massive tangle of ranges and very deep river valleys. The appearance of this region on a relief map suggests that the gods once removed a huge cork from the southeast corner of Tibet, and a great cascade of mountains plunged down into the adjoining lands of China and Southeast Asia. Here too are the beginnings of many great river systems: the Yangzi (Yangtse) and the Mekong are among them. The Zangbo, rushing down through some of the wildest geography on Earth, cuts a sharp U-turn to the southwest and then flows out to the sea through the northeastern section of the Indian subcontinent. After a journey of nearly two thousand miles from its source in the mountains of western Tibet, the Zangbo (Brahmaputra) joins the delta of the Ganges and mixes its waters in the Bay of Bengal.

All in all, the geography of the Tibetan plateau is truly awesome—great snowcapped mountains, high passes, roaring rivers, high desert plains, cold mountain lakes, vast distances of unspoiled natural beauty. Taken altogether, it conjures in the mind an image of a very special place.

"Tibet" is derived from an old Turkic word (more properly spelled "Tobo"). In Chinese, it is known as Xizang (Hsi-tang). To the people of Tibet, though, their mountain world is often referred to as Khang Yul, the "land of snow." The ancestors of the Tibetans were a Mongol people who long before the beginning of recorded history infiltrated the high country from the trackless lands to the north. Their migrations gradually carried them southward, eventually to the region of the Zangbo (Tsang-po) and its tributary valleys where most of the population would ultimately become concentrated. Over the generations, the Tibetans became a sturdy people, physically well-adapted to living at very high altitudes. Understandably, their economy also centered around what was suited to their high altitude way of life. For the most part, this has meant herding—especially yaks and sheep, and simple farming. The raising of barley was, and is, the mainstay of Tibetan agriculture.

The staple of the Tibetan diet is *tsampa*, a coarse flour made from roasted barley. Typically this is simply mixed in a bowl with a little yak butter and salt.* Tsampa is consumed with prodigious amounts of tea. The Tibetans are world-class tea-drinkers; twenty or more cups a day is not uncommon. Tibetan tea, brewed from hard cakes of

---

*Strictly speaking, the word *yak* (Tibetan *gyag*) refers to the bull of the Himalayan cattle species *Bos grunniens*. Thus "yak butter" is an impossibility. However, the world has come to refer to both males and females of the species as yaks.

compressed tea leaves, is liberally mixed with butter and salt. Butter made from yak's milk plays an important role in Tibetan life. Among its many uses, butter sometimes serves as a substitute for money. It is also used in place of clay for sculpting small religious statues which are then painted.

The original settlers of Tibet were loosely tied together along tribal lines and this pretty much remained the bond that defined them as a people. Over time, though, they developed a distinct "Tibetan" culture. The core around which early Tibetan culture developed was a shared set of religious beliefs. In common with folk cultures in virtually all parts of the world, the Tibetan people developed a highly animistic system of religious beliefs and practices in which the power of myriad good and evil spirits influenced every aspect of human life. This original religious tradition of Tibet is known as *Bon*. It would never die out completely. Over time, Buddhism assimilated much from Bon and became the unique tradition of Buddhism peculiar to Tibet and its neighboring Himalayan world.

Although Tibet has been richly influenced by the neighboring civilizations of India, Nepal, and especially China, it is nonetheless accurate to say that the Himalayan culture of Tibet developed in relative isolation from the rest of the world. Beyond their great mountain fortresses, the people of Tibet created and preserved a distinct culture and an autonomous feudal way of life. And so it remained until modern times, changing very little over the centuries.

The Western world became aware of Tibet in the nineteenth century. Its mysterious and isolated character appealed greatly to the romantic spirit of the time. The most unknown parts of the globe were being "discovered" by intrepid European adventurers, and Tibet in its unapproachable Himalayan remoteness was among the most unknown of all. Tibet took on a "Shangri-la" image in the mind of Westerners. It was a land of enchantment about which very little was known—imagination filled in where factual knowledge was scarce.

Factual knowledge about Tibet, though, began to accumulate gradually. One of the first to write knowledgeably about Tibet was L. Austine Waddell, a British military officer stationed on the Himalayan frontier of India. Drawing from his personal research—much of it controversial today—Waddell published a detailed account of the religion and history of Tibet, though he himself spent very little time within Tibet proper, which in the late nineteenth century was closed to Europeans. On his brief excursions into Tibet, he had to travel in disguise.

More widely read were the fascinating journals of the French woman, Alexandra David-Neel, who, in the company of a Tibetan monk from Sikkim, made five extensive journeys through Tibet in the early twentieth century. Like Waddell, she put her life at risk by entering Tibet, and sometimes found it prudent to travel disguised as a monk. She was an "adventurer" of the highest order. Though basically objective, David-Neel was clearly enchanted by the more mystical side of Tibetan Buddhism and offered her readers many accounts of supra-normal powers supposed to be had by those who had mastered the arcane arts. Her books remain very popular.

Of a more erudite nature were the studies of such men as the Oxford scholar W.Y. Evans-Wentz, who translated some of the principal Tibetan scriptural works into the English language, including the famous *Bardo Thodol*, to which he gave the name, *Tibetan Book of the Dead*. Also of significance has been Lama Govinda, a German Tibetologist who became a bona fide Tibetan Buddhist monk and authored many books that introduce the Western reader to the inner meaning of Tibetan Buddhism. These are only a few of the better-known names; as the twentieth century progressed, many others became active in the field of Tibetan studies, and gradually the fund of knowledge grew. Still, the Shangri-la image of Tibet prevailed in the West. This happy illusion was finally and abruptly shattered in 1959.

In the summer of 1959, army units of the People's Republic of China carried out an aggressive military operation within Tibet for the manifest purpose of suppressing a popular uprising and decisively establishing China's claim to rightful sovereignty over Tibet. This military action was the outcome of an enormously complex situation, and its roots go far back in history. Suffice it to say that the leaders of the People's Republic of China did not see their action as a ruthless land grab. In their own eyes it was a rightful action, a liberation of a sort, and was supported by some of the Tibetan population—some, perhaps, but certainly not all. Many Tibetans believed that Tibet was an independent nation and had been throughout its history. The Chinese "invasion" precipitated a mass exodus. As many as 100,000 Tibetan refugees fled over the mountain passes to neighboring Nepal and India. Among them were approximately 10,000 Buddhist monks, including the Dalai Lama, the spiritual (and formerly political) leader of Tibet. The Dalai Lama set up a headquarters in exile at the town of Dharamsala in the mountainous northwestern region of India. Operating from this base, he has traveled the world, enlightening people in all nations about the tradition of Tibetan Buddhism, and the desperate plight of the Tibetan refugees who are struggling to keep alive the ancient tradition, though faced with poverty and all the other problems of life in exile.

In the decade following 1959, the "The Great Proletarian Cultural Revolution" raged through China and swept into Tibet as well. What had started fundamentally as a political annexation became temporarily a fanatic crusade to wipe out the old ways altogether and transform Tibet into a collectivized Marxist utopia. Units of young Chinese Red Guards systematically destroyed many Buddhist temples and monasteries. Eventually, this Cultural Revolution was to be repudiated and more tolerant times would return to Tibet. But before that happened, many more refugees fled in despair, adding to the already swollen numbers in India and elsewhere.

The result of all of this was a Tibetan Diaspora. Refugee Tibetans, including Tibetan Buddhist monks, began to find new homes in places very different and very distant from the Himalayan world they had grown up in. Like a bursting seedpod, Tibet scattered its seeds to the four winds. Some fell on fertile ground in new and strange places. The ancient and intriguing Buddhist culture of Tibet, preserved and largely hidden in its remote Himalayan sanctuary, was suddenly out in the world, making itself known and offering its potential enrichment to all who might be interested. And thus we are brought back to Odiyan. It, and the numerous other Tibetan centers that have come into being around the world, plays an important part in the new life of Tibetan Buddhism—a new life thrust upon the ancient tradition by the tumultuous happenings of the twentieth century.

Our goal is to try to gain a general understanding of this very complex and mysterious subject. In a work of this scope, it is only possible to make a start in that direction; a full understanding of Tibetan Buddhism is the work of a lifetime. But a good start is a thing of much value. The place to begin, naturally, is at the beginning, the way in which Buddhism was first introduced into Tibet. We will then take a closer look at the philosophy and practices of Tibetan Buddhism. Following that is an exposition of the broad historical evolution of Buddhism in Tibet. That will bring us up to the present day, which I hope you will see is pregnant with exciting possibilities. Tibetan Buddhism, more properly known as

Vajrayana, is one of the major branches of Buddhism that is alive and well in the modern world. After many somnolent centuries, the ancient tradition of Tibetan Buddhism is fully awake and ready to make its impression on the future.

THE ESTABLISHMENT OF BUDDHISM IN TIBET

The first person to impose political unity on the Tibetan people was King Songtsen Gampo, who reigned from approximately 617 C.E. to 650 C.E. He was a feudal warlord who succeeded in uniting the clans of the south through a series of bloody conquests. His home turf was the Yarlung Valley, a tributary of the Zangbo southeast of Lhasa, and hence the "empire" that he created is known as the Yarlung Empire. Songtsen Gampo's domain, however, extended far beyond the Yarlung Valley proper; virtually all of southern Tibet came under his feudal rule. He established a new headquarters at a more centrally located place that would come to be known as Lhasa, and from that time to the present, Lhasa has remained the political capital and the spiritual center of Tibet.

Songtsen Gampo cemented his ties with some of the more powerful feudal barons of Tibet by the time-honored practice of marrying their daughters. Three Tibetan "princesses" became his wives. But Songtsen Gampo was looking farther afield than just the high country of Tibet. In addition to the three Tibetan wives, he married a Nepalese princess, and—an impressive accomplishment for a "barbarian" warlord—a Chinese princess as well. According to the story, more legend than history, we can thank these two ladies for the introduction of Buddhism into Tibet.

We are told that the Nepalese princess—known in Tibet as Tritsun, the "Royal Lady"—brought her Buddhist faith with her to Lhasa. Buddhism was strong in Nepal by this time, and Tritsun did not intend to leave it behind when she journeyed off to the wild lands of Lhasa. She continued to practice her faith and brought with her a variety of Buddhist art objects and writings. These caught the attention of her new husband who, wishing to be like his more sophisticated neighbors to the south, was persuaded to commission the building of a Buddhist temple in his new capital city. Nepalese craftsmen and artists were hired to carry out the project, and the result was the construction of the *Jokhang*, Tibet's first Buddhist temple.

The Jokhang was established right in the heart of Lhasa and has always been regarded as the spiritual center of Tibetan life; it is the navel of Tibet, the still-point around which the life of the entire nation revolves. In fact, the name Lhasa means "place of the gods" and was derived from the fact that it was the city that embraced the Jokhang. The Jokhang has been much modified and added to over the centuries, but some remnants of the original structure are still to be seen (or so they say). Amazingly, the Jokhang escaped destruction during the troubled days of the 1960s. Today, with its brilliant golden roof, the Jokhang is one of the most impressive sights in Lhasa. It attracts a never-ending stream of devout pilgrims who are ever circumambulating the temple, euphoric in the knowledge that they are at the exact center of Tibet's spiritual geography, and the very spot where it all began long ago.

The Chinese princess was named *Wencheng*. She too was Buddhist, and like Tritsun who had preceded her, Wencheng had her own Buddhist possessions in her baggage. In addition, as a gift for her new husband, Wencheng brought with her a large, bronze statue of Shakyamuni Buddha as a young prince. (This may actually have arrived later, after Wencheng wrote home to say, "They have no religion here.") The much-admired statue was housed in the new Jokhang. It must have given the temple a sort of official legitimacy; both the Nepalese and the Chinese had contributed to its completion.

The construction of the Jokhang marks the beginning of Buddhism in Tibet, but it must have remained only a novelty among the upper echelon of Lhasa during the time of Songtsen Gampo. The entrenched priesthood of the old Bon religion remained firmly in the ascendant for some time to come. Nevertheless, Buddhism had made its initial appearance in Tibet, and from this beginning, it would steadily grow. Whether or not the two princesses really had anything to do with it will probably always remain uncertain.

What is not uncertain, though, is that Songtsen Gampo sent a hand-picked group on a mission to Kashmir. They headed off on the long and difficult trip in 632 C.E. and were gone for four years. Ostensibly their charge was to study the Kashmiri alphabet and modify it as needed for their own language so that Tibet too could join the civilized nations in the arts of writing. Although this was accomplished, it is probable that they brought back far more than just a workable alphabet. These very receptive Tibetans may very well have felt the influence of the dynamic Buddhism of the Gandhara region and initiated the kind of connection that would have allowed Buddhist ideas to flow after them into Tibet. Perhaps this kind of influence, more than the machinations of exotic princesses, accounts for the germination of Buddhism in Tibet. Or perhaps it is some combination of all of these. In any case, by the end of the seventh century, Buddhism was in Tibet to stay.

The next important name in this story is that of King *Trisong Detsen*, who was born in 742 C.E. and is said to have lived to the age of fifty-five. He was an even greater warlord than Songtsen Gampo, extending his conquests throughout Tibet and even beyond its borders. Trisong Detsen's feudal war machine was so powerful that he even temporarily occupied the Chinese capital, Changan! But for all his successes on the warpath, Trisong Detsen was totally powerless to prevent a series of natural calamities that occurred in Tibet during his reign. In addition to a terrible plague, there was a series of floods that repeatedly wiped out the harvest. And on top of that the royal residence was struck by lightning, undoubtedly the work of an angry demon. In fact, it was assumed that all of these disasters were the work of angry demons. And why were the demons angry? Well, according to the leaders of the Bon priesthood, it was because Trisong Detsen, himself a devout Buddhist, had taken the extreme step of inviting to Tibet a renowned Indian Buddhist scholar named Shantarakshita and giving him a free hand to travel about the country teaching the Dharma.

The spirits of the ancient Bon were visiting havoc on the land because they were displeased by the growing interest in Buddhism. And things promised to get worse, not better. Many Tibetans, including some powerful nobles, were eager to uproot the new growth and exterminate it altogether. This presented King Trisong Detsen with a dilemma. He personally favored Buddhism and wanted to see it prosper in Tibet, but under the circumstances he could not openly oppose the hostile nobles. With great reluctance, Trisong Detsen was forced to ask Shantarakshita to give up his mission and depart from Tibet, at least temporarily. Shantarakshita agreed, but before he left he suggested to the king that he invite in his place the much-respected Vajrayana master, Padmasambhava (pronounced: Pahd-ma-sahm-BAH-va). He was known to be not only a very learned man, but a master of the arts of sorcery as well. If there was anyone with the power to control the demons, it was Padmasambhava, and if successful he would greatly advance the cause of Buddhism in Tibet.

It was a wonderful solution, and it turned out to be a total success. According to some chronicles, the venerable Padmasambhava arrived in Lhasa in the year 747 C.E., having made the long and difficult journey through the mountain passes of the west. Padmasambhava was his Sanskrit name, meaning "lotus-born one"; among the Tibetans, he is generally referred to as Guru Rinpoche, which means "very highly respected teacher." According to legend, Padmasambhava was a native of the Indian country of Oddiyana (from whence the name of Odiyan). His birth was rather spectacular. we are told that a large golden lotus bud rose miraculously from the center of a sacred lake. When the lotus opened, there stood Padmasambhava, already having the appearance of an eight-year-old boy and holding in his hands a vajra and a lotus.

In many important ways, the arrival of Padmasambhava (or Guru Rinpoche, if you prefer) marks the *real* beginning of Buddhism in Tibet; what came before amounts to something of a prelude. Before Padmasambhava, Buddhism was a small and disorganized movement; the traditional Bon was everywhere dominant. After Padmasambhava, Buddhism rapidly became dominant and assimilated much of Bon into itself.

Padmasambhava stayed in Tibet for about two years (though some legendary accounts put that figure at fifty). The first thing he did was to confront the angry demons. His power proved to be superior to theirs, and to everyone's great relief, he subdued them. The natural disasters ceased. The outcome, though, was more of a compromise than an unconditional surrender. Padmasambhava made a deal with the demons: they would desist from causing calamities and accept the superior position of the Buddhist powers in return for being incorporated into the system and permanently cared for with appropriate offerings and sacrificial rites. As a result of this arrangement, Bon was not vanquished but was assimilated; the ancient spirits of Bon, good and evil, would remain real to the common people of Tibet, and right down to modern times, they would demand and receive their share of religious attention.*

The most important thing that Padmasambhava did during his stay was to found the first of Tibet's Buddhist monasteries. It was officially consecrated about two years after his arrival in Tibet and was named *Samye Gompa* (Samye Monastery, after which California's Odiyan is fashioned). Padmasambhava—with the help of Shantarakshita, whose return to Tibet he had artfully managed—established Samye in a valley on the north bank of the Zangbo about sixty miles southeast of Lhasa. The monastery was built in the form of a great mandala, intended to replicate the Buddhist cosmological order of the universe. At the center of the mandala was the Utse, a pagoda-style temple which incorporated the architectural styles of Tibet, India, and China. It seems that King Trisong Detsen wanted the size of the monastery to be really impressive. With a kingly lack of practical self-limitation, he declared that each of the four sides of the monastery grounds should be equal to the distance he could shoot an arrow. Fortunately, some of his more practical-minded advisers smuggled some heavy mercury into the hollow shaft of the arrow he used. But Samye Monastery still turned out to be a huge—and wonderfully beautiful—new center for Buddhism in Tibet. Samye was home to the very first order of Buddhist monks established in Tibet, but it would

---

*Bon was not entirely assimilated into Tibetan Buddhism; to some extent it continued to exist side by side with it. Bon priests continued to exercise their shamanic work in the villages. In fact, even in the twentieth century, there were still large Bon monasteries to be found in some parts of Tibet.

be far from the last. What Padmasambhava started on a modest scale would grow to become enormous in scope, and, far more than anything else, would come to define the character of Tibetan civilization.*

THE GENERAL CHARACTER OF BUDDHISM IN TIBET

Padmasambhava was a Vajrayana Buddhist, and it was this great school of Mahayana Buddhism that became established in Tibet.[†] Vajrayana is derived from the Sanskrit word *vajra* (*dorje* in the Tibetan language). The *vajra* was originally an Indian term referring to the personal "weapon" associated with the god Indra. The vajra, a short shaft with a stylized trident head at each end, became the symbol that identified Indra. (See illustration on p. 310) It is often described as a "thunderbolt," but this is possibly a mistaken notion arising from the western association of the Hindu god Indra with the Greek god Zeus, whose personal weapon was indeed a thunderbolt.

FIGURE 16.1 Dorje. (P. Bresnan)

---

*Tibet's neighbor, Bhutan, also honors Padmasambhava (Guru Rinpoche). In Bhutan's folklore, Guru Rinpoche was the founder of the fabulous cliffside monastery, Taktshang, known as the "Tiger's Nest" to most of the world. According to the story, Guru Rinpoche transformed his consort into a flying tigress so that, flying about the Himalayas, he could more effectively carry out his mission to subdue the demons that were intent on destroying Buddhism. On one of these jaunts, he and the tigress landed at the site of Taktshang and stayed long enough to establish the monastery.

[†]Tibetan Buddhists in general feel that Vajrayana is far more than merely one of the divisions of Mahayana Buddhism—that it is, in fact, a third great branch of Buddhism in general: Theravada, Mahayana, and Vajrayana.

Indian Buddhists adopted the symbol of the vajra, but it took on a whole new meaning. The vajra became the symbol of Enlightenment. The word *vajra*, which literally means "diamond," came to be associated with the indestructible (that is, "diamondlike") union of wisdom and compassion. The Buddhist vajra, generally made of metal or bone, and small enough to be held in the hand, is a highly stylized art object. At the center of the short shaft is a simple circular ball. At each end, the shaft blossoms into a lotuslike form from which five prongs emerge, a straight central one and four curved prongs, all of which close back together at the tips. There is great beauty in the simplicity and symmetry of the vajra.

Vajrayana developed out of the Tantra movement that was growing strong in North India in the sixth century. From there it was carried to the highlands of Tibet. In large measure, Tantra grew out of the movement to incorporate into Mahayana Buddhism the rich variety of esoteric folk beliefs and rituals. This went so far as to include a great deal of what were frankly magical and superstitious elements. Allow me to quote from an earlier section in this book:

> What gave Tantra its special character, though, was its effort to involve the whole person in the adventure of spiritual growth. In place of the more traditional approach of self-discipline and transcendence of desire, Tantra developed a host of ritual practices that embraced the body, desires and all, and saw it as a wonderful vehicle that could be used to carry one to higher states of knowledge. Rather than regarding the pleasure-craving body as an impediment to growth, rather than renouncing desire, Tantra sought to harness the energy of desire, and use it to generate higher states of awareness. Of course, such an unorthodox approach could only hope to succeed if directed by a highly-skilled master. Consequently, in the spirit of the ashram tradition of India, Tantra originally took the form of small groups of disciples tightly bound to a guru.
>
> The term "tantra" referred to the various texts which formed the scriptural base of the movement. This Sanskrit word, taken originally from the weaving craft, refers literally to the weft, the horizontal strands that weave the yarn into a unified whole, a fabric. Tantra texts did the same sort of thing; they wove the various strands of the tradition into a unified whole, a philosophical system. (quoted from ps. 92–93 of this book)

Exponents of the Tantric movement claimed that most of these texts had been delivered by Shakyamuni Buddha and had been preserved in a secret oral tradition for a thousand years before finally being written down. For all practical purposes, the tantras amounted to a further addition to the body of Buddhist sutras, but the followers of "Tantrayana" regarded the traditional sutras to be inferior to the tantras. Not so, however, with regard to the great *Prajnaparamita*, which was much loved and became the very centerpiece of the Vajrayana system. Because of the central importance of the *Prajnaparamita*, the Doctrine of Shunyata, as enunciated by Nagarjuna, became the philosophical foundation of Vajrayana Buddhism. Awakening was (and is) seen as the opening of consciousness to the ultimate reality of "emptiness."

In Vajrayana, as in Mahayana Buddhism generally, the place of Shakyamuni Buddha was overshadowed by the various transcendent Buddhas, among whom Vairochana Buddha occupied the place of greatest importance. Each of the principle Buddhas was associated with various bodhisattvas, as well as with a specific female consort. All of these were properly venerated. As in Pure Land Buddhism, which strongly influenced Tibetan Buddhism, a special affection was felt for Amitabha, the Buddha of Sukhavati, the "western paradise." The great goal of awakening was commonly described as "rebirth" in the realm of Amitabha, where enlightenment was assured. Whether this was interpreted literally or metaphorically depended, then as now, on the particular mind-set of the individual.

The metaphorical interpretation of Mahayana teaching became profoundly important in the development of Vajrayana. It led to the creation of a very rich symbology, much of it frankly sexual in nature. This is an aspect of Vajrayana that has puzzled and even shocked many Westerners. Some have even grossly misinterpreted Vajrayana, confusing sexual symbolism with sexual practice. The widespread use of sexual symbolism results from the tradition of associating wisdom (*prajna*) with the female principle and compassion (*karuna*) with the male principle. Because enlightenment is synonymous with the union of perfect wisdom and compassion, it follows that the ecstatic sexual union of man and woman provides a wonderfully rich field of symbolic possibilities. Sexual union is something that most men and women are familiar with, and this most earthly of acts can thus be used metaphorically to represent knowledge of the perfect unity of all being.

The vajra itself, the symbol of Enlightenment, includes sexual symbolism. In a highly stylized way, the arrangement at each end of the vajra represents the union of male and female sexual organs, the central prong being the male enclosed within the lotus form, which is often employed to represent the female sexual organ. I want to emphasize that though this may be highly erotic in its essential meaning, it was not intended to arouse erotic feelings, at least not in the usual sense of the word. In Vajrayana, and in the Tantric tradition that produced it, the sexual theme was seen to be an excellent metaphor for the unity of being in which all duality is dissolved. To the puritanical mind this might seem shocking, but clearly the creators of Vajrayana were not troubled by that problem at all.

The most widely recognized employment of sexual symbolism in Vajrayana is to be found in the *yab–yum*. Whereas the symbolism may be subtle in the vajra, it's not subtle in the least in the yab–yum (See illustration on p. 91). The yab–yum (which literally means "father and mother") is a depiction of a man and woman joined together in the ecstasy of sexual union. Typically, the couple represented are a Buddha, or bodhisattva, and his female consort. They sit face to face in a yoga posture, their bodies intertwined. The theme of the yab–yum is very highly regarded; it appears over and over in sculpture and painting. Properly understood, it is an extremely powerful theme which symbolically represents the state of perfect union.

Awakening to knowledge of the perfect unity of being is, of course, what it's all about. This is enlightenment, which in the Tibetan language is called *tharpa*.* The ultimate goal of all practice is tharpa. But in the way of Vajrayana, this great goal was not to be ascended to slowly by denying the flesh-and-blood realities of human life. In contrast to non-Tantric schools of Buddhism, Vajrayana offered a dynamic path, an active "fast path" to enlightenment. Awakening was to be had by grappling with life, all of it, and bursting through the illusions and restraints created by the self-loving ego. Meditation, as in all Buddhist traditions, was seen as a most important part of the path; but in Vajrayana, meditation would become active, dynamic, involving the whole person. Consequently, a vast body of meditation techniques and ritual practices developed in Vajrayana.

---

*To be precise, the Tibetan word for enlightenment is *chang-chub*. *Tharpa* literally means liberation, but it is commonly used by Western writers to denote enlightenment.

Generally speaking, the various meditation practices of Vajrayana are derived from what are known as the *sadhanas*. These are lengthy and involved sections from the Tantric texts that the guru uses to initiate the student into successively higher states of meditative consciousness. The principle element of the practice of sadhana is what is called "visualization." In a visualization exercise, the meditator concentrates on visualizing, and identifying with, a particular Buddha or bodhisattva. In this way, the meditator seeks to instill within himself (or herself) the particular qualities of the one being visualized. The very popular bodhisattva Avalokiteshvara (pronounced Ah-va-loh-keet-esh-VAR-a), for example, is identified with perfect compassion. Skill in the visualization of Avalokiteshvara, it is believed, will increase the quality of compassion in the person practicing this exercise. It should be pointed out that in this exercise, the student does not believe that he has created an actual vision of Avalokiteshvara—not at all; it is accepted as a purely psychic experience, but an extremely powerful one.

Associated with the visualization exercise, and nurturing it, are many other elements of meditation practice. Chief among these is the recitation of *mantras*. The mantra plays a very big part in the life of Vajrayana Buddhism—so much so, in fact, that Vajrayana is sometimes referred to as Mantrayana, the "way of the mantra." A mantra is a spiritually powerful syllable, or string of syllables, that a person repeats (often chants) in order to forge a strong psychic connection between himself and the force or deity that the mantra represents. Om ("Aum"), for example, is the fundamental mantra of the Hindu tradition and was transported into Buddhism where it evolved into new forms. By far the most popular mantra of Tibetan Buddhism is *Om mani padme hum*. This mantra, an invocation to Avalokiteshvara, is repeated endlessly by all Tibetan Buddhists. It is ubiquitous in Tibet, inscribed everywhere in the arts, as well as in the minds and hearts of all Tibetans. *Om mani padme hum* is printed on prayer flags, amulets, and long chains of paper that fill the ever-turning prayer wheels. The mantra translates literally as, "Om—the jewel in the lotus—hum." The lotus can be seen as referring to human consciousness, and the jewel is the enlightened mind that is embraced within the lotus. And, of course, there is the possibility of sexual symbolism here too. The verbal meaning, though, is not terribly important; the power of a mantra transcends verbal meaning.

The recitation of a mantra is often accompanied by its appropriate *mudra*, which is a particular symbolic posture of the hands. It is intimately associated with the posture of the body and the expression of the mantra. The practice of mudra has evolved into a highly complex and refined art. There are specific mudras associated with virtually every important emotion and state of consciousness. Typically in the art of Vajrayana, every figure is represented in the form of a mudra appropriate to his or her role. This matter is often very subtle to the eye, but it is of essential importance to the meaning of the work. Each Buddha and bodhisattva is generally depicted in one of the mudras associated with him. Shakyamuni Buddha, for example, is often shown seated in meditation with the crossed hands in the lap in the position of the *dhyana mudra*. Sometimes, Shakyamuni Buddha is shown in the *bhumisparsha mudra*, which was the posture he assumed when, tempted by Mara, he summoned the Earth to be his witness and authority. In this mudra, the left hand remains in the lap while the right hand, palm inward, is extended over the knee and points at or touches the ground. Vairochana, the primordial Buddha, is often shown with his hands in the mudra of supreme wisdom. It is believed that skill in mudra, just as skill in mantra, will greatly intensify the effect of a meditation exercise, especially a visualization exercise.

Yet another highly important element in the performance of sadhanas—and the visualization exercise in particular—is the *mandala* (*kyilkor* in Tibetan) (see p. 315). The creation and use of mandalas are major features of Tibetan Buddhism; it can well be argued that no other tradition in human history has put so much emphasis on the value of the mandala. The use of the mandala goes well beyond the specific practices of meditation, but in sadhana practice the mandala plays a very powerful role.

In Tibetan Buddhism, the mandala that is designed to be an aid to meditation is often painted on a wall-hanging known as a *thangka*. A thangka is a symbolic representation, in mandala form, of a theme that is meaningful in the context of Tibetan Buddhism. This may be something as simple as a pictorial arrangement of scenes from the life of an important Buddha or bodhisattva. Often wrathful demons and mythological characters are included, each of them representing some particular psychic aspect of life. The Wheel of Life (*Bhavachakra*) is a popular thangka theme. Another very common theme is the "palace" of a celestial Buddha. The mandala-style architecture of the palace, and all of the beings which inhabit it, is a way of symbolically portraying the Buddha-realm of that particular Buddha, who is presented in the appropriate mudra at the center of the mandala. Use of a thangka such as this can profoundly influence a sadhana visualization exercise. The depiction, of course, need not be interpreted literally; the symbols and images are used to represent an enlightened state of mind. Through creative visualizations the meditator unites psychically with the mandala, becoming one with the state of consciousness that it represents:

> Practitioners are regularly reminded, however, that the figures in the mandala have no real ontological status; they are symbols of the mental qualities toward which tantric adepts aspire and are intended to provide templates for mental transformation, but they are empty of inherent existence. This is also true of demons and wrathful deities, which represent factors of human consciousness that are transmuted through meditation into virtuous qualities. (Powers, 228)

The production of thangkas has always been a highly skilled, busy profession within the monasteries of Tibet. They come in a great variety of sizes and types; some are entirely abstract and very complex. Thangkas are painted or inked usually on linen cloth, but sometimes on paper, silk, or wood. Some of the most elaborate are made entirely with sand of various colors. Only the most skilled (and patient) artists work on the sand mandalas, which are typically quite large, up to ten feet in diameter. The sand mandala originated as part of a sadhana ritual at the conclusion of which the mandala would be swept up and seen no more (which is true of all things eventually).

A dramatic event concerning a sand mandala occurred in San Francisco in 1993. Two Tibetan monks were constructing the highly complex Kalichakra sand mandala at the Asian Art Museum, at that time located in Golden Gate Park. It takes many days to complete a big mandala, and a large number of people would gather around the platform to watch its progress. All of a sudden a woman, apparently mentally disturbed, jumped up on the platform shouting angrily about witchcraft. Before the guards could seize her, she kicked the sand in all directions. To say the least, everyone was stunned—everyone, that is, except the two monks. The most interesting part of this little drama was their reaction. Without being flustered in the least, they both bowed deeply to the woman, who was by this time being held tightly by the guards, and began calmly sweeping up the remaining sand. Then, as if

FIGURE 16.2   A fine example of a modern thangka, painted in the
traditional style. (Photo by P. Bresnan)

nothing had happened at all, they patiently began work on the mandala again, starting at
square one. (That's unflappability!)

Vajras, mantras, mudras, thangkas, chanting, dancing, prayer flags, prayer wheels,
rosaries, bells, candles, incense, stupas, and on and on—Tibetan Buddhism is packed full

of wonderful and intriguing elements. And it all serves a lofty purpose in association with the performance of sadhana, the royal road to tharpa, the experience of awakening. But tharpa may lie at the end of a very long road. How does one know that he or she is making progress? Are there signs, or experiences, that indicate this? In the tradition of Tibetan Buddhism, it is widely believed that a person who is dedicated to the life of Vajrayana, and has acquired skill in its ritual practices, will come to exhibit certain supra-normal powers, and that this is evidence of spiritual progress. Such powers are said to be *supra*-normal, not *super*-natural: that is, not miraculous—a fine distinction, perhaps, but an important one. Tibetans believe that all powers, even the most amazing ones, are based on perfectly natural principles, even if these are not always understood.

Such powers can take many forms. Telepathy and clairvoyance are said to be fairly common, especially between a disciple and his guru. *Tumo* is another widely reported power. A master of tumo can sit outdoors for hours in the freezing Himalayan cold, wearing very little, and through only the power of concentration generate sufficient body heat to dry linen sheets that have been dipped in icy water and draped around his shoulders. *Lung-gompa* is yet another power said to be mastered by many Tibetan monks. One skilled in lung-gompa has mastered a specialized gait which permits him to walk at a truly incredible speed, covering (or so it is said) more than a hundred miles a day. In a country where the pilgrimage is a common part of life, and public transportation virtually nonexistent, this could indeed be a valuable power. Needless to say, many people out-side the fold of Tibetan Buddhism are understandably skeptical about such assertions as these. And obviously, it is a field that could lend itself to exaggeration, or even to self-deception. Perhaps the true meaning, and use, of such "powers" can only be understood within the monastic community that cherishes their existence.

By far the most important evidence of progress, though, is an entirely personal expe-rience, and it is an experience that cannot possibly be described in words. The real reward of adopting the monk's life is to be found in those rare and unexpected moments in which a vision of great truth, great beauty, takes form in consciousness. Such an experience—a moment of inexpressable joy—clarifies the meaning of the quest, and in a highly personal way it is all that one needs to be reassured that life is unfolding as it should.

But what if a monk (or a devout layperson), despite various profound experiences, dies before ever actually achieving the fullness of awakening? Tibetan Buddhism teaches—at least at the superficial, literal level—that when a person dies, the spirit of that person will be reborn after a passage of time that can last up to forty-nine days. Ideally, the person will be reborn in Sukhavati, the "western paradise" of Buddha Amitabha, where the realization of perfect enlightenment is assured; that is what most Tibetans yearn for. If this is not possible, the individual will be reborn in human or animal form, the specific type depend-ing on the condition of that person's karma at the time of death.

Naturally, in a discussion of this sort the question will keep arising in the reader's mind: How literally is all of this to be understood? We've already encountered this problem in the discussion of Pure Land Buddhism. All of this talk about reincarnation seems to contradict the basic teaching of Buddhism. Is it not a fundamental tenet of Buddhist philosophy that all is change, no thing exists, there is no substanding enduring entity—including "spirit"—which can be reincarnated? Indeed it is. Vajrayana Buddhism, solidly grounded as it is on the teaching of Madhyamaka, definitely does not contradict the basic teaching of Buddhism. But it must be remembered that Vajrayana is part of the evolution of Mahayana Buddhism, and in casting out its net to include everyone, Mahayana has no problem with a full spectrum of personal interpretations. Perhaps a better analogy would be Buddha's own, the lotus pond. There are many different levels of growth, and Mahayana wants to provide a meaningful interpretation that is appropriate to the level of understanding of all of them.

From the very beginning of the Mahayana tradition, it has been the custom to use rich metaphor and poetic license in attempting to express philosophical truths that simply cannot be stated objectively in words. We saw this clearly in the sutras, the scriptural foundation of Mahayana. This practice of using familiar imagery to suggest the meaning of that which is not familiar was well-developed in Hinduism and was carried over into Mahayana Buddhism. Whatever may have been the intention of the creators of the sutras, though, it is nonetheless true that a great many people in every age have chosen to accept such expressions as literally accurate, and so far as Mahayana Buddhism is concerned, that's just fine. Everyone is welcome to plug in at the level where he or she feels most comfortable. If one wishes to conceive of Avalokiteshvara as a distinct being— a distinct spiritual being—who in the company of Buddha Amitabha presides over the Pure Land of Sukhavati—a genuine paradise into which one's spirit may be reborn—then Mahayana Buddhism has not the slightest problem with that. If such belief, and the practices that go with it, helps one to grow in compassion in Buddha's lotus pond, where is the problem? Isn't this what it's really all about?

But there are some in that lotus pond who are receptive to the light of a different understanding. For them, the literal interpretation is not the best way. For these more philosophically minded ones, spiritual growth is nourished by following the path of metaphorical understanding. After all, a most fundamental understanding in Buddhism is the underlying unity of Being. If one understands this perfectly, then all talk of separate beings, including spiritual beings that can be reincarnated, must necessarily be metaphorical. To such a person, the Five Celestial Buddhas (including Buddha Amitabha) are not to be seen as distinct beings presiding over objectively real Buddha-realms; rather they are metaphorical ways of depicting the fundamental aspects of enlightenment, and the Buddha-realm is the interior state of consciousness that the disciple aspires to. Admittedly, this is the approach of a minority of the population; the common understanding is much more likely to be the literal one. Within the monastic tradition of Tibet, though, there have always been many who have inclined to the metaphorical understanding of Vajrayana teaching. The great Tibetan wonderland of myths and spirits and rituals can be seen to be a wonderfully rich way of expressing—and exploring—the complex psychology of the human mind, particularly the human mind that is searching for ultimate truth.

Again, though, the literal expression of the teaching holds that a person's "spirit" will be reborn following the death of the body. How it all turns out depends to a very large degree on how the person responds to a series of perceptions he will experience in the hours and days immediately after death. It is believed that the person, whose body is now dead, will nonetheless pass through several distinct planes of consciousness (called *bardos* in Tibetan). Some are alluring, some are terrifying, but all call for some kind of response, and, as mentioned, the quality of the rebirth is the direct result of how successful (or unsuccessful) the response is.

In this matter, the help of a trained spiritual assistant can be immensely valuable. Consequently, it has long been the custom in Tibet that many monks are trained to be expert guides whose task it is to help the dying prepare for the event of death, and after death to help the disembodied spirit successfully navigate the bardos and be reborn in the finest possible condition.* In the case of a layperson, the monks go to the home of the dying and conduct an elaborate ritual that may go on for days. The spirit is talked to, and given instructions, even though the body may be dead and cold. Eventually, the body is disposed of, also according to ritual. In the high country of Tibet, where firewood for cremation is scarce, the body is (or was) customarily taken to a place where it is cut up and offered to hungry vultures. Tibetans see nothing morbid or repulsive in this at all.

The character of the bardo experiences, and instructions for dealing with them, is discussed in an ancient Tibetan work known as the *Bardo Thodol*. It is widely believed that Padmasambhava himself was the author of this work. The Buddhologist W.Y. Evans-Wentz translated this work into English giving it the imaginative title, *The Tibetan Book of the Dead*. It's an intriguing work and has become very popular in the West. The most intriguing thing of all about the *Bardo Thodol* is the suggestion that at the deepest level of meaning, it is an esoteric work that is really directed at the living, not the dead. In this interpretation, death, as it is ordinarily understood, is a metaphor for death of another kind—death of the ego. The *Bardo Thodol*, then, becomes a powerful guidebook in the hands of a spiritual master to help the initiate die to his ego-self, pass successfully through the stages of psychic resistance (the bardos), and be reborn, "awakened," in the new life of enlightened consciousness.

> For all who are familiar with Buddhist philosophy, it is clear that birth and death are not phenomena that happen only once in a human life, but something that happens uninterruptedly within us. At every moment something within us dies and something is reborn. The different bardos, therefore, are nothing other than the different states of consciousness of our life . . . The Bardo Thodol is addressed not only to those who see the end of their life approaching, or who are very near death, but equally to those who are in the prime of life and who for the first time realize the full meaning of their existence as human beings . . . Under the guise of death it [the *Bardo Thodol*] reveals to the initiate the secret of life. He must go through the experience of death, in order to gain liberation within himself. (Govinda, 123–124)

Seen in this light, the *Bardo Thodol* provides the student of Tibetan Buddhism with a glimpse into the fabulous insights that this tradition has produced with regard to the nature of consciousness and the ways in which a person may overcome his own psychic fears. The *Bardo Thodol* becomes a guidebook for passing from ordinary ignorance to the freedom of perfect understanding.

While it is true to say that Tibetan Buddhism, Vajrayana, became the defining spirit of the entire culture of Tibet, and deeply affected the daily lives of all the people, it is also true that the wellspring of this culture, and the place where it all comes together, is the monastery, the *gompa*. Since Padmasambhava founded Samye Gompa in 747 C.E., the monastery has been the matrix of Vajrayana Buddhism in Tibet.

This would be an appropriate place to take a brief look at the character of the Tibetan Buddhist monastery. This picturesque structure is the only image that many people have of the Himalayan world. Unlike the early gompas, which were built after the

---

*Literally, the word *bardo* refers simply to the state between death and rebirth. It has become customary, though, to use the word in the plural, referring to the various stages that can be identified.

fashion of Indian and Chinese monasteries, the ones we see today are more representative of a native Tibetan style of architecture. Typically one pictures an attractive-looking jumble of multistoried buildings arranged in tiers on a hillside, the whitewashed walls sloping gently inward as they rise. The gleaming white of the walls is offset by dark wood trim and narrow balconies on the upper stories. The rooftops, sometimes gilt, are likely to be festooned in colorful pennants and prayer flags. It's a highly attractive sight. And—at least until recent times—it was a sight to be found with great frequency in the Himalayan world. Over the course of time, thousands of monasteries came into existence in all parts of Tibet and the neighboring Himalayan lands. At the beginning of the twentieth century, more than 3000 monasteries were functioning. Many of these, of course, were very small and local, but some were huge, counting thousands of monks in their membership.

Perhaps "monastery" is a misleading translation for gompa. Alexandra David-Neel commented, "Though for lack of another word in the English language we are compelled to refer to the gompas as monasteries, they do not in the least resemble a Christian monastery." This is undoubtedly true with respect to modern times. Western monasteries in this day and age tend to be purely religious communities that have withdrawn from the world in order to focus on the spiritual way of life. But it wasn't always this way. Western monasteries of an earlier time, especially during Europe's feudal age, took on many of the worldly functions of life that would later gravitate to the more secular part of society. At that time in history, Christian monasteries shared many features with the typical Tibetan Buddhist monastery.

Indeed, some of Tibet's monasteries became enormous in size, more like full-fledged towns than religious hermitages. Perhaps the best comparison of all would be to a university. In many important ways, the traditional gompa is like a university, albeit one that is solidly organized around a religious core. In addition to the pursuit of the spiritual life, all of the members of the community are involved to some extent in other fields of learning as well. Over time, several areas of study became standard, scriptural study being only one of them. Philosophy was another, and so was medicine. In Tibet, one of the most important fields of study—and to the Western mind the strangest one of all—is the field of ritual magic. Only the most prestigious monasteries have offered advanced study in the occult sciences. The masters of these mysterious arts became the ones charged with the crucial responsibility for controlling the wrathful spirits and attending to the needs of the Bon demons. Beyond these rather lofty offices, they also served the general population as sorcerers, exorcists, astrologers, diviners, prophesiers—whatever was needed in the daily lives of a population obsessively concerned with the machinations of a potentially threatening spirit world. In traditional Tibet, few undertakings were begun without first consulting an experienced sorcerer. For some Tibetan monks, mastery of ritual magic would become a full-time profession.

The gompa became the source of virtually all of the "professions" in traditional Tibet. It had to be; just as in feudal Europe, there was not yet any other social structure that could provide training and employment in the professions. Some members of the gompa specialized in the study of medicine, for example, though this, too, was heavily interfused with magical and occult elements. Those who showed promise were steered into the path of artistic studies, eventually becoming full-time professionals. Thangka production alone has always supported a multitude of artists.

It might seem surprising, but some monks were even trained in the worldly arts of business. This was necessary because the monasteries, except for the smallest and humblest, could not support themselves solely on the donations of the laity, no matter how generous. Not only did the bigger monasteries become very wealthy in land and serfs, but they also became active centers of a rough and ready capitalism, engaging in trade, simple banking, and lending money at interest. Waddell criticized the monasteries for growing rich on trade and lending money at usurious rates. He referred to the monks as "the chief traders and capitalists of the country." (Predictably, this state of affairs would attract the attention of Marxist reformers in the twentieth century.)

Undoubtedly, abuses did sometimes occur, and it is also true that many monasteries did become extremely powerful and wealthy. But this was inevitable in a feudal society, in which the monastery was the only institution that was capable of taking on the multifarious social and economic functions that in a more complex society would be spread out among many specialized sectors. In more recent times, Western monasteries have been able to focus exclusively on the core spiritual function, but only because other institutions have arisen to relieve them of their former, more secular, responsibilities.

One explanation for the great diversity within the monastery is to be found in the broad spectrum of the population from which the membership was drawn. In a modern Western monastery, most of the monks are recruited from the young-adult population, and only those sincerely willing to commit themselves to the spiritual life are accepted. The traditional Tibetan monastery, on the other hand, accepted its novices from virtually all families in its area, and boys were admitted at a very young age, often as young as eight. It was a common practice for the firstborn son in every family to enter the monastic life; many families would give more than one son. As a result of this, a significantly large proportion of the Tibetan population came to be concentrated in the monasteries. Not uncommonly in Tibetan history, a full quarter of the population were Buddhist monks. Given this situation, it should come as no surprise that many monks were more concerned with worldly professions than with the spiritual life. It's fair to say that in a modern society, many of these young men would have chosen to follow a more secular path, but in traditional Tibet, these opportunities simply did not exist; hence, in a way the monastery filled the void by attempting to be "all things to all people."

Let's not lose sight of the fact, though, that the monastery was, at its core, a monastery, a gompa, a community of men manifestly dedicated to following the path of Buddha in order to achieve awakening. The great goal of tharpa was unquestionably enshrined at the heart of every gompa. No matter how many secular activities the monastery might be involved in, no matter how many monks might as individuals be more interested in worldly pursuits than spiritual pursuits, it is nonetheless true that these were, and still remain, peripheral matters. The heart and soul of the Tibetan Buddhist gompa has always been the preservation of their unique tradition of Buddhist teachings and practices that lead to tharpa.

To at least some degree, all monks who have been accepted as members of a Tibetan gompa participate in the religious life of the community. This involves a large measure of communal ritual, often including the music and chanting that Tibetan monks are famous for in the West. This can be quite a joyous spectacle: pounding drums, blaring horns, clashing cymbals, deep droning voices. In the Vajrayana tradition, though, the individual monk has a great deal of personal freedom with regard to what constitutes his participation. This may range from only the bare minimum to total dedication to spiritual disciplines. In their zeal for spiritual growth, some few choose to become lonely anchorites living the solitary life in a tiny hermitage, dedicating all of their time to meditation and ascetic disciplines. The hermit monk is a part of every religious tradition, but in Tibet this exceptional life seems to have taken on an especially alluring value. The solitary hermit—searching for wisdom in the lonely isolation of his Himalayan cave—has become a veritable icon of the world's image of Tibet (and an endless setting for cartoon art).

There is a hierarchy of rank in the gompa. Properly speaking, only the highest-ranking monks are known as *lamas*. The name *lama* originated at Samye, the very first Buddhist monastery of Tibet. In founding Samye, Padmasambhava referred to the community as the "order of lamas." Literally this means "the superior ones," but it should be understood in the sense of ones who have chosen the "superior" path of Buddhist discipline. Within the Tibetan world, the word *lama* is used out of respect for all elderly and learned monks, regardless of rank, but outside of Tibet, it has become customary to refer to all Vajrayana monks as lamas. From this word also comes the term *Lamaism*, which is yet another popular name for Tibetan Buddhism.

In the Tibetan language, the fully-ordained monk is known as a *gelong*. This is the full-time professional monk whose life's work is bound up in the affairs of his monastery. He has studied and trained for a minimum of twelve years before becoming a gelong, at which time he publicly affirms the two-hundred and fifty-three vows which spell out the monastic rules of Vajrayana. The novice monks, the ones studying to become gelongs, are known as *trapas*. Generally these are young men under the age of twenty, but many trapas become entangled in a particular line of work and never go on to become ordained gelongs. Monks from poor families often fall into this category because the family is expected to pay a sizeable part of the tutoring cost that a student monk necessarily incurs.

Please bear in mind that these comments about the Tibetan monastery are very general and refer to an institution that grew and evolved over many centuries. The early gompas were very simple affairs compared to the huge and complex monastery-towns of later times. But from the beginning, the essential core of every monastery has been the tradition of Vajrayana Buddhist teaching.

Indeed, the monasteries have always been the wellsprings of Tibetan culture, and the entire land has been richly watered by their potent influence. Prayer flags flutter picturesquely around every village; and also to be found are the ubiquitous chortens, shrines, prayer wheels, and myriad other implements of a living Buddhism. (This, of course, is the picture of traditional Tibet. Much has changed since the Chinese annexation, but by no means has it all been eliminated, far from it.)

It must be remembered, though, that Tibetan Buddhism is an amalgam of Vajrayana Buddhism and the ancient tradition of Bon. The beliefs and practices of Bon were never exterminated. Rather, the outlook of Bon came to be something of a "ground" upon which the tradition of Tibetan Buddhism was built. At a deep level, the belief system of Bon continued to live on, especially among the common people. Fundamental to the belief system of Bon is the acceptance of a world of spirits. More than anything else this defines the basic worldview of the ordinary Tibetan:

> Their importance to ordinary people should not be underestimated, since in the consciousness of most Tibetans the world is full of multitudes of powers and spirits, and the welfare of humans requires that they be propitiated and sometimes subdued. Every part of the natural environment is believed to be alive with various types of sentient forces, who live in mountains, trees, rivers

and lakes, rocks, fields, the sky, and the earth. Every region has its own native supernatural beings, and people living in these areas are strongly aware of their presence. In order to stay in their good graces, Tibetans give them offerings, perform rituals to propitiate them, and sometimes refrain from going to particular places so as to avoid the more dangerous forces. (Powers, 432)

Nature spirits, demons, gods, ghosts, departed ancestors—the unsophisticated Tibetan has always earnestly believed that he lives his life surrounded by a vast number of spiritual beings (some benign, some malicious) and that they influence every aspect of daily life. The spirits must be dealt with; there is no question about that. The only question is, how best to deal with them. It is in this area, dealing with the spirit world, that the most significant contribution of the Buddhist tradition is to be found, at least among the common people.

The Buddhist establishment embraced this role from the earliest times, taking over (but never entirely replacing) the functions of the Bon priesthood. In a land where superstition pervades everything, perhaps it was only natural that some Buddhist monks would become specialists in astrology, necromancy, sorcery, and all of the occult arts. Propitiating the spirits, and holding at bay the dangerous ones, has always been an obsession with the people of Tibet. For this purpose, specialized charms are to be seen virtually everywhere:

> Their inveterate craving for material protection against those malignant gods and demons has caused them to pin their faith on charms and amulets, which are to be seen everywhere dangling from the dress of every man, woman, and child. (Waddell, 570)

The dependence on Buddhist rituals and objects as protective charms is an interesting aspect of grassroots Tibetan Buddhism. In addition to the ubiquitous rosaries and hand-held prayer wheels, printed thangkas are found everywhere among the common people. Certain ones are widely believed to have healing power and are actually eaten to ward off illness.

Illness, as well as every other kind of affliction, is believed to be caused by demons. The greatest affliction of all, naturally, is death. And here too the specialist monk stands ready to perform the proper ritual that will hold off the terrifying demons that await the deceased and guide his or her spirit through the awesome bardos to a satisfying rebirth. The most satisfying of all, of course, would be rebirth in Sukhavati, the last and greatest hope of all Tibetans.

When I say "all Tibetans," I do not mean to imply that every Tibetan understands rebirth in Sukhavati in a literal sense; indeed, as mentioned before, some interpret this metaphorically. Quite obviously, there is a huge difference between the understanding of the learned, philosophically minded Buddhist monk on the one hand and the common uneducated, unsophisticated Tibetan layperson on the other hand. To some, it is true to say that "Gods, demons, the whole universe are but a mirage which exists in the mind, springs from it, and sinks into it." And perhaps a great many Buddhists of Tibet would assent to that truth, at least verbally. But realistically speaking, the great majority of common people, including many of the monks, accept as undeniably true the assertion that spirits do in fact exist, that they affect the affairs of daily life in powerful ways, and that fundamentally each individual is essentially a spirit capable of a series of rebirths.

What it all comes down to is simply this: Each person will relate to the Dharma in the way that is appropriate for him or her. The teaching of Mahayana, in the spirit of Buddha's lotus pond, offers something for everyone.

A HISTORICAL OVERVIEW OF BUDDHISM IN TIBET

Buddhism in Tibet cannot be understood apart from its history; it has been an evolving story, and it is continuing to evolve in modern times. The object of this section is to present a broad overview of that history, a Big Picture, as it were. The fourteen centuries of the history of Tibetan Buddhism can be divided into three great eras. Each of these eras constitutes a cycle that begins with a stage of growth, followed by a time of flourishing, and then concludes in a period of decline.

The earliest era, during which time Buddhism was introduced into Tibet, is referred to as the Era of the Yarlung Empire. It spans the time from the beginnings of Tibetan Buddhism in the seventh century to the end of the tenth century. The second era, which may be called the Sakya Era, lasted from the early eleventh century to the end of the fourteenth century. The final of the three, the Era of the Dalai Lama, began in the fifteenth century and has continued down to the present time. It can well be argued that we are presently in the final stage of the third great era. (Though, of course, no one really knows for sure.) We will briefly examine each of these with an eye to understanding how the historical development of Tibetan Buddhism has shaped its special character.

THE FIRST PERIOD: THE ERA OF THE YARLUNG EMPIRE

As we have already seen, Buddhism was introduced into Tibet during the reign of Songtsen Gampo, the king who married the Chinese and Nepalese princesses and also sent the mission to Kashmir to acquire that region's alphabet. It was Songtsen Gampo who was responsible for establishing the Jokhang, Tibet's first Buddhist temple. During the next century, King Trisong Detsen invited Padmasambhava to Tibet, and that's where the story of Tibetan Buddhism really takes off. Padmasambhava, as you will remember, founded Samye Gompa, the first of Tibet's Buddhist monasteries.

After the founding of Samye Gompa in 747 C.E., Buddhism grew rapidly in Tibet. Monasteries were sprouting up in many places and were receiving the warm support of the royal court (a warmth not necessarily shared by all of the noble families). Many Indian Buddhist gurus were active in Tibet in those early days. For the most part, they were exponents of Vajrayana, the Tantric school of Indian Buddhism, and this became solidly and permanently established as the essential character of Tibetan Buddhism. As you might expect, these early years saw an intense interest in translating the corpus of Buddhist scripture into the Tibetan language. These most-treasured works were meticulously written out by hand on thin narrow sheets of parchment that were bound in stacks and lovingly preserved. Many exist even to this day.

The new tradition of Buddhism grew rapidly, but not without opposition. In fact, these two countervailing forces grew apace; the stronger Buddhism became, the stronger became the opposition. The principal opponent to Buddhism came, as you might expect, from the traditional Bon priesthood. They were allied with some of the old nobility and together they waited for their chance.

That opportunity came in 838 C.E. In that year the king, a friend of Buddhism, was assassinated by his brother, a man most definitely not a friend of Buddhism. The brother assumed the throne and is known in history as King Lang Darma. What is most remembered about his brief four-year reign is that he launched an all-out war against the Buddhist establishment. Clearly, his intention was to wipe out Buddhism altogether in Tibet, to use any means to end forever what he and others saw as a mortal threat to the ancient Bon tradition of the Tibetan people. He very nearly succeeded. There was a wholesale destruction of Buddhist temples, monasteries, and art objects; Buddhist monks were slaughtered or forced to return to their families. It might well have been the end of Buddhism in Tibet had not Lang Darma himself been murdered in 842 C.E. The assassin was a dagger-wielding Buddhist monk, and he claimed that his deed was actually an act of great kindness to Lang Darma who was thus spared the effects of further accumulation of negative karma generated by his brutal and ignorant persecution of the Buddhists.

Whether or not one sees it as an act of kindness, it certainly had the effect of saving Tibetan Buddhism from extinction. The new king quickly ended the persecution and began the long, slow process of repairing the damage. One very interesting, and significant, sidelight to the story of the persecution of Lang Darma is that the very same kind of persecution was occurring in China at just about the same time (discussed earlier in Chapter 15). In both realms, the persecution was intense but short-lived. And in both cases, the Buddhist establishment was badly damaged but not exterminated. The road back to health, though, was to be long and difficult.

In Tibet, a period of depression followed the persecution of Lang Darma. During the ninth and tenth centuries, the once-strong unity of the Yarlung Empire broke down. Tibet sank into a fragmented patchwork of small feuding principalities. It was something of a Dark Age in the history of Tibet. (European civilization was going through a similar era at the same time.) The fire of Tibetan Buddhism, formerly so strong, was now languishing and in danger of flickering out altogether. To a large degree, it was kept alive during this difficult time by the nurturing influence of Buddhist monasteries to the north of Tibet in the desert lands of the Takla Makan. But all things must change eventually, and the depression of the ninth and tenth centuries was no exception. With the coming of the eleventh century, a new day was about to dawn, but for Tibet this dawn would be in the west, not the east.

THE SECOND PERIOD: THE SAKYA ERA

The middle period in the unfolding history of Tibetan Buddhism takes its name from the great monastery of Sakya in southern Tibet. The abbots of Sakya dominated the religious and political life of Tibet for much of the twelfth, thirteenth, and fourteenth centuries. The revival, though, did not begin with Sakya, which was not founded until 1073. The revival began in the mountainous west of Tibet, in the region called Guge, which because of its location had close ties with the northwest Indian regions of Ladach and Kashmir.

Wishing to reinvigorate the Buddhism of their realm, the royal family of Guge sent delegations of students to Kashmir. Not only were they to study at the ancient centers of Buddhism, but hopefully they might attract learned Buddhist missionaries to Tibet as well. The most notable result of this effort was the arrival in Guge of the great Atisha in the year 1038 C.E. Atisha (pronounced a-TEE-sha) was a scholar-monk from northern

India who launched a reform movement sometimes referred to as the "second spreading" of Buddhism in Tibet. Already nearly sixty-years old when he arrived in Guge, Atisha spent the last twelve years of his life spreading the good word in Tibet, first in Guge and then on to the central parts, including the former capital, Lhasa. With the help of his devoted nephew, Dromton, Atisha founded many new monasteries in Tibet.

There is a wonderful legend concerning how it happened that Atisha accepted the invitation to restore the Dharma in Tibet. He was, after all, no young man when he made the journey, a journey that was by no means easy or lacking in danger. When he was first approached by the agents of Yeshe, the king of Guge, Atisha was offered a large amount of gold as an inducement. He politely declined, though, saying that he was needed in his Indian homeland. When informed of this, Yeshe concluded that he had not sent enough gold, so he personally scoured the kingdom trying to raise more from his nobles. In the process, he was captured by a rival king and held for ransom, which was to be nothing less than Yeshe's own weight in gold. If the ransom was not paid, Yeshe would be put to death. Yeshe frantically got word back to his court—forget the ransom; send the gold to Atisha. This is what they did, and poor Yeshe died in prison. When Atisha heard about this, he was deeply moved by this act of self-sacrifice and so decided to go to Tibet after all (after an account in Powers, 137).

The reform movement spearheaded by Atisha, and the monasteries he established, coalesced into what was in effect a new sect of Tibetan Buddhism. It would come to be called *Kadam-pa*.* The emphasis in Kadam-pa was placed on correct transmission and interpretation of the sacred texts. Before this time, there were no significant divisions within the world of Tibetan Buddhism; it was all one. But now, the formerly seamless fabric was rent. A distinct new reform sect had come into existence, and others would soon follow. "They arose in revolt against the depraved Lamaism then prevalent, which was little else than a priestly mixture of demonolatry and witchcraft. Abandoning the grosser charlatanism, the new sects returned to celibacy and many of the purer Mahayana rules." (Waddell, 74)

Eventually, four major Buddhist sects would take form in Tibet. By default, the traditional orthodox, pre-Atisha school of Buddhism would also be seen as a sect in its own right. They came to be called the *Nyingma-pa*, the "school of the ancients." Padmasambhava (Guru Rinpoche) is regarded as being the founder of Nyingma and thus Samye, the first of all Buddhist monasteries in Tibet, is a Nyingma monastery. (Therefore, California's Odiyan, the spiritual heir of Samye, is also a Nyingma monastery.)

The third of the sects is known as *Kagyu-pa*. This too was a reform sect and was distinguished by its special emphasis on the personal transmission of spiritual awakening from teacher to disciple. The Kagyu-pa was founded by Marpa and his disciple, Milarepa, one of the most loved and revered figures in all of Tibet's history. The story of Milarepa's life is well-known to all Tibetans; it is a classic example of the journey from youthful ignorance and hardship to ultimate perfection of enlightenment. He was inspired as a young man by Marpa, a scholarly layman who made several trips to India where he studied with Naropa, the abbot of the renowned monastery at Nalanda. In the process, he acquired a wealth of sacred texts which he devoted himself to translating into the Tibetan language. These texts were the vehicle for introducing the Mahamudra system of Tantric practices into Tibet.[†] Marpa is held in very high respect and is referred to simply as The Translator.

---

*The suffix *pa* in the Tibetan language means "sect" or "school" in English. It can also mean "man from."
[†]Each of the sects cherishes its own highly refined method for realizing the true nature of mind. In the Kagyu sect, it is Mahamudra. In the Nyingma, for example, the method is known as Dzogchen.

Marpa must have been an interesting character. He was much respected as a sorcerer. In fact, that's what originally attracted the young Milarepa to him. (At that time in his life, Milarepa was seething with desire for revenge against an uncle who had cheated his poor mother.) Marpa was said to be totally unattached to worldly wealth—an odd assertion considering that he charged wealthy "clients" as much as ten ounces of gold for protection against demons.

As a guru, Marpa was a harsh taskmaster and placed truly Herculean challenges before the young Milarepa, who would rather die than fail. Eventually, the highest success was Milarepa's, and he withdrew into the remoteness of the Himalayas, where he could find perfect serenity and devote his remaining years to expressing his wisdom in verse. These "songs" of Milarepa are some of the greatest treasures of Tibetan Buddhism. Milarepa became the epitome of the cave-dwelling hermit, blissfully happy in his solitude, but not really cut off from the world. By sharing his wisdom with others who sought him out, he made a mighty contribution to the development of the tradition of Tibetan Buddhism. Marpa and Milarepa were giants; they deserve much more attention than can be provided in a work of this scope. Unfortunately, their names can hardly more than be mentioned and we must move on. The student of Tibetan Buddhism, though, is well advised to search them out.

Marpa and Milarepa were the inspiration behind the founding of the Kagyu-pa sect, but the actual labor of establishing the monasteries of Kagyu-pa was the work of disciples. The various sects, of course, differed from one another with respect to a difference of emphasis placed on certain interpretations and practices, but this was not the whole story. There was a political dimension as well. Each sect—and in fact each monastery within a given sect—was the "protectorate" of a specific group of noble families, generally based on geographic location. They gave their monastery the support it needed, both financial and political, and, when necessary, even military. And too, as you might expect, sons of these families would by and large fill the higher posts within the monasteries.

The fourth great sect to concern us, the *Sakya-pa*, came into existence in the late eleventh century in south central Tibet in the region of the ancient city of Gyantze, which lay along a tributary of the Zangbo about one hundred miles southwest of Lhasa. The Sakya tradition, too, traces its roots to India, specifically to the legendary Tantric master, Virupa. Virupa also was a most interesting character; at least that's the way the stories describe him. Supposedly, he first attracted attention as an infant when he would scratch holy Sanskrit words in the sand and then refuse to crawl over them. He was said to have lived for seven hundred years, eventually achieving perfect enlightenment just before he died. Along the way, he mastered all the magical skills of a Tantric wizard. At one point, in order to increase his mastery, he dedicated twelve years to repeating an especially effective mantra twenty million times! (But when you live to be seven hundred, twelve years doesn't seem like all that much.)

Virupa was no ascetic. One of the most popular stories about him concerns a time when he stopped at an inn and promptly washed down flagon after flagon of wine. When the innkeeper became nervous about the bill, Virupa stuck his dagger in the table and said he would pay up as soon as the sunlight coming in the window reached the dagger. Well, Virupa thereupon used his magical powers to hold the sun still for several days, meanwhile putting away countless more flagons of wine. With everyone getting understandably frightened, and the unmoving sun scorching the nearby crops, the local king finally paid the bill just to get Virupa to move on.

The first temple of what would be the great Sakya monastery was erected on the outskirts of Gyantze in 1073 C.E. Gyantze, situated in the striking scenery of the northern foothills of the Himalayas—only about fifty miles from Everest—is described as gray earth country; Sakya means "gray earth." A powerful aristocratic family named Khon was largely responsible for its establishment, and members of that family have been the abbots of Sakya right down to modern times. Sakya would definitely have been a powerful monastery and very influential in the affairs of Tibetan life, but not necessarily the most powerful. The rise of Sakya to preeminence resulted from their unique connection with a dramatic new element in the isolated world of Tibet—the Mongols.

The northern parts of the Eurasian continent form a vast rolling ocean of grasslands trailing off to the tundra and ice of the far north. Since time immemorial this has been the homeland of immeasurable numbers of nomadic peoples. In the west, it was the Aryans; in the east, the Mongols. The horse gave them wings, and when they gathered as a fighting force, their power was awesome; it seemed that nothing could stop them. Aryan hordes invaded many regions of western Eurasia, and a similar force overwhelmed Han China in the third century C.E. Now it was happening again.

In the early thirteenth century, the great Mongol conqueror, Genghiz Khan, welded together an army of nomadic horsemen that burst out of the wild lands of the north, devastating and subduing everything in their path. It was the beginning of what history knows as the Mongol Empire. At its height, the Mongol Empire was one of the largest empires ever to be created. Under Genghiz's grandson, Kublai Khan, China would become the home of the central authority, and from his capital at Khanbalyk (the site of modern Beijing), Kublai ruled an empire that stretched all the way to Russia and included parts of the Islamic Middle East as well. Tibet too was included for a time in the Mongol Empire, but Tibet enjoyed something of a special status. After all, the Tibetan people were themselves descended from ancient Mongol clans.

Genghiz's son Godan Khan (father of Kublai Khan) was assigned the task of subduing Tibet. In 1239, his army began a series of sorties into the high country, throwing the feudal nobles of Tibet into an understandable fit of anxiety. Fearing that they lacked the strength to halt an all-out invasion, they prevailed on one of their own—Sakya Pandita, abbot of Sakya monastery—to meet with the Mongols in order to see if negotiations were possible. In the year 1247, Pandita traveled on horseback to the northern frontier town of Lanzhou to meet with Godan Khan. It must have been quite a scene! Apparently, the Mongol warlord was very impressed by the learned and spiritual leader of the great monastery. He offered Pandita a deal. If the warrior nobility of Tibet would accept the suzerainty of the Mongols, there would be no invasion. The abbot of Sakya monastery would become, in effect, the viceroy of the Great Khan who would rule Tibet through him. For all practical purposes, Tibet would become an autonomous state within the Mongol Empire; the Khan would be recognized as overlord, but within Tibet, supreme religious and political power would be united in the person of the Khan's viceroy, the abbot of Sakya monastery.

When Pandita returned, he gathered together the other nobles and made a little speech, ticking off the practical advantages to the proposed arrangement. He is supposed to have ended with a statement that might have begun: "Oh, by the way, the number of their horsemen is beyond counting." To say the least, this was the most practical consideration of all. Despite resistance on the part of many of the noble families, the plan was accepted and Sakya Pandita became something of a "Sakya pope." For almost a full century, his successors would hold, at least nominally, supreme temporal and religious authority within Tibet. It should be pointed out, though, that the Sakya authority was hotly challenged by many of the Tibetan nobles; they never enjoyed anything close to absolute power.

Pandita was succeeded by his nephew, Sakya Phagpa, a young man of great intelligence and charm. His position of "Imperial Perceptor" of Tibet was reconfirmed by Kublai Khan, who by this time was the emperor of a freshly conquered China (a significant precedent in light of modern history). For the investiture ceremony, Phagpa journeyed to Kublai's fabulous capital. Kublai was deeply impressed by Phagpa and wanted to hear all about his Tibetan religion. It is said that at that time Kublai was hunting around for a suitable religious philosophy that could be used to spiritually unite his vast and checkered empire (shades of Ashoka). There's a wonderful story—maybe even true—that he invited learned representatives of the major religions of the empire to engage in a debate about the merits of their respective systems. Kublai himself would judge which one was best. There were Moslems, Christians, Daoists, and, of course, Buddhists. Phagpa himself argued on behalf of "Lamaism." Apparently Kublai was more impressed by miracles than philosophical subtleties. According to the story, Phagpa was able to persuade a silver wine goblet, without a hand touching it, to rise from the table to the lips of the emperor. That settled it; Kublai decreed that henceforth Lamaism was to be promulgated as the "official" religion of the empire. At least among the Mongol people (if not the rest of the empire), Tibetan Buddhism did begin to spread its influence. Incidentally, the losers in the great debate called foul. But they didn't accuse Phagpa of sleight of hand; they said he summoned the help of devils.

Mighty though it was at its inception, the Mongol Empire did not last for a long time. Hardly were the conquests complete than the whole thing began to fall apart. In China, Mongol rule, known in history as the Yuan dynasty, lasted for less than a century. And in Tibet, the authority of the Sakya abbots weakened apace with the decline of Mongol power. The Tibetan nobility once again splintered into warring factions. Sakya leadership came to be largely rejected by the others, and during the latter half of the fourteenth century, Tibet degenerated as it had before into near-feudal anarchy. Naturally the vigor of Tibetan Buddhism suffered along with all else. But the dark of the later fourteenth century was again the dark before the dawn. The great wheel of history was about to begin yet another turn.

THE THIRD PERIOD: THE ERA OF THE DALAI LAMA

Once again a great man came to the rescue; his name was Tsong Khapa. Unlike Padmasambhava and Atisha, who both came to Tibet from India, Tsong Khapa was a fully home-grown Tibetan. (His name literally means man from the region of Tsong-kha.) According to a popular legend, in a previous life Tsong Khapa had known Shakyamuni Buddha, who predicted that one day his would be a powerful voice in the spreading of the Dharma. To say the least, a powerful voice was much needed in the early fifteenth century. Feeling that the existing sects were hopelessly mired in depravity and superstition, Tsong Khapa focused his reform effort on the establishment of an altogether new sect which would embody correct and rigorous principles of Buddhist monasticism, including the vow of celibacy. The new sect was called *Gelug-pa*, the "virtuous ones."

The traditional monk's robe and hat in Tibet was reddish-brown in color, but to distinguish themselves from these others, the Gelug-pa adopted a hat that was somewhat yellowish. Since the conical hat was the most identifiable part, this difference led to the

Gelug-pa being known as the "yellow hat" sect as opposed to the "red hats." Among the "red hats" were the men of Kadam-pa, the sect begun by Atisha three centuries before. As the Gelug-pa reform movement grew, the Kadam-pa was effectively absorbed into it; thus the number of major sects remained at four.

Tsong Khapa founded several new Gelug-pa monasteries, the first of these being Ganden, which was begun in 1409 C.E. in the mountainous country about twenty-five miles east of Lhasa. Ganden became the preeminent Gelug-pa monastery, and thus the place where the mortal remains of the founder were interred when he died ten years later. Before his death, though, Tsong Khapa created several other monasteries, among them Sera and Drepung, which were both close to Lhasa. Drepung grew to an incredible size. In the seventeenth century, Drepung Monastery was home to more than 10,000 monks, making it by far the largest monastic community ever to have existed anywhere.

Tsong Khapa also turned the first spade at what would become the large and beautiful monastery of Tashi Lhunpo. This famous center of Tibetan Buddhism was established on the south bank of the Zangbo near the city of Xigaze (Shigatze), about one hundred and thirty miles southwest of Lhasa. The Grand Lama of Tashi Lhunpo would later be known as the Panchen Lama and would rival the Dalai Lama in spiritual authority. (Much more about that later.) All of these historically important monasteries have survived into the modern day, though some were greatly damaged by Red Guards during the 1960s. (For political reasons, beautiful Tashi Lhunpo was left largely undamaged.)

Like Atisha, Tsong Khapa had a devoted nephew who was his right-hand man during the years of hard work. When Tsong Khapa died, the nephew, Gendun Grubpa, was given the title Grand Lama of Gelug-pa. He became the first Grand Lama of Gelug-pa. (Tsong Khapa, although he was the founder, had never been invested with the title.) When Gendun Grubpa died, the title was passed on to the second Grand Lama, Gendun Gyatso. Something else was passed on too; something that would have immense significance in the future. It seems that Gendun Gyatso was very young when he was chosen to be the Grand Lama. He was born shortly after the death of Gendun Grubpa, and the leaders of Gelug-pa decreed that the "spirit" of the first Grand Lama had been reincarnated in the infant Gyatso. Gendun Gyatso was thus a *tulku*, a reincarnated lama. This fascinating custom was to become widespread within the monastic orders of Tibet. We will have more to say about the process of selection shortly.

The third Grand Lama of Gelug-pa was Sonam Gyatso. He too was said to be the tulku of his predecessor, and he was something more as well. Sonam Gyatso was the first to be named Dalai Lama. This is how it happened. The great growth of Gelug-pa had understandably aroused some anxiety in the other sects. It must be remembered that the monasteries were intrinsically part of the feudal system of Tibet. Factions were constantly forming and re-forming; small-scale feudal warfare was a part of the way of life of the nobility. Gelug-pa faced growing opposition from some of the others, particularly from groups within the Kagyu-pa sect, which was supported by some of the most powerful nobles of the land. All-out civil war was by no means out of the question. In looking around for ways to build up their base of support, leaders of Gelug-pa went so far as to sound out the Mongol warlord Altan Khan, chief of the Tumed Mongols. Even though Mongol power had declined substantially from what it had been at its height—they were no longer the emperors of China—the Mongol homeland to the north was still a vast and powerful realm, and the Mongol horsemen were still very much a fighting force to be taken seriously.

As a result of these meetings, an alliance was concluded. In return for the promise of military help if needed, Sonam Gyatso officially recognized Altan Khan as "Ruler of Gods, and King of the Dharma." Altan Khan then bestowed upon Gyatso the brand-new title "Dalai Lama." In English, the word *dalai* translates as "vast ocean"; thus the term *Dalai Lama* means, more or less, the Grand Lama whose greatness is as "vast as the ocean." Sonam Gyatso, the third Grand Lama of Gelug-pa, was the one to receive the title, but he liked it so much that he wanted it to be more than merely his personal possession; he wanted it to become synonymous with being the Grand Lama of Gelug-pa. Consequently, he made the title retroactive to his two predecessors, and he, at least officially, became not the first Dalai Lama but the third.

Meanwhile, Altan Khan was so pleased with the Tibetan connection that he and all of his subjects became Tibetan Buddhists of the Gelug-pa ("yellow") sect. This was no half-hearted adoption; the Mongols became wildly zealous followers of their new way. They even made it clear to their Tibetan Gelug-pa allies that they would be profoundly happy should the reincarnated spirit of the next Dalai Lama be discovered residing in the body of a young Mongol lad. And, wonder of wonders, that's exactly what happened. Shortly after the death of Sonam Gyatso in 1589, those entrusted with the search for his reincarnated tulku claimed that they had found him. Not only was the boy a Mongol, but amazingly he was the great-grandson of Altan Khan himself. He took the name *Yontan Gyatso* and became the fourth Dalai Lama, the Grand Lama of Gelug-pa.

This matter of the search for the reincarnated spirit of the Dalai Lama would become one of the most intriguing aspects of Tibetan Buddhism. This would be a good place to look at how it's done. Tibetan men and women, just like everyone else, face the inevitability of death. As mentioned before, the common Tibetan yearns, though, to be reborn after death in Sukhavati, the "western paradise" of Buddha Amitabha. If this can't be, then the next best thing is to be reborn again in human form, but in the best possible human form. The best possible human form would be the one that is most likely to achieve rebirth in Sukhavati next time around. It may be necessary to try again and again. One of the most important services of the Buddhist priest, as we have seen, is to assist a person at the time of death so that his or her spirit will achieve either Sukhavati or the most favorable rebirth that can be had. In any case, the possibility of reincarnation is a common belief among the Tibetan people. It is an accepted fact that virtually everyone is a reincarnated being.

Some few, however, are very special reincarnations. They are already enlightened beings who out of deep compassion choose to be reincarnated in human form in order to be of help to their still-unenlightened brothers and sisters. Such a person, generally a lama, is called a *tulku*. A tulku, then, is a reincarnated lama who is reborn in order to help lead others to enlightenment, and, a tulku gives signs which others can use to identify the specific person in which the spirit has been reborn. In this way, a lineage can be established. The faithful can feel confident, for example, that over many generations the Grand Lama of a particular monastery has been one great spirit, reincarnated over and over, and each time successfully identified by the leading lamas of that monastery. For the past five centuries, the most important lineage in Tibet has been that of the Dalai Lama. There have been fourteen historical Dalai Lamas. But to the faithful, there has really been only one Dalai Lama, incarnated and re-incarnated fourteen times. And, in the case of the Dalai Lama, it is not merely the reincarnation of a highly enlightened lama, but of Avalokiteshvara himself, the bodhisattva of infinite compassion.

Here again, we confront the dichotomy between the basic Buddhist teaching that ultimately there is no "one" to be reborn and the custom of behaving as if reincarnation is real indeed. However one might choose to interpret the traditional teachings, the stated view is that when a Dalai Lama dies his "spirit" is shortly afterward reincarnated in the body of a newborn baby. It thus becomes a matter of prime importance to locate that child and see to it that he is properly groomed for the life that is his destiny. To this purpose, the leading lamas of Gelug-pa gather at the time of the death of a Dalai Lama. The very first order of business is to conduct an investigation of the deceased's words and activities in the days just preceding death. Perhaps there are some clues there that will help in the search—some repeated utterance, for example, or some unusual behavior. They will also examine the embalmed corpse carefully. In one case, we are told, the embalmed body kept realigning its position as if by magic. It was laid out each night so that the head was pointing to the north, but in the morning, the position of the body had changed so that the head was pointing east. This was interpreted as a clear sign that the search should be made to the east of Lhasa.

The search committee also consults with the official oracle of Tibet located at Nechung Monastery in Lhasa, and by long-standing tradition visits the sacred lake of Hlamo Latso approximately ninety miles southeast of Lhasa. They might spend several days at the lakeside, contemplating its surface with almost trancelike attention. It is believed that apparitions produced by mists rising from the lake can provide powerful clues. One might see a vision of particular kind of house, for instance, or a tree in bloom, or a geographic landmark. Finally, when all of the preliminary information has been gathered and studied, the real search is ready to begin. This might take many months or even years. Advance units of the search group are likely to travel in disguise, dressed as ordinary pilgrims. At last, a promising candidate is identified. This, of course, will be a little boy, often about two years old by the time he is found. Now he is put to the test.

The highest lamas conduct the examination of the child. They watch with the keenest interest to see if he exhibits any of the knowledge or personal traits of the recently deceased Dalai Lama. Part of the procedure is to place before the child various objects which had belonged to the deceased—such things as rosaries, scarves, prayer wheels, and perhaps a walking stick. Mixed in with these will be exact replicas. If the boy is truly the tulku they are looking for, he will, it is presumed, recognize his own things and pick up the right ones. The whole examination is quite elaborate, and the modern reader can't help but wonder how much unconscious prodding goes into it. In any case, when the little boy succeeds in convincing these visiting dignitaries that he is indeed the reincarnation of the Dalai Lama, it is a cause for great rejoicing.

When all is ready, an entourage of notables will escort the young tulku to Lhasa where, during a lengthy ceremony of investiture, he will be officially presented as the new Dalai Lama. (His family, by the way, will most likely accompany him and take up comfortable residence nearby.) Now begins the long process of grooming the child so that by the time he is a man, he will be fully able to take his place as the leader of the country. He will be thoroughly educated in all of the traditional disciplines, including philosophy and theology. Eventually, he must pass grueling oral examinations in order to win his scholarly degrees. In addition, he will be trained in all of the monastic disciplines. The Dalai Lama is a full-fledged ordained monk of the Gelug-pa order; it is expected that he will observe all of the vows, including celibacy. The young Dalai Lama grows up in a highly controlled environment, and if all goes well by the time he is a young adult, he will have been molded into a man of exceptional abilities. As Dalai Lama, he will be able to play the role of priest-king with wisdom and virtue.

Defenders of this unique way of producing a national leader argue that it is the best of all possible ways. To begin with, the risky problems of hereditary rule are totally avoided. From out of the rich variety of the general population, a child of sound mind and body is selected and then most carefully educated for the role of leadership. He is tutored by the best in every field, and is raised in an environment of Buddhist monastic discipline. From the time he is a little boy, he is encouraged to identify with the highest ideals of Buddhist teaching. Not only are the risks of hereditary rule avoided, but so also the risks of the elective system. There are no rival cliques promoting their candidates. No cliques, no political parties, no feuding aristocratic families—all of this is avoided. The entire system gets a fresh start each time. (It doesn't really matter whether one interprets the selection procedure literally or metaphorically. In either case, it can be reasoned that this is an excellent way to select and groom one for supreme leadership.)

One potential problem with the system, though, is that the new Dalai Lama must necessarily be a young child. For many years, the tasks of leadership will have to be in the hands of others. These others are called regents. And although every effort may be made to appoint dedicated and selfless men to the post of regent, there remains nonetheless the real possibility that self-serving individuals may come to occupy these powerful positions. Throughout much of the past five centuries, the regents, not the Dalai Lama, have been in control of Tibet's government, and this has not been a history entirely innocent of palace intrigues and feuding factions. For the most part, though, this very unusual system has worked well and has enjoyed the passionate support of the Tibetan people. Incidentally, the obvious advantages of the tulku system were not lost on the other sects. Before long, the leading lamas of virtually all monasteries were proclaimed to be tulkus. The Dalai Lama, however, has remained the paramount tulku of the land down to modern times.

The fourth Dalai Lama died in 1617, and the search began immediately for his successor. The fifth Dalai Lama was named *Nagwan Losang Gyatso*, but his reign was so tremendously important in the history of Tibetan Buddhism that he is generally referred to simply as the "Great Fifth." It was largely the work of his reign that established the character of Tibetan Buddhism that has come down to the present. He was born in 1617 C.E. and took over full personal responsibility of rule in 1640 at the age of twenty-three. The first order of business was to deal with the growing opposition of the other sects and their client noble families. The threat of civil war was again in the air. Losang dealt with this by taking the dramatic step of calling upon his Mongol allies for help. The Mongol response was an all-out invasion of Tibet. Under the warlord Gursi Khan, Tibetan resistance was crushed and the entire land was subjugated. But this was not a Mongol conquest; it was a military operation for the purpose of establishing the uncontested authority of their friend and ally, the Dalai Lama, who now became the undisputed all-powerful ruler of Tibet; temporal power and spiritual authority were united in the office of the Dalai Lama. In 1650, the Chinese emperor confirmed the supreme political and religious authority of the Dalai Lama within Tibet.

But the Great Fifth wanted even more. It was already accepted that he as the Grand Lama of Gelug-pa was a tulku, the reincarnation of his predecessor. What Losang added to this was the assertion that the spirit being reincarnated in the line of Dalai Lamas was none other than that of Avalokiteshvara, the great bodhisattva companion of Buddha Amitabha, the presiding Buddha of Sukhavati, the Western Paradise. He was saying, in effect, that he was the flesh-and-blood incarnation of Avalokiteshvara, and so was every other Dalai Lama, past and future. Quite a declaration, and it was received with enthusiastic acceptance. And it didn't stop there. Having declared himself to be the incarnation of Avalokiteshvara, Losang then went on to magnanimously declare the Panchen Lama, the Grand Lama of Tashi Lhunpo, to be the incarnation of Amitabha Buddha! This might seem to suggest that the Dalai Lama as the incarnation of Avalokiteshvara was actually inferior in status to the Panchen Lama. In the convoluted doctrinal logic of Tibetan Buddhism, however, this was not the case—at least not so far as worldly affairs were concerned. Thus could the people of Tibet celebrate the wonderful news that the spirit of both Amitabha and Avalokiteshvara were dwelling with them and leading them, not simply in a mystical religious sense, but in the flesh-and-blood persons of the Dalai Lama and the Panchen Lama.

It was a golden day for Tibetan Buddhism in general and for Gelug-pa in particular. And the Great Fifth used it to full advantage. He used his power and prestige to greatly expand the Gelug-pa establishment throughout Tibet. Fences were mended with his former opponents, and Tibetan Buddhism entered upon a new day of prosperity and growth. The symbol of the new age was the construction of that most fabulous symbol of Tibet, the Potala.

Rising in lofty tiers from its Lhasa hillside, the huge thirteen-story Potala is surely one of the architectural wonders of the world. Its magnificent white and red facade, crowned by golden rooftops, is synonymous with the charm and mystery of Tibet. It seems more like a beautiful dream than a real place. It is believed that the name *Potala* was derived from the name of the mystical south Indian hermitage of the Hindu deity Shiva. Tibetans regard Shiva to be closely related to Avalokiteshvara. From the beginning,

FIGURE 16.3   The Potala; Lhasa, Tibet. (P. Bresnan)

the Potala was intended to be much more than just a residence for the Dalai Lama. It housed as well a small monastery, a museum and archives of Tibetan Buddhist history, and a meeting hall for the Tibetan National Assembly. Don't let this last name mislead you. The National Assembly was in no way a democratic congress; it was a feudal assembly drawn from the great aristocratic families of Tibet whose only purpose was to advise the Dalai Lama.

Beginning with Nagwan Lobsang, the Great Fifth, every Dalai Lama down to the present time has, at least officially, occupied the splendid residence located at the top of the central section of the Potala. The current Dalai Lama, the fourteenth, fled to India in 1959, and since that time has occupied a considerably more modest residence in exile. The Potala today, stripped of its former sacredness, has become a national museum. Common footsteps now tread daily in places formerly forbidden to all but the gods, and those close to the gods.

The Great Fifth died in 1670, but oddly enough the news of his death was not made public until 1682. At the time of his death, the Potala was still unfinished, and supposedly the death was concealed so as to avoid any chance that the Potala might not be completed. During these twelve years, Tibet was governed by the regent Sangye Gyatso, a most unusual man. It is widely believed that he was actually the son of the Great Fifth, and he used his influential position in the palace to create a political clique that supported his own control of power. Eventually, a search for the new Dalai Lama was launched. We may assume that Sangye was fully in control of the procedure. And, if keeping real power in his own hands was what Sangye yearned for, he couldn't have been happier with the outcome.

The new Dalai Lama, Tsangyang Gyatso, installed in 1697, grew up with no interest whatsoever in the responsibilities of rule. In fact, he was said to be a libertine who spent much of his time carousing and drinking to excess. He and his drinking buddies were well known in the brothels and seamier establishments of Lhasa. Tsangyang Gyatso was not even a fully ordained monk of the Gelug-pa sect. He refused to take the final vows, preferring instead the life of wine, women, and song. Nevertheless, he was the Dalai Lama, and, we are told, he was accepted by the Tibetan people who rationalized his earthy lifestyle as being but a chimera. Others, however, were not in a mood to be so generous. In 1706, a Mongol force invaded Tibet, specifically to depose (and later murder) the completely intolerable Tsangyang Gyatso. The regent, Sangye, was also put to death.

At this point, the story takes an interesting and fateful turn. The rulership of China was again in foreign hands: this time the Manchus, a people related to the Mongols, whose vast homeland lay to the north and northeast of China. The Manchu emperors believed they had rights—and responsibilities—where Tibet was concerned. In 1720, the Manchu emperor, Kang Xi (K'ang Hsi), intervened in a big way, and, of course, he possessed a potentially sufficient military strength to fully back up his action. The first thing Kang Xi did was to brush aside the man that the Mongols had put in Tsangyang Gyatso's place, installing instead Kalzan Gyatso, who officially became the seventh Dalai Lama.

In name, Kalzan Gyatso was an independent ruler, but in reality, he was a puppet of the Chinese emperor, and this is essentially the way the relationship would remain until the fall of the Manchu dynasty in 1912. Kang Xi declared Tibet to be a Protectorate of the Chinese Empire, dispatching "ambans" to Lhasa, official Chinese representatives whose task it was to oversee the administration of Tibetan affairs and report back to the emperor's government. It was the beginning of a two-century-long period of Chinese control over the internal affairs of Tibet.

Insofar as Tibetan Buddhism was concerned, matters did not change substantially as a result of the closer Chinese connection. The Gelug-pa sect remained paramount and the Dalai Lama continued—at least so far as outward appearances were concerned—to exercise kingly rule over Tibet in both the worldly and the spiritual realms. The office of the Panchen Lama, however, grew steadily more powerful. The Chinese developed strong ties to both the Dalai Lama and the Panchen Lama and were not altogether averse to playing one against the other.

With the installation of Kalzan Gyatso, the seventh Dalai Lama, Tibet entered into a long and rather stagnant period characterized by strong ties to the Manchu government of China. In 1912, however, the aging Manchu regime finally collapsed. For a time, China became a democratic republic under the leadership of Sun Yat-sen and later under Chiang Kai-shek. But the republic was destined to know only a brief life. In 1949, Mao Zedong (Mao Tse-tung), leader of the People's Revolutionary Army, overthrew the democratic government, establishing in its place the People's Republic of China. A thoroughgoing Marxist system was established in China, and once again the ages-old connection with Tibet was restored by military force. Things might still have worked out reasonably well for Tibet. After all, Tibet had existed for centuries under Chinese suzerainty; so long as this arrangement was accepted, the old ways had been allowed to continue without much interference. Initially, the Marxist government seemed inclined to continue this policy. But all that was about to change—dramatically.

Fearing that the aging party leaders were straying far from the righteous path of Marxist revolution, Mao Zedong sought to inspire the youth of China with a new communist fervor; then, filled with revolutionary zeal, they were to be unleashed on the country. Their energy, he hoped, would reinvigorate the revolution. Their energy, however, gave birth to a monster totally out of control. By the millions they formed into paramilitary brigades known as Red Guards whose sole purpose was to cleanse China of every taint of "imperialist" corruption and to erect a thoroughgoing Marxist utopia. Beginning in October of 1966, the fire raged for a decade. During this time, China was convulsed in a revolutionary terror determined to destroy the old and create the new. The universities were closed; "intellectuals" were killed off or forced to go into the country and work on farms, most of which were collectivized according to the communist model. All traces of religious life were mercilessly persecuted. (It was a time in Chinese history suggestive of the years known as "The Terror" during the dark days of the French Revolution.)

Tibet felt the full brunt of the Cultural Revolution. Red Guards in Tibet sought to totally destroy what they saw as a corrupt feudal system in which the elite privileged class ruthlessly exploited the peasant masses, who were deliberately held in a degraded state of ignorance and poverty. The Red Guards saw the monastery system as the principal upholder of this depraved order. They would root it out altogether. Thousands of monasteries were destroyed, often systematically blown up with dynamite. Monks were slaughtered or forced to return to their families. Uncountable numbers of Buddhist art objects were demolished. Their destructive zeal was fierce; it's a wonder that anything is left! (If it weren't for all that dynamite, doesn't this seem like a *déjà vu* experience? Remember Lang Darma and the Great Persecution of the mid-ninth century?)

With the death of Mao in 1976, the Cultural Revolution quickly collapsed. More responsible figures within the Communist Party regained control of the People's Republic of China. The excesses were repudiated and the leaders of the Cultural Revolution (including Mao's wife) were jailed or executed. A new policy of tolerance replaced the hysteria. But the damage had been done—a great deal of damage. Nonetheless, the slow process of rebuilding began immediately. However, nothing would ever be the same again. Tibet was now wholly annexed to the People's Republic of China, and a full-scale policy of integration was put into action. The once-isolated and independent culture of Tibet, it would seem, had become a thing of the past. Like it or not, the days of the ancient culture were over.

So where does that leave us? Now that the dust has settled (or at least is settling), we can see that Tibetan Buddhism faces a whole new situation. Tibet itself is now a part of the People's Republic of China, which exercises tight control over the Buddhist establishment. Revolutionary changes have destroyed or swept away much of the traditional order. The monastery system has been enormously reduced in size and wealth and power. In effect, the feudal establishment that the monastery system was a part of has been abolished. The old aristocracy, both temporal and spiritual, has been largely killed off or driven out of the country. The Dalai Lama, along with thousands of others, is in exile, and the Potala has been converted into a people's museum.

But not all of the news is grim; there is a bright side to this picture too. Most important of all, Tibetan Buddhism is far from annihilated. However diminished, it is at least recovering to some degree within Tibet. And Tibet, please remember, is not the only home of "Tibetan" Buddhism. We might more properly speak of Himalayan Buddhism, or of the Vajrayana Buddhism of the Himalayan lands. Regions adjoining Tibet, such as Nepal, Sikkim, Bhutan, Mustang, and Ladach were not affected at all by the Chinese action, and here the old traditions still survive. Most significant, though, is the work of the Tibetan refugees who have taken up residence in many places around the globe. This Tibetan Diaspora has sown the seeds of new growth that may well usher in a new age in the long tradition of Tibetan Buddhism.

Perhaps that's what it's all about. When we step back and look at the Big Picture, it has all the earmarks of the beginning of a whole new era. The Rip Van Winkle of traditional Tibetan Buddhism was violently awakened in the mid-twentieth century. But it has come through the ordeal lean, reformed, and ready to take on the future. No one can say what that future will be. Perhaps someday the Dalai Lama will be welcomed back to Tibet. Or perhaps the Gelug-pa sect has run out its allotted time in history. The fourteenth Dalai Lama has let it be known that he is seriously considering the possibility of not being reincarnated again. It could be that the Nyingma-pa is poised to close the circle, restoring its own ancient lineage to preeminence. California's Odiyan may be the symbol of a reincarnate Samye, and Tibetan Buddhism may be about to take on a new life stemming from a resuscitated version of its own beginnings. Or it may be that the time is ripe for the founding of an altogether new sect. Perhaps a modern Tsong Khapa is waiting to make his (or her) entry onto the stage of history.

We can speculate on and on; many directions are possible. But one thing seems certain: Tibetan Buddhism shall remain firmly grounded in the teachings of Mahayana Buddhism in general and Vajrayana Buddhism in particular. The ancient tradition of Tibetan Buddhism is alive and well, and whatever form it takes in the years ahead, it will have much of value to offer the world of the twenty-first century.

Study Questions

1. In general terms, how would you describe the geography of Tibet? How has geography influenced the character of life in Tibet? Do you feel that Tibet's unusual geography in any way influences the character of "Tibetan" Buddhism?

2. What does it mean to say that the West has had a *Shangri-la* image of Tibet? What happened to change that image in modern times?

3. Why did a "Tibetan Diaspora" occur in the latter half of the twentieth century? Do you feel that you understand the position of both sides in this issue? Do you feel that one side has a stronger argument in its favor?

4. Who really deserves the credit for the founding of Buddhism in Tibet, the two princesses or Padmasambhava? Why do you suppose that Buddhism took root in Tibet at all, considering that Tibet already had a much-loved religion in Bon?

5. What kind of accommodation did Buddhism make with Bon? How do you feel about this? Was it perhaps a bad idea to make any accommodation at all? How has it worked out over time?

6. Why is Tibetan Buddhism more technically known as Vajrayana? What's this all about? Why the non-Tibetan name "Vajrayana"?

7. Why is there so much sexual symbolism in Tibetan Buddhism? Isn't this perhaps in conflict with the way of life recommended by Shakyamuni Buddha for one who would walk the path of Madhyamarga?

8. What is a yab–yum? In terms of Buddhist belief and practice, what is the purpose of a yab–yum? Many feel that the yab–yum is a beautiful expression of Vajrayana Buddhism. How do you feel about it?

9. The practice of sadhana is a very important part of Tibetan Buddhism. What is "sadhana," and what are the principal kinds of sadhana practice? Does this make sense to you, or do you perhaps think it's nothing more than a form of self-delusion?

10. What is a thangka?

11. What do you think is so significant about the monks bowing deeply before the woman who had just ruined days of work on their sand mandala?

12. In what ways does the "literal-versus-metaphorical" option apply with regard to the teachings of Tibetan Buddhism? Which option appeals more to you?

13. What is the *Bardo Thodol?* What is suggested as a possible esoteric interpretation of the real purpose of the *Bardo Thodol?* How do you feel about that suggestion?

14. What would it be like to visit a fully functioning Tibetan Buddhist monastery? What would you expect to find there? Does it seem like an attractive sort of place to you?

15. Don't you find it odd that the monk who assassinated Long Darma believed that he was performing an act of kindness to his victim? What could he have been thinking?

16. What do you make of the story about Virupa making the sun stand still while he finished off flagon after flagon of wine? Doesn't that seem like a rather odd thing for a Buddhist master to be doing? What's the real point of the story?

17. How do the Mongols enter into the developing story of Buddhism in Tibet? Do you feel that their influence was all in all a positive one, or a negative one? Why?

18. Who was Tsong Khapa? Why is he so highly revered by all Tibetans?

19. How did the title of Dalai Lama come into existence? What is the relationship of the Dalai Lama to the Panchen Lama?

20. What was so *great* about the "Great Fifth"? Do you feel that he really deserves such distinction?

21. On what does China base its claim to rightful suzerainty over Tibet?

22. What was the "Great Proletarian Cultural Revolution"? What effect did it have on Tibet in general and Tibetan Buddhism in particular?

23. Tenzin Gyatso is the fourteenth Dalai Lama. Why do you suppose that he is considering not undergoing "reincarnation"?

24. How do you assess the state of affairs of Tibetan Buddhism in the present day? What does the future hold?

CHAPTER 17

Chan Buddhism

Chan is the name of a school of Buddhism that developed in China. The word is derived from the Sanskrit *dhyana*, a term which refers to the practice of meditation. "Chan" is simply the Chinese version of the Sanskrit word. An emphasis on dhyana practice was introduced into China from India in the fifth century C.E. The school of Chan Buddhism was the result; it flourished for several centuries before declining and all but dying out in its Chinese homeland.

In the twelfth century, the school of Chan Buddhism was transplanted from China to Japan, where it also took root and flourished. In Japan, the tradition is known as *Zen* Buddhism. Just as *Chan* is the Chinese rendition of the Sanskrit *dhyana*, *Zen* is the Japanese rendition of the Chinese word *Chan*. Thus, *Chan* and *Zen* are fundamentally the same word; both are variants of the root word *dhyana*.

In essence, the Zen tradition is a continuation of the Chan tradition; there is a seamless flow between them. Because of the decline of the Chan tradition in China, though, the modern world is far more familiar with the tradition in its Japanese form, Zen. For this reason, many modern writers choose to avoid confusion by simply referring to the entire tradition by the name *Zen*, the Chinese part as well as the Japanese. There is logic in doing this. After all, it is one continuous tradition, and the names *Chan* and *Zen* both refer equally to that tradition. Zen has, in fact, become something of a universal word in modern times. Nevertheless, selecting the appropriate term presents something of a dilemma.

The aim of this study is to understand the tradition as a whole, viewed from the perspective of modern times. For this reason, I feel that, in order to avoid confusion, it is appropriate in this chapter to use the term *Zen* when referring to the tradition as a whole, and to use the term *Chan* only where it is needed to indicate historical aspects of the tradition peculiar to China alone.

Again, both Chan and Zen, derived from the Sanskrit *dhyana*, refer to the practice of meditation. Meditation is a matter of fundamental importance in this study. Considering its central place in the development of Eastern traditions, and especially in the development of Zen Buddhism, it would be appropriate to begin this chapter with a closer look at the nature of this often mysterious and elusive subject.

The practice of meditation was well established in Hindu culture by the time of Buddha, and though he rejected much from the Hindu tradition, Buddha loved and cherished meditation. Meditation was his last hope when, in the hour of his desperation, Buddha sat down beneath the bodhi tree resolved not to move until he found the truth he sought. Buddha stressed the importance of meditation in his teaching, and this is reflected in the high position that dhyana occupies in both the Eightfold Path of Theravada and the Six Paramitas of Mahayana. So, what precisely does this word mean? What is the proper place of meditation in the life of one who would follow in the footsteps of Buddha?

It must be emphasized that there is no single answer to this question. There are many different traditions, all of which have developed their own particular "schools" of meditation. Despite the differences, though, it is nonetheless possible to perceive some common elements in the various traditions, a sort of fundamental core that is shared by all.

The mind in meditation is the state of "no-mind"; that is, the customary thought-based processes that we associate with mental activity are temporarily suspended. When the talkative, thinking mind, and its close association with the ego-identity are allowed to become quiet, consciousness becomes very clear and absorbed in the reality of the present moment. The background dualities of thought evaporate. One who has mastered the art of meditation may experience, to some degree, what is generally described as the "unitive state." This simply means that the consciousness of one in a true state of meditation is freed from the usual human split between self and other. The underlying unity of being is perceived, not intellectually of course, but directly, experientially, in this moment. The experience of the unitive state can be more or less perfect. Perfect meditation is the perfect expression of the unitive state.

It is a common mistake to imagine that the mind in meditation is in some sort of trance state. Ideally, the meditative state of mind—even if far less than perfect—would be our normal state of consciousness, our ordinary state of mind. Many speculate that the consciousness of nonhuman beings is essentially like a meditative state. And that would be true of human infants too; all of us started out in life as perfect little meditation masters. A great divide was crossed when our distant human ancestors developed language. The significance of language cannot be exaggerated! Language gives one the power to create a conceptual world that represents the real world, but so easily becomes a substitute for it. The development of the language-based thinking process, and especially its great production, the ego-identity, has the effect of dislocating us far from our natural beginnings. In a sense, meditation disciplines are really nothing more than devices designed to loosen the grip of the ego-habit and help restore us to the natural state.

The *practice* of meditation is the practice of various techniques designed (hopefully) to help one achieve the state of mind-in-meditation—that is, the state of "no-mind." The state of mind-in-meditation, though, is by no means necessarily limited to those times set aside for "practicing" meditation techniques. Ideally it becomes the background condition of one's normal state of consciousness. Specific times for meditation practice are valuable in that the state of mind experienced at such times may expand to become more or less the continuous state of mind. A meditation master is a person who lives his or her ongoing daily life in a state of consciousness that can be accurately described as "mindfulness," that is to say, well rooted in the reality of the present moment. This, of course, is not an altered state of consciousness, nor is it something transcendent, something lofty that only a rare person can aspire to. It is actually the natural way to live.

Once again, meditation techniques are helps that one employs during a session of meditation practice. Myriad techniques have become popular over the centuries, many of them borrowed from the tradition of yoga. Probably the most widely recognized technique employed in the *practice* of meditation is what is called "sitting meditation." Typically, this involves the form of cross-legged sitting posture that has become virtually an icon in the art of Buddhism. The advantage of this posture, pure and simple, is that once mastered, it permits the meditator to remain comfortable, though sitting very still for long periods of time. One does not have to sit, though, to practice meditation. Many postures are possible. (Some people even claim to be able to make a meditation practice of jogging or swimming.)

To sum up, the practice of meditation is the deliberate practice of certain disciplines, often including the sitting posture, whose aim is to encourage the meditative state of mind, and ultimately the unitive state. Perfect meditation is the perfect expression of the unitive state. This is what the word *dhyana* refers to, and it is why dhyana occupies the summit position in Buddha's teaching. The word *dhyana*, like its English counterpart "meditation," refers to both the state and the practice. The Buddhist tradition holds that in the mastery of dhyana one ascends through four stages of growth, the fourth being synonymous with the opening of *prajna*, and thus the experience of awakening. To be in a state of perfect dhyana is to be an awakened person.

From the earliest days, many followers of Buddha found it reasonable to conclude that diligent practice of the disciplines—especially the practice of meditation—would lead slowly but inexorably to awakening. Given the amount of resistance normal in human beings, the process would most likely be long and slow, and, of course, some would never make it at all. By way of analogy, we could compare the process to the fashioning of a mirror for a great telescope. We start out with a large rough lump of glass, which is like the ordinary person before embarking on a life's work of Buddhist discipline. The perfect mirror is already there; it is inherent within the rough glass; it remains only to be brought out. Years of grinding and polishing will, if all goes well, bring out the mirror latent in the glass from the beginning. The improvement takes form gradually—no one can say at what moment perfection is achieved—but eventually the mirror does become perfect. In a similar vein, Michelangelo was once asked to explain the genius that made it possible for him to transform a block of rough stone into a lifelike replica of a horse. "It's easy," he said, "I just chip away everything that doesn't look like a horse." (No one knows for sure if he ever really said that, but it does sound like something Michelangelo might say.)

The aspirant himself is the large rough lump of glass. Years of grinding and polishing (yogic disciplines and meditation) will bring out the mirror (the Buddha-nature) and will eventually make it perfect. It's a gradual approach to the attainment of Enlightenment. In some ways, this gradual approach appeals to something basic in human nature. Perhaps it's because people want to feel that they are in control of their lives. Ironically, this is the very ego-centered problem that Buddhism seeks to solve, but there it sits nonetheless. If I can imagine that "awakening" (whatever that may be) is the payoff at the end of a clearly defined program of work, then I can apply myself to the disciplines involved and feel reasonably confident that the prize will ultimately be mine; I'm in control. Again, it's like polishing that telescope mirror. If I work hard at it, eventually I will see the truth of the universe. It's up to me.

This gradual approach to the goal of awakening pretty much sums up the general character of Buddhist meditation practice in China around 500 C.E. A thousand years had passed since Shakyamuni Buddha had started the ball rolling. Men and women were as passionate as ever in their determination to follow Buddha into the awakened state. Buddha had taught mankind how to do that, but his teaching needed to be interpreted. The prevalent interpretation emphasized a life organized around the disciplines of the vinaya, centered on attaining mastery in meditation practice. In this way, this *gradual* way, the obstacles would be removed, and the Buddha-nature would eventually be uncovered. This general state of affairs might not have changed much for a long time had it not been for one thing—a Buddhist revolutionary named Bodhidharma appeared on the scene. Bodhidharma is a semi-legendary figure whose name is associated with a very different approach to the role of meditation. Bodhidharma was destined to be the founder—at least the titular founder—of a powerful new movement that would coalesce into one of the major historical branches of Buddhism.

From the earliest times, those who favored the gradual approach to awakening were opposed by those who argued that awakening, by its very nature, must be a sudden experience. No amount of gradual "polishing" would ever *produce* awakening. It happened— if it happened at all—suddenly, all at once. This did not mean that the "sudden" school rejected the practice of meditation—not at all. What they rejected was the notion that one could *achieve* awakening gradually, through dedication to the discipline of meditation practice. In their eyes, the value of meditation was that it helped to foster the right state of consciousness—a fertile ground, you might say—out of which the sudden experience of awakening might be more likely to occur. Meditation practice was thus seen as a powerful help to the dedicated seeker, but by no means was it a necessity. The crucial difference between the "gradual" school and the "sudden" school was that the former regarded meditation practice as a *means* to awakening, whereas the latter regarded it as a *help*. Both, however, following the lead of Shakyamuni Buddha himself, held the practice of meditation in high regard.

Even though both schools, the gradual and the sudden, could trace their roots back to the beginnings of Buddhism, the gradual school had clearly dominated the Buddhist scene during its first millennium of development. Evidence of the existence of a minority "sudden" school continued to appear, however. Although seemingly not much emphasized in the Theravada tradition, those who favored the sudden approach would find new life in Mahayana. Some pointed references to sudden awakening are to be found in the Mahayana sutras.

Although evidence exists that some exponents of the sudden school were active in China as early as the third century, it remains apparent that the way of the gradual school was clearly the dominant approach, but its days of dominance were numbered. Beginning in the early fifth century, a new opposition movement began to come together. As mentioned before, the tradition holds that this movement became organized around the person of Bodhidharma, a Buddhist meditation master from India. The school of Buddhism associated with the name of *Bodhidharma* was known simply by the Sanskrit term *dhyana*. In Chinese this became *Channa*, ultimately shortened to *Chan*. And thus began Chan Buddhism, a wonderfully rich tradition within the great wheel of Mahayana. Chan Buddhism would flourish for many centuries in China, but eventually it would decline and nearly die out in its homeland, just as the original growth of Buddhism had declined in India. But like Indian Buddhism which had migrated to foreign lands, so too would Chan Buddhism find its way to new places—Viet Nam and Korea for example, and eventually to Japan, where the tradition would continue under the name Zen.

BODHIDHARMA

The story of Zen Buddhism (Chan Buddhism in China) first began to take on a coherent form around the teaching of a man named Bodhidharma. He was a semi-legendary meditation master from India who spread the good word of Buddhism in China during the early sixth century. It must be emphasized, though, that Bodhidharma is the *legendary* founder of Zen. Virtually all modern historians of Buddhism agree that the roots of the Zen tradition were in existence in China a full century or more before Bodhidharma.

In the Zen tradition, Bodhidharma is referred to as the first patriarch of Zen in China. Let me explain what this means. Shakyamuni Buddha freed himself forever from the prison ground of human misery. He selflessly gave the rest of his life to teaching others how to follow him to freedom. But how was his teaching to be preserved? The essence of it went far beyond anything that could be captured in mere words. If words could do it, Buddha would have simply written down the formula, and that would be that. But words can't do it; formulas can't do it; practicing certain disciplines can't do it. Then what *can* do it?

According to the tradition of Zen Buddhism, the reality of Buddha's enlightenment was transmitted personally and directly by him to his disciples. All other things might be helpful in clearing the way so that the experience could happen, but the experience itself is initiated in the disciple as the result of a sensed personal connection between disciple and

FIGURE 17.1 Bodhidharma. (photo by P. Bresnan)

master. This is commonly referred to as a "transmission," but it is not meant to be understood as a spiritual something that is given from one person to another. The awakening is personal; it arises within each individual, but it can be initiated by a "transmission," a deeply felt sense of shared consciousness, between an enlightened master and a disciple. The intimacy of the master–disciple relationship in Buddhism clearly has its roots in the Hindu tradition out of which Buddhism developed.

In the Zen tradition, the way that the purity of Buddha's enlightenment was to be preserved through the ages would be by direct personal transmission between teacher and student, master and disciple. Through his personal influence, Shakyamuni Buddha undoubtedly nudged many into that state of being wherein they were at last willing to let go completely, and become awakened. But, according to the tradition, when his life was nearing its end, Buddha made a point of identifying one of his disciples whose enlightenment was perfect. That disciple, Kasyapa by name, was chosen to be his personal successor; he would be the leader and unifying center of the sangha, the community of monks, after Buddha was gone. In time, he would name his own successor, choosing the person whom he deemed to be perfectly enlightened and best suited to be the custodian of the tradition.

Kasyapa was a loyal and much-loved disciple of Buddha. One day, Buddha called all of his close disciples together, something he did often in order to share his teaching with them. When they were all assembled, Buddha took his usual place before them. Ordinarily he would talk for a while and engage them in dialogue. But on this occasion, he just sat there saying nothing. At last, raising his eyes to the group, he drew out from under the folds of his robe a beautiful flower, perhaps a lotus in full bloom, and simply held it before the group. That's all; he just held out the flower, remaining silent and gazing peacefully at his disciples. There was some general uneasiness. Only one, Kasyapa, understood. Their eyes joined, and Kasyapa smiled; it was the smile of perfect recognition. Buddha knew beyond any doubt that this was the man he would entrust with the leadership of the sangha.

In selecting Kasyapa, Buddha was implicitly verifying the purity of Kasyapa's enlightenment. Kasyapa would take the place of Buddha in the sangha so that even death could not break the continuity. In a way, it was a device for preserving the presence of Buddha among them. In time, Kasyapa chose his own successor, who happened to be Ananda, the young disciple that Buddha had loved with great affection. Apparently Ananda was not yet ready for the role of successor during Buddha's lifetime; he achieved perfect enlightenment after the death of Buddha. As a symbol of Kasyapa's right to the succession, Buddha gave his own robe and begging bowl to him. And Kasyapa, when he selected Ananda, passed on to him these treasured personal items of Buddha. Ananda in turn would pass them on to his own chosen successor. And so it would go for generations to come.

In the Zen tradition, the designated successors of Buddha are called "patriarchs." Kasyapa, Buddha's immediate successor, was the first patriarch; Ananda the second patriarch, and so on. Altogether, the patriarchs formed an unbroken line of continuity, beginning with Buddha, and preserving over time the authenticity of Buddha's awakening. After all, that's what it's all about.

Although historical verifiability has to be stretched a little, the Zen tradition accounts for a line, a "lineage," of twenty-eight patriarchs from Buddha to Bodhidharma. Bodhidharma was the twenty-eighth patriarch of India, and when he began his mission in

China, he became the first patriarch of China. The line does not continue down to the present day; the numbering system came to an end with the sixth patriarch of China. Each of the twenty-eight patriarchs of India is listed by name in the archives of Zen history. The great second-century Indian philosopher, Nagarjuna, is designated the fourteenth patriarch.* Thus did Bodhidharma come to be known as the first patriarch of Zen. Although the living roots of Zen go directly back to Buddha himself, the distinct Buddhist tradition that bears the name Zen by common agreement is said to begin with Bodhidharma. Zen was an outgrowth of Mahayana, but the Zen tradition maintains that it alone has preserved the essential purity of Buddha's teaching.

As you might have guessed, not a whole lot is known for sure about Bodhidharma. The scant historical record we have comes from two brief accounts that were included in chronicles of Buddhist masters written about a century after his death. These give us some very basic facts, but most of the traditional story of Bodhidharma's life is based on conjecture and legend.

We can say with a fair degree of certainty that he was born in India, quite possibly in a noble or Brahmin family from the south of India. He was said to have died in 532 C.E. "at a ripe old age" (although presumably not quite so ripe as the one hundred and fifty years often cited). He may have been around eighty or ninety at the time of his death, which would put his birth sometime in the mid-fifth century. Bodhidharma's life coincided with the final collapse of the mighty Roman Empire in the far-off Mediterranean world. But in those days, that drama might as well have been happening on another planet.

Like Shakyamuni Buddha before him, Bodhidharma parted company with his family, choosing instead the spiritual path. Eventually he became a disciple of the Buddhist master, Prajnadhara, known in the Zen tradition as the twenty-seventh patriarch. There are some grounds for speculating that Prajnadhara was a woman, certainly an interesting element in the story if true. In any case, Prajnadhara selected Bodhidharma to be the successor and conferred on him the insignia of Buddha's robe and bowl. Prajnadhara also, according to the story, charged Bodhidharma with the mission of carrying the truth of Buddhism to China. Buddhist monks had been active in China for a long time, but that distant land had not yet been visited by one with the perfect enlightenment of Bodhidharma.

We don't know for certain how Bodhidharma traveled from India to China; some think it was by sea, but in those days an overland route was far more likely. Bodhidharma must have already been along in years when he began the arduous trek. Don't let the appearance of the map deceive you. In those days, there was no direct route from India to China; the mass of the great mountains of the north prevented that. A traveler would have to follow the passes of the northwest deep into the deserts of central Eurasia and then follow the winding Silk Road east into the land of China. It took Bodhidharma at least three years to reach his destination; presumably he stayed for periods of time at monasteries along the route. It would seem that he made his way slowly across southern China from west to east, and presumably he attracted a lot of attention. Bodhidharma was not just another Buddhist monk; he was a powerful and impressive figure. Bodhidharma was an Indian master of meditation, and he was teaching a new way and a new meaning for the practice of meditation.

---

*This matter of the lineage will strike a familiar note with anyone knowledgeable about the Roman Catholic Church. The "apostolic succession" of the popes seems to be very much the same sort of thing.

The chronicles tell us that in 520 C.E., Bodhidharma finally reached the region of modern Guangzhou (formerly known as Canton, about twenty miles upriver from present day Hong Kong). His fame preceded him, and Emperor Wu, wanting to meet this exotic foreigner, summoned him to the court at Nanjing. Emperor Wu was a pretty interesting character in his own right. He reminds one of Emperor Ashoka. Both were powerful monarchs who ruled vast empires, and both experienced a profound change of heart in adult life, which resulted in their embracing Buddhism. Wu had been a dedicated Confucian, but he gave that up when he discovered Buddhism; he even, we are told, became a monk himself for a short time. He lavished his kingly largesse on the Buddhist sects, supporting many temples and monasteries. He sponsored translations of Buddhist scriptures, paid for the upkeep of innumerable monks and nuns, and, like Ashoka, he earnestly encouraged a policy of nonviolence toward all animals. Emperor Wu was, to put it mildly, actively involved in promoting the Buddhist way of life in China even before the arrival of Bodhidharma.

No doubt Emperor Wu derived great personal satisfaction from his efforts on behalf of the Buddhist cause, but clearly he had another reason as well. Some of the Mahayana Buddhist sects (as discussed earlier in this work) held to a belief in personal reincarnation, including belief in the possibility of rebirth in a Buddha-realm such as Suhkhavati. It would seem that Emperor Wu had been won over to this school of thought. He believed that his impressive list of "good works" was piling up a mountain of positive karma that would guarantee him an excellent place among the gods in the next life. In his own mind, it was certainly no accident that he was a great king in this life. It was the working of karma, and it was his karmic destiny to be an even greater figure in the next life. Undoubtedly, a man of his wealth and power would have had no trouble finding others, even some Buddhist monks, who would be happy to reassure him in this belief. And now the great Bodhidharma himself was coming to visit the court. Confirmation from the lips of Bodhidharma would really gladden the emperor's heart. This was the setting into which Bodhidharma entered.

We can't say for sure what Bodhidharma looked like, but he is traditionally pictured as having a ferocious appearance: tall, dark, with deep-set penetrating eyes and bushy eyebrows—a gruff exterior, but a soft heart inside. He approached Emperor Wu, probably fixing his gaze on him instead of looking modestly downward. Bodhidharma said nothing, but Emperor Wu wanted to do the talking anyway. We can imagine him leaning back and ticking off the long list of his many charitable ventures. The litany was meant to impress Bodhidharma. What a noble and generous man! Finally he turned to Bodhidharma and asked, rhetorically, "So what do you think my reward will be for all of this?" This was supposed to be Bodhidharma's cue to start unctuously heaping flattery on the king, assuring him that he would be numbered among the gods in the next life. And then, of course, Wu would add another notch to his record by magnanimously bestowing some further generous gift on the monastery of Bodhidharma's choosing. Emperor Wu must have sat up straight when he heard Bodhidharma's reply.

"No merit at all," Bodhidharma said (probably in a gruff tone of voice).

"No merit?" the astonished Wu responded. "How can you say that! Why?"

We don't know precisely what Bodhidharma answered, but it's easy to guess what the gist of it would have been. If I may be permitted to speculate: "If you believe that all these so-called 'good works' are going to earn you some great reward, you totally fail to understand the basic principles of Buddha's teaching. Those who work for profit only intensify the stifling delusion of ego. The reward you speak of is in the doing, not separated from it. Not only do you deceive yourself about some future reward, you risk falling into a hell of your own making right here in this life."

"Then what," Wu asked, "*is* the merit of these generous acts of mine? Surely there is some kind of merit associated with the good things we do in life!"

Bodhidharma's response was cryptic. Wu wants to know what Bodhidharma regards to be the kind of action that is right action; the kind that is truly meritorious and adds to one's store of positive karma. The Buddhologist Heinrich Dumoulin puts Bodhidharma's response in these words: "It is pure knowing, wonderful and perfect. Its essence is emptiness. One cannot gain such merit by worldly means." (vol. 1, 91)

We can easily imagine that Emperor Wu was feeling somewhat tense at this point in the conversation, but that wouldn't faze Bodhidharma in the slightest. Having only muddied the water by going directly to his question about merit, Wu apparently decided that it might be a better course to drop that for the moment and start with first things first. "What is the first principle of this holy doctrine?" he asked.

"Vast emptiness," Bodhidharma answered bluntly, "and there is nothing holy about it."

"And who then is it who stands before me now?" Wu asked.

"I don't know."

With that the conversation ended, and Bodhidharma left the palace. It hadn't turned out quite the way that Wu expected. Bodhidharma withdrew to the monastery of Shaolinsi (Shao-lin-ssu), where he was a welcome guest, and he remained there for the next nine years of his life. During these years he spent a great deal of time practicing *piguan* (*pi-kuan*), which translates roughly as "wall-gazing." It is probable that Bodhidharma introduced a new technique in meditation practice. Traditional meditation exercises in India were generally practiced with the eyes closed. and often included chanting or other kinds of yogic techniques to still and center the mind. Bodhidharma's method was to sit before a blank wall with the eyes at least partly open, and to empty the mind of thought by concentrating on the simple nonverbal reality of the moment. One's ordinary mind—in perfect harmony with the oneness of the moment—is the mind that is truly in meditation.*

Bodhidharma spent long hours in meditation. But even this great dhyana-master could not prevent himself from occasionally nodding off to sleep (a universally annoying problem for those who practice meditation). This infuriated Bodhidharma, and according to one quaint little story, one day he got so upset that he tore off his eyelids and flung them on the ground. The sleepy eyes can't close if the eyelids are gone. The eyelids were nourished by the soil, and from them grew the first tea plants. Tea became the drink of

---

*The modern Buddhist scholar D. T. Suzuki has argued that a literal translation of *pi-kuan* is incorrect. How could mere wall-gazing start a revolutionary movement in the Buddhist world? Rather, Suzuki maintains, the term refers to the character of the state of consciousness of one who is practicing meditation in the proper way. In support of this, Suzuki refers to documentary sources that made reference to the manner in which Bodhidharma instructed his chief disciple in meditation. "Externally keep yourself away from all relationships, and internally, have no hankerings in your heart; when your mind is like unto a straight-standing wall you may enter into the Path." (*Zen Buddhism*, 63)

choice among Buddhist meditators; it tastes great, and it helps to keep sleepiness at bay. In a less gruesome version of the story, Bodhidharma plucked out his eyebrows, and it was from these that the first tea bushes grew. Whether or not Bodhidharma's eye parts had anything to do with it, the careful brewing and drinking of tea did, in fact, become almost synonymous with the practice of Zen. Strong green tea is said to exude "the flavor of Zen."

Certain of the monks at the monastery wished to become disciples of Bodhidharma, but the master seemed to be unapproachable. One of them, though, wouldn't take no for an answer. His name was Hui Ko (pronounced Wee-koh), and he was destined to become Bodhidharma's successor. Hui Ko was *very* persistent. He would sit patiently for hours, even days, in the presence of the master, waiting to be granted the opportunity to learn directly from him. But always he was rebuffed; Bhodidharma acted as if Hui Ko didn't even exist. The story gets really dramatic one cold and stormy winter night. The snow is swirling and the wind is howling at the monastery windows. Only a small oil-lamp lights the room where Bodhidharma sits; as usual he is quiet and immobile before the bare wall. Hui Ko can't bear it any longer. In desperation, he seizes a large cleaver and actually cuts off his left arm at the elbow. Blood dripping from the ragged stump, he interrupts Bodhidharma's meditation, presenting the severed arm. This, he shouts, is evidence of his determination. He'll do anything to receive instruction from the master. "If cutting off my arm doesn't move you, I will take this knife and cut off my head!" Now maybe Bodhidharma would pay attention to him.

And at last Bodhidharma did pay attention to Hui Ko. (Thank god!) He turned to Hui Ko, surveying the bloody scene, and asked almost in exasperation, "What is it you want from me?"

"I want to know the truth of my own nature," Hui Ko answered. "I know no peace of mind."

"Alright," said Bodhidharma, "bring your mind out here, and I'll pacify it for you."

"That's just the problem. My mind troubles me endlessly, but no matter how hard I search for it, I can never lay hold of it."

"There!" said Bodhidharma. "Your mind is pacified."

With those words, we are told, Hui Ko saw into the nature of the problem he had created, and he was instantly enlightened.

It is indeed a dramatic story. Unfortunately (at least for the sake of drama), it is undoubtedly fictitious. It's not that Hui Ko is fictitious, or that he did not achieve enlightenment as a disciple of Bodhidharma. But the part about cutting off his arm is unlikely, to say the least. The brief account in the chronicles gives a far more prosaic story. Hui Ko may have lost an arm, but a violent encounter with bandits is probably how it happened. Nevertheless, the story makes a couple of valuable points about Zen and uses sensational elements to emphasize them. It has long been a part of the tradition of Zen that one who seeks to be a disciple of a master can often expect to be ignored or brusquely turned away at first. This is not really a lack of interest; rather, the seeker must prove, must demonstrate, his genuine determination before being accepted. It may not be necessary to cut off one's arm, but some show of total sincerity is necessary. The second point concerns the abruptness of Hui Ko's enlightenment. It happened in a sudden flash of insight.

After Hui Ko, Bodhidharma accepted a few other monks as his disciples. When the ninth year was drawing to a close, Bodhidharma announced that he had become an old man, and he wished to return to his homeland while he could still make the journey. It was time to designate a successor. He gathered his four disciples together and posed a question: "What have you learned from me? What is the meaning of Buddha's teaching?"

The first person to answer was Dao Fu. "The ultimate truth of reality cannot be expressed in words. Words are concerned with dualities, but truth is beyond duality. Truth is Dao."

Bodhidharma listened carefully, and then said, "You speak well, but your understanding is not perfect. You shall inherit my skin."

The next disciple to speak was a woman named Zongji (Tsung-ch'ih). Her rather mysterious offering concerned a reference to a passage in the *Prajnaparamita*. "As I understand it, the truth can be likened to the time when Ananda experienced a glimpse of the Buddha-field of Akshobhya. It is perceived once, and then never again."

Bodhidhharma took it in intently, and then responded, "You too speak well, but your understanding lacks perfection. You shall inherit my flesh."

Dao Yu was the third to speak. "The four elements are empty. The five skandas don't really exist. In truth nothing can be said about the truth."

Bodhidharma probably smiled. "Your words are clever and well chosen, but you contradict yourself. You say that nothing can be said about the truth, but in so doing you try to say something about it. Your understanding too lacks perfection. You shall inherit my bones."

The last of the four was Hui Ko. He approached the master, bowed deeply, and spoke not a single word. Bodhidharma embraced Hui Ko, and whispered to him, "You shall inherit my marrow." (after an account in Dumoulin)

Hui Ko also inherited the robe and bowl of Buddha. He was to become the second patriarch of Zen (Chan) in China. Bodhidharma, feeling secure about the future of what he had begun, set off on the long journey home and was seen no more.

So what are we to make of Bodhidharma? Why, within the broad umbrella of Buddhism, is his teaching said to be the foundation stone of that distinct sect we know as Zen? The place to begin is with the following terse statement:

> A special transmission outside of scriptures;
> No dependence on words or letters;
> Direct pointing at the mind of man;
> Seeing into one's nature, and the attainment of Buddhahood.

The above verse (called a *gatha* in Japanese) is widely regarded as being the fundamental statement or definition of Zen Buddhism. This basic gatha (GAH-ta) says it all. And, according to tradition, Bodhidharma is credited with being its author. Modern Buddhist scholars almost unanimously agree that the precise wording of the gatha came later, but the spirit of its meaning derives from the time of Bodhidharma.

"Direct pointing at the mind of man; seeing into one's nature and the attainment of Buddhahood." The gatha is saying that true awakening is a sudden and direct experience; it is not simply the end result of a long process of mental cleansing. This point is all-important. The tradition of Zen teaches that the basic gatha gives expression to the central matter of Bodhidharma's revolutionary teaching. The function of Zen is to preserve and recreate the genuine experience of Buddha's awakening. Awakening is the great flash of insight in which one suddenly "sees into one's nature." Absolute Being is perfectly simple, one, indivisible. It can only be understood in its totality, all at once. Therefore, it makes no sense to talk about *gradual* enlightenment. "The fruit drops when it is ripe."

If it's the real thing, it happens all at once—*sudden* enlightenment. In Chinese "sudden enlightenment" is called *wu men*. Most people in the Western world are more familiar with the Japanese term, *satori*. It is the central and essential importance of satori that the teaching of Bodhidharma was all about. As D. T. Suzuki bluntly puts it: "The coming of Bodhidharma to China in the early sixth century was simply to introduce this satori element into the body of Buddhism."

It is not possible to exaggerate the importance of satori. Unfortunately, it is very possible to miscast the precise meaning of satori, because, once again, we are attempting to talk about that which, by definition, cannot be expressed in words or thoughts. The best policy is to keep it simple and allow the intuitional faculty an opportunity to sense the meaning.

Suzuki calls satori, "an intuitive looking into the nature of things," and more poetically, "the opening of the mind flower." In this sense, any sudden, powerful insight is a kind of satori. Everyone has had this sort of experience at one time or another. Even insights that relate to the meaning of life can be "great satoris" or "small satoris." But the experience that gives Zen its meaning is, of course, the ultimate insight that banishes all the clouds of unknowing—perfect awakening. This is perfect, unlimited satori and is usually what is being referred to when the word is used.

In focusing on the essential place of sudden enlightenment, Bodhidharma set the course of this new Buddhist teaching on a track different from the rest. As discussed at the beginning of the chapter, Buddhist teaching in China had emphasized the gradual approach to Buddhahood. The idea of sudden enlightenment, though, did not originate with Bodhidharma. In fact, we find both the sudden and the gradual approach discussed in the sutras. The gradual approach, though, had been dominant in the tradition of Buddhism, at least up to the time of Bodhidharma.

What made Bodhidharma something of a revolutionary, and the founder of a new way of Buddhism, is that he flatly disagreed with the traditionalist approach. This is not to say that Bodhidharma condemned the practice of the traditional disciplines. Far from it; he himself was an ardent practitioner of sitting meditation. All of the disciplines, he would argue, are good and helpful, but *by themselves* they are empty of value. They are lacking the central, essential element without which true awakening cannot occur.

Studying the sutras is a fine thing to do; such study brings great joy and enrichment. But, by itself, all of the intellectual knowledge of the human race is like but "a tiny hair dropped into the vastness of space." Not even kingly meditation, by itself, can transform consciousness into *prajna*. That would be like lifting yourself by your own bootstraps:

> The experience of enlightenment is not dependent on meditation; there is no causal connection between the two. Meditational practice is neither the cause nor the condition for coming to a realization. Once awakened to wisdom, the mind sees nature, its own nature, which is identical with the Buddha nature. (Dumoulin, 40)

Meditation practice is an excellent thing to do, but it is not by itself the means to awakening. Then what is? The answer to that question is given in the first two lines of the basic gatha: "A special transmission outside of scripture; no dependence on words or letters."

The gatha proclaims that the living experience of enlightenment can be awakened in one only by a direct, *personal transmission* from an already awakened man or woman. The master, in sharing his or her state of consciousness with the disciple, *arouses* awakening in that person. In other words, the influence of the master excites the satori experience in the disciple. The satori experience is the opening of the "mind flower" to the awakened state of consciousness. Bodhidharma, we may assume, would have taken the position that the "transmission" between master and student is the *only* reasonable way in which a genuinely perfect satori experience can be aroused. The master need not be physically present at the moment, though; it is the character of the relationship that matters. And that relationship will bear fruit when the person is ready—that is to say, when the person is finally willing to let go completely.

"The fruit drops when it is ripe." In other words, satori is not something that can be *achieved*, not something that can be *won* by diligent effort. It occurs when it occurs, if it occurs at all, just as the fruit drops when it is ripe. No amount of effort can have any effect at all. You can no more force yourself to "wake up" than you can force yourself to remember something. But when one is ready—just as when Buddha was ready—almost anything may trigger the dropping of the fruit. The simple sound of someone stepping on a dry leaf can do it; a long-forgotten aroma can do it; or, as was the case for Buddha, it can be triggered by the sight of the morning star in the predawn sky.

You may well be wondering at this point if Bodhidharma, and the Zen tradition in general, would insist that personal transmission is really the one and only way that true awakening can occur. Buddhism in general is not dogmatic; ultimately each individual must decide that question for himself. Buddha, of course, driven to the state of desperation, discovered the truth of his nature entirely on his own. But that's one reason why Buddha is so loved and honored, almost to the point of being regarded as a "savior" by some. Conceivably, others can and have had the same experience. But, at the very least, the Zen tradition would say that such a thing is very exceptional. However, there is no law preventing the transmission from taking many paths over time. "Zen Masters" are not necessarily confined to the grounds of Zen monasteries.

It is important to understand that Bodhidharma was not attacking the practice of meditation *per se*. Bodhidharma loved meditation; his awakening by no means put an end to it. He made an important place for it in his daily life, and so have innumerable men and women down through the history of Buddhism to the present day. Bodhidharma—or more precisely, the tradition associated with his name—was attacking only what was seen to be a wrong view, that is, that the discipline of meditation *by itself* can work as a means to the achievement of awakening.

What then might Bodhidharma say is the proper role of meditation in one's life? If the practice of meditation does not *of itself* constitute an effective means for achieving awakening, what value is there in this practice? Bodhidharma might begin by pointing out that meditation practice, in conjunction with the other disciplines, helps to prepare the person to become *receptive* to the influence of the master. It's not essential, but it certainly might be of help, in which case it would be a wonderful value. But this is still looking at meditation as a means to an end. The real value of meditation is, like dancing or singing, that it is an end unto itself. The practice of meditation has the capacity to greatly increase the joy of living.

It's a very reasonable question to ask: What good is it? Why deliberately give time to doing *nothing*, when you could be doing *something?** This is like asking what's so good about sleep. One could argue that we squander a third of our lives sleeping. But, of course, we know that in the total view of life sleep is not only enjoyable in itself, but is necessary to good health. And so are eating and exercising. Meditation is like these in that it is part of the natural balance of right living. It's healthy to pull the plug on the conceptualizing mind from time to time and give it a rest. But I don't want to give the impression that the value of meditation is because "it's good for you." Undoubtedly meditation *is* "good for you," especially if you are a reasonably normal modern man or woman (which is to say, a tightly wrapped storage chest of tensions and anxieties) but that's beside the point; that's simply an attractive bonus.

In the final analysis, meditation is its own reward. It may be good for you in a practical sense, but that's not why one does it. Sex is undeniably good for you; it's a fine aerobic exercise. But who in their right mind would engage in lovemaking simply because it's good for you? Does that make the point? The same can be said for dancing, or having dinner with friends, or hiking in the mountains. What's so good about the practice of meditation? It helps to relax the tyranny of the thinking mind and restore a more natural state of consciousness that is in harmony with the larger reality. In doing this, the practice of meditation increases the joy of living. In fact, meditation practice may well make the difference between the joy of living, and the agony of living.

Let's end this section where we began, with the basic gatha of *Zen Buddhism*:

> A special transmission outside of scriptures;
> No dependence on words or letters;
> Direct pointing at the mind of man;
> Seeing into one's nature, and the attainment of Buddhahood.

I hope that you see now that this is a beautifully terse statement of the essential character of Zen Buddhism. By declaring the two basic positions, the gatha sets the foundation for all that will come later. We are told that "a direct pointing at the mind of man" (satori) is the sudden way in which awakening shall happen. And also we are told that satori is aroused by "a special transmission outside of scripture." This has been the guiding light of the tradition of Zen Buddhism from the time of Bodhidharma to the present day.

HUINENG (HUI-NENG)

Two great masters shaped the development of Zen (Chan) in its early days: Bodhidharma and Huineng. Bodhidharma is honored as the first patriarch of Zen (Chan) in China. He brought the teaching from India, Buddha's homeland, and planted it in the soil of China. Huineng, the sixth patriarch, in a sense completed the work begun by Bodhidharma. Whereas Bodhidharma was something of a foreign missionary, Huineng was thoroughly Chinese. In the teaching of Huineng, we reach the mature expression of Zen Buddhism,

---

*A popular slogan among meditators these days: "Don't just *do* something; sit there!"

and it had become a decidedly Chinese creation. After Huineng, Zen Buddhism would continue to grow and evolve, but the essential philosophy would not change:

> The figure of the sixth patriarch came to embody a comprehensive and inspiring image of the perfection of Zen—what disciples came to call the "Zen of the Patriarchs." . . . It is the figure of Hui-neng that Zen has elevated to the stature of the Zen Master par excellence. His teachings stand at the source of all the widely diverse currents of Zen Buddhism. (Dumoulin, 123, 137)

The teachings of Huineng are to be found in a long discourse known as *The Sutra of the Sixth Patriarch* (more popularly known as *The Platform Sutra*). This work was lovingly copied and preserved through the early centuries of Zen history and has come down to us in a reasonably complete form. The fact that it is called a sutra is significant. Technically speaking, *sutra* refers to the words of Buddha that have been preserved and ultimately committed to writing. To identify Huineng's discourse as a sutra is to imply a belief that his teaching is perfectly in accord with the teaching of Buddha.

Presumably Bodhidharma departed from China around 530 C.E., turning over the role of patriarch to his chosen successor, Hui Ko. Huineng does not appear on the stage of Zen history until the year 662 C.E., at which time he was accepted as a young novice in the monastery of Hongren (Hung-jen), the fifth patriarch. In the intervening hundred and thirty years, Zen had been growing and establishing its place, but there had been no dramatic changes. The time was ripe for the work of a great leader.

Bodhidharma got the ball rolling in a new direction; he initiated a process of development that would continue through the sixth and seventh centuries, finally reaching completion in the time of the sixth patriarch, Huineng. The traditional way of gradual enlightenment had great appeal, however, and would remain strong well after the time of Bodhidharma. The brotherhood of Zen (Chan) was divided on the issue of gradual versus sudden. The seventh century progressed toward a showdown on this matter. It came to a head in the conflict between Shenxiu (Shen-hsiu) and Huineng. Both men were nominally disciples of Hongren, the fifth patriarch. It's possible that the chroniclers have exaggerated their personal roles in this conflict. They may stand as dramatic symbols of the two sides. In any case, the future of Zen was to be fundamentally shaped by the outcome of this controversy.

It must have looked as if the future belonged to Shenxiu (pronounced Shen-shoo). Shenxiu was a brilliant scholar and a dedicated Buddhist monk. He was the leader of a broadly popular movement within Zen known as the "Northern School." Essentially, though, the Northern School was a refitting of the gradual approach to enlightenment.

Shenxiu accepted without question that at the core of one's being is the Buddha-nature, pure and undefiled. He compared the Buddha-nature to an absolutely perfect mirror, so pure in fact that you don't even know it's there. (This mirror simile, by the way, was originally introduced by the Chinese Daoist philosopher Zhuang Zi.) The purity of the Buddha-nature becomes clouded over with the accumulating "dust" of the thinking mind's attachments, especially the passions of ego. The path to enlightenment is to clean the mind-mirror by long practice of the disciplines, especially meditation. And, once cleaned, it must be watched over and re-cleaned constantly through the continuous practice of meditation. Meditation becomes the all-important discipline. It gradually removes the obstacles—the "dust"—which prevents us from looking within and knowing the Buddha-nature (in other words, from achieving enlightenment). It's an appealing doctrine, especially so to those who had chosen the way of life of the Buddhist monk. Shenxiu's doctrine doesn't exactly negate the teaching of Bodhidharma. It leaves the door open, but clearly the emphasis is on the more traditional Buddhist approach of the gradual way to enlightenment through uncovering the obstacles to it.

The traditional way reached its finest expression in the teaching of Shenxiu. It was taken for granted by his admirers that Shenxiu would become the sixth patriarch; it was only a matter of time. Then, one day, modest little Huineng arrived at the monastery gate. No one would have paid much attention to him at the time. They should have, though; he was destined to win the struggle with the great Shenxiu. It was Huineng who would become the sixth, and last, of the patriarchs and would set the character of Zen Buddhism for all time to come—but not without a struggle.

Like Confucius, Huineng experienced poverty as a child. Both lost their fathers at the age of three, and as his mother was too poor to afford schooling, Huineng remained illiterate. They lived in a small rural village in the south of China, where Huineng helped out by gathering firewood which he sold in the village market. One day, when he was about twenty-four years old, he overheard someone in the marketplace reciting passages from the *Diamond Sutra* (part of the *Prajnaparamita*). One line in particular made a deep impression on him: "Let your mind rise freely, without attaching it to anything." These words had a profound effect on Huineng. Suddenly, the only thing that mattered in life was pursuing the deeper wisdom of the Buddhist scriptures. After seeing to it that his mother was cared for, Huineng set out on the long journey north to the monastery of the Zen Master Hongren, known in Zen history as the fifth patriarch. The monastery, known as Paolinsi, was located in a region of the north known as the Yellow Plum Mountain.

Hongren was a famous man. His monastery was home to five hundred monks. When the humble-looking Huineng arrived and asked to be admitted, he was rebuffed by Hongren. They had no room for an illiterate "barbarian" from the South. Could *anything* good come from the South? Hongren, of course, was following a common procedure in Zen by brusquely turning away someone seeking to become a disciple. It was up to Huineng to persuade the master that he was genuinely sincere. This he did by commenting that north and south is the kind of duality that Buddha taught has no real meaning. In Buddha's teaching, all people are the same. Hongren was immediately impressed by the young man before him and allowed him to join the community. He would not become a monk right away, though. Typically, a novice remained a layperson for several years before being initiated into the brotherhood of monks.

Compared to the others, Huineng was a very humble sort. He was poor, uneducated, couldn't even read or write, and as if that weren't bad enough, he was from the rural South, a region regarded as hillbilly country by the more sophisticated northerners. Presumably Huineng was treated poorly by the monks, who held him in disdain. He was put to work as a rice-pounder, the most menial task in the monastery. This was a job often done by animals, stomping on the dried rice kernels to separate the husks from the grain. Huineng was so small and light that he had to tie a heavy stone weight around his waist when he worked.

On the one hand, this picture of Huineng—the humble, illiterate farm boy despised by his betters—may be entirely accurate. On the other hand, it may be contrived to some extent. Zen has always set itself against the way of the intellectual, favoring instead the way of the innocent and natural person. Heinrich Dumoulin, a modern-day historian of Zen, suggests that the character of the young Huineng may be a carefully fashioned composite of desired elements:

> All the particular features of the story, whether factual or idealized, are fashioned into a composite whole. First we are shown the strong farm boy whose care for his aged mother manifests the filial piety that is so distinctive of the humanity of his people; then there is the image of the illiterate youth, untouched by book learning, a pure child of nature and at the same time a "seeker of Tao."

After Huineng had been working as a rice-pounder for about eight months, an event occurred that was to change the course of Zen. Hongren invited each of the monks to write out a gatha that would summarize his understanding of Zen. If one revealed true enlightenment, that person would be named Hongren's successor and would inherit the much-treasured robe and bowl of Buddha. At that time, the senior monk was Shenxiu. As mentioned before, he was brilliant, dedicated, and much admired by the other monks. Shenxiu was a true scholar, and apparently it was almost taken for granted that he would be Hongren's successor. Shenxiu was a star. None of the other monks even considered writing out a gatha; this was clearly the time for Shenxiu to demonstrate his brilliance and claim the prize that he rightly deserved.

Shenxiu may not have been quite so confident himself. According to one popular version of the story, he composed his gatha during the night and wrote it out with chalk on a monastery wall, but left it unsigned. Perhaps he wanted to see what the reaction would be before claiming it as his own. Here's what he wrote:

> The body is the Bodhi tree,
> The mind is like a clear mirror.
> At all times we must strive to polish it,
> And must not let the dust collect.

The following day everyone was awed by the gatha. There was no doubt who the author was, and praise of Shenxiu's wisdom was on everyone's lips. Hongren also praised Shenxiu, even going so far as to burn incense and conduct a brief ceremony before the gatha. That was for public display; privately he invited Shenxiu to his room for a little talk. Hongren said that the gatha was very good, but it revealed to him that Shenxiu had not yet really attained enlightenment. It were as if he was at the gate, but had not yet entered inside. He encouraged Shenxiu to keep striving and to try the gatha assignment again.

Why do you suppose that Hongren felt that Shenxiu's gatha revealed something less than real enlightenment? Clearly the theme of the gatha was in line with widely held beliefs at the time. Many of the other monks must have been experienced and knowledgeable, yet the general feeling was that Shenxiu had done a remarkable job of capturing the essence of Zen Buddhism.

There was one person, though, who did not agree with Shenxiu's statement at all. Huineng could not have read the gatha himself, but it was the talk of the monastery, and he overheard others repeating it aloud. In his mind, he had been thinking about the assignment, and after hearing what Shenxiu had written he couldn't restrain himself. It was a bold move for a rice-pounder, one who wasn't even a monk, but it was one of those things that just had to be done. He talked one of the monks into writing out his gatha for him in the middle of the night. The next morning the community discovered a new gatha, right there on the wall beside Shenxiu's gatha. It was a response to the statement of Shenxiu. This is what it said:

> Originally there is no tree of enlightenment,
> Nor is there a stand with a clear mirror.
> From the beginning not one thing exists;
> Where, then, is a grain of dust to cling?

The monks were more than a little shocked to discover that Huineng was its author. This time there was no ceremony, no burning of incense, no expressions of praise—but there was a little talk in Hongren's room. Hongren saw at once that modest little Huineng was a genuinely enlightened man. Illiterate rice-pounder though he was, he towered over all of the others in the perfection of his wisdom. And this could cause problems. Given the social politics of the monastery, it would be unthinkable for Hongren to openly declare that Huineng was to be his successor; such an announcement would provoke an uprising. It was almost as if Shenxiu was the leader of a party; his followers would never tolerate his being set aside in favor of this uneducated "barbarian" from the South.

On the other hand, Hongren couldn't deny the succession to the one truly enlightened man in the community, humble though he may be. To keep the peace, he devised a plan. There, in his tiny room in the middle of the night, Hongren invested Huineng with the legitimacy of the succession; Huineng was named the sixth patriarch. He was given the robe and bowl of Buddha, which Hongren had carefully preserved. And then Hongren told Huineng to leave the monastery at once; go back to the South, and stay there out of harm's way until things had cooled off. In time, Hongren hoped, he could persuade the others to accept his choice. Things would work out; Huineng was, after all, the rightful heir to the patriarchate.

Predictably, there was an uproar when the others discovered what Hongren had done. Certain monks, led by one Huiming (Hui-ming), took off immediately after Huineng, hoping to overtake him on the road south. Apparently, some of the followers of Shenxiu felt bold enough to openly defy the master of the monastery. Undoubtedly, there is much to this story that we will never know, but we can assume that the followers of Shenxiu were not willing to tolerate the idea of someone else inheriting the succession. Perhaps they perceived some sort of conflict between Hongren and Shenxiu. Maybe they thought that Hongren was envious of Shenxiu's popularity and had joined some sort of conspiracy to deprive him of what was rightfully his. Why else would he have sent the precious robe of Buddha off with that illiterate rice-pounder in the middle of the night? The insignia of the robe and the bowl were the all-important symbols of the right to preside as patriarch. They must be retrieved at all costs.

Huiming and his companions succeeded in catching up with Huineng. It was in a high pass of the Mount Da Yu region that the meeting took place. Huiming demanded that Huineng return the robe. Presumably the robe was no longer worn; it was a sacred relic, probably folded and wrapped in protective layers. Was it actually Buddha's robe? Who can say? It might have been, but it's doubtful that much would have been left of a simple cloth garment more than a thousand years old. Any old robe, symbolic of Buddha's robe, would have served the purpose just as well. Huineng remained calm. He placed the robe on a large rock, and said in so many words: "This robe is a symbol of our sacred tradition. It must not be an object of violence. It was given to me, and it's wrong for you to take it, but it would be worse still for us to fight over it. Take it, if you must, and go on your way."

According to the legendary story of this encounter, Huiming walked over to the robe and took hold of it, but he couldn't lift it. Try as he might he was unable to budge it from the rock. At last, shaking with fear, he turned to Huineng. "The robe is a symbol of the Truth. It's the Truth I want, not the robe. I thought I came here for the robe, but I see now that I came here for the Truth. Please; show me what it is that I seek."

Huineng's response to this dramatic turnabout was original. He didn't quote from the sutras or anything like that. Instead, he posed a question to Huiming that brought him up short. He asked Huiming a simple question that had the effect of turning his thinking inside out. It was the beginning of a technique that was to become very popular in the evolution of Zen. Huineng approached Huiming and said something like this: "If you wish to see the truth of your own nature, forget about these value judgments of who's right and who's wrong. Instead look deep inside yourself and tell me, what does your original face look like, before you were ever born?"

It's not important that these words do not seem to make sense literally. It was not Huineng's intention to be speaking rationally at that moment. The question was not *meant* to be answered rationally; its purpose was to provoke a certain kind of consciousness in Huiming, which could then open into a higher understanding. And that's exactly what happened. We are told that Huiming experienced enlightenment on the spot. Huineng, the simple man unfettered by scholarly learning, had devised a new and direct way of communicating. Zen would never be the same again.

Huiming returned without the robe, and Huineng continued on to a monastery at Cao Qi (T'sao-ch'i), which would be his new home for the next five years (some say it was closer to sixteen years). During this time, Huineng received full monastic ordination and began to attract a following. Huineng had a new way of getting at the truth of Buddha's teaching. He didn't depend on the sutras, nor on long hours of meditation practice. He focused on loosening the mental straitjacket of our customary way of thinking. A famous example of this occurred one time when Huineng was visiting the monastery of Zhi Zhi (Chih-chih). He encountered three young monks embroiled in a passionate argument concerning the true nature of a wind-ruffled pennant above the roof of one of the buildings. The first monk argued that it was the pennant itself that was flapping. The second monk claimed that it was the wind that was waving. The third monk argued that both were inanimate objects and that neither was flapping. Huineng interrupted them saying, "It is not the wind that flaps, nor is it the pennant that flaps. It is your mind that is flapping."

Eventually, Huineng would return in triumph to the monastery of Paolinsi (Pao-lin-ssu—known in Japanese as the monastery of Horin-ji). Hongren had died in the meantime, and Huineng became the master of the monastery. It was during this time that Huineng delivered his famous discourse known as *The Sutra of the Sixth Patriarch*. Some say that he returned again to the South to spend his last days at Cao Qi. In any case, his body was buried there in a splendid shrine. Huineng died, we are told, in 713 C.E. at about the age of seventy-five. His death was mourned by thousands; he had become a legend in his own time. Huineng was the epitome of what a Zen Master should be. As mentioned earlier, "It is the figure of Huineng that Zen has elevated to the stature of the

Zen Master par excellence. His teaching stands at the source of all the widely diverse currents of Zen Buddhism."

Huineng did not designate a successor; the line of patriarchs came to an end with him. The character of Zen was now fully formed; there was no longer seen to be a need for preserving a distinct line of development.* We may also speculate that Huineng was personally sensitive to the problems that the succession could cause. It could result in political divisions within the brotherhood, and this could lead to violent quarrels between the factions. And the robe of Buddha, meant to be an inspiring symbol of the tradition, could all too easily become a fetish in the minds of many. It had become something to be fought over, and venerated almost as if it possessed magical powers. Add to this the difficulty of caring for it—and the probability that it wasn't really Buddha's robe anyway—and the best course of action became clear to Huineng: Honor the traditions of the past, but allow a new way to open for the future of Zen. Put to rest the elements that could be divisive and misleading and encourage instead that which united the brotherhood, the way of Buddha as preserved in the teaching of Zen.

Hongren was once asked why he made the seemingly unlikely choice of Huineng as his successor. His answer was wonderful. "Of my five hundred disciples four hundred and ninety-nine possessed a remarkable understanding of Zen. Only Huineng did not understand Zen. That's why I chose him." Clearly a facetious reply, but not entirely. Hongren was distinguishing between rational understanding and intuitive understanding. The four hundred and ninety-nine had crafted an impressive intellectual understanding based on knowledge *about* Zen. They knew all about the history and the doctrine and were skillful in the disciplines. In other words, as Zen monks they made an excellent appearance. Huineng, on the other hand, would never be mistaken for a great intellectual. But his understanding transcended the rational and the discursive; his understanding was of the intuitive sort that spontaneously grasped the real nature of Zen consciousness.

It would be a mistake, though, to characterize Zen as antirational, anti-intellectual. Far from it; Zen has a rich tradition of historical and philosophical literature. In fact, it's ironic that Zen—with its "no dependence on words or letters"—in modern times enjoys almost an embarrassment of riches in this respect. It's very important to understand this point; the tradition of Zen Buddhism does not in any way damn the rational thinking mind. It is an excellent human faculty. In its proper sphere, the reasoning ability has much to contribute to life. But the rational thinking mind does have its limitations.

The object of thought is always "things," including ideas. The thinking mind can thus amass great conceptual knowledge concerning everything that may be an object of thought. But that which thinks can never be an object of its own thought, anymore than the eye can see itself. Real self-knowledge, therefore—not conceptual knowledge about the self—depends on a mode of knowing that transcends the limitations of the thinking mind. In the Zen tradition, as in Mahayana generally, this power is known as *prajna*. *Prajna* is the highest wisdom; it is the intuitive, experiential knowing of the seamless unity of being. As mentioned before, the eye of *prajna* opens only when we are willing to let go of our fixation on the activity of the thinking mind. The main thrust of Zen training is to help the student break free of the normal human attachment to discursive thinking. Zen

*Each of Huineng's five principal disciples was said to be the founder of a distinct school of Zen derived from the teaching of the master. Out of respect for their contribution, these men are often referred to as "patriarchs" in the history of Zen Buddhism.

teaches that one will never discover the truth of one's own nature (the Buddha-nature) through the thought processes of the reasoning mind. Awakening is an intuitive leap of insight that completely transcends thought; in fact, it can't occur until one is willing to let go of the grip of the thinking mind. Only when one does that is the eye of *prajna* free to see the truth. *Prajna* is intuitive wisdom. We might say that the opening of the eye of *prajna* is what satori is all about.

Establishing the central importance of the satori experience was the combined work of Bodhidharma and Huineng. Bodhidharma, the first patriarch of Zen in China, began the formative process. Huineng completed the work begun by Bodhidharma. By the time of Huineng's death in 713 C.E., the fundamental nature of Zen was established. Zen (Chan) had become a unique expression of Buddhism within the broad umbrella of Mahayana. Zen would continue to grow and evolve, and is evolving even today, but the original character laid down during the time of Bodhidharma and Huineng has remained a solid and unchanging foundation. This is known as the Zen of the Patriarchs.

Whereas Bodhidharma introduced into China the importance of satori, sudden enlightenment, and taught that this was the correct understanding of how awakening occurs, Huineng went on to clarify, in a sense, the nature of an authentic satori experience. One could conceivably be fooled by the dramatic impact of a powerful insight. Genuine awakening, genuine satori, has about it a particular character. Huineng said it best in his famous wall gatha:

> Originally there is no tree of enlightenment,
> Nor is there a stand with a clear mirror.
> From the beginning not one thing exists;
> Where, then, is a grain of dust to cling?

"From the beginning not one thing exists." Huineng, in opposition to the point of view expressed by Shenxiu, was giving expression to the Doctrine of Emptiness. In doing this, he was reviving a current of philosophical interpretation which the Zen tradition believes can be traced back to Buddha himself. We find elements of it in the *Prajnaparamita*, from which Nagarjuna developed the teaching of *shunyata*. Bodhidharma too was clearly in the spirit of shunyata, though we have only fragments of his words to base this on. One such fragment derives from his conversation with Emperor Wu. Perhaps you will recall his seemingly mysterious answer to Wu's question, "What is the first principle of this holy doctrine?" "Vast emptiness," was Bodhidharma's reply (and, he went on to say, there is nothing holy about it).

The matter of central importance in the teaching of emptiness (*shunyata*) is that nothing—*no-thing*—is real in a substanding sense. No thing is real unto itself. Yet the thinking mind eagerly conceptualizes an objective reality for all that it fastens upon. The thinking mind creates its own personal reality and then creates an attachment to it. (No wonder we have troubles!)

The idea of "mind" is itself one of the *things* that the thinking mind conceptualizes. In an insidious way, this is the strongest of all mental illusions. After all, this is home base. Mind ("my" mind) is what one ordinarily identifies as self and clings to with a psychological death grip. To deny the substanding reality of mind is to pull out the rug—the rug *and* the floor—from under one. There is nothing for the ego to stand on. But that is exactly what the Doctrine of Emptiness does. It flatly denies the independent, substanding reality of mind, thus removing this illusory psychological foundation. True, there is nothing left to stand on, but this is seen as the necessary condition for the awakening of true knowledge—knowledge of the interrelated oneness of all Being. Such knowledge is true wisdom.*

Huineng came to represent what would become the fundamental position of Zen with regard to the nature and attainment of satori. His wall gatha makes the point beautifully. Perhaps this whole matter of Huineng's doctrine of emptiness will make better sense if we look at both gathas side by side.

Shenxiu	*Huineng*
The body is the Bodhi tree,	Originally there is no tree of enlightenment,
The mind is like a clear mirror.	Nor is there a stand with a clear mirror.
At all times we must strive to polish it,	From the beginning not one thing exists;
And must not let the dust collect.	Where, then, is a grain of dust to cling?

In his gatha, Shenxiu clearly treats the mind as a thing; it is an unquestioned assumption. The goal is to see the mind in its original purity, and then continually clean it (wipe away the dust) so that it retains its original purity. In this gatha, Shenxiu was expressing the dominant belief prevailing up to his time:

The position of the Northern school is clearly expressed in Shen-hsiu's [Shenxiu's] metaphor. The mirror of the mind must be wiped clean continually lest the dust of erroneous notions collect on it. This is why one meditates. In such meditation an ongoing process of cleansing takes place until enlightenment is attained. (Dumoulin, 139)

Huineng's gatha was a response to Shenxiu's. As you can see, he flatly rejects the fundamental assumption of Shenxiu's position. One can practice meditation for a thousand years, but will never uncover the "clear mirror" of the mind for the simple reason that mind—as a something in itself—simply does not exist. It is only an idea, and so long as one clings to that illusory idea true awakening will remain forever elusive:

In the dust-wiping type of meditation it is not easy to go further than the tranquilization of the mind; it is so apt to stop short at the stage of quiet contemplation, which is designated by Huineng "the practice of keeping watch over purity." At best it ends in ecstasy, self-absorption, a temporary suspension of consciousness. There is no "seeing" in it, no knowing of itself, no active grasping of self-nature, no spontaneous functioning of it, no *chen-hsing* ("Seeing into Nature") whatever. The dust-wiping type is therefore the art of

---

*The late Alan Watts used to say that when the solid floor beneath us gives way and we are falling blindly with no place to stand, and we realize that we have absolutely no control at all; then, finally, we can just relax and enjoy the ride.

binding oneself with a self-created rope, an artificial construction which obstructs the way to emancipation. No wonder that Huineng and his followers attacked the Purity school. (D. T. Suzuki, 176)

Plainly, Huineng asserts that there is no causal connection whatsoever between meditation and awakening. Shenxiu and his followers in the Northern School are mistaken; the experience of awakening is not dependent on meditation. Awakening happens—if it happens—when the person is ripe for the experience. One can no more work to achieve awakening than can a sleeping person deliberately work at achieving the event of awakening in the morning. It simply happens when it happens—spontaneously.

Huineng dismissed the attitude of the Northern School regarding the practice of meditation, but he did not condemn meditation altogether. Presumably Huineng did not personally find satisfaction in long hours of sitting meditation—certainly not to the extent that Bodhidharma did—but he, and the Southern School generally, were open to the possibility that under the right conditions meditation practice could be very valuable. And in fact, meditation practice (*zazen*) has always been a highly important part of Zen practice.

The lifestyle of a Zen Buddhist, in accord with the general principles laid down by Shakyamuni Buddha himself, is geared to freeing oneself from bondage to the ego-attachments and aversions generated by the thinking mind. The whole Zen Buddhist way of life works to achieve this transformation of consciousness. Properly understood, everything becomes a meditation exercise: working, eating, walking, studying, sweeping, *everything*! Little by little one is loosening the grip of the ego-centered thinking mind and thus creating a more receptive condition for the occasion of satori. This may or may not occur; one has no control over that, but one does have a measure of control with regard to a lifestyle that is more or less receptive to it. I would compare it to the matter of love. There is nothing in the world that you can do to *make* love happen. It springs into being, or it doesn't; it's not under your control. But there are many things you can do to influence the environment (so to speak), to improve the conditions right for it.

Meditation practice must be seen in this light. Again, everything becomes a meditation practice. But sometimes—not all the time, but some of the time—it is appropriate, and profoundly enjoyable, to just sit quietly for a while doing nothing, allowing your consciousness to turn deeply inward. Not everyone responds in the same way to this, but most people, once they get used to it, find the daily practice of sitting meditation to be a wonderful part of the total lifestyle of Zen Buddhism. The goal, of course, is not to find that "mind-mirror" down there beneath all the rubble of the thinking mind; Huineng took care of that misconception long ago. In fact, there is no goal; it is an experience that can be a boundless joy unto itself. "The fruit drops when it is ripe." The entire way of life of Zen Buddhism, including the practice of meditation, has the effect of nourishing the soil, and thus the tree—and thus the fruit.

AFTER HUINENG

This would be a good place to step back for a moment and take in the broad view, the Big Picture, that shows the relationship of Zen Buddhism to the larger story that it is a part of. The Asia map (p. 130) will be helpful in doing this.

Over many centuries, the people of China had developed the arts of civilization to a high level and had evolved a society that was culturally and politically united. Chinese civilization had spread out to establish its homeland throughout the great river valleys of the far eastern part of the Eurasian continent. The land area of China was vast, but it was nonetheless defined rather clearly by geography. In all directions, the land of China ultimately gave way to the mountains of the south, more mountains as well as forests and deserts to the west, the high plains of the north, and, of course, the ocean to the east. So far as the people of China were concerned, these frontiers marked the limits of the civilized world. Beyond the pale were the "barbarian" lands. These neighboring people, however, borrowed much from Chinese civilization; it was the cultural fountainhead whose waters nourished everyone. Thus the Chinese came to regard their own land as the "Central Kingdom." Chinese civilization could go about its way of life, serene, superior, and securely situated at the center of the universe. Well, not entirely secure. As we have seen, one of those "barbarian" frontiers refused to remain obligingly peaceful and subordinate.

To the north of China were the vast steppe lands of northcentral and northeastern Eurasia. This was the trackless homeland of the people known to history as the Mongols. They were a conglomerate of nomadic tribal peoples, and their numbers were beyond counting. The Mongols' way of life was much like that of the nomadic Aryans, with whom this story began many pages ago. From time to time, mounting pressures would unleash migrating waves of these nomadic people onto the lands of their agricultural neighbors. Whereas Aryan predations were directed toward India and the western parts of Eurasia, the Mongols' land of opportunity was southward into the great civilization of China. The Huns had been a Mongol people, and the Great Wall of China was constructed to hold them back. It helped the Han emperors keep the peace for more than four hundred years before finally being overwhelmed. Eventually peace and order returned to China, and the northern defenses were reconstructed. But the pressure began to build again, and in the twelfth century, Mongol horsemen again swept down from the north. Within about a century, they had extended their rule over much of China, bringing down the curtain on a particular era of Chinese history. It had been during this era, more specifically known as the Tang and the Song dynasties, that the great story of the early development of Zen Buddhism in China had been played out.

The historical dates of the Tang (T'ang) dynasty are 618 C.E. to 907 C.E. Bodhidharma had set the course of Zen (Chan) in the century preceding the formation of Tang, but for the most part, the initial developmental stage of Zen, the "Age of the Patriarchs," was in the time of Tang. This was a wonderfully creative period; some regard it as the high-water mark of Chinese civilization. The late Tang was the "golden age" of Zen Buddhism (Chan Buddhism) as well. After a brief time of internal disorder in the early tenth century, the more military-oriented Song dynasty became established in 960 C.E. Among other things, the Song emperors had the job of holding back the Mongol hordes, which they succeeded in doing until 1129 C.E., at which time the dam broke and the entire northern part of the empire was lost to the invaders. The court retreated to the south where the dynasty, known as the "Southern Song," continued to rule for another century and a half. The Mongols, though, eventually conquered much of the south as well, creating a new Chinese-Mongol empire known in history as the Yuan dynasty.

Yuan came into existence in 1280 C.E. and would rule China for a century. The first of the Yuan emperors was that intriguing character we know as Kublai Khan. Kublai Khan, being essentially a foreign conqueror, found it expedient to employ many non-Chinese in high government posts. Perhaps he felt more secure that way. One of his highly placed foreigners, incidentally, was a young merchant traveler named Marco Polo from a very, very faraway place named Venice. Marco Polo was one of the first Europeans to visit the empire of China, and when he finally returned to Venice, his countrymen found it hard to believe his stories about the dazzling refinements of Chinese civilization.* Only two centuries later, though, another of his countrymen, Christopher Columbus by name, took Polo's stories very seriously and risked everything on a daring sea voyage which hopefully would find a direct route to the rich land of China. In addition to Polo's book, Columbus carried with him a letter from the Queen of Spain, introducing him to the emperor of China. It's a wonderful story; all the strands are woven together like a tapestry. But now let's get back to that part of this history which we call Zen Buddhism.

Once again, Zen as a distinct school of Buddhism took form in China during the six centuries prior to the Mongol conquest—that is to say, during the time of the Tang and Song Dynasties. During the first part of this period, the time of the six patriarchs, the basic character of Zen (Chan) was established. By the time of the death of Huineng in 713 C.E., the various factions within Zen had come together. The controversies that had formerly divided the Zen movement into a Northern School and a Southern School had been resolved, and what came to be called the "Zen of the Patriarchs" gave a unity of doctrine and practice to all men and women who followed the way of Zen.

There were several features that gave Zen its distinct character within the broad umbrella of Buddhism. Most fundamental of all was the Zen emphasis on satori, sudden awakening. Various Buddhist disciplines, including meditation, might have a role to play, but no practice can *achieve* awakening. Through the guidance of an already awakened teacher, an individual can be urged to the state wherein he or she may be willing to let go of attachment-to-self and suddenly and spontaneously see the real truth of one's nature. The real truth is, of course, the Buddha-nature, which is the common essence of all beings, hidden from us only by our ignorance and the fear born of that ignorance.

The time following the death of Huineng was a time of consolidation and enrichment for Zen Buddhism. Daoist influences, always strong within the culture of China, were richly woven into the fabric of Zen during this time. Zen experienced near-explosive growth during the late Tang and Song periods. Zen was far from being the only Buddhist sect in China, though. Early Zen itself had been richly influenced by Tiantai Buddhism, the most prominent school of Buddhism in China at that time. In fact, Buddhist groups were so numerous and diverse as to be likened to the trees of a forest. Zen was only one part of the forest—an important part to be sure—but just one part nonetheless.

Not all Buddhists were (or are) monks. One of the great attractions of Mahayana Buddhism was that it offered something for everyone. Laymen and women could also enjoy a rich Buddhist way of life. But those few who were willing to give up everything and dedicate their lives one hundred percent to practicing the Buddhist disciplines—in other words, the monks—would remain at the core of the movement.

From the very beginning of Buddhism in China, dedicated men and women formed themselves into monastic communities.† We have encountered references to monasteries

---

*Some wonder if Marco Polo ever really made his famous trip to China at all. Perhaps he made up the whole thing, basing the story on accounts he heard from other travelers. Doesn't it seem odd that he would have so much to say about food and never even mention the use of chopsticks (*kuaizi*)?

†By the way, the word *monk* can refer to either a man or a woman, but it has become customary to use the more familiar word *nun* when referring to a woman. This too can carry some unfortunately misleading connotations.

often in the story of Buddhism's evolution in China. Bodhidharma, for example, stayed for nine years at the "monastery" of Shaolinsi. But the early monasteries were little more than loosely organized communities of men (or, in some cases, women) who shared a common interest in following the Buddhist way of life as best they understood it. As in the ashram, the role of the leader was all-important. Undoubtedly, there was a large amount of personal freedom in such communities. During the late Tang, and especially during the Song periods, there was a great proliferation of Buddhist monasteries throughout China. Hilltops were favored sites, as often as not to leave the more fertile low regions available for agriculture. Hilltops throughout China were blossoming forth in Buddhist monasteries. With this increase in the number of monasteries came, for better or for worse, a general tightening of monastic discipline. Zen monastic discipline also underwent a transformation at this time.

In the late eighth century, a Zen Master named Paijing (Pai-Jing) formulated a discipline for his own monastery that was soon being adopted by virtually all Zen monasteries. It was known as the "Pure Rule of Paijing," and it did for Zen Buddhism in China what the "Rule of Saint Benedict," the founder of the Benedictine Order, did for Christian monasticism in far-off Europe. (There is an interesting similarity between these monastic rules, but it is due only to coincidence. There is no reasonable possibility that at that time they could have influenced one another.) The Rule of Paijing adapted the traditional Buddhist vinaya to a fully worked-out regimen for daily life in the monastery. It was the beginning of the monastic system that is still followed today in most Zen monasteries. Paijing gave special emphasis to the importance of manual labor. The Zen community must be fully self-supporting. Mendicancy would cease to have a necessary place in the life of a Zen Buddhist monk, although a purely ritualized mendicancy would continue to be practiced by most Zen monasteries. Paijing is credited with laying down the maxim, "A day without working is a day without eating." But it wasn't just the practical need for labor that Paijing emphasized. He made work an important and dignified part of a monk's normal daily life. Instead of being something to be despised, something seen as appropriate only for the humbler classes of society, manual labor of all kinds became an excellent form of active meditation. From that day to this, physical work became an essential part of the daily organization of every Zen monastic community; it is looked upon as honorable and joyful.

During this time of expansion, the "forest" of Buddhism spread not only throughout China, but began to spread as well into some of the lands beyond China. To the south, Chinese Buddhism spread into Viet Nam and in the northwest into Korea. It was from Korea that Chinese-style Buddhism would first begin to influence the world of Japan. Japan, at this time in its history, was hungrily absorbing all that it could from the civilization of China. The Japanese cultural appetite was insatiable, and Buddhist ideas became an important part of the feast. In the year 801 C.E., a Japanese Buddhist named Saicho arrived in China for a four-year stay. He visited many monasteries, studying the teachings of different schools of Buddhism. His focus of study, though, was Tiantai, and when he returned to Japan he founded what came to be known as Tendai Buddhism. This was something of a syncretism of Chinese Buddhism with a strong emphasis on the more "religious" and supernatural aspects then common in some schools of Chinese Buddhism. Tendai with its strong mass appeal laid the foundation of the Buddhist tradition in Japan; Zen would later have to compete with it. Japan was home to many Tendai monasteries when Zen first began to sink roots in that country in the twelfth century. But that's getting ahead of the story.

The Zen emphasis on self-sufficiency turned out to be a lifesaver. In the middle of the ninth century, something unexpected and horrible happened to Buddhism in China. The Tang emperor Wu Zung ascended to the throne in 841 C.E., and he immediately launched what Buddhists refer to as the Great Persecution. (Recall that very much the same sort of thing had happened almost exactly four hundred years before.) The Great Persecution of Wu Zung occurred at the same time that the persecution of Lang Darma was raging in Tibet. Perhaps the Tibetan persecution helped to evoke its companion in China.

It seems that Wu Zung was determined to wipe out Buddhism altogether in the land that he ruled. His reign, mercifully, lasted for only five years, and his successor quickly put an end to the persecution, but in those few years, Wu Zung clear-cut the forest of Buddhism in China, and many Buddhist organizations never recovered from the devastation. He forced more than 200,000 monks to give up the monastic way of life and return to their families. More than 4,000 monasteries were closed, most of the land being confiscated and sold. These are staggering numbers! However, much as Wu Zung was determined to stamp out Buddhism, there was at least some civilized touch in his method. For one thing, the monks were not slaughtered as they had been in the fifth century; they were simply required to go back to their family homes. And monks who were too old or too sick to be able to work were allowed to live out their final years in a few special monasteries that were spared for this purpose. So, it would seem that real hatred was not the motivating force behind the persecution.

Why, then, did Wu Zung so fervently wish to expunge Buddhism from China? We can only guess, but some things seem pretty clear. In the first place, Wu Zung was not acting entirely alone in this matter. He was the leader of an anti-Buddhist movement made up of some Daoists, some Confucians, and probably a fair percentage of the common people as well. This group within the Chinese population perceived Buddhism as a threat: a threat to themselves personally and to the much-loved traditions of Chinese culture. When one of their own became emperor, the time to act was at hand.

As we have seen, from the very beginning there had been tension between the Buddhists on the one hand and the Chinese Daoists and Confucians on the other. Despite the strong cross-fertilizing influences between Buddhism and Daoism, and even between Buddhism and Confucianism, there remained many Daoists and Confucians who harbored negative feelings toward this "foreign" philosophy. This was especially true among Confucian scholars who enjoyed a virtual monopoly of government positions. So long as the Buddhist movement remained relatively small in China, the conflict could be contained. But during the Tang period, Buddhism began to grow very rapidly in China.

More specifically, it was Buddhist *monasticism* that was growing rapidly. Confucians in government, and leaders of Daoist organizations, probably did not feel threatened by the philosophy of Buddhism in general, but rather by the "institutional" power of the Buddhist monasteries. These were specifically defined centers of Buddhist influence and potential political power. At least that's how non-Buddhists might well have seen them. And the Buddhists were increasing in numbers at an alarming rate. In the eyes of the anti-Buddhists, the Buddhist monastery system threatened to overwhelm the traditional institutions of Chinese culture. The movement must be halted before it was too late. Wu Zung and company looked upon Buddhist monasticism as if it were an unhealthy foreign weed that had invaded the soil of China. Exterminate it, and the soil could once again nourish the native plants (Confucianism and Daoism, for example) that were age-old products of Chinese culture and were thus much better suited to meet the needs of society. Better work fast, though; exterminate it quickly before its defenders could mount a counterattack, as had happened in the fifth century.

That was the setting in which the Great Persecution occurred. All that was needed was a rationale that would (hopefully) find broad support among the common people. To justify the closings of the monasteries, Wu Zung focused on the alleged threat they posed to the social order. (As we have seen in recent history, this was an argument that would prove useful again in the twentieth century.) This is not to say that the rationale was insincere. Ardent Daoist that he was, Wu Zung was presumably fully sincere in arguing that the Buddhist movement posed a threat to the social order. How reasonable that point of view was, though, is another matter altogether.

Wu Zung's argument, somewhat of a replay of 445 C.E., would have gone something like this. Above all else, the Buddhist monastery system posed a dire threat to the institution of the family. Absolutely nothing in Chinese civilization (then as now) is of greater fundamental importance than the family. It is the bedrock foundation of the culture. The birth of children is what maintains a family over the generations. They are lovingly raised and nourished in the culture, and the expectation is that they will play a role for life in the support and maintenance of the family. The family is what gives the individual identity. This is especially important in an agricultural economy. The loss of a son through war or illness is a severe blow.

And then another sort of sinister influence entered the scene. Sons in many families were being lured away by the appeal of the monastic life. (The reason for such appeal is not easily defined; it resides deep in the heart of each individual who answers the call.) The Buddhist monk gives up the ties to his family completely; he becomes literally a "homeless" person. He voluntarily departs, depriving his loved ones not only of the warmth of his company, but also of his contribution to the work of the family. Off he goes to join another "family," a community of monks. Their life of celibacy assures that they won't even replace themselves, but will forever drain away a percentage of the productive young men from the families and villages of China.

And what of the monasteries themselves? These were not productive centers, viable alternatives to the agricultural villages they drew their membership from. With few exceptions (such as Zen monasteries), the monastic communities were actually parasitic. They depended on the generosity of others for their sustenance. And what did they give in return? Many were exempt even from paying taxes. Their members, arguing that they had "left society," claimed that they were thus exempt from rendering homage to the ruler and also that they were exempt from levies for providing military or social services. To the cold eye of an outsider, a typical Buddhist monastery might appear to be a totally unproductive institution made up only of individuals who wished to escape from reality and the work of human life. The seeming preoccupation with meditation practice would only reinforce this prejudice. Only one thing to do—strike it out. And Wu Zung struck.

When the dust finally settled after Wu Zung's death in 846 C.E., Buddhist monasticism in China had been dealt a devastating blow. Perhaps his crusade went too far too fast. There was a countermove when Wu Zung died, and as mentioned before, his successor quickly clamped the lid on the campaign against the monasteries. But it was too late for many; their membership was scattered, their property confiscated or destroyed. Zen, however, came through the ordeal without being badly injured at all. Only Zen Buddhism and Pure Land Buddhism, the two extremes of the Buddhist movement, escaped devastation during the Great Persecution.

Zen monasteries had been able to keep a low profile, partly because they preferred very remote locations, and also because the Zen discipline emphasized self-sufficiency. Since Zen monasteries were accustomed to providing all of their own needs, they could more or less pull into their shells and wait out bad times. We can also speculate that Zen monasteries were well-respected by the general population in the areas where they were located.

In any case, Chinese Buddhism in general experienced a major die-off as a result of the Great Persecution and thus went through something of an "evolutionary bottleneck" in the mid-ninth century. The principal survivors—again, Pure Land Buddhism and Zen Buddhism—did the natural thing and began to expand rapidly to fill the void. This helps to explain why Zen played such an important role in Chinese Buddhism by the time of the late Tang period. In early Tang, Zen was only one small part of the forest, but by late Tang, much of the forest consisted of the various "schools" of Zen.

It would not be appropriate to the scope of this work to go into detail regarding the various divisions that evolved within Zen Buddhism in the Tang and Song periods. Suffice it to say, for the record, that five major "schools" of Zen emerged. All were derived from the teaching of Huineng. These five were not in conflict; they got along together quite well, but each emphasized a somewhat different philosophical approach. The five would ultimately be reduced to two, and these two would flourish and come to dominate the world of Zen Buddhism up to the present time. This twofold division seems, mysteriously, to represent something basic in nature; it keeps re-emerging. It seems that whenever one side manages to conquer the other and absorb it—as the Southern School did to the Northern School—before long, the resultant unity splits itself into a new twosome. Perhaps it accords to some fundamental duality in the nature of the human psyche.

The split in Zen was expressed in the formation of *Soto Zen* and *Rinzai Zen*. Soto and Rinzai are the Japanese names, which are more familiar to the modern reader. The development of Soto and Rinzai, though, began in China during the late Tang period where they were, of course, known by their original Chinese names. (In Chinese, *Soto* becomes *Caodao* in the pinyin system; *Ts'ao-tao* in the Wade-Giles system. *Rinzai* becomes *Linji* in pinyin; *Lin-chi* in Wade-Giles.)

The split between Soto and Rinzai is suggestive of the earlier division between the Northern School and the Southern School. In this comparison, Soto would be more akin to the Northern School and Rinzai to the Southern School. The resemblance, though, is only superficial. Soto and Rinzai have always been in fundamental agreement as to the nature of enlightenment. The differences between the two are almost entirely concerned with what are seen to be appropriate disciplines, especially with regard to the place of meditation practice.

Soto's resemblance to the Northern School is due largely to the great importance placed on sitting meditation, zazen, in daily life. But Soto did not revert to the "dust-wiping" interpretation of meditation practice that we found in the Northern School. Rather, Soto emphasized what was called "quiet illumination," meaning simply that long practice of zazen could create the perfectly "quiet" state of consciousness most conducive to the arising of satori. The rival (if I may call it that) Rinzai school took very strong exception to this position. They contended that a preoccupation with zazen did not encourage illumination, "quiet" or otherwise; it produced only a state of peaceful tranquilization. Here's what the Rinzai monk, Ta-Hui, had to say about Soto:

> Recently a type of heterodox Zen has grown up in the forest of Zen. By confusing the sickness with the remedy, they have denied the experience of enlightenment. . . . Because they have not experienced enlightenment, they think others have not either. Stubbornly they contend that an empty silence and a musty state of unconsciousness is the original realm of the absolute. To eat their rice twice a day and to sit without thoughts in meditation is what they call complete peace. (quoted in Dumoulin, 257)

And so the argument continues: to sit or not to sit? Perhaps, as mentioned before, the controversy ultimately boils down to a basic difference in human personalities. One type, which benefits tremendously from the more contemplative and introverted approach, will incline toward Soto. Another, which prefers a more active approach, will choose Rinzai. Both Soto and Rinzai, though, respect the elementary power of zazen; it's a matter of emphasis. The debate is as much alive today as it ever was. By coincidence, two modern Japanese Zen Masters who have had much to do with transplanting Zen to the West were both named Suzuki. Daisetz T. Suzuki, of the Rinzai school, was a Zen scholar whose writings have greatly influenced Western students of Zen. He was personally much opposed to the practice of sitting meditation and may have inadvertently created a somewhat mistaken impression regarding the attitude of Zen in general on this matter. Shunryu Suzuki Roshi, a modern Soto Zen Master and founder of the Zen Center of San Francisco, very nicely put the whole matter of zazen in perspective:

> If you think you will get something from practicing zazen, already you are involved in impure practice. . . . When you practice zazen, just practice zazen. If enlightenment comes, it just comes. We should not attach to the attainment. The true quality of zazen is always there, even if you are not aware of it. Just do it. (155)

Soto and Rinzai are the right and left hands of Zen Buddhism. It would be seriously missing the point to think of one as better or more correct than the other. It comes down to a matter of where a given individual fits best. We will have more to say about Soto Zen later on. For now, let's turn to the development of the Rinzai tradition, which played a more dynamic role in the story of Zen's evolution in China.

The putative founder of the Rinzai school was one of the truly great characters in the history of Zen Buddhism. His name was Linji (Lin-chi). (To be more technically accurate, his name was Yi Xuan; Linji was the name of the monastery he headed, but he is universally referred to by the name Linji. "Rinzai" is simply our spelling for the way in which the Chinese name *Linji* was rendered in Japanese.) Linji was also a product of the ninth century, the end-time of the formerly splendid Tang dynasty. He died, probably in his mid-fifties, in 867 C.E. Most of what we know about his teachings are preserved in the *Rinzairoku*, the Japanese name for a collection of Linji's discourses.

Linji was interested in nothing less than creating a new kind of person—a genuine man or woman of Zen. He used the term *true human*. Linji borrowed this term from Daoism, which philosophy heavily influenced his thinking. In a way, Linji brought to fruition the long Buddhist love affair with Daoism. Zen Buddhism, as a way of daily life, was seen to be an excellent vehicle for becoming a true human—a man or woman of Dao.

According to the teaching of Linji, the true human was first and foremost an ordinary person. Linji insisted that "in no way is the true human anything special." Special, in this sense, means that he (or she) was not interested in such artificial things as wealth or rank in society. The true human was free of attachments, natural and simple in lifestyle, moving through daily life in a relaxed, cheerful manner. Linji further described such a person as "without root, without source, and without any dwelling place, yet brisk and lively." Linji's true human was a natural man (or natural woman) at peace with the ultimate emptiness of reality and thus free to wander cheerfully through the mysterious adventure of human life.

Linji's true human was the beginning of that characteristically Zen type which even to this day gives a special and refreshing kind of charm to Zen Buddhism. (More than anything else it was the ideal of this "Zen hobo" that inspired an interest in Zen among the younger generation of the West in the mid-twentieth century. Jack Kerouac is an excellent example.) This Zen *bikkhu* was a very different kind of person from the more traditional monk, who by comparison was something of a monastic recluse withdrawn into an interior world of meditation. The character of the traditional Buddhist monk, including Zen monks, may well have played a part in the negative attitude that allowed Wu Zung's persecution to occur. And that very attitude may have influenced Linji's eagerness to fashion a "new man": a Buddhist monk who *really was* an embodiment of the Daoist ideal. Linji's dates would certainly support this speculation.

> The way of the true human (the "Zen person") was, of course, opened up through awakening to the truth of one's nature; through seeing experientially that one's personal being is one with the universal Buddha-nature. Linji played down the use of such terms as "enlightenment" and "satori." Awakening, however, whether talked about or not, was naturally a matter of prime concern to Linji. He, though, would employ a very different approach where his own students were concerned. Linji felt only scorn for those schools of Zen (including the newly forming Soto) which emphasized long hours of meditation. "Having stuffed themselves with food, [they] sit down to meditate and practice contemplation; arresting the flow of thought they don't let it rise; they hate noise and seek stillness. This is the method of the heretics!" (quoted in Dumoulin, 194)

Well, "heretics" may be overstating it, but it certainly wasn't overstating the intensity of Linji's personal feelings on the subject. He wanted a dynamic approach to Zen, as opposed to what he saw as quietism in others. Linji kept urging his disciples to believe in themselves, to give up running around searching for truth outside themselves. His way of encouraging his students was also new and was the beginning of a tradition in Zen instruction that is often rather shocking to a person new to Zen study. Linji was not at all reluctant to strike his students with his staff, strike them hard. Or, he would come up close and shout at them, shout so loudly that one student complained that he couldn't hear anything but a ringing in his ears for three days. Linji really loved the technique of shouting. Consider this passage from the *Rinzairoku*:

> Sometimes a shout is like the jeweled sword of the Vajra King;
> Sometimes a shout is like the golden-haired lion crouching on the ground;
> Sometimes a shout is like a weed-tipped fishing pole;
> Sometimes a shout doesn't function as a shout.

A shout "doesn't function as a shout," presumably, when it's intended that it function as something else. The real purpose of the blows and the shouts was to jolt the student out of his state of ego self-hypnosis. Naturally, this had to be artfully timed and delivered. Only a Zen Master like Linji could work such a technique effectively. Actually, Linji learned to use the rough stuff from his own guru, Ma Zi (Ma-tsu). Ma Zi is another interesting personality who was said to be able to stick out his tongue so far that he could cover his nose. (If you're not impressed, try doing it.) In addition to kicks and shouts, Ma Zi would sometimes grab a student's nose and twist it so hard that the person would cry out in pain.

I'm sure you're wondering if all this violence is really necessary. And the answer, of course, is no. But it was a specialized technique that became enormously popular as Linji's reputation spread. It was a dramatic way of emphasizing the new active approach to Zen as opposed to the more traditional passive approach. One can't help but assume that to some degree Linchi's dynamic approach was a response to the recent Great Persecution. A big part of the problem had been the popular perception of Buddhism. It probably appeared to outsiders to be far to quiescent, empty of vital energy. Linchi was moved to change that image entirely.

There is something intriguing about Linchi's approach. Direct physical involvement can break through in a way that mere words never will. Sometimes a student can be on the verge of awakening, but somehow unable to go the final step. The discomfort of a blow from the master's staff is a trifling matter if it succeeds in breaking the mental knot of ego-frustration. Let's face it; nothing jolts one into the here and now more abruptly than a sudden kick or a blow on the head. This technique remained popular, particularly in Rinzai monasteries, when Zen spread to Japan, but the modern Western world would seem to want no part of it.

Beginning in the time of Linji, the Rinzai tradition was grounded solidly on the basic Zen premise of satori, sudden enlightenment. Thus Rinzai teachers were interested in methods that would get at satori in a more direct way than the path of meditation. They preferred techniques that would jolt the mind out of its customary fixation on discursive thought. Blows and shouts could be helpful in this, but there was another method which in the long run was seen to be far more effective. In time, it would become the very trademark of the Rinzai approach. We can most simply describe this method as the "Zen paradox." The Zen Master, by skillfully employing paradoxical statements and questions, attempts to suddenly jolt the mind of the student out of its normal rational mode of thinking and open it to an insight of a higher truth. This can be a progressive process, culminating ultimately in the opening of *prajna*, perfect satori.

The finest form of the "Zen paradox" is the *koan* (*gongan* in Chinese), a particular kind of question or riddle which cannot be solved rationally. In the hands of a skillful master, the koan (pronounced "koh-ahn") becomes a razor-sharp knife for cutting through the knots of the thinking mind. The "Zen paradox," though, includes much more than the koan; there is a great wealth of Zen stories and one-liners out of which most of the popular koans have evolved. Before examining this matter of the koan, let's look at a few representative Zen stories. Again, these are popular tales, drawn from the long tradition of Zen, which are paradoxical in nature. They might seem ridiculous in the everyday rational sense, but it is that very nonsensical feature which attempts to open the mind to a meaning *outside* the rational. It is truly said that the essence of Zen is condensed in the Zen story.

Huineng's encounter with the three students who were arguing about the flapping pennant is an excellent example of a Zen story. In another story involving three students, a Zen Master approached the monks to test their understanding of Zen. He picked up a ricecake, and holding it out to the first monk said, "What is this?" The flustered monk replied, "It's a ricecake, sir." The master shouted, "You fool!" and cracked him on the head with his staff. Then he asked the second monk, "What's this?" The second monk didn't say anything. He simply picked up the ricecake and took a big bite out of it. "Not bad; not bad," the master muttered. Then he turned to the third monk, who without waiting to be asked, took the ricecake and placing it on the top of his head walked out of the room like a duck. "Now that man understands Zen," the master said.

Don't feel dismayed if you don't "get it." Zen stories are not jokes with punch lines (although that's another genre in itself). These stories are *meant* to be illogical. In each case, the Zen Master is looking for an expression, a *demonstration* of the other person's understanding of Zen. Seemingly strange behavior or words can be that demonstration. In a way, we are eavesdropping on the Zen Master's conversation.

Zen Master Nanchuan (Nan-ch'uan), a contemporary of Linji, called his disciples together in order to test their understanding of Zen. Nanchuan was sitting in front of the group, holding one of the monastery cats in his lap. Suddenly he stood up, holding the cat high in one hand and a large knife in the other. "Anyone: Give me a true expression of Zen, or I will kill the cat!" The startled group of disciples remained silent. After a long moment, the master sliced the cat in two. That evening, Nanchuan was telling the story of the cat to Zhao Zhou, one of his more advanced disciples, who had been away for the day. Without saying anything, Zhao Zhou took off his sandals, and putting them on top of his head walked out of the room. "Oh, if only you had been there this afternoon," Nanchuan sighed. "That cat would still be alive."

I don't mean to give the impression that the "right" thing to do is to put something on your head and walk out of the room. These two stories just happen to end that way. Nor do I mean to suggest that Nanchuan really killed a cat to make his point. Maybe he did, but it's not likely that a Zen Master would do a thing like that. It makes a good story, though.

Zen Master Zhu Zhi (Chu-chih) was a quiet sort of person. When a student would ask him a question, he would often answer by simply smiling and raising his index finger; that's all, just slightly raising the finger. One day he caught one of his disciples imitating him. Zhu Zhi grabbed a kitchen knife and cut off the offending finger. In shock and pain the disciple howled, "Why did you do that?" Zhu Zhi's answer was simply to smile and raise his finger. In that instant, the disciple achieved awakening.

Zen Master Bozhang (Po-chang) was very popular. His monastery grew so large that he decided to split the group in two, opening a new monastery not far away. He called his disciples together in order to select a master for the new monastery. He placed a large water pitcher on the floor in front of the group. "What is this?" he asked. The head monk was the first to speak. "Well, it's definitely not a piece of wood." The master was not impressed. The monastery cook, who had been standing at the back of the group, walked up to the pitcher and kicked it over; then he left the room. Bozhang made him the master of the new monastery (after an account in Watts, 129).

Many Zen stories include humor. In fact, the love of laughter is one of the most significant characteristics of Zen—and one of the most unusual. As R. H. Blythe points out, "It is possible to read the Bible without a smile and the Koran without a chuckle; no one has died laughing while reading Buddhist sutras. But Zen abounds in anecdotes that stimulate the diaphragm. Enlightenment is frequently accompanied by laughter of a transcendental kind which may further be described as a laughter of surprised approval." Throughout the ages, one of the best authentic demonstrations of Zen has been simply to break out in a genuine hard laugh. (Better even than putting your shoes on your head and walking out of the room like a duck.) A very popular pair in the Zen tradition are the two monks Kanzen and Jittoku. These two "happy lunatics" would bum around together laughing uproariously at everything they encountered: falling leaves, birds, broken chairs, even the full moon. No, they did not have the help of drugs; it was just their nature to see the humor in everything. This attitude is much admired in Zen.

Do you remember Ma Zi, the one who could cover his nose with his tongue? One of his monks asked him for help with the koan he had been working on. Ma Zi reminded him that he was supposed to bow deeply before addressing the master. The monk immediately bowed very deeply, and Ma Zi snuck around behind him and gave him a hard kick in the pants. The kick did the trick; the monk attained immediate enlightenment. It was the humor of it, though, that made it effective. "Since I received that kick from Ma Zi," the monk told everyone, "I haven't been able to stop laughing."

In their search for ways to jolt the student into satori, no device has served Rinzai masters better than the koan. This is the most unusual and intriguing aspect of Rinzai Zen Buddhism. As mentioned, the word *koan* is the Japanese form of the Chinese term *gongan*, which originally referred to a "public announcement." In the Zen tradition, though, the word came to refer to a sort of riddle that was designed to defeat the dominance of the discursive intellect and thus allow the student to open up to an insight of the greater nonrational nature of reality. A koan exercise is given to a student by a Zen teacher. In "solving" the koan the student, in effect, comes to share the state of mind of the teacher. The koan, therefore, is a dynamic tool that the skilled teacher uses to bring the student to satori.

To a large degree, the Rinzai tradition developed out of an effort to put new life— new direction—into the Zen movement and prevent it from slipping into the "quietism" that could lead to stagnation. Masters such as Linji scoured the accumulated lore of the Zen tradition looking for stories and insightful sayings that could be used as pointers in the guidance of Zen disciples. Items that emphasized the "Zen paradox" were particularly favored, and out of this, the way of the Zen koan was born.

A koan can be a simple question, such as the one that has become a veritable cliche, "What is the sound of one hand clapping?" One of Huineng's questions became a very popular koan, often assigned to beginning students in Rinzai monasteries. "What is your original face, even before your parents were born?" Much more often, though, a koan is a combination of a question and the response. The question may be quite reasonable, but the response is what makes it a koan. For example, Zhao Zhou (Chao-chou) was asked, "What is the Buddha-nature?" His reply, "Three pounds of flax." Another one, even more obscure: "In what way do my feet resemble the feet of a donkey?" And the answer: "When the heron stands in the snow, its color is not the same."

A vast number of "official" koans have been collected in the Rinzai tradition, perhaps more than 2,000. The ones noted above are just a few representative samples. They illustrate, though, the essential feature of all koans. There is absolutely no way that the rational mind can "make sense" of a koan, and a serious effort to do so will drive the rational mind into a fit of anxiety. Dumoulin refers to the koan as a "perplexing puzzle":

> One becomes confused, and the more one tries to come up with an answer and search for a solution, the more confused one gets. The essence of the koan is to be rationally unresolvable and thus to point to what is irrational. The koan urges us to abandon our rational thought structures and step beyond our usual state of consciousness in order to press into new and unknown dimensions. This is the common purpose of all koan, no matter how much they may differ in content or literary form. (246)

The koan exercise may seem harmless, but it's not meant to be fun and games at all. The appropriate place for it is within the monastic community where the master can personally monitor the student's progress. In the routine of the monastery, each student meets privately from time to time with the master. This is called *dokusan* in Japanese. The master may choose a koan exercise for the student, one that he judges to be appropriate to that particular student's state of mind. The student is then expected to give all of his time and energy to trying to understand the meaning of the koan. The master will check his progress during dokusan. It can be a terribly frustrating and exhausting ordeal for the student. For days, or weeks, the rational mind tries to "figure out" a solution. No amount of cleverness, though, will ever fool the master, who insists that the student demonstrate in some fashion his understanding of the koan. Eventually the discursive mind may give up and collapse in despair. And then—eureka!—the thing is had (maybe).

The whole point of the koan exercise rests on the premise that the rational thinking mind is capable, at best, of giving us a very imperfect knowledge of true reality. This is not to say that the rational thought process does not have an important role to play in the practical affairs of daily life—of course it does—but it is to say that when we allow ourselves to become transfixed on thought, believing that the world of thought encompasses the whole of reality, we are very, very much self-deluded.

> Zen holds that the so-called rational mind is incapable of solving an individual's deepest problem: his meaning to himself and to life. There is no way, in the Zen view, that conclusive answers to existential questions can be found by discussion, dialectic, or even ordinary thought. Final awareness, lasting freedom, and true psychological equilibrium come only when the deepest intuitional faculties of the human being have been tapped. It follows that, in Zen, reason is never permitted the unquestioned place of rulership it has occupied for centuries in Western philosophy. Zen holds that the reasoning process's function is separation, discrimination and the division of "this" from "that," thus making it impossible ever to see life's wholeness and oneself in relation to it. In Zen, since All-is-One, knowledge of one's own true nature predicates knowledge of all nature, or the universe itself. (Ross, 144)

The role of the koan exercise, then, is to grapple with the rational mind, wrestle it to the floor, and pin it there. Only then can consciousness break free from its self-imposed prison. Another way of putting it is to see the mental process as analogous to what happens when gazing at an autostereogram (aka "magic eye illusion"), one of those intriguing computer-generated pictures that initially looks like nothing more than a repeating pattern of abstract lines and wiggles. But all of a sudden, as if completely on its own, a three-dimensional dinosaur or palm tree or whatever will jump into form. There's no way you can force it to happen. To the ordinary eye the picture looks flat and meaningless. But if you can relax and just "let go," all of a sudden you see what was always there but was hidden from the rational eye.

Perhaps the most famous and best-loved of all the koans is the one that is offered first in the *Momunkan,* a prominent collection of Zen koans. In the *Momunkan,* it is titled "Zhao Zhou's dog," but usually it is simply referred to as the koan on *Mu.* A monk once asked Zhao-Zhou, "Does a dog have Buddha-nature?" Zhao-Zhou replied, "Mu!" Actually he replied, "Wu!" which is the Chinese equivalent of the Japanese "Mu." Both words literally mean "nothing," but the literal meaning is not necessarily important (though, of course, it could be). Countless Zen students have struggled with Mu over the ages. Wu Men, the compiler of the *Momunkan,* called "Mu" the "gateless barrier of the Zen school." The character *mu* is, as he explains,

" . . . the gateless barrier of the Zen school. Do you not wish to pass through this barrier?" If so, "then concentrate yourself into this 'Mu,' with your 360 bones and 84,000 pores, making your whole body one great inquiry. Day and night work intently at it. Do not attempt nihilistic or dualistic interpretations. It is like having bolted a red hot iron ball. You try to vomit it but cannot. . . . Now how should one strive? With might and main work at this 'Mu' and be 'Mu.' If you do not stop or waver in your striving, then behold, when the Dharma candle is lighted, darkness is at once enlightened." (quoted in Dumoulin, 259)

Well, this is only a tantalizing glimpse into the mysterious world of the koan. We will have more to say about the subject later. But all of the words in the world wouldn't begin to really *explain* it. That's the way it is with the koan. We must not underestimate its importance, though, in the evolution of Zen Buddhism. D. T. Suzuki maintained that the koan exercise was critical to the success of Zen Buddhism. "To my mind it was the technique of the koan exercise that saved Zen as a unique heritage of Far Eastern culture."

We've come a long way from the time when Bodhidharma stood before Emperor Wu and answered, "I don't know" to the question, "Who are you?" It's quite a journey from Bodhidharma to Linji—four long centuries of development and refinement. Out of this development, though, emerged a mature Zen Buddhism, one of the finest creations of the human spirit in all of history.

The essential character of Zen Buddhism was established during the Age of the Patriarchs. In the period following the death of Huineng, the essential character was filled out; flesh was added to the bones. By the death of Linji in 867 C.E., a mature Zen Buddhism had been achieved. Zen (Chan) would continue to flourish in China for another three centuries before it would enter upon a slow decline in the land of its birth. There is something of a life cycle to any great cultural movement, and Buddhism is no exception. Constant renewal is the secret of life. Buddhism began in India, where it grew and flourished for a time, and like a flower it spread its seeds before beginning to decline. Some of the seeds took root in China, where a new Buddhism grew and blossomed, also spreading its seeds before going into decline. Some of these seeds took root in Japan, where yet another flowering occurred. And today, perhaps, we are witnessing the same process once again. The seeds of Japanese Zen Buddhism have been cast throughout the globe and are sinking healthy roots in places that are very new to Buddhism.

I hope you now see that the development of Zen Buddhism in Japan began with the importation of an already mature form of Zen from China. Zen Buddhism—or more properly speaking, Chan Buddhism—was originally a creation of the civilization of China. The next stage of the story, though, will be worked out in Japan, and to say the very least, it is a great story in itself.

I would like to end this section by repeating the very beautiful quote from the Chinese Zen Master, Ching Yuan. It perfectly captures the essential spirit of the experience of Zen Buddhism:

> Before I had studied Zen for thirty years, I saw mountains as mountains, and waters as waters. When I arrived at a more intimate knowledge, I came to the point where I saw that mountains are not mountains, and waters are not waters. But now that I have got its very substance I am at rest. For it's just that I see mountains once again as mountains, and waters once again as waters.

Study Questions

1. What is the origin of the word *Chan*?
2. "The mind in meditation is a state of 'no-mind.'" What does this mean?
3. What is the reasoning behind the metaphor in which the gradual way to enlightenment is compared to the making of a perfect telescope mirror?
4. Who was Bodhidharma? Why is he referred to as a "patriarch"? What does it mean to say that Bodhidharma was both the twenty-eighth patriarch and the first patriarch?
5. Why does the Zen tradition insist on the reality of the "lineage" from Buddha to Bodhidharma and beyond?
6. How do you interpret Bodhidharma's responses to the questions of Emperor Wu? In particular, what did he mean by answering, "I don't know" to Wu's question, "Who then is it who stands before me now?"
7. According to legend, what did Bodhidharma have to do with the origin of tea drinking? Why did it become so popular in the Zen tradition?
8. How are we to understand Bodhidharma's exchange with Hui Ko, right after Hui Ko had severed his arm? Why did this exchange result in Hui Ko's sudden enlightenment?
9. When Bodhidharma chose Hui Ko to be his successor he whispered to him, "You shall inherit my marrow." What do you suppose he meant by this?
10. The basic gatha of Zen (attributed to Bodhidharma) is said to sum up the special character of the Zen way. How so? What is it that makes Zen different from other schools of Buddhism?
11. What is satori?
12. According to the tradition of Zen Buddhism, how does one actually come to know the experience of satori? Do you believe this is possible?
13. Why did the monastery's master, Hongren, privately reject Shenxiu's gatha and tell him that he had not yet entered into real awakening?
14. What is the essential difference in meaning between the wall gathas of Shenxiu and Huineng?
15. Why do you suppose that Huiming was unable to lift the robe of Buddha when he encountered Huineng in the mountain pass?

16. What is the meaning of Hongren's comment; "Of my five hundred disciples four hundred and ninety nine possessed a remarkable understanding of Zen. Only Huineng did not understand Zen. That's why I chose him." (?)

17. "The main thrust of Zen training is to help the student break free of the normal human attachment to discursive thinking." What does this mean?

18. In what way is it correct to say that Huineng *completed* the work of Bodhidharma?

19. What was Huineng's attitude with regard to the proper role of meditation?

20. Why in the world did Emperor Wu Zung fervently attempt to extinguish Buddhism in China? How could such a peaceful philosophy of life give rise to such wrath?

21. Distinguish between Soto Zen and Rinzai Zen. Which of these appeals more to you? Why?

22. Does it make any sense to you that Zen masters such as Linji and Ma Zi would strike and kick their students? Doesn't this seem like the antithesis of the Zen way?

23. What exactly is a koan? How does a skilled teacher use a koan to help bring a student to satori?

24. Why do you suppose that Zhao Zhou's putting his sandals on his head and walking out of the room made such an impression on Zen master Nanchuan? Doesn't that response seem a bit crazy to you?

25. Explain the meaning of the quoted passage from Zen master Ching Yuan at the very end of the chapter.

CHAPTER 18

Zen Buddhism

JAPAN BEFORE ZEN

Early Japanese society was organized by clans. Eventually one of the clans succeeded in creating a measure of unity among them all by conquering and welding together a part of Honshu at the eastern end of the Inland Sea. This region, including one of Japan's few arable river valleys, came to be called Yamato. The chief of Yamato became Japan's first "emperor." (The Japanese have always preferred "emperor" to "king.") According to legend, the first emperor of Japan was named Jimmu Tenno, and we are even given a very precise date for his accession to the throne, February 11, 660 B.C.E. As we have seen in Chapter 14, he was believed to be descended from the sun goddess, Amaterasu. One account holds that with the help of his many wives he produced seventy-seven sons, who became the chiefs of the various clans. Thus could all of the Japanese nobility claim some measure of divine descent.

Legend aside, the reality is much more mundane (as always seems to be the case). We don't know the name of that first clan chief who established unified rule in the region of Yamato; it was probably a process that took several generations to complete. That process, though, would have been worked out during the fourth century C.E., a full thousand years after the legendary date of 660 B.C.E. The clans were unified within a sort of confederacy, and all accepted the legitimacy of the "emperor" at Yamato. Yamato, please remember, refers to a region, not to a city. During the early centuries, there was no capital city. The entire court, such as it was, moved to a new location and constructed a new palace each time one emperor died and was succeeded by a new one. This practice was probably derived from traditional religious rites of purification. But as the size of the court grew, creating a new home could get expensive. At last, in the year 710 C.E., a permanent capital was established. The site selected was the place we know as Nara. They chose a beautiful location, a hilly, sparsely wooded area about twenty miles up from the head of Osaka Bay at the eastern end of the Inland Sea.

Nara, on a much humbler scale, was patterned after Changan, the splendid capital of Tang dynasty China. The Chinese-style grid pattern of streets was only the beginning.

The Japanese ruling class hungrily borrowed all that they could from Chinese civilization. Among other things, the Japanese adopted the Chinese system of writing, as they had none of their own. With the adoption of a system of writing, and hence the keeping of written records, the true history of Japan begins.

Perhaps China's most important contribution to nascent Japanese civilization was Buddhism. Actually, the very first recorded incident regarding Buddhism in Japan dates back to 538 C.E. At that time, one of the regional "kings" of Korea sent a present to Emperor Kinmei of Japan; it was a small gilt statue of Buddha. The emperor, not quite sure what to do with it, entrusted it to the care of an important noble family, the Soga, which had extensive relationships with the noble families of the Korean mainland. The Soga preserved the statue and began to develop an interest in the religious teachings it represented. Before long, Buddhist monks from Korea were preaching the Dharma in Japan.

Buddhism did not enter into a religious void in Japan. As we have seen, the Japanese people from very early times had followed a rather loosely organized religious system known as Shinto. The word *Shinto*, however, did not come into use until after the rise of Buddhism. It then became necessary to distinguish between the two. *Shinto* referred to the "way of the gods"; *bukkyo* referred to the "way of Buddha."

Shinto began as a primitive animistic collection of beliefs and practices, focusing on reverence for the spirits (*kami*) of natural phenomena, such as mountains, waterfalls, great trees, and also the spirits of departed ancestors. These practices tied the Japanese clans together, encouraging a belief that they were a unique and superior people ruled by an emperor of divine descent. The fundamental character of Shinto has survived even to the present day. The foreign traveler in Japan is often surprised to discover how ubiquitous are the shrines (*jinja*) and temples of Shinto. It seems that almost everyone is connected, however casually, with a local Shinto shrine. For many, these have an important association with the ritual events of life and are important for honoring the spirits of departed family members.

No real conflict developed between Buddhism and Shinto when Buddhism entered on the scene. You might expect that there would have been some conflict, but Buddhism and Shinto have coexisted very peacefully right from the beginning. In fact, early Buddhism in Japan absorbed into itself many Shinto beliefs and practices. It is quite possible for a Japanese man or woman to be both a Buddhist and an active member of a Shinto jinja.

During the Nara Period, which occupied almost all of the eighth century, Buddhism continued to grow in southern Japan, especially at the capital itself. There were frequent visits and exchanges between Japan and Tang China, but there was no effort to fashion a native Buddhism; it was strictly Chinese Buddhism transplanted to Japanese soil. (This suggests a modern parallel. Buddhism in the West is still in its infancy; Zen Buddhist monasteries in America, for example, are to a large degree careful replicas of the Japanese model.) It's a somewhat amazing fact that we can still see the evidence of the early Chinese influence in Japan. Some of the earliest Buddhist temples still exist in the city of Nara. They have been carefully maintained and still appear today much as they did in the eighth century. They show clearly the Chinese architectural style that inspired them, though their counterparts from Tang China have disappeared centuries ago. One of these, the "Golden Hall" from the monastery Horyu-ji is said to be by far the oldest extant all-wood structure in the world. Not only do we have the oldest, but also the largest wooden building under one roof, the "Buddha Hall" of the monastery Todai-ji. This building houses an enormous, fifty-three-foot-high bronze and gilt statue of a seated Vairochana Buddha. The gilt alone is said to weigh in at more than half a ton.

In 784 C.E., the imperial court abandoned Nara and moved about thirty miles north to the brand-new imperial capital, which we know as Kyoto. Kyoto (pronounced as two syllables, "Kyoh-toh") was also laid out according the Chinese grid system and quickly became the greatest city in Japan. It would remain the seat of the imperial residence until 1868, at which time the first of the Meiji emperors would move the imperial residence to Tokyo. The emperor, although honored as a divine being by the people, gradually lost the real power of rule. The emperor became something of a grand but powerless figurehead, while real power was exercised by the *shogun*, a hereditary post that controlled military power. It was an unusual arrangement, almost suggestive of the relationship between the papacy and the Holy Roman Empire in medieval Europe.

It was at Kyoto that we find the beginnings of a truly Japanese Buddhism.* In the year 805 C.E., a Japanese monk named Saicho was received at court in the still-new imperial palace at Kyoto. Saicho had just returned from a four-year visit to China (as mentioned in Chapter 17), during which time he had studied the ways of several different Buddhist sects. He was now ready to weave together various strands of Buddhist practice, and some aspects of Shinto as well, and fashion a new distinctively Japanese school of Buddhism. It would be called *Tendai*, the Japanese rendering of the name of the Chinese monastery, Tiantai, which had been the major base of Saicho's study while abroad. Tendai, with its emphasis on the magical and the supernatural, was a far cry from Zen, but it appealed to the needs of the people of the time.

With the help of the imperial court, Saicho established the first Tendai monastery, Enryakou-ji on Mount Hiei just to the northeast of Kyoto. It was popularly believed in those days that evil spirits controlled the northeasterly direction, and a Buddhist monastery on Mount Hiei could protect the city from their demonic influence. The power and prestige of Tendai Buddhism grew rapidly. Before long, the numerous monks of Mount Hiei became a political force—and even, oddly enough, something of a paramilitary force—to be reckoned with in Kyoto. Tendai monasteries began to proliferate, especially in the south and west of Japan. Although influenced by Chinese Tiantai, Tendai was fundamentally the first truly native Japanese school of Buddhism. A rival school, known as Shingon Buddhism, was founded by the monk, Kukai, only a year after Saicho began work on his monastery. Kukai too had studied in China, and established his monastery on Mount Koya in the southwestern sector of the Kyoto area. *Shingon* is derived from the Chinese *Zhenyan*, the name for an esoteric school of Buddhism greatly influenced by Vajrayana. Shingon too spread beyond the Kyoto area, but never enjoyed anything near the growth experienced by Tendai.

Buddhism in Japan, especially Tendai Buddhism, developed slowly but steadily in the centuries following the founding of the imperial capital of Kyoto. As mentioned before, the emperor became more and more a figurehead, while real power was exercised by the

---

*Kegon Buddhism—which was essentially Chinese Huayen transplanted to Japan—flourished in eighth-century Nara, but this was an unmodified Chinese school of Buddhism. A native "Japanese" Buddhism first developed at Kyoto. Incidentally, the Nara monastery of Todai-ji was a Kegon monastery, and its great gilt Buddha is a representation of Vairochana Buddha, not Shakyamuni Buddha.

military dictator, the shogun. The shogun presided over a class of warrior nobles known as the *samurai*. Endless divisions among the samurai led to civil war on many occasions. The shogunate, a hereditary office, passed from one dynasty to another as a result of these civil wars. In 1185 c.e., Minamoto Yoritomo, the first to hold the title of shogun, succeeded in defeating his rivals in an especially bloody civil war. He thereupon abandoned Kyoto, leaving its opulent imperial court there, but moving the seat of his own military government to Kamakura, a small coastal city just south of modern Tokyo. The "Kamakura Shogunate" would rule Japan until 1338 c.e., when the shogun would again return to Kyoto.

It was during the time of the Kamakura Shogunate that Japan was nearly invaded and conquered by the huge Mongol armies of Kublai Khan. Not content with the conquest of China only, Kublai Khan on two occasions (1274 and 1281) sent enormous invasion forces against Japan, landing both times on the shore of the island of Kyushu. The Japanese beat back the first invasion, but would surely have been overwhelmed by the second had it not been for the fortuitous help of a typhoon. Of more than 4,000 ships in the Mongol force, only 200 returned, and only 30,000 men survived out of an invasion force of 140,000. Naturally, the Japanese interpreted the typhoon as a heaven-sent answer to their prayers; it was a *kami-kaze*, a "divine wind."*

What this adds up to is that the relatively simple life of Japanese society in its earlier days had given way to times that were more complex and unstable. Tendai Buddhism, which had the field pretty much to itself for four centuries, was being challenged at the end of the twelfth century by new Buddhist sects that were more in tune with the needs of the Japanese people. During the thirteenth century, three new schools of Buddhism would become firmly established in Japan: Nichiren Buddhism, Pure Land Buddhism, and Zen Buddhism.

Closest to traditional Tendai was Nichiren Buddhism, named after the monk who began the movement in the thirteenth century. He was a fiery, messianic sort of person who was determined to save Japanese society from what he perceived to be the corrupt state it had fallen into. He gave his new version of Tendai Buddhism a highly nationalistic spirit, which had great appeal among the common people. About the only doctrinal innovation that he introduced was an intense emphasis on the recitation of the sutras, especially the *Lotus Sutra*. At odds with the usually tolerant attitude of Buddhism, Nichiren argued that all other Buddhist sects were heretical; he alone held the key to the truth of Buddha's teaching.

Unlike Nichiren, which was a home-grown sect, Pure Land Buddhism (known as *Jodo* in Japanese) was an import from China. In the long run, it would prove to be vastly more popular with the common people and is still a very popular sect within the umbrella of Buddhism. In modern times, about half of the Japanese people classify themselves as Buddhists, and most of these identify with the Pure Land sect.

Pure Land Buddhism was founded in Japan in the late twelfth century by the monk Honen, who preached a very simple, unsophisticated doctrine that quickly became

---

*In 1945, threatened with another great invasion, the Japanese military leaders revived the idea of *kamikaze*. The spirits of the ancient gods were to work through the minds and bodies of aviators who would form a "divine wind" of suicide-planes that would destroy the American warships by deliberately crashing into them, thus saving Japan once again from imminent invasion. This time, though, the fleet was not destroyed. However, the threatened invasion never did take place.

enormously popular with the common people. As we have seen, Pure Land Buddhism is the most "religious" of Buddhist sects in the ordinary sense of the word. Following the tradition of Chinese Pure Land Buddhism, Honen taught that one can achieve salvation simply through the ceaseless invocation of the name of the loving and compassionate Buddha Amida (from the Sanskrit and Chinese Amitabha). This ceaseless chanting of the name, referred to as *nembutsu*, was said to result in a spiritually meditative state of mind which would lead to one being reborn after death in the western paradise of the "Pure Land" of Buddha Amida. Much like the early Protestant reformers, Honen taught that all that is required is faith—faith in the compassionate Buddha and the consequent ritual practice of the repetition of the sacred nembutsu.

RINZAI AND SOTO ZEN

The seeds of Zen would fall on extremely fertile ground in Japan and would reproduce the two great schools already existing in China. In Japan, they would come to be known as Rinzai and Soto. We will examine these by looking at the contributions of three historically great figures: Eisai, Dogen, and Hakuin.

Eisai

A Tendai scholar-monk named Myoan Eisai (pronounced "Ay [as in 'day']-sigh") is credited with introducing Zen Buddhism into Japan. Troubled by what he perceived to be a decline in the vigor of Japanese Buddhism, Eisai concocted a wonderful plan. His dream was to trace the development of Buddhism backward in time from his own age in Japan, through the stages of evolution in China, all the way to its roots in India. And he would do this not through books, but *on foot*. Eisai would travel through China all the way to India, leisurely studying the developmental stages of Buddhism at important sites along the route. In this way, he hoped to gain a deep personal understanding of the true nature of the Dharma practice. Ultimately, he would drink from the very wellspring of the tradition. Finally, he would return to Japan prepared to reinvigorate the Buddhism of his native land.

Well, Eisai never got as far as India, sad to say, but he did make two trips to China, and in the process, he fell deeply in love with the teaching and practice of Zen (Chan) Buddhism—specifically, the Linji school (which would come to be known as Rinzai in Japan). During his second Chinese trip, a four-year sojourn from 1187 to 1191, he studied "Rinzai" extensively, finally receiving the Dharma-seal at the monastery of Tiandong. When Eisai returned to Japan in 1191, he was determined to recast the character of Buddhist practice. His goal was to reinvigorate Japanese Buddhism by emphasizing the strict adherence to the precepts that he had observed among Chinese Buddhists.

Eisai, as the legitimate Dharma-heir of a recognized Zen Master, was in effect, introducing a new Buddhist sect into Japan, but it seems that he wanted to play down that fact. Eisai did not seek to replace Tendai; what he wanted most of all was to launch a genuine reform movement that would reinvigorate all of Buddhism in Japan. Perhaps he naively believed that Tendai could be absorbed into the reform movement and integrated into a new Zen-oriented Buddhism. In any case, he avoided using the term *Zen*, speaking instead of the "school of the Buddha mind." Also, he remained technically a Tendai monk.

But none of this could long hide the fact that something new was in the air; Zen Buddhism had at long last arrived in Japan.

Eisai's reform movement caught fire immediately, and he lost no time in organizing Buddhist monasteries on the new model. The honor of being the first Zen monastery in Japan goes to Shofuku-ji, established in 1195 at Hakata (now known as Fukuoka) on the north shore of the island of Kyushu (ironically, the very place where Kublai Kahn's invaders had tried unsuccessfully to penetrate Japan). Before long, though, Eisai was back at Kyoto; the center of the nation was to be the center of the Zen movement. With the help of the royal family, he established Kennin-ji, the first Zen monastery at Kyoto. (Kennin-ji still stands and, like almost all of the many famous Zen monasteries of the Kyoto area, is open to the public.)

To mollify worried Tendai leaders, Kennin-ji was "officially" designated a Tendai monastery, and Eisai even agreed to include both Tendai and Shingon shrines on the grounds. Another little addition to the grounds of Kennin-ji was to have far-reaching effects. It was a tea garden, presumably the first to be planted in the soil of Japan. Eisai had acquired a taste for tea while studying in China and brought this home with him. Not only did he find tea an excellent aid for Zen practice, but he was also impressed by its general medicinal qualities. Technically speaking, the monk Kukai, the founder of Shingon Buddhism, introduced tea into Japan, but nothing much came of his efforts. The real credit belongs to Eisai. His little tea garden launched a thirst that soon engulfed Japan.

It did not take long for Zen Buddhism to usurp Tendai's favored position at Kyoto. Both the emperor's court and the shogun's government favored close ties with Zen. Specifically, it was the Rinzai school of Zen that was favored. Both Rinzai Zen and Soto Zen would be transplanted to Japan, and both would flourish there, but it was Rinzai Zen that developed a close association with the government. In fact, the association was so close that Rinzai Zen, in a sense, could be said to have become an operative organ of the government. Skilled Rinzai monks were often enlisted to perform diplomatic tasks for the government. To give just one example, in 1342, a Zen monk led a delegation to China seeking financial help for a planned memorial to the recently deceased emperor, Go-Daigo. He succeeded not only in raising the funds, but also in negotiating a rich and complicated trade agreement with China.

Many Rinzai monasteries were generously underwritten by government funding. Kyoto continued to be the headquarters of Rinzai activity, and several impressive Zen monasteries began to take form in the countryside ringing the city. During the time that the shogun governed at Kamakura, important Rinzai monasteries were founded there as well. The various Zen monasteries of Japan were organized by rank into systems that resembled a mountain or a pyramid. Altogether such a complex was known as a "Gozan System." The entire complex included even the *rinka*, small, semi-independent monasteries in rural areas. Ranking at the top of the Rinzai system were the "Five Mountains," the leading Rinzai monasteries of Kyoto. (In Japanese, *go* is five, and *zan* is a word for mountain.) Presiding at the very peak of the pyramid was the great Nanzen-ji, constructed in the countryside just southeast of the city in the late thirteenth century. Kennin-ji continued to be important, but its place at the top was taken over by the much larger Nanzen-ji.*

---

*As mentioned before, many of these great monasteries, as well as the former imperial palace, still exist and are open to the public. Kyoto and its environs were off-limits to saturation bombing during World War II, and for this reason, there were some who pushed hard to make Kyoto a target for one of the atomic bombs. Nothing would be left if they had had their way. The world can be eternally thankful that they were overruled.

It might seem somewhat puzzling to the modern reader that these Zen monasteries were so closely connected with the government. We must remember that "government" is not being used in anything like the modern sense of the word. In those days, Japan was a feudal society; there were really only two great classes. The common people made up the vast majority of the population and were engaged for the most part in a farming way of life. The feudal ruling class, relatively small in numbers, was a warrior nobility, the samurai. The noble families of the samurai controlled virtually all of the land and all of the power.

The life of a samurai nobleman was the life of a warrior, and true to the spirit of all feudal societies, the samurai were often on the field of battle. Endless interclan quarrels were the order of the day; sometimes very large in scale, usually small and local. Whatever the case, the samurai must always be ready to fight, and to fight well. Out of this way of life arose the tradition of *bushido*, the "way of the warrior," an uncompromising code of conduct that defined the character of the samurai warrior.

Bushido has caught the imagination of modern society, especially with respect to skill in the martial arts. According to the code of bushido, a samurai was to give absolute, unswerving loyalty to his feudal lord and to his peers, and to show reverence to the divinity of the emperor. These could not be compromised for any reason. To do so would be to bring dishonor on himself and his family, and such a thing was unthinkable. A samurai warrior was expected to always accept death before dishonor, even if it meant taking his own life, the highly dramatic act of *seppuku*. When it came to a fight, the samurai was expected to be both brave and highly skilled. Typically the samurai fought with a sword that was a masterpiece of the steelmaker's craft. About three-feet long (approximately one meter), slightly curved, and sharp as a razor, it was a deadly weapon in the hands of a skilled fighter. Supposedly, the samurai sword was capable of taking off the head of an opponent with a single lightning blow.

The sword was the symbol of the samurai, but so was the cherry blossom. The two make an interesting contrast. The code of bushido maintained that great gentleness is the evidence of great strength. When challenged, the samurai would fight like a tiger, but in the ordinary course of life he was to be a model of modesty and simplicity. In addition to its concern with the martial arts, the code of bushido emphasized the basic virtues of honesty, directness, protection of the weak, and respect for traditional institutions. (In many ways, the Japanese samurai was a kindred spirit to the Spartan warrior of ancient Greece.)

Zen Buddhism, with its emphasis on simple virtues, self-discipline, and self-reliance, was speaking right to the heart of the samurai. This helps to explain the close association that developed between the ruling class—that is, the warrior class—and Zen Buddhism. Rinzai Zen monasteries became, among other things, the training grounds of the samurai. This is certainly not to say that that was the only function they served, but it definitely was an important one. Samurai families were typically associated with a particular Rinzai monastery, at which the man trained from time to time in the disciplines of Zen, especially when young. Zen discipline was seen to provide an excellent foundation for training and mastery in all of the skills that made up the samurai way of life. And for this reason, Rinzai Zen monasteries were generously supported by the ruling class.

Rinzai Zen became the Buddhism of the aristocracy, whereas Pure Land (Jodo in Japanese) became the Buddhism of the common people. To say that the Gozan System became a network of "military academies" for the samurai is overstating it, but there is a measure of truth in it. Our use of the word *monastery* is a little misleading. The Zen monastery was not a "religious" institution in the present-day sense of the word; it was a specialized community dedicated to a highly disciplined manner of living aimed at perfection of the human character. As such, it is easy to see why such an institution would have great appeal to the samurai class.

Dogen

One of the great figures in the history of Japanese Zen Buddhism is Dogen Kigen, the founder of Soto Zen in Japan. Dogen was a disciple of Eisai. Whereas Eisai is something of a shadowy figure, Dogen stands out as a strong personality, and we know a good deal more about him. Much of our knowledge about Dogen and his thinking comes from his extensive writings, collectively known as the *Shobogenzo*, a ninety-two book compendium of his thoughts on a great variety of subjects. Dogen was a brilliant philosopher; he has often been compared to the great Western philosopher Martin Heidegger.*

Dogen was born in the year 1200 C.E. His father, a nobleman, died when Dogen was only two, and he lost his mother when he was just seven. The mother's deathbed wish was that the young Dogen should become a Buddhist monk, and after her death, the family made arrangements for her wish to be honored. While still just a boy, Dogen was admitted to the community of Tendai monks at the monastery on Mount Hiei near Kyoto.

New things were in the air. The reform movement launched by Eisai excited the interest of the young Dogen, and while still in his teens, he abandoned the old-fashioned ways of Mount Hiei, becoming instead a disciple of Eisai, whose approach to Buddhism was far more to Dogen's liking. He loved the spirit of Zen, but his hunger to know more could only be partially satisfied at this brand-new little outpost of the tradition. As a result, he planned a trip to China, the seemingly indispensable journey that every ardent seeker had to experience in those days. He wanted to study the tradition of Zen in its homeland and seek enlightenment in the company of a certified master.

Dogen departed for China in 1223 and remained there for four years. During this time, he visited many Zen monasteries, but finally settled down at the monastery at Mount Tiantong (T'ien-t'ung), presided over by the elderly Zen Master Rujing (Ju-Jing), a man very much established in the school of Cao Dong (Ts'ao-tao) (from which name is derived the Japanese word "Soto"). In Rujing, Dogen found exactly the kind of master his heart craved. Rujing was totally committed to the practice of *zazen*, sitting meditation. He, and the monks under his supervision, would sit until eleven o'clock in the evening, and then he'd be back at it again at three in the morning. Sitting meditation was the dedicated work of Rujing's monks. He wanted no one to be able to say that they worked less hard at their vocation than did the farmer, or the soldier, or anyone else outside the monastery.

Dogen fell in love with this total dedication to zazen, and he believed that it finally resolved his struggle for enlightenment. It happened one evening when one of the monks in the meditation hall fell asleep. Rujing gently chastised him, saying (in a rather koan-like way), "If your mind and body are sloughed off in meditation, how can it be

---

*For an excellent examination of this linkage, see Steven Heine, *Existential and Ontological Dimensions of Time in Heidegger and Dogen* (Albany, New York: State University of New York Press, 1985).

that you sleep?" These words, according to Dogen, jarred him out of his ego-illusion, and he became instantly enlightened. This was later verified by Rujing, who gave Dogen a document "certifying" his enlightenment and naming him a Dharma-heir in the house of Caodao. The followers of Dogen regard this event as the official beginning of the school of Japanese Soto Zen.

While in China, Dogen learned a very important lesson, and the unlikely teacher was an old cook at one of the monasteries he visited. The man was totally absorbed in his endless work as a cook and laughed out loud when Dogen asked him why he didn't spend more time in his final years practicing zazen and reading the sutras. In so many words, the old cook replied, "If you think Zen practice consists only in those kinds of things, you haven't yet learned *anything*!" Dogen was deeply impressed by this cheerful old man and came to realize that the real evidence of enlightenment is loving service to others. Done in the right spirit, anything at all can be Zen practice. One's ordinary daily life can be a beautiful expression of Zen practice.

In his own opinion, the Dogen who returned from China in 1227 was a very different man from the one who had embarked on the journey of discovery four years earlier. His struggle for enlightenment had now matured, and as evidence, he carried with him the Dharma-seal of the master, Rujing. Here were his credentials, so to speak, which gave him the authority to found a monastic community in Japan that would be in the legitimate succession of the house of Caodao. Dogen made his way to Kyoto, where, in 1236, he established the new monastery of Kosho-ji. His teaching at Kosho-ji, naturally, placed great emphasis on the practice of zazen. Like those before him, Dogen earnestly hoped to heal the divisions within Buddhism in Japan, uniting all in the way of Caodao (Soto).

Before the China trip, Dogen had been active in the Tendai community, and also in the nascent Rinzai movement begun by Eisai. He hoped to absorb both of these, especially his former Rinzai fellow-monks, into the Zen Buddhism that he was proclaiming. Quite possibly, Dogen imagined himself to be something of a messiah, the "one they were waiting for" who would unite all in a transcendent new movement based on his teachings. To his dismay, though, Dogen experienced only rivalry and criticism from the others. The Rinzai monks were particularly vociferous in their criticism, denouncing Dogen's attachment to sitting meditation. And with their growing closeness to the impe- rial court, Rinzai opposition became an unendurable burden for Dogen. With a heavy heart, he finally gave up his great dream of reforming all of Japanese Buddhism under his banner and made the decision to abandon Kyoto altogether. He would go off to the wilds where at least he and his monks could live in peace. He was further encouraged in this decision by remembering the words of his master, Rujing, to "shun cities, and dwell deep in mountains and valleys."

In 1243, Dogen and his band of loyal disciples relocated to an out-of-the-way rural area about sixty miles northeast of Kyoto, not far from the desolate north coast of Honshu. There, on property given to them by a wealthy landowner, they founded the monastery of Eihei-ji (pronounced "Ay [as in 'day']-hay-jee"). Dogen was to live another ten years, and it was during this time at Eihei-ji that he nailed down the particulars of his teaching, establishing the foundation of the school of Japanese Soto Zen. Most of this is to be found in the collection of his writings known as the *Shobogenzo*.

The practice of sitting meditation was, of course, the heart of Dogen's discipline. And why should it not be central? Had not Buddha himself treasured meditation? It was the setting of his awakening. And throughout the evolution of Buddhism, great bodhisattvas had made a special place for meditation. Bodhidharma, for example, the titular founder of Zen, had spent nine long years in sitting meditation at Shaolinsi, and that was *after* his enlightenment.

The monks at Eihei-ji spent many hours in zazen; it was the core around which the daily routine was built. Normally, much of the day was also given over to other tasks, such as work projects and study, but at certain times of year, all other activities were temporarily suspended so that the monks could devote almost all of their waking hours to zazen. Such a period of concentration in zazen came to be called a *sesshin*. At Eihei-ji, a sesshin typically lasted for seven days, and there were at least four of them, corresponding to the seasons of the year. A sesshin, still very much a part of the Zen calendar, offers a special opportunity to make some kind of breakthrough on the path to satori.

Dogen was very precise about the way zazen was to be practiced. His method, fundamentally, is still the method practiced in Soto Zen. If we could enter his meditation hall, we would see rows of monks dressed in the familiar black, loose-fitting monk's robe. Unlike a Rinzai meditation hall, in which the monks sit facing inward, Dogen's monks would be facing the wall. They would sit on long low platforms, in the cross-legged posture, using only a tatami mat and a small firm cushion, known as a *zafu*, to sit on. Their posture would be upright but not tense, and the hands would rest above the lap formed by the crossed legs. Dogen took exception to the traditional yogic practice of closing the eyes in meditation. His monks were to keep the eyes open, but downcast. The wall covering was bare straw mat or shoji screen, so there was nothing especially visual to catch the eye. Dogen emphasized the importance of regulated easy breathing, but only to help relax and center the body–mind. He had no interest in yogic breathing exercises in which the exercise was itself the meditation practice.

Chanting, repetition of a mantra, koan, and all other kinds of activity were ruled out in Dogen's method of zazen. They might have a place at other times, but not at the time specifically set aside for zazen. The meditator was to do one thing, and one thing only: He was to completely focus his consciousness on the existential reality of the moment, and *stay with that*. Consciousness was to be keenly observed, in the moment, but never "managed." Thoughts, images, feelings of desire, etc. might come and go; that in itself didn't matter, so long as the meditator was fully mindful of them, but did not enter into them. This practice, which requires great energy and can be totally exhausting for the novice, is called *shikantaza*; it is to fully grasp the moment. Basically, shikantaza is an intense version of what is called "Mindfulness Meditation." The dedicated practice of shikantaza, so Dogen believed, was the way par excellence for "seeing into one's nature."

Dogen was in full accord with the tradition of Zen in emphasizing that "seeing into one's nature" is the very essence of Buddhism. One's nature is the Buddha-nature. There is nothing to be acquired in meditation; it remains only for the individual to see through the illusions of his own making that prevent him from knowing the truth of his own Buddha-nature. Dogen was convinced that zazen was the royal road that could take one to the place where he or she was at last able and willing to completely let go of all attachments, including the iron grip of the attachment to self, and "see the true nature of the self."

Although Dogen's primary concern was with the monastery and his immediate disciples, he was determined that Eihei-ji not become some sort of Buddhist ivory tower isolated from the common people of the area. All who lived within its environs were welcome to join to some extent in the life of the monastery. Dogen himself often preached a simplified version of his discipline to the laypeople, encouraging them to make meditation and other Buddhist disciplines a part of their daily lives. The more typically "religious" elements of traditional Buddhism were emphasized where the common people were concerned, perhaps as a concession to the popularity of Pure Land Buddhism.

In addition to welcoming the neighboring people into the life of the monastery, Dogen encouraged his monks to go out to them too. The monks of Eihei-ji were always available to help out in times of need. Dogen's monks were a familiar sight helping with the harvest, lending a hand at a barn-raising, or joining a work party to repair a bridge. This close association with the common people set the pattern for Soto Zen communities that would eventually spread throughout Japan, and in this way, Soto Zen in time came to permeate the lives of the ordinary men and women of Japan.

To sum up, both Soto and Rinzai became firmly established in Japan during the thirteenth century. Their beautiful monasteries were being constructed at the same time that the great Gothic cathedrals were rising in distant Europe. I wish to emphasize again that Rinzai and Soto were not so much antagonistic rivals as they were different alternatives. Both were solidly grounded in the fundamentals of Zen Buddhism, growing from the Zen of the Patriarchs as funneled through the teaching of Huineng. The basic character of each school had matured in China during the Tang and Song periods and had been transplanted to Japan where a distinctively Japanese style had developed.

This difference in style was expressed in three primary ways. First, of course, was the matter of social class. Speaking very generally, Rinzai was the Zen of the aristocratic class, and Soto was the Zen more favored by common people. This was broadly true, but there was room for lots of exceptions in both cases. The second difference concerns the place of meditation. Both Soto and Rinzai held zazen in high regard, but Soto emphasized the practice of zazen to a far greater degree than did Rinzai. In fact, Rinzai masters often gently (and sometimes not so gently) ridiculed Soto monks for their "excessive" love of sitting meditation. And the Soto people returned the favor, chastising Rinzai for its attachment to the koan exercise: "wall-gazing" versus "koan-gazing"; "quiet illumination" versus "dynamic enlightenment." The word *dynamic* identifies the third difference. Rinzai took a dynamic, energetic approach to Zen, whereas Soto was more contemplative. A person might join a Rinzai community for a short period, but the Soto monastery was more likely to attract the dedicated person who wished to make the way of the monk his life's work.*

Rinzai and Soto became established in Japan during the thirteenth century. From that time to the present, both have continued to grow and develop, and in modern times have begun to take root in places far beyond the borders of Japan. Many important names have been added to the history of Zen Buddhism since the time of Eisai and Dogen, but one stands out in a special way. It is the name of Hakuin. Even in a broad survey such as this, it would be unthinkable not to pause and consider the contribution of this very significant man.

---

*In the Zen tradition, there is a wonderful way of describing the difference between Rinzai and Soto. A Rinzai monk wishes to get an apple on a limb just out of reach (a metaphorical way of describing enlightenment). He leaps and lunges until finally he snatches it. A Soto monk also wants the apple, but his method is simply to sit quietly beneath the tree and wait for the ripe fruit to drop into his lap.

Hakuin

Hakuin (pronounced "Hah-koo-in") was born in 1685, the same year as Johann Sebastian Bach, and lived until 1768. He died at the age of eighty-three, outliving his famous German contemporary by eighteen years. Hakuin never knew Bach, which is unfortunate, but he was well aware of the existence of European culture; the civilizations of Europe and the Far East had begun to make contact and to influence one another. Hakuin lived during the Tokugawa Period, often referred to as the Edo Period (1603–1867), a time in history when Japanese civilization had to adjust to the wrenching changes brought about by the coming of the Europeans. Eventually Japan would deal with the challenge by barring all foreigners, exterminating the new growth of Christianity, and withdrawing into a self-imposed isolation that would have nearly devastating results. When Japan was persuaded to emerge from its isolation in the nineteenth century, the country was seriously behind the times with respect to the progress of technology. To say the least, though, Japan amazed the world by the speed with which it caught up. As a result, Japan was the only Asian country, other than Thailand, never to be colonized and/or ruthlessly exploited by European empire builders. That, however, is another story. Back to Hakuin.

Hakuin is often said to represent the culmination of the development of Rinzai Zen in Japan. Although he was a Rinzai master, and his contribution was specifically directed to the Rinzai tradition, his teaching has profoundly affected all of Zen Buddhism, in fact all of Buddhism generally. Hakuin reaffirmed the fundamentals of Buddhism, but he did it in a new way.

Hakuin spent most of his life in the region of Shizuoka on the southern side of Honshu within sight of the great Mount Fuji. The ethereal beauty of snow-capped Fuji is truly awesome. Passengers on the train to Tokyo, even though they may make the trip regularly, typically come alive and move toward the windows when Fuji first comes into view. Maybe the beauty of Fuji and the surrounding countryside worked its spell on the young Hakuin. His was an intense, deeply emotional personality. He loved beauty, and in addition to being a Zen philosopher, he was a gifted artist. Some of his work, such as the self-portrait and the portrait of Bodhidharma, have become masterpieces in the tradition of Zen art.

Hakuin was a true mystic. He longed for the joy of the transcendent experience, and he found myriad opportunities in the ordinary events of daily life. By his own account, Hakuin experienced rapture in such mundane things as the sound of gentle rain, the sight of freshly fallen snow, the song of a bird, or even the slow movement of a spider weaving its web. In other words, contact with *anything*, if the experience were entered into completely, could give rise to a transcendent moment. For Hakuin, these were the many gateways that opened the way to *kensho*, the experience of "seeing into one's nature."*

Achieving kensho was all that mattered to Hakuin—achieving it and deepening it. That was his idea of a life well spent. It seems that in the earlier years of this lifelong quest, Hakuin was most affected by the deeply emotional experience. As his life matured, though,

---

*Literally speaking, *kensho* is synonymous with *satori*. In customary usage, though, kensho refers to a "little satori," a powerful insight into the nature of reality, but one that is still short of full awakening.

the intuitive experience came to be even more important. In this respect, he was very much like that European contemporary of his, Johann Sebastian Bach. Both men followed similar paths, and each gave expression to his discoveries in his own way: Bach in the language of the musical forms of his age, and Hakuin in the language of Zen mysticism. What a profound influence they might have had on one another.

Hakuin was totally immersed in the Zen Buddhism of his age. He gave all of his time and energy to deepening the Zen experience, to understanding it in the marrow of his bones. This quest included a lifelong succession of pilgrimages to the numerous Rinzai monasteries of Japan in order to share the experience of many Zen masters. He did not, however, travel beyond the islands of Japan. The sojourn to China, a nearly obligatory mission in an earlier age, was no longer seen as necessary. The vigor of Zen Buddhism had declined markedly in China since the golden age of Tang and Song, more than four centuries in the past by the time of Hakuin. The future of Zen Buddhism had passed from China to the hands of others, most notably the Japanese.

As Hakuin's experience matured, he came to see a comprehensive order to it all, which became the basis of his teaching. He would focus on the fundamentals, just as Buddha himself had done. He would restate the essence of Buddha's teaching through the language and experience of Zen Buddhism. Hakuin began where Buddha began, with an assessment of the human condition in general, *sarvam duhkha*. To a very large degree, the general condition of humankind is fear, insecurity, and suffering. We start out in life as perfectly fine natural little beings, but something goes horribly wrong. What is it that goes wrong? It is, Buddhism proclaims, the nearly irresistible tendency of the ego-centered human mind to create a prison of self-delusion. Once fashioned, this self-absorbed state of consciousness leads inevitably to the all-too familiar human life of anxiety and dissatisfaction. But it doesn't have to be that way. Human life can be—and in fact *should* be—a state of abiding joy. Abiding joy is the truly natural state for men and women; the more familiar alternative is an aberration.

It is possible for every person to free himself or herself from the prison of ego—to awaken to the real truth of one's nature and thus to know freedom from fear, the basis of abiding joy. Buddha long ago showed the way to freedom. The tradition that he founded preserved that teaching. But the way to freedom is very difficult. Once hardened into our world of self-created delusions, we humans resist mightily any effort to change the situation. "Many are called, but few are chosen." Nonetheless, every person at least has the inner capacity to achieve liberation. The person who chooses to take up the great challenge must, as Buddha declared, become totally dedicated to the effort. Nothing short of total dedication can hope to succeed. A prisoner attempting an escape from jail doesn't dawdle along the way—at least, not one who make good the escape.

The quest for liberation is a process of total immersion. At the end of it is the great awakening to the truth of one's nature. It is the ultimate satori that sweeps away all delusions, opening consciousness to the clear knowledge of the "identity of one's own nature with all reality in an eternal now." In this state of freedom is found the abiding joy that is the natural fulfillment of human existence. But before this can occur, it is necessary that the unenlightened person experience a kind of death—a "Great Dying" as Hakuin put it. Satori, in fact, is the character of the "rebirth" that follows the act of finally letting go of everything, of "dying" to the old person and being "reborn" as the new person. In the words of Hakuin: "If you wish to know the true self beyond ego, you must be prepared to let go your hold as if hanging from a sheer precipice, to die and return again to life."

The Great Dying is itself preceded, and in fact brought to fruition, by what Hakuin called the "Great Doubt." This is a matter of the most profound importance. Whatever the trials and tribulations of ordinary life may be, at least a person normally feels some measure of security regarding the things he believes in and takes for granted. Most of all, his strong sense of self seems solid, inflexible, enduring. There is comfort in this; it is at least a dependable home base. But when one "leaves home" to follow instead the path of Buddha, one truly becomes a homeless person in the deep inner sense of the word. Whatever may be the pleasing initial experiences of this choice, the path must ultimately lead into a dark interior forest where the demons of fear reside. A genuine seeker of enlightenment has to face the fact that undreamed-of dreads—even terror—await the pilgrim who abandons the artificial comforts and securities of ordinary life and ventures into the realm where that artificiality comes to be revealed. It is no easy matter to give up the deep-seated sense of substantiality that we unconsciously associate with familiar things, most of all with one's self. A growing sense of uncertainty and lack of control can result in a terrible anxiety, even in some cases leading to suicidal thoughts. And there's no turning back! In the Zen tradition, this familiar condition is referred to as the "Zen sickness." Given the normal character of human consciousness, it is to some degree the necessary and inevitable precondition of enlightenment. Hakuin called it the Great Doubt.

So what's to be done? Hakuin would answer that first of all—and it is absolutely essential—the seeker must have the guidance of a genuinely enlightened teacher. Buddha could go it alone, and perhaps a few others have done so, but only a very few. The vast majority of men and women need the close and personal guidance of an already awakened teacher. But a Zen Master who employs only the techniques of meditation will not, in Hakuin's judgment, be successful. Hakuin fired many arrows at the Soto school. He denounced what he considered to be their excessive dependence on zazen. He called them tree stumps. Hakuin wanted a person to grapple with the Great Doubt in a dynamic way, to be like a blazing fire, not cold ashes:

> They foolishly take the dead teachings of no-thought and no-mind, where the mind is like dead ashes with wisdom obliterated, and make these into the essential doctrines of Zen. They practice silent, dead sitting as though they were incense burners in some old mausoleum and take this to be the treasure place of the true practice of the patriarchs. (quoted in Dumoulin, vol. 2, 384)

What, then, would Hakuin have the Zen Master do in properly guiding the student into and through the Great Doubt? He would have the Zen Master skillfully employ the koan exercise. In Hakuin's judgment, the koan exercise is the perfect solution; it is a wonderful tool that can be used in a series of stages to adroitly navigate the student into and all the way through the Great Doubt. The Great Doubt after all is a product of the rational mind struggling hopelessly with new experiences that it can't comprehend. The special beauty of the koan exercise is that it produces a state of psychological tension that finally bursts through the blockage created by discursive thought, thus dissolving the Great Doubt. The solution of the koan clears consciousness of the rational mind's doubts and tension, thus opening the way to satori.

Hakuin, fully immersed in the traditions of Rinzai Zen, was convinced that the koan exercise was the key to success in the quest of enlightenment. He reinvigorated the artful use of the koan, gathering together the best from the tradition and formulating a system that could be used by other Zen Masters. In Hakuin's system, the koans are hierarchically arranged in a series of gradations that correspond to the stages of growth that a Zen student will experience. The student starts at the beginning, usually with Mu, and then progressively moves through more and more difficult koans. Each solution produces a greater kensho experience, but thereby sets the stage for that much greater doubt, until finally the teacher guides the student into the koan exercise that results in perfect satori, the perfect "seeing into one's nature."

It's a wonderful ideal, and undoubtedly in the hands of skillful Zen Masters Hakuin's system has produced impressive results over the centuries. Hakuin certainly did much to establish the koan exercise as an important and fundamental part of Zen Buddhism. As mentioned earlier, the modern Zen scholar D. T. Suzuki has said, "To my mind it was the technique of the koan exercise that saved Zen as a unique heritage of Far Eastern culture." To the degree that that statement is accurate, Hakuin deserves much of the credit.

In addition to establishing the central place of the koan exercise in Rinzai discipline—and thus developing the orthodox line of Rinzai Zen—Hakuin also did much to free Rinzai from its aristocratic exclusivity and bring it to the common people. Rinzai would not match Soto in this respect, but at least Hakuin began some movement in the direction of a universal appeal. Undoubtedly his personal style had a lot to do with this. We are told that he was a congenial and tolerant man who cared nothing about distinctions of rank and wealth.

Hakuin was a great Zen Master; his contribution would affect the course of Zen for all time to come. Hakuin in the Rinzai tradition and Dogen in the Soto tradition, are the two tall mountains of the historical landscape of Zen Buddhism in Japan.

THE ZEN MONASTERY

The Zen monastery, like a Hindu ashram, is not a specific place, nor is it a group of buildings; it is a living organism.* Specifically, a Zen monastery is a community of monks living and working together under the guidance of a *roshi*. They have come together in the belief that the communal way of living offers the richest possible environment within which to follow Buddha's path leading to enlightenment. The roshi, an already awakened man or woman, will oversee the life of the community and personally guide the development of each of the monks.

Zen monasteries in China developed out of the monastic tradition of Buddhism generally, which, in turn, had its roots in the ashram tradition of India. When Zen became established in Japan, the Chinese monastic system was adopted and was gradually modified to fit the more characteristic Japanese way of life. In modern times, as Zen Buddhism takes root in the West it is only natural that the Japanese monastic system would be adopted and faithfully recreated, at least initially.[†] Already, though, significant adaptations can be discerned.

---

*It should be pointed out that a "monastery" includes some technical aspects that may not always be present. In the West, the term "Zen Center" is more likely to be used.

[†]Zen Buddhism has a long history in Korea and Viet Nam as well as in Japan, and some Zen monasteries in the West are the products of these traditions, but the great majority are based on Japanese Zen Buddhism.

Although a Zen monastery is a group of people, not a group of buildings, it is normal for the mind to think of a monastery in terms of its physical layout, the place where the community resides and practices the Zen way of life. A Zen monastery can be located in virtually any kind of environment. We ordinarily think of Zen monasteries, though, as being located in very remote, out-of-the-way places—and often this is the case—but many Zen centers are situated right in the heart of busy cities. The original Rinzai monasteries were clustered around the outskirts of Kyoto and were actively involved in the life of the capital. And still today, Zen centers are to be found in many urban areas of Japan, as well as in cities throughout the world. It is often the case, though, that urban-centered Zen communities will own, in addition to the city address, a remote location that offers a serene alternative.*

For the most part, though, the founders of Zen monasteries have from the very beginning sought out relatively remote locations. Ideally a Zen monastery would be found in an out-of-the-way place, far removed from the hustle and bustle of ordinary life, a place passed over by others where the environment has retained its natural character and beauty. In this serene and natural setting, the monastery can go about its daily life in a peaceful way, undisturbed by the usual distractions of human life. This, of course, is the description of an ideal; compromises often have to be made. Nevertheless, wherever it is located, the Zen monastery is a place of great tranquility and beauty. Whether it be large or small, richly endowed or very humble, city-centered or nestled in the farthest part of the mountains, a Zen monastery is one of the truly great achievements of the human spirit. To better understand its character, let's mentally visit a traditional country monastery and explore the parts that make up the whole.

Traditionally, the entry to a Zen monastery is through some sort of gateway. This is important because the space that makes up the monastery grounds is a special place. It is distinctly set aside for the practice of Zen; in a way it is a "sacred precinct." When one passes through the gateway, one has the feeling of entering another realm. The earliest monasteries in Japan, inspired by the Chinese model, had huge, elaborate gateways. They were ornate buildings in their own right, sometimes with several rooms. Examples of this type of architecture can still be seen at Nara and Kyoto. Over time, gateways became increasingly modest. (Some modern monasteries don't have distinctive gateways at all, which seems to me to be an unfortunate omission.)

The grounds of a traditional Zen monastery are not left in a wild state, far from it—the grounds are cultivated into a garden-like setting and lovingly maintained. But everything—grounds, buildings, and other structures—all fit together with the surrounding environment in a perfect harmony. A traditional Zen monastery is not in conflict with its surroundings; it looks almost as if it had grown in that place along with the trees and the grass.

Within the grounds of the monastery precinct are a collection of buildings that serve the needs of the members of the community. The most important building by far is the

---

*This practice has become popular in the West. The Zen Centers of San Francisco and Los Angeles, for example, are located right in the heart of their respective cities. Both, however, maintain fully developed monastic centers in remote locations. The San Francisco Zen Center operates an excellent monastic retreat in a remote part of the coastal mountains near the Big Sur area. And the Los Angeles Zen Center maintains a retreat high in the San Jacinto Mountains, southeast of the Los Angeles area urban sprawl. Many other urban Zen Centers do the same sort of thing.

Zendo. This structure, the core of the monastery, is the place where the community gathers for zazen. In many cases, the Zendo is used solely for meditation practice, but it is not uncommon for it to have other uses as well. The Zendo, for example, may double as a Buddha Hall, the place where "services" honoring Buddha are held. Monasteries that can afford it have a separate Buddha Hall and not uncommonly it is a very elaborate room. The Zendo, though, is the pride and joy of the community. Typically the whole community will lavish its very best work on the construction and upkeep of the Zendo. Zendos represent some of the finest expressions of traditional Japanese architecture, and this tradition has spread to other parts of the world where Zen Buddhism has taken root.

In the early days, it was popular to arrange the buildings of the monastery, according to the Chinese custom, to conform loosely to the shape of a human body, the "body of Buddha." The Zendo, naturally, would be located at the position of the heart. This custom gradually died out, but the Zendo, wherever it may be located, remains the heart of the physical layout.

Every Zen monastery has a Zendo, but other buildings will vary widely from one monastery to another. One building likely to be found in modern times is a dormitory or residence hall for the monks. This is quite common today, but in the past it was often the custom, especially in Soto monasteries, for the monks to sleep and eat their meals right in the Zendo. The roshi, however, would not sleep with the rest. Typically he would have a simple hut of some kind separate from the others. In the roshi's quarters would be found a small room where the monks could meet individually with him for *dokusan,* a private conversation which gives the roshi an opportunity to check and guide the progress of each member of the community.

A dining hall with adjacent kitchen would be another commonly found building. And in connection with this would be some kind of barn or shed where needed gardening equipment could be stored. All traditional Zen monasteries, at least those located in a country setting, could be expected to have a large fruit and vegetable garden that would provide most of the food needs of the community. It is a distinctive feature of the Zen monastery that it strives to achieve the greatest possible degree of self-sufficiency. Work in the garden, and in the kitchen, is a major part of the productive activity of a Zen community.

Another building, sure to be found in all of the monasteries of Japan, is the bathhouse. The hot soaking tub (*onsen* in Japanese) is so deeply ingrained in Japanese culture that it was regarded as an indispensable part of monastery life as well. The Japanese bath is not for washing; it is for soaking the body in extremely hot water. Cleaning the body is a separate operation that precedes the bath. No soap ever reaches the soaking tub. (God help the person who makes that mistake!)* It's probably not going too far to say that the locations of many Zen monasteries were chosen primarily because of nearness to natural hot springs. The Japanese hot bath is a wonderful custom that, happy to say, has largely followed the migration of Zen Buddhism to other lands.

There are several other possible buildings that might be located within a Zen monastery: a monastery office, for example, an infirmary, or a library. In addition to

---

*I once committed this mortal sin, but it *really* was an accident. I was staying in a *riyokan* (a traditional style inn) in a remote part of Honshu. Alone in the bathhouse, I was washing off before getting into the soaking tub. Suddenly the slippery bar of soap shot out of my hand, and made a long, time-stopping arc. *Plop!*—right into the tub. My tender Western arms took a long time searching around in the scorching water to find it, and I had to half empty the tub. They all knew, of course, but no one ever said a word to me about it.

buildings, there are certain other structures that are likely to be found. *Ogane*, the great monastery bell, ranks second only to the Zendo in the loving attention it receives. Every Zen monastic community—just like every Christian monastic community—yearns to have the special beauty of a great monastery bell marking out the divisions of the day. But this is one of the few things that the community cannot produce for itself. The craft of bronze casting became a specialized kind of work that was elevated to a fine art in Japan, just as it was in the West.

A great bell is a masterpiece of the bronzecaster's art; a Zen community might have to save for generations before being able to afford such a commission. But, great or small, some kind of bell would occupy an important place within the monastery grounds. By custom, it is usually placed near the Zendo and is hung within a large wooden scaffolding constructed specifically for this purpose. The Zen bell has no clapper; it is struck on the lower outside rim with a wooden piece which is ordinarily suspended by ropes. The sound of a Zen bell is typically very, very deep and resonating. It's more of a boom than a clang—the type of sound you feel as much as hear. The deep vibrating waves continue for a long time, finally trailing off to merge with the natural sounds of the environment. Usually it is struck just once or twice. The Zen bell is a sound that is never forgotten; in a way its sound ties together all of the disparate elements of the monastery.

Another thing certain to be found somewhere on the grounds of a traditional Zen monastery is a small shrine containing a statue of Shakyamuni Buddha. This too would probably represent a major purchase, but an indispensable one. The statue of Buddha is honored, not venerated in the usual religious sense. It is a visible and much-loved reminder of the founder and his teaching. The teaching of Buddha is, after all, what the monastery is all about. In addition to the statue of Shakyamuni Buddha, there may be other shrines as well, honoring, for example, esteemed bodhisattvas such as Avalokiteshvara.

All of these things that taken together make up the fabric of a Zen monastery are woven together in its garden-like setting. The art of Japanese gardening reaches its finest expression in the grounds of some Zen monasteries. This is not formal gardening, nothing flamboyant or overstated. Though much care is given to detail, the grounds have a natural feel, much in harmony with the surrounding environment. Through patient care and planting, the gardeners have over many generations created a place of great tranquility and natural beauty. Everything about a Zen monastery is designed to promote serenity and the meditative state of mind. The Daoist love of nature is everywhere to be seen, and heard. If you have an opportunity to visit a traditional Zen monastery, I'm sure that you will be struck by the many touches, some of them very humble, that give rise to feelings of beauty and harmony with nature. Let me mention just a couple examples from my own experience.

Picture a small water basin made from natural rock. It is filled with clear cold water. The water, diverted from a nearby rippling stream, trickles into a gourdlike structure above the basin, to which is attached a short length of hollow bamboo. The gourd is fixed to a swivel, and when the water fills it, the increased weight tips the structure forward spilling the water into the basin through the bamboo pipe. Empty of water, a counterweight returns the gourd to the original position, and the cycle begins again. At the end of each cycle, approximately one or two minutes, any nearby ear is treated to the sound of a hollow thwunk followed by a brief rush of spilling water. It might seem as if this would be distracting, but it's not at all. It's a beautiful sound, almost hypnotizing in a way. (And it also has the practical effect of keeping the deer from munching too much of the garden. In fact, it is called a *shishi-odoshi*, which originally meant "deer chaser.") I suspect that a great many satori experiences have been triggered over the ages by such Zen garden sounds as this.

The same little stream that feeds the basin has been crossed by a large wooden beam similar to a railroad tie. It has been placed in the stream to help step it down from a higher to a lower level. The running water spills over the beam, making a wonderful rippling sound that never stops. In autumn, leaves falling into the stream back up behind the wooden beam, creating something of a tangled mass of wet leaves. One's first impulse might be to get a rake and clean it out, but what a mistake that would be! To the relaxed eye, the natural pattern of these many-colored leaves, shimmering in the dappled sunlight, becomes a sight of such great beauty as to be nearly overwhelming. This is the kind of experience that Hakuin, and countless other lovers of Zen, would want to cherish. These humble little "natural accidents" are filled with beauty and are capable of lifting the heart and the mind to a new and higher vision of reality.

A place of serene natural beauty, highly conducive to the meditative state of mind—that is the Zen monastery. The traditional arts of Japan have shown themselves to be very well suited to this. The physical layout of the monastery, however beautiful it may be, is of course only the setting for the practice of Zen. It is the community of monks that really makes it a monastery. The daily life which the setting supports is what it's all about. And it matters not in the least whether the monastery be a fully developed center in a beautiful mountain setting or merely a converted warehouse in the middle of a modern city. The daily routine of the members of the community is the lifeblood of Zen Buddhism.

The daily routine of the Zen community has a grand simplicity about it. The cycle of the day begins before dawn and unfolds slowly and peacefully. There is never the feeling of hurry or anxiety that is so typical of modern life in general. Although there is room for much variation, there is also much similarity in daily life from one monastery to another. In very general terms, a typical day would begin early, usually before dawn. The community is summoned to the Zendo where the day begins with the recitation of passages from the sutras. This is followed by a period of sitting meditation, typically for about an hour.* There may be an opportunity during the morning meditation period for dokusan, a brief private meeting with the roshi, whose experienced eye can quickly check on each person's progress. A simple breakfast (vegetarian, of course) would be available after zazen, and then the monks would spend about half an hour thoroughly sweeping and cleaning the entire monastery. The bulk of the day is given over to work or study, with a brief break for a light lunch. In the late afternoon, the monks are likely to gather again for recitation of the sutras, followed by the evening meal. The day closes with another session of sitting meditation, which again includes the opportunity for dokusan. The community retires around nine or ten o'clock. Sleep comes easily after a day such as this. Soon the morning bell will rouse them all for another turn of the cycle.

---

*Many Rinzai Zen centers follow a wonderful old custom of serving tea to the meditators at the beginning of the morning meditation session. I came to love this tradition some years ago when I was a guest at a Zen Center in the mountains of New Mexico. It was still dark and *very* cold when we assembled each morning in the Zendo. That cup of steaming tea was almost a little satori in itself.

Clearly the practice of zazen occupies a central place in the daily life of a Zen monastery. This is true in both Soto and Rinzai monasteries, although there will be a greater emphasis on zazen in the Soto tradition. It's not uncommon for several hours of each day to be given to zazen, and this is just the normal daily routine. In addition to the normal routine, there are throughout the year times of intensive work known as "practice periods," or even more intense periods of work known as sesshins. During a sesshin, the normal routine is suspended and the monks sit almost continuously in zazen. Twelve hours a day or more is not uncommon. In a Zen monastery, zazen is king.

Zazen is practiced in the Zendo. This is typically a large airy room, or sometimes two or three rooms that open into one another. In the traditional Japanese-style Zendo, the platformed sitting areas are covered with tatami mats and the walls are bare; doorways are sliding shoji screens. Its simplicity is the essence of its beauty. In the central part of the room will be an altar-like structure which holds a statue of Shakyamuni Buddha and perhaps some other items such as a floral arrangement and an incense burner. This is not an altar for the worship of a god in the customary religious sense. Again, it is a visible reminder of the teaching, the Dharma, and one's link through that teaching to Buddha himself and all that have come after him.

Near the altar, one will likely find one or more bowl-shaped gongs resting on cushions. Next to these will be a wooden striker and perhaps other implements such as wooden clappers. These are used by the senior monk who presides over the meditation session. In a large group, the senior monk may be assisted by one or two others.

The beginning of a meditation session is ordinarily announced by the striking of a wooden clapper that hangs just outside the Zendo. As the monks arrive, they leave their shoes (or more likely sandals) in wooden cases designed for that purpose. No one ever walks in the Zendo with shoes on. In a traditional monastery, there is a ritual right way to do practically everything. One enters the Zendo slowly, in a dignified manner, stepping through the doorway with the left foot first. When leaving it is the right foot first. The monk walks to his or her place and bows deeply before sitting down. The deep bow with the palms pressed together is called *gassho*. The monks sit in rows along the walls, unless the group is too large, in which case interior rows are also formed. Generally, each person sits facing the bare wall, although in the Rinzai tradition, it is common to sit facing the interior of the room. Each monk sits on a firm round black cushion called a *zafu*, which may be centered on a thin cloth mat which may be placed directly on the tatami floor covering, or as is more likely the case, on long wooden platforms built up about two feet from the floor. Unless there is some physical problem that prevents it, each person is expected to sit in the cross-legged posture, with the hands together above the lap. As mentioned before, there are variations to this posture so that almost everyone can master it in time. The great value of this posture is that, once mastered, it permits one to sit still for long periods of time without feeling the need to change the position of the body. It is very solid and balanced, and allows the blood to circulate freely and the breathing to be deep and easy. The spine is held upright, with the chin brought in toward the chest just a little. The eyes are open but downcast, not focusing on anything.

So what's really going on here? Why is *so much* time given to simply sitting motionless? What are they *doing* when they practice zazen? These are legitimate questions. A person raised in the culture of the West can't help but find it puzzling, to say the least. And, as has been noted, there have been more than a few throughout the tradition of Zen itself who have criticized what they regarded to be an excessive affection for sitting meditation. The great Hakuin referred to the rows of sitting monks as tree stumps. Nonetheless, from the time of Buddha himself to the present day, sitting meditation has enjoyed a place of special importance in the tradition of Buddhism.

If nothing else, sitting meditation provides an excellent opportunity to set aside the usual distractions of life and turn inward for a little while to focus on the flow of consciousness, and thus in a dispassionate way to get to know one's personal state of consciousness. There is great value in this. Growing intuitive self-knowledge can go far to loosen the grip of the ego-delusion. Also, sitting meditation, by emphasizing a concentration on the flow of the present moment, can have the effect of increasing one's sensitivity to the present, to the larger reality that one is always a part of, but often fails to perceive. In the Rinzai tradition, a sitting meditation period provides an ideal opportunity for one to concentrate on the present koan exercise.

The above-mentioned applications are all undeniably valuable. But there is something which many in Zen Buddhism, especially in the Soto tradition, hold to be vastly more valuable. The art of sitting meditation, when mastered, holds forth the possibility of giving one the ability to enter into a state of consciousness in which the thinking mind is completely put to rest, the grip of ego is loosened, and the individual experiences, for a while at least, that state of consciousness known as *samadhi* in Sanskrit. "Samadhi" becomes *zanmai* in Japanese. Zanmai, a profound experience in its own right, is held by many to be a most fertile condition for the rising of satori, the perfect intuition of awakening in which one "sees the truth of one's nature." Zanmai does not *cause* satori—no one would argue that—but it well may provide an ideal condition for its spontaneous emergence.

Words become such frail things when we direct our attention to the nature of that which we call transcendent truth. One thing is clear, though; we must "get out of our own way" before we can be open to a new way of knowing. By this, I mean that we must be willing to let go of the way of the thinking mind. Learning to do this is one of the things that sitting meditation is all about.

Of course, developing skill in achieving the state of zanmai is no simple matter. Mastery of the art of meditation is essentially not different from mastery of a musical instrument, a violin for instance. No one would expect to achieve mastery quickly; it takes many years and much dedication. And that is one reason why so many hours are given to zazen practice. One may develop skill in the posture of zazen relatively quickly. Thus, from the outside, the student may *appear* to be very calm, very "meditative." But inside it may well be a very different story. The tranquil exterior can often disguise the war going on inside. As Hakuin emphasized in his teaching, one must pass through various stages, especially the Great Doubt, on his or her journey to liberation. For many Zen students, meditation practice is the primary way in which this journey is walked. And that, once again, is why the continual guidance of an already enlightened roshi is so valuable.

Just as there are stages in the overall life of the Zen student, there are stages in each individual meditation session as well. Everyone has a contemporary "edge" (a "cutting edge"), which represents the farthest limit so far achieved in his or her progress toward experiencing the unitive state—or maybe a better way of putting it, the farthest limit so far achieved in being able and willing to totally let go. Real zazen is practiced "at the edge." But one cannot hope to sit down, assume the right posture, and immediately be at one's edge. It takes time to relax and become centered, to get past one's peculiar distractions— and everyone has his or her own personal collection of distractions. We could compare a meditation session to a diamond mine. Each time you go into the mine you must descend past the earlier levels and corridors before you reach the cutting face. This is why zazen sessions tend to be somewhat long. In a short session, too much of the time is spent just getting back to where the diamonds are.

There are many "schools" of meditation, and each one has its own collection of meditation techniques (ways of getting you to the diamonds). Traditional yoga meditation emphasizes the creation of a totally interiorized state of consciousness. Zen meditation, for the most part, emphasizes the practice of shikantaza—fully experiencing, as a focused observer only, whatever the conscious reality of the moment may be; completely attentive concentration on whatever the form of consciousness may be, at this moment, and even if it takes no form at all. Doing this takes great power of concentration, and this power does not come quickly or easily. Consciousness is so mysterious. Why does it exist at all? Some modern researchers speculate that consciousness is a *tool* of the brain, one of the means it uses to successfully manage the survival and reproduction of a given genome. That's a pretty humbling thought, but there does seem to be a lot of truth in it— most of the time, perhaps, but not all the time. Meditation reveals that at least the *potential* exists for ordinary consciousness to transcend itself.

The great journey to liberation begins, like everything, at the beginning. A novice in a Zen monastery will often be assigned the exercise of "counting the breath" while practicing zazen. In this exercise, the student concentrates his or her attention as fully as possible on the simple act of breathing. Each outbreath is silently given a number, usually only from one to ten and then repeated. "Counting the breath" is an excellent exercise for developing skill in centering and concentration.*

There is one little problem in the practice of sitting meditation that seems to plague almost everyone. If you have had experience with meditation practice, you'll know what I mean. It is the tendency, especially when sitting for a long time, to fall asleep. Some are bothered by this more than others—and perhaps a few rise above it altogether—but most meditators will sometimes know the experience. That is the reason why the drinking of tea became popular in Zen.

There is also another interesting way of dealing with this problem. In a traditional Zendo, a senior monk patrols the room during a meditation session. He carries with him the *kyosaku*, a long thin stick broadened at one end. When he encounters a person who is slouching, or who has fallen asleep, the kyosaku comes into play. As with everything else, this is a highly ritualized act. He will first lightly touch the person's shoulder with the kyosaku, then whack the same spot four times. The blow will be administered on both sides of the neck. Don't let this shock you. Please don't get the idea that this is violent or painful, or even embarrassing. It's none of these things. The kyosaku blow is not meant to hurt, but it does dramatically invigorate a body and mind much in need of some invigoration. It's not uncommon for a person to use a silent gesture to ask for a blow from the kyosaku. In a strange way, its occasional sound, far from being a distraction, actually adds to the meditative ambience of the Zendo and helps to keep everyone alert. Incidentally, when one is struck by the kyosaku the only permitted response is gassho (bowing respectfully with the palms pressed together). There are indeed some aspects of

---

*Kobun Chino Otagawa Roshi, founder of Jikoji Zen Center in California, was once asked if counting the breath was a good practice. "Sure," he said, "One, one, one . . ."

traditional Zen that seem somewhat violent to the modern world and have thus gradually disappeared. Perhaps, unfortunately, this is coming to include the use of the kyosaku. In many non-Japanese monasteries, it has become merely a Zen ornament left to hang unused on the Zendo wall.

In addition to sleepiness of mind, there is the problem of sleepiness of body during a long meditation session. This is dealt with through the practice of *kinhin*. After approximately an hour of sitting, a signal is given from a wooden clapper and everyone stands. The monks form a line and walk around the periphery of the room, or outside the Zendo, for about ten minutes. Naturally, this too is a highly ritualized affair. The line moves—in silence, of course—always in a clockwise direction. Soto monks walk rather slowly; Rinzai monks walk briskly. But all Zen monks walk in a very distinctive way, holding the closed hands pressed against the solar plexus. When the time is up the clapper is again sounded and everyone returns to the seated posture.

And so it goes, seemingly without end. The appearance of the monks seated in zazen seems so tranquil. The room seems to be the epitome of serenity. But each is vividly absorbed in his or her own great adventure. And occasionally that adventure breaks through in the miracle of new vision. Consider this description by Kosen Imakita:

> One night as I sat absorbed in meditation, I suddenly fell into a strange state. It was as if I were dead and everything had been totally cut off. There was no longer a before or an after and both the object of my meditation and my Self had disappeared. The only remaining feeling was that my innermost Self was completely filled by and at one with everything above, below and around me. An infinite light shone within me. After a while I came back to myself like one risen from the dead. Seeing, hearing, speaking, movements and thoughts all seemed completely transformed from what they had previously been. As I tentatively pondered the truth of the world and tried to make sense of the inconceivable, everything was at once understood. It appeared to me clear and real. Without thinking about it, overjoyed, I began to throw my hands into the air and to dance around. Then suddenly I cried out: one million sutras are as but a single candle before the sun. Wonderful, truly wonderful. (quoted in Dumoulin, vol. 2, 408)

In the traditional Zen monastery, each member of the community meets privately from time to time with the roshi in dokusan. This does not necessarily occur every day; it may be very infrequent or no more often than once a week. Although any time of day may be appropriate for dokusan, it is often convenient to arrange these meetings during zazen periods. After being admitted to the roshi's room, he (or she) bows deeply and waits for the roshi's questions. Within the Zen community, it is believed that an experienced master can quickly and intuitively determine the state of mind of the student, and can thus recommend exactly the right thing for that person to be working on. Dokusan is typically quite brief, two or three minutes is often sufficient, seldom more than ten minutes. This is not a "confession" period, nor is it meant to be a counseling session; it is simply an opportunity for the roshi to check each person's progress and recommend appropriate disciplines.

In the Rinzai tradition, the usual purpose of dokusan is for the roshi to check the students' progress with their koan. He will ask the student to explain the meaning of the koan currently being worked with. No amount of cleverness can ever fool an experienced roshi. If the response is not completely authentic and spontaneous, the student will be dismissed and told to work harder. In traditional Japanese monasteries, it would seem that it was customary for the roshi to affect a very gruff exterior manner. There are endless stories of roshis shouting at students, kicking them, or hitting them with a stick. The roshi might say, for example, "Alright, tell me now, what was your original face before you were born?" (or, an even more perplexing version: "What *is* your original face before *your parents* were born?") If the student's response did not show evidence of real Zen understanding, the master was likely to shout his disapproval, and the student might be driven from the room. This is a cultural difference that is simply incomprehensible to most of the modern world, and dokusan has correspondingly become a much more peaceful affair in today's Zen monasteries.

Three activities are of primary importance in the ongoing life of a Zen monastic: *sanzen* (meeting in dokusan with the roshi), *samu* (participating in the work of the monastery), and *zazen* (sitting meditation). Zazen occupies several hours of each day, and during periods of sesshin, it takes up practically all of the monk's waking hours. But in a normal routine, zazen is far from being the only activity of the day. A number of other things are included. Chief among these is samu. The word *samu* refers to the ongoing work of the monastery. Remember, a Zen community seeks to be as self-sufficient as it possibly can be. Everyone works, and works hard, whether it be manual labor or some other kind of useful work. This has always been the case. It was the eighth-century Chinese master Paijing, the creator of the basic monastic rule, who said, "A day without working is a day without eating." And Dogen, the founder of Japanese Soto Zen, elevated work to a place of profound importance by insisting that the real practice of Zen consists in loving service to others.

Samu is not to be thought of as toil or as a necessary evil. Work for the good of the community is an expression of the mutual support and love that the individual members share with one another. Seen in this way, samu is a source of joy, and when entered into in the right spirit it is a genuine form of meditation. In fact, samu is really the other side of zazen; together they form a whole. Both are ways of achieving the state of consciousness in which one transcends the delusion of the separated ego and experiences the undivided reality of being, as it is. Zazen is the physically passive side of this experience, in which one turns inward. Samu is the physically active side of the experience. In a full Zen lifestyle, each implies the other.

Although samu is concerned with physical activity, the mind can still be fully absorbed in the present moment. This all-important state of consciousness is called "mindfulness" in modern times. It is the wonderful skill of being able to enter fully into the being of this moment's activity. No distractions, no chattering thoughts about other things, no hurrying, no fretting about the clock's time, nothing but the undivided being of what exists, as it exists, here and now. If you are chopping lettuce, you chop lettuce—nothing more and nothing less. If you are raking the garden, you rake; you do not rake soil with the hands while raking old memories with the mind. Mindfulness is to samu what shikantaza is to zazen. In a way, "mindfulness" is the bottom line of the life of Zen; it is the distinguishing characteristic of a Zen man, a Zen woman. A famous Zen saying puts it this way: "When you stand, stand. When you walk, walk. Just don't wobble."

Individual members of the community may have specialized skills—such as cooking, carpentry, or calligraphy—and will therefore usually work at these crafts during times of samu. But some things, such as general cleaning and helping in the kitchen, are shared by everyone. Work details are assigned by a senior monk delegated for this task by the roshi. It would be unthinkable that anyone would ever object, or do less than his or her very best work. Once again, samu is not toil; it is an act of love. There is always work that needs to be done—gardening, fixing a leaky roof, preparing meals, tending to a sick person, paying the bills, shopping, chopping firewood, and on and on and on. I'm sure most of these things sound pretty familiar; the basic needs of life don't change much from one environment to another. But what could be thought of a drudgery in another context becomes a joy in the daily routine of a Zen monastery.

Samu, like its counterpart zazen, is meant to be done in silence. Outer silence helps to quiet the habitual inner chatter of the thinking mind. Speaking is not forbidden, but by mutual agreement, talking is limited to only what is necessary. This, in fact, is true throughout the whole day in a Zen monastery. The usual background buzz of chattering voices is noticeably (and enjoyably) absent within a Zen community. Mindfulness and verbosity are mutually exclusive. And this applies equally to that inner verbosity that plagues almost all of us humans. Mindfulness is indeed a wonderful skill, but it is not acquired easily. The beginner must struggle against the habits of self-distracting thought. An experienced roshi knows this and keeps an eye on the novices; one can easily be overwhelmed both physically and mentally by the volcanolike power set free by the effort to adopt the Zen state of mind.

In the traditional Japanese monastery, afternoon was the customary time for samu. In the modern West, it is more likely to be mornings, or, depending on need, both mornings and afternoons. Other necessary activities compete with samu and are scheduled on a regular recurring basis, but not every day. One of these is the roshi's informal lecture to the community. Occasionally the talk will be delivered by a senior monk or an honored guest, but usually it is the roshi himself (or herself, as is sometimes the case in modern times outside of Japan). Zen Masters have always taken seriously their responsibility to educate their disciples in the deeper meaning of Zen. In this, the roshi is following the example of Buddha himself who often called the sangha together and spoke to them from his own experience. The importance of this cannot be exaggerated. Zen tradition holds that above all else it is the special personal transmission from master to student that effects awakening. Recall that the fundamental gatha of Zen Buddhism states that enlightenment is "a special transmission outside of words and scriptures."

Personal transmission may be key, but words and scriptures are far from being unimportant. From the earliest times, the Zen tradition has maintained a loving regard for its accumulated lore, especially the sutras. It has always been the expectation that Zen monks will be knowledgeable regarding this heritage of traditional wisdom. Consequently, periods of individual study have long had a place in the ongoing routine. These may not be every day, but they would be at frequent intervals nonetheless. One excellent way of studying is to copy by hand the text being studied. In this way, Zen monks—just like their monastic counterparts in the West—have kept alive the literary treasures of the past. Even though the invention of printing ended the need for this, the practice continues still to some extent—unfortunately, only a small extent.

A brief general cleaning is done every morning, but by tradition on certain days— days of the month with a 4 or a 9 in their number—a very thorough cleaning is scheduled. These days also include the much-loved hot bath. On "bath days" the bathhouse fire is stoked up, and the water in the soaking tub raised to its customary scorching temperature.

Even the bath has its necessary ritual. Monks use the bathhouse in small groups according to rank, with the roshi going first. As a rule, there is a small statue of Batsudabara, the mythical god of the bath, somewhere near the entry. In the really orthodox tradition, each monk would not only bow in reverence to this statue, but would do three full prostrations in front of it before entering!

Bath days are also the days for shaving one another's heads, a task best performed by someone other than oneself. The shaved head, a universal badge of monkhood, is another of the changes occurring in modern times. It is still very popular, both in and out of Japan, but it is generally not required in Western monasteries and is by no means universal any longer.

One of the most profound changes concerns mendicancy. Mendicancy refers to begging. Until the time of Paijing, it was customary for monastic communities to support themselves almost entirely through begging. This was already a long-established tradition in India when Buddhism began to spread to China. The Rule of Paijing, though, stressed self-sufficiency. Mendicancy, however, continued to be practiced in Zen communities, but it became a ritualized activity with a higher purpose than merely acquiring the essentials of life from generous donors. In the traditional Japanese Zen monastery, mendicancy was preserved and became a regularly scheduled activity. The monks would leave the monastery in the morning and walk to the nearby villages. That is probably the reason for samu being an afternoon activity.

The ritual of mendicancy was quite a spectacle. It can still be seen occasionally in rural parts of Japan, but is fast dying out in modern times, and hardly exists at all any longer in Zen communities outside of Japan.* The monks would assemble dressed in the customary white inner kimono and black outer robe tied at the waist with a cord, straw sandals on the feet, and a broad flat straw hat on the head or carried in the right hand. In addition, there was the cloth mendicant's bag slung around the neck. They would form a long line, and in a quiet and dignified manner, march off single file through the bamboo groves and rice fields to the villages, where each would silently canvass in separate areas. Townspeople considered it an honor to share something, perhaps some cooked rice or a small coin, with the monks of the local monastery. After about an hour or so, they would reassemble and silently return to the monastery. Undoubtedly, what they collected would be useful, but that was not the point of begging in a Zen community. Mendicancy was seen as a powerful exercise in humility; that was its real value. As the *Hoju Sutra* puts it, "If a man practice mendicancy, all arrogance will be destroyed."

The above examples are just some of the more important activities that help to make up the daily routine. What ties it all together is the strong sense of community. A Zen monastery is, once again, a living organism made up of the men and women who have come together to share a way of life based on the teaching of Buddha and the long tradition of Zen Buddhism. The grounds of the monastery constitute the place that the community calls home. That place is the matrix within which the community brings to life the teaching of Buddha. Although all Zen communities share the same tradition, each monastery is, of course, unique; each has its own special way of enlivening the teaching. For this reason, the custom of the pilgrimage has a long history in Zen.

---

*One unlikely place where the tradition of mendicancy is alive and well is in the English village of West Sussex. A small group of Theravadin Buddhist monks from the nearby Chithurst Forest Monastery make their daily rounds. This very interesting center was described in a 1994 article written for the Buddhist periodical *Tricycle* (Steven Batchelor, "A Thai Forest Tradition Grows in England," *Tricycle*: Summer, 1994, p. 39).

It has always been the custom in Japan, especially in the Rinzai tradition, for the younger monks to enrich their practice by taking to the road from time to time in order to seek out other masters to study under for a while. Every monastery could expect to have a certain number of "guest monks" among the community. This constant shuffling around undoubtedly helped to preserve a certain amount of uniformity within the tradition. It should come as no surprise that this too was a highly ritualized procedure. And how strange this particular ritual seems to the modern mind. The Zen Master Tsuguo Miyajima has given us a vivid description of what it was like.

In Miyajima's illustration, the monk—traveling on foot, of course—would arrive at the gate of the monastery he hoped to visit. After making his request to enter, he would be kept waiting, usually for two whole days, in a little room near the entry. During this time, he must show his sincerity and humility by remaining constantly in a kneeling position with his head bowed all the way to the floor where it would rest on his small traveling rucksack. His only break from this position would be for brief periods of eating and sleeping. Meanwhile, people would enter the room from time to time and heap abuse on him, telling him that he's not wanted and perhaps even attempting to physically throw him out. Of course, all parties know that this behavior is prescribed by tradition; nevertheless, the young monk had better not even for a minute cease to play the part expected of him, or he really will be thrown out.

If he gets past this initial period, the visiting monk is allowed to enter another special room called the *tankaryo* where he must ceaselessly practice zazen for as long as a week. He will be carefully watched, and if everyone is satisfied with his earnestness, the visitor will at last be allowed to join the community. How different it is today! But still it is not uncommon to encounter at least a little ritual resistance at first. The discipline is demanding, to say the least, and not everyone is cut out for it. It's important to know that the person seeking admission does sincerely feel some measure of dedication.

I hope that this brief overview of the character of a Zen monastery helps to make it seem more real to you. And I also hope that you haven't gotten the impression that a Zen monastery is too much of a formidable and serious sort of place. It's not that way at all. All of the members of the community are flesh-and-blood human beings who typically have an especially rich appreciation of the joy, and humor, of life.

Before we leave the monastery, there is one more thing to be aware of. It's not a part of all Zen monasteries, but it was a much-loved addition to the early ones, and when means permitted has been included in many down through the ages. It is a unique masterpiece of Zen art with strong roots in the Daoist tradition. The Japanese name for it is *kare-sansui*, which in English means "dry—mountains and water," but it is usually referred to as a "rock and gravel garden." The kare-sansui has a spellbinding beauty that no words can describe; it must be experienced. Fortunately, some of the greatest ones still exist, particularly in the Kyoto area, and are open to the public.

The special value of the kare-sansui lies in its having an unusual and potent influence on the meditative state of mind. Its beauty is something to be contemplated, slowly and quietly. Perhaps for this reason, the kare-sansui is usually located directly beside the Zendo. In fact, it is ordinarily attached to the Zendo by a low wall that encloses the garden on the three open sides. Just outside the wall, one would likely find a planting of ornamental trees. On the Zendo side, there is generally a long wooden veranda where people can sit and contemplate the garden scene.

FIGURE 18.1   Kare-sansui, Ryoan-ji Monastery; Kyoto, Japan. (P. Bresnan)

    Each kare-sansui is a unique creation and can be any size and shape, but most are large rectangles. The masterpiece at Ryoan-ji, a monastery near Kyoto, is approximately one hundred feet by forty-six feet. Picture this broad, flat piece of ground completely carpeted with a deep layer of coarse, snow-white gravel. It is made from a special white rock found only in one mountainous part of Japan. Actually, if you look closely, you will see that the gravel pieces contain tiny flecks of black, but from a distance it has a snowy appearance. Gravel covers almost all of the surface, but a few small boulders have been carefully placed within it. These too have been chosen with great care; the eroded texture is especially beautiful and may appear to have a wood-like grain about it. Although the placement is most carefully chosen, if it is done well, the rock has a completely natural feeling about it, as if it had always been just there. A velvety green moss is allowed to grow on the rock surface. This is the only vegetation to be found in this "garden." Nothing else will be included.*

    The most unique feature of the kare-sansui is the raking; this is what gives it its special beauty. In the early morning, one or two skilled monks have the highly honored task of "raking" the garden. This is done with a special wooden rake that has about six widely spaced large wooden teeth. The monks use the rakes to create a fresh pattern of parallel rows in the gravel. For the most part, these are long straight furrows that may stretch the entire length of the garden. In the vicinity of the boulders, though, the raking becomes

---

*There is no absolute rule regarding the kare-sansui. The Hoko-ji (Zen monastery) at Hamamatsu has a very beautiful kare-sansui that even includes a small tree.

more liquid and swirling, as if the lines of gravel were the waves of the ocean and the rocks were mountainous islands. Raking the whole garden this way is a high art, and very much a Zen art. If the raking is to look right, it must be a completely spontaneous action, just like Zen painting or Zen archery.

The total effect of the kare-sansui is mesmerizing. The rational mind may at first try to interpret it in terms of symbolism—the way it at first wrestles with a koan—but if one stays with it the thinking mind eventually settles down and allows the deeper consciousness to enjoy it simply for what it is. Many visitors sit quietly for a very long time. The kare-sansui provides the setting for a fine meditation exercise.

From this description, you may get the impression that a kare-sansui is a static sort of thing. It's not static at all. The character of the garden is changing all the time, but in very subtle ways. Shadows play slowly across the surface—shadows from nearby trees and from passing clouds. And leaves will occasionally drop onto the gravel surface. Far from being out of place, the leaves add a wonderful, very Daoist, touch to it all. Birds will come and go, leaving their footprints. All of this is perfectly natural, and therefore perfectly in accord with the nature of a kare-sansui. But how ghastly it would be if a person walked across the gravel or left a beer can lying there. (No doubt this would be ugly, and yet, strangely enough, it could be just as natural as the bird. Perhaps it would be different if a baby got loose and toddled across the gravel.)

Beautiful as the kare-sansui is in the soft sunlight, it becomes even more enchanting in the moonlight. And when it's covered by a light snowfall the beauty is indescribable. In fact, everything about it is indescribable; one must sit there for a while and personally experience it. To see the best of these, one must travel to the Zen monasteries of Japan. However, some excellent ones can be found outside of Japan. There is, for example, a very beautifully maintained kare-sansui on the grounds of the Huntington Library in southern California. But for the most part, this delicate artform doesn't travel well beyond the limits of the monastery grounds.

ZEN AND THE ARTS

The kare-sansui may not have traveled well beyond the confines of the monastery, but the influence of Zen in general has traveled very well indeed beyond the monastery grounds. Japanese culture has been powerfully influenced by Zen Buddhism; it has affected all of the arts, including the humbler arts of practical everyday things. It's a two-way street, of course; from the beginning, Zen in Japan has been shaped by the existing culture. But, in return, Zen has also been a creative force, influencing in its own way the arts of Japanese life. We see this in the emphasis on simplicity and naturalness and in that "disciplined spontaneity" that is the hallmark of Zen.

Nowhere is this more obvious than in the art of *sumi-e,* the wonderfully beautiful art whose name means simply "ink painting." In a way, sumi-e is much like the art of kare-sansui; both depend on a sudden spontaneous expression that reveals the unspeakable "suchness" of the beauty of nature. Some of the finest kare-sansui were, in fact, created by renowned ink painters.

The sumi-e artist uses just three things: a finely tapered soft brush with a long wooden or bamboo handle, long pieces of finely made white paper (or occasionally white silk), and black ink that is mixed with water for different shades and textures. Sometimes colored inks, such as pink, will be used, but in the pure tradition of sumi-e only black ink on white paper is allowed. The ink starts out as a hard stick. A little water is poured into a slightly concave stone dish, and the ink stick is rubbed in it until the desired consistency is achieved. The artist can create a great variety of shades by altering the amount of water in the ink.

The brush stroke must be completely spontaneous and without analytical thought. It is often the case that just a few well-executed strokes are all that the artist needs to capture the essence of the subject, whether this be a mountain, a face, or whatever. In sumi-e, the painting is not meant to be *about* nature; it is an act *of* nature. The artist, the subject, and the action of the brush are all one reality. There are many good stories that illustrate this point.

Once upon a time, the emperor wished to have a painting of a bamboo grove, so he called in his favorite court artist and, paying the man his usual commission in advance, he asked the artist to produce such a work. Weeks stretched into months and still there was no painting. It began to look as if the artist had taken the money and fled. After three long years, he finally reappeared at court. "Where is my painting?" the emperor shouted. "After making me wait so long it had better be good!"

"I haven't started it yet," the artist answered, but before anyone could react, he offered to do it right then and there. Supplies were brought to him, and in just a matter of seconds, his fast brush strokes had finished the painting. Needless to say, it was perfect. The bamboo seemed to sway in the breeze.

The emperor was nonplussed. At last he spoke, "This is magnificent, and it took you only seconds. Why did you make me wait three long years?"

"I was not ready until now," the artist replied. "For the past three years I have been living with the bamboo; feeling what the bamboo feels, thinking what bamboo thinks. At last I became bamboo myself. Only when I and the bamboo became one could I express its inner essence. Once that unity is achieved, it takes no time to do the painting."

The art of sumi-e, like Zen itself, came to Japan from China. It was already a highly developed art form in the Tang and Song periods. The Daoist love of nature was obvious from the beginning. Many of these masterpieces have survived in museums and are familiar to us today. They are the large "nature paintings"—sometimes done on a series of folding panels—that display great landscapes, often including mist-shrouded mountains and plunging waterfalls. They were often done in a progression of scenes portraying the changing of the seasons. People are likely to be in the picture too, but you might not notice them at first. Instead of dominating the picture, as would be likely in traditional Western art, people fit into these great landscapes at the appropriate scale. They are a part of the whole; their activity is in harmony with this great scene of nature that they are a part of. By looking closely, you might discover two or three figures standing on a small bridge or wending their way along a mountain trail. They fit into the scene as just one of its many elements. Again, this is not to say that human life was seen as unimportant, not at all, but what was most important was to show the grand harmony of nature, within which human life takes its meaning.

The art of Chinese landscape painting took root in Japan and flourished there. This form of expression became especially popular with Rinzai artists, who often decorated the walls of their Zendos with beautiful landscape murals. These paintings, some of which can still be seen, reveal that Japanese artists preferred an even sparer style than the Chinese masters, limiting brush strokes to only what was essential. Beautiful though the landscape paintings may have been, the practice of decorating Zendo walls eventually died out in favor of leaving them simple and bare.

One of the most intriguing aspects of the sumi-e style is what it doesn't do. The artist feels no need to "fill the canvas." In fact, what the brush does not do is just as important as what it does do. "Painting by not painting," as it is sometimes called. This can be disconcerting to a person raised in the Western tradition. Empty space plays a profoundly important role in the art of sumi-e. It's not uncommon for most of the paper to be left bare; sometimes the inked work occupies only one small corner. Far from appearing incomplete, though, this display of clean white emptiness is very powerful; it gives life and energy to whatever *is* portrayed. It is another way—another potential way—of grasping intuitively the perception of reality that is at the heart of Zen Buddhism.

Japanese artists, like the Chinese, favored scenes from nature in which the great harmony of nature is emphasized. It is that harmony that most interested the artist. The greatest of all the Japanese ink-painters was the Zen Master, Sesshu Toyo (1420–1506). In his hands, sumi-e landscape painting reached perfection. But he is also deservedly admired for his portraits. That side of sumi-e was also inherited from the Chinese. You may recall that Japanese Buddhist monks who studied in China often returned home with treasured portraits of their Chinese teachers. It is interesting to compare Sesshu's portrait of Bodhidharma with da Vinci's "Mona Lisa." Both are works of great genius; both are transcendent in that they really portray the universal rather than the particular; but what an immeasurable difference there is in technique. Da Vinci's creation was meticulously constructed over many months. Attention was given to the tiniest details, and the painting fills the whole canvas. Sesshu's portrait, on the other hand, was probably completed in minutes; attention to detail would have ruined it. One is not better than the other because of this. They are simply different expressions of different philosophies. The brush stroke of a sumi-e master is Zen in action.

There is yet a third area of ink-painting that the Japanese inherited from China, the art of calligraphy. In every way, calligraphy is the equal of nature painting and portraiture. Chinese characters are such beautiful creations in themselves; it must have been only natural to elevate the practice of writing to a fine art. When the Japanese adopted modified Chinese characters, they understandably continued the tradition. To find any sort of parallel in the West, we would have to go back to medieval times when the production of illuminated manuscripts was a flourishing art. The invention of printing put an end to that tradition. How ironic it is that printing—moveable type carved on wooden blocks—was invented in China so as to facilitate the reproduction of whole characters. In China, though, printing did not lessen the love of the art of calligraphy. The Japanese certainly have shared this love. A paper panel containing only inked characters is seen as a fine piece of art in and of itself. Often a much-admired scroll of this sort will be hung on the wall, to be appreciated for its artistic value in the same way that a painting or a flower arrangement would be.

The special thing about calligraphy, though, is that it *is* writing; it's not only beautiful to look at, but it also communicates the written thoughts of its creator. The art of calligraphy is thus ideally suited to unite with the art of poetry. And in the art of poetry, Zen Buddhism found yet another magnificent vehicle for the expression of its essential spirit. This is especially true with regard to that unique style of Japanese poetry known as *haiku*.

A haiku is one short verse—only seventeen syllables long—that is meant to evoke a specific feeling or state of mind. It has been nicely described as "a pebble thrown into the pool of the listener's mind." The plop of the pebble creates a brief ripple of consciousness that is more intuitive than rational. It grasps the immediate "suchness" of an experience:

> The old pond, ah!
> A frog jumps in:
> The water's sound. (All haiku are from Blyth.)

Do you see what I mean? Haiku does not aim to stimulate the thinking mind. It evokes feelings and impressions from the memory:

> On a withered branch
> A crow is perched—
> Autumn evening.

How different this kind of poetry is from what became the traditional style in the West. The haiku is to traditional Western poetry what sumi-e is to traditional Western painting. Both, however, have profoundly influenced Western styles in modern times. Haiku is much like sumi-e. In haiku, the "brush strokes" are done with words, or more accurately, with sounds and rhythm. For this reason, haiku loses much in translation. But a well done translation still preserves the essence of it:

> A fallen flower
> Returning to the branch?
> It was a butterfly.

Haiku generally focuses on very mundane things, the ordinary sights and sounds of daily life:

> The sound of the scouring
> of the saucepan blends
> With the tree-frog's voices.

The greatest name in haiku is Matsuo Basho, a Zen Master who lived during the latter half of the seventeenth century. (*Basho*, which means banana tree in Japanese, was his pen name.) Basho is to haiku what Sesshu is to sumi-e. It's tempting to imagine that Basho was inspired to verse by some of Sesshu's ink-paintings:

> Ishiyama no   White shines the stone
> ishi yori shiroshi   Of the mountain rock; whiter yet
> aki no kaze.   The autumn wind.

The spirit of Zen affects many of the arts of Japanese culture, and they all come together in the "Tea Ceremony." It is a sort of grand opera of all the elements influenced by Zen. What we know as the Tea Ceremony is called *Chado* in Japanese (the "way of tea"). Like the kare-sansui gardens, Chado is uniquely Japanese. Both of these art forms, so deep and filled with beauty, are difficult for the Western mind to understand. Both, however, have been honed to perfection over many centuries. When understood even a little, they can easily be seen to be profound expressions of Japanese culture in general and Zen in particular.

The "cha" in Chado is tea, a plant known in botany as *camellia sinensis*. It is a bushy green shrub whose leaves contain small amounts of caffeine. It was first domesticated in the warm hilly regions of southern China and became a highly popular drink with all classes of Chinese society. Tea keeps the mind alert, but without causing intoxication. Of course, the amount consumed does make a difference. Consider this comment by the Tang period poet Lo Dong (Lo-tung):

> The first cup moistens my lips and throat, the second cup breaks my loneliness, the third cup searches my barren entrail but to find therein some five thousand volumes of odd ideographs. The fourth cup raises a slight perspiration—all the wrong of life passes away through my pores. At the fifth cup I am purified; the sixth cup calls me to the realms of immortals. The seventh cup—ah, but I could take no more! (And this is *tea* he's drinking!) (Okakura, 48)

Lo Dong's comment is revealing. Tea was not just an early version of soda-pop among the Chinese; they felt a deep affection for the mysterious beauty of tea in all of its aspects—not only the brewing and drinking of tea, but even the very appearance of the tea leaves. This point is made by a wonderful comment from the same time as Lo Dong. Here another Tang poet, Lu Wu by name, is describing the nature of the best tea leaves. According to Lu Wu, the best quality of the leaves must have "creases like the leather boot of Tartar horsemen, curl like the dewlap of a mighty bullock, unfold like a mist rising out of a ravine, gleam like a lake touched by a zephyr, and be wet and soft like fine earth newly swept by rain." (Okakura, 47)

Zen monks in particular were attracted to *tcha*, as the Chinese called it. The sipping of tea could ward off sleepiness during long hours of meditation practice. As a result, the ritual drinking of tea was introduced into the monastic routine. The origin of the Tea Ceremony is said to go back to Zen monasteries in China, where monks would gather to sip tea before a portrait of Bodhidharma. Legend had it, you may remember, that the first tea plants grew from the eyelids (or eyebrows) of Bodhidharma when he tore them off and flung them on the ground. A certain amount of ritual grew up around this shared act of tea drinking, but it was still a rather modest affair when it was transported from Chinese to Japanese Zen monasteries. The ritual of the Tea Ceremony was transformed and perfected in the sixteenth century by Sen-no-Rikyu, the first great tea master of Japan. He was a counselor to the *daimyo*, Oda Nobunaga, a powerful military leader who unified the country. On the grounds of Nobunaga's estate, Sen-no-Rikyu constructed the first fully developed tea garden. The mature form of Chado created by Sen-no-Rikyu has been carefully preserved down to the present time with only refinements being added.

Chado is a carefully designed ritual activity in which a small group of people participate. Every act, every movement in Chado is prescribed by ritual. This may seem excessive to the uninitiated, but in fact it is very liberating; ritual permits the participants to temporarily set aside the role-playing of the ego. The procedure is led by a man or woman called a *teishu*, "master of tea," who prepares and serves tea to the others. But there is so much more involved here than simply getting together to drink some tea. This is in no way a "tea party" in the conventional sense; it is a highly refined group activity in which each person plays an important role. In the course of the ceremony, *all* of the senses will be gently stimulated, creating in the participants an aesthetic experience of the highest order. Mindfulness, the Zen love of total immersion in the present moment, permeates the whole experience.

The ceremony of Chado can be conducted almost anywhere; a small room set off for this purpose can be perfectly adequate. But ideally the ceremony of tea will have its own special setting, a teahouse, known as a *chashitsu*, set within a tea garden. By custom, a tea garden should be small and modest. The important thing is that it promotes a sense of naturalness and serenity, and that it be separated from the ordinary environment of daily life.

The guests arrive at the *machiai*, which is just a simple little gathering place, perhaps a trellis-covered porch. When all are assembled, the teishu will summon them to the teahouse. Most likely, they will pause along the way and admire the beauty of the garden; its arrangement is meant to encourage a contemplative frame of mind. The path through the garden, the *roji*, signifies the first stage in the practice of meditation. The teahouse is simplicity itself, and therein lies its special beauty. It is a small squarish building, a hut really, by tradition ten feet on a side. The roof is likely to be straw thatch in the old rural style of Japan; it overhangs the walls which are made of bare lath and shoji paper. The building nestles into the garden in perfect harmony; it appears to have grown there.

Before entering the chashitsu, each guest pauses at the *tsukubai*, the "stone water basin," to purify the inner self by ritually cleansing the hands and mouth. Certain guests may be especially honored, but all social rank is left outside. In the old days, when the samurai entered the teahouse they had to leave their swords behind, the insignia of their class. Entry is made through a low sliding door (the *nijiriguchi*). The doorway is deliberately made low so that one must bow or even kneel in the act of entering. Of course all shoes will be left outside. The interior of the teahouse is spotlessly clean and simple; there is a complete absence of clutter. Soft light filters into the room through the shoji covered windows, and a subtle aroma of incense may fill the air. The floor is covered in tatami mats, and near one end of the room is an opening in the floor for a small fire pit where a charcoal fire will heat the water in a heavy cast iron kettle. In one of the walls there will be an alcove called a *tokonoma*. Here an object of art will be displayed, probably a hanging scroll with calligraphy, and on a shelf beneath it there is likely to be a naturally beautiful rock or a very simple arrangement of flowers, or perhaps a small bare branch. And most likely it will have been placed slightly off-center on the shelf.

The display of natural objects has been raised to a fine art in Japanese culture. This has been much influenced by the spirit of Zen. Objects displayed in the tea room will be selected with great care. In arranging the room, the tea master carefully avoids the clutter of repetition and the dullness of symmetry. "Uniformity of design is considered fatal to the freshness of the imagination."

The guests will sit directly on the tatami-covered floor, forming a small square or circle around the perimeter of the room. Cushions may be used, but Japanese people are more likely to prefer a posture called *seiza*, in which one kneels and then sits back on the heels. It's a very comfortable position when you get used to it. After the guests are seated, the tea master (the teishu) will enter the room and take his or her place near one end of the circle beside the fire pit. While the teishu cleans the utensils, the guests may chat among themselves. Silence is not required, but it is expected that conversation will be friendly and will be limited to appropriate subjects. Sports and politics would definitely be out of place. Particularly appropriate would be expressions of appreciation regarding the beauty of the things in the room. Everything has been selected with great care by the teishu. By no means are the guests merely passive receivers. Chado is a ritual event in which each participant plays an important role. There is an art to being a good guest. An atmosphere of relaxed formality characterizes the Tea Ceremony.

While they are waiting, the guests may take note of the beauty of the tokonoma or the tea utensils. At the same time, they will be enjoying the sound of the steaming water, which is sometimes described as being like the sound of wind passing through a bamboo grove. Not infrequently, all will fall silent for a while in order to enjoy its sound. Other sounds too may be enjoyed, such as the song of a bird in the garden, or the patter of lightly falling rain, or the wonderful sound of the wind in the trees just outside the teahouse.

Chado is a word with broad meaning. It refers not only to the Tea Ceremony, but to the whole philosophy behind it. The Tea Ceremony is a very refined expression of a way of life based on tranquility and acceptance. Within the Tea Ceremony itself, the actual preparation and sipping of the tea is known by the name *temae*. The tea used in temae is a strong green tea that has been finely powdered. It has a rich aroma and an almost bitter taste. It is sipped, not from tea cups, but from small ceramic bowls that are held lightly in both hands.

You might expect that only perfect and costly teaware would be used. In fact, it's quite the opposite. A person who attempts to impress his guests by showing off expensive items completely misses the point of Chado. The beauty of the humble and the natural is what is most appreciated. A tea master will search in unlikely places for his wares. He is looking for those wonderfully rare accidents that transform the ordinary into a master-piece. Of course, such "flaws" may not be appreciated by everyone, but the experienced eye of a lover of Chado sees it easily. Prized tea bowls are often surprisingly humble pieces of ceramic. The glaze may drip unevenly, or there may be a crack on one side, or the whole thing may even be misshapen. But the knowing guest will smile in appreciation. Ceramic tea caddies are delicate and sometimes will be accidentally broken (and maybe, on occasion, not so accidentally). It is believed that the way the pieces are glued back together adds greatly to its beauty. This sense of seeing beauty in spontaneous "mishaps" is very much in the spirit of Zen.

The tea is prepared one bowl at a time by the tea master. This ritual absorbs the full attention of the guests. Using a thin bamboo strip, the teishu will spoon a measured amount of powdered tea into a bowl and add a little steaming water from the kettle. He then briskly stirs them together with a bamboo whisk until the mixture becomes "a froth of liquid jade." The bowl is then placed before one of the guests. Even this act is done in such a way as to show off the bowl's best appearance. What is regarded to be its most beautiful side will be placed facing the guest. Each guest lifts the bowl and courteously addresses those near him. Turning first to the person on his, or her, right he says, "Allow me to share tea with you." Then turning to the person to his left he says, "Excuse me for going before you." And finally, addressing the tea master he says, "Thank you for making tea." Only then does the guest begin to sip the wonderful concoction. At the first sip, all of the taste buds will be stimulated to full attention.

The tea invigorates the senses. When the sipping is done, it is customary to pass each of the implements around the circle so that they can be admired by the guests. No matter how humble its use, each utensil is a work of art. The whisk is a thing of simple beauty, and so is the bamboo dipping spoon, the small towel, and so on. This love of perfection in the most ordinary things of life is one of the distinguishing characteristics of

Japanese culture in general. In the Tea Ceremony, it becomes the focus of attention. The Zen attitude of mindfulness is fully employed in Chado.

Temae does indeed refresh and stimulate all of the senses, but it is a very mistaken impression to see the Tea Ceremony as nothing more than a relaxing and pleasurable experience. It is this, of course, but it is much more as well. Above all else, the special appeal of Chado is to be found in the state of mind that it encourages. This is where the connection to Zen is most obvious and most profound. The ritual, the implements, and the sensory pleasures are the raw material out of which a particular state of consciousness is subtly constructed. Tradition identifies four aspects to this state of mind; they are the principles that give definition to the Tea Ceremony. In Japanese these four are known as *wa, kei, sei,* and *jaku.* It should come as no surprise that these words do not translate easily into English. *Wa* is usually rendered as "harmony," *kei* as "reverence," *sei* as "purity," and *jaku* as "tranquility." It is said that these four qualities bring together the spirit of Confucianism, of Daoism, and of Buddhism. The tea master seeks to use temae in the way a gifted musician uses an instrument, to create a state of mind in his guests that exemplifies these virtues.

But there is still more, at least potentially. A gifted tea master brings it all together in a subtle but transcendent state of consciousness that cannot really be named. It has to be called something, though, and the Japanese use the word *wabi. Wabi* is another word that defies translation, and maybe it's better that way. Let's be satisfied with saying only that wabi suggests a deep and serene state of mind that is in tune with the great beauty of emptiness. *Wabi* is sometimes called "poverty," but it is poverty in the sense of an acceptance of the fact that nothing is ever owned, nothing endures. Out of this kind of poverty can arise a deeply felt aesthetic appreciation of emptiness. This spirit is best expressed in poetry:

> In the woods, over there, deeply buried in snow,
> Last night a lone branch of the plum tree burst out in bloom.

All is fleeting; all is transitory; nothing endures. But, like the plum tree blossoming in the snow, every moment—if only we would stop and look—is filled with an awesome beauty that can lift the spirit to an experience of transcendent joy. The curling steam of the tea kettle, the momentary scent of the incense, the fleeting taste of the tea—everything about temae is evanescent, transitory. And therein is its excellence. In the hands of a true tea master, temae becomes a beautiful expression of the meaning of *shunyata.* There is a wonderful verse by the poet Rikyu that reveals the very heart of Chado:

> When tea is made with water drawn from the depths of mind,
> Whose bottom is beyond measure,
> We really have what is called cha-no-yu [Chado].

When the tea has been consumed and everything has been admired and put away, the teishu will invite everyone to return to the garden where the guests will graciously take their leave. For a while they have set aside the usual responsibilities of ordinary life and entered the state of mind which the Daoists called "the world of carefree hermits, wandering through the mountains like wind-blown clouds, with nothing to do but cultivate a row of vegetables, gaze at the drifting mist, and listen to the waterfalls."

Like all things, Buddhism too is transitory; it must be reborn each moment. Shakyamuni Buddha initiated a process, a wave of development which has known flourishing times and times of decline. Like a flowering plant, Buddhism in India blossomed and then declined. But by this time, the seeds were in the ground outside of India. In China, a new flowering occurred, and then began to decline. Again, though, the seeds had been carried to new lands. In Japan, Buddhism—especially Zen Buddhism—would experience yet another magnificent flowering, and alas, this was followed by still another period of decline.

By the beginning of the twentieth century, it must have seemed to many that the golden age of Zen Buddhism in Japan was a thing of the past. But again, the flower had broadcast its seeds, this time very far afield. Seedlings were taking root in the most unlikely places. The ancient tradition of Buddhism had at last spread to the West. The new growth is strong and healthy. Yet another flowering—this time worldwide in scope—would seem certain to be an exciting part of the not-too-distant future.

Study Questions

1. Distinguish between the various schools of Buddhism to be found in Japan during the early days: Kegon; Tendai; Shingon; Nichirin; and Pure Land.

2. What was the character of Buddhism in Japan before the arrival of Zen? Was Zen just one more variety of Buddhism, or would it be accurate to say that in some ways it was a revolutionary new movement?

3. In what fundamental ways do Rinzai and Soto Zen differ?

4. Why do you suppose that the samurai aristocracy in Japan took so fervently to Rinzai Buddhism? For that matter, why did they *not* feel just as fervent about Soto?

5. What do you make of Dogen Kigen? What did he actually *do* to earn a place of great esteem in the history of Japan?

6. Do you feel that you understand the meaning of *shikantaza*? Why do you suppose it is said that *shikantaza* "requires great energy, and can be totally exhausting for the novice"?

7. Hakuin must have been an unusual sort of person. What do you imagine he was like?

8. Why do you think Hakuin was so infatuated with the koan? How would Hakuin want to see the koan used?

9. What do you understand to be the meaning of Suzuki's arresting statement: "To my mind it was the technique of the koan exercise that saved Zen as a unique heritage of Far Eastern culture."?

10. The "Great Doubt" and the "Great Dying"— these are extremely powerful insights. What's it all about? Do you feel that you understand why these two matters hold a place of supreme importance in the teaching of Hakuin?

11. What is a Zen monastery like? What are its rhythms during the day, and the year? Do you find it an appealing sort of place? Could you imagine yourself staying at a Zen monastery sometime?

12. Which do you feel is greatest in importance: zazen, sanzen, or samu? Why?

13. What is a kare-sansui? Why do you suppose it is suggested that the kare-sansui "has a spellbinding beauty that no words can describe; it has to be experienced"?

14. Do you remember the story about the artist that the emperor hired to do a painting of a bamboo grove? What's the point of that story? Why is it said that it's a fine example of the Zen mind?

15. Do you agree that sumi-e and haiku are very similar art forms. What makes them so similar? What makes them "so Zen"?

16. It is said that Chado brings together all of the elements of Zen? What are those elements, and how does Chado bring them together? Would you like to participate in a Chado ceremony?

WORKS CITED

Anthony, Carol K. 1988. *A Guide to the I Ching*. Stowe, MA: Anthony Publications.

Aurobindo, Sri. 1995. *Secret of the Vedas*. Twin Lakes, WI: Lotus Light Publications.

Blofeld, John. 1985. *Taoism; The Road to Immortality*. Boston: Shambala.

Blyth, R. H. 1981. *Haiku*. Tokyo: Heian International Publishing.

Bryant, Edwin. 2001. *The Quest for the Origins of Vedic Culture*. New York: Oxford University Press.

Chai, Ch'u, and Chai, Winberg. 1973. *Confucianism*. Hauppauge, NY: Barrons Educational Series.

Chakrabarti, Kisor Kumar. 1999. *Classical Indian Philosophy of Mind*. Albany: State University of New York Press.

Ch'en, Kenneth. 1968. *Buddhism*. New York: Barrons.

Creel, Herrlee G. 1953. *Chinese Thought from Confucius to Mao Tse-tung*. Chicago: University of Chicago Press.

Danielou, Alain. 1964. *The Myths and Gods of India* (originally published as: *Hindu Polytheism*). New York: Bollinger Foundation.

Dumoulin, Heinrich. *Zen Buddhism: A History*, 2 vols. (translated by James W. Hesig and Paul Knitter). New York: Macmillan.

Easwaren, Eknath. 1985. *The Bhagavad Gita*. Petaluma, CA: Nilgiri.

——1986. *The Dhammapada*. Petaluma, CA: Nilgiri.

——1987. *The Upanishads*. Petaluma, CA: Nilgiri.

Eliade, Mircea. 1969. *Yoga: Immortality and Freedom*, 2nd ed. Princeton, NJ: Princeton University Press.

Ellwood, Robert S. 1973. *The Feast of Kingship: Accession Ceremonies in Ancient Japan*. Tokyo: Sophia University Press.

Feuerstein, George. 1983. *Introduction to the Bhagavad Gita: Philosophy and Cultural Setting*. Wheaton, IL: Quest.

Govinda, Lama Anagarika. 1960. *Fundamentals of Tibetan Mysticism*. New York: Samuel Weisner.

Henricks, Robert G. (trans.) 1993. *Te-Tao Ching*. New York: Modern Library.

Herman, A. L. 1976. *An Introduction to Indian Thought*. Englewood Cliffs, NJ: Prentice-Hall.

Hixon, Lex. 1993. *Mother of the Buddhas*. Wheaton, IL: Quest Books.

Holton, C. 1938. *The National Faith of Japan: A Study in Modern Shinto*. London: Trench, Tulsner.

Johnston, E. H. (trans.) reprint 1988. *Ashvaghosa's Buddhacarita*. Delhi: Montalil Baranasidass Publications.

Kaltenmark, Max. 1969. *Lao Tzu and Taoism* (translated from French by Roger Greaves). Stanford, CA: Stanford University Press.

Kardash, Ted. "Ageless Wisdom for a Modern World Part : Te – The Principle of Inner Nature." Jade Dragon Online. http://www.jadedragon.com/tao_heal/taopart2.html

Koller, John M. 1985. *Oriental Philosophies*, 2nd ed. New York: Macmillan.

LaFleur, William. 1988. *Buddhism*. Englewood Cliffs, NJ: Prentice-Hall.

Lau, D. C. (trans.) 1970. *Mencius*. London: Penguin Books.

Majumdar, R. C. ed. 1971. *The Vedic Age*. Bombay: Bharatiya Vidya Bhavan.

Mallory, J. P. 1989. *In Search of the Indo-Europeans*. London: Thames and Hudson.

Michell, George. 1988. *The Hindu Temple*. Chicago: The University of Chicago Press.

Mitchell, Stephen. (trans.) 1988. *Tao Te Ching*. New York: HarperCollins.

Murti, T. R. V. 1955. *The Central Philosophy of Buddhism: A Study of the Madhyamika System*. London: George Allen and Unwin.

O'Flaherty, Wendy Doniger. (trans.) 1981. *The Rig Veda*. London: Penguin Classics (Reproduced by permission of Penguin Books Ltd.).

Okakura, Kakuzo. 1989 (reprint). *The Book of Tea*. Tokyo: Kodansha.

Powers, John. 1995. *Introduction to Tibetan Buddhism*. Ithica, NY: Snow Lion Publications.

Rahula,Walpola. 1983. *What the Buddha Taught*. New York: Grove Press.

Ross, Nancy Wilson. 1981. *Buddhism; A Way of Life and Thought*. New York: Vintage Books.

Schirokauer, Conrad. 1989. *A Brief History of Chinese and Japanese Civilizations*. Fort Worth, TX: Harcourt Brace Jovanovich.

Schumann, H. W. 1989. *The Historical Buddha*. London: Arkana.

Suzuki, D. T. 1956. *Zen Buddhism: Selected Writing of D. T. Suzuki*. Garden City, NJ: Doubleday.

——1973. "The Development of the Pure Land Doctrine in Buddhism," *Collected Writings on Shin Buddhism*. Kyoto: Shinshu Otanika.

Suzuki, Shunryu. 1970. *Zen Mind, Beginner's Mind*. New York and Tokyo: Weatherhill.

Thapar, Romila. 2002. *Early India: From the Origins to A.D. 1300*. Berkeley: University of California Press.

Thompson, Evan. 2007. *Mind in Life*. Cambridge, MA: Belknap Press of Harvard University Press.

Verma, Hari N. and Amrit. 1992. *100 Great Indians Through the Ages*. Campbell, CA: GIP Books.

Waddell, L. Austine. 1972. *Tibetan Buddhism*. New York: Dover.

Watson, Burton. (trans.) 1964. *Chuang Tzu*. New York: Columbia University Press.

——1993. *The Lotus Sutra*. New York: Columbia University Press.

Watts, Alan W. 1957. *The Way of Zen*. New York: Vintage Books.

Wong, Eva. 1997. *The Shambala Guide to Taoism*. Boston: Shambala.

Zimmer, Heinrich. 1946. *Myths and Symbols in Indian Art and Civilization*. Princeton, NJ: Princeton University Press.

——1951. *Philosophies of India*. Princeton, NJ: Princeton University Press.

INDEX